Real Estate Law

Unlike existing textbooks written for law students on specific subjects affecting real estate transactions, *Real Estate Law: Fundamentals for The Development Process* uses "The Development Process" as a framework for understanding how the U.S. legal system regulates, facilitates, and generally impacts real estate transactions and their outcomes.

This book not only addresses the nature of specific legal issues directly relating to real estate transactions but also how those issues may best be identified and addressed in advance. This book breaks down the myriad of laws influencing the selection, acquisition, development, financing, ownership, and management of real estate, and presents them in context.

Readers of *Real Estate Law* will gain a practical understanding, from the perspective of a real property developer or real estate executive, investor, or lender, of:

* *how* to identify potential legal issues before they arise;
* *when* to involve a real estate attorney;
* *how* to select an attorney with the appropriate, relevant experience; and
* *how* to efficiently and economically engage and manage legal counsel in addressing real estate issues.

Written as a graduate-level textbook, *Real Estate Law* comes with numerous useful features including a glossary of terms, chapter summaries, discussion questions, further reading, and a companion website with instructor resources. It is a resource of great value to real estate and finance professionals, both with and without law degrees, engaged in one aspect or another of real estate development and finance, who want to become more conversant in the legal issues impacting these transactions.

Peter E. Smirniotopoulos is Adjunct Professor of Real Estate in the MBA program at The George Washington University and in the School of Business at George Mason University, USA.

"Better than any other book I know, *Real Estate Law: Fundamentals for The Development Process* communicates to real estate business people how they may effectively utilize law and lawyers to add value in achieving their real estate objectives. I only wish I had been armed with Peter's book when I began practicing real estate law 30 years ago, and before I began teaching real estate law 10 years ago. If I were a student today, I would want to learn real estate law from this splendid work."

Charles Schilke, Professor, University of Maryland Colvin Institute of Real Estate Development and former Director, Georgetown and Johns Hopkins University Real Estate Programs, USA

"Peter Smirniotopoulos' book, *Real Estate Law: Fundamentals for The Development Process*, is the first I have seen specifically written for developers. It covers the full range of legal issues that developers confront from land acquisition to entitlements, financing, design, construction, leasing, and operations. He does so in a forthright, easy-to-read manner, explaining what the legal issues are, and when and how to obtain efficient, cost-effective legal advice. Active developers as well as students of the development game will find Peter's book a must-have addition to their libraries."

Richard Peiser, Michael D. Spear Professor of Real Estate Development, Harvard University, USA

"When hiring recent graduates from real estate master's programs, we expect to see candidates who possess the kind of broad-based yet subject-matter specific knowledge that Professor Smirniotopoulos conveys through his MBA real estate law course and this companion textbook. This textbook represents a new standard for how real estate law should be taught. It is also the only textbook on real estate law that focuses on walkable urban places or WalkUPs - a project type for which Forest City is a nationally recognized leader. WalkUPs have become a national focus throughout the U.S., making this textbook of particular value."

Deborah Ratner Salzberg, President, Forest City Washington, Inc. Board Member, Center for Real Estate and Urban Analysis, G.W. School of Business, USA

"Real estate development is an exceedingly complex process with many constantly moving parts but also many parts that involve different aspects of the law. *Real Estate Law: Fundamentals For The Development Process* is the first to use the development process as the structure for a textbook on this topic, which makes comprehension far easier and more organized. Professor Smirniotopoulos also takes the enlightened approach that there are appropriate times to use a lawyer and times that having a comprehensive knowledge of the law by the developer is sufficient…necessary to keep pursuit and soft costs under control. Finally, this textbook recognizes, for the first time, that today's real estate development is predominantly "walkable urban", a far more complex development process than the "drivable sub-urban" development of the past century. This textbook is destined to be the standard for real estate law for many years to come."

Christopher B. Leinberger, Charles Bendit Distinguished Scholar and Research Professor of Urban Real Estate, Chair, Center for Real Estate and Urban Analysis, USA

"Peter's book provides students with a disciplined introduction to the topic combined with a fool for how it all comes together in practice."

Peter Linneman, Principal and Founder of Linneman Associates and Professor Emeritus at the Wharton School of Business, University of Pennsylvania, USA

Real Estate Law
Fundamentals for The Development Process

Peter E. Smirniotopoulos

Routledge
Taylor & Francis Group

LONDON AND NEW YORK

First published 2017
by Routledge
2 Park Square, Milton Park, Abingdon, Oxon OX14 4RN

and by Routledge
711 Third Avenue, New York, NY 10017

Routledge is an imprint of the Taylor & Francis Group, an informa business

British Library Cataloguing in Publication Data
A catalogue record for this book is available from the British Library

Library of Congress Cataloging-in-Publication Data
A catalog record for this book has been requested

ISBN: 978-1-138-79098-8 (hbk)
ISBN: 978-1-315-76306-4 (ebk)

Typeset in Helvetica Neue
by Apex CoVantage, LLC

Visit the companion website: www.routledge.com/cw/Smirniotopoulos

Printed and bound in the United States of America by
Edwards Brothers Malloy on sustainably sourced paper

This book is dedicated to my parents—Lieutenant Colonel Eleftherios D. Smirniotopoulos (RHAF, Ret.) and Panayiota Athanasiadou, M.D.—who taught me the importance of hard work, perseverance, and an excellent education (even though, to this day, when they call me in the middle of a work day, they ask want *"Peter, are you at work?"*), but who also remind me to *"Have Always Good Time"* (which my father had inscribed on the pocket watch he gave me for my wedding); to my, two, wonderful and amazing, adult children— Casey Lynn Smirniotopoulos and Nicholas Alexander Smirniotopoulos—who've taught me so much more than I have them, and from whom I learn something new almost every, single day; to our beloved five-year-old mixed-breed, Zoe (known to my *Real Estate Development* students as the *EVP of Thought Leadership*), who, throughout the eighteen months required to research and write this textbook, on our daily walks, listened attentively to whatever legal issue I was grappling with at the time; and, most-importantly, to my beautiful wife of 32 years, Lauren Lynn Smirniotopoulos, who makes everything and anything possible, and without whom I would truly be lost.

– In Memoriam –

Patrick Lyman Kelsey
Oxon Hill Sr. High School Class of 1974

Mark Henry Quattro, Esq.
Georgetown University Law Center, 1981

Myron P. "Mike" Curzan
Founder & CEO, UniDev, LLC

Each of whom, in their own way, would have been exceptionally proud
of this accomplishment.

Contents

Detailed Table of Contents

Figures

Tables

Foreword

IN NOVEMBER 1941, David Tishman's two sons were on top of the world. Both were recent Ivy League college graduates, newly married, with bright career prospects in the family company.[1] Bob was lanky and thoughtful; Alan, two years his junior, was similarly tall but broader and more outgoing, a born salesman. While working, Alan was taking accounting and law courses at New York University, as his father had done thirty years earlier. Bob had just finished a law course at Columbia. "You don't have to get a law degree," Alan remembers his father advising, even though David had one. "Just take enough courses to know when to hire a lawyer."[2]

To paraphrase this David Tishman quote: "You don't have to have a law degree; you just need to know enough about real estate law to know when to hire a lawyer." This is, arguably, the foundational theme of *Real Estate Law: Fundamentals for The Development Process*. However, even someone with a law degree, but who has not been exposed to real estate law as a professional discipline, will benefit from what's presented in this textbook.[3]

Nothing occurs in a vacuum

The purpose of this textbook is to teach real estate law not as some amalgamation of abstract, static legal concepts but within the context of the dynamics of real estate development and finance, through a framework I have developed and refer to throughout this book as **The Development Process**. What is presented in this textbook is not what is taught in most American law schools, with curricula offering a range of related topics, such as Real Property Law, Contracts, Federal Taxation, and Environmental Law, among others, that provide little context for law students as to how these disciplines intersect with and impact The Development Process.

Rather than offering in-depth discussions of law school subjects such as "servitudes" and "estates in land" in Real Property Law or "fraud in the inducement" in Contracts, this textbook instead offers a much broader treatment of real estate law as an overarching discipline impacting and driving the development and financing of real estate projects. This is done with considerable intention, to facilitate an understanding of the true breadth of the subject matter by graduate students seeking a master's degree in real estate development and finance or an MBA with a concentration in real estate (to whom this textbook is specifically targeted), as well as to assist the real estate executive or professional in gaining a more comprehensive understanding of how real estate law impacts their endeavors.

Neither real estate development nor The Development Process is ever about just one thing: *Real estate development is always about 1,000 different things, big and small, occurring simultaneously*; some within the developer's control but many occurring independently of the developer and its project. Part of the allure and the challenge of real estate development – as a process and a profession – is the need to keep a number of balls in the air at the same time, always knowing where each ball is and to where it is heading next. In this respect, real estate development and finance can be one of the most rewarding – and most maddening – professional endeavors one can pursue.

It bears repeating: *Nothing occurs in a vacuum*. It would be hypocritical of this emphasis on the critical importance of context to deny that The Development Process and every real estate development project takes shape within a larger context of time, capital, culture, and societal evolution. Accordingly, this textbook presents three principal themes sprinkled throughout each chapter and threaded among them. That is in addition to providing a pragmatic, transactional approach to teaching real estate law using The Development Process, as I have developed this construct, as a teaching tool and organizational framework for laying out how real estate law can support, impede, and/or otherwise impact the development and financing of real property.

By way of providing larger contexts within which the subject matter of this textbook should be considered, these three broad themes are offered throughout this text:

1. *The emergence of walkable urban places as the predominant real estate development form in the United States in the twenty-first century.* My friend and colleague at The George Washington University School of Business's Center for Real Estate and Urban Analysis (CREUA), Chris Leinberger,[4] through his extensive research and writing through CREUA, has denominated walkable urban places as "WalkUPs". Some of Professor Leinberger's research, and the CREUA reports it has generated, is presented in a very extensive online Appendix to this textbook, which also includes Case Briefs, Case Studies, and illustrative Project Profiles, all created specifically for this textbook.
2. *The cycle of real estate development in the United States for almost 100 years*, from the evolution of streetcar suburbs providing the first "escape" from city life in the United States, to the "white flight" to the suburbs commencing in the 1940s and continuing unabated to the end of the past century. This almost sixty-year exodus from American cities has, in the past fifteen years, shown promising signs of reversal; a return to cities that has been led and will continue to be characterized primarily through the creation of WalkUPs throughout America in the twenty-first century.
3. *The critical role and evolution of cities throughout civilization*, beginning with ancient Greece; how the role of cities in civilization, and their evolution over time, shapes modern American cities in the twenty-first century; and how that evolution has shaped the real estate laws prevailing today.

To this end of presenting real estate law within three, increasingly more-expansive (at least chronologically) contexts, each chapter begins by looking through one of these larger lenses before delving into its technical subject matter. Additionally, wherever appropriate or otherwise instructive, these larger contexts are offered throughout this text as unique points of view on what might otherwise mistakenly be viewed as exclusively contemporary issues.

What this textbook doesn't cover. A number of real estate law topics, as well as several genres of real estate development types, are both well-covered by other textbooks and treatises and, more important, are either incompatible with the transactional theme of this book's use of The Development Process as a pedagogical construct or incongruous with this book's emphasis on the development of walkable urban places (WalkUPs) and the evolution of modern cities. For example, this book does not spend an inordinate amount of time covering, in detail, the different estates in land, for which there are several, worthy treatises on Real Property Law.

Additionally, with the exception of residential development in connection with Mixed-Use projects, this book does not cover garden-variety issues relating to the construction, marketing, purchase and sale, or taxation of single-family homes, the creation of suburban bedroom communities or "subdivisions," or the typical sale-and-purchase transactions ordinarily handled by Realtors© through the Multiple-Listing Service (MLS) (although the section of this book on "Agency," in Chapter 11, does cover Agency Law in the context of Commercial Real Estate Services (CRES) firms, which may have limited utility in the residential sales context as well).

Finally, at least by way of example, this book does not cover greenfield development generally – that is, the acquisition of raw land, generally located in suburban and exurban locations, the process of securing all necessary entitlements, including a plat of subdivision, and bringing in the requisite infrastructure, including roads, sewers, water, and general utilities to serve the site. There are, of course, exceptions to this limitation in the coverage of this textbook, as is the case with the development and financing of greenfield-specific WalkUPs, such as Easton Town Center in Columbus, Ohio, and National Harbor in my childhood hometown of Oxon Hill, Maryland, and greenfield-brownfield WalkUPs, such as Atlantic Station in the Midtown community of Atlanta, Georgia, and The Brewery Blocks in Portland, Oregon's Pearl District, each of which is presented in a Case Study or Project Profile, as the case may be, available online through the companion website for this textbook).

To assist the reader in fully comprehending what's offered between the covers of this textbook, as supplemented by the material on the companion website, two final notes regarding the genesis of this textbook are in order. First, this textbook – having evolved out of a course I specifically created as a means of teaching real estate law to graduate students matriculating through Georgetown University master's in real estate program – sometimes devolves into classroom anecdotes and, consequently, mixes the third-person narrative with an occasional lapse into the first-person voice. With apologies to every English teacher and professor I've ever had, this is sometimes necessary as a way of emphasizing a particular point. I trust it will not be overly distracting or, worse yet, annoying. I'm sorry for this, Mrs. Murphy; I truly am.

Second, I have taught a variety of courses on real estate development, finance, urban regeneration, and housing policy in three different graduate programs and one undergraduate program in the Washington, DC, area since 1999. There is a fundamental truth that is oftentimes not fully absorbed by my students early enough in the course to keep them out of trouble. This is an issue with which, even after more than fifteen years of teaching about real estate development and finance, I find some of my students struggle mightily: *Real estate development and finance is, by its very nature, an extremely detail-oriented endeavor.*

Real estate development and finance is, by its very nature, an extremely detail-oriented endeavor.

As William Poorvu, author of *The Real Estate Game: The Intelligent Guide to Decision Making and Investing*, states so eloquently, yet so directly:

> If you're not interested in paying attention to a plethora of small but important details, in getting your hands dirty, in mixing it up with a wide range of people, then real estate is almost certainly not for you.[5]

Accordingly, and fully buying into the sage guidance architect Robert Venturi offered long ago, this textbook endeavors to be *both* broad-based *and* detail-oriented in its approach. Real estate law, as presented within the framework of The Development Process, is a subject not only made up of a panoply of very specific subjects, but each such specific subject is *extremely detail-oriented in its own right*. As a consequence, the likelihood that the subject of "real estate law" may be narrowly viewed, at least by the uninitiated, as "tedious and boring" is extremely high. Great pains have been taken in the research and writing of this textbook to bring the subject matter of each chapter to life in novel ways, in hopes of fostering both a genuine respect for and interest in real estate law in students and readers alike.

Having said that, and having made the aforementioned considerable effort to back up the promise of excitement by sharing my unbridled enthusiasm for the subject matter throughout this book, I must nevertheless forewarn students and other readers: There is no way around the fact that an incredible amount of minutia is involved in real estate development and finance. Real estate development and finance is, by its very nature, an extremely detail-oriented endeavor.

Resistance is futile.

Peter E. Smirniotopoulos
Adjunct Professor of Real Estate
Department of Finance
School of Business
Funger Hall
The George Washington University
Washington, DC 20052
        and
Adjunct Professor of Real Estate
Finance Unit
School of Business
Enterprise Hall
George Mason University
Fairfax, VA 22030

March 2016

Notes

1. For those uninitiated in the elite real estate development families in the United States who trace their beginnings to New York City, David Tishman's father, Julius, started building in the city in 1898. He was the patriarch of what has grown into one of the greatest real estate enterprises in the country, including Tishman-Speyer and Tishman Realty & Construction, Inc.

2. Shachtman, Tom, *Skyscraper Dreams: The Great Real Estate Dynasties of New York*, Little, Brown & Company, Boston, MA (1991), pg. 189. Emphasis added.

3. To be able to refer to oneself as "a real estate lawyer," someone with a law degree should have five to ten years of involvement in an intensive, transactional real estate practice, being exposed to the full range of legal disciplines covered in this textbook.

4. Christopher B. Leinberger is the Charles Bendit Distinguished Scholar and research professor of urban real estate at the George Washington University School of Business (GWSB) and chairman of GWSB's Center for Real Estate and Urban Analysis.

5. Poorvu, William J., with Jeffrey L. Cruikshank, *The Real Estate Game: The Intelligent Guide to Decision-Making and Investment*, The Free Press, a Division of Simon & Schuster Inc., New York, NY (1999), pg. ix.

Acknowledgments

Warren, Vermont, architect John Connell, a former faculty member in the Yale School of Architecture, is the founder, former director, and long-standing Board member of the Yestermorrow Design/Build School, also in Warren, Vermont. I met John when I took Yestermorrow's two-week Design-Build course in the summer of 1990, the ten-year anniversary of this ground-breaking school. John, along with design/build collaborators and architects L. Macrae "Mac" Rood and Robert S. Bast (now in an architecture practice together), and newly minted architect Kathy Meyer, taught our two-week design/build program: It was one of the most-rewarding educational experiences of my life. In our farewell message at the end of the program, John told our class a story about an old Vermont builder, who was talking with a satisfied client upon completing a home addition. After the client lavished praise on the builder for the quality of his and his crew's work, the builder looked earnestly at his client and said *"Well, if we had to do it again, I'm sure it would be cheaper and take a lot less time."* Such is the ethos of Vermont's candid-to-a-fault, indigenous culture; such is the nature of any complex undertaking, like building a home addition or, in this case, writing one's first textbook.

Having now finished researching and writing *Real Estate Law: Fundamentals for The Development Process*, I can relate to the candid sentiment expressed by that old Vermont builder: If I had to do this over again, I would likely do things differently and certainly take less than eighteen months to do it. Among other things, I might farm out some of the chapters to real estate lawyers whom I know and respect, in specific disciplines, collaborating with them in editing their draft chapter submissions, rather than researching and writing each chapter myself. I also might use my graduate students to undertake legal research on specific issues in real estate development and finance, as well as to prepare detailed case studies, for incorporation into the textbook. I also might employ my legendary powers of persuasion with my many professional, collegial, and personal relationships in the local, regional, and national real estate development companies, to secure substantive contributions to the textbook and its companion website from them.

However, given the evolution of my own pedagogy in teaching graduate programs in real estate development and finance since joining the Johns Hopkins Real Estate Program faculty in 1999, I have developed a unique—some might say idiosyncratic—approach to teaching real estate law to non-lawyer future developers, real estate executives, investors, and lenders. I felt very strongly that this textbook would best reflect my unique approach if I did almost everything myself: So I did. As a consequence, however, the number of people deserving of acknowledgement in the creation of this textbook is much shorter than the book's length, depth, and breadth might imply; however, I am no less indebted to those who have contributed to the completion of this Herculean endeavor.

In the order of the magnitude of the contributions they made to *Real Estate Law: Fundamentals for The Development Process*, I want to acknowledge and thank the following people who made direct contributions of content to the textbook. First, I acknowledge, and express my sincere gratitude to, Nicole Lane, Senior Analyst, Hospitality, in the Washington, D.C. Office of Savills Studley. A former graduate student of mine in Georgetown University's master's of real estate program (MPRE), Nicole served as my Research Assistant in 2014, after I left the Georgetown real estate faculty to become Adjunct Professor of Real Estate in the MBA program at The George Washington University School of Business in Washington, D.C. Nicole made significant contributions to my 2014 research study for the Center for Real Estate and Urban Analysis (CREUA) on conflicts of interest in commercial real estate transactions. My CREUA research study report and executive summary are both included on the companion website for the textbook. Nicole authored the Feature Box, Crowdfunding: The Future of Real Estate Investment, in Chapter 9 – Financing real estate transactions, as well as the Hospitality Case Study: Trump Post Office Pavilion, which appears on the companion website.

Second, and also deserving of acknowledgement and my appreciation are Richard Abramson, Esq. and Robert M. DiPisa, Esq., who co-authored the Shopping Center Case Study, which also appears on the companion website. Richard is a Member, and Co-Chairman of both the Real Estate Department and the Real Estate Special Opportunities Group, at Cole Schotz, P.C. Richard also serves on the Board of the Center for Real Estate and Urban Analysis at The George Washington University School of Business; GW's real estate think tank. Rob DiPisa is a senior associate working with Richard in these practice areas. Cole Schotz is a real estate law firm with offices in the greater New York City area and in New Jersey, and it was Rob with whom I worked most-closely in framing that Case Study.

Third and finally, Dr. Peter Linneman, Professor Emeritus of the real estate program at the University of Pennsylvania's Wharton School of Business, is also deserving of acknowledgement and my thanks for making a direct contribution to the textbook. Peter authored the Feature Box in Chapter 9 – Financing real estate transactions, titled WHAT DETERMINES CAP RATES? Peter is a Principal and Founder of Linneman Associates in Philadelphia, Pennsylvania, and the author of a leading textbook on real estate finance: Real Estate Finance and Investments: Risks and Opportunities. Linneman Associates publishes the highly acclaimed real estate industry newsletter, The Linneman Letter, which may be found at www.linnemanassociates.com. Students and readers alike are encouraged to Follow Peter on Twitter: @P_Linneman.

While not making a direct contribution to the textbook per se, Thomas E. Hogan, Esq., Counsel to the Washington, DC, office of Baker Hostetler, is equally worthy of being singled out for my appreciation and praise for his various contributions to Chapter 3 – Environmental Law. Tom was the very first practitioner to accept my invitation to serve as a Guest Lecturer, on Environmental Law, for my inaugural Foundations of Real Estate Law course in Georgetown's MPRE; he was gracious and generous enough with his time to follow me to GW, when I moved that course to, and adapted it for, the real estate concentration in the University's MBA program. Among other things, Tom created the initial Environmental Law Problem Statement, which I edited and adapted for my Foundations of Real Estate Law MPRE course at Georgetown, and which appears in its modified form as part of Chapter 3. Tom also served as a critical reviewer of an early manuscript draft of Chapter 3, providing substantive and invaluable input into its final version delivered to the publisher.

Similarly, I want to thank the other Guest Lecturers I sought out and secured for the Georgetown MPRE Foundations of Real Estate Law course, each of whom contributed, albeit indirectly, to this volume: Richard J. Melnick, Esq. and Tara K. Gorman, Esq., Shareholders in the national real estate law firm Greenberg Traurig, practicing in the firm's Tyson's Corner and Washington, D.C. Offices, respectively; M. Catherine Puskar, Esq. and G. Evan Pritchard, Esq., Shareholders in the Arlington, Virginia, Office of the D.C. area land use law firm, Walsh, Colucci, Lubeley & Walsh, P.C.; and C. Allen Foster, Esq., a nationally recognized construction claims attorney, formerly with Greenberg Traurig's D.C. Office and now Senior Counsel with the Washington, D.C. Office of Whiteford, Taylor & Preston, one of Maryland's largest law firms. In addition to the specific expertise each Guest Lecturer provided to my Georgetown MPRE students, which in turn influenced specific chapters in the textbook in various ways, the outline used by Rick Mclnick to organize his lecture on the federal income tax impacts on real estate development and finance transactions, provided helpful guidance as I began researching and writing Chapter 8 - Tax considerations of real estate transactions. Rick was also kind enough to follow me to GW, serving again as a Guest Lecturer in my real estate law course, after I joined the Finance Department faculty at GWSB.

Finally, I want to acknowledge the important role Myron P. "Mike" Curzan played in the Georgetown MPRE *Foundations of Real Estate Law* course. Mike, who was the founder and CEO of UniDev, LLC, where I worked with him as the company's Senior Vice President, served as "Kibitzer-in-Chief" for most of the Spring 2013 lectures at Georgetown, providing episodic counterpoint to my unique lecture style; always ready to challenge my students with a penetrating question or regale them with an interesting story (sometimes with the former immediately following the latter). Sadly, Mike passed away March 18, 2016. He would be especially proud to see what the 2013 *Foundations of Real Estate Law* course has become, through this textbook.

Among those of my Georgetown MPRE students from the Spring 2013 Semester, a handfull or two stood out both in their in-class participation as well as the quality and clarity of their written work product. Some of their papers provided useful guidance in the research and writing of the substantive chapters of this textbook but were not excerpted in the writing of the chapters; others warranted having excerpts from their papers included as part of specific sections of the textbook. In those instances in which I chose to quote directly from this collection of student papers, the authors are fully credited, in each instance, in the End Notes for their specific contributions. I would like to recognize each such student, regardless of the extent to which their papers were utilized, by listing each such paper, and its author, below:

- Arnold, Jason, *"Early Contractor Involvement (ECI) In Federal Procurements,"* April 28, 2013 (Georgetown MPRE-601-01, Spring 2013)
- Brennan, Joseph, *"Hardrock Development Corporation's 200 Acre Bay View Development – a New Direction?"* April 3, 2013 (Georgetown MPRE-601-01, Spring 2013)
- Corea, Juan Camilo, *"Federal Statutory and Regulatory Changes in the Post-Great Recession Recovery of the U.S. Real Estate Market: How Expanding Capital Formation While Limiting Debt Availability Will Impact Real Estate Development Projects,"* April 5, 2013 (Georgetown MPRE-601–01, Spring 2013).
- Holiday, Will, *"Kelo's Aftermath and The Impacts on Large-Scale Revitalization Projects,"* dated April 26, 2013 (Georgetown MPRE-610–02, Spring 2013)
- Luke, Ben, *"Unbreak My HART: Honolulu's Rail Line Fiasco and Eminent Domain "* dated February 13, 2013 (Georgetown MPRE-610–02, Spring 2013)
- Martinelli, Christin, *"The PUD Process: Know the Rules, Roles, and the Right People,"* dated April 26, 2013 (Georgetown MPRE-601–01, Spring 2013)
- Kessler, Paul, *"Too Big to Fail: U.S. Financial Regulatory Framework & Real Estate,"* April 23, 2013 (Georgetown MPRE-601–01, Spring 2013)
- Sekander, Yama, *"Problem Statement Paper: When Bad Things Happen to Good People"* dated April 26, 2013 (Georgetown MPRE-610–02, Spring 2013)
- Stover, Danny, *"A 'TIF' Story,"* dated April 13, 2013 (Georgetown MPRE-610–01, Spring 2013)

I would also like to recognize and thank my colleague, friend, and Real Estate Program Chair (i.e., my "boss"), Christopher B. Leinberger, Charles Bendit Distinguished Scholar and Research Professor of Urban Real Estate, and Chair, Center for Real Estate and Urban Analysis (CREUA), The George Washington University School of Business, for generously allowing me to include substantial portions of his WalkUP Wake-Up Call Reports for Atlanta, Boston, and Washington, D.C., respectively, in Chapter 1 of the textbook, and also for allowing me to reproduce each of the aforementioned reports, in their entirety, as part of the companion website materials for the textbook. Also in this regard, I want to thank Christine Patton of Patton Creative, who produced all three WalkUP Wake-Up Call Reports for CREUA, whose assistance was invaluable in providing me access in to the images and graphics presented in those reports, thereby providing what little "eye-candy" this textbook has to offer, almost all of it in presented in Chapter 1.

I also want to thank Ed Needle, Commissioning Editor for Construction and Real Estate, whose initial, misplaced faith in me and my proposal for this textbook has been, hopefully, finally rewarded with its completion. I also want to acknowledge the rest of the Routledge executive editorial team in the Taylor & Francis Group's Oxfordshire, U.K. offices, working with and for Ed, including Matt Turpie, Editorial Assistant for Construction and Real Estate, Helena Hurd, Editor for Development Studies, and Sade Lee, Senior Editorial Assistant for Landscape Architecture and Built Environment Research, each of whom exhibited remarkable patience with me throughout this arduous process, and none of whom ever gave up on me despite numerous twists and turns along the way, most of them self-induced. I also want to thank and acknowledge the production team, particularly Marie Louise Roberts at Apex CoVantage, and Elizabeth Spicer with Taylor & Francis.

Last but certainly not least, I want to thank my lovely wife, Lauren Lynn Smirniotopoulos, who came to my rescue upon the electronic delivery of the galley proof. After researching and writing a textbook on real estate law, the last thing the author of such tome would want to do is read the entire book to prepare it for printing, regardless of how scintillating and engaging that author believes his writing to be. Lauren generously volunteered to proof-read and edit the entire, 520-page galley proof—from cover to cover—saving my sanity or, at least, what little of it there was left given the process of getting that point in the production process. Laruen's diligent and dedicated assistance helped me greatly, making a number of corrections to the galleys. Her three-week commitment also gave me the comfort of knowing that the textbook would not only be eminently readable but also comprehensible to a well-educated audience. Lauren's insights were invaluable, and I will forever be in her debt for this remarkable contribution of her valuable time.

CHAPTER 1

Introduction
Asset classes, property classifications, ownership types, and The Development Process

In the Boston metropolitan area, walkable urbanism adds value. On average, all of the product types studied, including office, retail, hotel, rental apartments, and for-sale housing, have higher values per square foot in walkable urban places than in low-density drivable locations. These price premiums of 20 to 134 percent per square foot are strong indicators of pent-up demand for walkable urbanism.

Walkable urban places are now gaining market share over drivable locations for the first time in at least half a century in hotel, office and rental apartment development. This is good news for people moving to those locations, since households in walkable urban places spent less on housing and transportation (43 percent of total household budget) than households in drivable locations (48 percent), primarily due to lower transportation costs. In addition, property tax revenues generated in walkable urban places are substantially higher than in drivable locations on a per acre basis.

Previous research has demonstrated the correlation between walkable urban places and both the education of the metropolitan work force and the GDP per capita. The current research confirms this finding: for example, since 2000, 70 percent of the population growth of young, educated workers has occurred in the walkable urban places of the Boston region.

Despite the strong momentum toward a more walkable urban future for the region, there are challenges and causes for concern. In many walkable urban places, proximity to transit is a major requirement for households and employers. However, increasing congestion in the core transit system and system fragility in the face of extreme events (such as was experienced during the blizzards of 2015) diminish the value of the system and present substantial risks that may deter investors. As a result, public sector investments in [Metropolitan Boston Transit Authority] capacity and resiliency are prerequisites for the billions of dollars of private sector capital seeking to flow into walkable urban places over the coming decades. Public transit, especially rail transit, activates walkable urbanism's potential for adding real estate value, and as this report demonstrates, that potential is ample. Therefore, policymakers must weigh the costs of funding transit against its power to increase tax revenues. With the right value capture tools in place, the increased value that transit supports could be used to fund at least a portion of the system's maintenance and future expansion.[1]

It is fitting, in beginning this introductory chapter, to **Asset Classes** in general and to asset categories within the real estate asset class in particular, to consider whether the twenty-first century will mark the advent of an entirely new classification of real estate development: walkable urban places or "WalkUPs." Just as a neighborhood retail center is not the same as a regional mall – despite the fact each falls within the "Retail" category of real estate asset classification – it would be equally wrong to characterize a downtown office building with ground-floor retail as the same thing as a Mixed-Use development project, occupying one or more full city blocks, with a broad mix of commercial office, residential (rental and for-sale), retail, entertainment, and hospitality uses. In addition to offering an in-depth exploration of real estate as an asset class, and the many classifications of real estate product within that single asset class, this chapter proposes that the WalkUP should be considered as its own classification, particularly when examined through the prism of The Development Process.

Chapter outline

Real estate as an asset class
Asset classes in real estate
    Commercial office
    Residential
    Retail
    Hospitality
    Entertainment/restaurant
    Mixed-Use
    Walkable urban places (WalkUPs)
    Industrial
    Special-use properties
    Institutional/academic
    Government
    Agricultural
"Ownership" of real estate: estates in real property
Types of estates in land
    1. Fee simple
    2. Fee simple determinable with possibility of reverter
    3. Fee simple subject to or on a condition subsequent
    4. Fee simple subject to a shifting or springing executory interest
    5. Fee tail
    6. Life estate for the life of the tenant
    7. Life estate for the life of one other than the tenant
    8. Life estate created by fee tail after possibility of issue extinct
    9. Dower
    10. Curtesy
    11. Life estate by and during coverture
    12. Estate (or term) for years
    13. Periodic tenancy
    14. Tenancy at will
    15. Tenancy at or by sufferance
"Ownership" of real estate: concurrent estates
    Joint tenancy
    Joint tenancy with right of survivorship (JTWROS)
    Tenancy by the entirety
    Tenancy in common (TIC)
The Development Process
    A brief introduction to "The Development Process"

Chapter introduction

To understand and apply real estate law to The Development Process (see Chapter 2), one must first understand that not all real estate is the same. Merely because land and the "improvements" (e.g., one or more buildings) thereon may be generically described as "real estate" or "real property," they are by no means fungible. Different types of real estate are categorized into separate classes by property type, and such classifications impact their treatment under the law.

Similarly, legal mechanisms reflect different ownership interests in real estate. The legal rights, obligations, and liabilities of owners of interests in real estate depend on how such ownership interests are defined under the law. Consequently, explaining The Development Process as *a framework for learning about and understanding real estate law* requires that the reader first have a baseline understanding of real estate property types, as well as the different ownership interests in real property recognized under the law.

Real estate as an asset class

In order to understand "real estate as an asset class," one must first understand that the classification of investments or investment securities has traditionally recognized only two asset classes – equities (i.e., stocks) and fixed-income securities (i.e., bonds) – with a third class – cash-equivalents – added to the list only in the latter half of the twentieth century.[2] Essentially, "asset class" defines a group of financial instruments with similar characteristics – such as an ownership interest, which entitles the holder to a ratable share of a corporation's assets – that tend to respond in a somewhat similar manner to prevailing market characteristics, and that generally are treated the same under the law. Depending on whom you ask, in addition to what were, by the 1970s, the three main asset classes – equities, fixed-income securities, and cash-equivalents – two or three additional asset classes are recognized by investors and fund managers in the twenty-first century: guaranteed securities, commodities, and real estate.

Asset allocation, as an axiom of investing, has as a principal goal *spreading the risk of loss in a portfolio through diversification*, as well as *optimizing returns from one asset class* at a time when the return performance of another asset class or classes may not be as robust. While not among the troika of primary asset classes – stocks, bonds, and cash-equivalents – real estate is an important asset class for investors. The percentage of an investor's portfolio of assets allocated to real estate will depend on that investor's tolerance for risk (low, moderate, or high). The risk associated with a particular investment in real estate will be balanced against its potential return to the investor through anticipated, periodic cash distributions, projected increases in the value of the original investment, or some combination of the two.

In his master-work on Value Investing, *The Intelligent Investor*, Benjamin Graham, the "Father of Value Investing,"[3] describes the advantages and disadvantages of including real estate assets in an investment portfolio:

> The outright ownership of real estate has long been considered as a sound long-term investment, carrying with it a goodly amount of protection against inflation. Unfortunately, real-estate values are also subject to wide fluctuations; serious errors can be made in location, price paid, etc.; there are

pitfalls in salesmen's wiles. Finally, diversification is not practical for the investor of moderate means, except by various types of participations with others and with the specialized hazards that attach to new flotations – not too different from common-stock ownership. This too is not our field. All we should say to the investor is, "Be sure it's yours before you go into it."[4]

Roy Hilton March, a director of Real Estate Roundtable and chief executive officer of Eastdil Secured LLC, a subsidiary of Wells Fargo & Company, offers this perspective of the emergence of real estate as a separate asset class.

With the advent of Modern Portfolio Theory in the 1950s and its subsequent adoption by institutional investors in the 1960s to 1980s, commercial real estate went from cottage industry to bona fide asset class. But the obstacles to its ownership (including capital intensity, lack of transparency, operational requirements, geographic specificity and illiquidity) made real estate largely inaccessible to all but the largest investors. Twenty years ago, a remarkable transformation occurred: liquidity in real estate brought on by the rise of public REITs, CMBS, real estate private equity funds and the abundance of capital sources. Today, real estate competes directly with stocks, bonds, currencies, commodities and other financial assets. The evolution of the sector occurred much as evolution does in nature: life-threatening conditions forced inhabitants to adapt or perish and introduced new entrants to the ecosystem. As Charles Darwin famously observed, "It is not the strongest of the species that survives, nor the most intelligent . . . it is the one that is most adaptable to change." The creative destruction of the late 1980s and early 1990s forged a new species of real estate industry – more resilient than its ancestors but, as recent years attest, still vulnerable to threats old and new. Understanding the factors that catalyzed the industry's transformation, and the lessons learned along the way, is the key to preparing for the many exciting challenges and opportunities that lie ahead.[5]

Additionally, a varying number of liabilities and duties arise during The Development Process, as well as in the ownership and management of operating properties, each with its own peculiar nature, depending on the category of property in the real estate asset class. Consequently, certain direct investments in real estate may entail a greater amount of risk than what is most commonly associated with evaluating an asset class in order to assess properly the risk/reward balance.

Generally speaking, in investment analysis, the risk of loss of the entire investment is the worst-case risk scenario. However, depending on how they are structured, direct investments in real estate – as contrasted with indirect investments through vehicles such as the purchase of shares in a real estate investment trust or REIT (see Chapter 9) – may result in the loss of 100% of the investment *and also impose* additional monetary liabilities on the investor. (See Chapters 3 and 7.)

Finally, depending on the structure of the particular investment, interests in real estate may generate losses the investor may use to offset income and gains from other investments in a portfolio. Such "tax benefits" from real estate investments are dictated largely by the Internal Revenue Code of 1986, 26 C.F.R. § 1, et. seq. and, to a lesser extent, by applicable state laws. Federal tax rules governing the distribution and availability of losses to owners of certain interests in real estate have changed dramatically over the years, owing to a number of significant tax reform laws amending the Internal Revenue Code, beginning with the Economic Recovery Tax Act of 1981 (ERTA Public Law 97–34), and are covered extensively in Chapters 8 and 9. Nonetheless, there are still investment vehicles in real estate assets, such as various forms of federal tax credits, which allow for sheltering of income from other investments.

The need to differentiate specific types of real property into categories is not merely limited to an investor's perspective on real estate as an asset class. Just as different asset classes reflect "different risk and return investment characteristics," different types of real property within the real estate asset class not only present similar differentials in risk and return because of the very nature of the product type and use, respectively, but the trajectory of The Development Process is often very different. A number of property classifications exist within the real estate asset class. Each property classification is predicated on particular aspects in the character and use of real property that differentiate its treatment *under the law*.

For example, typical uses for and users of properties falling within the **Commercial Office** property classification are very different from typical uses for and users of properties in the Industrial property classification. These different uses and users present substantively different legal issues. Similarly, as a function of zoning and land use laws (see Chapter 5), properties classified as Commercial Office are generally not co-located with properties included in the Industrial asset class, presenting further differences in their treatment under the law.

Interesting, with the importance of property classifications being beyond peradventure, there is no generally accepted, industry standard listing of property classifications or definitions for such classifications. Some sources advocate a very simple, three-part system of categorization: Commercial (i.e., all income-producing uses other than Industrial); Industrial; and Residential. However, this approach may cause conflicts in how certain real estate assets are classified. Should multifamily rental housing (i.e., rental apartments), as contrasted with multifamily ownership units (i.e., condominium buildings) be included under Commercial because they are "income-producing," or should they be included under Residential because of their underlying use and categorization for zoning and land use purposes?

Other sources have embraced a more fine-grained approach, which is much more instructive in learning and understanding the legal framework impacting each. Accordingly, based on real property classifications from various sources, including interpolating from various zoning and land use codes and reviewing definitions used by REITs and other investment vehicles focused on investing in only specified property types, a comprehensive list can be ascertained, as follows:

Asset classes in real estate

Commercial office
Residential
Retail
Hospitality
Entertainment/restaurant
Mixed-Use
Walkable urban places (WalkUPs)
Industrial
Special-use properties
Institutional/academic
Government
Agricultural

The Mixed-Use category is generally the most complicated property type, and it involves the greatest intensity of uses and the greatest diversity of potential users. It is listed after the listing of the other urban property types because the mix of uses in a particular project may involve some permutation of all of the listed uses preceding it. In other words, conventional wisdom aside, Mixed-Use properties are not limited to Commercial Office, Retail, and Residential. In order for students and readers to fully understand the legal issues peculiar to Mixed-Use properties, they need to first understand the legal issues specific to each of the property types comprising the "mix of uses" in each Mixed-Use property.

However, depending on prevailing zoning and land use codes, and the ability of a developer to modify the same through Planned Unit Developments (PUDs), updated master plans, and other land use devices and frameworks facilitating innovative combinations of property types, the Mixed-Use category may include various combinations of the other uses, and serve diverse types of users. For example, an Academic/Healthcare/Industrial mix of uses created for the purpose of facilitating academic and medical research and medical diagnosis and treatment might be made possible through the zoning and land use process, even though at the outset of that process even light industrial uses are strictly prohibited.

Finally, and as suggested at the outset of this introductory chapter to The Development Process, following detailed descriptions of the real estate classifications outlined earlier, this chapter offers WalkUPs and its seven subcategories as a much more fine-grained analysis of the Mixed-Use classification:

- Downtown
- Downtown adjacent
- Urban commercial
- Urban university
- Suburban town center
- Strip commercial redevelopment
- Greenfield

What is most important to understand at this very nascent stage of presenting The Development Process is that different property types contemplate different uses, intensities of uses, and users, and that each of these things is generally subject to its own regulating framework dictating the permissibility, form, and operation of each specific property type. Once that's well understood, modifications to the existing zoning and land use framework to permit innovative combinations of property types become better grasped and, more important, possible. The concepts of "different uses, intensities of uses, and users" will be explored more fully in Chapters 4 and 5.

Accordingly, as a prefatory matter, each real estate property classification, described briefly later, provides the reader with a basic understanding of the breadth of the real estate asset class. As suggested earlier, real estate is primarily defined by its usage or proposed usage. Three simple, yet somewhat broad categories for real estate are widely accepted:

1. Residential
2. Commercial
3. Agricultural

However, as also suggested earlier, real estate is much more nuanced than that; the utility of such simple categorization quickly breaks down in the contexts of conceiving, developing, financing, constructing, operating, and buying and selling real property building types for purposes of understanding real estate law.

Additionally, it is important to note that the components of real estate *as an asset class* may also be categorized based on other characteristics of real property, including:

- Geographic location
- Broadly defined risk and return parameters
- Susceptibility to particular types of risk
- Manner/method by which cash flow and value are generated
- Regulatory framework within which it is developed and operated

By way of example, geographic location may be an important characteristic for investors in real estate assets. A portfolio of real estate assets may be composed exclusively of a particular use type – say, Hospitality – because of the investor's understanding and acceptance of the general risk and return profile of that property type. However, despite making all of its investments in Hospitality properties, such a limited focus on a single property type may be somewhat ameliorated through geographical diversity among the properties purchased. Through the geographic distribution of its assets, such a portfolio may achieve a hedge against specific market downturns.

Similarly, the investment focus of another portfolio may be on a mix of income-producing properties that work synergistically when located in "24/7 markets." Since a limited number of such 24/7 markets exists in the United States, with New York City the prime example, such a portfolio would also be driven by the geographic locations of the properties purchased.

The main point here is that the traditional property characteristics used to identify, categorize, and define different real estate assets is not, by any means, the only method for categorizing real property.

For purposes of this introduction, however, the following, commonly used, functional categories for organizing and understanding the components of the **Real Estate Asset Class** will be used throughout this book and are described next:

Commercial Office (Figure 1.1). The Commercial Office classification is, at first blush, very straightforward: any improvements to real property (i.e., "building or buildings") dedicated

Figure 1.1 Commercial office space and Virginia Tech Research Center on N. Glebe Road in Ballston Area, Arlington, VA

to "general office use." Depending on local land use and zoning laws and regulations, however, "general office use" varies from jurisdiction to jurisdiction. For example, a daycare facility or early childhood development center in the ground floor of a downtown office building may or may not be a by-right use in a Commercial Office property, requiring additional approvals other than a **Certificate of Occupancy** or **C of O** as a condition precedent to such uses being permitted. Similarly, many ground-floor retail uses – such as convenience stores, sandwich shops, sit-down restaurants, office supply stores, and apparel retailers – are the rule rather than the exception in downtown office buildings, although additional legal hurdles may need to be overcome prior to such occupancies and uses being permitted. However, their presence does not change the fundamental use and, therefore, classification, of the building as Commercial Office.

The Commercial Office classification may be further defined, however, based on the legal basis for its occupancy between tenants (i.e., renters) and owners.

Rental. The vast majority of Commercial Office properties make their premises available for occupancy by Tenants through a Lease or Lease Agreement with the **Landlord**. The legal relationships between Tenants and Landlords are addressed in detail in Chapter 11. For the sake of simplicity, the terms "Commercial Office" and "Commercial Office Building," whenever used in this book, mean a rental building.

Ownership. While making up a very small percentage of the total Commercial Office classification, the Office Condominium is a widely recognized form of ownership for Commercial Office properties. Office Condominiums are much more prevalent in suburban contexts than in urban office cores, and may be structured as such either with the intent of attracting Owner-Occupants or merely as a different way of structuring an investment property that is nonetheless intended to serve as a Commercial Rental property. In other words, each office condominium unit will be rented out by the Unit Owner to a Tenant. In the 1980s, many medical office buildings were developed in suburban markets to facilitate medical practices, the principals in which wanted to own their offices and rent them to their medical practices. These arrangements not only eliminated the prospects of the medical practices not being able to renew a lease on favorable terms down the road, but also were structured in a manner that allowed the investors in these medical office buildings (i.e., the principals in the medical practice) substantial deductions to offset the income they earned from their medical practices, as well as other income. In other words, these are perhaps primarily "tax shelter" transactions, providing the investors/occupants with multiple benefits: the security of permanent office space; an income stream from the rental; and depreciation and interest deductions to offset income from their professional practices. The enactment of the Tax Reform Act of 1986 ushered in a number of rules limiting the use of tax shelters, including the "Passive Activity Loss Rules," discussed in great length in Chapter 8. The Office Condominium functions completely differently from the Commercial Office because of the vastly different ownership regimes of the two.

Residential (Figures 1.2 and 1.3). The federal government has extensive involvement in various programs involving "housing." These include but are not limited to the regulation of various types of financial institutions making housing-related loans, the **U.S. Department of Housing and Urban Development (HUD)**, the creation of government-sponsored entities (**GSEs**) such as **Fannie Mae** and **Freddie Mac**, and numerous provisions in the **Internal Revenue Code** relating to housing (including but not limited to the **mortgage interest deduction** and the **low-income housing tax credit program** or "**LIHTC**"). Consequently, federal statutes and regulations contain a variety of definitions relating to the Residential property classification.

Figure 1.2 Inman Park rowhouses in Atlanta, GA

For example, U.S. Code §1464(c)(6)(A) provides, regarding the making of loans by federal savings banks, the following definition:

(A) Residential property

The terms "residential real property" or "residential real estate" mean leaseholds, homes (including condominiums and co-operatives, except that in connection with loans on individual cooperative units, such loans shall be adequately secured as defined by the Director), and combinations of homes or dwelling units and business property, involving only minor or incidental business use, or property to be improved by construction of such structures.

The far simpler and arguably more functional definition of Residential property is *any place where people live* other than on a very temporary or interim basis, so as to exclude, by intention, lodging properties (see **Hospitality** classification), campgrounds, homeless shelters, jails and prisons, and the like.

As with the Commercial Office classification, the Residential property classification may be further subdivided by **Tenure Type**; that is, ownership versus rental.

Rental: It is worth noting that the Residential Rental Property sub-classification of the real estate asset class presents a definitional morass. As alluded to early on in this section on definitions, in rejecting the overly simplistic, three-category subdivision of the real estate asset class into Commercial, Residential, and Industrial categories, multifamily rental property straddles both the Commercial and Residential categories:

Should multifamily rental housing (i.e., rental apartments), as contrasted with multifamily ownership units (i.e., condominium buildings) be included under Commercial because they are "income-

Figure 1.3A Single-family detached (SFD) home at University Glen, Ventura County, CA, developed by UniDev, LLC for California State University, Channel Islands

Figure 1.3B Semi-attached home at University Glen, Ventura County, CA, developed by UniDev, LLC for California State University, Channel Islands

Figure 1.3C Townhomes (attached single-family) at University Glen, Ventura County, CA, developed by UniDev, LLC for California State University, Channel Islands

Figure 1.3D Multifamily (MF) homes at University Glen, Ventura County, CA, developed by UniDev, LLC for California State University, Channel Islands

producing," or should they be included under Residential because of their underlying use and categorization for zoning and land use purposes?

This dilemma is further compounded by the fact that the term "multifamily housing" is universally intended to be synonymous with "rental housing," despite the fact that multifamily housing can be organized and owned as a single building devoted to residential rentals, as a condominium, where individual residential units are independently owned, separate and apart from the Common Elements of the building or property, and cooperatives, where the Owner-Occupants own "interests" in the property entitling them to certain benefits in the occupancy of their respective residential units. Yet multifamily housing excludes a variety of Residential Rental property types, including renter-occupied, single-family detached structures and student housing. Consequently, it is very important to be able to separate out from the legal definitions of various classifications of the real estate asset class the built form and focus more on the use and occupancy.

Having said all that, the definition of the Residential Rental property sub-classification of Residential property is very similar to the definition of the sub-classification Commercial Office under the Commercial property classification: it is characterized by the use and occupancy of a "**Premises**," owned by a Landlord, for a limited duration by a Tenant, generally through a Lease or Lease Agreement, but not necessarily. In this regard, many states have adopted, in one form or another, the Residential Landlord and Tenant Act (RLTA), a model code intended to govern the relationships between residential landlords and their tenants in the absence of a written and signed lease (see, e.g., Virginia Residential Landlord and Tenant Act, Effective July 1, 2011, Va. Code Annotated § 55–248.2. through 55–248.40.) Not surprising, no analog to the RLTA exists in the Commercial Office context.

Ownership. Although the rate of owner-occupied versus renter-occupied housing (aka the "homeownership rate") has been around 67% for an extended period of time – starting in 1999 and reaching just more than 69% in 2005 – it dropped to 63.7% in the first quarter of 2015. As suggested in the discussion of rental housing, such ownership may take a variety of forms, including what is referred to as "fee simple ownership" of a single-family detached home, condominium ownership, and ownership of an "interest" in a cooperative. All of the various ownership forms are discussed in greater detail in the section Tenure Types in Real Estate.

Retail (Figures 1.4A, B, C). Any commercially zoned property engaged in the marketing and selling of consumer goods and services may be considered a Retail Property. This runs the gamut from a stand-alone retail business, such as a 7-Eleven, to community shopping centers to regional mega-malls, and everything in between. Interesting, the advent and proliferation of online marketing and sales have eliminated some of the brick-and-mortar retail locations in favor of an online presence plus a distribution network facilitating the execution of sales transacted completely over the Internet. However, few brick-and-mortar retailers are willing to abandon their physical locations in strong retail markets in favor of an online-only presence, and some online retailers, such as Levenger, have gone from online only to having both physical locations and a virtual, online presence. In addition to the impact such trends have on real estate development nationally, they also change the fundamental property categories on which certain retail businesses rely, placing increased emphasis on Industrial Properties (see later), particularly warehouse and distribution facilities for online retailers endeavoring to provide an ever-shorter period of time from mouse click to delivery.

Hospitality (Figures 1.5A, B). The hospitality industry is not the same as "the hotel industry." It is comprised of every business sector relating to (i) travel and (ii) the activities in which travelers engage on their way to, while at, and on their way from their destination. Accordingly, the hospitality industry includes the hotel industry, which is itself comprised of a variety of players, from the international lodging companies like Marriott and Hilton, to the boutique hotel groups, to the interval-ownership industry (formerly known as "time-sharing"), to one-off accommodations including niche hotels and bed-and-breakfasts, to the emergence of new lodging options and new players in the sector through their participation in The Sharing Economy, such as Airbnb.[6] However, the hospitality industry includes the airline industry, which requires airports and a network of transportation connections to and from airports to function; public and private transportation networks, including taxi cab companies and their emergent competitors – again a function of The Sharing Economy – such as Uber and Lyft; restaurants catering to business and resort travelers; the gaming industry, which creates entire destinations for business and pleasure travel alike; and a network of service providers, primarily driven by online operators, who assist travelers in knitting together all of the components for a successful or enjoyable (or both) trip.

Figure 1.4A Street-level retail at M St. in Georgetown, Washington, DC

Figure 1.4B Street-level retail at Atlantic Station, Atlanta, GA

Figure 1.4C Street-level retail in Back Bay, Boston, MA

Figure 1.5A Royal Palm Hotel in South Beach, Miami, FL

Figure 1.5B Waldorf-Astoria Hotel in New York, NY

Entertainment/Restaurant (Figure 1.6A, B). Although arguably a sub-classification of Retail Properties, Mixed-Use Properties (discussed later), or both, the Entertainment/Restaurant classification in the real estate asset class is warranted in the context of real estate law because the intensity of use is so much greater and, as a consequence, involves additional legal hurdles in securing local land use and zoning approvals, as well as additional regulatory compliance in their operation. This classification encompasses everything from the free-standing, fast food restaurant with drive-through service, to white-tablecloth dining establishments, to night clubs offering food, dancing, and music, to stand-alone concert venues. The intensity of the use, in each case, is likely to be addressed in a variety of legal requirements, ranging from where they may be located to specific limitations on their operations.

Figure 1.6A The Bond 45 restaurant, one of a number of signature restaurants at National Harbor, Oxon Hill, MD

Figure 1.6B Regal Cinema 16, Atlantic Station, Atlanta, GA

Mixed-Use (Figure 1.7A, B). Mixed-Use Properties is a classification that has gained in importance and complexity over the past thirty years or so, with interest in this property classification increasing exponentially over the past ten years. Whereas the first fifty years of real estate development in the United States following World War II focused on suburban and exurban development, starting in the 1980s urban planning and real estate development

Figure 1.7A Upstairs Bethesda Row, retail-lines passage between Bethesda Avenue and Elm Street at Federal Realty's Bethesda Row

Figure 1.7B Gallery Place and Chinatown Friendship Gate, anchoring the Downtown DC Business Improvement District (DCBID)

began to refocus attention on the country's urban cores. Cities had lost substantial populations of both residents and daytime workers to the suburbs, beginning with the "white flight" from city centers in the 1950s, spawning the precipitous growth of suburbs throughout the United States. In the auto-dominated world of the suburbs, each use could be, and usually was, segregated: bedroom communities here; strip malls and community shopping centers over there; office parks over there; and so on and so forth. The birth of the national interstate highway system; new methods for constructing relatively inexpensive single-family detached houses (e.g., the shift away from horsehair plaster applied by craftsmen, to the new invention known then as "sheetrock"); low-interest-rate mortgages made available to G.I.s returning home from the war; these things all contributed to an explosion in bedroom communities away from cities, which remained – for a time, anyway – the employment centers of their respective regions. Once a critical mass of workers had relocated to the pristine, new suburbs, employers and services followed.

While the reasons are not particularly germane to the subject of real estate law, in the early 1980s urban theorists and planners started to focus on revitalizing cities, some of which had been left moribund by the mass exodus to the suburbs but also by fundamental, structural changes in the U.S. economy (particularly away from manufacturing and toward services and, more recently, the advent of "the Knowledge Economy"). At the same time, the inherent disconnectedness of suburban development, where different uses had to be located away from each other and all required a passenger vehicle to patronize or participate in, drove a desire among some suburban residents to relocate to a place where different life functions (what's commonly today referred to as "live/work/play," "live/learn/work/play," and similar permutations and extrapolations), could be co-located. Because this resurgence in interest in "living downtown" required an intensity of uses co-located such that they were all accessible by foot or public transit, most city zoning codes were ill-equipped to facilitate the development of Mixed-Use Property types for which there was increasing demand among developers and their customers.

In 2006, as part of the 2006 Conference on Mixed-Use Development, four well-established, widely recognized real estate industry groups – the International Council of Shopping Centers, Inc. (ICSC), the National Association of Industrial and Office Properties (NAIOP), the Building Owners and Managers Association International (BOMA), and the National Multi Housing Council (NMHC), each with its own peculiar interest in this property category on behalf of its membership – unveiled a joint definition of "Mixed-Use Property"[7]:

> Mixed-Use is quickly establishing itself as a unique type of development and a trend that is revolutionizing the real estate landscape. Combining the elements of residential, retail, office and entertainment, Mixed-Use projects are being developed in both urban and suburban markets and on a global scale. But what constitutes a "mixed-use development" project in today's development environment?
>
> In an effort to formulate an industry-wide definition, the International Council of Shopping Centers, Inc. (ICSC), the National Association of Industrial and Office Properties (NAIOP), the Building Owners and Managers Association International (BOMA), and the National Multi Housing Council (NMHC) collaborated on an ambitious cross-organizational member survey to identify the characteristics among mixed-use developments. The survey was conducted from July 11, 2006 through August 3, 2006 and featured 1,004 respondents. Though mixed-use is commonly defined as a project that features the mixing of at least three significant revenue-producing uses, i.e. retail, residential and commercial, today the definition represents a collection of components working together simultaneously – and the project may include a non-revenue-producing – though traffic-generating –

element. Thus, as a result of the survey, the new working definition for mixed-use development for these four associations is:

> A mixed-use development is a real estate project with planned integration of some combination of retail, office, residential, hotel, recreation or other functions. It is pedestrian-oriented and contains elements of a live-work-play environment. It maximizes space usage, has amenities and architectural expression and tends to mitigate traffic and sprawl.

Today, a Mixed-Use Property may run the gamut from a Commercial Office property with ground-floor Retail and Entertainment/Restaurant uses to town centers that accommodate and facilitate interaction among Residential (both Ownership and Rental), Commercial Office (again, both rental and ownership), and Retail, Entertainment/Restaurant uses, to industry-specific projects, such as properties combining commercial office, residential, retail, restaurant, and entertainment uses in combination with research, testing, and production facilities promoting medical technology and treatment breakthroughs. New categories of land use and zoning statutes and regulations have been promulgated and adopted to facilitate the creation of Mixed-Use Properties, and this trend may be reasonably expected to continue for the foreseeable future. And while the ownership of various real property categories of real estate assets may be disparate, the management of Mixed-Use Properties generally cannot be accomplished efficiently and effectively through the segregated management of such uses, such that the initial land developer of such projects may also be expected to own and operate one or more specific uses, as well as to provide overall property management, raising a host of legal issues not presented by any other single property category discussed herein.

As suggested in the introduction to this chapter, walkable urban places, or WalkUPs, offer a much more fine-grained understanding of the "Mixed-Use" classification. Accordingly, following is a general description of the WalkUPs real estate classification, along with detailed descriptions of the seven subcategories of WalkUPs. An argument can be made that these seven subcategories of WalkUPs could be added as subcategories of the "Mixed-Use" real estate classification. Alternatively, WalkUPs might be offered as a separate category altogether, differentiating them from the catch-all of Mixed-Use.

Walkable urban places or "WalkUPs" are best understood in the context of the predominant development pattern in the United States in the second half of the twentieth century: suburban Euclidian development, aka "suburban sprawl."

> Walkable urban development calls for dramatically different approaches to urban design and planning, regulation, financing and construction. Most importantly, it also requires the introduction of a new industry: place management. This new field develops the strategy and provides the day-to-day management for walkable urban places (referred to in shorthand as WalkUPs), creating a distinctive "could only be here" place in which investors and residents seem willing to invest for the long term.
>
> This new research defines – for the first time – where most existing WalkUPs are in the metropolitan D.C. region. It shows specific locations, the physical size of the places, the product mix, the transportation options and so forth.[8]

In addition to the functional importance of Mixed-Use Properties as a real estate asset class category, Mixed-Use projects and, more particularly, WalkUPs comprise an ever-larger proportion of total real estate development and real estate asset value in the United States, as demonstrated in **Figure 1.8**.

> During the second half of the 20th century, the dominant development model has been the familiar drivable suburban approach. Most real estate developers and investors, government regulators and financiers have come to understand this model extremely well, turning it into a successful development formula and economic driver.
>
> However, starting in the mid-1990s, the pendulum has been slowly moving back toward building WalkUPs, which was the approach embraced by the Washington, D.C., metro area and virtually every other metropolitan area prior to World War II. In recent years, real estate developers, investors, government regulators and financiers in the metropolitan D.C. area have become quite comfortable developing and managing walkable urban projects – distinguishing the nation's capital region from most other metro areas that have not yet recognized the importance of WalkUPs in their future development.
>
> In fact, metropolitan Washington, D.C., has emerged as the model for how the nation should develop the built environment, according to a 2007 Brookings Institution study, as will be expanded on in this report.[9]

In order to better understand this property classification of WalkUPs, as well as the seven sub-classifications, it is instructive to grasp some of the methodology behind the WalkUPs classification and its sub-classifications. The creation or designation of a separate property category for "walkable urban places" was first posited by Professor Leinberger, along with his coauthor, Mariela Alfonzo, in their Brookings Institution report *Walk this Way: The Economic Promise of Walkable Places in Metropolitan Washington, D.C.*[10] Regional and local serving places play complementary but distinct roles within the metropolitan economy. The former,

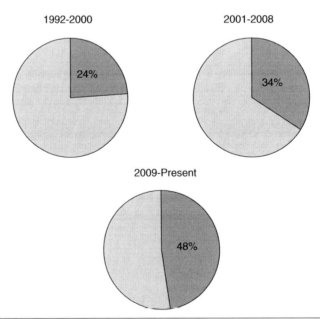

Figure 1.8 Share of commercial real estate investments allocated to WalkUPs during the past three real estate cycles: 1992–2000, 2001–2008, and 2009–present

with a higher concentration of jobs that generate income from outside the region, and regional-serving jobs (e.g., lawyers, bankers, hospital workers), act as significant economic engines for the region, while the latter, with a larger proportion of local-serving jobs (teachers, pharmacists, dentists), may support a region's day-to-day activities and contribute to overall quality of life. Classifying places based on their roles within the metropolitan region may help the private and public real estate industry and urban planners tailor their investment, lending, policy, planning, and design intervention strategies based on their needs and interests.

There is a lack of consensus, however, regarding what indicators – and at what thresholds – best serve to delineate between regional- and local-serving places. Conceptually, regional-serving places may contain one or more of the following: a significant amount of retail with a large catchment area; regional employment centers; industrial hubs; high concentrations of government activity; higher education uses; medical institutions; cultural/sport/recreational activities; civic uses; transportation hubs; or entertainment (e.g. theaters, movie theaters) uses. Local-serving places tend to contain a higher percentage of residential uses than do regional-serving places; [they] primarily have neighborhood-oriented retail uses and services such as grocery stores and medical offices; and have primary and secondary educational uses, post offices, libraries and other neighborhood supporting services.

Building on the literature and findings from the advisory panels, we established a working definition for regional-serving places: A place that is a key economic contributor to a metropolitan area in terms of employment, entertainment, retail, education, or other institutional production, and has reached critical mass (or the point at which a place is self-sustaining and does not need government subsidies for subsequent development).

Based on that, we developed a classification system for regional- and local-serving places. First, we classified a place as regional serving based on the presence of any of the following non-commercial uses: educational (e.g. Georgetown University), regional entertainment (e.g. Nationals Ballpark), or civic use (e.g. Superior Court of D.C.). Next, we considered the concentration of commercial uses. We identified two tiers of regional-serving places based on the total rentable building area for both office and retail.[32] Specifically, we found the tipping point for office and retail concentrations at which a statistically significant difference in office rents and retail sales, respectively, was observed as these are considered to be important indicators of real estate and economic performance.[33]

32. The differences between these categories are statistically significant. For example, tier one regional-serving office places are significantly different from tier two regional-serving office places with respect to office rents; tier one regional-serving office places are also significantly different from local-serving places. Tier 1 regional-serving retail places are significantly different from tier two regional-serving retail places with respect to retail revenues.

33. Throughout this study, the term statistically significant refers to a finding that has less than a 5 percent probability of being attributed to chance. In other words, the finding is not random.[11]

- Downtown (See **Figure 1.9** for Washington, DC's downtown product mix.)

Downtown WalkUPs are the original downtown sections off a metro area's principal city. Downtown WalkUPs are dominated by office space (83 percent of total square footage) and have modest though fast-growing residential (6 percent). Only one percent of the space is occupied by retail, although one-of-a-kind regional assets (convention center, Verizon Center, museums, etc.) account for 10 percent of all space.[12]

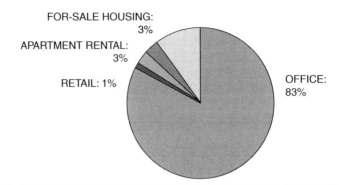

Product Mix: Downtown
Average % of Total Square Footage

FOR-SALE HOUSING: 3%

APARTMENT RENTAL: 3%

RETAIL: 1%

OFFICE: 83%

Figure 1.9 Distribution of total square feet of commercial space in Washington, DC's "Downtown" WalkUPs among office, for-sale housing, rental housing, and retail uses

- **Downtown Adjacent** (See **Figure 1.10** for Washington, DC's downtown adjacent product mix.)
  Immediately adjacent to downtown, these WalkUPs usually have a lower density than downtown and possess unique character.

  Downtown Adjacent WalkUPs have a substantial amount of office space (58 percent), but they also have significant residential (24 percent) and four times the relative retail of downtown (4 percent). The result is generally a lively, 24-hour environment.[13]

Product Mix: Downtown-Adjacent
Average % of Total Square Footage

FOR-SALE HOUSING: 16%

APARTMENT RENTAL: 8%

RETAIL: 4%

OFFICE: 58%

Figure 1.10 Distribution of total square feet of commercial space in Washington, DC's "Downtown-Adjacent" WalkUPs among office, for-sale housing, rental housing, and retail uses

- **Urban Commercial** (See **Figure 1.11** for Washington, DC's urban commercial product mix.)

  Historically local-serving neighborhood commercial, these places declined after World War II but, in recent years, have found a new economic role.

  Urban Commercial WalkUPs in metro D.C. are dominated by residential property (56 percent) and are marked by more retail (15 percent) and less office space (20 percent)

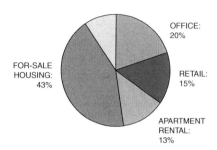

Product Mix: Urban Commercial
Average % of Total Square Footage

OFFICE: 20%
FOR-SALE HOUSING: 43%
RETAIL: 15%
APARTMENT RENTAL: 13%

Figure 1.11 Distribution of total square feet of commercial space in Washington, DC's "Urban-Commercial Mix" WalkUPs among office, for-sale housing, rental housing, and retail uses

than downtown or downtown adjacent. The retail in urban commercial WalkUPs is generally characterized as urban entertainment, such as restaurants and nightclubs, as well as boutique shops and furniture and home décor stores.[14]

- **Urban University** (See **Figure 1.12** for Boston's urban university product mix.)

In these WalkUPs, universities and other institutional owners, such as medical facilities or government research centers, are the dominant landowners. These landowners gauge the "success" of their development not in terms of rent they may be able to collect, but in their ability to attract talent (professors, students, administrators, etc.).

The presence of these anchor institutions can also present opportunities for Innovation Districts to develop. As mentioned earlier, MIT/Kendall Square is one of the country's

Product Mix: Urban University
Average % of Total Square Footage

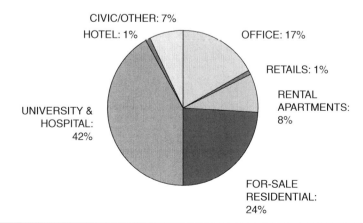

CIVIC/OTHER: 7%
HOTEL: 1%
OFFICE: 17%
RETAILS: 1%
RENTAL APARTMENTS: 8%
UNIVERSITY & HOSPITAL: 42%
FOR-SALE RESIDENTIAL: 24%

Figure 1.12 Distribution of total square feet of commercial space in Boston's "Urban University" WalkUPs among office, for-sale housing, rental housing, and retail uses

leading examples of an Innovation District. University space (classrooms, laboratories, hospitals, general office, and dorms) is the largest use, followed by off-campus housing, both rental and for-sale. Office space represents 17 percent, showing the commercialization of university research and desire to be near the university campus. Retail is very small (one percent), which is an opportunity; only Harvard Square has created a critical mass of retail in this type of WalkUP.[15]

- **Suburban Town Center** (See **Figure 1.13** for Washington, DC's suburban town center product mix.)
  Typical Suburban Town Centers are eighteenth- or nineteenth-century towns that were swept up in the sprawl of the metropolitan area after World War II. Following decades of decline, they have found a new economic role.

  Suburban Town Centers have relatively less office space than in downtowns or downtown adjacent areas (although offices still occupy 46 percent of all space), more residential (30 percent) and significantly more retail (16 percent).[16]

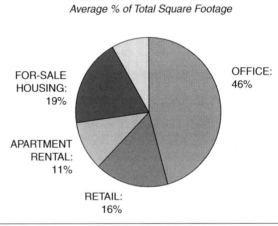

Product Mix: Suburban Town Center
Average % of Total Square Footage

FOR-SALE HOUSING: 19%

OFFICE: 46%

APARTMENT RENTAL: 11%

RETAIL: 16%

Figure 1.13 Distribution of total square feet of commercial space in Washington, DC's "Suburban Town Center" WalkUPs among office, for-sale housing, rental housing, and retail uses

- **Strip Commercial Redevelopment** (See **Figure 1.14** for Washington, DC's strip commercial redevelopment product mix.)

  These WalkUPs were mid-to-late twentieth-century strip commercial that became obsolete and then evolved into higher density development.

  Somewhat similar to suburban town centers, Strip Commercial Redevelopment WalkUPs have relatively less office space than in downtowns or downtown adjacent areas (46 percent of all space), more residential (31 percent), and significantly more retail (16 percent). Many of these WalkUPs include regional malls that have been or will be urbanized. This type of WalkUP will be the major focus of walkable urban development over the next generation.[17]

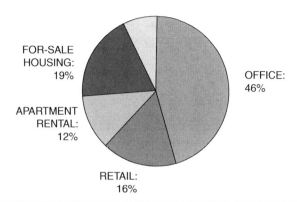

Product Mix: Strip Commercial Redevelopment
Average % of Total Square Footage

FOR-SALE HOUSING: 19%

OFFICE: 46%

APARTMENT RENTAL: 12%

RETAIL: 16%

Figure 1.14 Distribution of total square feet of commercial space in Washington, DC's "Strip Commercial" WalkUPs among office, for-sale housing, rental housing, and retail uses

- **Greenfield** (See **Figure 1.15** for Washington, DC's greenfield product mix.)

Often criticized as being sterile, Greenfield WalkUPs are situated where major investment has quickly turned formerly undeveloped land into a walkable urban place.

Greenfield WalkUPs have among the most balanced product mix. Office (45 percent) is in balance with rental and for-sale residential (33 percent), while retail (6 percent) tends to be urban entertainment and boutiques. The large upfront capital costs required for Greenfield WalkUPs and high market risk mean few will probably be attempted in the next generation.[18]

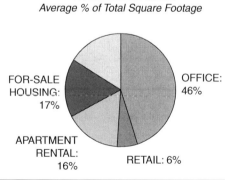

Product Mix: Greenfield
Average % of Total Square Footage

FOR-SALE HOUSING: 17%

OFFICE: 46%

APARTMENT RENTAL: 16%

RETAIL: 6%

Figure 1.15 Distribution of total square feet of commercial space in Washington, DC's "greenfield" WalkUPs among office, for-sale housing, rental housing, and retail uses

Industrial (Figures 1.16A, B). Industrial Properties range from generic warehouse space to light industrial/manufacturing (mostly assembly work), to distribution facilities, to heavy manufacturing including things like smelting ore and refining crude oil. And as the combination of air pollution, noise pollution, tractor-trailer and delivery truck traffic, toxic waste discharge and disposal, and other by-products of such industrial activities increase, depending on what

Figure 1.16A Renovated, adaptive reuse of a warehouse in Boston's Charlestown Navy Yard

Figure 1.16B Original boilermaker shop at the Washington Navy Yard in Washington, DC, before its adaptive reuse as a retail building housing primarily restaurant uses

they are, the greater the zoning, land use, and operational legal barriers are interposed to limit the number and nature of such uses, or to exclude some altogether from particular locations. Technically, a gas station is both a retail and an industrial use; they are generally specifically provided for in zoning and land use codes or grandfathered in as such. Gas stations and consumer storage rental facilities are fairly commonplace industrial-type uses intermingled with or near less-noxious uses such as car dealerships (also primarily a retail activity but with industrial components, such as large service departments) and auto repair facilities.

Special-Use Properties (Figures 1.17A, B). Special-Use Properties include airports; hospitals and healthcare facilities; dedicated sports stadiums and baseball parks; convention

Figure 1.17A 2013 BB&T Atlanta Open tennis tournament, Atlantic Station, Atlanta, GA

Figure 1.17B Fenway Ballpark, home of the Boston Red Sox, Boston, MA

centers; performing arts centers; multiuse entertainment complexes designed to host NBA and NHL franchises' home games, A-list concerts, extreme sports events, and WWE spectacles; and publicly financed private utilities facilities, such as water treatment plants and pumping stations. Special-Use Properties are increasingly the result of public-private partnerships (P3s), generally require some combination of public and private financing, and are almost always the result of specific statutes and local ordinances permitting them, the specifics for which evolve out of the overall process of negotiating and structuring the P3 arrangements among the key participants and stakeholders. The larger the scale and land area footprint of such Special-Use Properties, the greater the likelihood that government powers of condemnation may need to be exercised to acquire land from recalcitrant landowners, the exercise of which has been dramatically constrained in the aftermath of the 2005 U.S. Supreme Court decision in *Kelo v. City of New London*.[19] Other than Mixed-Use Properties, which are, perhaps, a close second, Special-Use Properties involve the greatest amount of complexity that must be navigated successfully in terms of the applicable real estate laws impacting their development and finance.

Institutional/Academic (Figures 1.18A, B). Institutional/Academic Properties include college and university campuses and their facilities thereon; museums and art galleries; and academic and not-for-profit research buildings and campuses.

Government (Figures 1.19A, B). Government Properties include any and all area of land and facilities owned by any unit of government, whether local, state, or federal, and include municipal, state, and federal buildings; parklands and any and all improvements thereon; community centers; recreational facilities and complexes, including local, regional, and national parks; libraries; jails and prisons; vehicle maintenance and storage lots; landfills and garbage collection and disposal facilities, including co-generation plants; and, to the extent owned and funded by a governmental entity, colleges and universities, hospitals and healthcare facilities, and other Special-Use Properties described earlier.

Figure 1.18A Campus of Georgia Tech University, Atlanta, GA

Figure 1.18B Trinity Church, on Copley Square, H. H. Richardson, architect, Boston, MA

Agricultural Property (Figures 1.20A, B). Any land, including farmland, ranches, pastureland, and the like, specifically designated for and dedicated to the production of food and food-related products, apparel, and the breeding of working animals used in agricultural production, such as livestock (including dairy cows, sheep for the production of wool, beef cattle, and breeding domesticated animals such as dogs), permanent crops (orchards and vineyards), arable land for the production of staples, produce, and crops such as cotton used

Figure 1.19A Dome of the Georgia State Capitol, Atlanta, GA

Figure 1.19B National Archives and Navy Memorial, Washington, DC

Figure 1.20A Governors Island Teaching Garden, Governors Island, New York, NY

Figure 1.20B Potrero del Sol Community Garden, San Francisco, CA

in the apparel industry. While Agricultural Land may seem to provide the greatest bright-line contrast with the other real estate asset class categories, consider the following example of a commonplace fact pattern raising legal issues when the bright lines become blurred. In Napa Valley, California, vineyards have gone from merely producing grapes and, from those grapes, fermenting wines, to an area that is a significant tourist destination within the state, with vineyards constructing increasingly elaborate facilities, some including Hospitality, Entertainment/Restaurant, and Retail Properties. Do these Napa Valley vineyards constitute Agricultural Land or do they comprise Mixed-Use Properties, combining Agricultural Land, Hospitality Properties, Entertainment/Restaurant Properties, and Retail Properties?

"Ownership" of real estate: estates in real property

While real estate – *terra firma* – is a real, tangible thing, *rights in and to real estate* may take many forms. Even the purest form or ownership of real estate, fee simple title to real property issued in the name of a single individual, may still be encumbered by things like easements, subterranean mineral rights, and air rights across, under, and over such property, respectively.

Despite the passage of almost nine and a half centuries since the Battle of Hastings (1066), real estate law in the twenty-first century perpetuates some of the vestiges of the complex and now seemingly arcane edifices of the feudal system of real property William the Conqueror imposed after successfully invading England. This system, which first ushered into usage the temporary, possessory right of serfs to work the land with the consent and at the will of the noble lord, evolved into English common law principles of real property, which were largely exported to the colonies, serving as the foundation for our modern real estate laws.

This legacy includes the concept of an estate in land. Essentially, an estate in land describes the nature, extent, duration, and quality of someone's interest in real property. That estate in land may range from fee simple ownership to a temporary, possessory right such as a month-to-month lease in the improvements (i.e., a building) constructed on land.

Estates in land are perhaps best understood as variations on the fee simple estate owned by a single individual (a "single individual" refers here only to one person and does not refer to that person's marital status, as under some state laws that may, in and of itself, imply joint ownership of the fee simple estate). A fee simple ownership is an estate of an indefinite duration. That is, the ownership lasts forever or until such time as the owner decides to transfer or otherwise modify this undivided estate. Fee simple ownership may be freely transferred, in whole or in part.

Fee simple ownership by a single individual is the most comprehensive ownership of real property, because the estate is neither limited by time nor constrained by the ownership interests of others, such as would be the case with a joint tenancy (see later). The owner of an estate in fee simple has unfettered discretion in the use and disposal of her estate, other than compliance with applicable laws and regulations (such as zoning and land use laws). Because the fee simple estate is comprised of a number of severable rights – such as the right to use and possess the real property; the right to lease all or some portion of the property; the right to subdivide the property; the right to develop; the right to pledge as security for debt or other obligations; and the right to extract subsurface minerals and other valuable commodities such as oil and gas – the fee simple estate is characterized by the fact that the owner may grant or sell these severable rights as she sees fit, thereby intentionally limiting her estate and, presumably, receiving compensation (as in the case of granting a leasehold estate on the property), personal satisfaction (as in the case of transferring an estate in the land after the fee simple owner's death or incapacity), or some combination of the two.

For example, the Owner of a fee simple estate in Parcel A, assuming compliance with local land use and zoning laws, might subdivide the fee simple into Parcels A-1, A-2, and A-3, with Parcel A-1 containing the Owner's personal residence. Again, assuming full compliance with all local laws, the owner could construct a second residential dwelling unit on Parcel A-2, with a fence along the back wall of the structure demising the structure and front yard from the back yard. The Owner could then enter into a one-year lease with a tenant, and that lease could conceivably convey only the right to possess and use the rental unit and the front yard, but not the rear yard, even though the front and rear yards comprise new Parcel A-2. The Owner could grant subterranean rights to everything that can be extracted from the entirety of what was originally Parcel A without disturbing the structural integrity of any of the improvements to Parcel A (i.e., the Owner's personal residence on new Parcel A-1 and the rental property the Owner constructed on Parcel A-2), and allow access to the rear yard of Parcel A-2 over an easement adjacent to the boundary between Parcels A-2 and A-3. Finally, subject to such easement allowing access to the rear yard of Parcel A-2, the Owner could sell grazing rights to Parcel A-3 to the rancher whose ranch is located adjacent to Parcel A-3.

In this example, the Owner still owns Parcel A in fee simple. However, her rights are now constrained by the possessory and use rights of the tenant occupying the improvements on, and the front portion of, Parcel A-2; the subterranean rights to the entirety of Parcel A and the rights of ingress and egress permitted therewith; and the grazing rights granted on Parcel A-3. These are all temporary rights of possession and use, presumably with defined, limited terms. In fact, it is conceivable that after all such possessory and use rights have expired or are otherwise terminated according to their respective terms, the Owner may be able to merge Parcels A-1, A-2, and A-3 back into a single parcel of land under fee simple ownership. It is also possible that the Owner could have undertaken all of these transfers of rights without ever having subdivided Parcel A, although it would have arguably been more difficult to do so.

Many of the English common law estates of land that evolved out of William the Conqueror's desire to facilitate the feudal system in England, and that were incorporated into the laws of the colonies and, ultimately, the American states, have by and large been transcended by state statutes governing the ownership, use, and transfer of real property and various rights and interest therein. For example, the law of intestate succession, governing the transfers of property to heirs when someone dies without a will, in essence creates a "life estate" in the fee simple owner, because any fee simple estates owned will automatically pass to those heirs as designated in the state statutes where each such fee simple estate is owned. Statutes of frauds, requiring that certain rights must be in writing in order to be enforceable, may render moot certain types of "tenancies" recognized under common law. In other words, a large portion of the multitude of "estates in land" recognized under common law have little to no influence in real estate development today.

For the sake of completeness, however, here is a fairly comprehensive list of typical "estates in land":

1. Fee simple
2. Fee simple determinable with possibility of reverter
3. Fee simple subject to or on a condition subsequent
4. Fee simple subject to a shifting or springing executory interest
5. Fee tail
6. Life estate for the life of the tenant
7. Life estate for the life of one other than the tenant
8. Life estate created by fee tail after possibility of issue extinct

9. Dower
10. Curtesy
11. Life estate by and during coverture
12. Estate (or term) for years
13. Periodic tenancy
14. Tenancy at will
15. Tenancy at or by sufferance[20]

"Ownership" of real estate: concurrent estates

Unlike common law "estates in land," concurrent estates continue to be relevant to the ownership and disposition of rights to and interests in real property. A concurrent estate exists whenever two or more persons have the same rights in an estate in land at the same time (i.e., concurrently). The four forms of concurrent estates are as follows:

Joint tenancy

A joint tenancy is any concurrent estate in land (as contrasted, for example, with a future interest), by two or more people, with each person having such concurrent interest having an independent right of possession.

Joint tenancy with right of survivorship (JTWROS)

In a joint tenancy with right of survivorship (JTWROS), joint tenants must receive their interest at the same time and through the same instrument, such as a deed conveying title; their interests must be ratable (i.e., each owns identical percentage interests in the property); each has the same rights of possession; and ownership in the property passes automatically to the remaining (i.e., surviving) tenant upon the passing of other joint tenants, with the final, surviving joint tenant becoming the fee simple owner of title to the property because all others having claim to it are no longer living. This is the "right of survivorship" provision in this form of concurrent estate. A JTWROS may convey its joint tenancy interest in the property; however, such conveyance automatically terminates the right of survivorship.

Tenancy by the entirety

Tenancy by the entirety is limited to legally married couples, adding the "unity of marriage" to the unities of possession, interest, title, and temporality. Accordingly, a married couple acquiring property in their names automatically becomes tenants by the entirety in that property. A tenant by the entirety does not have a unilateral right to dispose of her or his interest, and this tenancy is only severable upon the dissolution of the marriage.

Tenancy in common

In a tenancy in common (TIC), each tenant owns a divisible interest in the property, which interest may be freely conveyed and may also be passed on to the interest owner's heirs.

Tenants in common may own non-ratable interests (i.e., they are not required to each own an equal interest in the property). In many respects, a tenancy in common in real property is identical to a general partnership in real property. See Chapter 8 for more information about general partnerships in real property.

The Development Process

A brief introduction to "The Development Process"

Real estate development is both a linear process and an iterative process. It is a linear process in that, in each Phase of The Development Process (see Chapter 2), certain critical path items must be completed before other steps can be taken. For example, jurisdictions generally require that an applicant for any type of zoning approval (e.g., a Special-Use Permit, Variance, Master Plan Amendment, or Planned Unit Development Ordinance) must have control of the Subject Property. This is commonly known as "**Site Control**."

Consequently, the **Developer** will not likely be allowed to submit the requisite application for the necessary land use approvals without evidencing Site Control, the definition of which may be contained in the zoning and land use code itself or be the result of a series of legal decisions regarding the meaning of Site Control in that jurisdiction. In this regard, The Development Process is linear. The process cannot continue unless/until certain milestones have been reached.

However, in order to get to a point where the Developer will be comfortable securing Site Control (which generally entails some type of financial commitment to ultimately proceed with the acquisition of the Subject Property and a legal transfer of **Title**), such as the local jurisdiction and/or legal precedent in that jurisdiction define it, the Developer will need to make certain determinations during the Project Conception Phase, defined later, regarding the suitability of the Subject Property for the Developer's intentions therefore.

Some of these early steps in determining **project viability** and **financial feasibility** will likely require revisions to the earliest conception about what Property Categories, Total Development Costs, specific product types, sizes, and end-product pricing are appropriate for the Subject Site. In this regard, The Development Process is iterative, in that as information is refined and tested, the Program for the Subject Property is likely to change. By way of example, a Preliminary Land Use Analysis may yield limitations for the Preliminary Program for the Subject Property, while a **Preliminary Market Survey** may support a modification to an envisioned product type in terms of gross and net square footages of the proposed improvements and possibly improved projected revenues generated from such product types, such that overall the yield from the Subject Property is enhanced.

So long as neither individually nor collectively such iterative changes materially alter the envisioned end product on the Subject Site and its projected value, or render the Project financially infeasible (or simply not sufficiently profitable to warrant the inherent risks in the earliest phases of The Development Process), such "adjustments" along the way will assure the completion and ultimate success of the undertaking. Combining the two, The Development Process may be viewed as *a linear process along a trajectory and in its totality, with a series of iterative steps within each Development Phase.*

By using The Development Process as the framework within which legal issues are presented, understood, and resolved, *Real Estate Law: Fundamentals for The Development Process* seeks to convey each intersection of "the law" and real estate development in context. For example, the understanding that a Developer needs to have about permitted land uses and the zoning and land use approval process generally during the Project Conception Phase is very different than the actual land use and approval process the Developer may be required to pursue in order to secure all necessary approvals for the Project, which will be preconditions to, among other things, the construction financing for all proposed improvements. Accordingly, local government and land use laws are addressed in each Development Phase of The Development Process, rather than simply being presented as an abstract concept in its entirety without relation to (i) where it arises in each Development Phase and (ii) the differences in how such issues should be addressed.

Outline of The Development Process. The Development Process, from beginning to end, is set forth next and is depicted in **Figure 1.21**. A detailed explanation of each of the five Phases of The Development Process follows in Chapter 2.

Project Conception Phase

Site identification
Community outreach
Assemble and engage development team
Preliminary program
Market overview or survey
Preliminary infrastructure assessment
Updated program
Land use analysis
Schematic design
Negotiate acquisition and development (A&D) financing commitment
Secure site control

Pre-Development Phase

Closing on A&D financing
Market analysis
Site due diligence
Civil engineering
Design development (DD)
Value engineering
Close on land acquisition

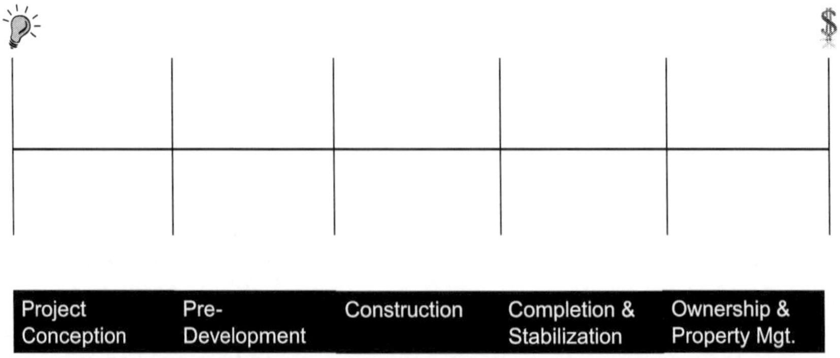

| Project Conception | Pre-Development | Construction | Completion & Stabilization | Ownership & Property Mgt. |

Figure 1.21 The Development Process, including five Development Phases

Develop construction documents (CDs)
Creation of any necessary entities (e.g., GPs, LPs, and LLCs)
Identify and secure take-out (permanent) financing commitment
Identify and secure construction loan commitment
Pricing and bidding for general contractors (GCs) and subs
Negotiate and document construction loan docs
Engage construction manager (CM), if required
Close on construction financing
Execute construction contracts
Identify/engage marketing/pre-leasing company

Construction Phase

Construction administration
Horizontal construction
Horizontal construction disbursement process
Horizontal construction close-out*
Vertical construction
Vertical construction disbursement process
Identify/engage property management company
Marketing and pre-leasing

Project Completion and Stabilization Phase

Vertical construction close-out
Construction claims resolution
On-site property manager in place
Lease-up and move-in

Ownership and Property Management Phase

Ongoing property management
Closing on permanent financing
Sale or refinancing

Notes

1. Leinberger, Christopher B. and Patrick Lynch, *The WalkUP Wake-Up Call: Boston*, Center for Real Estate and Urban Analysis, The George Washington University School of Business, Washington, DC (2015), pg. 4.

2. In a diversified portfolio, cash-equivalents allow an investor the option to earn a relatively low but safe rate of return, generally based on interest rates set by the U.S. Treasury or on LIBOR rates. Generally speaking, an investor will "park" in cash-equivalents money the investor believes she'll need in the short term or that is waiting to be invested in another asset class, such as stocks or bonds. The primary characteristics of cash-equivalents are liquidity, safety, and ease of access. Although commonly considered one leg of the three-legged asset class stool, the first money market fund was not created in the United States until 1971, at which time depository accounts did not pay interest, whereas stocks and bonds – the other two principal asset classes – have existed for

centuries. Money market funds are regulated under the Investment Company Act of 1940.

3. In his tribute to Benjamin Graham shortly after his death in 1976, published in *Financial Analysts Journal* (November/December 1976), Warren Buffett offered the following perspective on Graham's contribution to the field of securities analysis and investment:

> It is rare that the founder of a discipline does not find his work eclipsed in rather short order by successors. But over forty years after publication of [*The Intelligent Investor*, which] brought structure and logic to a disorderly and confused activity, it is difficult to think of possible candidates for even the runner-up position in the field of security analysis.

4. Graham, Benjamin, *The Intelligent Investor: A Book of Practical Counsel*, Revised Edition, First Collins Business Essentials Edition, Harper-Collins (Reprint © 2006; original Revised Edition © Benjamin Graham, 1973), pg. 56.

5. March, Roy Hilton, "The Making of an Asset Class." *Wharton Real Estate Review*, Spring 2012. Found at http://realestate.wharton.upenn.edu/review/index.php?article=229.

6. Benkler, Yochai, "'Sharing Nicely': On Shareable Goods and the Emergence of Sharing as a Modality of Economic Production." *Yale Law School Legal Scholarship Repository*, January 1, 2004; Swallow, Erica, "The Rise of the Sharing Economy." *Mashable*, February 7, 2012. Found at http://mashable.com/2012/02/07/sharing-economy/.

7. Press release dated November 17, 2006, issued by the 2006 Conference on Mixed-Use Development. Found at www.icsc.org/uploads/research/general/Mixed-use_Definition.pdf.

8. Leinberger, Christopher B., *The WalkUP Wake-Up Call: D.C.*, Center for Real Estate and Urban Analysis, The George Washington University School of Business, Washington, DC (2012), pg. 4.

9. Ibid., pg. 6. Footnote omitted.

10. Leinberger, Christopher B. and Mariela Alfonzo, *Walk This Way: The Economic Promise of Walkable Places in Metropolitan Washington, D.C.*, Brookings Institution, Washington, DC (May 2012).

11. Ibid., pgs. 6 (text) and 20 (referenced footnotes in the excerpt), respectively.

12. Leinberger, *The WalkUP Wake-Up Call: D.C.*, pg. 8.

13. Ibid., pg. 9.

14. Ibid., pg. 10.

15. Leinberger and Lynch, *The WalkUP Wake-Up Call: Boston*, pg. 16.

16. Ibid., pg. 11.

17. Leinberger, *The WalkUP Wake-Up Call: D.C.*, pg. 12.

18. Ibid., pg. 13.

19. *Kelo v. City of New London*, 545 U.S. 1158 (2005).

20. Hovenkamp, Herbert and Sheldon F. Kurtz, *Principles of Property Law*, Sixth Edition, Thompson/West, St. Paul, MN, 2005, pgs. 90–95.

Introduction to The Development Process

For centuries, probably everyone who has thought about cities at all has noticed that there seems to be some *connection between the concentration of people and the specialties they support*. Samuel Johnson, for one, remarked on this relationship back in 1785. "Men, thinly scattered," he said to Boswell, "make a shift, but a bad shift, without many things. . . . It is being concentrated which produces convenience."[1]

The keen observations of urbanist Jane Jacobs, in her landmark book, *The Death and Life of Great American Cities*, have found renewed meaning in the urban renaissance that has taken place after more than half a century of devastating population decline. Starting in the last decade of the twentieth century and accelerating into the first decade and a half of the twenty-first, American cities are experiencing an unprecedented repopulation of their cores. This has been accomplished primarily with a plethora of walkable urban place-making projects or "WalkUPs," discussed in the Idea Generation Sub-Phase of the Project Conception Phase of The Development Process and throughout this chapter. These new walkable places are proposed and developed with ever-more complex mixes of uses and presenting intensities of development never before imagined. How The Development Process is shaping new urban development, and how WalkUPs are reshaping The Development Process, are considered in this chapter.

Chapter outline
Chapter introduction
    Real estate development is both a linear process and an iterative process.
Functional components of The Development Process
    Selection
    Acquisition
    Development
    Financing
    Ownership and property management
    Sale or refinancing
Understanding each Development Phase in The Development Process
    Project Conception Phase
    Pre-Development Phase
    Construction Phase
    Project Completion and Stabilization Phase
    Ownership and Property Management Phase
Detailed descriptions of the Sub-Phases in each Development Phase

Chapter introduction

Real estate development is both a linear process and an iterative process

Real estate development is a linear process in that, in each of the five Phases of The Development Process detailed in this chapter, certain critical path tasks must be completed before other steps can be taken. For example, jurisdictions generally require that an applicant for any type of zoning approval (e.g., a Special-Use Permit, Variance, Master Plan Amendment or Planned Unit Development Ordinance) must have *control* of the Subject Property ("control" does not necessarily mean fee simple ownership of the subject property). Consequently, the Developer will not be allowed to submit the requisite application for the necessary land use approvals without evidencing "site control," the definition of which may be contained in the zoning and land use code itself. In this regard, *The Development Process is linear* because it cannot move forward unless and until certain legal hurdles are overcome or milestones achieved. **Figure 2.1** depicts The Development Process and its five Phases. **Figure 2.2** demonstrates the linearity of The Development Process, with specific milestones marking the end of one Phase and the beginning of the next Phase. In this way The Development Process is very linear.

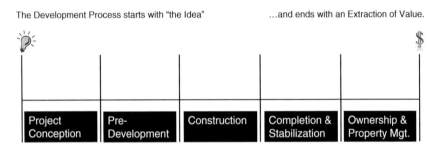

Figure 2.1 The Five Phases of The Development Process

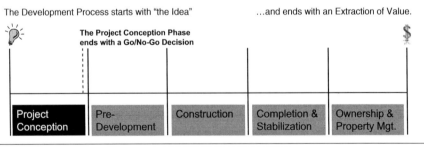

Figure 2.2 The Development Process is LINEAR: Project Conception

However, *real estate development is also an iterative process* when one examines the flow among and between various Sub-Phases in each Phase of The Development Process. **Figure 2.3** provides a simple example of how several of the Project Conception Phase Sub-Tasks – Site Selection, Preliminary Program, and Site Analysis – operate iteratively, in this instance sending the Project Conception Phase back to Site Selection.

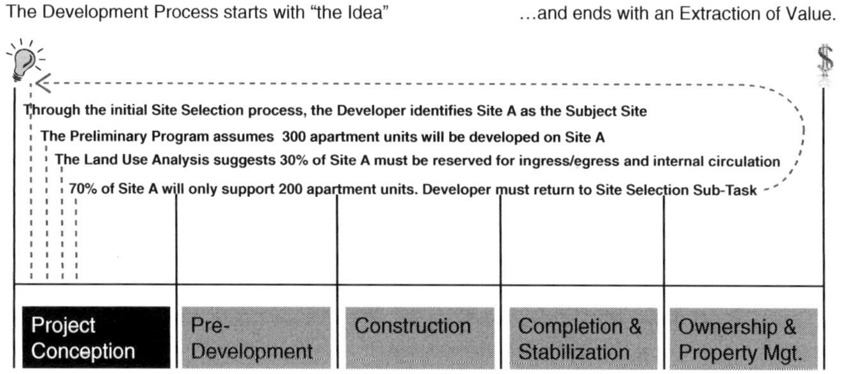

The Development Process starts with "the Idea"   ...and ends with an Extraction of Value.

Through the initial Site Selection process, the Developer identifies Site A as the Subject Site

The Preliminary Program assumes 300 apartment units will be developed on Site A

The Land Use Analysis suggests 30% of Site A must be reserved for ingress/egress and internal circulation

70% of Site A will only support 200 apartment units. Developer must return to Site Selection Sub-Task

| Project Conception | Pre-Development | Construction | Completion & Stabilization | Ownership & Property Mgt. |

Figure 2.3 The Development Process is ITERATIVE: Project Conception Phase example

To continue the example, in order to get to a point where the Developer will be comfortable securing "site control" as the local jurisdiction defines it, the Developer will need to make certain determinations regarding the suitability of the Subject Property during the first Phase of The Development Process: the **Project Conception Phase**. In **Figure 2.3**, information gathered and analyzed after initially selecting Site A as the Subject Site sends the Developer back to the beginning of the Site Selection Sub-Phase. However, it is perhaps more likely that some of the early Sub-Phases during the Project Conception Phase contributing to a determination of a project's viability and financial feasibility will likely require revisions to one or more of the previously completed Sub-Phases, such as the Initial or Preliminary Program for how the Subject Site should be developed:

- What asset class(es) are most suitable for the Project (see Chapter 1);
- The **Total Development Cost ("TDC")** of the Project;
- The tenure type of each asset class to be constructed; and
- The specific product types, sizes, and end-product pricing within the selected asset class(es).

In this regard, The Development Process is *iterative*: As information is refined and tested through the interplay of the Sub-Phases within Phase 1 of The Development Process, the Initial or Preliminary Program for the Subject Property is likely to be revised and improved along the way. By way of example, a Preliminary Land Use Analysis may yield limitations for the Preliminary Program for the Subject Property, while a Preliminary Market Survey may support a modification to an envisioned product type in terms of gross and net square footages of the proposed Improvements and possibly improved projected revenues generated from such product types, such that overall the yield from the Subject Property is enhanced.

So long as, neither individually nor collectively, such iterative changes do not materially alter the envisioned end product on the Subject Site and its projected value, or render the Project financially infeasible (or simply not sufficiently profitable to warrant the inherent risks in the earliest phases of The Development Process), such "adjustments" along the way should assure the completion and ultimate success of the undertaking. Combining the two, The Development Process may be considered a *linear process* along a trajectory and in its totality, *with a series of iterative steps* within each Development Phase.

Functional components of The Development Process

In addition to providing a complete, detailed timeline for the series of five **Development Phases** and the Sub-Phases within each Phase, The Development Process also focuses students' and readers' attention on the following, functional aspects of real estate development, which – with the exception of Development and Financing, which have some iterative aspects between them – occur in relative chronological order:

- Selection
- Acquisition
- Development
- Financing
- Ownership and property management
- Sale or refinancing

By using The Development Process as the framework within which legal issues are presented, understood, and resolved, this textbook seeks to convey each intersection of "the law" and real estate development in context. For example, the understanding a Developer needs to have about permitted land uses, and the zoning and **Land Use Approval Process** generally during the Project Conception Phase of The Development Process, is very different than the actual land use and approval process the Developer may be required to pursue during the Pre-Development Phase of The Development Process, in order to secure all necessary approvals for the Project (which regulatory land use approvals will be preconditions to, among other things, the construction financing for all proposed Improvements to be undertaken during the Construction Phase of The Development Process). Accordingly, Local Government and Land Use Law are addressed in each Development Phase of The Development Process, rather than simply presented as an abstract concept in its entirely, without relation to (i) how and where it arises in each Development Phase and (ii) the differences in how such issues should be addressed.

In order to use The Development Process as a framework for learning real estate law, one must first understand The Development Process itself. Accordingly, this chapter is devoted to detailing The Development Process without regard to the real estate law implications for each Phase of The Development Process and each component of each Phase. How legal issues manifest themselves or, better yet, are anticipated and planned for during The Development Process are addressed in Chapter 3.

In its most elemental form, The Development Process begins with an Idea and ends with the Extraction of Value (what may also be referred to herein as the "Exit Strategy") from the successful execution of the Idea (or some version of the Idea that has evolved and, hopefully, improved over time while retaining its inherent value). **See Figure 2.1.** The Idea may be as simple as the repetition of a development formula with which the Developer is very familiar and extremely comfortable. In the fifty or so years of suburban and exurban commercial development in the United States, certain types of real estate development activities became very formulaic and, therefore, somewhat immune to specific development risks:

- bedroom communities of single-family detached homes;
- neighborhood strip shopping centers providing community-serving retail;
- surface-parked, garden-apartment projects; speculative and build-to-suit office buildings in corporate office parks; warehouses in industrial parks; and

- the ubiquitous, enclosed, regional shopping mall, the risks of which ultimately *did* manifest themselves as retail shopping patterns in the United States began to shift to other, brick-and-mortar shopping venues, such as new Power Centers and Town Centers, stand-alone "value" department stores like Target, and apparel retailers like H&M – although some are in malls – as well as to online "**etailers**" such as amazon.com and eBay.[2]

In the case of creating walkable urban places (aka "WalkUPs"), however, the Idea is more likely to be a one-off rather than a cookie-cutter Project, taking advantage of some particular opportunity in a specific (as opposed to the generic homogeneity of many suburban locations) geographic marketplace. A WalkUPs Project, by definition, involves the development and integration of more than one asset class into a single Project, creating a mix of uses that is internally and externally synergistic to the Project and its surrounding context.

WHAT MAKES A CITY?

Observers are forever rediscovering this relationship [between the concentration of people and the specialties they support] in new times and places. Thus, in 1959, John H. Denton, a professor of business at the University of Arizona, after studying American suburbs and British "new towns" came to the conclusion that such places must rely on ready access to a city for protection and cultural opportunities. "He based his findings," reported the New York *Times*, "on the lack of a sufficient density of population to support cultural facilities. Mr. Denton . . . said that decentralization produced such a thin population spread that the only effective economic demand that could exist in suburbs was that of the majority. The only goods and cultural activities available will be those that the majority requires, he observed," and so on.

   But this relationship between concentration and diversity is very little considered when it comes to city districts where residence is a chief use. Yet dwellings form a large part of most city districts. The people who live in a district also form a large share, usually, of the people who use the streets, the parks and the enterprises of the place. Without help from the concentration of the people who live there, there can be little convenience or diversity where people live, and where they require it.[3]

Commercial office space, retail and entertainment components, and one or more types of residential products are becoming increasingly common components in true, Mixed-Use projects in the downtowns and central business districts (CBDs) of first-tier U.S. cities. New CBD commercial buildings are no longer limited to a single, at-grade floor of users representing a very narrow range of retail offerings, with the balance of the upper floors devoted to general office use. In this regard, *for WalkUPs, the "Ideas" have become much more elaborate and complex* and, as a consequence, The Development Process has become more drawn out and more prone to challenges.

   The Extraction of Value or Exit Strategy marks either *a milestone in or the conclusion of* The Development Process, depending on whether this is done periodically throughout the Ownership and Property Management Development Phase (in the case of a portfolio property, the Developer embarks upon creating with the intention of long-term ownership), or if the Developer's intention is to sell the Project or 100% of the Developer's interest therein. The Developer's Exit Strategy generally follows one of several alternative formulations:

- Partnering on the front end with an institutional investor that intends to acquire the Project once it has reached its **Stabilized Net Operating Income (SNOI)**;

- mini-perm financing used to take out the construction financing and allow the Developer to own and operate the Project for a sufficient period of time – generally three to five years – to not only reach operating stabilization but also market the building for sale at an optimal time in the market cycle for the asset class and geographic market; or
- portfolio ownership utilizing long-term financing or a mini-perm with the intention of pursuing periodic refinancings at each interval when a sufficiently large increase in the Project's value may be extracted through such refinancing.

With the increasing complexity of downtown WalkUPs, the opportunities for extracting value at different times in The Development Process from each of the different asset classes comprising the Project have multiplied as well. The ownership regime for a Project may be divided up in ways that facilitate selling one or more components of the Project while retaining other components for long-term value realization. For example, developing a hotel as part of a Mixed-Use project, with the intention of selling the hotel to a hospitality property group or fund, which then enters into a Hotel Management Agreement with a particular hotel chain or "flag," allows the Developer of that project to extract some of the value created by the overall project while meeting other return objectives of the overall undertaking. A similar approach may be taken in including a component of residential units in a condominium ownership regime, with the Developer's return on that component of a Mixed-Use project coming serially, as each condominium unit is sold and the outstanding construction financing incrementally curtailed, similar to how for-sale, single-family detached homes in bedroom communities are released from the security interest held by the construction lender in that context.

THE IMPORTANCE OF DENSITY IN MAKING MIXED-USE DEVELOPMENT FUNCTION PROPERLY

To be sure, the dwellings of a district (like any other use of the land) need to be supplemented by other primary uses so people on the streets will be well spread through the hours of the day, for the economic reasons explained in Chapter Eight. These other uses (work, entertainment, or whatever) must make intensive use of city land if they are to contribute effectively to concentration. If they simply take up physical room and involve few people, they will do little or nothing for diversity or liveliness. I think it is hardly necessary to belabor that point.

This same point is just as important, however, about dwellings. City dwellings have to be intensive in their use of the land too, for reasons that go much deeper than cost of land. On the other hand, this does not mean that everyone can or should be put into elevator apartment houses to live – or into any other one or two types of dwellings. That kind of solution kills diversity by obstructing it from another direction.[4]

Understanding each Development Phase in The Development Process

The Development Process is presented as a series of five Development Phases (see **Figure 2.1**), with each Project Phase representing a discrete set of tasks or Sub-Phases, each of which must be accomplished before the Project can move forward into the next Phase. Accordingly, each Development Phase concludes with a critical milestone marking the end of one Development Phase and the beginning of the next one (see, e.g., **Figure 2.2**. Additional descriptions of The Development Process milestones, by Phase, are provided in **Figures 2.4** through **2.7**). The five Development Phases are listed next, and then each is briefly described in the following, five subsections:

Project Conception Phase
Pre-Development Phase
Construction Phase
Project Completion and Stabilization Phase
Ownership and Property Management Phase

   Project Conception Phase (Figure 2.2). The Project Conception Phase marks the beginning, or genesis, of every development project. The Developer is seeking to decide what to do, and where. While limiting, to the greatest extent possible, the expenditure of funds, the Developer seeks to identify any impediments to a potential project. Any number of obstacles, such as an inflexible zoning code or problematic environmental conditions, may be identified during the Project Conception Phase. Additionally, the financial feasibility or infeasibility will be assessed during this initial Phase of The Development Process.
   The Project Conception Phase starts with an Idea. As suggested earlier, the Idea will either blossom following its genesis or die at some point during The Development Process. In a perfect world, if the Idea is going to die, it should do so relatively quickly during the Project Conception Phase; the death of the Idea during the Pre-Development Phase or, worse yet, the Construction Phase, could spell financial disaster for the Developer, as well as for the Developer's Equity Investors and Lenders.
   The Project Conception Phase represents the highest risk profile to the Developer, because it is the most speculative activity in which the Developer engages. Paradoxically, the Project Conception Phase also entails the lowest risk profile to the Developer, because the Developer assumes the lowest amount of risk presented throughout The Development Process. If the Developer never proceeds from the Project Conception Phase to the Pre-Development Phase, there is little if any ongoing liability for the Developer attendant a decision not to proceed with the Project, for whatever reason(s).
   During the Project Conception Phase, the Developer seeks to make a baseline determination as to whether the Subject Property will be suitable for the purposes for which the Developer initially intended to acquire it (i.e., does it support and facilitate "the Idea"). The Developer's initial interest in the Subject Site may be very simplistic or even crude. The Subject Site would be "good" for a housing project, for example, because it is already located adjacent to an existing residential neighborhood. At the initial germination of the Idea, there is perhaps little consideration given to what residential building type or types would be best suited to the surrounding community and/or the Developer's return model: The initial Idea, in this scenario, is "Hey, let's build some kind of housing here."
   The 80:2 Solution. Because the Project Conception Phase is very speculative, the Developer seeks to minimize the funds invested in the process while maximizing the level of certitude to be achieved through the various tasks or Sub-Phases the Developer and its **Development Team** undertake during the Project Conception Phase. One way to think about the Project Conception Phase is that the Developer wants to find the 80:2 Solution, expending *no more than 2%* of the Project's projected Total Development Cost, while getting *80% of the way* to the final formulation of the Project; getting 80% of the way toward figuring out precisely what can be developed on the Subject Site, before committing further to purchase or otherwise secure legal control of the Subject Property.

If, in getting to the 80:2 Solution, it is determined that the Subject Property is, in fact, *not suitable* for the Developer's intended purposes or that the projected return from the completed project does not warrant the risks associated with developing the Subject Property (or for any of dozens of other potential reasons that may be ferreted out during the Project Conception Phase, ranging from title issues to environmental liabilities to having to run an expensive and time-consuming gauntlet to secure the needed land use approvals), the Developer won't be bound to purchase the Subject Property from the **Seller**. All that will be lost is the Developer's out-of-pocket expenditures incurred during the Project Conception Phase, including the cost of specific tasks performed by third-party professional services firms, and, of course, the value of the Developer's time and that of the Developer's staff. If the Developer is a large corporate enterprise with full-time land acquisition and development staff, that lost time has a specific cost associated with it, and becomes part of the Developer's ongoing cost of doing business.

At the end of the Project Conception Phase, the Developer expects to get to **a Go** or **No-Go Decision**. A "no-go" decision means walking away from the opportunity, hopefully in a manner that doesn't preclude or render more difficult in the future the Developer returning to the same community with a different project proposal for the Subject Property or a different project on a different Subject Site. If, however, the decision is a "go," then the Project Conception Phase will conclude with the Developer acquiring Site Control and moving into the Pre-Development Phase.

The chronological tasks or Sub-Phases of the Project Conception Phase are as follows:

Project Conception Phase

Idea generation
Site identification
Develop exit and funding strategies: How will "the idea" pay off?
Analysis and selection of project delivery method
Community outreach
Assemble and engage development team
Preliminary program
Market overview or survey
Preliminary infrastructure assessment
Updated program
Preliminary development budget pro forma
Land use analysis
Schematic design
Preliminary project pro forma
Negotiate acquisition and development (A&D) financing commitment
Secure site control

Pre-Development Phase (Figure 2.4). In the **Pre-Development Phase**, the process of moving forward with the Project goes *from merely conceptual to buildable*. Every aspect of the Project that was explored conceptually during the Project Conception Phase has to be taken to a level of sufficient certitude that the Project will be able to move forward. This means, among other things, that the market survey undertaken during the Project Conception Phase will be replaced by a full Market Study; the Schematic Design will go through Design Development, leading ultimately to the creation of a full set of Construction Documents (also referred to as "Construction Drawings" or, simply, CDs), and the Land Analysis will be replaced by a formal Site Evaluation Report by the civil engineering firm, from which it will develop Site Construction Plans for all horizontal construction on the Subject Site.

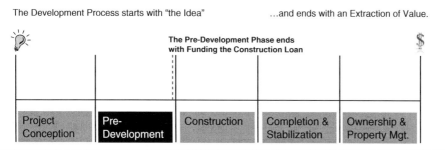

Figure 2.4 The Development Process is LINEAR: Pre-Development

The Preliminary Program for the Subject Property – a detailed description of each of the components that will comprise the Project once everything has been completed – must be tested, refined, and finalized. The level of detail of all of the work the Development Team undertakes must be able to support, among other things, entering into one or more contracts for the construction of the planned Improvements to the Subject Site, as well as securing both acquisition and construction financing to pay for such construction activity. As will be learned in the Construction Phase, the process for entering into contracts for the construction of the Improvements to the Subject Site will depend, to a great extent, on the Construction Delivery Method that the Developer and its **Design Team** (a subset of the Development Team) select.

Whatever the form of Site Control the Developer attained in order to be able to move the Project from the Project Conception Phase into the Pre-Development Phase – whether an **Option Contract** purchased from the Seller by the Developer or a **Purchase and Sale Agreement** entered into by the parties, requiring a substantial good faith deposit from the Developer (but also providing the comfort of a substantial Feasibility Study and Due Diligence Period) – the Developer, or a **Development Entity** or Special Purpose Entity (SPE) created by the Developer for that purpose, will need to consummate a purchase of the Subject Property, effecting the full transfer of title from the Seller to the Purchaser.

Before the Developer or Development Entity acquires title to the Subject Property, all critical zoning and land use approvals necessary to support the Final Program for the Project must be secured. Taking title to the Subject Property, by making full payment therefore as agreed to between the Seller and the Buyer, without having all necessary local jurisdictional approvals, will put the Project's financing at risk, and may leave the Developer with undeveloped land far less valuable than what the purchase price reflected. Additionally, if the zoning and land use approvals secured from the local jurisdiction do not support the proposed Improvements and the Subject Property ends up with a lower fair market value than its purchase price, the collateral value of the Subject Property from the perspective of the **Construction Lender** may not allow the requested **Construction Loan** to be underwritten. For these reasons, the Purchase and Sale Agreement must provide an absolute out of the obligation to close on the Subject Property if, for any reasons, the Developer cannot secure the necessary land use and zoning approvals for the development of the property.

The final steps in the Pre-Development Phase generally involve **Closing** on the Subject Property and taking title thereto, entering into the **Construction Contracts**, and Construction Loan Closing, marking the end of this second phase of The Development Process and commencing the next phase in the process: the Construction Phase.

The chronological tasks or Sub-Phases of the Pre-Development Phase are as follows:

Pre-Development Phase

Closing on acquisition and development (A&D) financing
Market study
Site due diligence
Civil engineering analysis and site evaluation report
Design development (DD)
Value engineering
Revised and expanded project pro forma
Secure land use approvals
Close on land acquisition
Site work construction documents
Construction documents (CDs)
Creation of all necessary entities (e.g., GPs, LPs, and LLCs)
Creation of all necessary authorities (e.g., TIF District, CFDs)
Identify and secure take-out (permanent) financing commitment
Identify and secure construction loan commitment
Pricing and bidding for general contractors (GCs) and subs[5]
Negotiate and document construction loan docs
Engage construction manager (CM), if required
Close on construction financing
Execute construction contracts
Identify/engage marketing/pre-leasing company

Construction Phase (Figure 2.5). The Construction Phase is very straightforward: it represents the period during which all of the Improvements are constructed. It arguably involves the greatest amount of risk for the Project, given the dangers inherent in the construction process itself, but also considering the opportunities for conflict between the **Construction Documents** and their implementation by the **General Contractor**, potentially leading to delays and cost-overruns negatively impacting the Development Budget on which everything is based.

Project construction will generally involve both **Horizontal Construction**, which is comprised of all tasks necessary to prepare the Subject Property for the construction of the Improvements, and then the construction of the Improvements themselves, referred to as **Vertical Construction**. Depending on the size, scale, and complexity of the Project, both Horizontal Construction and Vertical Construction may be phased, such that one section or

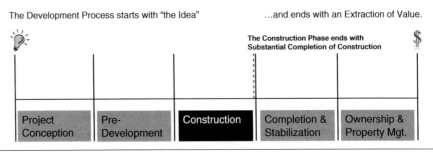

Figure 2.5 The Development Process is LINEAR: Construction

phase of the Project may be completed and ready for occupancy before any other phases are completed, as would be the case with large-scale subdivision development.

Horizontal Construction and Vertical Construction may be funded differently, with different **Draw Schedules**, conditions precedent, and approvals necessary to make payments to the General Contractor. Additionally, large-scale, Mixed-Use projects may rely on sophisticated financing techniques for massive infrastructure improvements, such as the creation of a **Community Facilities District** in the case of development projects in California, to fund all Horizontal Construction costs using bonds.[6] The Construction Documents, the Construction Contracts (including the General Conditions, in the case of the families of construction documents produced by the American Institute of Architects), and the Construction Loan Agreement govern the conduct, rights, duties, obligations, and liabilities of the various parties during the Construction Phase.

The chronological tasks or Sub-Phases of the Construction Phase are as follows:

Construction Phase

Construction administration
Horizontal construction
    Request for information (RFI) process
    Change order (CO) process
    Draw request process
    Close-out*
Vertical construction
    Request for information (RFI) process
    Change order (CO) process
    Draw request process
Identify/engage property management company
Marketing and pre-leasing

Project Completion and Stabilization Phase (Figure 2.6). The Project Completion and Stabilization Phase covers the period between the **Substantial Completion** of all activities that occurred during the Construction Phase and the commencement of normal operations of the completed Project. What constitutes Substantial Completion, as well as the timely disposition of all **Punch-List Items**, may be contentious and lead to litigation, although it is more likely than not that substantial disagreements between the Developer and the General Contractor, the **Architect/Engineer** and the Construction Lender will have manifested themselves long before the General Contractor claims that the Construction Contract has been substantially completed. Depending on the language in the Construction

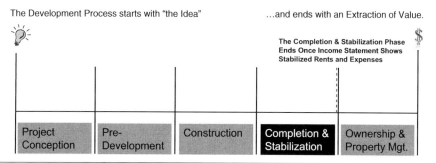

Figure 2.6 The Development Process is LINEAR: Completion and stabilization

Contract, the General Contractor may not be able to hold up construction for matters that are in dispute while the parties seek to resolve certain issues, but, instead, may be required to defer *until the end of the construction process* the resolution of who bears the economic burden of any such disputes. The Project Completion and Stabilization Phase marks the winding down of all construction activity, other than addressing Punch-List Items, and the ramping up of the move-in process (assuming that **Pre-Leasing** and/or pre-sales activities were vigorously and successfully pursued during the Construction Phase).

Getting facilities, such as a Resident Manager's or Sales Office, Community Center, and other **Common Areas** and Project amenities and facilities, furnished, equipped, appointed, and fully staffed are a critical part of the Project Completion and Stabilization Phase. In the case of rental buildings, including Commercial Office, Retail, and multifamily rental buildings, either the take-out financing or the investment parameters of the intended, ultimate owner of the Project (such as a pension fund or insurance company) will dictate what constitutes an appropriate **Stabilization Period**, which may be determined by the passage of time, the achievement of specified **Occupancy Rates**, or some combination of the two.

In the case of the development of various types of for-sale products, such as single-family homes and condominium units, there is no take-out financing: Individual unit sales allow for the serial curtailment of the outstanding principal amount, and any attendant, accrued but unpaid interest of the Construction Loan. How and when the **Developer's Fee** is earned and paid during the completion of sale transactions of the units will depend on the terms and conditions of the Construction Loan. For example, the Developer may be entitled to incrementally receive its Developer's Fee out of the net proceeds from each sale. Alternatively, the Developer may have to meet certain sales thresholds – in number of units sold, the aggregate square footage of units sold, or the dollar value of gross, aggregate sales proceeds – before any portion of the Developer's Fee is included in the disbursements at the Closing on subsequently completed sales transactions.

In an exclusively for-sale context, the Project Completion and Stabilization Phase marks the end of The Development Process. However, for the kind of large-scale, Mixed-Use projects that typify WalkUPs, with substantial Common Elements, the Developer may have to actively engage in the management of the Project and the Property until such time as a Condominium Owners' Association or Homeowners' Association is required, in accordance with the Condominium Documents, to take over such property management functions. This is still considered the Stabilization Period, even though it may well exceed what is commonly required to reach Project Stabilization in a rental context. In making this comparison of and contrast between the development of exclusively for-sale units versus developing exclusively rental products or some mix of the two, it should be noted that, in the former situation, the Developer may still be formally engaged as the **Property Manager** after all for-sale units, or substantially all such units, have been sold.

The chronological tasks or Sub-Phases of the Project Completion and Stabilization Phase are as follows:

Project Completion and Stabilization Phase

Vertical construction close-out
Construction claims resolution
On-site property manager in place
Lease-up and move-in

Ownership and Property Management Phase (Figure 2.7). This is the operational phase of the Project, and assumes that the Exit Strategy for the Developer, and the Developer's

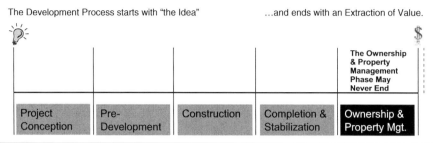

The Development Process starts with "the Idea"　　…and ends with an Extraction of Value.

The Ownership & Property Management Phase May Never End

| Project Conception | Pre-Development | Construction | Completion & Stabilization | Ownership & Property Mgt. |

Figure 2.7 The Development Process is LINEAR: Ownership and property management

Investors, is to hold the Project as a **Portfolio Asset** until such time as the capital value of the Project may be fully realized through a **Sale or Refinancing** of the Project. A **Fully Integrated Real Estate Development Company** will earn **Property Management Fees** during the **Management Period**, as well as benefit from whatever allocations of **Tax Attributes**, such as **Depreciation** and **Operating Losses,** and **Distributable Cash** are provided for under the Project ownership documents. However, the largest part of the Developer's return on the Project, other than through the Developer's Fee, may be through the distribution of net cash proceeds from a sale or periodic refinancing of the Project.

During the Ownership and Property Management Phase, all of the duties, obligations, and liabilities of being both a Property Owner and a Landlord must be fully addressed. This includes maintaining all of the Common Areas and keeping them safe and secure, renewing or securing competitive leases for all Premises in the Project, and making **Repairs and Capital Replacements** consistent with the useful life of each component of the Improvements. The legal obligations during the Ownership and Property Management Phase may range from dealing with slip-and-fall and other tort-related claims and cases arising from activities and conditions on the Project grounds to making sure **Loan Covenants** under the **Permanent Financing** for the Project are not violated (such as allowing the Occupancy Rate to fall below a specified level) to properly funding all **Reserve Accounts**.

The chronological tasks or Sub-Phases of the Ownership and Property Management Phase are as follows:

Ownership and Property Management Phase

Ongoing property management
Closing on permanent financing
Sale or refinancing

The tasks or Sub-Phases in each of the five Phases of The Development Process are described in greater detail next:

Project Conception Phase

Idea Generation (Figure 2.8). As mentioned at the beginning of this chapter, The Development Process begins with an Idea. That Idea or Project Concept (or, simply, the Concept) may be the same Idea the Developer has always followed, modified only by whatever externalities warrant its modification in order to be developed successfully in a different location and that location's locally imposed constraints. However, the Idea may be something completely different, not only for the Developer but also for the Market Area in

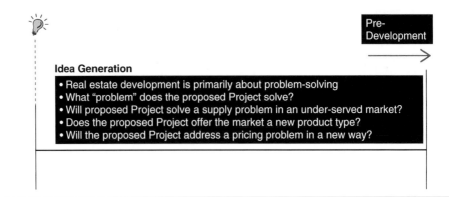

Figure 2.8 The Development Process: The Project Conception Phase

which the Developer is considering implementing (i.e., developing) the Project Concept. Idea Generation may be viewed as an intellectual exercise intended to answer a set of questions:

- Is there demand in the market for a real estate product that hasn't been offered before?
- Do current commercial property typologies take full advantage of potential synergies among various users of existing commercial property types?
- Are consumers willing to pay a premium for conveniences, features, and amenities not available to them in the market's current offerings of commercial property types?

Consider some of the product types that are perhaps commonplace today, at least in metropolitan areas, but that no one had conceived of only twenty, thirty, and forty years ago. The following might well fall into this category:

- Town Center retail complexes
- Highly amenitized, renter-by-choice projects
- Mixed-density, Mixed-Use, New Urbanist communities
- Urban, Mixed-Use developments
- Luxury condominium and hotel buildings offering concierge services for residents

How can a Developer tap into consumers' unmet needs and demands by developing the next, new real estate product type? That is what the Idea Generation Sub-Phase is all about.

Site Identification (Figure 2.9). Generally, a Developer will have "the Idea" before identifying the ideal property (i.e., the "Subject Site") on which to develop the Idea. However, that may not always be the case. An opportunistic property acquisition – or, at least, the identification of a property that may eventually constitute an opportunistic acquisition – may present itself and then generate the Idea. What ultimately becomes the Subject Site may be identified through a number of methods. First, the Developer may already own the property and be waiting for the right market timing, optimum approvals environment, or other external condition or event (or some combination of prevailing conditions and/or occurrence of events) to develop it profitably and within the Developer's comfort zone of expertise. Alternatively, the Developer may have a business or other relationship with the owner of the property, the acquisition and development of which meets the Developer's risk and reward parameters for proceeding with Project Conception. Absent the first or second scenarios, the Developer will need to employ one or more methods for seeking out and vetting one or more potential

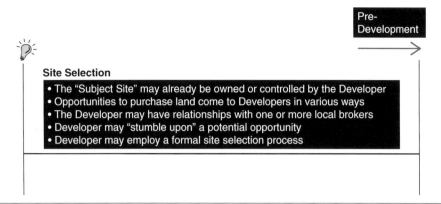

Site Selection
- The "Subject Site" may already be owned or controlled by the Developer
- Opportunities to purchase land come to Developers in various ways
- The Developer may have relationships with one or more local brokers
- Developer may "stumble upon" a potential opportunity
- Developer may employ a formal site selection process

Figure 2.9 The Development Process: The Project Conception Phase

properties on which the Idea may be executed. In that case, the site search and selection process, also known as "Site Selection," may involve the principal(s) of the Developer, the Developer's staff, and/or one or more third parties engaged for such a purpose, such as a commercial property broker. Once a particular property has been identified, then the Developer will proceed with the other tasks or Sub-Phases of the Project Conception Phase, except as noted in the Community Outreach Sub-Phase.

Develop Exit and Funding Strategies: How Will "the Idea" Pay Off (Figure 2.10)?
A Developer should never embark upon The Development Process without first knowing, or at least having an inkling about the **Exit Strategy**: the specific manner in which the Developer will receive compensation or otherwise extract value from the Project in a way that properly compensates the Developer for the value created. This Exit Strategy may or may not involve actually exiting from the transaction. Similarly, inasmuch as the Developer most likely will be seeking various sources of equity and debt to fund the Project at various phases in The Development Process, a **Funding Strategy** premised on the Developer's Exit Strategy will be an essential framework for seeking and securing various sources of funding, with a view toward avoiding, to the greatest extent possible, conflicts between different funding sources and their respective, idiosyncratic funding requirements. Even though it is very early in the Project Conception Phase of The Development Process, and knowing that the Funding Strategy will need to adapt as the Idea evolves well into the Pre-Development Phase,

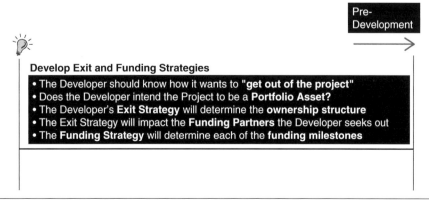

Develop Exit and Funding Strategies
- The Developer should know how it wants to **"get out of the project"**
- Does the Developer intend the Project to be a **Portfolio Asset?**
- The Developer's **Exit Strategy** will determine the **ownership structure**
- The Exit Strategy will impact the **Funding Partners** the Developer seeks out
- The **Funding Strategy** will determine each of the **funding milestones**

Figure 2.10 The Development Process: The Project Conception Phase

having the Funding Strategy as a guide during the Project Conception Phase will be critical to the feasibility and overall success of the Project.

Analysis and Selection of Project Delivery Method (Figure 2.11). It might seem counterintuitive to start thinking about how to build a Project that hasn't even been fully conceived, must less have a potential site for development. However, inasmuch as **Project Delivery Methods** are no longer limited to variants of the traditional **Design/Bid/Build** method of pricing and securing a Construction Contract and General Contractor, new, more innovative Project Delivery Methods demand that the method by which the Developer intends to have the Project constructed be considered very early in the Project Conception Phase of The Development Process. At a minimum, both the Design/Bid/Build and the **Integrated Project Delivery** methods require the early identification of the General Contractor or "GC" to participate as a member of the Development Team. Identifying and selecting the GC under either the Design/Bid/Build or Integrated Project Delivery method, and making that GC an integral part of the Development Team, is crucial to the success of either of these two Project Delivery Methods.

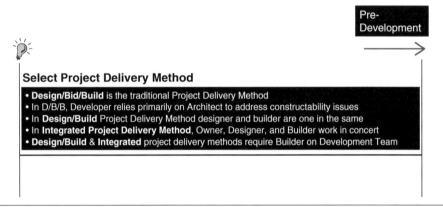

Figure 2.11 **The Development Process**: The Project Conception Phase

Community Outreach (Figure 2.12). Generally speaking, some form of Community Outreach needs to be undertaken once the potential Subject Site has been identified through the Site identification Sub-Phase. However, and as alluded to in the preceding paragraph, under some circumstances it may be prudent for the Developer to refrain from *any* activities whatsoever unless and until a Community Outreach strategy has been developed and is ready for implementation. This is in part due to the fact that in many communities, particularly those with existing and politically active residential neighborhoods, real estate developers are held in less than high regard. In close-knit and politically active residential communities, the grapevine works exceedingly well but almost never to a developer's advantage. A developer getting out too far ahead of potentially impacted neighborhoods may generate so much community distrust that the project may never secure necessary zoning and land use approvals. As a consequence, even the mere whiff that a developer is "poking around" in a particular jurisdiction, in search of real property to develop or redevelop, may by itself set off an opposition movement. Under such circumstances, some form of community outreach may be warranted, introducing the Developer to the potentially impacted communities. This approach, however, must be balanced against having local planning staff and elected officials feel slighted or, worse yet, giving the impression that the Developer is working and plotting

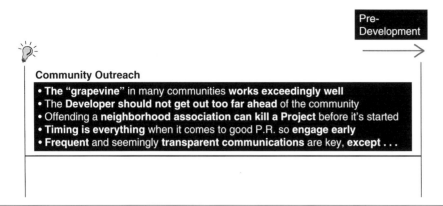

Community Outreach
- **The "grapevine"** in many communities **works exceedingly well**
- The **Developer should not get out too far ahead** of the community
- Offending a **neighborhood association can kill a Project** before it's started
- **Timing is everything** when it comes to good P.R. so **engage early**
- **Frequent** and seemingly **transparent communications** are key, **except . . .**

Figure 2.12 The Development Process: The Project Conception Phase

with local residents to game the system against the jurisdiction's normal process for civic engagement as part of the planning approvals process.

Assemble and Engage Development Team (Figure 2.13). Getting to the 80:2 Solution, means engaging third-party professionals very early on in the process, well before the Developer is in any position to know whether the Idea is financially feasible or even viable at all. Hiring professionals means spending money or at least committing to expend funds in the future. In a depressed market for professional services, participation on the Development Team, particularly for an existing or attractive prospective client, may be undertaken as a loss-leader for many firms, particularly if such participation is the best way to assure the opportunity to continue as part of the Development Team as a Project moves from the Project Conception Phase to the Pre-Development Phase. Additionally, for the vast majority of tasks third-party professional services firms undertake during the Project Conception Phase, little to no professional liability is incurred. Consequently, covering actual costs to be incurred, such as the fully loaded staff costs of all personnel to be involved in the engagement and any out-of-pocket expenses to be incurred, may comprise the threshold for agreeing to participate on the Development Team. For most real estate development projects in the Project Conception Phase, the Development Team will be comprised of the following experts: a design or design and engineering firm; a civil engineering or land planning firm; an environmental assessment vendor; a local law firm specializing in zoning and land use in the jurisdiction where the

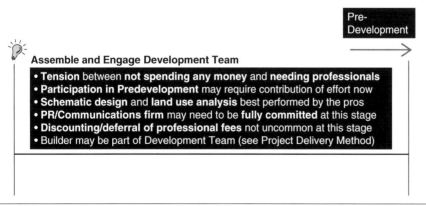

Assemble and Engage Development Team
- **Tension** between **not spending any money** and **needing professionals**
- **Participation in Predevelopment** may require contribution of effort now
- **Schematic design** and **land use analysis** best performed by the pros
- **PR/Communications firm** may need to be **fully committed** at this stage
- **Discounting/deferral of professional fees** not uncommon at this stage
- Builder may be part of Development Team (see Project Delivery Method)

Figure 2.13 The Development Process: The Project Conception Phase

property is located; a market analysis firm experienced in the market and submarket where the property is located; and a communications and public relations firm. Additionally, and as suggested elsewhere in this chapter, the General Contractor for the Project, if an Integrated Project Delivery or Design/Bid/Build project delivery system is to be used to construct the Improvements on the property to be acquired and developed, will also need to be included as part of the Development Team very early on in the Project Conception Phase.

Preliminary Program (Figure 2.14). The Preliminary Program represents the Developer's first attempt to quantify the Idea, providing a relatively simple framework for determining the potential scale of the Project and making some very crude, very early projections about costs and gross revenues. The Preliminary Program may be expressed narratively but more often than not is a quantitative, tabular description of the Idea. For example, the Preliminary Program for a multifamily rental project could be narratively described as "a 300-unit rental project comprised of one, two, and three-bedroom units."

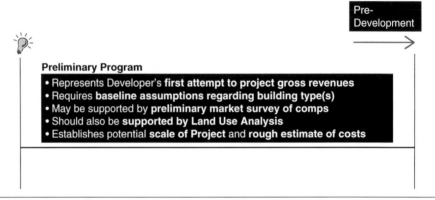

Figure 2.14 The Development Process: The Project Conception Phase

Alternatively, this hypothetical, multifamily rental project might be more specifically articulated as follows:

Preliminary program for hypothetical, 300-unit multifamily rental project (Figure 2.15)

The Preliminary Program may drive the Site Selection Sub-Phase or vice versa. For example, if the Developer builds, owns, and manages a portfolio of renter-by-choice, upper-market, multifamily properties (adding very important detail to the earlier, narrative description), many of the components in the Preliminary Program will be givens, dictating the search parameters for Site Selection purposes.

Continuing with this hypothetical, assuming the Developer's experience with the luxury, renter-by-choice product type and market indicates that an additional 20% of the building envelope will be taken up by its Core Factor (i.e., 43,200 sq. ft.), to account for common areas including building entrance lobbies, hallways, elevator cores, stairwells, fitness and community rooms, and the like, the gross square footage of the building or buildings comprising the Improvements will be 216,000 sq. ft. (i.e., 172,800 sq. ft. of gross leasable area plus a 43,200 sq. ft. Core Area). Accordingly, the maximum allowable F.A.R. (i.e., the maximum amount of floor area that may be constructed as a multiple of the gross area of the land on which it's constructed, hence the acronym "Floor Area Ratio) will eliminate some properties while putting others into sharper focus.

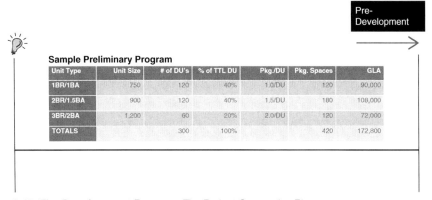

Sample Preliminary Program

Unit Type	Unit Size	# of DU's	% of TTL DU	Pkg./DU	Pkg. Spaces	GLA
1BR/1BA	750	120	40%	1.0/DU	120	90,000
2BR/1.5BA	900	120	40%	1.5/DU	180	108,000
3BR/2BA	1,200	60	20%	2.0/DU	120	72,000
TOTALS		300	100%		420	172,800

Figure 2.15 The Development Process: The Project Conception Phase

The application of the foregoing parameters isn't the end of the analysis, however, because the 420 parking spaces identified in the Preliminary Program also need to be taken into account. And it's not enough to provide just for how resident, guest, staff, and service vehicles will be parked on the Subject Site. Properties on which the Site Selection process will be focused must also manage how a variety of vehicles, including but not limited to emergency and refuse collection and disposal vehicles, gain access to and exit from the property. This is commonly known by planners and other real estate professionals as "ingress and egress."

In fact, other than the relationship of the proposed projected gross floor area of Improvements to a specific property's F.A.R., nothing so impacts the development feasibility of real property as how vehicular traffic and vehicles themselves are managed on-site. Returning to the hypothetical example relating to the Preliminary Program presented in the table, assuming the Developer's preferred product type involves wrapping residential buildings around multistory, structured parking with pedestrian walkways connecting the two (what's commonly referred to as a "Texas donut," because the product type was pioneered in Texas and, in plan, resembles a donut), then the number of parking spaces projected in the Preliminary Program will need to be translated into the number of spaces per floor, the number of floors required to meet the total parking requirement, and the footprint, expressed in square feet, of the parking structure.

In moving forward with the Project Conception Phase of The Development Process the Preliminary Program will be tested by the Market Overview, the Preliminary Infrastructure Assessment, and the Land Use Analysis, and either confirmed are revised. Rarely, however, does the Site Selection process turn up a potential property to be considered for acquisition and development that *perfectly* matches the Preliminary Program. Consequently, the most likely outcome of moving into the Sub-Phases following the Preliminary Program is that the Preliminary Program will be revised specifically in response to what is learned by the Development Team from one or more of the subsequent Sub-Phases of the Project Conception Phase. The interplay between the Preliminary Program, Market Overview, Preliminary Infrastructure Assessment, and Land Use Analysis, Sub-Phases may, in fact, be one of the best examples of how The Development Process is both linear and iterative. As new information generated through a series of seemingly sequential Sub-Phases prompts a series of tweaks to or even the complete recasting of the Preliminary Program, the iterative nature of The Development Process becomes clear.

Market Overview or Survey (Figure 2.16). One area from which the Preliminary Program most likely will benefit is attaching market pricing to the product or products the

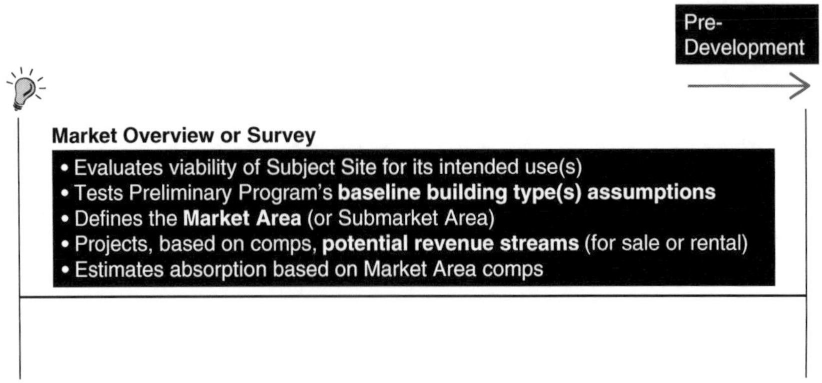

Pre-Development

Market Overview or Survey
- Evaluates viability of Subject Site for its intended use(s)
- Tests Preliminary Program's **baseline building type(s) assumptions**
- Defines the **Market Area** (or Submarket Area)
- Projects, based on comps, **potential revenue streams** (for sale or rental)
- Estimates absorption based on Market Area comps

Figure 2.16 The Development Process: The Project Conception Phase

Developer contemplated when first generating the Idea, and then refined in developing the Preliminary Program. In the hypothetical example given earlier, how much should each of the three unit types – 1BR/1BA, 2BR/1.5BA, and 3BR/2BA – command as asking rents in that particular market and geographic submarket? A threshold question, before getting to pricing, however, is: *What is the Market Area for the Project?* Below are some of the questions that the **Market Overview or Survey** may ask and answer:

- From where is the Project most likely to draw potential renters?
- Which existing and planned projects will the marketplace view as competing with the Developer's proposed Project?
- Is the Market Area one that the target tenants – luxury apartment renters by choice (i.e., individuals and households that can afford to be buyers and owners of for-sale housing but, for various reasons, choose to rent instead) – view as desirable?
- What amenities, unit configurations, and unit sizes does this target audience find most appealing?

While falling far short of, and costing substantially less than a comprehensive Market Study, the Market Overview or Survey should answer some or all of these and other questions about the market and geographic submarket. Relating to the Preliminary Program in the hypothetical presented earlier, the answers to questions about the market that the Market Overview or Survey should answer, the Developer may decide to change the proportions of the different unit configurations and sizes presented, and may even modify or eliminate entirely one or more unit type. For example, should the 3BR/2BA units be eliminated entirely or retained in modified form but at a different percentage of the Project total? Given that the total number of units contemplated is fairly large, would a broader range of unit configurations and sizes benefit the Developer by decreasing the amount of time required for the market to absorb all 300 units (the Absorption Rate), such that the changes detailed later may be warranted to the Preliminary Program?

Revised Preliminary Program (Figure 2.17). As suggested in the preceding section, one scenario in which The Development Process is most likely to prove itself both linear and iterative is in the evolution of the Preliminary Program.

Revised Preliminary Program for Hypothetical, 300-unit Multifamily Rental Project (Figure 2.18). Using the example of the 300-unit multifamily rental project, described

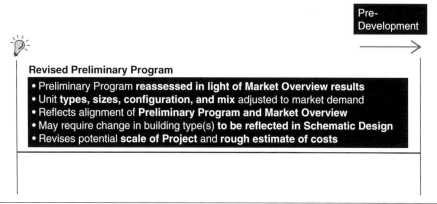

Revised Preliminary Program

- Preliminary Program **reassessed in light of Market Overview results**
- Unit **types, sizes, configuration, and mix** adjusted to market demand
- Reflects alignment of **Preliminary Program and Market Overview**
- May require change in building type(s) **to be reflected in Schematic Design**
- Revises potential **scale of Project** and **rough estimate of costs**

Pre-Development

Figure 2.17 The Development Process: The Project Conception Phase

Pre-Development

Sample Revised Preliminary Program

Unit Type	Unit Size	# of DU's	% of TTL DU	Pkg./DU	Pkg. Spaces	GLA
Studio	500	60	20%	0.5/DU	30	30,000
1BR/1BA	650	60	20%	1.0/DU	60	39,000
1BR+Den/1.5BA	850	60	20%	1.5/DU	90	51,000
2BR/1.5BA	900	60	20%	1.5/DU	90	54,000
2BR+DEN/2BA	1,150	30	10%	2.0/DU	60	34,500
3BR/2.5BA	1,350	30	10%	2.5/DU	75	40,500
TOTALS		300	100%		405	249,000

Figure 2.18 The Development Process: The Project Conception Phase

in the Preliminary Program, the Revised Preliminary Program shown later demonstrates how the Market Overview or Survey information may change how the Project is comprised:

Under the Revised Preliminary Program, the gross leasable area (GLA) for the building, without taking into account the Core Factor or the parking structure, is 249,000 square feet, versus 172,000 square feet for the Improvements originally contemplated and reflected in the Preliminary Program. Accordingly, the GLA has increased by 44 per cent Naturally, after factoring in the same 25 per cent Core Factor and the 465 parking spaces (versus 420 parking spaces in the Preliminary Program), the Developer will be looking for a substantially larger property given these revisions to the program. Any properties initially identified in the Site Selection process will more than likely need to be rejected or the Developer will need to scale down the overall size of the project. However, if the Developer's past experience in developing such projects, and its ongoing experience in providing property management to completed projects, is that 300 units is the ideal size to achieve certain economies of scale in property management, it is possible that no properties are available in the geographic area where the Developer's Site Selection process has been concentrated. Clearly, then, in the scenario posited earlier, the Market Overview or Survey has a huge impact on the Project Conception Phase of The Development Process **(Figure 2.19)**.

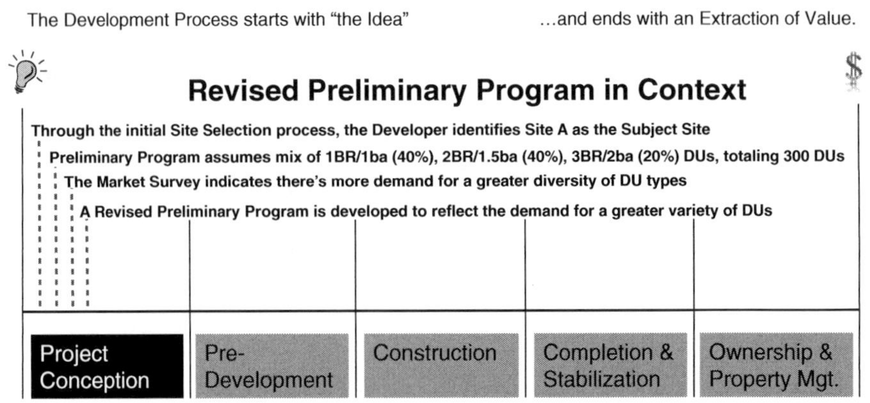

The Development Process starts with "the Idea"   ...and ends with an Extraction of Value.

Revised Preliminary Program in Context

Through the initial Site Selection process, the Developer identifies Site A as the Subject Site

Preliminary Program assumes mix of 1BR/1ba (40%), 2BR/1.5ba (40%), 3BR/2ba (20%) DUs, totaling 300 DUs

The Market Survey indicates there's more demand for a greater diversity of DU types

A Revised Preliminary Program is developed to reflect the demand for a greater variety of DUs

Project Conception	Pre-Development	Construction	Completion & Stabilization	Ownership & Property Mgt.

Figure 2.19 The Development Process

Preliminary Infrastructure Assessment (Figure 2.20). A Preliminary Infrastructure Assessment can generally be conducted by a civil engineer's examination of public records available in the department of public works of the jurisdiction in which the Site Selection Process is being undertaken. Engaging on the Development Team a local civil engineer whose firm has experience with recent projects in that same jurisdiction is prudent, as that firm may have identified and resolved infrastructure issues that may also pose challenges on one or more potential properties identified during the Site Selection process. Such a firm may also have a sense for the path of least resistance within the jurisdiction to getting infrastructure issues resolved in the most efficient manner possible.

The Preliminary Infrastructure Assessment should determine what utilities (water, electrical, high-capacity data lines, natural gas, sewage, and storm water runoff) are already *provided to* or are already *accessible from* the proposed site, and where the nearest connections are located. It may also reveal whether any such utilities present any capacity issues relevant to the Preliminary or Revised Preliminary Program, such as whether the age and diameters of water and sewage lines are sufficient, without being upgraded, to handle the increased requirements presented by the contemplated project or whether the nearest electrical substation can handle the increased demand for electricity without being upgraded.

Depending on the policies of the jurisdiction and the utility provider involved, increasing the capacities of utilities necessary to the success of the contemplated Project may involve capital outlays well beyond the allocable cost of the increase in capacity requirements of any particular, proposed project. However, it's impractical for utilities to increase their capacity in such small increments, to accommodate *only* the demands of the next project. Consequently, accommodating the next incremental step in the capacity of a utility – such as increasing a water supply line from twelve inches to sixteen inches – will inevitably involve an increase in capacity well beyond what the contemplated Project will require. Moreover, if a utility can reasonably project future demand for increased capacity for any number of reasons, it may decide to leapfrog past the next incremental increase in capacity, in anticipation of the future increase in demand. Using the example of needing to increase the water supply line serving the potential site and other properties as well, the utility may determine that the twelve-inch water supply line needs to be upgraded to a twenty-inch line instead of a sixteen-inch line.

In addition to assessing off-site capacity issues, the Preliminary Infrastructure Assessment will determine, again based on existing records, the types, sizes, and locations of on-site utilities. Learning from public records where the sanitary sewage system connection is located

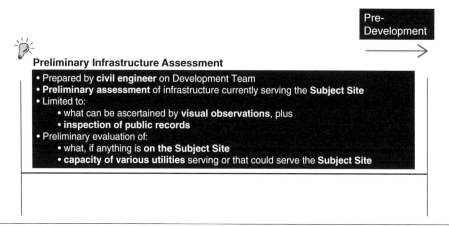

Pre-Development

Preliminary Infrastructure Assessment
- Prepared by **civil engineer** on Development Team
- **Preliminary assessment** of infrastructure currently serving the **Subject Site**
- Limited to:
    - what can be ascertained by **visual observations**, plus
    - **inspection of public records**
- Preliminary evaluation of:
    - what, if anything is **on the Subject Site**
    - **capacity of various utilities** serving or that could serve the **Subject Site**

Figure 2.20 The Development Process: The Project Conception Phase

under a boundary street is one thing; knowing how existing improvements on the potential site are served by that utility on-site is another matter. However, if neither the owner and prospective seller of a property nor the local utility have as-built plans showing the on-site location of utility runs to the nearest off-site connection, the civil engineer may have to make a physical inspection of the prospective site using techniques and equipment designed to locate underground utilities. Such an effort may not, however, be included in whatever arrangements the Developer and the civil engineering firm have regarding the latter's participation and performance of services on the Development Team during the Project Conception Phase of The Development Process.

Land Use Analysis (Figure 2.21). As contrasted with the Preliminary Infrastructure Assessment, the Land Use Analysis reviews and assesses a number of characteristics of a property, including but not limited to site conditions such as slope, the presence of still or moving water, biological and cultural resources, known or reasonably predictable soils conditions (in lieu of actual soils testing, normally conducted during the Pre-Development Phase), ingress and egress issues, and any observable endangered species or endangered species habitats. The Land Use Analysis is the first step in identifying what portions of the potential site may be developed and what portions of that site will or should be restricted

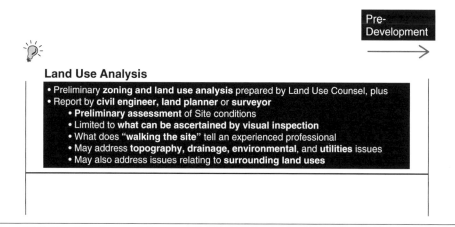

Pre-Development

Land Use Analysis
- Preliminary **zoning and land use analysis** prepared by Land Use Counsel, plus
- Report by **civil engineer, land planner** or **surveyor**
    - **Preliminary assessment** of Site conditions
    - Limited to **what can be ascertained by visual inspection**
    - What does **"walking the site"** tell an experienced professional
    - May address **topography, drainage, environmental**, and **utilities** issues
    - May also address issues relating to **surrounding land uses**

Figure 2.21 The Development Process: The Project Conception Phase

in terms of the construction of Improvements thereon. For example, steep slopes present challenges for both the construction of improvements and managing water runoff on a property. Depending on the location, direction of pitch, and severity of the incline of a steep slope, normal grading techniques may not be sufficient and building retaining walls may prove too costly a solution to create more buildable area. The presence of either still or moving water (e.g., a pond or lake or a stream or creek, respectively) may present both flooding and environmental issues. Either may also provide on its shoreline habitats for critical botanicals and/or endangered species. The Land Use Analysis is intended to provide the Developer with a threshold set of constraints on how the Subject Site may be developed with Improvements beyond any that may already be present on the property.

Schematic Design (Figure 2.22). Based on all of the inputs the Developer and the Development Team receive from the Preliminary Infrastructure Analysis and the Land Use Analysis, a Schematic Design will be created, depicting, in at least a Site Plan format, how the latest iteration of the Revised Preliminary Program will be constructed on the Subject Site if the Project were to proceed based on all the information at the Developer's disposal. Depending on how the Developer has composed the Development Team, the Schematic Design may be prepared by a land planning firm, a landscape architecture firm, or a full-service architecture and design firm. In other words, the firm preparing the Schematic Design for the Subject Site may not be the same firm that prepares the designs and construction documents for the building comprising the Improvements on the Subject Site.

The Schematic Design will show the footprints of all buildings (existing, if applicable, and to be constructed); each point of ingress onto and egress from the property, as well as all internal roads and walkways; surface parking lots and/or parking structures on the site, including all parking lot and garage entryways and exits; and any site amenities, including but not limited to all active and passive-use outdoor spaces. In addition to providing, in plan view, the first graphic depiction of how the proposed site would be developed in order to implement the Developer's Idea, the Schematic Design allows the Developer and its planners or designers to test how the potential site meets certain land use requirements and restrictions on which land use approvals will be conditioned, such as setbacks from public sidewalks and other buildings, and any requirements that a minimum percentage of the total area of a developed property be dedicated to Open Space. The Schematic Design also allows the Development Team to assess how effectively vehicular traffic will be managed on-site, as well as how efficiently vehicular traffic flows into and out of the Subject Site.

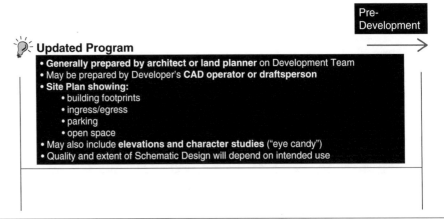

Figure 2.22 The Development Process: The Project Conception Phase

Updated Program (Figure 2.23). It is somewhat misleading, by attempting to provide this chronological list of Sub-Phases in the Project Conception Phases of The Development Process, to suggest that there is a single opportunity or point in time during this Phase to update the Preliminary Program. As suggested in the earlier discussion about the Market Overview or Survey, the continuous feedback loop about "the Idea" may prompt many iterations of the program as it is adjusted to accommodate the challenges and opportunities presented by each property identified and examined as part of the Site Selection process. The foregoing discussion suggests how the Market Overview or Survey could prompt the development of a Revised Preliminary Program. Similarly, while not addressed specifically in the discussion about the Preliminary Infrastructure Assessment, limitations on the capacities of existing utility services, and a narrow range of options for addressing those capacity issues, could prompt substantial changes to the Preliminary Program.

Pre-Development

Updated Program

- Represents **further refinements** to Revised Preliminary Program
- Reflects re-assessment of all **baseline assumptions**
- Continues to reflect **Market Survey**
- Land yield assumption must be **supported by Land Use Analysis**
- Takes **Preliminary Infrastructure Assessment** into account
- Makes Program adjustments **informed by Schematic Design**

Figure 2.23 The Development Process: The Project Conception Phase

For example, if a proposed property offers strong fundamentals in other respects, such as competitive pricing and strong locational characteristics, but is less than ideal for a 300-unit, luxury, renter-by-choice product based on the demand such project would likely place on the existing capacity of utilities services, would scaling back the project allow such a project to proceed without the Developer having to make a contribution to the capital expenditures necessary to increase such capacity **(Figure 2.24)**? Can the Developer make the Project

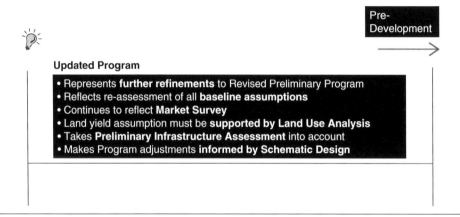

The Development Process starts with "the Idea"   ...and ends with an Extraction of Value.

Updated Program in Context

Revised Preliminary Program reflects Market Survey demand for a greater variety of DUs than Preliminary Program

Land Use Analysis shows constraints on buildable portion of Subject Site requiring change in building type

Preliminary Infrastructure Assessment shows that 300 DU program will require expensive capacity upgrades

Updated Program adjusts to examine simplified 200 DU program to keep Total Development Costs down

| Project Conception | Pre-Development | Construction | Completion & Stabilization | Ownership & Property Mgt. |

Figure 2.24 The Development Process: The Project Conception Phase

successful from an operational standpoint with fewer than 300 units to manage (for example, does the Developer have an existing project within a reasonable distance from the potential site that the two projects could share some operational staff, making a 200-unit project feasible)?

Pre-Development

Sample Updated Program

Unit Type	Unit Size	# of DU's	% of TTL DU	Pkg./DU	Pkg. Spaces	GLA
1BR/1BA	750	80	40%	1.0/DU	80	60,000
2BR/1.5BA	900	80	40%	1.5/DU	120	72,000
3BR/2BA	1,200	40	20%	2.0/DU	80	48,000
		200	100%		280	115,800

Figure 2.25 The Development Process: The Project Conception Phase

　　The Updated Program for a hypothetical, 200-unit multifamily rental project requires only 115,800 square feet of gross leasable area and 280 parking spaces, instead of 172,800 GLA and 420 parking spaces. Assuming that the Preliminary Program could have been physically accommodated on the potential site, this reduction in the total number of units to develop could change the building type and allow for other changes in the program as well, depending on how detailed the Market Overview or Study is. For example, perhaps the renter-by-choice market contains a niche for larger and more luxurious units, which would command higher rents on a per-square-foot basis. Further, if the Market Overview or Survey indicates that, regardless of the unit configurations, the market demands only one covered parking space per unit, could the building type be changed from a Texas donut configuration to a podium-style building, where the ground floor accommodates only the building lobby and the remainder is one level of structured parking, with all of the units constructed above? The additional land area of the potential site could be used for (i) surface parking for eighty vehicles and (ii) a separate community building, providing enhanced amenities that the renter-by-choice market expects/demands for the higher rents the Project would be expected to command.

　　The process of updating and revising the program will continue until all inputs expected to be elicited through the Project Conception Phase have been exhausted, including the three Sub-phases: **Preliminary Development Budget pro forma**, Land Use Analysis, and **Schematic Design**, respectively. Additionally, as more information is revealed about the potential property and how and with what it may be developed, additional and/or more specific inputs may be sought from various members of the Development Team. Again, this process of continuous, ongoing feedback loops illustrates how The Development Process is both linear and iterative.

　　Preliminary Development Budget pro forma (Figure 2.26). The Preliminary Development Budget pro forma will be developed based on all new inputs from the preceding Sub-Phases in the Project Conception Phase. As noted later, eventually a new document, the Preliminary Operating Budget pro forma, will be created, and these two sets of financial projections will together constitute the Preliminary Project pro forma on which requests for

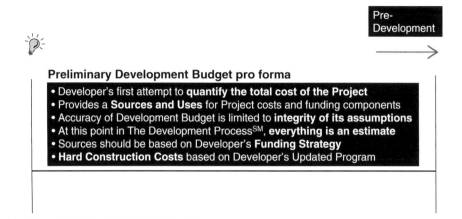

Pre-Development

Preliminary Development Budget pro forma
- Developer's first attempt to **quantify the total cost of the Project**
- Provides a **Sources and Uses** for Project costs and funding components
- Accuracy of Development Budget is limited to **integrity of its assumptions**
- At this point in The Development Process^{SM}, **everything is an estimate**
- Sources should be based on Developer's **Funding Strategy**
- **Hard Construction Costs** based on Developer's Updated Program

Figure 2.26 The Development Process: The Project Conception Phase

financing commitments will be based. An additional iteration of the Revised Program, showing rental rates and annual projected Gross Rental Income, is provided in the Supplemental Materials on the companion website for this textbook.

Once the Revised Preliminary Program has evolved sufficiently that the basic parameters and building type(s) are relatively certain (as certain as they can be when pursuing the 80:2 Solution), the Developer will be in a position to develop a Preliminary Project pro forma. Among other things, this means that as a function of the Site Selection process the Developer has decided to focus on one particular potential property for the implementation of the Idea and is no longer actively pursuing other alternatives (the Subject Site), at least for the time being.

The Developer should have enough information from the Market Overview or Survey and from the Preliminary Infrastructure Assessment to know what product type(s) will work best on the Subject Site, and through the Revised Preliminary Program, have an estimate of the total square feet of building or buildings that need to be constructed. The Developer should be in a position to apply standards in that market for dollars per square feet of **Hard Construction Costs (HCC)** for each type of product proposed, and also apply reasonable assumptions for soft costs and financing costs to be incurred, as well as the Land Cost based on the seller's asking price for the potential site. The Updated Preliminary Development Budget pro forma is used to test the financial feasibility of the Idea. Additionally, the Updated Preliminary Development Budget pro forma, when evaluated in the context of the Preliminary Operating Budget pro forma, will yield valuable insights into the potential profitability of the Project after stabilization, as well as the projected value of the completed Project based on its **Net Operating Income**.

Similar to the Preliminary Program, the Preliminary Development Budget pro forma is not intended to be a static document. Like the Preliminary Program, the Preliminary Development Budget pro forma will go through a series of iterations, with both greater detail and increasing certitude attached to the values and underlying assumptions of the pro forma. This is another excellent example of how The Development Process is both linear and iterative. For example, if the Developer has decided, at the outset of the Project Conception Phase of The Development Process, to use the traditional Design/Bid/Build Project Delivery System for the construction of the Improvements, then the Preliminary Development Budget pro forma may rely on a commonly accepted cost-per-square-foot number to project the cost of the Improvements. Using the information already provided in the Preliminary Program for the 300-unit multifamily rental hypothetical, for example, if the **Residential** Building Type, excluding the cost of designing and constructing the parking structure, generally costs $150/square foot in hard construction costs (HCC), then constructing the residential buildings will be $32.4 million (216,000 sq. ft. X $150/sq. ft.). That does not include the cost of the land, soft costs (design and building engineering, civil engineering, accounting, legal, etc.), carrying costs or capitalized interest, furniture, fixtures, and equipment (FF&E) needed to outfit the Project, and contingency funds. As with each of the preceding Sub-Phases in the Project Conception Phase of The Development Process, the evolution of the Preliminary Program and the Preliminary Development Budget will proceed down parallel tracks, demonstrating the linear yet iterative nature of The Development Process.

Preliminary Project pro forma (Figure 2.27). As mentioned earlier, like the Preliminary Program, the Preliminary Development Budget pro forma is a dynamic document, going through a series of revisions every time new information is obtained throughout the Project Conception Phase of The Development Process. At this point in the Project Conception Phase, all of the inputs from the preceding Sub-Phases should have been received, other than (i) any remaining negotiations with the Seller of the Subject Site that would impact the acquisition price and, therefore, the Land Cost in the Development Budget, and (ii) the financing structure for the Project, including any equity contributions beyond what the Developer has already or plans to contribute to the venture, and debt financing for the Construction Loan and subsequent construction take-out financing (i.e., Permanent Financing). An Updated Preliminary Development Budget pro forma will be prepared, taking into account all new information not previously available when the Preliminary Development Budget pro forma was prepared, as well as reflecting any changes made to the most recently updated Revised Preliminary Program as the result of new information obtained since the last update of the Revised Preliminary Program. Students and readers are encouraged to consider additional information on the evolution of the aforementioned documents, and the iterative nature between them, in the Supplementary Materials on the companion website for this textbook.

Additionally, an Operating Budget pro forma will be prepared, based on the best information available to the Developer at the time. Inasmuch as the only way to project the Net Operating Income (NOI) from the Project following its completion and income stabilization is through an Operating Budget, and considering, further, that most income-producing property is valued based on applying a capitalization rate (commonly known as a "cap rate") to the Project's projected NOI, it would be difficult to seek, much less secure, Permanent Financing for the Project without some rational, supportable estimation of the its value. Accordingly, the Updated

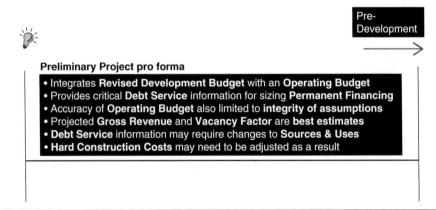

Preliminary Project pro forma

- Integrates **Revised Development Budget** with an **Operating Budget**
- Provides critical **Debt Service** information for sizing **Permanent Financing**
- Accuracy of **Operating Budget** also limited to **integrity of assumptions**
- Projected **Gross Revenue** and **Vacancy Factor** are **best estimates**
- **Debt Service** information may require changes to **Sources & Uses**
- **Hard Construction Costs** may need to be adjusted as a result

Pre-Development

Figure 2.27 The Development Process: The Project Conception Phase

Development Budget pro forma and the Operating Budget pro forma are referred to collectively as the Preliminary Project pro forma.

Among other inputs into the Operating Budget pro forma are the projected rents based on the Revised Preliminary Program, which in turn are based on the Market Overview or Survey, relying on comparable rental product in the Market Area, adjusted up or down based on any unique characteristics of the Project that support a higher or lower rent per square foot. Larger unit sizes, a higher quality of fit and finish, more and better community amenities, and easy access to public transit could contribute to a higher asking rent than otherwise comparable properties in the Market Area. An inferior location, fewer amenities, and smaller unit sizes than comparable properties could warrant a downward adjustment on the asking rents in the Revised Preliminary Program.

The Updated Preliminary Project pro forma will be critical in seeking and securing all forms of financing for the Project. The better substantiated the numbers are and the more rational the underlying assumptions, such as the absorption schedule projecting how much time will be required between the issuance of the Certificate of Occupancy and the achievement of the projected full occupancy rate, the more credence will be accorded this document.

Negotiate Acquisition and Development (A&D) Financing Commitment (Figure 2.28). Before the financial collapse of the savings and loan industry in the late 1980s and early 1990s (the "S&L Crisis"), precipitating the most recent nationwide real estate recession prior to the Great Recession of 2008, and ushering in the Financial Institutions Reform, Recovery, and Enforcement Act of 1989 (FIRREA) and the Resolution Trust Corporation (RTC), savings and loan financial institutions commonly engaged in "relationship banking," which was particularly useful to the home-building boom at the time but also for commercial real estate lending generally. During the late 1970s and early 1980s, it was not uncommon for savings and loans and other financial institutions to make what were commonly known as "A&D Loans," providing developers with the funding necessary to acquire properties for development and to fund Pre-Development activities. Such loans were made to good customers who had a track record of repaying such A&D loans out of their construction financing, oftentimes provided by the same institution.

Following the S&L Crisis, and primarily as the result of greater restrictions on lending of this type under FIRREA, at the beginning of the twenty-first century, this type of lending became more and more scarce, with financial institutions having become very reluctant to place any

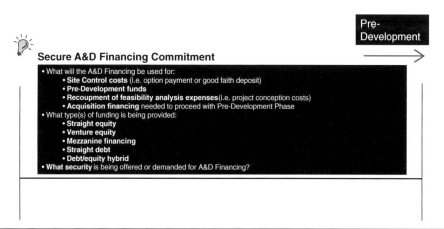

Figure 2.28 The Development Process: The Project Conception Phase

value whatsoever on raw (i.e., undeveloped) land as security for an A&D loan. So, despite retaining in the Project Conception Phase Sub-Phases this anachronistic nomenclature from the pre–S&L Crisis real estate development boom in the United States, "Negotiate Acquisition and Development (A&D) Financing Commitment" could translate to "Secure Early Stage Debt and Equity to Fund Pre-Development." Such funds no longer come from financial institutions but, instead, from institutional investors who are active in commercial real estate development financing. And such early stage financing may come in many forms, running the gamut from pure debt with a very high risk premium attached to debt–equity hybrids to straight equity, and may also include funding of the Developer itself instead of the Developer's Project, with the Developer then contributing such funds as its equity contribution to the endeavor.

Without such early stage commitment of funding, the Project might not proceed for a number of reasons. The Developer may have the resources to invest its own funds as an equity contribution, but making such a commitment may unreasonably constrain the Developer's capacity to engage in other transactions, thereby constraining the pipeline of potential new projects. The Developer may be using all or some portion of its liquid assets to backstop its land development activities and/or fund its ability to warehouse potentially lucrative properties for future development. Finally, the Developer may merely be used to financing its projects using OPM – Other People's Money – and prefer to leverage the capital of interested investors in whatever financing structure works best for that investor without making the project financing overly cumbersome.

Secure Site Control (Figure 2.29). Up to this point, the Developer's exposure to risk is limited to the costs incurred in engaging and compensating the members of the Development Team, on whatever basis the Developer can negotiate with each one. Walking away from a potential project that is not financially feasible or that is not projected to return a profit sufficient to warrant the risks involved may involve walking away from sunk costs that, in the aggregate, represent a mere fraction of potential losses if the project proves infeasible farther down the road, say halfway through the Pre-Development Phase of The Development Process. Making the commitment to Secure Site Control could quickly commit the Developer to out-of-pocket expenses that, in the aggregate, represent a substantial multiple of what the Developer just expended getting to the 80:2 Solution. Accordingly, this decision to proceed from the Project Conception Phase to the Pre-Development Phase is not undertaken lightly.

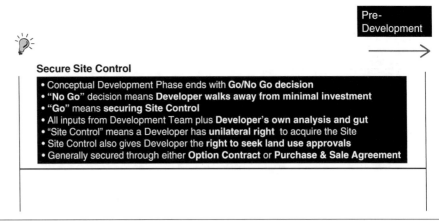

Figure 2.29 The Development Process: The Project Conception Phase

Securing Site Control may be accomplished in one of three ways. First, the Developer may make an outright purchase of the Subject Site, which is not going to happen because there is still too much that's not known about the property that could derail the execution of the Developer's Idea.

Second, the Developer may purchase an option for a specified period of time at an agreed-upon price – and perhaps including other terms favoring the Developer – but if that Option to Purchase the Property is not exercised in accordance with its terms and conditions, and the Option expires, the purchase price for the Option is not recoverable, even if the Developer has sound reasons for not completing the transaction.

Third and finally, the Developer may enter into a Purchase and Sale Agreement (PSA), conditioning the purchase upon a number of subjectively determined events affording the Developer considerable flexibility in determining whether to proceed with the acquisition after more information has been obtained and analyzed. One of the most common such conditions precedent to the Developer's obligation to purchase the Subject Site is the completion of a Due Diligence Period during which the Developer may walk away from the purchase contract and be entitled to a full refund of its good faith deposit accompanying the execution of the PSA, for any number of reasonable events subjectively assessed by the Developer. Because PSAs are generally structured in this manner, while the good faith deposit will be exponentially larger than the payment for a Purchase Option, the conditions under which the good faith deposit may be refunded to the Developer under a broad range of circumstances makes the PSA the preferred choice for securing legal control of the Subject Site with limited exposure for risk of losing the value of the good faith deposit.

Pre-Development Phase (Figure 2.30)

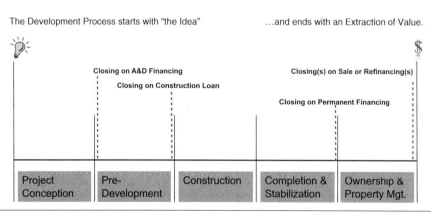

Figure 2.30 The Development Process

Closing on Acquisition and Development (A&D) Financing (Figure 2.31). All of the funds necessary to undertake the Project come in during the Pre-Development Phase **(Figure 2.32)**. Although a commitment for the Construction Loan will not be provided from the Construction Lender without a forward commitment on the Permanent Financing, the latter will eventually replace the former after certain preconditions are met (e.g., completion of the Construction Contract followed by occupancy of the Project and a period of Stabilized Rents). As suggested in the Project Conception Phase breakdown of Sub-Phases, this Sub-Phase could just as reasonably be referred to as "Closing on Early Stage Debt and Equity to

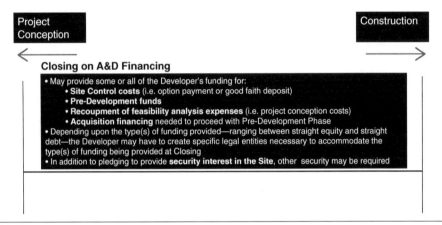

Figure 2.31 The Development Process: The Pre-Development Phase

| Project Conception | Pre-Development | Construction | Completion & Stabilization | Ownership & Property Mgt. |

Closing on A&D Financing

- May provide some or all of the Developer's funding for:
  - **Site Control costs** (i.e. option payment or good faith deposit)
  - **Pre-Development funds**
  - **Recoupment of feasibility analysis expenses** (i.e. project conception costs)
  - **Acquisition financing** needed to proceed with Pre-Development Phase
- Depending upon the type(s) of funding provided—ranging between straight equity and straight debt—the Developer may have to create specific legal entities necessary to accommodate the type(s) of funding being provided at Closing
- In addition to pledging to provide **security interest in the Site**, other security may be required

Figure 2.32 The Development Process: The Pre-Development Phase

Fund Pre-Development." Chapter 8 explains the impact of Entity Choice on the ability to bring financing into The Development Process, within the following context:

> [D]ifferent types of funding, with different risk and return expectations, need to come into the transaction at different points during The Development Process. As demonstrated in **Figure 2.31**, the timing of closing on each stage of Project Financing is critical to moving from one phase of The Development Process to the next.

In the current real estate lending environment, it is unlikely debt financing will provide much if any of the cash needed to fund Pre-Development Phase expenses. As also discussed in Chapter 8, early stage financing of the Project received during the Project Conception Phase of The Development Process is most likely only to be offered in the form of high-cost mezzanine financing, debt or hybrid financing coming in at the Developer rather than the Development Entity level.

> Although historically the banking community was willing to provide A&D Financing for Projects, particularly to Developers with whom a Lender had a positive, prior lending experiences, following the S&L Crisis starting in the late 1980s and continuing into the early 1990s and the subsequent enactment by the U.S. Congress of the Financial Institutions Reform, Recovery and Enforcement Act of 1989, commonly referred to as "FIRREA" (pronounced "fye-ree-ah"), and the creation of the

Resolution Trust Corporation or RTC, charged with responsibility, many of the savings and loans that commonly made A&D loans, as well as the practice itself, largely disappeared.

This historical aspect of the evolution of early stage, essentially exploratory funding for real estate development projects is relevant here for the same reason that the All-Debt **Take-Out Financing** scenario is relevant to an understanding about **Choice of Entity**. As long as this early stage funding came in the form of loans, even if they had to be guaranteed by the Developer and/or its individual principals, these loans did not present serious entity structuring issues for tax purposes because the tax treatment of loans, as discussed above, is very straightforward. However, once early stage, Project Conception Phase lending went away in the wake of FIRREA following the S&L Crisis, pure equity investments or debt plus equity investments, looking more like start-up venture capital than like the A&D loans of old became the only game in town. And introducing equity concepts changes the dynamics of Choice of Entity significantly.

See, in this regard, the discussion in the section titled Taxation of Transactions Involving, and Investments in, Real Estate, and the section that follows it – Equity vs. Debt: An Overview of Structuring Options for the Development Entity – in Chapter 8.

Some of the professional firms on the Development Team, such as those for design and engineering services, the fees for which the Construction Loan is expected to fund, may be willing to defer near-term fees until after the Closing on the Construction Loan (assuming, of course, such retroactive expenses are permitted to be paid from the Construction Loan draws).

Other expenses, however, such as for professional services that are *not* expected to continue past the Closing on the Construction Loan – including, without limitation, legal fees associated with securing all necessary land use approvals, the cost of the Market Study, and the performance of Value Engineering or "VE" prior to the completion of the Construction Documents – are rarely deferred by the respective professional service providers. Consequently, all such fees will need to be paid as they are earned.

Additionally, a critical milestone in the Pre-Development Phase of The Development Process is the Closing on the acquisition of the Subject Site. Up until that point, the Developer will have "Site Control" but will not actually be the title owner to that property. Depending on how this early stage funding is structured, a Special Purpose Entity (SPE) will most likely be taking title to the Subject Property rather than the Developer itself. Depending on the valuation and fundamentals of the Subject Site, as well as the source of the A&D financing secured in this initial Sub-Phase of the Pre-Development Phase, the lender will take a security interest in the Subject Site to the full extent of any financing provided at the Closing table on the land acquisition.

Market Study (Figure 2.33). Early on in the Project Conception Phase, the market analysis firm the Developer commissioned as part of the Development Team was tasked with performing a Market Overview or Survey. The primary purpose of that market research is to preliminarily identify the Market Area and provide the Developer with sufficient feedback to allow refinement of the Preliminary Program, leading to one or perhaps a series of increasingly refined Revised Preliminary Programs. The Market Overview or Survey is also intended to provide market-based support for the projected rents or sales prices for each and every product type contained in the Revised Program, which information feeds into the development of both the Revised Development Budget pro forma and the Operating Budget pro forma, which together comprise the Preliminary Project pro forma. Once Site Control has been secured, marking the end of the Project Conception Phase and the beginning of the Pre-Development Phase, all aspects of the Project must achieve new levels of exactitude as a predicate to securing a Permanent Financing Commitment and closing on the Construction

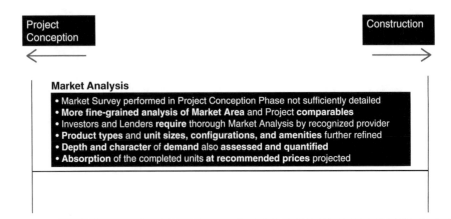

Figure 2.33 The Development Process: The Pre-Development Phase

Loan. In other words, in the Pre-Development Phase, the 80:2 Solution is no longer sufficient to serve as the financial basis for making the final decision to proceed to Closing on the Subject Site and becoming the record owner of title to the property, and then moving forward with construction.

Getting beyond the Market Overview or Survey with a formal Market Study is the first step in this Pre-Development Phase's incremental improvement in all of the inputs generated during the Project Conception Phase. Among other things, the Market Study will (i) further examine and, if necessary, make adjustments to the Market Area; (ii) identify, with particularity, the prospect base for each product type proposed as part of the Project and assess the breadth and depth of market demand for each product; and (iii) identify and examine, in detail, all comparable properties in the Market Area, whether existing or in the development pipeline, with which the Project will be competing. The increased depth of scrutiny of the Market Study in these areas will allow the market analysis firm to make projections on both the proper pricing of and absorption rate for each of the product types comprising the Project, both of which will be critical to Identify and Secure Take-Out (Permanent) Financing Commitment, a critical step toward the end of the Pre-Development Phase, and to Identify and Secure Construction Loan Commitment, for which having a "Take-Out Commitment" is a precondition. Additionally, the Market Study will likely inform additional changes to the Revised and Updated Program, including but not limited to requiring changes to product design.

Site Due Diligence (Figure 2.34). One of the most critical Sub-Phases of the Pre-Development Phase is conducting extensive due diligence on the Subject Site. This basically means learning everything the Developer can about the Subject Site that neither the time nor cost constraints the Project Conception Phase imposed would allow.

Site due diligence tasks may include but are not necessarily limited to:

(i) **Commissioning and examining carefully an ALTA Title Survey of the Subject Site.** The **American Land Title Association (ALTA)** and the American Congress on Surveying and Mapping (ACSM) provide the standards for "an **ALTA Title Survey**," which is a prerequisite to secure title insurance on real property. Together with an **ALTA Preliminary Title Report** [see paragraph (ii)], the ALTA Title Survey provides a complete picture of the property being acquired and any recorded claims, including constraints on title and claims of rights of use or possession, against the property. The ALTA Title Survey is a scaled map showing the property boundaries, the footprints of all improvements

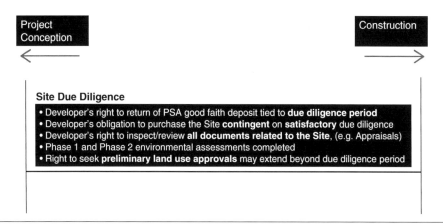

Figure 2.34 The Development Process: The Pre-Development Phase

on the property, all means of ingress to and egress from the property, and any and all easements on the property.

(ii) **Commissioning and examining carefully an ALTA Preliminary Title Report.** Just as with the ALTA Title Survey, a satisfactory (to the Lender), an ALTA Preliminary Title Report is a precondition of Closing on the property acquisition for any mortgage financing used to acquire the Property. The ALTA Preliminary Title Report provides narrative descriptions of the title history of the Property, up to and including the current Seller of the Property, as well as any restrictive covenants, easements, limitations, or restrictions on the Seller's use and possession of the Property. As suggested in the preceding paragraph, these two documents – the ALTA Title Survey and the ALTA Preliminary Title Report – must be read together to get a complete picture about the quality of the title to the Property that is proposed to be conveyed from Seller to Buyer, as well as any constraints on the Buyer's post-Closing use of the Property. For instance, an easement depicted on the ALTA Title Survey may show the physical location or boundaries, within the legal Property boundaries, but would not explain the nature of the easement, by whom it is held, and its terms and conditions, including but not limited to its tenure. Both documents are needed to fully understand the complete impact of any such constraints on the Seller's title to the Property being conveyed.

(iii) **Securing a Title Commitment.** Unless the Buyer of the Property is willing to pay the additional premium amount to an Owner's Title Insurance Policy, the Title Commitment is generally written only in favor of the Lender (i.e., the policy to be issued at Closing is a Lender's Title Insurance Policy) and, consequently, the Lender must be satisfied with the terms and conditions of the Title Commitment. A Title Commitment is not the same as a policy of title insurance: it is merely a promise to issue a Title Policy – in most cases, as already noted, a Lender's Title Insurance Policy – within a specified number of days from the date of the Title Commitment, in connection with the parties' Closing on the transfer of title to the Property.

(iv) **Commissioning Environmental Assessments.** Although Environmental Assessments are generally required as a precondition for removing an Exception to the Title Commitment for environmental liabilities [and, arguably, may be argued as being more appropriately included as part of the ALTA Preliminary Title Report described in paragraph (ii)], under certain circumstances the Developer may deem it prudent to commission a Phase I Environmental Assessment during the Project Conception Phase of The Development

Process. For this reason, both the Phase I and Phase II Environmental Site Assessments are treated separately in this section.

a. **Phase I Environmental Site Assessment.** A Phase I Environmental Site Assessment has two essential components: a physical inspection of the Property and a search of the land records for the Property to determine if any prior uses – for example, it was formerly a gas station; a dry cleaners where certain hazardous fluids were used and dumped; agricultural land on which certain pesticides were used; machine storage and/or repair facility or yard, where PCBs are likely present – would indicate the need for a Phase II Environmental Site Assessment. Based on the collection of these data, the engineering or environmental services firm conducting the Phase I Environmental Site Assessment will make a recommendation that a Phase II Environmental Site Assessment be performed or, alternatively, indicate that hazardous materials are not likely present on the Property based on its history and current physical condition.

b. **Phase II Environmental Assessment.** Based on the nature, scope, and extent of historical uses of the Property, as determined from the Phase I Environmental Site Assessment, the engineering or environmental services firm that conducted the Phase I Environmental Site Assessment will take soils, water, and/or air samplings to determine the presence of any hazardous materials on the Property. Based on the testing and analysis of the samples taken, the engineering or environmental services firm conducting the Phase II Environmental Site Assessment will provide an assessment of the presence, location, and severity of hazardous materials found on the property, as well as recommendations for how each hazardous material found may be acceptably mitigated.

Civil Engineering Analysis and Site Evaluation Report (Figure 2.35). Construction may generally be divided into two, fundamental components: Horizontal Construction and Vertical Construction. Horizontal Construction involves everything necessary to prepare the Subject Site for Vertical Construction (i.e., everything constructed from the horizontal plane of the land, up). Horizontal Construction, also known as Site Preparation, includes general grading; cutting and filling an uneven site; mass excavation; providing for site drainage; accessing, laying out, and providing for all utilities necessary to serve the entire Site (water,

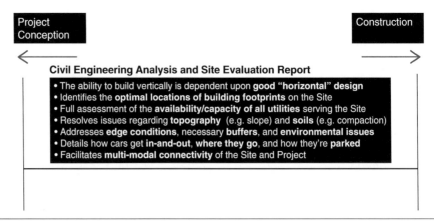

Figure 2.35 The Development Process: The Pre-Development Phase

sewer, electrical, natural gas, coaxial or fiber-optic cable; telephone lines); excavating for below-grade facilities such as parking garages, basements, and foundations; and grading for and laying out streets, curbs and gutters, and sidewalks. Depending on the size of the Subject Site and complexity of the Final Program, Horizontal Construction may need to be completed throughout the Subject Site before any Vertical Construction can begin, or both can proceed in phases, with the first phase of Horizontal Construction preceding the first phase of Vertical Construction, and so on. Regardless of the manner and phasing of Horizontal Construction, however, before any Site Preparation work can be undertaken, it must be planned. And before Horizontal Construction can be planned, a civil engineering firm must conduct a comprehensive and thorough analysis of the Subject Site to assess its opportunities and challenges. This Civil Engineering Analysis, leading to the Site Evaluation Report, may be comprised of but is not necessarily limited to the following components:

Design Development (DD) (Figure 2.36). The Project Conception Phase of The Development Process relied exclusively on Schematic Designs for the Site Plan and the Improvements thereon. The process of transforming Schematic Designs to Construction Documents or CDs is referred to as "Design Development." In Design Development, the architecture firm researches and identifies the methods, materials, and details for the Improvements to be constructed on the Subject Site, based on what the Schematic Design depicts. This includes, among other things, the construction method(s) for each of the Improvements in the Schematic Design, researching and incorporating into the design all of the required, specific design details, and specifying material to incorporate into the exterior and interiors of each of the Improvements. For example, if the Schematic Design calls for an eight-story office building with ground-floor retail comprising the first story:

- What construction method will be used to erect that commercial building?
- Will the building utilize a curtain wall or window wall construction between floors (and, if the latter, what kind of windows will be installed in the window wall)?
- What types of mechanical systems will be used to service the building and where will they be located to avoid conflicts between them and facilitate their installation by different subcontractors?
- What kinds of mechanical conveyancing systems (i.e., elevators) will be used to serve each of the floors in the building?

Figure 2.36 The Development Process: The Pre-Development Phase

- How many feet of clearance must be allowed between the ground-floor slab and the underside of the floor above to meet retailers' finished-height needs inside their respective spaces and how will the exteriors of retail spaces be finished?

With WalkUPs, particularly those proposed and developed in densely populated and intensely developed downtowns, the mix of uses in a single building may be much more complex than the typical office building with ground-floor retail uses. A single WalkUP building in a downtown in a major city like New York, Chicago, or Boston may have ground-floor retail, a number of floors of commercial office, a number of floors of residential (rental or ownership), and even a number of floors of hospitality. Just determining the fenestration[7] for such a complicated program may require resolving a number of conflicting demands of the various user groups. For example, ground-floor retail uses favor glazed storefronts to maximize their visibility to customers and passersby, which is inconsistent with a curtainwall, which essentially hangs from the building's structural, exterior frame from the top of the building to the ground. Similarly, mid- and high-rise residential occupants prefer to have operable windows, requiring the use of window wall construction rather than the curtainwall customary to commercial office and hospitality buildings. This is just one of hundreds of issues that must be identified and resolved in designing and constructing a complex, Mixed-Use WalkUPs building.

Thousands of details – both great and small (e.g., what faucet assemblies will be specified for the common bathrooms on the commercial office floors) – need to be addressed and incorporated into the CDs before they go out for bid, assuming the Developer adopted the Design/Bid/Bid Project Delivery Method early in the Project Conception Phase of The Development Process.

Value Engineering (Figure 2.37). "Value Engineering" is the process through which a qualified third party not involved in the Design Development process – usually an engineering and design firm specializing in Value Engineering – thoroughly reviews the CDs before they are finalized and then either makes recommendations to the Developer and the architecture firm or collaborates with them to make the construction of the building less expensive and take a shorter period of time, and/or to reduce operating costs and/or maintenance and replacement costs.

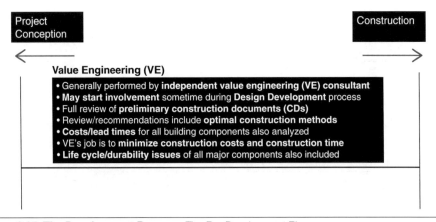

Figure 2.37 The Development Process: The Pre-Development Phase

Applied in its most robust form, as expressed in this quote, VE is a holistic and comprehensive methodology incorporated at the outset of Design Development:

> Value Engineering is a conscious and explicit set of disciplined procedures designed to seek out optimum value for both initial and long-term investment. First utilized in the manufacturing industry during World War II, it has been widely used in the construction industry for many years.
>
> Value Engineering (VE) is not a design/peer review or a cost-cutting exercise. VE is a creative, organized effort, which analyzes the requirements of a project for the purpose of achieving the essential functions at the lowest total costs (capital, staffing, energy, maintenance) over the life of the project. Through a group investigation, using experienced, multi-disciplinary teams, value and economy are improved through the study of alternate design concepts, materials, and methods without compromising the functional and value objectives of the client.[8]

Revised and Expanded Project pro forma. As previously discussed regarding the development and refinement of the Project pro forma documents during the Project Conception Phase of The Development Process, these internal financial projections are constantly updated as new and more accurate information comes in and the assumptions underlying the projections are refined. Without undercutting the notion of continual improvement being made to these pro forma projections, toward the end of the Design Development process – before the completion of final CDs but after the completion of Value Engineering – a substantial number of updated cost estimates for the construction of all Improvements will warrant a comprehensive updating of the Project pro forma. This would include not only updated construction costs to incorporate into the Development Budget pro forma, but also updated projections for repair and replacement costs for capital components of the Improvements that would, among other things, better inform the reserve accounts in the Operating Budget pro forma.

Secure Land Use Approvals (Figures 2.38 and 2.39). Almost nothing of significance is built in the United States "by right." "By right" development means that the land on which Improvements are to be constructed *already has* the necessary local land use approvals to permit what the Developer is contemplating – constructing "the Idea" – without any further process before or approval of the local unit of government with jurisdiction over the property. Even in forward-thinking jurisdictions that have undertaken a master-planning process with

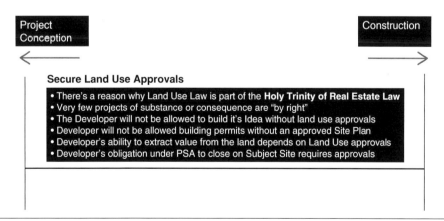

Project Conception

←

Construction

→

Secure Land Use Approvals

- There's a reason why Land Use Law is part of the **Holy Trinity of Real Estate Law**
- Very few projects of substance or consequence are "by right"
- The Developer will not be allowed to build it's Idea without land use approvals
- Developer will not be allowed building permits without an approved Site Plan
- Developer's ability to extract value from the land depends on Land Use approvals
- Developer's obligation under PSA to close on Subject Site requires approvals

Figure 2.38 The Development Process: The Pre-Development Phase

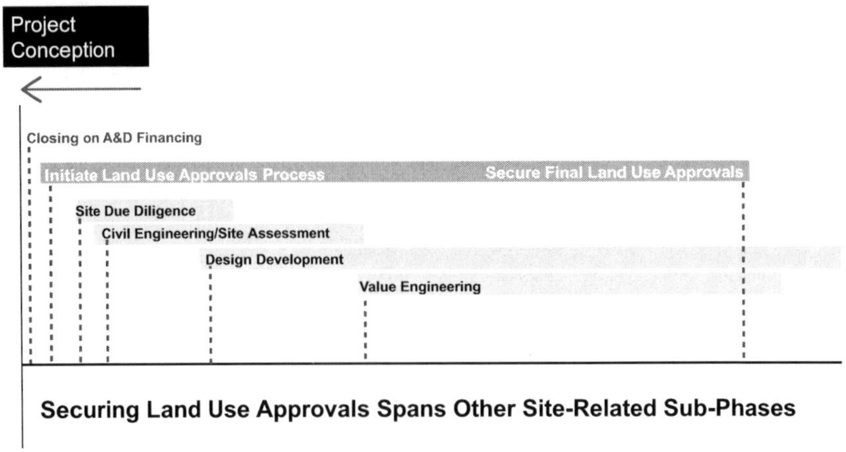

Securing Land Use Approvals Spans Other Site-Related Sub-Phases

Figure 2.39 The Development Process: The Pre-Development Phase

extensive community input, with a view toward encouraging the most enlightened, high-density, walkable, connected, Mixed-Use projects, chances are very good one or two things will preclude such "by right" development from allowing the Developer to act on "the Idea."

First, no matter how broadly written a zoning ordinance designed to encourage WalkUPs may be, it's impossible to anticipate completely and precisely what the next Developer may want to create in the area newly zoned for such WalkUP, much less write that into the zoning ordinance such that it creates a "by right" opportunity for the next Developer. Second, between the passage of time between when a flexible and enlightened Mixed-Use zoning ordinance is enacted for the express purpose of encouraging WalkUPs, and the time when a Developer can secure Site Control of the property or an assemblage of properties, successfully navigate the Project Conception Phase and a substantial portion of the Pre-Development Phase of The Development Process, and line up the necessary financing components to support the Developer's Project, *things inevitably will have changed.*

The demand for X number of hotel rooms in the area, on which that portion of the Mixed-Use ordinance was based, will have been filled by nearby projects now already in the development pipeline; "thereby reducing demand for those rooms below underwriting standards for financing." retail demand for the area will have increased because other projects anticipated to deliver the necessary retail square footage will have fallen short; "but the new Mixed-Use ordinance doesn't allow sufficient new, retail square footage to take advantage of the increased demand in the area;" the destination restaurant or entertainment venue key to the Developer's overall Mixed-Use program will have fallen through (the movie theater business, for example, oftentimes seems overly susceptible to market forces, including an overbuilding of screens or a rash of poor box-office performances); or, even more likely, the financing parameters of the Developer's equity funders or the underwriting standards for the lender will have changed, making one type of Mixed-Use project financeable but the original concept not. As the poet Robert Burns put it somewhat more succinctly:

But Mousie, thou are no thy-lane,
In proving foresight may be vain:
The best laid schemes o' Mice an' Men,
Gang aft agley,
An' lea'e us nought but grief an' pain,
For promis'd joy![9]

Regardless of the amount of advance planning, forethought, and good intention that may *"oft go awry"* on the part of those drafting such enlightened zoning ordinances, it is indeed a true rarity for any Project proposed under the end product of such endeavors to not require the submission of an application and a review and approval process following a prolonged series of public hearings. Accordingly, only a madman would acquire the Subject Site – actually go to Closing to take full legal title to the property, as distinguished from securing Site Control – without first having in hand all necessary land use approvals needed to proceed with the Project as conceived by the Developer. Securing land use approvals, therefore, should always be a condition precedent to going to Closing on the land acquisition, which is the next Sub-Phase in the Pre-Development Phase of The Development Process.

Zoning and land use laws are such a critical aspect of The Development Process that this textbook devotes both Chapters 4 and 5 to the subject.

Close on Land Acquisition (Figure 2.40). This is the Moment of Truth for the Developer; win or go home. Every Phase, Sub-Phase, Task and Sub-Task in The Development Process has led to this point. Once the Developer or the Development Entity takes legal title to the Subject Site, there's no turning back. Having, presumably, determined the Purchase Price for the Subject Site based on the Developer's Idea – or, more accurately, at least not paying more for the Subject Site than bringing the Idea to fruition will support – the economic imperative for the Developer to proceed as expeditiously as possible toward the successful completion of the Project will be very compelling. Unless the Developer can do that, or convince another developer to purchase from the Developer the Subject Site and all of the work product that's been produced up to that point in support of the purchase of the Subject Site, the Developer will never recoup its investment in the Project. Once the Closing on the acquisition of the Subject Site is concluded, and the Development Entity takes title to the property, the Developer must proceed with all due speed with The Development Process.

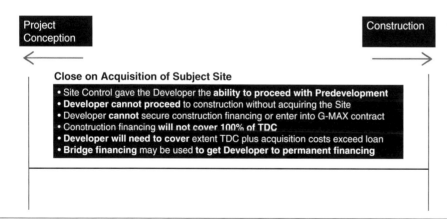

Figure 2.40 The Development Process: The Pre-Development Phase

Construction Documents (CDs) (Figure 2.41). The Design Development Sub-Phase culminates in the completion of the Construction Documents. If the Developer, early in the Project Conception Phase of The Development Process, selected either the Design/Bid/Build or the Integrated Project Delivery as the Project Delivery Method for building the Improvements, the General Contractor (GC) will have been an active participant in Design Development (and, in the case of the Design/Bid/Build GC, an active participant in the Schematic Design

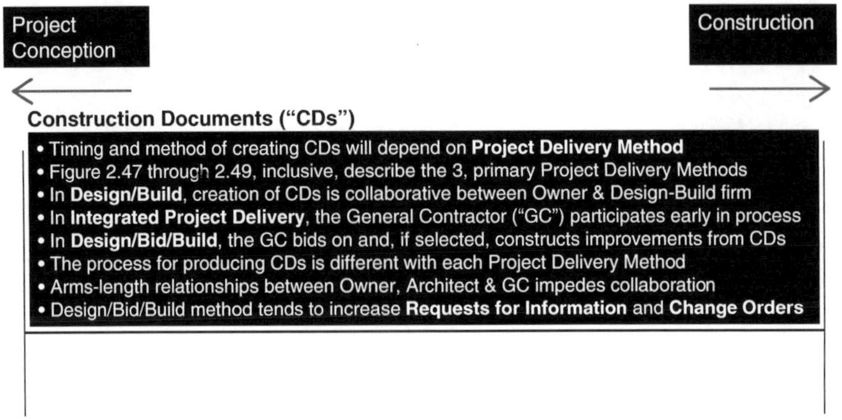

Project
Conception

Construction

⟵

⟶

Construction Documents ("CDs")

- Timing and method of creating CDs will depend on **Project Delivery Method**
- Figure 2.47 through 2.49, inclusive, describe the 3, primary Project Delivery Methods
- In **Design/Build**, creation of CDs is collaborative between Owner & Design-Build firm
- In **Integrated Project Delivery**, the General Contractor ("GC") participates early in process
- In **Design/Bid/Build**, the GC bids on and, if selected, constructs improvements from CDs
- The process for producing CDs is different with each Project Delivery Method
- Arms-length relationships between Owner, Architect & GC impedes collaboration
- Design/Bid/Build method tends to increase **Requests for Information** and **Change Orders**

Figure 2.41 The Development Process: The Pre-Development Phase

Sub-Phase of the Project Conception Phase of The Development Process). Among other things, such early participation of the GC under either of these two Project Delivery Methods in the evolution of the CDs should, in theory at least, lead to a minimum of Requests for Information (RFIs), requests for Change Orders (COs), and Draw Request disputes, all of which increase the cost of a Project and delay the completion date (which, of course, delays everything else in The Development Process). However, for the vast majority of commercial construction projects, which are undertaken using the traditional Design/Bid/Build Project Delivery Method, the completion of the CDs marks the beginning of the Developer's process for recruiting qualified GCs to bid on the Project; informing them through the Bid Package and, if appropriate, the Pre-Bid Conference; and finally selecting the winning bid, presumably by striking the optimal balance between price, value, quality, and experience. The quality and completeness of the CDs and the Bid Package may determine, to a great extent, the frequency and substance of the submission of RFIs, CO requests, and Draw Request disputes. Accordingly, the CDs are critically important. However, regardless of the Project Delivery Method, CDs are critically important to any project's success because they tell the GC and all of its Subcontractors how the Project is to be built.

    Creation of all Necessary Entities (Figure 2.42). This Sub-Phase has moved around considerably since the author first conceived and articulated The Development Process, not only in terms of its chronological position within the Pre-Development Phase, but also as between the Project Conception Phase and the Pre-Development Phase. On one hand, up to this point in The Development Process, certain acts such as incurring and paying expenses to third parties, entering into contracts, and Closing on the acquisition of the Subject Site would all be facilitated by having these transactions undertaken by the proper entity for tax, liability, and structured financing purposes (in these regards, see, among others, Chapters 5, 8, and 9). On the other hand, unless all anticipated equity and debt sources that will participate in the funding of the Project are known as early as the Project Conception Sub-Phase (see Develop Exit and Funding Strategies: How Will "the Idea" Pay Off?), it may be impossible to know the optimal Development Entity and transaction structure to facilitate and support the investment and loan parameters, respectively, of the equity and debt participants in Project Financing. This current iteration of The Development Process has too many variables – including whether the equity participants and/or proposed structure envisioned early on in the Project Conception Phase will still be "in the game" at this Sub-Phase of the Pre-Development Phase – to allow the identification and creation of these necessary entities (e.g., GPs, LPs, and LLCs)

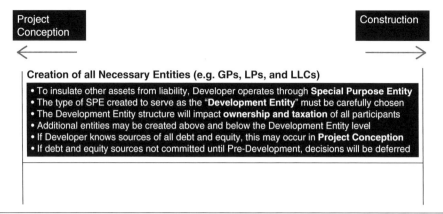

Figure 2.42 The Development Process: The Pre-Development Phase

earlier than at this stage in The Development Process. No doubt, this tension between the benefits of creating such entities early in the process and the benefits of creating them once more is known with certitude will continue, making the Creation of all **Necessary Entities** somewhat of a moving target in subsequent editions of this textbook. An extensive discussion about **General Partnerships (GPs)**, **Limited Partnerships (LPs)**, **Limited Liability Companies (LLPs)**, and other entities that may serve the Developer and the Project is contained in the Entity Choice section of Chapter 8 and elsewhere in that chapter.

Creation of all Necessary Authorities (Figure 2.43). As contrasted with the subject matter of the preceding section, relating to the creation of the Development Entity and directly related or ancillary entities to facilitate the financing structure for the Project, there is a range of quasi-public authorities (e.g., TIF District, Community Facilities District, a Business Improvement District), determined on a state-by-state basis or even a jurisdiction-by-jurisdiction basis, that may also facilitate the overall funding available for the Project and/or provide a range of quasi-public services supporting the Project. This includes tax increment finance (TIF) districts providing a source of Development Budget funding for public facilities serving the Project; community facility and analogous districts (e.g., Georgia's Community Improvement Districts or "CIDs," California's Community Facilities Districts[10] or "CFDs," and

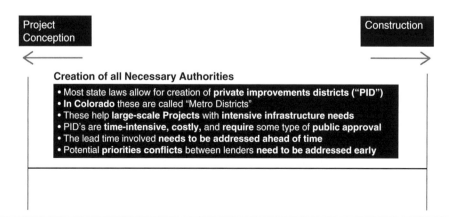

Figure 2.43 The Development Process: The Pre-Development Phase

New Mexico's Public Improvement Districts or "PIDs"), providing mechanisms to fund the up-front costs of public infrastructure serving the Project; and quasi-governmental authorities that will operate the Project in the same way a Local Governmental Unit (LGU) might otherwise, if one had the broad powers to do so and the Developer could get comfortable with that LGU's capabilities and commitment to do so (e.g., Colorado metropolitan districts). These various quasi-governmental entities are addressed in detail in Chapter 10.

Identify and Secure Take-Out (Permanent) Financing Commitment (Figure 2.44). As suggested elsewhere in this chapter, early in the Project Conception Phase of The Development Process, the Developer should have formulated its Exit Strategy, which, in turn, should inform its Funding Strategy (see Project Conception Phase, Sub-Phase titled Develop Exit and Funding Strategies: How Will "the Idea" Pay Off?). The Exit Strategy should determine to what extent the Developer will continue to participate in the ownership and management of the Project after the Project has reached and maintained Stabilization (as defined in the Project Completion and Stabilization Phase of The Development Process). The Developer's Exit Strategy may run the gamut from an outright sale of the Project to a Buyer identified very early in The Development Process, to continuing to own or hold an ownership interest in the Project, deriving periodic Management Fees in consideration of the Developer providing Property Management Services to the Project, receiving periodic distributions of Distributable Cash from the Development Entity, and receiving additional, episodic distributions of Distributable Cash upon strategic refinancings of the Project's Permanent Financing. Whatever the mechanism for realizing the Developer's Exit Strategy, it will also serve as the exit strategy for the Construction Lender. Accordingly, the form and substance of the commitment from the entity providing the Take-Out Financing for the Project must be satisfactory to the Construction Lender, which will be relying on that Take-Out Financing Commitment in making its own commitment for the Construction Loan.

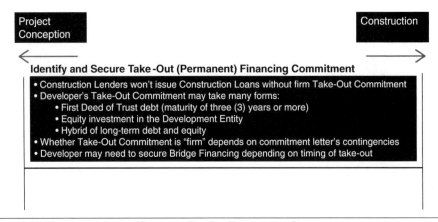

Figure 2.44 The Development Process: The Pre-Development Phase

Identify and Secure Construction Loan Commitment (Figure 2.45). As referenced in the preceding section regarding the Take-Out Financing Commitment, the Construction Lender will issue to the Developer or the Development Entity a **Construction Loan Commitment**. That commitment will be based on, among other things, the Take-Out Financing Commitment, as well as the Construction Lender's review of the CDs, Bid-Package, and proposed construction contract. Although this Sub-Phase suggests that, at this point in the Pre-Development Phase chronology, the Developer will just be beginning

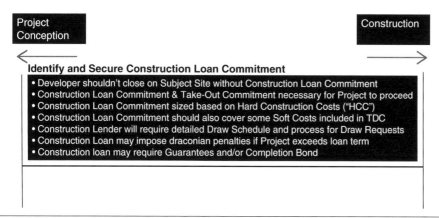

Figure 2.45 The Development Process: The Pre-Development Phase

the process of identifying potential Construction Lenders, the reality is that the process of cultivating potential Construction Lenders will commence much earlier than this point in time – as early as the completion of Schematic Design in the Project Conception Phase – and that sometime during Design Development the Developer will begin the process, in earnest, of identifying the Construction Lender with which the Developer intends to submit an application for a construction loan. As a practical matter, the Developer or Development Entity will need to have a firm Construction Loan Commitment in hand before negotiating and executing the Construction Documents with the GC to be selected to construct the Improvements comprising the Project.

  Pricing and Bidding for General Contractors (GCs) and Subs[11] (Figure 2.46). The Integrated Project Delivery (IPD) (**Figure 2.49**) and Design/Bid/Build Project Delivery (**Figure 2.48**). Methods contemplate different levels of collaboration at different times throughout The Development Process, with Design/Bid/Build collaboration beginning immediately after the Design/Bid/Build GC is selected, while IPD collaboration begins during Design Development. This early collaboration informs the pricing process. However, using the traditional Design/Bid/Build Project Delivery Method (**Figure 2.47**), the Developer relies on construction cost estimates from its architectural firm to gauge costs, with the pre-bid and/

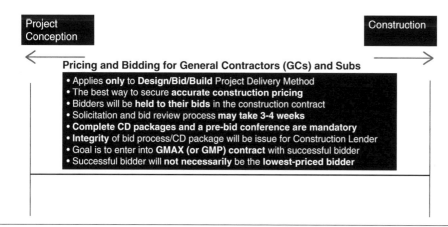

Figure 2.46 The Development Process: The Pre-Development Phase

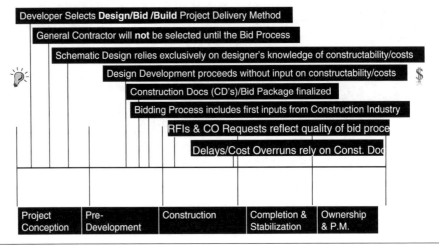

Figure 2.47 The Development Process: Adopting Design/Bid/Build PDM

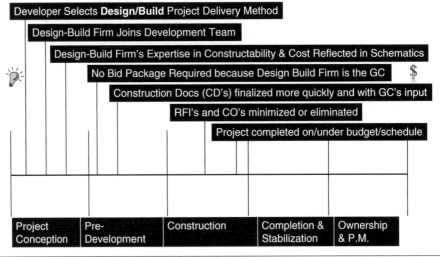

Figure 2.48 The Development Process: Adopting Design/Bid/Build PDM

or bid process later providing more accurate cost projections from those firms making up the General Contractor's construction team. Cost estimating is notoriously unreliable during Design Development, such that it is not usual for the Developer to be subjected to a number of unpleasant surprises when bids are opened following the submittal of bid proposals in response to the bid package. While there are accepted strategies for evaluating multiple bids submitted in response to a bid package (e.g., excluding outliers from consideration), if a majority of the bid responses are well grouped in terms of overall costs and time frames, the Developer may be placed in the position of having to rework the Project or rework the financing to the extent the bulk of the bids suggest the same order of magnitude for Project costs. Through this process, the Developer may create a short list – usually only two or three General Contractors – and focus on their bid proposals as well as the quality of their construction teams. For certain types of projects, it is not unusual for different GCs to include the same subcontractor on their respective construction teams.

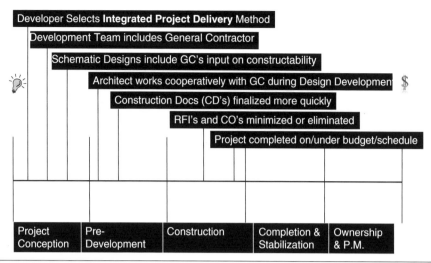

Figure 2.49 The Development Process: Adopting Integrated Project Delivery PDM

Negotiate and document Construction Loan Docs (Figure 2.50). While the Developer and the architecture and engineering firms participating on the Development Team are managing the process for Pricing and Bidding for General Contractors (GCs) and Subs, discussed in the preceding section, the Developer will be simultaneously negotiating the terms and conditions of the **Construction Loan Documents**, based on the Construction Loan Commitment the Developer secured from the Construction Lender (see earlier discussion). Selected legal issues regarding the Construction Loan Documents are highlighted in Chapter 9. For additional information regarding the negotiation of construction loan documents, see the Supplementary Materials on the companion website under Construction Phase Issues, Documentation, and Claims.

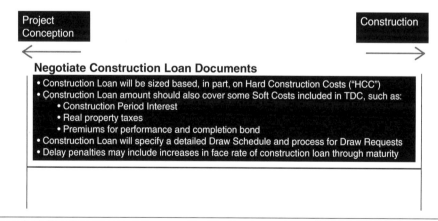

Figure 2.50 The Development Process: The Pre-Development Phase

Engage Construction Manager (CM), if required (Figure 2.51). There is no one way or "right way" for the Developer to manage the Construction Phase of The Development Process. A Developer may be "fully integrated," meaning that the General Contractor is either a division or wholly or partially owned subsidiary of the Developer. Alternatively, the Developer

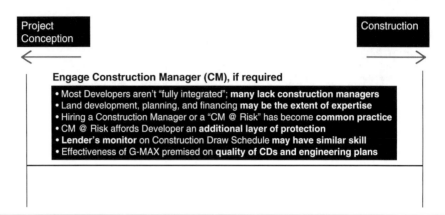

Figure 2.51 The Development Process: The Pre-Development Phase

may not have a captive construction company but may have in-house capabilities to serve as **Construction Manager** for the Project. If the Developer does not have such in-house capabilities, a third-party Construction Manager may be engaged as part of the Development Team. It is not only possible but recommended that, early in the Project Conception Phase of The Development Process, during the Select Project Delivery Method Sub-Phase, the Developer will have considered all of the options for Construction Management under whichever Project Delivery Method the Developer selected, and made key decisions about how to handle Construction Management, with or without actually engaging a Construction Manager (CM) for the Project at that time and making the CM part of the Development Team. However, certainly at this stage in the Pre-Development Phase of The Development Process, immediately preceding Closing on the Construction Loan and entering into the Construction Contract with the GC, the Developer will need to have a CM on board, regardless of whether that CM is in-house or a third-party contractor. If a third-party CM is to be engaged, the Developer will need to decide whether to hire a CM only or a "**CM at Risk**."

Identify/Engage Marketing/Pre-Leasing Company (Figure 2.52). As with some of the other third-party professional services providers whose roles are not activated until a later phase in The Development Process, a compelling argument can be made for including the Property Management Company (see Identify/ Engage Property Management Company under the Construction Phase) and a Sales and/or Leasing Agent(s), depending on the number and nature of the various categories of real estate products included in the Product Mix of the Project (see Marketing and Pre-Leasing, also under the Construction Phase) to the Development Team very early in the Project Conception Phase of The Development Process, rather than waiting until during or after the Pre-Development Phase. For example, an experienced Property Management Company can help the Development Team in general, and the architects and land planners in particular, with avoiding design solutions that may look good on paper but tend to cause property management issues. In the same way, involving experienced Sales and/or Leasing Agent(s) on the Development Team early in the Project Conception Phase may provide valuable input to the Market Analysis Firm, as well as the architecture firm, in Product Mix, Product Configuration, Amenities, and other programmatic design decisions that will accelerate the absorption of various unit types. Inasmuch as both of these types of third-party professional services providers work on a percentage fee basis, they may be willing to participate on and contribute to the Development Team early on in the Project Conception Phase, knowing that their contributions may make their respective jobs easier and, therefore, more profitable.

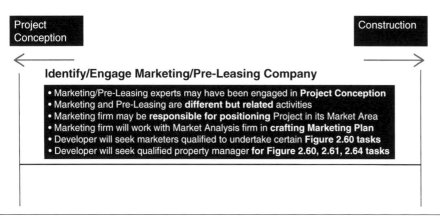

Figure 2.52 The Development Process: The Pre-Development Phase

Close on Construction Financing (Figure 2.53). By the time the Developer, the Construction Lender, and other parties (e.g., the Surety Bond provider) get to the Closing table for the Construction Loan, all of the tough issues should have been worked out. However, that's not always the case, and the Developer, the Developer's Counsel, and any related members of the Development Team need to prepare to make last-minute adjustments to the Project based on the requirements of the Construction Lender and Construction Lender's Counsel. Among other things, in responding to any such last-minute requirements from the Construction Lender, the Developer must bear in mind the priorities, requirements, and conditions of any financing already in place, so as not to agree to a Construction Lender's demand at the Closing table that will violate an existing covenant, condition, or requirement of an equity or debt provider already in the deal.

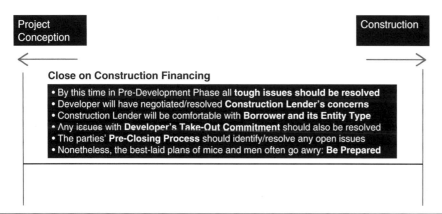

Figure 2.53 The Development Process: The Pre-Development Phase

Execute Construction Contracts (Figure 2.54). Although Execute Construction Contracts is listed here as a separate Sub-Phase of the Pre-Development Phase of The Development Process, the Construction Lender will most likely insist that all of the Construction Contract Documents be executed simultaneously with the execution of all of the Construction Loan Documents at the Construction Loan Closing, such that these two Sub-Phases would occur at the same time. That is because, among other reasons, the Construction Loan is not

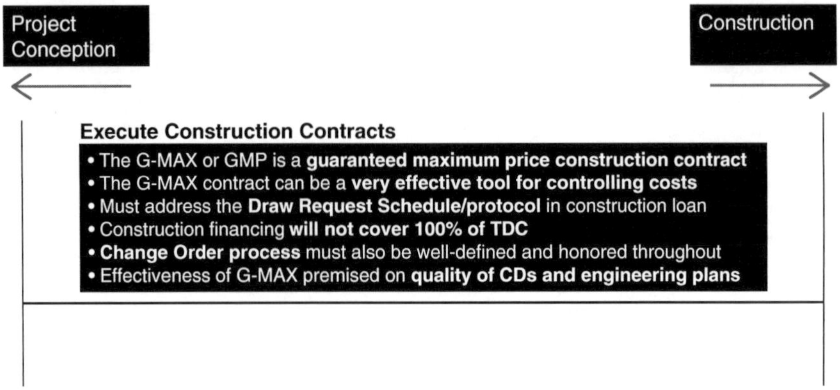

Project Conception		Construction
←		→

Execute Construction Contracts
- The G-MAX or GMP is a **guaranteed maximum price construction contract**
- The G-MAX contract can be a **very effective tool for controlling costs**
- Must address the **Draw Request Schedule/protocol** in construction loan
- Construction financing **will not cover 100% of TDC**
- **Change Order process** must also be well-defined and honored throughout
- Effectiveness of G-MAX premised on **quality of CDs and engineering plans**

Figure 2.54 The Development Process: The Pre-Development Phase

being made by the Construction Lender to the Development Entity for the latter to do with the net funds from Closing as the Developer sees fit. The Construction Lender is funding the payment of Construction Draws specific to the Construction Contract and specifically related to the percentage of completion of the Project based on the CDs and the Construction Contract, as defined in the Construction Contract.

Construction Phase (Figure 2.55). Although the Project Conception Phase of The Development Process is, arguably, the highest-risk portion of the trajectory of any Project – because there is no telling at the outset whether there will even be "a Project" (which is why the Developer has an imperative to spend as little money as possible until there is greater certitude that the Developer's Idea may come to fruition, in one form or another, invoking the 80:2 Rule) – more can go wrong, and greater monetary consequences accrue to the Developer, the Development Entity, and the Project when things go wrong during the Construction Phase than in any other. Every once in a while on a construction site, something goes horribly wrong: a utilities trench or wall in a foundation or underground garage excavation collapses, with fatal consequences for construction workers; an improperly supported crane tips over, causing damage to surrounding buildings (and construction worker fatalities); a construction worker who's not properly harnessed falls from an upper floor of a steel frame being erected or, more commonly, some large, heavy object falls from an upper floor to the ground below (and, once again, there are construction worker fatalities).

The fact is that both the Development Entity and the General Contractor may have adequate insurance to cover the monetary consequences of such construction site accidents; they take their toll in other ways. Simply put: a construction site is an inherently dangerous place to work. At the same time, the potential for Project losses, in the form of costly construction over-runs and extensive construction delays resulting in a domino effect of cascading delays, sometimes with severe, adverse consequences for the Project, is ever-present. Consequently, active and detailed Construction Management or Construction Administration on the part of the Developer and on behalf of the Development Entity is critically important for the Developer to successfully navigate the Construction Phase of The Development Process.

In addition to making sure that the timeliness and quality of the construction of the Project is maintained by the General Contractor, the Developer must make sure that there's complete alignment with what the Construction Loan Documents, the CDs, and the Construction Contract Documents say about the incremental progress of the Project and payment to the General Contractor of its periodic Construction Draws. Many of the details supporting the foregoing introduction to the Construction Phase of The Development Process are covered

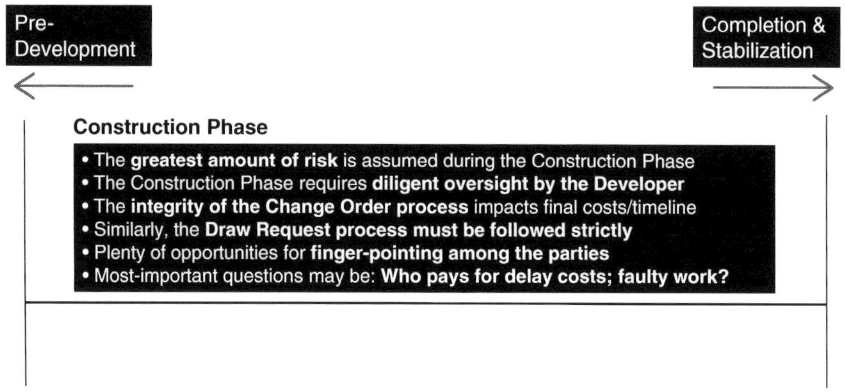

Pre-Development		Completion & Stabilization
←		→

Construction Phase

- The **greatest amount of risk** is assumed during the Construction Phase
- The Construction Phase requires **diligent oversight by the Developer**
- The **integrity of the Change Order process** impacts final costs/timeline
- Similarly, the **Draw Request process must be followed strictly**
- Plenty of opportunities for **finger-pointing among the parties**
- Most-important questions may be: **Who pays for delay costs; faulty work?**

Figure 2.55 The Development Process: The Construction Phase

in Chapter 9, as well as being addressed in the Supplementary Materials on the companion website under Construction Phase Issues, The Draw Request Process, respectively. However, a few of the basics of the Construction Phase are covered next.

Construction Administration (Figure 2.56). Regardless of the Project Delivery Method the Developer selects (presumably in the very early stage of the Project Conception Phase), for the reasons articulated in the introductory paragraph to this section, the Developer will want and need to pay close attention to all construction activity, from the time various construction permits are issued by the building, code enforcement and/or public works department of the Local Governmental Unit having jurisdiction over the Subject Site, to the issuance of COs (Certificates of Occupancy) for each Improvement to the Property. Specifically who within the Development Team or outside of it (e.g., the local Code Enforcement Office of the Local Governmental Unit) will be held accountable for monitoring the progress of construction will be determined as a matter of Contract Law (see, in this regard, Chapter 7, generally). For additional information relating to construction administration, see the Supplementary Materials on the companion website under Construction Phase Issues, Documentation, and Claims.

It should be noted, in this regard, that architecture firms, which used to be responsible for "Inspecting" the General Contractor's work at specific points in the construction process, some decades ago made a decision, as a profession, that providing "Inspections" imposed too much liability on architects. As a consequence, as part of the contract between Owners and their Architects (using the defined terms from the standard form documents created by the American Institute of Architects or AIA), as part of their fee for taking a Project through Design Development to CDs to completion (i.e., issuance of COs), Architects only provide "Observations" of the job site and the progress, completion, or failure to complete specific components of the Project. Such "Observations" may or may not be sufficient to satisfy the Construction Lender's requirement that the Developer or its designee sign off on each Draw Request the General Contractor submits. It is also worth noting that even if the Architect's "Observations" are sufficient for purposes of the Construction Lender's Draw Request procedures, the Architect's sign-off on Draw Requests does not extend the Architect's liability to the Developer or the Development Entity for any other aspect of the specific items enumerated in the following paragraph.

The fact that the architecture profession, through its representative body – the American Institute of Architects – long ago ceded responsibility to the Owner for the quality and progress

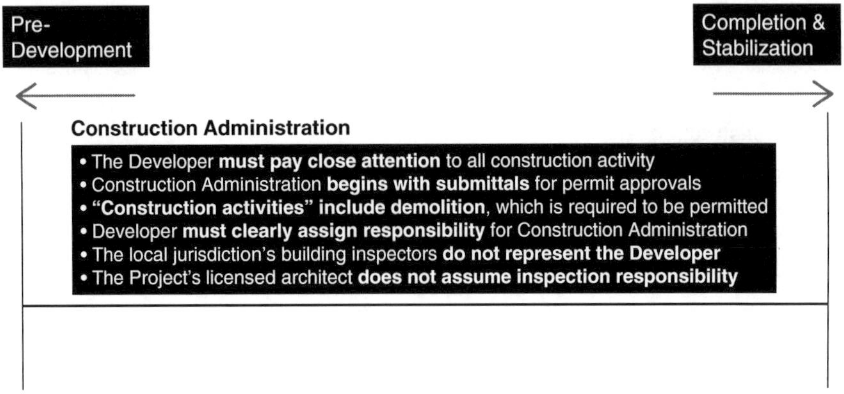

Figure 2.56 The Development Process: The Construction Phase

of construction designed by architects, through its standard form document sets, the AIA remains the primary source for Construction Contract Documents. Accordingly, and as discussed in the Supplementary Materials on the companion website under Construction Phase Issues, Documentation, and Claims, in 2007 a consortium of twenty construction industry organizations and trade groups decided to challenge the preeminence of the AIA construction document sets by developing its own. Now known as **ConsensusDOCS**, the premise for this undertaking is that form documents for construction shouldn't favor the "Owner" but, instead, should be neutral.[12] For a discussion of some of the differences between key documents in the AIA document sets and their ConsensusDOCS counterparts, see the Supplementary Materials on the companion website under Construction Phase Issues, Documentation, and Claims. Regardless of the source of the contract forms the parties use, almost all construction disputes involve the interpretation of specific provisions in documents negotiated and entered into by the parties.

As suggested earlier, the Developer will be seeking continuous assurances, through its Construction Manager or Construction Administrator, of the following:

1. That the Project is being constructed in accordance with:
   a. the CDs (also sometimes referred to as "the Plans and Specifications");
   b. the **Building Code** adopted and administered by the Local Governmental Unit;
   c. the Construction Contract Documents; and
   d. the Construction Loan Documents.
2. That the Project is being constructed on budget.
3. That the Project is being constructed on time.
4. That each Draw Request the General Contractor submits for payment out of the Construction Loan meets all of the requirements of the Construction Loan Documents and is consistent with items 1 through 3.

Horizontal Construction (Figure 2.57). As mentioned in the section titled Civil Engineering Analysis and Site Evaluation Report, Horizontal Construction may need to be started and completed before any Vertical Construction is commenced, or both Horizontal and Vertical Construction will be phased, with the phases of each carefully sequenced. Inasmuch as the definition of Horizontal Construction is to prepare the Subject Site for Vertical Construction, the latter cannot commence without the former. And in a scenario such as the construction of a single, Mixed-Use building on the Subject Site, general site preparation work;

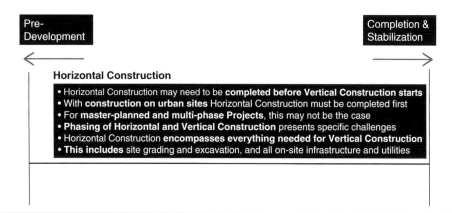

Horizontal Construction

- Horizontal Construction may need to be **completed before Vertical Construction starts**
- With **construction on urban sites** Horizontal Construction must be completed first
- For **master-planned and multi-phase Projects**, this may not be the case
- **Phasing of Horizontal and Vertical Construction** presents specific challenges
- Horizontal Construction **encompasses everything needed for Vertical Construction**
- **This includes** site grading and excavation, and all on-site infrastructure and utilities

Figure 2.57 The Development Process: The Construction Phase

bringing in and routing all utilities; excavation for underground garage parking and/or building basement; and providing for the building foundation will all have to be completed before any Vertical Construction commences. However, on a Subject Site where the Developer has planned multiple buildings, it is possible (but not necessarily optimal from either a schedule or cost standpoint) to have both the Horizontal Construction and the Vertical Construction proceed in phased, synchronized sequences. The relationship of and timing for Horizontal Construction vis-à-vis Vertical Construction will presumably have been largely worked out by the civil engineering firm on the Development Team during the Civil Engineering Analysis and Site Evaluation Report Sub-Phase, and revised and refined during the Design Development and Value Engineering Sub-Phases.

Regardless of whether Horizontal Construction and Vertical Construction are sequenced – that is the former must be completed before the latter can be started – or each is phased and the phases are sequenced, if issues arise during Horizontal Construction the Construction Documents will provide specific procedures for addressing and resolving them as follows:

Request for Information (RFI) Process. If the General Contractor or one of its subcontractors finds something in the CDs that doesn't make sense or they don't understand, their primary obligation is to inquire about that item by submitting a Request for Information or RFI to the Architect. This contractual obligation of inquiry is contained in the Construction Documents and is discussed in the Supplementary Materials on the companion website under Construction Phase Issues, Documentation, and Claims, including in a discussion comparing differences between the AIA document sets and their counterpart ConsensusDOCS construction contract documents. Generally speaking, the General Contractor's submission of an RFI starts the clock ticking on the Architect's Response to RFI, which should be intended to clarify the General Contractor or subcontractor's question about the CDs or, alternatively, providing a correction to the CDs to the extent the RFI has called attention to an error or conflict in the CDs with another section or sections of the CDs. If the Architect's Response to the RFI requires, in the professional opinion of the General Contractor, the General Contractor or subcontractor to use materials, equipment or personnel over and above what the GC or its sub put in their cost proposal in response to the Bid Package, based on a reasonable reading of the CDs contained therein, the General Contractor or the subcontractor, through the General Contractor, may request an increase in the Contract Price based on the added materials, equipment, and/or personnel required based on the Architect's Response to the RFI. Of course, as the representative of the Owner, with which the Architect has a separate contract for the architectural services to be performed, the Architect's natural inclination is to take the position, in the Architect's

Response to the RFI, that such a response is merely providing additional clarification based on the General Contractor's inquiry, and that such clarification does *not* materially add to the cost to the General Contractor and/or its subcontractor in performing the Construction Contract as it was bid. If, however, the General Contractor is not satisfied with the Architect's Response to the RFI (e.g., the additional information does not clarify the ambiguity or other infirmity with the section(s) of the Construction Documents that are the subject of the RFI in the first place), or with the Architect's position that the Architect's Response to the RFI should not occasion any increase in the Contract Price, the General Contractor may seek such incremental increase in the Contract Price through a Request for Change Order (CO).

Change Order (CO) Process. The **Change Order** process is set forth in several sections of the AIA's A201 General Conditions document, which is discussed in the Supplementary Materials on the companion website under Construction Phase Issues, Documentation, and Claims, along with a discussion comparing differences between the AIA document sets and their counterpart ConsensusDOCS construction contract documents. In addition to the reasons set forth earlier, emanating from the RFI process for the GC's submittal of a Change Order Request, the Developer may also initiate Change Orders for any number of reasons. Under the A201 General Conditions document, changes may not be made without a written and approved Change Order. Because the Construction Lender is not a party to the Construction Contract Documents and, therefore, there is no privity of contract (see, in this regard, Chapter 7), the Construction Loan Documents should provide protections for the Construction Lender in the Change Order process, including the advance review and approval of any Change Orders, regardless of by whom they are requested, if the cost increases occasioned by such Change Orders are expected to be paid through Draw Requests.

Draw Request Process. In addition to whatever collateral security the Construction Lender the Construction Lender has insisted on receiving as a condition of Closing on the Construction Loan, the Construction Lender's best protection for the preservation of its security interests in the Project itself is the **Draw Request Process**. Although the Draw Request Process is discussed in the Supplementary Materials on the companion website under Construction Phase Issues, Documentation, and Claims, it is instructive to understand a few key points in this introduction to The Development Process. First, the GC submits Draw Requests for work already performed, which includes materials delivered to and secured at the Site. Second, the GC certifies that the work that has been performed and the materials that have been delivered to and secured at the Site, which is the subject of the Draw Request, represents a specific percentage of the total work to be performed under the Construction Contract Documents (i.e., "Percentage of Completion"). Third, the Developer is required, in accordance with the Construction Loan Documents, to provide its independent certification or verification that the GC's certification of the Percentage of Completion represented in the Draw Request is, in fact, correct. Fourth, a specific amount of the Draw Request, usually 10 percent, is "retained," meaning that it is not paid to the GC but is held in a Retaining Account, which may be a separate, physical bank account for retaining or may be an accounting entry relating to the Construction Loan. The final reconciliation and disposition of the Retaining Account is handled as the final act in Close-Out, discussed in the next subsection.

Close-Out*. Close-Out takes place at the point at which the GC has notified the Developer that the Horizontal Construction is "Substantially Completed." In the case of Horizontal Construction, this means that Vertical Construction can proceed but that non-structural issues remain to be resolved. This might include "Punch-List Items," any Warranty Issues, and any unresolved Change Order Issues. These are all addressed, in detail, in the Supplementary Materials on the companion website under Construction Phase Issues, Documentation, and Claims. It is noteworthy that, in the case of Vertical Construction, this concluding phase of the construction process is addressed in the Project Completion and Stabilization Phase of The Development Process, which follows the Construction Phase.

Vertical Construction **(Figure 2.58).** (See Horizontal Construction.)

    Request for Information (RFI) Process. (See Request for Information (RFI) Process in Horizontal Construction.)

    Change Order (CO) Process. (See Change Order (CO) Process in Horizontal Construction.)

    Draw Request Process. (See Draw Request Process in Horizontal Construction.)

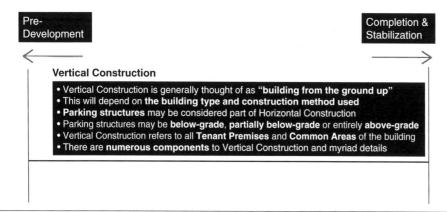

Figure 2.58 The Development Process: The Construction Phase

Identify/Engage Property Management Company (Figure 2.59). As mentioned in the discussion at the end of the Pre-Development Phase of The Development Process on the Identify/Engage Marketing/Pre-Leasing Company Sub-Phase, there are some third-party professional services providers whose roles do not become activated until a later phase in The Development Process. Notwithstanding that the roles and responsibilities of such third-party service providers do not become actuated until much later in The Development Process, there are many sound reasons for having the Property Management Company join the Development Team very early in the Project Conception Phase of The Development Process, rather than waiting until during or after the Pre-Development Phase. Until the Project Completion and

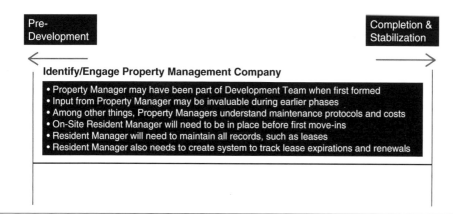

Figure 2.59 The Development Process: The Construction Phase

Stabilization Phase of The Development Process, there is no Project to manage. However, once the Local Governmental Unit issues a Certificate of Occupancy and tenants or owners start moving into and occupying the Project, assuming the Marketing/Pre-Leasing Company did its job during the Construction Phase (see Marketing and Pre-Leasing), the Development Entity will be counting on the Property Management Company to fully engage in managing the project. See, in this regard, Chapter 11.

Marketing and Pre-Leasing (Figure 2.60). Marketing and Pre-Leasing could easily have been placed first among the Sub-Phases of the Construction Phase of The Development Process, because the marketing and pre-leasing of the Project should be actively pursued throughout the Construction Phase. Among other things, the Construction Loan Documents or the Construction Loan Commitment may contain thresholds for pre-leasing that the Project must meet as a condition of funding. This may seem like somewhat of a Catch-22 situation for the Developer: How can the Developer convince tenants to sign onto the Project when it isn't even under construction yet? However, particularly in the case of critical anchor tenants, without which the entire Program for the Project won't be viable, such advance commitments are essential to the success of the Project, and the Developer itself may have to pin them down as a condition precedent to the Close on Land Acquisition Sub-Phase of the Pre-Development Phase of The Development Process. For large, specialty commercial users, they are just as interested in securing a commitment for their space as are the Developers of the Projects that host them. Commercial office tenants, on the other hand, are not as forward-looking, although – once again, dependent on the space needs of the tenant – getting a commitment twenty-four or even thirty-six months out might not be unusual. At the shorter end of the lead-time spectrum for advance marketing and pre-leasing activities, home buyers, in the case of condominium products, may start their search as much as twelve months in advance of when they expect to close and take occupancy on their unit, but may be constrained by the process of selling an existing residential unit if they are not first-time homebuyers. At the shortest end of the advance marketing and pre-leasing activities are residential renters, who are generally constrained by the termination of their existing lease, although there are always exceptions.

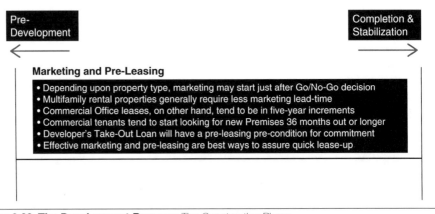

Figure 2.60 **The Development Process**: The Construction Phase

Project Completion and Stabilization Phase (Figure 2.61). The Project Completion and Stabilization Phase of The Development Process marks the period during which the Construction Phase is winding down and the Ownership and Property Management Phase is

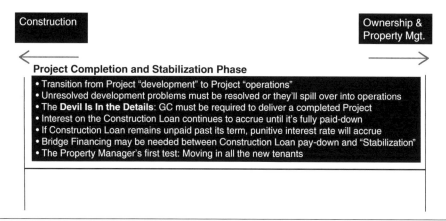

Figure 2.61 The Development Process: Project Completion and Stabilization Phase

ramping up. It is neither fish nor fowl: neither construction nor operations. There is a very short list of Sub-Phases during the Project Completion and Stabilization Phase. However, each Sub-Phase is critical to moving the Project completely out of the Construction Phase and getting it over the finish line to becoming a stabilized, operating property.

Vertical Construction Close-Out (Figure 2.62). See discussion of Horizontal Construction Close-Out in Horizontal Construction. See also Chapter 9 and Supplementary Materials on the companion website, under Construction Phase Issues, The Draw Request Process.

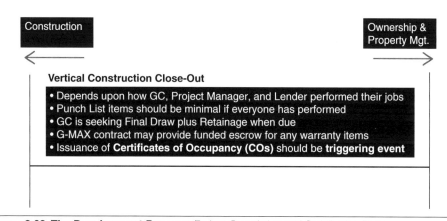

Figure 2.62 The Development Process: Project Completion and Stabilization Phase

Construction Claims Resolution (Figure 2.63). To the extent unresolved disputes remain outstanding between the Owner (i.e., the Development Entity) and the General Contractor, the parties will be obligated to follow whatever dispute resolution procedure is set forth in the Construction Contract Documents. Dispute resolution of claims may include all or some of the following, and may require the parties to pursue the least onerous resolution mechanism before proceeding to the next most onerous, or may limit the parties to only one or a few of these options: Mediation; Nonbinding Arbitration; Binding Arbitration; Civil Litigation. The dispute resolution provisions in the AIA's A201 General Conditions document

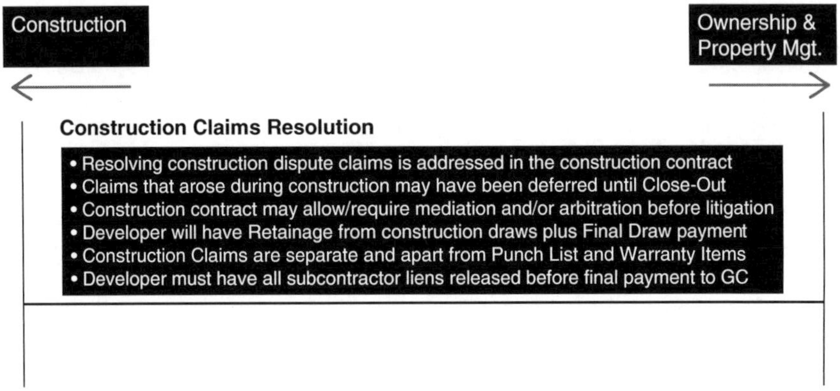

Construction | Ownership & Property Mgt.

Construction Claims Resolution

- Resolving construction dispute claims is addressed in the construction contract
- Claims that arose during construction may have been deferred until Close-Out
- Construction contract may allow/require mediation and/or arbitration before litigation
- Developer will have Retainage from construction draws plus Final Draw payment
- Construction Claims are separate and apart from Punch List and Warranty Items
- Developer must have all subcontractor liens released before final payment to GC

Figure 2.63 The Development Process: Project Completion and Stabilization Phase

are addressed in the Supplementary Materials on the companion website under Construction Phase Issues, Documentation, and Claims, as well as in the discussion in the Supplementary Materials about the differences between the AIA document sets and their ConsensusDOCS counterparts.

On-Site Property Manager in Place (Figure 2.64). At some point prior to the first scheduled tenant move-in, the Property Management Company referenced in Identify/ Engage Property Management Company will need to be installed in the Project. The Property Management Company will need enough lead time to hire necessary on-site staff (generally, at minimum, a Property Manager, an Assistant Property Manager, and a Maintenance Staff sufficient to serve the needs of all tenants of the Project, including janitorial staff and mechanics). They will also need enough time, before the first tenant is scheduled to move in to the Project, to train all staff and get the Property Management Office and the Maintenance Office set up and fully outfitted with tools and equipment. Accordingly, the Property Management Company will need to back into its official Start Date for the Property Management Agreement and the installation of Property Management Staff from the date the first tenant is scheduled to move into its Premises.

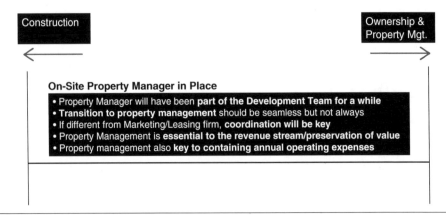

Construction | Ownership & Property Mgt.

On-Site Property Manager in Place

- Property Manager will have been **part of the Development Team for a while**
- **Transition to property management** should be seamless but not always
- If different from Marketing/Leasing firm, **coordination will be key**
- Property Management is **essential to the revenue stream/preservation of value**
- Property management also **key to containing annual operating expenses**

Figure 2.64 The Development Process: Project Completion and Stabilization Phase

Lease-Up and Move-In (Figure 2.65). The larger and more complex the Project and its Program, the greater the attention to detail in scheduling move-ins and the longer the overall timeframe will need to be. As suggested in the Marketing and Pre-Leasing Sub-Task in the Construction Phase of The Development Process, the lease-up process may have been completed months before this Sub-Task commences (as is the case with tenants that have complex build-outs of their Premises and long lead times in their search for Commercial space), or – particularly in the case of residential rental properties – may be ongoing well into the **Ownership and Property Management Phase**. Coordinating move-ins is critical to avoiding aggravation among different tenants and minimizing damage to the Project in the process. Additionally, as move-ins may be staggered over months and even years, again depending on the size, scope, and complexity of the Project and its Program, the need to minimize disruptions to existing tenants who previously moved in when new tenants arrive becomes particularly acute the longer the Project has been operational.

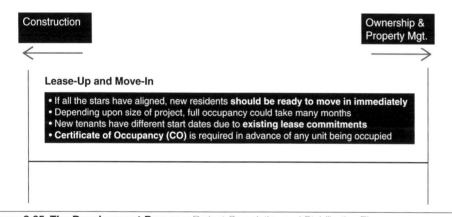

Construction

Ownership & Property Mgt.

Lease-Up and Move-In

- If all the stars have aligned, new residents **should be ready to move in immediately**
- Depending upon size of project, full occupancy could take many months
- New tenants have different start dates due to **existing lease commitments**
- **Certificate of Occupancy (CO)** is required in advance of any unit being occupied

Figure 2.65 The Development Process: Project Completion and Stabilization Phase

Project Stabilization (Figure 2.66). Project Stabilization is whatever the Developer and the Permanent Lender (or other Financing Partner) agree it is. Stabilization refers to the Project operating at or above agreed parameters over an extended period of time. That period of time could be as short as six months and as long as two years or longer, but will generally be between twelve and eighteen months (the "Operating Period"). However the parties end up quantifying the Operating Period, it will not commence until the Project has hit its "Target Occupancy Rate," which again will be something the parties agree to and will differ among Product Types in the Project. By Product Type, the Target Occupancy Rate should reflect what is ordinary and customary in the marketplace where the Project is located. For example, a high-end residential rental building may be expected to achieve and maintain a 95% Occupancy Rate. In this case, when such a building reaches 95% occupancy, its Operating Period will commence, and one of the indicia of Project Stabilization will be maintaining that Occupancy Rate. For a Mixed-Use Project or WalkUP, each Product Type will have its own Operating Period and its own Target Occupancy Rate, as well as its own set of metrics that must be continuously met in order for the Project to be deemed to have reached Project Stabilization.

Construction

⟵

**Ownership &
Property Mgt.**

⟶

Project Stabilization

- Developer will define "Project Stabilization" from its Preliminary Pro Forma
- Definition evolves as Project progresses through Project Conception and Pre-Development
- Definition of Project Stabilization will include definition of "Full Occupancy"
- "Full Occupancy" is defined as 100% Occupancy less the "Vacancy Rate"
- The "Vacancy Rate" should be based on the market for the product type being developed
- Developer also determine how long the Project must maintain its Full Occupancy

Figure 2.66 The Development Process: Project Completion and Stabilization Phase

Ongoing Property Management (Figure 2.67). The end of the Project Completion and Stabilization Phase and the beginning of the Ownership and Property Management Phase of The Development Process marks a truly dramatic shift in the process. Many, if not all, of the inherent risks at various Phases in The Development Process up to this point have either not materialized or have and have been resolved. The Project is now in its operational phase – a Property Management and Ownership – and may remain there for decades, depending on the Exit Strategy the Developer settled on very early in the Project Conception Phase (see Sale or Refinancing). As is demonstrated, in detail, in Chapter 11, the Developer will be faced with an entirely new set of risks and challenges during the Ownership and Property Management Phase of The Development Process.

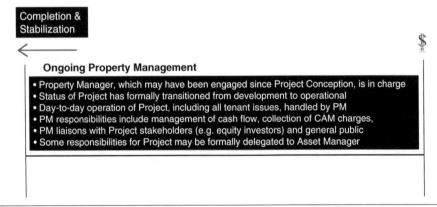

**Completion &
Stabilization**

⟵

$

Ongoing Property Management

- Property Manager, which may have been engaged since Project Conception, is in charge
- Status of Project has formally transitioned from development to operational
- Day-to-day operation of Project, including all tenant issues, handled by PM
- PM responsibilities include management of cash flow, collection of CAM charges,
- PM liaisons with Project stakeholders (e.g. equity investors) and general public
- Some responsibilities for Project may be formally delegated to Asset Manager

Figure 2.67 The Development Process: Ownership and Property Management

Closing on Permanent Financing (Figure 2.68). This Sub-Phase is exactly what it sounds like: the Developer once again finds itself at a Closing table, where all of the documents necessary to effect the Permanent Financing and pay down the outstanding principal amount, plus any accrued but unpaid interest thereon, of the Construction Loan, and secure clean, unencumbered title to the Project, will, as part of the Closing process, be

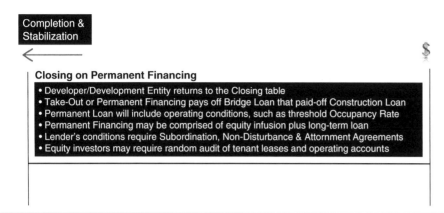

Figure 2.68 The Development Process: Ownership and Property Management

pledged to the Permanent Lender as collateral security for the repayment of the principal, plus accrued interest, on the Permanent Financing.

Sale or Refinancing (Figure 2.69). For a Developer that, early in the Project Conception Phase of The Development Process during the Develop Exit and Funding Strategies Sub-Phase, decided to make the Project a portfolio asset, the sale or refinancing of the Permanent Financing of the Project is the event through which the enhanced or increased value of the Project is tangibly realized.

Sale: Strategic, Opportunistic, and Distressed Dispositions. For a portfolio owner of operating, commercial real property, the sale of a performing asset would most likely only come about in one of three scenarios: a strategic disposition of the Project; an opportunistic disposition of the Project to support a new, potentially more valuable real estate development opportunity; or a distressed disposition of the Project.

Strategic Disposition. In the event of a strategic decision to no longer continue to hold (i) the Project, (ii) all real estate assets in the geographic market, which real estate assets include the Project – in which case other portfolio assets may also be marketed for sale – or (iii) real estate assets in a particular real estate asset category that includes the Project (e.g., hospitality, which tends to be more susceptible to market volatilities than other real estate asset categories), the Project, either alone

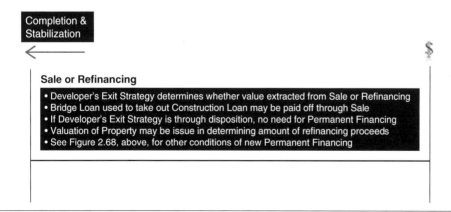

Figure 2.69 The Development Process: Ownership and Property Management

or as part of a portfolio of properties identified by geographic location or property types will be sold or otherwise disposed. In other words, a **Portfolio Developer** or its Asset Manager may make a strategic decision to divest the Project by itself or a package of properties including the Project, either because the Developer foresees problems on the horizon that may negatively impact the future operating performance of each such property in the portfolio to be made available for a Strategic Sale, or because the Developer or its Asset Manager perceives the Project and any other related, real estate assets bundled for disposition out of the portfolio have reached a price premium not expected to be seen again for a prolonged period of time. Although these alternative scenarios may sound similar – sell at a peak in value before problems foreseen on the horizon erode that value – these are, in reality, two different scenarios. It is, however, easy to understand how, under certain circumstances, there might be some convergence of the two scenarios.

Opportunistic Disposition. Additionally, however, unrelated to the market value of the Project and other similarly situated assets in the Developer's portfolio, the Developer may be presented with an unusual, new real estate development opportunity requiring substantial liquid resources, warranting the disposition of currently held and profitably operated portfolio assets to actuate such a new opportunity. In the case of such Opportunistic Disposition including the Project, the new opportunity trumps whether the timing and market dynamics at the time impacting the disposition of existing portfolio assets are ideal, based on the return model the new opportunity presents. Presumably, in the case of an Opportunistic Disposition, the Developer's analysis takes into account both (i) potential loss in value by selling portfolio assets, including the Project, under such circumstances and (ii) the likelihood that the new real estate development opportunity may not pan out in the manner projected that is prompting the Opportunistic Sale.

Distressed Sale. In a distressed sale situation, the Developer, for whatever reason, isn't given the choice of whether to dispose of the Project; the Developer must sell the asset. Among other things, a Distressed Sale generally means that the Developer is unlikely to receive full value for the Project, and may also have to accept other disadvantageous terms and conditions in order to expedite the disposition.

Refinancing. In a refinancing, the Development Entity replaces existing debt with new debt. The assumption is, so long as the term of the existing debt is long enough, that the Development Entity can choose the timing of the refinancing to coincide with a period of low interest rates. The other assumption is that the Project will increase in value over time, such that the value of the Project supports a larger amount for the refinancing, which is sufficient to pay down 100% of the outstanding premium amount of the existing financing, plus any accrued but unpaid interest thereon, plus all transaction costs, and still leave a substantial amount of Distributable Cash for the owners of interests in the Development Entity. In this way, the Developer, presumed to be the exclusive or a majority owner of the outstanding interests in the Development Entity, can periodically extract the increased value of the Project without having to dispose of any portion of its interest in order to realize that increased value.

Notes

1. Jacobs, Jane, *The Death and Life of Great American Cities*, Modern Library Edition, Random House, New York, NY (1993), originally published in 1961, pgs. 261–262. Emphasis added.
2. Underhill, Paco, *Why We Buy: The Science of Shopping*, Simon & Schuster, New York, NY (1999) and Underhill, Paco, *Call of the Mall*, Simon & Schuster, New York, NY (2004).

3. Jacobs, *The Death and Life of Great American Cities*, pgs. 262–263.

4. Ibid., pgs. 262–263.

5. This assumes the Developer, early on in the Project Conception Phase, decided to use the traditional Design/Bid/Build form of Construction Delivery System. The substance and timing of construction-related Sub-Phases in each of the first two Development Phases of The Development Process will be fundamentally different in the Project Conception and Pre-Development Phases if either the Design/Build or the Integrated Project Delivery system is selected as the Construction Delivery System for the Project.

6. Mello-Roos Community Facilities Act of 1982, added to the California Government Code by Statutes 1982, Ch. 1451, Sec. 1., California Government Code §§53311–53317.5.

7. Definition of "fenestration," Merriam-Webster Dictionary, found at: www.merriam-webster. com/dictionary/fenestration

    Fenestration – noun fen·es·tra·tion \ˌfe-nə-ˈstrā-shən\

    1: the arrangement, proportioning, and design of windows and doors in a building

    2: an opening in a surface (as a wall or membrane)

8. Cullen, Scott, "Value Engineering." *Whole Building Design Guide, a Program of the National Institute of Building Sciences*, last updated December 15, 2010. Found at www. wbdg.org/resources/value_engineering.php.

9. Burns, Robert, "To a Mouse, on Turning Her Up in Her Nest with the Plough." *From Poems, Chiefly in the Scottish Dialect*, Kilmarnock, 1786. Emphasis added.

10. Mello-Roos Community Facilities Act of 1982, added to the California Government Code by Statutes 1982, Ch. 1451, Sec. 1., California Government Code §§53311–53317.5.

11. This assumes the Developer, early on in the Project Conception Phase, decided to use the traditional Design/Bid/Build Project Delivery Method. The substance and timing of construction-related Sub-Phases in each of the first two Phases of The Development Process will be fundamentally different in the Project Conception and Pre-Development Phases if either the Design/Bid/Build or the Integrated Project Delivery approaches is selected as the Project Delivery Method for the Project.

12. There has always been a criticism of the AIA document sets that, in addition to favoring the Owner vis-à-vis the other parties to these form documents, the AIA-drafted and -controlled document sets favor architects, by relieving them, as the design representatives of owners generally, of liabilities that a more neutral position might not accept.

3

How legal issues arise in The Development Process

Two approaches invariably conflict in each story of downtown change. The first and foremost is the project approach to rebirth, what I call Project Planning. The fundamentals are always recognizable.

This approach assumes that a void exists that can be filled with a project. The planning process is designed to achieve the project, market it, sell it, and involve the public in selecting a predetermined solution – in other words, the project. The Project Planning process should not be confused with a problem-solving process. A problem-solving process may or may not involve a project. Project-based Planning does. The problem, if there was one, remains unsolved.

Under Project-based Planning, a project must be big to be meaningful. Big projects require big, experienced developers, big contractors, big government agencies, big public financial support, and lots of investment banking and legal fees. Under this Project-based Planning, the new is added at a large enough scale to overwhelm and alter what exists. What exists may be wiped out entirely, as with urban renewal. Something radically replaced it. Few clues are left as to what has been lost and what alternative strategy has been missed.[1]

Opponents of Project Planning recognize and celebrate the complexity about which [Jane] Jacobs writes. We call them Urban Husbanders. Urban Husbanders is a term I introduced and summarized in The Living City.[4] Urban Husbanders assume that assets are already in place to be reinvigorated and built onto in order to stimulate place-based rejuvenation that adds to the long-evolving, existing strengths, instead of replacing them. Planning is meant to be about problem solving, relying heavily on the expertise of citizen users, the accumulated experience and wisdom of the community. Building on resources to diminish or overcome problems is the chosen route, instead of projects that obliterate those worthy resources. Urban Husbanders advocate introducing change incrementally and monitoring it carefully, providing a great opportunity to learn from each step. Urban Husbanders are the initiators of most of the downtown successes in this book.[2]

> Chapter 6: "Urban Husbandry: The Economy of Wisdom," was contrasted with "Planned Shrinkage (an early form of Project Planning): The Economy of Waste."[3]

When *Cities Back from the Edge* was first published in 1998, from a demographic perspective the urban renaissance that has firmly taken hold in most, if not all, U.S. cities by the second decade of the twenty-first century was only just beginning. The specter of Robert Moses' open disdain for citizen participation in the planning process, as well as the urban scars of 1960s-style urban renewal, still loomed large in the psyches of those who had not previously fled their homes in the cities. In the intervening period, however, Developers have become more receptive and sensitive to citizen input in the planning process, and have developed a greater appreciation for preserving the history and authenticity of the places they create in our downtowns as a selling point for the Projects they create. Still, there are always going to be tensions between what Developers propose to do with their Projects and what citizens are willing to tolerate. This tension may manifest itself in a variety of ways throughout The Development Process.

Chapter outline
Chapter introduction
Introduction to "the Law"
The Development Process
Legal Components of Almost Every Real Estate–Related Transaction
Understanding "the Law"
How the law impacts real estate transactions and ownership
Laws that are:
Prohibitive
Permissive
Prescriptive
Laws that impose liabilities
Laws that confer rights
Laws that act as:
Incentives
Disincentives
Laws that set the default option
Understanding the hierarchies of laws of the U.S. court systems

Chapter introduction

Introduction to *"the Law."* Creating an authoritative textbook – or, at least, one that claims to be so – on the subject of "real estate law" is either a Herculean or a Sisyphean task. The subject of real estate law encompasses, as the Table of Contents suggests, a number of complex areas of legal specialty – such as Land Use Law (Chapter 5) and Financing Real Estate Transactions (Chapter 9) – as well as areas of the law that are vast, at least in part, because their history harkens back not only to English common law but all the way back to its feudal antecedents, as Local Government Law (Chapter 4) and Contract Law (Chapter 7). These challenges provide, in large measure, the principal rationale for teaching real estate law within the framework of The Development Process, providing students and other readers with a practical context within contemporary real estate development and finance for understanding and applying this expanding network of laws and practices.

The fact that "real estate law" sounds like such a dry, technical, and boring subject presents a threshold challenge to effectively teach it. There aren't any popular cable series devoted to the subject (at least not yet); it is not the subject of cocktail party conversation; a YouTube video search of "real estate law" does not reveal anything substantively worthwhile unless you consider cute cat videos substantively worthwhile (as they are impossible to avoid no matter how narrowly drawn a YouTube video search is constructed). And yet, while having acknowledged, as early as the Foreword to this textbook, that the subject of real estate law, as well as The Development Process, is inherently detail-oriented (which readers may equate with being "technical"), the subject matter of this textbook is neither dry nor boring when viewed and understood in the context of The Development Process.

Given the enormous popularity and near universality of cable series – *Breaking Bad*, *The Walking Dead*, *Dexter*, *Homeland*, *House of Cards*, *Orange Is the New Black*, *Scandal*, *Sons of Anarchy*, *Dr. Who*, *True Detective*, *American Horror Story*, *Downton Abbey*, and the rest – any fan of one or more of such cable series may better understand and appreciate real estate law through a similar lens. The Development Process is:

- A framework through which
- an interesting story
- with fascinating characters
- plays itself out.

The Development Process is riddled with plenty of drama, intrigue, manipulation, self-serving conduct, and uncertain outcomes. No one who's a fan of *The Walking Dead* or *Breaking Bad* believes those shows are merely about a Zombie apocalypse or a high school chemistry professor dying of cancer, respectively. Each of those premises provides the framework through which human behaviors are explored. The same is true, essentially, about The Development Process. Embracing this parallel makes learning about and understanding real estate law infinitely more enjoyable and memorable.

This textbook was developed on the premise that students and readers alike do not have any grounding in the law, much less in real estate law. And even those readers and students, respectively, who may have a law degree or some form of legal background will nonetheless benefit from exposure to real estate law through The Development Process. Accordingly, Chapter 3 marks the transition between The Development Process itself and the panoply of statutes, ordinances, regulations, court cases, administrative rulings, contracts and other agreements comprising "real estate law," the principal components of which are covered, in great detail, in Chapters 4 through 11.

Legal Components of Almost Every Real Estate–Related Transaction. It is important to invite to the student's or reader's attention at this juncture that not everything that falls into the category of "real estate law" involves a federal law, state statute or local ordinance, or a dispute requiring resolution by a court. In fact, the vast majority of "things" comprising real estate law involve legal relationships or arrangements that must or should be reduced to an enforceable, written document, such as a contract, a Limited Partnership Agreement, a promissory note, a deed of trust, or an agreement of lease. Even without the benefit of a law degree plus the legal training allowing someone to refer to herself as "a real estate lawyer," the student or reader will benefit greatly from an initial understanding of the principal components of nearly every relationship or transaction undertaken during The Development Process.

Purpose. It is difficult to think of any relationship or transaction that occurs during The Development Process that doesn't have some fundamental, underlying purpose of a Purchase and Sale Agreement; one such purpose, for example, is to effect the conveyance of title to real property from one party, the Seller, to another party, the Buyer. Similarly, the underlying purpose of a Lease Agreement is to grant one party, the "Tenant," legal rights to occupy a physical location (the "Premises") for a finite period of time for a particular, monthly rent. Understanding the underlying Purpose of each relationship or transaction that is part of The Development Process helps make sense of everything else characterizing that relationship or transaction.

Goals. Goals are the means by which the Purpose of a relationship or transaction is effected. For example, one of the Goals of the Purchase and Sale Agreement is to assure the Buyer that the Seller has good title in and to the Property to be conveyed. In the context of the

Lease Agreement, one of the Goals is to accurately define the Premises that the Tenant seeks to occupy.

Parties. Every relationship or transaction in The Development Process has to have more than one Party. More often than not, each relationship or transaction that is part of The Development Process has multiple parties (i.e., more than two). In fact, two of the aspects of The Development Process that makes it analogous to all of those great cable series is (i) the multiplicity of parties involved and (ii) the extent to which the interests of each of these parties diverge from and need to be resolved with the conflicting interests of other Parties to the overall subject matter of The Development Process. For example, take the Construction Lender for a Project. The Construction Lender wants the Developer and the Development Entity to succeed: otherwise, the Construction Lender may never see the return of the full amount loaned, much less all of the accrued but unpaid interest on the Construction Loan. On the other hand, there has to be a certain level of distrust in order for the Construction Lender to protect its financial interests in the transaction.[4] In this respect, the Lender's perspective in negotiating the Loan Documents may best be analogized to a nation negotiating a nuclear arms reduction agreement with another nation: "Trust but Verify" must be the governing axiom. Additionally, although the Construction Lender and the General Contractor do not have "privity of contract," because neither is party to the other's contracts, their fates are nonetheless tied. The same goes for the General Contractor's subcontractors, who must rely on the GC's relationships with the Development Entity and the Construction Lender in order to enjoy timely payment of their invoices to the GC.[5] The General Contractor won't receive its payments under the Construction Contract unless the Lender is satisfied with the accuracy and quality of the former's Draw Requests, and the Lender is less likely to be made whole on the outstanding principal amount of its Construction Loan, plus any and all accrued but unpaid interest thereon, unless the General Contractor completes the Project on time and on budget. As such, these two Parties in The Development Process are not Parties to the same contracts and, as a consequence, have no rights to proceed in court in the event one fails one or more of its contractual commitments to other parties, such as the Development Entity, with which they have direct contractual relationships, despite the fact that all such contracts, regardless of the Parties thereto, impact the outcomes relating to the Project.

Definitions. Creating relationships and effecting transactions, which are accomplished primarily through written agreements – although some relationships and transactions may be effected by either oral agreements or even merely by the conduct of the Parties, and yet other agreements and transactions may only be effected through written agreements – almost always involve creating a set of Definitions to which the Parties are agreeing as well. In a Purchase and Sale Agreement, for example, the "Definitions" or "Defined Terms" section may run several pages. Using Definitions or Defined Terms makes the drafting or legal agreements much easier, but they may also have substantive meaning.

Relationships. One of the key questions in understanding and evaluating each component of The Development Process is, in any given instance, "what are the Relationships of the Parties?" Legal Relationships by and between specific Parties may be imputed, under Common Law, by their conduct and/or oral agreements, or may be specifically defined in written contracts. The latter approach is by far the most common method within The Development Process, which is why Contract Law (Chapter 7) is treated in this textbook as a principal component of the **Holy Trinity of Real Estate Law** (i.e., Land Use, Environmental, and Contract Law). Understanding the nature of the Relationships by, among, and between Parties is an essential element in navigating The Development Process.

Duties. A "Duty" is a legal obligation one Party owes to another Party or Parties. Under common law (although much of the common law in this area has been codified under state statutes), agents owe specific Duties to their principals. For more on this, see the section on the Law of Principal and Agent in Chapter 11. For purposes of this framework for understanding the law generally, a Duty may be distinguished from a Responsibility because the former exists independently of any other action on the part of another Party while the latter is usually predicated on some other obligation on the part of another Party or is directly tied to a benefit received or conferred upon the Party that owes the Responsibility.

Rights and Responsibilities. As suggested earlier, Rights and Responsibilities imply a mutuality. For example, a Party may have an obligation of "fair dealing" with another Party but may have a concomitant expectation of "fair dealing" from that other Party.

Without the benefit of a law degree and years of practice as a real estate lawyer, the student or reader may, nonetheless, develop a working understanding of many if not all of the components and aspects of The Development Process by making inquiries in each Phase, Sub-Phase, Task, and Sub-Task in The Development Process as follows:

1. What is the Purpose?
2. What are the Goals supporting that Purpose?
3. Who or what are the Parties?
4. What are the relevant Definitions?
5. What is or are the Relationships of the Parties?
6. What Duties does one Party owe to another Party?
7. What are the respective Rights and Responsibilities of the Parties to each other?

The student or reader should keep this inquiry in mind throughout this textbook as a layperson's approach to understanding and assessing real estate law within the framework of The Development Process.

Understanding "the Law." In order to fully understand and be able to apply the panoply of statutes, ordinances, regulations, court cases, administrative rulings, contracts, and other agreements comprising "real estate law" to The Development Process, it is instructive to accept, at the outset, that laws are not fungible commodities. Each law has its own intent and purpose, as well as its own intended and unintended consequences. This premise, providing yet another layperson's construct for understanding "real estate law" as a body of individual statutes, ordinances, regulations, court cases, administrative rulings, contracts and other agreements, is provided next.

How the law impacts real estate transactions and ownership

Laws that are:

Prohibitive. A Prohibitive law is a law that says: *"You may not do X."* These are laws making certain actions or conduct illegal per se. An example of a Prohibitive law would be an environmental statute, ordinance, or regulation prohibiting wetlands from being destroyed or jeopardized as the result of a development project.

Permissive. A Permissive law is a law that says: *"You may do X."* These laws make clear that certain actions or conduct are, in fact, legal per se. Permissive laws are somewhat unusual in that, generally speaking, any conduct not expressly prohibited or contrary to some general law is deemed permissible. An example of a Permissive law would be a zoning code that allows a proposed use to deviate from a master plan if the applicant seeking that proposed use successfully completes a modification process (e.g., Variance or Master Plan Amendment).

Prescriptive. A Prescriptive law is a law that says: *"You may do X, but only if you do it this way."* An example of a Prescriptive law would be a zoning ordinance that *only allows* the operation of certain types of uses (e.g., a restaurant or bar) *if* they conform to a specific set of guidelines (e.g. operating hours; ratio of food to alcohol sales).

Liabilities. A law that imposes Liabilities says: *"If you do X, you'll be responsible for Y."* An example of a law that imposes Liabilities would be a law imposing Liabilities on residential property owners with swimming pools, requiring them to take reasonable, affirmative precautions to prevent tragic accidents from occurring (e.g., erecting a fenced enclosure versus merely posting a sign that young children may not be able to read), under the doctrine of attractive nuisance.

Rights. There are many examples of laws conferring rights that impact real estate development and finance in one form or another. Some are federal statutes, such as 2010's post–Great Recession Dodd-Frank reform bill that, among other things, created the Consumer Finance Protection Bureau, which has promulgated a number of consumer rights for mortgage loan applicants. Others are decisions made by administrative authorities whose powers are granted by state statutes or constitutions, such as the granting of a Site Permit to an applicant by a municipal planning commission, city council, or county board, which grants development rights to that applicant. Still others may be decisions by federal agencies, such as the Environmental Protection Agency, in implementing the panoply of federal statutes enacted to protect the environment, such as in response to a Property Owner's application for and compliance with all EPA requirements regarding securing a No Action or "comfort letter" regarding the agency's decision not to enforce CERCLA owner's liability under specified circumstances where previously contaminated land is proposed for reclamation, giving that Property Owner the right to proceed with its development plans without fear of an EPA enforcement action.

Laws that act as:

Incentives. A law that acts as an Incentive says: *"If you do X, you'll receive reward Y."* An example of a law that acts as an Incentive would be the mortgage interest deduction, which allows a taxpayer to deduct from gross income the amount of interest paid on a purchase money mortgage or other indebtedness (e.g., a home equity loan) on the taxpayer's primary residence, thereby incentivizing taxpayers to purchase, rather than rent, their homes.

Disincentives. A law that acts as a Disincentive says: *"If you do X, you'll receive penalty Y."* An example of a law that acts as an Disincentive would be a zoning code provision that *only allows* certain types of uses, deemed socially undesirable, in geographic areas that are physically removed or otherwise segregated from residential and commercial uses, such as industrial uses producing toxic or nauseous fumes or strip clubs and adult bookstores, punishing business operators by placing their business locations in an undesirable part of the jurisdiction.

The Default Option. A law that serves as the Default Option says: *"X will be done in a particular way unless you opt out."* An example of a law that serves as the Default Option would be the law of intestate succession, which provides for how property passes from a decedent to her/his heirs in the absence of a formal, written intention expressing the decedent's wishes (i.e., a Will). In other words, the law of intestate succession is the Default Option, unless a resident of the jurisdiction overrides the Default Option by preparing and duly executing a Will.

Understanding the hierarchies of laws of the U.S. court systems

Limited only by the U.S. Constitution, Congress can pass a seemingly limitless breadth of laws with which U.S. residents, non-person, resident entities, and visitors and guests must comply. Under the doctrine of federal preemption, such laws may take precedence over state statutes, although there is a recognized bias under the federal preemption to give deference to state laws in interpreting acts of Congress.

There are other areas, however, in which local governments are deemed to have authority, again subject to limitations on what government generally may do, as proscribed by the Constitution. The enactment and collection of state and local taxes, for example, as well as local land use planning, are two such areas in which states and particularly their localities are granted great deference. Again, all such municipal ordinances and state statutes, respectively, must not run afoul of protections afforded under the Constitution. For a very detailed discussion about the relationship of municipal governments with their state government, and how that relationship impacts the authority of municipal governments to pass ordinances and regulations, see the discussion in Chapter 4 regarding Dillon's Rule and the Cooley Doctrine, respectively.

Accordingly, whenever a party's compliance with, or alleged violation of, a specific ordinance or statute (state or federal) is at issue in connection or with respect to The Development Process, it is important to understand the origin of such an ordinance or statute, and the power of the authority that enacted such a law to do so.

Sources of law

Legislative branch

> U.S. Congress (U.S. Code)
>
> State legislatures (state statutes)
>
> Municipal ordinances (county, city, township, etc.)

Executive branch

> Executive involvement in legislative process (e.g., veto power)
>
> Promulgation of interpretive rules and regulations
>
> Executive orders
>
> Federal examples include:
>
> > Agency regulations
> >
> > Private letter rulings (IRS)

Judicial branch

> Interpretation and invalidation of
>
> > Legislation
> >
> > Executive decisions

Decisions based on common law

> Rights
>
> Remedies

Understanding the hierarchies within court systems. Generally speaking, court systems, whether federal or state, have a hierarchy consisting of:

- A trial court or "court of first impression." Among other things, a trial court is "the trier of facts." Anything presented in the course of trial, as well as the manner in which the trial itself is conducted, provided a timely objection thereto is properly made, may be preserved for appeal.
- Appellate courts. As suggested earlier, provided matters are the subject of timely and proper objection at trial, they may be "preserved" for an appeals process. Appellate courts *do not* retry the facts in a case; they solely consider the basis of each matter as to which one party objected during the trial and with respect to which a proper and timely appeal has been filed. In other words, the fact that a proper objection was made at trial – whether that objection was sustained or denied; whether the judge at the trial court level made the correct decision; and whether the judge's decision prejudiced the party against whose interests it was decided – does not automatically put the objection before the appellate court. A detailed appeal must be filed on behalf of the party claiming to have been prejudiced by each such objection put at issue by the Appellant, and that appeal must justify each such decision being subject to such appeal. In the event the appellate court determines that the Appellant was prejudiced regarding the ruling of the trial court, the appellate court does not substitute its judgment for that of the trial court: The case is "remanded" or sent back to the trial court for rehearing on that specific issue. Under certain circumstances, the appellate court may order a new trial. However, the appellate court does not retry the case based on the appeals that are filed and make its own decision about the outcome of the case on appeal.
- Supreme courts. Matters heard by an appellate court, on which the appellate court rules, may – before being remanded for the appropriate procedural disposition by the court of first impression – be appealed to the highest court, commonly referred to as the Supreme Court of the state over which it has jurisdiction. In the state of New York, however, the Supreme Court of New York is actually the lower or trial court, with the New York Court of Appeals serving as the final arbiter of all appellate proceedings.

The Real Estate Development Process in Detail. Having been described and explained in Chapter 2, each Phase of The Development Process is presented here, along with each of the Sub-Phases in each Phase, illuminated by (i) a discussion of the real estate law issues that may arise during each such Sub-Phase, and (ii) a discussion of other Sub-Phases that the subject Sub-Phase may impact or by which it may be impacted. In this way, Chapter 3 provides a comprehensive approach to navigating the substantive chapters of this textbook (Chapters 4 through 11) and understanding the linear but iterative nature of The Development Process.

The chronological Sub-Phases of each of the five Phases of The Development Process are as follows:

Project Conception Phase

Idea Generation. Inasmuch as Idea Generation represents the earliest Sub-Phase of The Development Process, it might arguably be the only Sub-Phase in which no real estate law issues are presented at such a nascent stage in the process. However, depending on the Idea or Ideas being generated, it is not wholly inconceivable that some legal issues may be known and relevant enough to the immediate Idea to warrant being raised, at least preliminarily, even at the very beginning of The Development Process. For example, a Developer that is interested in trying to develop, in a new jurisdiction, a product type (e.g., a WalkUP) that was successfully developed in a different jurisdiction will likely have some notion of the land use issues likely to arise during the course of The Development Process; more so, perhaps, if both jurisdictions are in the same state. See **Figure 2.1**. The legal issues relating to the financing of such product types are even more likely to be repeated the second time around (e.g., whether each component in a WalkUP should be separately financed, because it was harder the first time around to find a single lender or equity investor willing to take on the entire Project versus individual components of the Project), and, as a consequence, hinting at structural modifications from the first iteration may facilitate both the Construction Financing and the Permanent Financing. See **Figure 2.2**.

Site Identification. The primary real estate law issues during Site Identification relate to (i) who owns record title to real property and what type of title is held; (ii) the process by which properties are found by or brought to the Developer's attention; and (iii) honoring the current owner's possessory rights to their property, including the right to exclude others from entering the property. See **Figures 2.3, 2.4**, and **2.5**, respectively. The first issue is addressed in the section on "Ownership" of Real Estate: Estates in Real Property in Chapter 1; legal issues attendant to the search for properties are addressed in the discussion of Brokers and Agents in Chapter 11; and the legal issues impacting the right to exclude others from the property are addressed in both the first and final chapters of this textbook (not surprisingly, of course, inasmuch as in Chapter 11, the Development Entity is in the same, relative position as the owner of property seeking or entertaining a Buyer in Chapter 1).

Select Project Delivery Method. On one hand, the Project Delivery Method selected at this early Sub-Phase in the Project Conception Phase of The Development Process may not require any immediate actions on the part of the Developer that give rise to taking any binding action. Only in the instance in which the Developer selects the Design/Bid Project Delivery Method will the Developer need to take any short-term actions (see Assemble and Engage Development Team in this regard). However, selecting the Project Delivery Method to be used by the Development Entity in designing and constructing the Project has wide-ranging implications for The Development Process and will impact a number of legal relationships and transactions throughout the process, perhaps well into the Ownership and Property Management Phase of The Development Process. See **Figures 2.6** through **2.12**. Accordingly, the process of selecting the Developer's preferred Project Delivery Method requires examining all of the legal issues and relationships arising in connection with the Construction Phase of The Development Process, and touches on fundamental aspects of Construction Law. This decision will impact the legal relationships between the Developer and the Development Entity, on one hand, and key members of the Development Team, on the other. The implications of each Project Delivery Method are addressed in more detail in the discussion about the Construction Phase of The Development Process, and in the section of the Supplementary Material on the companion website for this textbook titled Construction Phase Issues, Documentation, and Claims.

Develop Exit and Funding Strategies. Just as with the selection of the Project Delivery Method, crafting the Developer's Exit Strategy, as well as the Funding Strategy for the Development Entity and the Project, respectively, has wide-ranging implications for many critical steps in The Development Process. So, while completing this task may not have any short-term implications for the Developer in the early part of the Project Conception Phase, every Phase of The Development Process will be impacted, starting with the Negotiate Acquisition and Development (A&D) Financing Commitment of the

Project Conception Phase. See **Figures 2.13** through **Figure 2.17**. The type of funding coming into the Project and/or the Development Entity, if it's already been created, whether equity, debt, a combination and/or hybrid of the two, and how those investments in the Project are expected to be paid a return and repaid, will be expressed initially in the Developer's Exit Strategy and Funding Strategy, respectively. Each participant in the Acquisition and Development (A&D) Financing will have tax implications from the nature and extent of their investment (see Chapter 8 in this regard), and will insist that the documentation evidencing their investment, in whatever form, reflects their investment intent and return expectations (see, in this regard, Chapter 9). Additionally, the Preliminary Development Budget pro forma of the Project Conception Phase should reflect both the Exit Strategy and the Funding Strategy, respectively.

Community Outreach. Engaging a communications and/or public relations firm to handle the Developer's communications, including the development of a Communications Strategy or Plan, and implementing each of its components, means that the Developer or the Development Entity will need to engage these third-party services through a contract or contracts (see, in this regard, Chapter 7). Among other things, this means developing a comprehensive Scope of Work or Scope of Services to define the third-party services to be performed (see Defining and Drafting a Scope of Work in the Supplementary Materials on the companion website for the textbook), as well as contract provisions relating to the timing of and other terms of payment; provisions regarding the Developer's acceptance of the Work as being in accordance with the contract; and circumstances under which either party, or only the Developer, may terminate services prior to the completion of the Scope of Work under the contract. Other than a brokerage or agency agreement the Developer may decide to negotiate and enter into in connection with the Site Identification Sub-Phase, the contract(s) for communications and public relations services (which may be two separate arrangements with two separate third-party providers, may be the first legally binding documents the Developer enters into as part of The Development Process.

Assemble and Engage Development Team. As described in Chapter 2, for most real estate development projects in the Project Conception Phase, the Development Team will be comprised of the following experts:

- A design or design and engineering firm;
- a civil engineering or land planning firm;
- an environmental assessment vendor;
- a local law firm specializing in zoning and land use in the jurisdiction where the property is located;
- a market analysis firm experienced in the market and submarket where the property is located; and
- a communications and/or public relations firm (as mentioned in the section addressing the **Community Outreach** Sub-Phase).

Additionally, and as suggested in the section addressing the selection of the Project Delivery Method for the Project, if the Developer selects an Integrated Project Delivery or **Design/Build Project Delivery Method** to use to construct the Improvements on the Subject Site identified through the Project Conception Phase, the General Contractor for the Project will also need to be included as part of the Development Team very early on in the Project Conception Phase.

Accordingly, the Developer will need to have a contract with each member of the Development Team. At a minimum this means the Developer and each member of the

Development Team will be legally bound to a written agreement setting forth a Scope of Work, terms of payment, provisions regarding the early termination of the agreement (which may not necessarily provide mutual rights to effect such termination), and other essential contractual provisions necessary to effect the intent of the parties. Some of the members of the Development Team will be providing professional services with respect to which professional liabilities do not inure to their detriment, as is the case with design professionals providing Schematic Design. Others, such as Local Counsel, may not have that luxury unless the contract for providing professional services by Local Counsel to the Developer expressly exempts the former from professional liability, which would make the value of the professional services rendered almost nil. Additionally, and as suggested in Chapter 2 regarding the engagement of the Development Team, these professional services firms may be willing to provide their services at less than full market value because they want the opportunity to continue on the Development Team through the completion of The Development Process. Accordingly, these contracts must be drafted in such a way that the Developer is committed to keeping each member part of the Development Team, provided there aren't any failures of performance that would warrant their replacement prior to the commencement of the Pre-Development Phase of The Development Process. Accordingly, these professional services contracts must be carefully crafted, with the terms and conditions very much reflecting the bargaining position of each professional services provider vis-à-vis the Developer.

Preliminary Program. The Preliminary Program is the first quantification of the Idea articulated in the Idea Generation Sub-Phase of the Project Conception Phase of The Development Process. At least initially, and for the most part of the Project Conception Phase, this is an internal planning document that is likely to change often and, quite possibly, dramatically throughout the Project Conception Phase and well into the Pre-Development Phase of The Development Process. However, at some point, possibly as part of the Negotiate Acquisition and Development (A&D) Financing Commitment Sub-Phase of the Project Conception Phase of The Development Process, the Updated Program, along with other important internal planning documents, including but not limited to the Preliminary Development Budget pro forma and the Preliminary Project pro forma, are going to be shared with potential Investors and Lenders to the Developer, the Development Entity, and/or the Project, at which point, absent the appropriate disclosures, disclaimers, and waivers, the Developer will be legally bound by the substance of these "merely internal" documents. Accordingly, it is instructive to invite to the student's and the reader's attention at this juncture that seemingly benign, internal planning documents and other materials, when provided to particular parties in connection with particular types of transactions taking place during The Development Process, may impose legal liabilities on the Developer. See, in this regard, Chapters 8 and 9.

Market Overview or Survey. The implications for and impacts from real estate law emanating from the Market Overview or Survey are much more subtle than they are for Project Conception Phase Sub-Phases such as the Select Project Delivery Method and Assemble and Engage Development Team. For example, the results of even just a Market Overview or Survey may push the Preliminary Program initially devised by the Developer into product types and uses on the Subject Site that will require land use approvals that are fundamentally different from – and, potentially, much less certain as the final outcome – what the Developer initially contemplated. Similarly, the Market Overview or Survey may recommend product types requiring the Developer to alter its Funding Strategy for the Project, as might be the case in the event the Market Overview or Survey recommends a shift or mixing of tenure types as part of the Project, such as adding condominium units to the residential product mix in a WalkUP project. Additionally, it bears repeating that the Market Overview or Survey report will be a function of the

Scope of Work contained in the Developer's engagement letter or other contract document used to bring the Market Analysis Firm on board the Development Team.

Revised Preliminary Program. Aside from potential changes in land use approvals occasioned by changes in the Revised Preliminary Program, discussed in detail in the Market Overview or Survey and Land Use Analysis Sub-Phases, respectively, the principal real estate law issue the Revised Preliminary Program presents may relate to its inclusion in any materials used to seek and/or secure financing for the Project. As suggested in the discussion of the Preliminary Program Sub-Phase, absent the appropriate disclosures, disclaimers, and waivers in sharing such "internal planning documents" with third parties – particularly those asked to participate in the financing of the Project – the Developer may be legally bound by the substance of these documents. This raises the "doctrine of detrimental reliance" and whether an Investor or Lender could subsequently revoke a financing commitment upon fundamental changes occurring in the Revised Preliminary Program. See Chapter 7 regarding the doctrine of detrimental reliance.

Land Use Analysis. The Land Use Analysis may have a variety of direct and immediate real estate law implications, from the land use approvals the Developer will need to secure during the Pre-Development Phase of The Development Process (see Chapter 5), to Environmental Law compliance in the proposed uses of the Subject Site and the Improvements proposed thereon (see Chapter 6). By way of example, as prefatory as it is in scope (again, referring to the Scope of Work that will be incorporated into the Developer's contract with the professional services firm to be engaged as part of the Development Team in the Assemble and Engage Development Team Sub-Phase), the Land Use Analysis may nonetheless delineate constraints on the buildable area of the Subject Site, forcing the Developer to consider more intensive product types and building types, respectively, for the Schematic Design (see the Schematic Design Sub-Phase). As with the discussion in the Market Overview or Survey Sub-Phase, such changes in the Developer's Preliminary Program will require land use approvals that are fundamentally different from what the Developer initially contemplated, the ultimate outcome of which land use approval process may be significantly less certain than the land use approvals necessary to proceed with what is contemplated in the Preliminary Program.

Schematic Design. The chronological appearance of the Schematic Design Sub-Phase at this point in the Project Conception Phase of The Development Process is intended to allow the Schematic Design to be informed by the Market Overview or Survey, the Land Use Analysis, and the Revised Preliminary Program, respectively. As a graphic depiction of how the proposed Improvements to the Subject Site might appear in plan view, the Schematic Design itself does not create any of the real estate law issues already discussed, in detail, in relation to the aforementioned Sub-Tasks. Additionally, because the definition of Schematic Design is that it cannot be relied on to actually build anything, no professional liability attaches to the design firm providing the schematic designs. As such, the only real estate law implication for this Sub-Phase is that the contract between the Developer and the design firm regarding the latter's performance of Schematic Design services will, among other things, make clear that the design firm is not assuming any professional liability whatsoever for the work product to be delivered.

Preliminary Infrastructure Assessment. In addition to highlighting potential cost areas for connecting the Subject Site and its proposed Improvements to various utilities, the Preliminary Infrastructure Assessment may indicate capacity issues impeding the ability of exiting utilities to adequately serve the Subject Site. A proposed Project that requires the Local Governmental Unit to increase the capacity of one or more public utilities will have the power to require the Developer to pay for the increased capacity. This may entail a relatively nominal (when compared to the projected Total Development Cost for the Project) additional expense – as would be the case of the Developer having to pay the cost of replacing 500 feet of an eight-inch water supply line under the street to a twelve-inch water supply line because the connection to a twelve-inch or larger water supply line is 500 feet away from where that new water supply line would logically be brought onto the Subject Site – or it may require a substantial capital investment by the local government or utility district that will benefit not only the Subject Site but a substantial number of property owners served by that infrastructure upgrade. Accordingly, the Developer will have to enter into a Memorandum of Understanding or some other binding agreement covering (i) the local government or utility district's commitment to make the necessary capacity upgrade and (ii) the Developer's quid pro quo commitment to pay all or some portion of the cost to make that upgrade. Naturally, a number of details need to be incorporated into such an agreement or contract, whether it's called a "Memorandum of Understanding" or something else. See Chapters 4 and 7 regarding this issue.

Updated Program. See Preliminary Program Sub-Phase regarding real estate law issues raised during the Updated Program.

Preliminary development budget pro forma. As with other internal planning documents, such as the Preliminary Program and Revised Preliminary Program described in Chapter 2, the Preliminary Development Budget pro forma does not, in and of itself, generate real estate law issues. However, this first-look pro forma will rely on assumptions that eventually will need to be finalized and formalized through various contract documents. Accordingly, in this regard, the Preliminary Development Budget pro forma will need to anticipate terms and conditions for various forms of financing, as well as the terms and conditions for the Construction Loan to be negotiated and closed during the Pre-Development Phase of The Development Process. For example, anticipated application and/or origination fees, as well as a rate of interest and/or any preferred equity return anticipated in connection with the Acquisition and Development (A&D) Financing, will be assumed, pending the finalization of the Acquisition and Development (A&D) Financing Commitment discussed later. Once the Developer has negotiated and secured a commitment for Acquisition and Development (A&D) Financing, then the Preliminary Development Budget pro forma will need to be updated, replacing various pro forma assumptions about this early stage financing with the *express terms and conditions of the commitment* itself. However, as is the case with other internal planning documents, absent the appropriate disclosures, disclaimers, and waivers in sharing internal planning documents with third parties, the manner in which the Preliminary Development Budget pro forma is used outside the Developer and the Development Team may give rise to real estate law issues down the road. In particular, if the Preliminary Project pro forma is used to support or backstop financing proposals (i.e., solicitations for investor financing) and/or loan applications, this could give rise to the *doctrine of detrimental reliance*, mentioned earlier, allowing an Investor or Lender to subsequently revoke financing commitments upon fundamental changes occurring in the Preliminary Development Budget pro forma. See Chapter 7 regarding the doctrine of detrimental reliance.

Preliminary project pro forma. See Preliminary Development Budget pro forma Sub-Phase regarding real estate law issues raised during the Preliminary Project pro forma Sub-Phase.

Negotiate Acquisition and Development (A&D) Financing Commitment. If the Acquisition and Development (A&D) Financing being sought is consistent with the Funding Strategy the Developer developed very early in the Project Conception Phase of The Development Process, presumably the Developer will have taken a number of steps to facilitate this first tranche of financing for the Project and/or the Development Entity. However, regardless of how well prepared the Developer is for the type of early stage financing it has anticipated through this commitment, it will still be negotiating a document that the Developer hopes to make as legally binding as possible while the Investor or Lender offering to make the commitment will want to make it as contingent as possible. As described in Chapter 2 and elaborated in Chapter 8, it is unlikely debt financing will provide much if any of the cash needed to fund Pre-Development Phase expenses, which is a principal component of A&D financing. As also discussed in Chapter 8, early stage financing of the Project received during the Project Conception Phase of The Development Process is most likely to be offered in the form of high-cost mezzanine financing or debt or hybrid financing coming in at the Developer level, rather than the Development Entity level. As such, the Developer will be keenly focused on the terms and conditions of such a financing commitment, as a Project failure during the Pre-Development Phase of The Development Process could result in the return of the entire principal amount of the equity investment or loan, plus what will mostly likely be a premium return for the Investor or Lender owning a portion of the Developer, as is often the case with mezzanine financing. Accordingly, the terms and conditions set forth in the financing commitment document are not to be taken lightly.

Secure site control. As suggested in Chapter 2, up to this point in the Project Conception Phase of The Development Process, the Developer's exposure to risk is limited to the costs incurred in engaging and compensating the members of the Development Team, on whatever basis the Developer can negotiate with each one (see Assemble and Engage Development Team). Walking away from a potential project that is not financially feasible or that is not projected to return a profit sufficient to warrant the risks involved may require abandoning certain sunk costs that, in the aggregate, represent a mere fraction of potential losses if the project proves infeasible farther down the road. Securing Site Control – meaning creating, for the benefit of the Developer, an unfettered right to acquire the Subject Site based on the specific terms and conditions to which the parties have agreed – involves the use of one of two legal documents: a Purchase and Sale Agreement (PSA) or an Option Contract (Option). The pros and cons of each method of securing Site Control are discussed in detail in Chapter 7. Under the Option Contract, the Developer purchases an option, giving the Developer the legal right to purchase the Subject Site. This purchase option may be exercised for a specified period of time (the Option Period), provided the Developer pays the agreed-upon price (the Exercise Price) – and perhaps including other terms favoring the Developer. If that Option to purchase the Property is not exercised in accordance with its terms and conditions and the Option expires, the purchase price paid to the Seller for the Option is not recoverable, even if the Developer has sound reasons for not completing the transaction. Under the Purchase and Sale Agreement, the Developer's obligation to purchase the Subject Site is conditioned on a number of subjectively determined events, thereby affording the Developer considerable flexibility in determining whether to proceed with the acquisition after more information has been obtained and analyzed. One of the most common such conditions precedent to the Developer's obligation to purchase the Subject Site is the completion of a Due Diligence Period, during which the Developer may walk away from the purchase contract and be entitled to a full refund of its good faith deposit that accompanied the execution of the PSA, for any number of reasonable events subjectively assessed by the Developer. Because PSAs are generally structured in this manner, while the good faith deposit will be exponentially larger than the payment for a Purchase Option, the conditions under which the good faith deposit may be refunded to the Developer, in full, under a broad range of circumstances makes the PSA the preferred choice for securing legal control of the Subject Site.

Pre-Development Phase

Closing on acquisition and development (A&D) financing. This is the first of several "Closings" that will take place throughout The Development Process. The parties providing the financing, in whatever form, will be ready to disburse the funds being contributed to the Developer and/or the Development Entity. The Developer and/or the Development Entity, for their respective parts, will have documentation prepared providing evidence of Investors' equity stakes that will be issued in exchange for such investments being made in the Developer or the Development Entity, as the case may be. If the A&D financing involves a loan, the parties will have negotiated and finalized the loan documents and security instruments setting forth the terms and conditions of the loan being made and the collateral security being provided to the Lender to assure repayment, in full, of the principal amount of that loan, plus accrued but unpaid interest. Generally a law firm or title company will serve as the Escrow Agent, holding all of the monies to be paid at (or prior to), and disbursed at, the Closing, and each party will have their respective legal counsel present to make their final review of the documents, negotiated and finalized ahead of the Closing, before each document is circulated around the Closing table for execution by each required party. Once each and every "Closing Document" has been "duly executed" by each required party, the Escrow Agent will disburse funds as appropriate. For example, if the Developer used a broker to find and secure the A&D funding commitment(s), that broker will be entitled to its commission or "finder's fee" out of the Closing proceeds. See Chapters 7, 8, and 9 for various aspects of the Closing Documents.

   Market Study. See the Market Overview or Survey Sub-Phase of the Project Conception Phase of The Development Process regarding the real estate law implications and impacts of the Market Study Sub-Phase in the Pre-Development Phase. Consonant with that discussion, note the inherent tension between the Market Study, which the Market Analysis Firm will make clear is "issued for the exclusive use of the [Development Entity], and may not be used or relied upon by any other party involved in the transaction," and the Developer's natural inclination or necessity to use the Market Study to persuade the Permanent Lender of the merits and soundness of the Project. To the extent that the application and/or underwriting process of the Permanent Lender (or any other entity providing the Take-Out Financing Commitment on which the Construction Loan Commitment will necessarily rely) specifically requires a Market Study "in form and substance acceptable to Lender," this fact and any specific parameters or requirements of that Lender for the required Market Study need to be worked out with the Market Analysis Firm by the Developer at the time the Developer is negotiating the Scope of Work of and costs for the Market Analysis. Otherwise, the Developer may find itself in the position of needing to commission – and pay for – a second, independent Market Analysis.

   Site Due Diligence. The Developer generally has its work cut out for it in managing the things and processes that are (relatively) within its control during The Development Process in order to end up with a successful Project, without inheriting any additional problems. Accordingly, a good way of looking at the Site Due Diligence Sub-Phase of the Pre-Development Phase is that this is the Developer and the Development Team's best, and only, opportunity to carefully scrutinize every aspect of the Subject Site, to assure the Developer that, in acquiring title to the Subject Site and proceeding with the rest of the Sub-Phases of the Pre-Development Phase of The Development Process, the Developer is not inheriting any additional problems, the resolution of which may be well out of the Developer's control. Accordingly, given the significance of Site Due Diligence when viewed in this manner, it is worthwhile to review briefly what's entailed in the Site Due Diligence Sub-Phase of the Pre-Development Phase of The Development Process.

The Site Due Diligence Sub-Phase is truly emblematic of real estate law at its most technically intensive during The Development Process. As stated in Chapter 2, one of the most critical Sub-Phases of the Pre-Development Phase is conducting extensive due diligence on the Subject Site. This basically means learning everything the Developer can about the Subject Site that neither the time nor cost constraints imposed by the Project Conception Phase would allow. Site due diligence tasks may include but are not necessarily limited to:

Commissioning and examining carefully an ALTA Title Survey of the Subject Site
Commissioning and examining carefully an ALTA Preliminary Title Report
Securing a Title Commitment
Commissioning Environmental Assessments, which may be comprised of:

- Phase I Environmental Site Assessment, and
- Phase II Environmental Assessment.

Each of these documents is described in detail in Chapter 2. The ALTA Title Survey, ALTA Preliminary Title Report, and Title Commitment will determine the quality and character of the title to be conveyed at the Closing on the Acquisition of the Subject Site to occur later, if at all, in the Pre-Development Phase of The Development Process. The ALTA Title Survey will also determine any constraints on the Developer's or the Development Entity's use of the Subject Site, particularly whether 100% of the Subject Site may be used for the construction of Improvements, as well as means of ingress and egress onto and from the Subject Site. Finally, the Environmental Assessments will determine whether the Developer should (i) terminate the Purchase and Sale Agreement due to the presence of previously undisclosed or unidentified environmental hazards present on the Subject Site, (ii) accept the Subject Property only after the Seller has undertaken and completed, to the satisfaction of the U.S. **Environmental Protection Agency (EPA)**, remediation efforts to remove any and all such environmental hazards, or insist on a substantial reduction in the Purchase Price of the Subject Site under the Purchase and Sale Agreement to account for the clean-up costs, as well as any time that will be lost during the clean-up effort. See discussion of "Ownership" of Real Estate: Estates in Real Property in Chapter 1 and, generally, Chapter 6 regarding real estate law issues in connection with the Site Due Diligence Sub-Phase.

Civil engineering analysis and site evaluation report. Unlike the Project Conception Phase of The Development Process, in which the professional services firms on the Development Team (other than, perhaps, Local Counsel) were not incurring professional liabilities for the work being performed, in the Pre-Development Phase each professional services firm will be held to account for the work performed (and will be compensated accordingly). Accordingly, making a mistake in the Civil Engineering Analysis and Site Evaluation Report may give rise to one or more legal claims by the Developer or the Development Entity, depending on who contracted with the civil engineering firm. Additionally, the parties will be held to their contractual commitments under whatever contract document the Developer or Development Entity uses to engage the services of the civil engineering firm. As suggested in the Assemble and Engage Development Team Sub-Phase of the Pre-Development Phase of The Development Process, how clearly and completely the Scope of Work is written in each of the professional services agreements will determine the Developer's or Development Entity's enforcement rights in the event of a breach of the contract. In addition to real estate law issues relating to the performance of the civil engineering firm under its contract with the Developer or the Development Entity, it is possible that the Civil Engineering Analysis and Site Evaluation Report will reveal site conditions requiring changes to one or more aspects of the Updated Program, which may not only then require substantive modifications to the Preliminary Development Budget pro forma and the Preliminary Project pro forma (see those Sub-Phases in the Project Conception Phase of The Development Process for possible real estate law implications of changes in these internal planning documents), but such site conditions may require changes in the Product Types and Product Mix planned for the Subject Site, which changes may, in turn, require changes to the Zoning and **Land Use Approvals** to be sought in connection with the Subject Site (see **Secure All Necessary Zoning and Land Use Approvals**).

Design development (DD). A number of decisions will be made between the Developer, the Project's architect, and the Development Team during Design Development that will change the Project, and these changes may have real estate law implications, such as changes in the Secure All Necessary Zoning and Land Use Approvals Sub-Phase. However, beyond these collateral real estate law implications, and the same kinds of potential legal issues the Developer may have with any of the Development Team members regarding the performance of their respective professional services contracts (see, e.g., the discussion in the Civil Engineering Analysis and Site Evaluation Report Sub-Phase), there are very limited real estate law implications during the Design Development Sub-Phase.

Value Engineering. See previous discussions regarding the Civil Engineering Analysis and Site Evaluation Report and Design Development Sub-Phases, respectively, regarding the very limited real estate law implications during the Value Engineering Sub-Phase.

Revised and Expanded Development and Operating Budget pro formas.

Secure All Necessary Zoning and Land Use Approvals. There is a reason Land Use Law is part of the "Holy Trinity of Real Estate Law." Without securing All Necessary Zoning and Land Use Approvals, the Developer will not be able to proceed with the next Sub-Phase, Close on Land Acquisition, but remain at a point in The Development Process where the Developer will have expended an enormous amount of money, possibly running in the millions of dollars for a complex WalkUP awarded by a public entity through a competitive, public procurement process. See Chapters 4, 5, and 10 regarding the details of this Sub-Phase of the Pre-Development Phase of The Development Process.

Close on land acquisition. See discussion under the Closing on Acquisition and Development (A&D) Financing Sub-Phase of the Pre-Development Phase of The Development Process regarding how a Closing reflects the culmination of a variety of issues and transactions involving real estate law. The Closing by the Developer or the Development Entity on the acquisition of the Subject Site marks a dramatic change in both the Developer's and the Development Entity's posture vis-à-vis the Subject Site and the Project. Once title transfers, options will be very limited for realizing the Developer's Exit Strategy for the Project. Equity Investors will have claims to the title to the Subject Site by virtue of their ownership of a ratable share of the assets of the Development Entity, and the Lender will hold a security interest in the Subject Site. See Entity Choice discussion in Chapter 8. Additionally, if environmental liabilities are associated with the Subject Site, which went undetected despite the successful completion of the Site Due Diligence Sub-Phase of the Pre-Development Phase of The Development Process, the Developer or Development Entity will, under most environmental laws, inherit those environmental liabilities despite not having actual knowledge of them, by virtue of being in "the chain of title." See Chapter 6 in this regard. Finally, it is incumbent upon the Developer to make sure that the financing supporting the Closing on the acquisition of the Subject Site does not constrain the Developer or Development Entity's ability to grant security interests required by subsequent Lenders to and Equity Investors in the Project. See Chapter 9 in this regard.

Construction documents (CDs). The Construction Documents provide the definitive instructions to all parties involved as to how the Improvements are to be constructed. To the extent they are required to be filed with the **Building Department**, Code Enforcement Division, or other department or office of the Local Governmental Unit charged with responsibility for issuing building permits, CDs are required to be stamped by an Architect or Engineer licensed to practice in the state in which the jurisdiction is located. In preparing and stamping CDs, the architecture or engineering firm that prepared them is putting its professional reputation and liability at risk. Some of the real estate law issues arising out of the development of and reliance on the Construction Documents for a Project are mentioned in the discussion about the Construction Phase of The Development Process, and in the Supplementary Materials on the companion website for this textbook under Construction Phase Issues, Documentation, and Claims.

Creation of all necessary entities (e.g. GPs, LPs, and LLCs). Readers should note the discussion about Creation of all Necessary Entities (e.g., GPs, LPs, and LLCs) in Chapter 2, in the Pre-Development Phase of The Development Process, as to whether this Sub-Phase should appear much earlier in the Pre-Development Process, toward the end of the Project Conception Phase of The Development Process, or even as part of the Develop Exit and Funding Strategies Sub-Phase at the beginning of the Project Conception Phase. As mentioned in Chapter 2, it could greatly facilitate certain actions, such as incurring and paying expenses to third parties, entering into contracts, and Closing on the acquisition of the Subject Site to have them undertaken by the proper entity for tax, liability, and structured financing purposes. See, among others, Chapters 5, 8, and 9 regarding the specifics). On the other hand, unless all anticipated equity and debt sources that will be participating in the funding of the Project are identified or even identifiable as early as the Project Conception Sub-Phase Develop Exit and Funding Strategies, it may be impossible to know what are the optimal Development Entity and transaction structures, respectively, to facilitate and support the investment and loan parameters for the equity and debt participants that will be engaged in the Project Financing. Substantively, as noted in the parenthetical, this Sub-Phase of the Pre-Development Phase holds wide-ranging implications for real estate law, and Chapters 5, 8, and 9 should be consulted regarding the variety of real estate law issues in creating the entities necessary to support the Project.

Creation of all necessary authorities (e.g., TIF district, community facilities district). Depending on the location and nature of the Project, and the state within which the jurisdiction of the Subject Site is located, a range of "quasi-public," governmental, and "quasi-governmental" authorities may be created to facilitate the overall funding available for the Project and/or provide a range of quasi-public services supporting the Project. These run the gamut from tax increment finance (TIF) districts, public infrastructure improvements districts, special tax credit investment districts, business improvement districts, and special-purpose governing districts funded through assessments on some or all of the Improvements to be constructed on the Subject Site. These quasi-public and quasi-governmental entities are all creatures of state statute, and oftentimes have long-lead procedural approval processes that must be followed in order to be created. Accordingly, and as is the case with the discussion about the proper timing of the Creation of all Necessary Entities (e.g., GPs, LPs, and LLCs) Sub-Phase, creating some or all of such "necessary authorities" may need to be commenced well in advance of where this Sub-Phase is shown in this listing of the Pre-Development Phase.

Identify and secure take-out (permanent) financing commitment. Parties seeking "forward commitments" – a promise today to do something specific tomorrow or some other time in the future – want such commitments to be as iron-clad as possible. Parties making forward commitments seek exactly the opposite: a contingent promise to "maybe do something in the future" (the equivalent of "I don't know; we'll see"), which may be abrogated for almost any reason the party making the commitment deems fit in its sole, unconditional, and unfettered discretion. Accordingly, the terms and conditions of the Take-Out Financing Commitment are absolutely critical. It is instructive to understand, at this point, that the issuer of the Take-Out Financing Commitment is being asked to loan money against or to purchase an interest in something that does not yet exist and might not exist for several years. Moreover, even if the promised Improvements do, in fact, materialize, neither their overall and specific quality nor their ability to command the revenues the Developer projected can be 100% assured. Accordingly, the "qualifications" in a financing commitment – those specific conditions that, if not present at the time the Developer or Development Entity seeks to secure the permanent financing that is the subject of the forward commitment – will be critical to the effectiveness and enforceability of the Take-Out Financing Commitment. See Chapter 9 for further detailed information about Take-Out Financing Commitments.

Identify and secure construction loan commitment. Although technically also a "forward commitment," as discussed in the preceding Sub-Phase of the Pre-Development Phase of The Development Process, and, therefore, susceptible to the same legal infirmities as the Take-Out (Permanent) Financing Commitment, the Construction Loan Commitment relates to a Construction Loan expected to be closed within three to six months from the Loan Commitment's date of issuance. It is important to recognize at this point in The Development Process that the Development Entity needs to secure the Construction Loan Commitment prior to commencing the Pricing and Bidding for General Contractors (GCs) and Subcontractors, which is a subsequent Sub-Phase of the Pre-Development Process. To assure potential bidders that, if selected, the Development Entity will have the construction funds available to commence the work. Nonetheless, the Construction Loan Commitment will still present significant preconditions the Construction Lender needs to have satisfied before the Construction Loan will be issued. These preconditions will, accordingly, appear as qualifications to the Construction Lender's Loan Commitment. See Chapter 9.

Solicit bids and pricing from general contractors (GCs) and subcontractors.[6] The intended outcome of the process of soliciting bids, with pricing, from qualified General Contractors to undertake the construction of the Improvements on the Subject Site in accordance with the CDs is to identify the best combination of quality and price embodied in the winning bid. If the process is well organized and well thought out, and if adequate time is allowed to the bidders in responding to the solicitation for bids, the bidding process may also ferret out interpretation issues in the CDs that may be reconciled through the bidding process or contract negotiations with short-listed bidders, potentially minimizing RFIs and COs later in the construction process. The real estate law impacts of and for the solicitation of bids and pricing for the CDs is very much internalized to the Construction Contract and the processes described in that contract. To the extent collateral real estate law issues come out of this process, they relate primarily to timing and cost issues with regard to contracts or commitments between the Development Entity and various users of the completed Improvements. For example, if the delivery of a completed building is delayed for six months because of a dispute between the General Contractor and the Development Entity regarding the interpretation of the CDs and/or the respective liabilities of the Development Entity, the architecture or engineering firm that prepared the CDs, and the General Contractor for resolving such interpretation, such delay may negatively impact a tenant with a signed lease for completed Improvements that was promised delivery of its completed Premises on a date that may now be exceeded because of the delay. To the extent that the Tenant must pay a punitive, holdover rent to its current Landlord because it cannot vacate its existing Premises in accordance with its current lease, who among the Development Entity, the architect or engineering firm responsible for the CDs, and the General Contractor will be held liable for compensating the Tenant for the additional expenses of occupying its existing Premises as a Holdover Tenant? Similarly, what if delays in the construction of the Improvements are so substantial that some or all of the components of a Mixed-Use or WalkUPs Project "miss the market," such that the Project pro formas appear overly optimistic when comparing projected revenues with actual revenues once the Project is completed and occupied? See Chapter 9. For additional information regarding the bidding process, see the Supplementary Materials on the companion website under Construction Phase Issues, Documentation, and Claims.

Negotiate and document construction loan docs. Real estate executives may be both accustomed to and very adept at negotiating the "business terms" of many real estate development and finance agreements. Nonetheless, it is an increasing rarity for even these "business terms" negotiations to be undertaken without the benefit and presence of legal counsel, whether in-house (i.e., employed by the Developer directly) or outside counsel. However, even if legal counsel is not present for the negotiation of the business terms of a transaction – in this case, the Construction Documents – all agreements will be drafted, modified, and finalized by lawyers on both sides of the transaction. This is not an area in which laypeople should be entrusted with responsibility for the final outcome. The forms of contracts commonly used to develop the Construction Documents are fairly well established, with the document sets developed and maintained by the American Institute of Architects (AIA) being the industry standard. The AIA document sets have been the industry standard for construction documentation for decades. However, in 2007, a consortium of twenty construction industry organizations and trade groups decided to challenge the preeminence of the AIA construction document sets by developing its own. Now known as ConsensusDOCS, the premise for this undertaking is that form documents for construction shouldn't favor the "Owner" but, instead, should be neutral.[7] For a discussion of some of the differences between key documents in the AIA document sets and their ConsensusDOCS counterparts, see the Supplementary Materials on the companion website under Construction Phase Issues, Documentation, and Claims.

It is critical to recognize that "form documents," as the name suggests, are intended to be customized and revised to meet the needs of the parties. Accordingly, a General Contractor that is actively engaged in construction in the immediate jurisdiction or even the region where the Subject Site is located most likely maintains a version of the AIA's A201 General Conditions document that has been customized over the years to meet the GC's needs and concerns. For a detailed discussion of some of the clauses in the AIA A201 General Conditions document, see the Supplementary Materials on the companion website under Construction Phase Issues, Documentation, and Claims.

Similarly, an active Developer that has focused its business on ground-up projects (as contrasted with acquiring operating properties, whether or not they require renovation) will also have its own preferred form of the A201 document. The Developer's preferred forms of Construction Contracts will be included in the Bid Package made available to all qualified GCs intending to submit a bid and pricing on the Developer's Project, and the Bid Requirements more than likely will require each Respondent to specifically identify any provisions in any proposed forms of contract included in the Bid Package that the Respondent requires be modified or removed. This gives the Developer the opportunity to identify any potential conflicts in the Construction Documents between what the Developer prefers and what the GC indicates it needs in terms of relief from the Developer's preferred forms.

Engage Construction Manager (CM), if required. As with most relationships and transactions forged or occurring during the Pre-Development Phase of The Development

Process, the engagement of a Construction Manager by the Development Entity will be the subject of a binding written agreement. And, as with almost every contract the Developer negotiates and has drafted by its legal counsel in connection with The Development Process, a principal focus of this contract will be the Scope of Work. See the discussion in the Assemble and Engage Development Team Sub-Phase as well as Chapter 7 regarding the nature of such legal agreements. Because of the multiplicity of parties involved across the various agreements and other documents supporting the construction of the Improvements – General Contractor and its Subcontractors; architecture or engineering firm; Lender and Lender's designee for approving Draw Requests, local building code enforcement officials; surety bond provider – it is critical that the agreement between the Development Entity and its Construction Manager clearly set forth the specific responsibilities of the CM with regard to the construction process, including the review and approval of Draw Requests, as well as how RFIs and COs are managed. If the Construction Manager to be hired will be a CM at Risk, additional requirements will need to be addressed in the contract. See Chapter 7. See also the discussion of project management responsibilities generally in the Supplementary Materials on the companion website under Construction Phase Issues, Documentation, and Claims.

Close on construction financing. For those students and readers keeping count, this is the third Closing that will take place during The Development Process, the Closing on Acquisition and Development (A&D) Financing and the Closing on the Land Acquisition having occurred at the beginning and approximate midpoint of the Pre-Development Phase of The Development Process, respectively. Again, readers and students are encouraged to review the discussion under the Closing on Acquisition and Development (A&D) Financing Sub-Phase of the Pre-Development Phase of The Development Process regarding how a Closing reflects the culmination of a variety of issues and transactions involving real estate law. Along those lines, another Closing means another long list of Closing Documents that will have been extensively negotiated, revised, and finalized by the counsel to the respective signatories to each such document. Because of the nature of the Construction Loan, however, the "disbursement of funds" from this Closing will be fundamentally different, because the Construction Lender retains control of the Construction Loan funds throughout the process of construction, making disbursements according to the percentage of completion of the Project as evidenced by Draw Requests submitted by the GC along the way. See the discussion of construction loan disbursement procedures in the Supplementary Materials on the companion website under Construction Phase Issues, Documentation, and Claims.

Execute construction contracts. This Sub-Phase may occur simultaneously with the Closing on the Construction Loan. In fact, the Construction Lender's Closing process is likely to insist that the Construction Contract be duly executed during the Construction Loan Closing, inasmuch as the Construction Lender is relying on the Development Entity's contractual relationship with the GC. Beyond the formalities of the Construction Loan Closing at which this takes place, however, by the time the Development Entity and the GC are prepared to execute the Construction Contract, all legal issues have been negotiated and finalized between their respective legal counsel.

Identify/engage marketing/pre-leasing company. As should be clear from all of the preceding Sub-Phases of the Pre-Development Phase of The Development Process, and as specifically discussed in the Engage Construction Manager (CM) Sub-Phase of the Pre-Development Phase, specific contracts will establish and govern all relationships and transactions. The identification and engagement of the Marketing and Pre-Leasing Company will be no exception. And, as with most of the legal agreements the Developer or Development Entity will enter into throughout The Development Process, this contract will be governed by a detailed Scope of Work. See Chapters 7 and 11 for more information about the Real Estate

Law implications of the identification and engagement of the Marketing and Pre-Leasing Company.

Construction Phase. Through the negotiation, drafting, execution, and administration of a series of related documents – in particular, the Construction Documents (CDs), the Construction Bid Package, the Construction Loan Documents, and the Construction Contract Documents – the Developer, through the Development Entity, has the legal authority to assure the timeliness, cost containment, and quality of the construction of the Project in accordance with the terms and conditions of these agreements and related materials. In order for things to go as smoothly as possible during the Construction Phase of The Development Process, the Developer, through its legal counsel, must have focused considerable attention during the Pre-Development Process that there is complete alignment with what the Construction Loan Documents, the CDs, and the Construction Contract Documents say about the incremental progress of the Project (this includes issues of quality control) and payment to the General Contractor of its periodic Construction Draws. Perhaps no other Phase in The Development Process demonstrates more clearly how real estate law impacts real estate development and finance. At the same time, the Construction Phase is emblematic of why Contract Law is part of the Holy Trinity of real estate law, as the relationships, duties, and obligations of the respective parties engaged in various activities during the Construction Phase are governed by private contracts and not by other, principal components comprising real estate law.

As referenced earlier, the Supplementary Materials on the companion website under Construction Phase Issues, Documentation, and Claims include further discussion of the relationships, duties, and obligations of the parties involved in the Construction Phase, including but not limited to examinations of the competing Project Delivery Methods; specific clauses in the A201 General Conditions document; key differences between some of the documents in the AIA construction document sets and their ConsensusDOCS counterpart; the Draw Request Process; and the resolution of conflicts in the interpretation of the CDs, including RFIs and COs. These materials are provided in the Supplemental Materials on the companion website to better accommodate the use of graphics, including animate graphics, to convey the substance of the content presented, and to accommodate the dynamic nature of these legal issues. All of the following activities, transactions, and events occurring during the Construction Phase of The Development Process are addressed in such Supplementary Material, as well as in textbook chapters specifically referenced in the previous sections. For introductory, background information on the Construction Phase of The Development Process, see the following topics and subtopics in Chapter 2.

Construction administration
    Horizontal construction
        Request for information (RFI) process
        Change order (CO) process
        Draw request process
        Close-out
    Vertical construction
        Request for information (RFI) process
        Change order (CO) process
        Draw request process
        Vertical construction close-out (see Project Completion and Stabilization Phase)
Identify/engage property management company
Marketing and pre-leasing

Project completion and stabilization phase

The Project Completion and Stabilization Phase of The Development Process begins with two carryover Sub-Phases from the Construction Phase: Vertical Construction Close-Out and Construction Claims Resolution, respectively. As with the discussion about the Construction Phase, trying to summarize real estate law implications in, of, and to that phase in The Development Process may do more harm than good, considering the detailed coverage of all of these issues elsewhere in this textbook and in the Supplementary Materials section of the companion website under Construction Phase Issues, Documentation, and Claims.

> **Vertical construction close-out.** See the Supplementary Materials section of the companion website under Construction Phase Issues, Documentation, and Claims.
>
> **Construction Claims Resolution.** See the Supplementary Materials section of the companion website under Construction Phase Issues, Documentation, and Claims.
>
> **On-Site Property Manager in Place.** Once a Certificate of Occupancy is issued by the Local Governmental Unit for the Improvements – which will be done on a building-by-building basis for multi-building WalkUPs and other Mixed-Use Projects – and tenants or owners of those Improvements start moving into and occupying the Project, the Development Entity will be counting on the Property Management Company to fully engage in managing the project. As with all other third-party services providers, the relationship between the Property Management Company and the Development Entity will be governed by a Property Management Agreement with a defined Scope of Work and other terms and conditions (including the amount, terms, and mechanics of payment), which will govern the legal relationship of these two parties. For more detailed information about the Property Management Agreement and the relationship, duties, and obligations of these parties created by that contract, see Chapter 11.
>
> **Lease-Up and Move-In.** Assuming the Marketing/Pre-Leasing Company did its job during the Construction Phase (see the Marketing and Pre-Leasing Sub-Phase of the Pre-Development Phase of The Development Process), on the day the Certificate of Occupancy is issued for each residential building comprising a portion of the Project, there should be duly executed Residential Leases in place[8] consistent with the Pre-Leasing target or assumption contained in the latest Project pro forma immediately preceding the Developer's securing the Construction and Take-Out Financing Commitments (also see those Sub-Phases of the Pre-Development Phase of The Development Process). Accordingly, coordinating with the Marketing/Pre-Leasing Company, the Property Management Company should have already scheduled move-ins into each completed residential building, based on the anticipated issuance date of the Certificate of Occupancy, to assure a smooth move-in experience for each new tenant. This level of coordination must be required and specified in both the Marketing Agreement between the Development Entity and the third-party vendor in charge of marketing and pre-leasing the residential components of the Project, and the Property Management Agreement between the Development Entity and the Property Management Company. For more detailed information about each of these contracts, see Chapter 11.

Ownership and Property Management Phase. As discussed in Chapter 2, the end of the Project Completion and Stabilization Phase and the beginning of the Ownership and Property Management Phase of The Development Process marks a truly dramatic shift in The Development Process. The Project is now in its operational phase and may remain in that phase for decades in the hands of the Developer, depending on the Developer's Exit Strategy. As is demonstrated in detail in Chapter 11, the Developer will be faced with an entirely new set of risks and challenges during the Ownership and Property Management Phase of The Development Process.

Ongoing property management. As mentioned in the On-Site Property Manager in Place Sub-Phase of the Project Completion and Stabilization Phase of The Development Process, the relationship between the Property Management Company and the Development Entity will be governed by the Property Management Agreement. In addition to having a defined Scope of Work, the Property Management Agreement will include other essential terms and conditions, including the amount, terms, and mechanics of payment of the Property Management Company's compensation. The Property Management Agreement governs the entirety of the legal relationship between these two parties, with the exception of certain common law principles impacting their relationship in the absence of specific language to the contrary contained in the contract. See Chapter 11 regarding the Property Management Agreement.

Closing on Permanent Financing. This represents the final Closing in The Development Process, unless and until there is either a refinancing of the Project or an outright disposition. See the Sale or Refinancing Sub-Phase in this regard. As suggested in the other Closing-related Sub-Phases of The Development Process, discussed in the Pre-Development Phase, the Closing on Permanent Financing should reflect the culmination of a variety of commitments, obligations, and transactions involving real estate law, taking into account the qualifications contained in the Take-Out Financing Commitment, as well as the collective body of documents governing the Construction Phase of The Development Process: The Construction Documents (CDs), the Construction Bid Package, the Construction Loan Documents, and the Construction Contract Documents. The Closing by the Developer or the Development Entity on the Permanent Financing, the majority of the net proceeds from which will be used to pay off the entirety of the outstanding balance of Construction Loan, as well as payment of any accrued but outstanding interest on the Construction Loan through the date of the Closing (or the anticipated date of the disbursement of Closing proceeds, whichever last occurs), marks yet another dramatic change in both the Developer's and the Development Entity's posture vis-à-vis the Subject Site and the Project: the introduction of new Equity Investors and/or a new Lender. Accordingly, while title to the Subject Site and all Improvements thereon most likely will remain with the Development Entity, and any remaining liens or other title claims relating to the Construction will be released, the ownership structure of the Development Entity may change dramatically, and a new security interest or mortgage will be recorded against the title to the Property. Finally, the Closing on Permanent Financing Sub-Phase should mark the final implementation step in the Developer's Exit Strategy for the Project, determining, among other things, the manner in which the proceeds from a Sale or Refinancing will be distributed to the Developer and other principals in the Development Entity.

Sale or Refinancing. Chapter 2 offers several different scenarios in which the Development Entity may be inclined to dispose of its assets (i.e., the Project) or the owners of 100% of the ownership interests in the Development Entity may find it advantageous to sell those interests, such that the operating assets remain in the Development Entity, which ends up with a different ownership group. The best way to conceptualize the range of real estate law issues in a Sale is to picture the Developer or the Development Entity in the opposite position it has held throughout The Development Process: the Developer will now be the "Seller" rather than the "Buyer" in the Purchase and Sale Agreement; the Developer or Development Entity will be expected to make the Representations and Warranties rather than receiving them; the Developer or Development Entity will have to be the party providing its good faith compliance with all of the requirements of the Buyer's Due Diligence Period. See Chapters 7, 8, and 9 regarding the real estate law issues and, in particular, the contract documents and potential tax implications involved in a Sale of the Development Entity or a Sale of the Ownership Interests in the Development Entity.

In a refinancing, the Development Entity replaces existing debt with new debt. Under certain circumstances, as part of a refinancing the Developer could be required to make changes in the relative ownership interests in the Development Entity (for example, if one or more parties having equity interests in the Development Entity and the remaining equity owners prefer to use a refinancing as the vehicle for "cashing out" those equity owners, leveraging the unencumbered value of the Development Entity's assets – that is, the Project – to finance the resulting increase in the remaining equity owners' ownership interests). The assumption is, so long as the term of the existing debt is long enough, the Development Entity will be able to choose the timing of the refinancing to coincide with a period of low interest rates combined with an optimal valuation of the Project (i.e., "optimal market timing"). The other assumption is that the Project will incrementally increase in value over time, such that the value of the Project will periodically support a sufficiently large enough amount for the refinancing that is sufficient to pay down 100% of the outstanding principal amount of the existing financing, plus any accrued but unpaid interest thereon, plus all transaction costs, and still leave a material amount of Distributable Cash for the owners of interests in the Development Entity. In this way, the Developer, which is presumed to be the exclusive or a majority owner of the outstanding interests in the Development Entity, can periodically extract the increased value of the Project without having to dispose of any portion of its interest in order to realize that increased value. See Chapter 9.

Notes

1. Gratz, Roberta Brandes, with Norman Mintz, *Cities Back from the Edge*, Preservation Press, John Wiley & Sons, Inc., New York, NY (1998), pg. 59.

2. Ibid., pg. 61.

3. Ibid., pg. 83.

4. See, e.g., almost every relationship in which President Francis Underwood is involved in *House of Cards*.

5. This is somewhat similar to the fifth season of *The Walking Dead*, in which the members of Sheriff Rick Grimes' group owe their lives and allegiance to Rick, and have to rely on Rick's interactions with Deanna Monroe, the leader of New Alexandria, at the same time that Deanna is trying to establish separate relationships with the members of Rick's group to serve New Alexandria under her leadership.

6. This assumes the Developer, early on in the Project Conception Phase, decided to use the traditional Design/Bid/Build form of Construction Delivery System. The substance and timing of construction-related Sub-Phases in each of the first two Development Phases of The Development Process will be fundamentally different in the Project Conception and Pre-Development Phases if either the Design/Build or the Integrated Project Delivery systems is selected as the Construction Delivery System for the Project.

7. There has always been a criticism of the AIA document sets that, in addition to favoring the Owner vis-à-vis the other parties to these form documents, the AIA-drafted and controlled document sets favor architects by relieving them, as the design representatives of owners generally, of liabilities that a more neutral position might not accept.

8. This assumes that not only are effective residential leases in place but that, with regard to each such lease, credit and criminal background checks, respectively, have been satisfactorily completed; security deposits required under the residential lease have been received; parking spaces, if applicable, have been assigned; and procedures for move-ins have been provided to and acknowledged by each tenant in advance.

CHAPTER 4

Local governments and land use law

"Most of human history has been made in cities. It is no accident that the word "civilization" is derived from the city, as the word "politics" is derived from the ancient Greek word for the city state, the polis. The centers of wealth and military power, of government and culture, have always been cities, and the human societies complex enough to have a history have been designated civilizations. It is worthwhile to spell out the reasons for this, since they go as deep as the city's reason for being."[1]

Like politics, all real estate is local. And in no area of real estate law is that axiom more relevant than with local land use and zoning regulation, sometimes referred to herein, and elsewhere in this textbook, collectively as "Land Use Controls." Land Use Controls, however, as important as they are to the ultimate outcomes of The Development Process, represent only one aspect of a Project's and its Developer's near-term and long-term relationship with the local government of the jurisdiction in which that Developer's Project is located.

Local government input into and/or control over various other aspects of and impacts on a Project – various taxes levied on the Project, its tenants, and/or its tenants' customers; the capacity and availability of local protective services (police, fire, and EMS) to assure a safe and secure environment; the availability and capacities of critical utilities serving the Project; the panoply of transportation systems, running the gamut from public transit to dedicated bike lanes; and a host of other potential benefits to and burdens on the \Project – will play a critical role in that Project's ultimate success and may greatly influence the path that Project takes through The Development Process. Consequently, *fully understanding the powers of local government, and the sources and limits of each of those powers*, is critical to understanding real estate law within the framework of The Development Process.

In order to understand local government powers, one must first know from where and how local government derives its powers, as well as the full extent of those powers. Accordingly, this chapter begins with an analysis of the sources of local government authority, followed by a brief discussion about the different forms of localized governmental entities (i.e., anything smaller than, but not necessarily a subset of, state government) and an examination of the most commonly held powers of local government impacting The Development Process and real estate Projects, before delving into the general framework within which Land Use Controls are enacted and administered. Several of these topics are expanded in Chapter 10, which takes up contemporary questions such as "What, and Who, Is "the Government"; considers a number of variants on traditional municipal government, including the impact of hybrid versions of local government created through public-private partnerships, and then examines one of the most powerful actions municipal government may take, condemnation of private property.[2]

Chapter 4 concludes with a comprehensive review of various forms of exactions local governments commonly require of Developers as part of the normal approval process – a system some Developers derisively refer to as "Pay-to-Play" – the successful navigation and completion of which is a condition precedent to commencing the process of securing construction financing, much less actually beginning to build something.

Chapter outline
Chapter introduction
Local governments as creatures of state governments
Forms of municipal government
General powers of local government that impact The Development Process
Specific powers of local government that impact The Development Process
Land Use and Zoning Law generally
The community participation process (informal and formal)
Eminent domain and the U.S. Constitution
Public exactions for private development

Chapter introduction

Early in the Chapter 2 discussion introducing The Development Process, the notion of the Developer having an "Idea" involving real estate development, and moving forward with refining and determining how to finance and implement that Idea, were presented for the first time. Chapter 2 provided, in pertinent part, as follows in this regard:

> During the Project Conception Phase, the Developer seeks to make a baseline determination as to whether the Subject Property will be suitable for the purposes for which the Developer initially intended to acquire it (i.e., does it support and facilitate "the Idea"). The Developer's initial interest in the Subject Site may be very simplistic or even crude. The Subject Site would be "good" for a housing project, for example, because it is already located adjacent to an existing residential neighborhood. At the initial germination of the Idea, there is perhaps little consideration given to what residential building type or types would be best suited to the surrounding community and/or the Developer's return model: the initial Idea is "let's build *some kind* of housing here."

If the Developer's *"initial Idea is 'let's build some kind of housing here,'"* one of the earliest questions to be answered during the Project Conception Phase will be *"will the local jurisdiction allow the Developer to build that, there?"* And, if so, what kind of "that" will the local government allow? And how many units of "that" are permitted under the zoning code? And within what limitations and restrictions? And this line of inquiry is focused solely on the process of securing the necessary development approvals or "entitlements," as they're sometimes called, to proceed with "the Idea." The Developer must pursue countless other questions and dozens of other areas of inquiry to gain a fulsome understanding of the powers, capabilities, interests, and political will the local government has at its disposal to support the Project. However, before pursuing any one among this manifold inquiry, two, related, threshold questions must be answered: From where does this local government derive its powers, and what is the full scope and extent of those powers?

Local governments as creatures of state governments

Is *local self-governance* an "inherent right" of all citizens, or is local government merely a "creature of the state" in which it's located, having only those powers its state government expressly grants to it? This issue dates back to well before the Civil War, yet it is still the subject of real estate–related litigation to this day.

But, first, a brief history lesson

In *Governing the Metropolis*, Professor Greer's 1962 book about politics and social change in American cities, a quote from which opens this chapter, the author posits that the authority of the state actually emanated originally from the city. Professor Greer reviews the historical evolution of cities, suggesting that "the state" was loosely defined as everything else that wasn't "the city." However, before expounding on the prominence of cities in the evolution of cultures and societies, Professor Greer acknowledges the historical tensions between cities through history and their non-urban surroundings.

> As a consequence of their economies, the great societies of the past never became really urban. Though the city of Rome may have reached a population of one million at the height of the Empire, the great mass of the Empire's population (probably 90 per cent or more) lived as it had for thousands of years in peasant villages far from the coasts. While a sophisticated culture developed in the "world cities," most human beings through most of history lived in what Turner calls the "daemonic universe of the peasant village."[1] Their thought and social behavior were dominated by tradition, superstition, and fear of the unknown.[3]

While the dominance of cities in the United States is a foregone conclusion in the twenty-first century, looking at the whole of human history this period of supremacy, if it can rightly be called that, is of extremely recent vintage; representing little more than a century compared to millennia of human, cultural, and societal evolution.

> As late as the 1890s [in the United States] most people lived outside the cities, while a very large proportion of urban dwellers today were born and raised in open country neighborhoods or in small towns permeated by the atmosphere of the countryside.

More important in the context of real estate law in the United States, this sociological and anthropological view of states as creatures of the cities they surround is the complete opposite of how American jurisprudence has interpreted the role and authority of cities vis-à-vis the states that, through their constitutions, created them.

The intentional irony, of course, in quoting extensively from and relying too heavily on Professor Greer's 1962 *Governing the Metropolis* as a lens through which to first examine the tensions between state and local governing authority, is his book's publication extremely early in the prolonged "white flight" from the majority of American cities. Although white flight is believed to have begun in major U.S. cities in the late 1940s, not until better computing power and demographic methodologies in the late 1950s could scholars conduct any kind of precise analysis of the 1950 U.S. Census regarding changing demographics between cities and their suburbs by identifiable racial components. This white flight was exacerbated by the race riots in various U.S. cities in the mid-1960s, culminating in riots occurring in approximately 125 U.S. cities following the assassination of Dr. Martin Luther King Jr. on April 4, 1968.

Moreover, the outmigration of predominantly white middle- and upper-income households from cities to their surrounding suburbs persisted well into the 1990s, after nearly decimating some urban population centers – the City of Baltimore, for example, has yet to fully recover its lost population from the early 1960s – shifting the focus of political power in most states from their cities to their suburban counties, which in turn shifted the focus of political power from the cities back to their counties and, of course, back to the states.

Since around the turn of the twenty-first century, however, this dramatic outmigration of populations from cities to suburbs, and from suburbs to exurbs, started to reverse. And it has been this reversal, with broad demographic cohorts repopulating urban centers – in many cases to occupy new Mixed-Use projects created in parts of U.S. cities that had not fully recovered from the race riots of the mid-to-late 1960s – that has once again shifted the focus of political power from the states back to the cities.

The one thing we know about history is that it is destined to repeat itself. Starting with the civil unrest in Ferguson, Missouri, following a police shooting of an unarmed, African American youth, Michael Brown, on August 9, 2014, and continuing through and including race riots in the Sandtown-Winchester neighborhood west of downtown Baltimore, Maryland, that ensued following the death on April 19, 2015, while in police custody, of twenty-five-year-old African American resident, Freddie Gray, with a spate of similar incidents in between across the country, the proper exercise of police power by local governments has been a topic of national debate in the United States.

Determining how local governments derive or are conferred their powers shapes any discussion about, and forms the fundamental premise for challenges to, how those powers are exercised legitimately. One of the most effective challenges to local ordinances and regulations – including, in particular, zoning and land use regulations – involves making the argument that *the law being challenged is beyond the power or authority of the locality.* Accordingly, it is essential to start any consideration of Local Government and Land Use Law with a firm understanding of how local governments derive their powers in the first place.

When the State of Maryland adopted its second constitution in June 1851 (the first Maryland constitution having been adopted in November 1776, at the time of the Revolutionary War, by the Ninth Provincial Convention),[4] it mandated the separation of Baltimore City from Baltimore County, creating an "independent city," one of the very few in the United States at that time. Baltimore City was given all of the same privileges and powers of Maryland's twenty-three counties, granting the city limited "home rule" authority *separate from the authority of the General Assembly of Maryland.* This concept of a "home rule city" is at variance with another prevailing theory about the source of powers of local government, which came to be expressed as "Dillon's Rule." The Commonwealth of Virginia, for example, on the other side of the Potomac River from Maryland, is a Dillon's Rule state.

Dillon's Rule vs. the Cooley Doctrine

The theory of state preeminence over local governments came to be known as "Dillon's Rule" based on an 1868 Iowa Supreme Court case authored by Chief Justice John Forrest Dillon: "Municipal corporations owe their origin to, and derive their powers and rights wholly from, the legislature. It breathes into them the breath of life, without which they cannot exist. As it creates, so may it destroy. If it may destroy, it may abridge and control."[5] Dillon went on to write a treatise, titled *Municipal Corporations*, in which he elaborated on his legal analysis of the limited powers of local government.

By contrast, the Cooley Doctrine expressed the theory that an inherent right to local self-determination could and did exist within the confines of the Constitution of the United States. The Cooley Doctrine derived from a concurring opinion authored by Michigan Supreme Court Judge Thomas M. Cooley in 1871, in which he stated: "[L]ocal government is a matter of absolute right; and the state cannot take it away."[6]

In *Municipal Corporations*, Dillon explained that, in contrast to the powers of states, which are limited only by either express restrictions under the state's constitution or the U.S. Constitution, municipalities *only have* those powers the state *expressly grants to them*. This formulation of the scope of municipal power came to be known as Dillon's Rule or the Dillon Rule:

- that municipal governments have only those powers the state legislature expressly grants to them,
- those that are necessarily implied from that grant of power, and
- those that are essential and indispensable to the municipality's existence and functioning.

As a matter of judicial construction, Dillon's Rule holds that any ambiguities in the state's legislative grant of power to municipal governments are to be resolved in favor of the state and adversely toward the municipality, to assure that municipal powers are narrowly construed. Dillon's Rule also holds that when the state has not specifically directed a specific method for implementing the power it has granted to the municipality, the municipality may implement that power in whatever manner it may *reasonably* choose.

Hundreds of U.S. court decisions have interpreted Dillon's Rule to limit the scope of municipal powers and rights. Critics of the rule have argued that it imposes unreasonable constraints on the ability of communities to govern themselves, which is the level of government closest to the people and in which they are most likely to participate regularly and effectively. As such, these critics argue, Dillon's Rule undermines democracy. Critics of Dillon's Rule also argue in favor of the Cooley Doctrine: that local self-government is a matter of natural right that does not need to be conferred by higher political structures. Some have suggested that Dillon's approach derived from the contemporary view, at the time the rule was formulated, that cities were inherently corrupt political organs. Nonetheless, departures from Dillon's Rule remain in the minority, despite the significant decrease in the public perception of municipal corruption (except in Florida, Illinois, New Jersey, and New York, to name just a few where the perception and reality of government corruption persist).[7]

The Supreme Court of the United States took up the issue of municipal authority in *Merrill v. Monticello*, 138 U.S. 673 (1891), specifically considering the authority of the Town of Monticello, Indiana, to issue municipal bonds whose proceeds would be used to construct a schoolhouse:

> The implied power of a municipal corporation to borrow money to enable it to execute the powers expressly conferred upon it by law, if it exists at all, does not authorize it to create and issue negotiable securities to be sold in the market and to be taken by a purchaser freed from equities that might be set up by the maker.
>
> To borrow money, and to give a bond or obligation therefore which may circulate in the market as a negotiable security freed from any equities that may be set up by the maker of it, are essentially different transactions in their nature and legal effect.[8]

As with all case law, the facts are of critical importance. Even subtly different facts between one case and the next may distinguish the two to the extent that the legal precedent established by the former will not automatically be applied to the latter. In the *Merrill* case, the salient facts are as follows:

> A municipal corporation in Indiana issued its negotiable bonds having ten years to run, to the amount of $20,000, the proceeds to be used to aid in the construction of a school house, and sold them in open market. When they matured, a new issue of like bonds to the amount of $21,000 was made, which were sold in open market, and a part of the proceeds converted by a trustee of the corporation to his own use. Held that the new issue was void for want of authority, and that the municipality was not estopped from setting up that defense.[9]

The lower court heard a complaint from Abner Merrill, a resident of Massachusetts, who had purchased some of the Town of Monticello's "refunding bonds" (see following discussion), whose proceeds never went to refund the town's original issuance of school bonds that had come due, thereby requiring the refunding bonds to pay the outstanding indebtedness, because the trustee of the refunding bond issuance absconded with some of the proceeds of the bond sales. Merrill sued the town for payment in full, outstanding but unpaid interest, plus the full, principal amount, after Merrill's first interest payment coupon was presented to the bank specified for payment and that bank refused payment. One of the defenses the town raised to Merrill's claim for payment in full was that the town lacked authority from the state legislature to issue the refunding bonds and, therefore, could not be compelled by the court to pay an outstanding debt that was not authorized by the state legislature.

After a detailed recitation of the facts, Justice Lamar opened the opinion of the court:

> The decisive question presented by the record in this case is did the Town of Monticello have authority under the laws of Indiana to issue for sale in open market negotiable securities in the forms of the bonds and coupons on which recovery is here sought?
>
> Chancellor Kent, in his Commentaries, vol. 2, pp. 298–299, referring to the strictness with which corporate powers are construed, irrespective of the distinction between public and private corporations, uses the following language:
>
> "The modern doctrine is to consider corporations as having such powers as are specifically granted by the act of incorporation or as are necessary for the purpose of carrying into effect the powers expressly granted, and as not having any other. The Supreme Court of the United States declared this obvious doctrine, and it has been repeated in the decisions of the state courts. . . . As corporations are the mere creatures of law, established for special purposes, and derive all their powers from the acts creating them, it is perfectly just and proper that they should be obliged strictly to show their authority for the business they assume, and be confined in their operations to the mode and manner and subject matter prescribed."

In his opinion, Justice Lamar refers specifically to two Indiana statutory provisions expressly authorizing *"any city or incorporated town in the state"* to borrow funds for the exclusive purposes of buying land on which to build a school, buying improved land for purposes of using the improvements thereon to operate a school building, or to erect a school building on land already owned. These sections of Indiana law did not expressly authorize *"any city or incorporated town"* in Indiana to issue what are commonly referred to today as "refunding bonds," the proceeds of which are used, in whole or in part, to pay interest and outstanding principal due on previously issued and outstanding debt instruments. Merrill's counsel argued in the original action that given the Town of Monticello's authority to issue such bonds in the first place, its authority to issue refunding bonds to retire the original issuance once it matured was implied by the state legislature's original grant of authority to issue the original bonds in the first place.

After reciting, verbatim, the Indiana statutes authorizing the borrowing of money by an Indiana municipality for purposes of acquiring and/or building schools, the court's opinion turns to Dillon's treatise:

> Section 119, Dillon on Munic. Corp., lays down the Indiana law on this subject substantially as is contended for by the plaintiff in error. That section is as follows:
>
> "In Indiana, the doctrine is that corporations, along with the express and substantive powers conferred by their charters, take by implication all the reasonable modes of executing such powers which a natural person may adopt. It is a power incident to corporations, in the absence of positive restriction, to borrow money as means of executing the express powers."
>
> A large number of cases from the Supreme Court of Indiana are cited in a note to support the doctrine of the text. We think the proposition that under the laws of Indiana a town has an implied authority to borrow money or contract a loan under the conditions and in the manner expressly prescribed cannot be controverted.[10]

Continuing, the opinion of the court, in pertinent part relating to the relevance of Dillon's *Municipal Corporations* treatise, states:

Judge Dillon, in his work on Municipal Corporations, § 89, says:

> It is a general and undisputed proposition of law that *a municipal corporation possesses and can exercise the following powers, and no others*: first, those *granted in express words*? second, those necessarily or fairly implied in or *incident to the powers expressly granted*? third, *those essential to the declared objects and purposes of the corporation* not simply convenient, but indispensable. Any fair reasonable doubt concerning the existence of power is resolved by the courts against the corporation, and the power is denied.[11]

Earlier in the court's opinion, Judge Lamar relies on a detailed analysis of Indiana statutes regarding the express authority given to Indiana cities and incorporated towns to issue debt for the purpose of buying or building schools, as interpreted by Indiana state courts:

> In *Gause v. Clarksville*, 5 Dillon 165, the court, in an able discussion of the inherent and incidental authority of municipal corporations, holds that whether a municipal corporation possesses the power to borrow money and to issue negotiable securities therefore depends upon a true construction of its charter and the legislation of the state applicable to it.
>
> In order to determine the question before us, recourse must be had to the statutory enactments applicable to the subject that were in force at the time the bonds in this suit were issued in May 1878. These enactments are contained in sections 3333, 3342, 3344, 3345, 4488, and 4489 of the Revised Statutes of Indiana of 1881. Section 3333 is a section of the act of 1852 for the incorporation of towns in that state, and contains the usual grant of municipal powers. Section 3342, which was also section 27 of the same act of 1852, provides as follows:
>
> "No incorporated town under this act shall have power to borrow money or incur any debt or liability unless the citizen owners of fiveeighths [sic] of the taxable property of such town, as evidenced by the assessment roll of the preceding year, petition the board of trustees to contract such debt or loan. And such petition shall have attached thereto an affidavit verifying the genuineness of the signatures to the same. And for any debt created thereby, the trustees shall add to the tax duplicate of each year, successively, a levy sufficient to pay the annual interest on such debt or loan, with an addition of not less than five cents on the hundred dollars, to create a sinking fund for the liquidation of the principal thereof."[12]

In the 1907 U.S. Supreme Court case *Hunter v. City of Pittsburgh*, 207 U.S. 161 (1907), the Court held that the power of the Commonwealth of Pennsylvania to facilitate the consolidation of cities through a state statute providing the procedures that much be followed to do so, violated neither Article 1 of the U.S. Constitution or the Fourteenth Amendment's prohibition of state action with due process of law (the "Due Process" clause).[13] In the *Hunter* case, the City of Allegheny, across the river from the City of Pittsburgh, was annexed by the latter, under the Commonwealth of Pennsylvania's annexation statute, despite the fact that a majority of Allegheny's residents voted against the measure.

The Court's ruling relied, in part, on the distinction between public, municipal corporations, on one hand, and private corporations, on the other, as previously articulated by Judge Dillon, holding that states could alter or abolish, at will, the charters of municipal corporations because all such municipal corporations are creatures of the state, which has the power to create or destroy them.

University of Pittsburgh Professor David Y. Miller argues that Justice Dillon hit on a central paradox defining local government in America: political philosophers, such as Alexis de Tocqueville, and Founding Fathers like Thomas Jefferson, who well preceded Dillon, marveled at the efficiency and effectiveness of governing at the local level, yet in his own court decisions and writings, Justice Dillon declared that local governments have no independent legal legitimacy.[14] Justice Dillon as referred to municipal governments as "mere tenants at will of their respective state legislatures" that could be "eliminated by the legislature with a stroke of the pen."[15]

WHY DOES THIS MATTER?

The critical importance of zoning and land use to a Developer's ability to implement successfully "the Idea" to build something somewhere is likely obvious even to those new to The Development Process. The rest of the contents of this chapter may not seem quite so important but they, indeed, are. Here are a few reasons why:

- Sometimes municipal government will be a Developer's best friend in moving a Project forward; other times, however, it will seem to be an intractable obstacle. When an LGU plays that latter role, the Developer may have only two, dichotomous options: abandon the Project or sue the LGU. In order to pursue that latter option, it's critically important to know from where the LGU's power derives and what the limits of that power are. Whether the LGU is in a Home Rule State or a Dillon's Rule State may loom large in making these important determinations.
- Particularly in the largest cities in the United States, the activities of quasi-governmental authorities and metropolitan area governing structures may have profound impacts – both directly and in terms of their ripple-effects – on development generally. Because these municipal governmental entities operate in the open, at least for the most part, their plans are formulated through public processes that may take years, and sometimes decades, to evolve. This offers Developers opportunities to both (i) make land acquisition decisions well ahead of when final decisions, plans, and proposed projects drive up the price of nearby parcels of land and (ii) participate actively in these processes to steer them in a direction favorable to the Developer's plans and business model.
- Various powers of LGUs beyond those regarding zoning and land use may offer benefits for and impose burdens on a Developer's proposed Project. Understanding what powers the LGU has and how the LGU is willing to employ those powers may allow the

Developer to rely on services the LGU provides as a general public benefit that may serve as substitutes for things the Developer might otherwise need to build into the Project's Operating Budget.

- Municipal governments at all levels collect and analyze statistics, keep track of development activities within their boundaries, and love to fund studies of various kinds. Some of this data, analysis, and information may provide important insights to a Developer. See, for example, the discussion on Forms of Municipal Government, regarding how the findings and recommendations from a primarily federally funded study undertaken by the Houston-Galveston Area Council, the metropolitan planning organization for the greater Houston, Texas, metropolitan area, is being translated into land use guidelines for the City of Houston, which does not have a zoning or land use code, that will promote more sustainable and cohesive development.

Forms of municipal government

At the risk of making a list that is not sufficiently comprehensive, the following is an attempt to generically identify different types of municipal governmental units, ranking them from smallest to largest, with the understanding that the names used as identifiers may mean different things to different people. Commonly used names – such as "village" or "town" – may have different meanings in different states that have nonetheless identified each type as a lawful unit of municipal government. Additionally, states may differentiate among different types of municipal government – such as "village" or "town" – based on the powers and obligations of each, further classifying each type by relative population or land area. As suggested in the listing that follows, the "Borough of Manhattan" is a very different Local Governmental Unit than the independent borough of Germantown, Pennsylvania, which borders the City of Philadelphia, even though they are both, technically, boroughs.

Units of Local General Government

Unincorporated village, town, or township
Incorporated village, town, or township
Borough (each of the five Boroughs of New York City is larger than many U.S. cities,[16]
City (which may be part of the County in which it's located or may be an independent
    jurisdiction)
County

Special-purpose governmental and quasi-governmental units

Single-jurisdiction School District, Water District, Sanitation District, or other public utilities district
Multi-jurisdiction Special-Purpose Governmental and Quasi-governmental Units (see previous list)
City-County Special-Purpose Governmental and Quasi-governmental Units
Multi-County Special-Purpose Governmental and Quasi-governmental Units
Single-State Regional Special-Purpose Governmental and Quasi-Governmental Units
Multi-State Regional Special-Purpose Governmental and Quasi-governmental Units

In addition to metrics such as population size, population density, and geographic area, municipal governments may be distinguished by the type of governing structure employed and the range of services offered to residents. The type of deliberative body and how its members are elected, that deliberative body's relationship with a chief executive, how that chief executive is elected or selected, and how lawful, binding decisions are made are all characteristics of municipal government that help to further classify different types of Local Governmental Units.

As is suggested elsewhere throughout this textbook, the early colonial villages or towns that evolved into some of America's largest and most influential cities have arguably played a much larger collective role in the creation and refinement of the law generally, and real estate law in particular, than have the states. Understanding the historical trajectory of the size, importance, and influence of American cities since their inception as colonial villages in the late seventeenth century is critical to understanding the role of municipal government in contemporary real estate law today. However, understanding this trajectory may also prove critical to envisioning how real estate law, as a function of municipal government, may evolve over the next 50 to 100 years.

Arguably, two of the most recent (at least in relative terms) phenomena of municipal government having a tremendous impact on real estate development in the twenty-first century are:

(i) the rise in importance of quasi-governmental authorities – such as the Port Authority of New York and New Jersey, operating in the New York City, New Jersey, Connecticut metropolitan area, as well as the Washington Metropolitan Transit Authority (WMATA) and the Metropolitan Washington Airports Authority (WMAA), providing ground and air transportation, respectively, serving the District of Columbia, Maryland, and Virginia metro area; and

(ii) the establishment of new, metropolitan-level governmental organizations, agencies, and instrumentalities, such as the Metropolitan Planning Organizations ushered into existence by the Federal Aid Highway Act of 1962, Public Law 87–866, and reinvigorated by the Intermodal Surface Transportation Efficiency Act of 1991 (ISTEA, pronounced "iced tea"), Public Law 102–240, of which there were still 381 in 2015, including the Houston-Galveston Area Council (H-GAC), the Atlanta Regional Commission (ARC), and the Association of Bay Area Governments (ABAG).

The growth in number, size, and influence/impact of regional or metropolitan forms of governmental agencies and cooperative, multi-jurisdictional initiatives has had dramatic impacts on real estate development in the areas over which these metropolitan-scaled units of municipal governance have power and/or influence. Such impacts are only expected to increase as metropolitan regions continue to gain population, as well as in domestic and global influence. See Chapter 10, sections What, and Who, Is "the Government?" and Examples of Special Purpose Taxing and Management Districts.

For example, one of the key stakeholders in what is considered the United States' largest real estate development project to date, projected at a total of 2 billion square feet when completed, Hudson Yards in Manhattan, includes as key stakeholders the Metropolitan Transit Authority or MTA, which provides mass transit services to New York City, New Jersey, and Connecticut (see Hudson Yards Case Study in the companion website to this textbook). Similarly, the co-Developer of the tallest building in North America, One World Trade Center, is the Port Authority of New York and New Jersey.

In Houston, the Houston-Galveston Area Council (H-GAC), which is the Metropolitan Planning Organization for the metropolitan Houston area, has provided U.S. Department of Transportation funding and project guidance and leadership for a smart growth planning initiative intended to directly influence city policy making to incentivize sustainable development proposals within the City of Houston. The *Urban Houston Framework Report*, April 2013, prepared by a multidisciplinary team of planning and development professionals led by Design Workshop,[17] is part of a series of H-GAC Sustainability Case Studies. The *Urban Houston Framework Report* made a series of specific recommendations to the City of Houston Planning Department for encouraging and facilitating more sustainable development patterns and projects in the city. For a more detailed discussion about how H-GAC's *Urban Houston Framework* study and report are shaping the City of Houston's historic inaugural General Plan, see the Supplementary Materials on the companion website for this textbook.

General powers of local government that impact The Development Process

The irony should not be lost on anyone that local units of government must derive their powers and authority for governing from the states (see the section titled Local Governments as Creatures of State Government), despite the fact that the earliest towns formed after the discovery of North America established the basis for self-government through the provision of necessary services. Writing about the emergence of the five largest towns in colonial America in 1760 – Philadelphia (pop. 23,750), New York (pop. 23,750), Boston (15,631), Charles Town, eventually renamed Charleston (pop. 8,000), and Newport (pop. 7,500)[18] – University of Wisconsin professor, historian, and author Charles N. Glaab, PhD, offers some specifics in how these "urban enclaves" became critically important to the success of a new nation by providing essential services to their respective residents:

> From their first years as primitive villages, cities had to find means to provide essential services collectively. Housing and building regulations, fire-fighting, and water supply early became fundamental concerns of town leaders. Sometimes reluctantly as in Charleston, sometimes willingly as in Boston, these first cities met the pressing demand for new streets, paving, wharves, and ferries and provided for the poor and criminals. Although for many years the removal of garbage was left to roving herds of swine and goats, and dead animals were allowed to putrefy in city streets, public health became a matter for local legislation. Carl Bridenbaugh, the historian of the colonial American city, defined "urban" partly in terms of this collective response to distinct problems. "In these problems of town living, which affected the entire community," he wrote, "lay one of the vast differences between town and country society, and out of the collective efforts to solve these urban problems arose a sense of community responsibility and power that was further to differentiate the two ways of life."[19]

It is not surprising, then, that the evolution of municipal government has been concerned with gaining and exercising control over "the public realm." Given this foundational imperative to provide the collective of urban residents, business interests, and visitors with essential services, plus the trajectory of rapid urban growth of American cities following the War of 1812, it was inevitable that municipal governments would grow into claiming and exercising a number of powers that impact, in very real ways, The Development Process, and the development projects shaped by that process.

Putting aside, for the moment, whether a local government exists and operates in a Home Rule State or a state that follows Dillon's Rule (again, see Local Governments as Creatures of State Government), the powers of local government generally include, although they may not be limited to, the list that follows. Each of these powers is subject to established limitations and constraints peculiar to the jurisdiction and the state within which it is located. Some of the local government powers enumerated later – such as the Land Use Powers, the Power to Regulate, the Power to Tax, the Power to Spend, and the Power to Educate – have direct and considerable consequences impacting The Development Process. Other powers of local government have more subtle yet important influences on The Development Process.

What are the "general powers of local government?"

1. **Power to Tax**. The power of a Local Governmental Unit (LGU) to assess and collect taxes from its residents and persons within the LGU's jurisdiction is generally expressly conferred on the LGU by the state.[20] As made clear in the detailed discussion on the taxing powers of LGUs, every state has a somewhat different taxing scheme, and that taxing scheme is followed by its LGUs.[21]

2. **Power to Spend**. An LGU's power to spend is generally broad but constrained by processes imposed by the state, by the LGU's own adopted ordinances and procedures, or some combination of both. LGUs generally are required to adopt annual budgets for their operating expenses during each fiscal year, as well as a separate budget for capital improvements, all or some significant portion of which will be financed through the government's Power to Borrow (see later). Additionally, the process for submitting for approval and adopting an annual budget for the ordinary expenses of running the LGU and its apparatus – such as the aggregate salaries and benefits of the jurisdiction's full-time and part-time salaries and benefits – may be very different from the procurement procedures for the LGU to engage private-sector entities to perform specific services under a contract with the LGU (see Power to Contract), with local and/or state ordinances and statutes imposing restrictions and procedures in the procurement of goods and services from the private sector. By and large, these rules and regulations governing public procurement of privately sourced goods and services are intended to assure open and fair procurement and avoid even the appearance of government providing special favors to private-sector entities through such contracts.

3. **Power to Contract**. An LGU's power to enter into contracts is ancillary to many of its other, substantive powers. For example, LGUs often enter into collective bargaining agreements in instances in which groups of its employees are represented by a collective bargaining unit, also referred to as a public employees' union. In the event a local government chooses to have some of its services performed by the private sector, such as having the collection of refuse and recyclables undertaken by a private contractor instead of waste management personnel employed by the jurisdiction (which is becoming an increasingly common practice), the LGU will be required to enter into a contract for such services. The same goes for purchasing and leasing contracts for goods and equipment, as well as services contracts for things such as telecommunications, email, and Internet services. As with the foregoing discussion regarding protocols and procedures involved when an LGU desires to exercise its Power to Spend where the vendor is a private-sector entity, most local jurisdictions have very specific rules and regulations regarding soliciting and receiving bids for contracts. Unless the total value

of the contract is deemed *diminimus* under the LGU's rules and regulations regarding contractual authority (this may range anywhere between $1,000 and $100,000, depending on the size of the jurisdiction and the nature of the contract), the LGU is required to go through a public procurement process for identifying the best vendor or provider for the subject matter of the contract.

4. **Police Powers Generally**. It is universally recognized that local governments need "general police powers" to protect the health, safety, morals, and "general welfare" of their citizens. In the United States, this axiom is contained in the Tenth Amendment to the U.S. Constitution, which reserves such police powers to the states. Each state, in turn, confers police powers on Local Governmental Units within the state. Many of the powers of local government contained in this listing derive their specific authority from the general police powers conferred on them.

5. **Power to Adjudicate**. LGUs generally but do not always have their own adjudicatory branch of government. Smaller jurisdictions oftentimes enter into cooperation agreements with larger, neighboring jurisdictions to provide a court system to adjudicate offenses committed within the smaller jurisdiction's boundaries. This highlights the difference between having the Power to Adjudicate and the apparatus of local government necessary to exercise such power.

6. **Power to Detain and Incarcerate**. Whether as an exercise of authority by the local law enforcement agency of the LGU (i.e., a police department) or as a separate function of a sheriff's office that is also part of the same LGU, the power to detain and arrest those suspected of engaging in unlawful activities is an essential local government function. As with smaller jurisdictions that don't find it efficient to organize and support a court system and, consequently, rely on a neighboring court system to adjudicate disputes and criminal matters, some small jurisdictions may not have a jail and rely on cooperation agreements with neighboring jurisdictions for the detention of persons accused of committing criminal acts within the smaller jurisdiction's borders.

7. **Power to Regulate.** LGUs have broad, general powers to regulate many aspects of life and commerce within their respective jurisdictions provided such regulations are not infringing upon rights guaranteed to the regulated under either the U.S. Constitution or the constitution of the state within which the LGU is located. Such regulations generally fall within the LGU's duties, obligations, and powers relating to the protection and facilitation of the public "health, safety, and welfare." The powers of LGUs over matters of public health, safety, and welfare were well established centuries ago in the United States, to which the courts later added the power of LGUs to have authority over the "morals" of their residents. For additional information regarding an LGU's Power to Regulate, see the discussion in item 13 regarding Power to Protect (Health, Safety, Welfare, and Morals). See also General Police Powers.

8. **Land Use Powers**. As is discussed in greater detail later in this chapter, and explored in even greater detail in Chapter 5, one of the principal and most important powers of an LGU is the power to enact and enforce Land Use Controls. Most, if not all, LGUs have an inferior decision-making body charged with responsibility for the enactment, interpretation, and enforcement of Land Use Controls, usually in the form of a Planning Commission or similarly named deliberative body. The members of an LGU's Planning Commission are generally appointed by the LGU's elected officials and not elected by the residents of the LGU. Planning Commissions may have decision-making authority or merely recommendation authority. In the larger, urban LGUs, it is common to also have lower-level deliberative bodies reporting to the Planning Commission in the LGU, such as a Board of Equalization (addressing claims and disparities in the assessment and

taxation of real property in the LGU) or a Board of Zoning Appeals (handling minor zoning and land use issues, such as relief from land use regulations such as side-yard and rear-yard setbacks or height limitations in residential neighborhoods). It is also common in major metropolitan areas to have a system of neighborhood or community advisory governance, such as the system of Area Neighborhood Councils (ANCs) in the District of Columbia, with such bodies having formal roles in the enactment, evolution, and enforcement of the LGU's Land Use Controls.

9. **Power of Condemnation**. As is addressed in great detail later in "Public Takings for Private Purposes," in Chapter 10, LGUs have the power of eminent domain – that is, the power to take private property for public purposes – the exercise of which power is referred to as the "condemnation of land." Among other things, the power of condemnation is the ultimate enforcement power to assure an LGU's collection of taxes, fees, and other monies due to it from a property owner within its jurisdiction, even if the money being sought is not outstanding real property taxes. The liens of LGUs against property within its legal jurisdiction is generally superior to most other liens, other than those of the federal government for outstanding debts owed to it by the property's owner. The power of eminent domain, and its exercise through condemnation, is guaranteed to LGUs, by negative implication, in the Fifth Amendment to the U.S. Constitution. The Fifth Amendment states, in pertinent part, that *"[N]o person shall be . . . deprived of life, liberty, or property, without due process of law; nor shall private property be taken for public use, without just compensation."*[22]

10. **Power to Educate**. Most LGUs operate school districts. Oftentimes the elected officials of the LGU appoint the members of the local school board, who serve at the pleasure of the LGU, and the LGU provides the operating funds for the school district out of the operating budget of the LGU. In other instances, although the LGU and the school district have congruent boundaries, the school board members are elected officials but the school district is still reliant on the elected officials of the LGU for budgetary approval and appropriation. In still other jurisdictions the public school district operates completely independently of the LGU, with both an elected school board and the power to assess and collect real property taxes (or have them collected and paid over to the school district by the LGU); in some of these cases, the geographic boundaries of the school district are not congruent with those of the LGU and may, in fact cross over into and cover more than one LGU.

11. **Power to Build**. LGUs own real property within the boundaries of the jurisdictions they own and use those properties for various purposes. At various times, and for various reasons, they may acquire new real properties – undeveloped and improved – as well as selectively and, one would assume, strategically dispose of properties owned. By way of recent example of the former activity, the City of Detroit has its power of condemnation to acquire and demolish blighted properties, primarily abandoned and distressed houses, as a way of helping to revitalize the city's distressed neighborhoods. In addition to activities involving the acquisition or disposition of real property within its jurisdiction, and spurring development by the private sector and/or through public-private partnerships (discussed in greater detail in Chapter 10), LGUs build facilities on the real property they own that serve their basic governmental functions, including city halls and maintenance facilities; police and fire and rescue stations; schools and public libraries; parks and community and recreation centers; water and waste treatment facilities; and jails. LGUs also are responsible for building at least some of the infrastructure network within their jurisdictions – including local streets, sidewalks, cubs, and gutters; sanitary and wastewater distribution systems; arterial and highway systems; and components of

mass transit systems (from bus shelters to multimodal transportation stations to subway stations) – or to contribute along with state, regional, and federal sources of funding.

12. **Power to House**. It has long been a fundamental duty and obligation of LGUs to house the poor, although this task has been undertaken with varying degrees of compassion, efficacy, and success since performed by the early colonial settlements that ultimately grew to become the East Coast's great cities. In the twenty-first century, the commitment to provide housing for those unable to afford it – often referred to as "low-income housing" or "public housing" – is discharged by LGUs administering programs funded and managed by the U.S. Department of Housing and Urban Development (HUD) and sometimes but not always state low-income or public housing programs.

13. **Power to Develop**. As mentioned in Power to Build, LGUs often own substantial amounts of real property within their jurisdictional boundaries, which they hold and use for a variety of purposes directly related to their principal governmental activities. LGUs may acquire new real properties – undeveloped or improved – as well as dispose of properties they own. Regarding the disposition of surplus or excess properties, LGUs appear increasingly inclined to use such land deemed excess to the goals and objectives of the LGU to strategically, through some form of public procurement process – generally a Request for Information (RFI), a Request for Qualifications (RFQ), or a Request for Proposals (RFP) – make such real property available to private-sector developers, oftentimes combining the availability of the land with additional benefits the LGU may offer, to spur the kind of development the LGU believes will have a broader impact on its residents and the jurisdiction as a whole. Several of the Case Studies included in this textbook, most notably Hudson Yards, New York City (related Hudson Yards), and Washington Navy Yard, Washington, DC (Forest City, Washington), are the product of a public solicitation and procurement process through which the private sector submitted proposals for development of underdeveloped sites with tremendous potential value if properly redeveloped.

14. **Power to Promote**. Perhaps as early as the rivalry that arose in the early nineteenth century between the City of Philadelphia, Pennsylvania, and the City of Baltimore, Maryland, LGUs have devoted an increasing amount of attention and political will, annual budgetary and spending authority, staff time, and capital expenditures to the promotion of the LGU for economic development purposes. Convention centers (which have become increasingly large in scale, broad in scope, and complex in program), visitors' centers, and attractions intended to boost tourism and trade (the Torpedo Factory, housing artists' studios and gallery spaces, in Old Town in the City of Alexandria is a good example) are among the primary edifices LGUs design, develop, fund, and construct to promote their jurisdictions. Economic development departments or divisions, convention and visitors' bureaus, and tourism offices, complete with annual budgets and staffs, have become the rule, rather than the exception, even for relatively modest units of local government. Such ongoing activities to promote LGUs run the gamut from the Fairfax County Economic Development Authority of Fairfax County, Virginia (just outside Washington, DC), with a population of more than 1.1 million, which is one of the best-funded, most active and effective, internationally recognized economic development authorities (EDAs) in the United States; to the Muncie Visitors' Bureau in Muncie, Indiana, a city of just more than 70,000, and the subject of a series of sociological case studies undertaken in the mid-1920s by husband-and-wife sociologists Robert Staughton Lynd and Helen Merrell Lynd leading to the publication in 1929 of *Middletown: A Study in Modern American Culture*; to the South Haven/Van Buren County Convention and Visitors Bureau of South Haven, MI, a resort town on Lake Michigan with a population of less than 5,000.

15. **Power to Facilitate Transportation**. In addition to providing infrastructure improvements critical to the free flow of people and commerce, as mentioned in item 11, LGUs often participate directly in making transportation options available to residents, businesses, and visitors. In addition to providing sidewalks and safe streets promoting walkability, the activities of LGUs in facilitating transportation range from implementing dedicated bike lanes to participating in the planning and funding of mass transit systems and stations serving the jurisdiction. As increasing emphasis is being placed on walkability and Mixed-Use development in America's cities, the opportunities for LGUs to participate in the facilitation of transportation alternatives are ever increasing. Two relatively recent examples of this type of activity may be found in the Project Profile for the Silver Spring Transit Station in Montgomery County, Maryland (see Appendix) and the decision of the City of Alexandria City Council on May 19, 2015, of the citing of a new metro station to be incorporated into the existing Yellow Line of the metro subway system operating in the greater Washington, DC, area by the Washington Metropolitan Transit Authority (WMATA) (see discussion under Forms of Municipal Government regarding regional governmental entities).

16. **Power to Borrow**. LGUs generally have the power to borrow money, to the extent expressly granted to them by the state or by inference to the powers granted to it by the state. However, when a unit of local government needs to borrow money – which LGUs do with consistent frequency – the City Controller or County Treasurer doesn't stroll down the street from their office to the local bank to fill out a loan application on behalf of the unit of local government. LGUs borrow money by selling bonds, most often done in the form of General Obligation Bonds, "Special Purpose" Bonds, and Revenue Bonds. Generally speaking, different types of bonds have to follow different rules; some of these rules are set by the state in which the LGU is located, some by the locality itself, some by a federal agency such as the **Internal Revenue Service**, and some by the debt markets. Because a General Obligation or "GO" Bond pledges the full faith and credit of the LGU issuing it, their issuance generally has to be approved by the registered voters in the LGU, granting the LGU specific authority for those bonds. A Revenue Bond, on the other hand, because it does not rely on the full faith and credit of the issuing LGU, does not have to follow the same procedural requirements as the issuance of GO Bonds.

17. **Power to Encumber**. As suggested in the discussion regarding an LGU's Power to Borrow, LGUs require a concomitant Power to Encumber in order to provide the requisite security to assure bond buyers that their principal, plus all accrued but unpaid interest, are repaid in full in accordance with the terms and conditions of the bond instruments. Unlike most real estate financing transactions, where the principal asset pledged to secure debt is improved real estate, in the case of bonds, LGUs, to one extent or another, are pledging their ability to collect tax revenues and an attendant commitment to pay those collected tax revenues over the bondholders should an uncured Event of Default occur under the bond instruments. This is an essential power providing the foundation for "full faith and credit" borrowing by any entity of government, federal, state, or local. As suggested earlier, however, there are varying degrees of what a municipal bond issuance is pledging as security for the repayment of principal and payment of accrued but unpaid interest depending on the nature of the type of bond being issued. Various types of "Special Purpose" Bonds and Revenue Bonds generally will have something less than the full faith and credit of the municipal bond issuer pledged, and in the case of conduit financing, where the underlying bond instrument is secured by revenues pledged from the asset being created through the net bond proceeds, the issuer may not be offering anything at all in terms of security for the bond's repayment.

18. **Power to Collaborate and Cooperate**. Most cities have the power to enter into public-private partnerships, as well as to enter into Memoranda of Understanding with other jurisdictions. Intergovernmental agreements run the gamut from allowing law enforcement agencies from one jurisdiction to enter a neighboring jurisdiction to continue the pursuit of a suspect, to sharing services, such as a waste water treatment plant, to jointly marketing a multi-jurisdiction area for tourism or economic development purposes. As with all municipal powers, the fundamental question, in the event of a challenge to any such collaborative or cooperative undertakings, is whether the parties had the authority to do so in the first place. Beyond that, the interpretation and enforcement of such arrangements will largely depend on the language of the documents to which the respective jurisdictions have indicated their willingness to be bound.

19. **Power to Provide Health Services**. Most major cities operate at least one public hospital. The provision of health services, at some level, is deemed fundamental to an LGU's Power to Protect Health, Safety, Welfare, and Morals.

Specific powers of local government that impact The Development Process

Although it is arguable that each of the nineteen featured powers of Local Governmental Units has the potential to impact The Development Process and specific development Projects in fundamental ways, a handful or so of LGU powers deserve more detailed treatment in this chapter. These LGU powers, and their impact on The Development Process, are addressed next.

The power to tax

Local Governmental Units (LGUs), ranging in size from multi-county or multi-jurisdiction metropolitan-scaled districts to boroughs, towns, and villages – with the most common LGUs, counties and cities, filling in the middle – generally derive the vast *majority* of their general tax revenues from two sources: Real Property Taxes and Sales and Use Taxes.[23] The level of control over and amount of these taxes, both in their application and as a percentage of local revenue, vary greatly throughout the United States and are primarily controlled through state constitutions and/or statutes. In other words, LGUs have delegated, not inherent taxing powers.

Real property taxes supporting a Local Governmental Unit. The assessment and collection of Real Property Taxes are generally the primary source of annual operating revenues for LGUs. Local taxes on property date back to ancient times and have a long history leading up to the systems of property taxation commonly employed in the United States to fund local government.

> Taxes based on ownership of property were used in ancient times, but the modern tax has roots in feudal obligations owed to British and European kings or landlords. In the fourteenth and fifteenth century, British tax assessors used ownership or occupancy of property to estimate a taxpayer's ability to pay. In time the tax came to be regarded as a tax on the property itself (in rem). In the United Kingdom the tax developed into a system of "rates" based on the annual (rental) value of property.
>
> The growth of the property tax in America was closely related to economic and political conditions on the frontier. In pre-commercial agricultural areas the property tax was a feasible source of local

government revenue and equal taxation of wealth was consistent with the prevailing equalitarian ideology.[24]

In one of the newspaper essays by Alexander Hamilton collectively comprising what came to be known as "The Federalist Papers," of which Hamilton, James Madison, and John Jay were the anonymous (at the time) authors, under the nom-de-plume "Publius," in an effort to win popular support for the proposed Constitution of the United States of America particularly in his home "state" of New York, Hamilton takes up the argument about taxes on commerce versus taxes on real property. In Federalist Paper No. 12, from which excerpts are provided later in this chapter, Hamilton makes the case for excises, duties, and – to a limited extent – sales taxes as superior forms of taxation than taxes on the value of real property, referring specifically to the "houses and lands" of farmers as susceptible to only modest taxes. From even a casual reading of Federalist Paper No. 12, it is easy to make the case that the use of real property taxes as a means of supporting government has been well at issue since before the formation of the thirteen original colonies as "the United States." Not surprising, the arguments about the utility and fairness of real property taxes have not, by any means, gone away.[25]

In Federalist Paper No. 12 – "The Utility of the Union in Respect to Revenue" – Hamilton wrote:

> The prosperity of commerce is now perceived and acknowledged by all enlightened statesmen to be the most useful as well as the most productive source of national wealth, and has accordingly become a primary object of their political cares. By multiplying the means of gratification, promoting the introduction and circulation of the precious metals, those darling objects of human avarice and enterprise, it serves to vivify and invigorate all the channels of industry and to make them flow with greater activity and copiousness.[26]
>
> In so opulent a nation as that of Britain, where direct taxes from superior wealth must be much more tolerable, and from the vigor of the government, much more practicable than in America, far the greatest part of the national revenue is derived from taxes of the indirect kind, from imposts and from excises. Duties on imported articles form a large branch of this latter description.
>
> In America it is evident that we must a long time depend for the means of revenue chiefly on such duties. In most parts of it excises must be confined within a narrow compass. The genius of the people will ill brook the inquisitive and peremptory spirit of excise laws. The pockets of the farmers, on the other hand, will reluctantly yield but scanty supplies in the unwelcome shape of impositions on their houses and lands; and personal property is too precarious and invisible a fund to be laid hold of in any other way than by the imperceptible agency of taxes on consumption.[27]

Having made the argument for the superiority of excise taxes and import duties as a source of funding for government over that of real property taxes, Hamilton goes on, in Federalist Paper No. 12, to then argue that only a union of the colonies will be in a position to efficiently and effectively manage such a taxation system.

Putting both ideological and policy critiques of real property taxes aside, however, it is a nearly ubiquitous method of funding local government. And so long as an LGU stays true to its statutory authority to assess and collect real property taxes, there is little basis for a legal challenge to the obligation to pay local property taxes based on the assessed value of real property owned in a jurisdiction. Accordingly, such challenges tend to be limited to whether the taxing jurisdiction has properly followed its own procedures for assessing the "fair market value" of the property being taxed. To a lesser extent, legal challenges may be mounted based on whether the taxing jurisdiction has followed its procedures for establishing or adjusting the "mil rate" of the tax being assessed, including honoring any statutory caps on how much the mil rate may be raised from year to year.

The fact that LGUs administer and collect Real Property Taxes has given rise to three Project financing techniques to support or facilitate projects that meet specific policy imperatives: tax abatement programs, payment-in-lieu-of taxes (PILOT) arrangements, and tax increment financing districts (TIF Districts) and TIF Bonds. This subject area is discussed in greater depth in Chapter 10.

Real property taxes supporting other municipal governmental functions. Unlike the double-jeopardy clause in the Constitution,[28] precluding the same person from being tried more than once for the same capital crime, no analogous protection exists in the Constitution precluding more than one jurisdiction from taxing the same parcel of real property. Accordingly, in addition to taxes imposed by the local unit of government on the assessed value of real property within its jurisdiction, it is possible for the same parcel of land to be taxed by *other governmental units* on the value of that real property, provided the aggregate amount of all such taxes do not exceed any statutory limitations imposed by the state in which the property is located. The most common example of this occurs where the local public school district in which the parcel of land is situated exists independently of the LGU, such that each must rely on its independent taxing authority to generate annual operating revenues for its respective operations. In this regard, it is not uncommon for the boundaries of the LGU and an independent school district to be noncontiguous, such that the latter may include all or portions of more than one LGU. For a discussion of taxes other than real property taxes imposed by different LGUs in different states, such as ad valorem taxes, personal property taxes, and sales and excise taxes, see the Supplementary Materials on the companion website for this textbook.

Powers of Local Government: The Power to Spend

As discussed in the comprehensive listing of the Powers of Local Governmental Units, LGUs adopt annual budgets, which are used both to gauge the amount of revenues they need to raise each fiscal year but also to guide their spending in that fiscal year. Additionally, LGUs develop and adopt what are commonly referred to as Capital Improvement Plans (CIPs), which are used to project and make spending decisions for capital improvements to the jurisdiction. CIP expenditures are generally financed through the issuance of municipal debt obligations, the interest and debt-service payments on which are programmed into the Annual Operating Budgets in each fiscal year in which the debt obligation will be outstanding. Government spending through the annual budget process, as well as through its CIP projections, may have profound impacts on and implications for a development project within the LGU's boundaries. Such spending may range from where and how the LGU plans to spend its Community Development Block Grant (CDBG) funds to CIP line-items ranging from public transit to community facilities such as recreation centers, libraries, and multimodal terminals. In deciding on the specific location, size, and programming of such public facilities and/or infrastructure improvements (such as the kind of streetscape and infrastructure improvements on which LGUs typically spend their federal CDBG funds), the Developer may consider and possibly rely on the LGU's spending commitments. The power of an LGU to spend money will impact The Development Process *only to the extent* the Development Budget and/or Operating Budget are *dependent*, directly or indirectly, on the timeliness and reliability of any such spending commitments. One might construct an unlimited number of scenarios in which the LGU makes a spending commitment intended to support the Developer's Project, from a funding commitment from the jurisdiction for its ratable share of the contribution to expand a regional transit system that is or will serve the Project (see, for example, the discussion in *The Impact and Growth of Public-Private Partnerships (P3s)* in **Chapter 10**, regarding the addition of the Silver Line to the Washington Metropolitan Transit Authority's metro subway system, and the development opportunities it spawned), to making much-needed street and sidewalk repairs serving the Subject Site, to a spec office building the tenanting of which depends on the success of the LGU's economic development efforts, which itself depends on the LGU fully funding the budget for its economic development office or department. Powers of Local Government: The Power to Spend. The power of an LGU to spend money will impact The Development Process only to the extent the Development Budget and/or Operating Budget are *dependent*, directly or indirectly, on the timeliness and reliability of any such spending commitments. One might construct an unlimited number of scenarios in which the LGU makes a spending commitment intended to support the Developer's Project, from a funding commitment from the jurisdiction for its ratable share of the contribution to expand a regional transit system that is or will serve the Project (see, for example, the discussion in The Impact and Growth of Public-Private Partnerships (P3s) in Chapter 10, regarding the addition of the Silver Line to the Washington Metropolitan Transit Authority's metro subway system, and the development opportunities it spawned), to making much-needed street and sidewalk repairs serving the Subject Site, to a spec office building the tenanting of which depends on the success of the LGU's economic development efforts, which itself depends on the LGU fully funding the budget for its economic development office or department.

Powers of Local Government: The Power to Contract

As mentioned in General Powers of Local Government, an LGU's power to enter into contracts is ancillary to many of its other substantive powers. Municipalities often find valid public purposes to be served by cooperating or partnering with the private sector on specific real estate development projects. See, in this regard, several substantive sections in Chapter 10 on public/private partnerships.

Powers of Local Government: Land Use Powers

The scope, nature, purpose, and administration of a local jurisdiction's Land Use Controls will determine whether a proposed real estate development project will or won't be allowed. That is why Land Use Law is one of the Holy Trinity of real estate law. That is also why Purchase and Sale Agreements for real property intended by the Purchaser to serve a specific real estate development project should always provide that the Purchaser is not legally obligated to close on the purchase of the Subject Site unless and until the Purchaser can secure the necessary land use approvals from the decision-making body for the LGU on all land use matters – generally a Planning Commission and a city council or county board of supervisors, as the case may be. For this reason, a separate chapter of this textbook – Chapter 5 – is devoted to this topic.

Powers of Local Government: The Power of Condemnation

An LGU's Power of Condemnation, and *its willingness to use that power*, can be an extremely powerful and effective tool for a Developer working in partnership or through some other formal relationship with an LGU toward the successful completion of the Developer's Project.

In particular, the mere threat of condemnation may be used effectively to leverage current property owners needing to be "persuaded" to sell their land and improvements thereon to the Developer in situations where the property owner or owners want to hold the Developer "over a barrel" to hold out for a purchase price that appears more grounded in extortion than in market realities. The Power of Condemnation, the authority for which is contained in the Fourth Amendment of the U.S. Constitution, has been the subject of considerable controversy in the twenty-first century, even rising to the level of a campaign issue in the Republican Primary process in the United States involving real estate developer and GOP candidate for president Donald J. Trump. To fully understand the importance and limits of eminent domain law in the context of The Development Process, see Public Takings for Private Purposes in Chapter 10.

Powers of Local Government: The Power to Develop

In some instances, the path of least resistance for the Developer may be to enter into a public-private partnership with the LGU and rely on the local jurisdictions authority to proceed with the developer. Given the constraints the vast majority of states impose on their own ability to use eminent domain to acquire land through condemnation to then be made available for private-sector development, creating such a P3 could provide a solution to such constraints on acquiring key parcels of land through condemnation. In such a scenario, challenging the LGU's authority to act as the lead developer in a P3 with the Developer could prove an effective deterrent to the LGU's exercise of its limited condemnation powers.

Powers of Local Government: The Power to Facilitate Transportation

As new development projects become increasingly grand in scale and ambition, and as WalkUPs continue to represent an increasing proportion of all commercial real estate value in the United States, multimodal access to new projects will increase their cash flow and long-term value. Accordingly, the greater the power the LGU has over maintaining and expanding existing modes of mass transit and adding new modes as new technologies are embraced by those who live, work, play, and learn in the jurisdiction, the greater the Developer may rely on commitments from the LGU to expand and support a panoply of transit modes. For example, many LGUs are experiencing a newfound but intense interest in streetcars. However, because of the costs of planning, installing, and operating streetcar lines, and vigorous challenges to streetcars as an economically viable, alternative form of mass transit, some local jurisdictions, such as Arlington County, Virginia, the Borough of Brooklyn in New York City, and Washington, DC, have abandoned, delayed or scaled back what were initially ambitious plans for new streetcar lines. A multifamily developer in the Columbia Pike corridor of Arlington County who made development decisions, including capital cost decisions, based on the Arlington County Board's approval of a dedicated streetcar line may not recoup such costs in the aftermath of newly elected County Board members overturning the prior Board's approval. Additionally, as mass transit systems become more robust and require a consortium of neighboring jurisdictions to share the costs, as well as sharing the decision making, it may become completely unrealistic to rely on the plans or intentions of the LGU in which the Subject Site is located when that LGU represents only one voice – and one vote – on the decision-making board for the entire system.

Powers of Local Government: The Power to Borrow

Municipal Finance is completely different from structured financing for a real estate development project. Yet the former could impact the latter to the extent the LGU is relying on its debt capacity and credit rating to provide funding directly or indirectly to the Project, or the Project depends on the LGU financing and completing some other capital improvements that are deemed integral to the Project. Besides the addition of the Silver Line to WMATA's metro subway system serving the greater Washington, DC, area, WMATA recently approved the construction of a new Potomac Yard metro station in the City of Alexandria that will, when completed, change the face and property values of the entire 300-acre former RF&P Potomac Yard redevelopment site. These are instances in which numerous private-sector real estate development projects will depend on the completion of very ambitious and extremely costly public improvement projects for their success. An additional concern may be that because municipal finance benefits from economies of scale, an LGU may have to wait until it can package several smaller-scale capital improvement projects into a single bond offering, taking the timing of when such municipal funding may be available largely out of the hands of the Developer and even the LGU itself. At the time, during the Project Conception Phase, the Developer reasonably relied on an LGU's proposed funding of one or more components of the Project, the Developer would have included such line-item into the preliminary Development Budget. However, twelve months later, during the Pre-Development Phase, be (i) much more illusory, (ii) more expensive to issue, and (iii) more costly to carry than originally projected during the Project Conception Phase of The Development Process.

Land Use and Zoning Law generally

Like real estate markets and investing generally, urban trends tend to be cyclical

Looking over the course of history in the evolution of American cities, since their very modest, colonial beginnings in the late seventeenth century, "government" with a capital "G" – including what came to be a fairly robust federal government in Washington, DC, despite the Founding Fathers' clear intentions to the contrary – has been alternately accused of *doing too little* or *doing too much* to impact the physical development of the urban built environment. In the 1950s and 1960s era of urban renewal, referred to by numerous critics as "Urban Removal," powerful city officials like Robert Moses in New York City and Edmund Bacon in Philadelphia demolished wide swaths of their respective domains with an indiscriminate "out with the old and in with the new" approach to remaking city life. While displacing millions of African American households nationwide, with few plans for how they would be rehoused other than in sterile-block-after-sterile-block of faceless, high-rise public housing projects, these efforts put nary a dent in the white flight from America's cities that began in the late 1940s and continued to the end of the century. In the 1970s, 1980s, and into the 1990s, during which period, among other things, New York City had to be bailed out by the federal government and Congress passed the District of Columbia Financial Responsibility and Management Assistance Act of 1995, ushering in the District of Columbia Financial Control Board to take over the city's operations from its duly elected government, "Government" was accused of doing far too little to save the cities, many of which fell into various stages of distress.

Through its zoning code, providing definitions for different types of permitted uses within the jurisdiction, together with a zoning map, showing precisely where each such use is allowed to be located (and, by negative implication, where they are not), municipal government attempts to organize real estate development into a logical and orderly configuration to maximize specific benefits to the public and minimize specific detriments. Most cities, at least those on the East Coast – many of the largest of which started out very modestly as those colonial enclaves referenced earlier, like Boston, New York (nee "New Amsterdam"), Philadelphia, Newport, and Charleston (nee "Charles Town"), aka the original "Big Five" towns in Colonial America – grew organically, without the benefits or burdens of zoning regulations. New York City, for example, claims to have enacted the nation's first municipal land use code, with its passage of the Zoning Resolution of 1916. Today, 100 years later, New York City has one of the most comprehensive and most complex systems of Land Use Controls in the United States. Its most recent Zoning Resolution was adopted December 15, 1961, and has been substantially and comprehensively amended since that time, comprised of thirteen Articles, plus Appendices, and totaling 3,773 pages in its online version as of May 28, 2015. By stark contrast, the City of Houston to this day does not have a zoning code.

Zoning and land use generally tend to be both proscriptive and prescriptive. You may not put X usage over there. However, if you put Y usage over here, you will be rewarded in some tangible way (e.g., some bonus density; an expedited application process; something else of value in time, money, or both). Planners, with the best of intentions and more often than not in contemporary planning practice using a variety of community participation techniques, strive to create the future by planning it within an inch of its life. Sometimes they get it mostly right, but that's the exception and not the rule. Things change: the economy changes; market demands change; market preferences change; demographics change. Suddenly, the master plan from ten years ago, which took more than two years of planning, visioning, community input, and a lot of political maneuvering (because local government must listen to the residents who are present now, because future residents won't be around yet to vote in the next election cycle, and residents generally prefer the devil they know to the devil they don't know), just isn't attracting the kind of redevelopment fervor the master plan was intended to encourage when it was finally approved after all those meetings. The end result, of course, is that the intrepid Developer who now has a vision for what Parcel X could become if only that pesky master plan wasn't calling for something completely different, must now go through some form of torturous exception, exemption, or variance process of, worse yet, requesting a Master Plan Amendment, in essence saying to everyone who led, drove or participated in hundreds of hours of community meetings, "What you have here is wrong."

Planners, senior government staffs, and – most important – local elected leaders finally caught on to the fact that those best able to anticipate and respond to the demands of the commercial market were the ones who made their livings doing so: commercial real estate Developers. Even when they were willing to come to the table to participate in the well-intentioned visioning and long-range planning intended to yield the foolproof master plan, their expertise was often overshadowed by louder, local voices who didn't want "their" master plan "railroaded" by some real estate Developer who was like a carpetbagger, merely interested in making a fortune and moving on to the next town. So, somewhere along the way those responsible for the process, and ultimately the master plan, realized that perhaps things would work better all the way around if a mechanism could be created that allowed the development community a little more flexibility to come in and propose something "bankable"; something it could raise the necessary debt and equity to finance and that, when completed, would be occupied and used. Enter the Planned Unit Development (PUD).

Local jurisdictions of various sizes, from those with populations of less than 25,000 to those with more than 1 million residents have embraced the PUD process. It is particularly well suited to the WalkUPs that require a complex and finely tuned balance of two or more uses and at least as many alternative forms of transit connectivity. Accordingly, and given this textbook's focus on WalkUPs, the balance of this chapter will be devoted to a case study of sorts: the PUD process in the District of Columbia. These materials will be supplemented by two Case Studies in the Supplementary Materials in the companion website of two different commercial real estate development projects in Washington, DC, that navigated the District's PUD process: the Adams Morgan Church Hotel and the West End Library.

THE IMPORTANCE OF A COMPREHENSIVE PLAN: LAND USE PLANNING IN WASHINGTON, DC[29]

The L'Enfant Plan of 1791 for the nation's capital

Washington, DC's sentiments still run strong for the Frenchman artist turned engineer who, under George Washington, drafted the city's first urban plan. Characterized as Baroque-inspired because of its broad horizontality, L'Enfant's vision was primarily grid based with a complementary system of intersecting diagonal avenues layered over top. The terrain's natural topography was integrated into his design, and informed the positioning of the Capitol, the Mall, and the White House. Said esteemed landscape architect Frederick Law Olmsted Jr., "Here is a plan not hastily sketched, not by a man of narrow view and little foresight. It is a plan with the authority of a century behind it, to which we can all demand undeviating adherence in the future; a plan prepared by the hand of L'Enfant, but under the constant, direct, personal guidance of one whose technical knowledge of surveying placed the problem completely within his grasp, and who brought to its solution the same clear insight, deep wisdom, and forethought that gave pre-eminence in the broader fields of war and statesmanship to the name of George Washington."[30]

L'Enfant naturally took his design cues from the Paris and London he grew up in while simultaneously considering the potential of Washington as the nation's newly recognized national seat of power. He considered the future possibilities of a nation that was just beginning to burgeon in wealth and world influence. Worthy elements otherwise found at the Palace of Versailles; wide avenues, tree-lined streets, plentiful monuments, and strategically oriented views were drafted into his revered 1791 city plan.

The next 100 years

The city's 100th anniversary, in 1891, was cause to reflect, study, celebrate, and improve the development efforts that had taken place since Washington's master plan had first been adopted. Though L'Enfant had provided the vision, the city had yet to fully implement his strategies, and so Senator James McMillian, who was particularly concerned with the city's trajectory, decided to take action. He formed the McMillan Commission in 1901, which was comprised of architects and planners and whose goals were to see through those of L'Enfant in making Washington an astute and sophisticated capital city exemplary of a strong, prosperous and unified nation. The Senate Park Commission (as it was formally known) most notably dedicated its efforts to creating a robust public park system whose green spaces were connected by deliberate nodes of memorial buildings, statues and public spaces. The overarching axial orientation to government buildings (i.e., the Capitol, White House, etc.) and its most prominent monuments was finally established and captured the grandeur of space L'Enfant had conceptualized from the beginning.

Over the subsequent years, the master plan was fully realized and constructed. During the execution, Congress delegated oversight to the National Capital Park Commission. Soon after, Congress expanded the Commission's original mandate, endowing it with responsibility for the "*comprehensive, systematic, and continuous development of the park, parkway, and playground systems of the National Capital and its environs.*"[31] By 1952, the National Capital Planning Act established what still exists today – a federal agency with responsibility to maintain and promote the L'Enfant plan, to provide an advisory role to city agencies when determining land use decisions, and to continue the development of urban planning strategies applicable to the DC metro area.

Comprehensive planning in the shadows of L'Enfant and MacMillan

Priorities with regard to urban renewal and redevelopment are carefully laid out within the Comprehensive Plan, as is the overarching guidance for future planning and new development within the city. As previously mentioned in the Separation of Duties, two separate entities, one municipal and one federal, write individual reports that when combined, make up Washington, DC's Comprehensive Plan. The Office of Planning details District Elements while the National Capital Planning Commission reports on Federal Elements – these pertain to areas on which federal government operations have a direct impact.

The District Elements

As the nation's capital, Washington, DC, is unique among all other cities. As a result of its role, the necessity of an uncommon legal authority has been developed. Even though municipal responsibly lies within the mayoral office, the mayor's plans and policies and their implementation are reviewed at the federal level. The result is a much more broad approach to the Comprehensive Plan, but also an added layer of bureaucracy that can have significant effects on land use decisions. The advisory and approval role at the local level alone is an arduous process, but the addition of a secondary and more even powerful legislative body is often exhaustive. Together, however, they mandate within Section 1–302.62 of the DC Code that:

The purposes of the District Elements of the Comprehensive Plan for the National Capital are to:

(a) Define the requirements and aspirations of District residents, and accordingly influence social, economic, and physical development;
(b) Guide executive and legislative decisions on matters affecting the District and its citizens;
(c) Promote economic growth and jobs for District residents;

(d) Guide private and public development in order to achieve District and community goals;

(e) Maintain and enhance the natural and architectural assets of the District; and

(f) Assist in the conservation, stabilization, and improvement of each neighborhood and community in the District.[32]

The District Elements are comprised of thirteen Citywide Elements and ten Area Elements. Most of the Citywide Elements will affect a Planned Unit Development in some capacity, therefore it's important to understand how a particular project will either contribute to or exhaust each of the categories. Knowing the difference and having solutions in advance can help propel a project through approvals.

The Citywide Elements

1. Framework (setting the plan's guiding principles and vision)
2. Land Use (the cornerstone of the Citywide Elements)
3. Transportation
4. Housing
5. Economic Development
6. Parks, Recreation, and Open Space
7. Educational Facilities
8. Environmental Protection
9. Infrastructure
10. Urban Design
11. Historic Preservation
12. Community Services and Facilities
13. Arts and Culture

Of the ten Area Elements, a Planned Unit Development project will lie in its respective location. Though each of the ten areas is within the District, they all have distinct needs with regard to development.

The Area Elements

1. Capitol Hill
2. Central Washington
3. Far Northeast and Southeast
4. Far Northwest and Southwest
5. Lower Anacostia Waterfront and Near Southwest
6. Mid-City
7. Near Northwest
8. Rock Creek East
9. Rock Creek West
10. Upper Northeast

Here, the purpose of the Comprehensive Plan is to break down each zone using demographic, historical and geographic information at a myopic scale. "Many of the policies are place-based, referencing specific neighborhoods, corridors, business districts and local landmarks."[33] For purposes of this discussion, the focus will be the Mid-City for Planned Unit Development case study one and Near Northwest for Planned Unit Development case study two. Both areas will be defined in the subsequent pages to analyze whether the projects put forth responded accurately to the specific needs of the area or challenged the findings of the Comprehensive Plan.

The Federal Elements

Federal Elements of the Comprehensive Plan for the National Capital are to (in summary): promote the efficient operation of the federal government while reinforcing Smart Growth principles and supporting local and regional planning objectives. Smart Growth is defined by the American Planning Association as "that which supports choice and opportunity by promoting efficient and sustainable land development, incorporates redevelopment patterns that optimize prior infrastructure investments, and consumes less land than is otherwise available for agriculture, open space, natural systems, and rural lifestyles."[34] The seven elements are titled:

1. Federal Workplace
2. Foreign Missions and International Organizations
3. Transportation
4. Parks and Open Space
5. Federal Environment
6. Preservation and Historic Features
7. Visitors

The National Capital Planning Commission is in the process of receiving public comment on its federal Urban Design Element 2015, which will eventually be adopted as an integral element of the Comprehensive Plan for the National Capital. The proposed Element will establish new policies and combine existing policies about design and physical character into a unified section. The draft element was released in November 2012 and circulated for initial public comment. It was drafted in response to Washington DC's surge in recent redevelopment and overall spike in population, median income, and real estate market values. NCPC staff prepared the updated and expanded 2015 draft element reflecting the public comments received in response to the November 2012 draft, the Height Master Plan study, as well as more recent staff studies of viewsheds, public realm, image, and form in the Nation's Capital.

   Like the November 2012 draft, the federal Urban Design Element 2015 addresses, among other things, the importance of recognizing and preserving mid-century designs, such as Eero Saarinen's Dulles Airport Terminal Building (1962); the horizontality of the city, which has been carefully controlled since enactment of the 1910 Federal Height of Buildings Act (see "Dispelling the Urban Legend about Washington, DC's Building Height Limit," and "The Power of a Strong Vision" Feature Box in Chapter 5); and the necessity to preserve its classically designed civic structures while fostering creativity, perhaps best reflected in the Smithsonian Institution's penchant for one-off designs for its buildings, including: James Renwick Jr.'s Smithsonian Institution Building, aka "The Castle" (1855); Adolph Cluss and Paul Schulze's Arts and Industries Building (1881); Hornblower and Marshall's National Museum of Natural History (1911); John Russell Pope/Eggers and Higgins' National Gallery of Art, West Building (1941); Hellmuth, Obata + Kassabaum's Air and Space Museum (1976); and I.M. Pei and Partner's National Gallery of Art, East Building (1978).

   In all, the National Capital Planning Commission is responsible to draft the federal portion of the Comprehensive Plan, which includes such priorities as locating federal facilities, providing guidance to foreign governments (embassy integration), implementing strategies for transit-oriented development, drafting historic preservation best practices, ensuring visitors to the region are provided with educational and memorable experiences, all the while constantly espousing history of place with references to and reverence for L'Enfant's original vision for the capital city of a young nation.

The community participation process (informal and formal)[35]

Ten critical stages in the Planned Unit Development (PUD) approval process

1. Developer meets with Advisory Neighborhood Commission (ANC), community, Office of Planning (OP), District of Columbia Department of Transportation (DDOT), Office of Zoning (OZ)
2. File a Notice of Intent to Office of Zoning and Advisory Neighborhood Commission
3. File application with Office of Zoning
4. Office of Planning Setdown Report
5. Zoning Commission Public Meeting
6. Developer meets with impacted ANC(s) and community groups
7. Developer meets with Office of Planning and all other District agencies
8. Applicant files "Pre-Hearing" Statement with Office of Zoning
9. Office of Planning Final Report
10. Public Hearing

The ten stages of the PUD approval process are each a mini-process in and of themselves. Each involves multiple parties and, therefore, extensive scheduling to make meetings work for both the project and each of its stakeholders.

Each step is further complicated because the District is the seat of the federal government. The federal government has representation on the District's zoning administrative bodies: Office of Planning, Historic Preservation and Renovation Board, Zoning Commission, National Capital Planning Commission, Fire and Emergency Medical Services Department, to name a few. This makes zoning in the District unique compared to any other local government in the nation.[36] It also makes it much more complex. Agencies must carry out due process or trial-type protections at hearings, provide the opportunity for sworn testimony and rebuttal, grant the chance to cross-examine, and accommodate requests to continue and/or appeal hearings and decisions. Because they are both legislative and quasi-judicial and mandated by statute, each agency must follow a broad framework in which to structure their meetings. They include:

1. Fairness – cannot prejudge or have biases on the matter
2. Decisions – must be made based on the record
3. Notification – must inform the public by way of local newspaper, physical posting at project site, and mailings to affected parties

Beyond this general framework, each agency conducts business with varying degrees of formality. While the ANC meetings feel personal and collaborative in nature (due in part to location and venue within the affected neighborhood), the Zoning Commission manages its procedures similar to court proceedings in courtroom-like settings. Whether an informal ANC meeting or a more formalized zoning procedure, the physical time commitment is extraordinary.

The application must capture the essence of the project in an extensive written document whereby revisions and updates should be addressed on an ongoing basis. In turn, those corrections should be circulated to the affected party, which takes an additional level of effort and coordination to ensure the project is being reviewed in its most current state. Final reports do not get drafted or decided on until the project has been set down and public hearings have commenced and concluded.

Of all the critical stages, most important are the meetings made in advance of the actual filing. All of the participating District offices agree that proactive discussion of the intended PUD provides valuable feedback for an applicant. These meetings can drive a project in the right direction almost from its inception. Developers can better assess budgets' financial outcomes and potential approvals based on these Pre-Development conversations. Similarly, developers can help themselves by making sure their application speaks to the municipal and federal rules laid out in the Comprehensive Plan. And they can assemble a team of experienced, well-connected, informed, and detail-oriented experts to see them through the PUD process.

Eminent domain and the U.S. Constitution

Two amendments to the Constitution of the United States provide the framework for when government, at any level, may exercise its rights of eminent domain to take private property for a public purpose through a condemnation proceeding. Eminent domain as a constitutional right, as well as the exercise of the power of condemnation by states and localities, is taken up in great detail in Public Takings for Private Purposes in Chapter 10.

Public exactions for private development

Public benefits and amenities packages in the context of the District's PUD process[37]

Developers, planners, and ANC participants all understand the intention of the Public Benefits and Amenities portion of the application, and most agree with its inclusion but in all are uncertain what and how much to offer. There is no mathematical equation that informs the developer if granted "x" then he is to supply "y" Public Benefits and Amenities.

Looking at the table, anyone would be hard-pressed to objectively equate zoning relief for the height of a building to the 4,000-square-foot community meeting space contained in its floor plan. Similarly, the relief requested from having to provide a particular number of loading docks for the promise of a job training program and small facility is difficult to rationalize. *Because an objective system has yet to be developed, uncertainty remains between the give and take.*

Interviews with planners revealed most would prefer a method of objectively quantifying and evaluating the strengths of proffers (i.e., community meeting spaces and job training programs)

Table 4.1 Detailed summary of current zoning conditions (columns two and three), requested changes (column four), and categories requiring relief (column five)

Item	R-5-B MOR	RC / C-2-B MOR	C-2-B PUD	Proposed
Height	50'	40'	90'	92' Relief Required
Lot Area	n/a	n/a	15,000 sf	42,279 sf
Lot Width	n/a	n/a	n/a	~140'
FAR	1.8 (76,102.2 sf)	3.5 max (147,976.5 sf) 1.5 non-res (63,418.5 sf)	6.0 max 2.0 non-res (84,558 sf)	Rooms/ Service 149,093 sf (3.53 FAR) Adjunct 38,033 sf (0.9 FAR) Total 187,296 sf (4.43 FAR)
Lot Occ	60%	100% (commercial)	100% (commercial)	75%
Rear Yard	4"/ft. at rear 15' min.	15' (below 20' in height may be measured to CL of alley)	15' (below 20' in height may be measured to CL of alley)	Below 20' in height – 8' Above 20' in height – 0' Relief Required
Side Yard	None required	None required	None required	0'
Courts	Open Court 3"/ft. of height, 10' min	Open and Closed Court 3"/ft. of height, 12' min	Open and Closed Court 3"/ft. of height, 12' min	Information required
	Closed Court 4"/ft of height, 15' min area = 2*(w^2), 350 sf min	Closed Court area = 2*(w^2), 250 sf min	Closed Court area = 2*(w^2), 250 sf min	Information required

Item	R-5-B MOR	RC / C-2-B MOR	C-2-B PUD	Proposed
Parking			1 per 2 rooms (227/2 = 114) 1 per 150 sf of largest function room (2,861 sf / 150 sf = 19) 114+ 19 = 133	174
Loading			2 berths @ 30' 1 berth @ 55' 1 delivery @ 20' 2 platforms @ 200 sf 1 platform @200 sf	3 loading spaces and a loading platform Relief Required

The information presented in the table is typical of a setdown report drafted by the Office of Planning. This information is specific to the Adams Morgan Historic Hotel PUD application and shows how the project is quantified prior to final approval. Requests for relief (variance) are bolded.[38]

in order to more easily and directly compare projects. Some planners do support employing a more mathematical formula between proffers and the variances received by Developers.[39] Since ambiguity is a large portion of the rub, many developers conceded that perhaps, though not ideal, numerical equations provide some framework for the Public Benefits and Amenities (PBA) package. They indicated reliability is of great value to a PUD.

With little consistency citywide, each PBA package varies in reach and complexity, making it nearly impossible for a developer to conclude how much time or money it will cost. It is mainly recommended to study similar projects in similar neighborhoods to help provide some clarity. In the forthcoming case studies, the range is quite dramatic and is more evidence that a formula still does not exist. Regardless of content uncertainty, it's essential to designate contingency funds and build in extra time within the project's schedule in order to achieve success.

According to the District of Columbia Municipal Regulations, Title 11, Section 2403.9, public benefits and project amenities of the proposed Planned Use Development may be exhibited and documented in any of the following or additional categories:

(a) Urban design, architecture, landscaping, or creation or preservation of open spaces;
(b) Site planning, and efficient and economical land utilization;
(c) Effective and safe vehicular and pedestrian access, transportation management measures, connections to public transit service, and other measures to mitigate adverse traffic impacts;
(d) Historic preservation of private or public structures, places, or parks;
(e) Employment and training opportunities;
(f) Housing and affordable housing;
(g) Social services/facilities;
(h) Environmental benefits, such as storm water runoff controls and preservation of open space or trees;
(i) Uses of special value to the neighborhood or the District of Columbia as a whole; and
(j) Other public benefits and project amenities and other ways in which the proposed PUD substantially advances the major themes and other policies and objectives of any of the elements of the Comprehensive Plan.[40]

As previously mentioned, the Public Amenities and Benefits package will vary widely from project to project. "Each ward, each neighborhood, each site, and each proposed project is so unique that it would be difficult to predict and/or equalize proffers across projects. Most developers also note that doing so would override the very purpose of the PUD process: negotiating the details of a project, based on its specifics, in order to make it truly superior."[41]

Students and readers interested in other examples of Developer concessions made in exchange for the requisite development approvals for their projects in the greater Washington, DC, area, as well as from elsewhere in the United States, are encouraged to review the selected examples provided in the Supplementary Materials on the companion website to this textbook.

Notes

1. Greer, Scott, *Governing the Metropolis*, John Wiley and Sons, Inc., New York, NY (1962), pg. 3.

2. Chapter 10 includes a thorough consideration of the power of eminent domain, and attendant exercise of the power of condemnation, as shaped by Article V and Article XIV of the U.S. Constitution and the interpretation of those constitutional protections in the aftermath of the U.S. Supreme Court's decision in *Kelo v. City of New London*, 545 U.S. 1158 (2005).

3. Greer, *Governing the Metropolis*, pg. 6. The footnoted material in the excerpt refers to Chapter XX of Ralph Turner's *The Great Cultural Traditions*, published by McGraw-Hill Book Company, New York, NY (1941).

4. Maryland's fourth and final constitution was adopted on September 18, 1867, replacing a short-lived third constitution adopted in 1864, during the Civil War.

5. *Clinton v. Cedar Rapids and the Missouri River Railroad* (24 Iowa 455; 1868).

6. *People v. Hurlbut*, 24 Mich. 44, 108 (1871).

7. Wilson, Reid, "The Most Corrupt State(s) in America." *The Washington Post*, January 22, 2014. Found at www.washingtonpost.com/blogs/govbeat/wp/2014/01/22/the-most-corrupt-states-in-america.

8. *Merrill v. Monticello*, 138 U.S. 673 (1891), pg. 138.

9. Ibid., pg. 137.

10. Ibid., pg. 686.

11. Ibid., pg. 681. Emphasis added.

12. Ibid., pg. 682.

13. *Hunter v. City of Pittsburgh*, 207 U.S. 161 (1907), pg. 180.

14. Miller, David Y., *The Regional Governing of Metropolitan America*, Westview Press (a member of Perseus Book Group), Boulder, CO (2002), pg. 2.

15. Ibid., pgs. 59–60.

16. U.S. Census Bureau population estimates for the State of New York, New York City, and the city's five Boroughs, respectively, based on projected growth since the 2010 Census, as of July 1, 2014, are as follows:

New York State:	19,746,227
New York City:	8,491,079
Bronx:.	1,438,159
Brooklyn:.	2,621,793
Manhattan:	1,636,268
Queens:.	2,321,580
Staten Island:	473,279

17. The author served as the housing strategist for this study.

18. Glaab, Charles N., *The American City: A Documentary History*, The Dorsey Press, Inc., Homewood, IL (1963), pgs. 2–3.

19. Ibid., pg. 3.

20. Dillon, John F., LL.D, *Treatise on the Law of Municipal Corporations*, James Cockroft & Company, Chicago, IL (1872), §89:

It is a general and undisputed proposition of law that a municipal corporation possesses and can exercise the following powers, and no others: first, those granted in express words; second, those necessarily or fairly implied in or incident to the powers expressly granted; third, those essential to the accomplishment of the declared objects and purposes of the corporation – not simply convenient, but indispensable. Any fair, reasonable, substantial doubt concerning the existence of power is resolved by the courts against the corporation, and the power is denied.

21. See, e.g., Forster, Ryan and Kail Padgitt, "Where Do State and Local Governments Get Their Tax Revenue?" Fiscal Fact No. 242, August 27, 2010, Tax Foundation, Washington, DC. Found at http://taxfoundation.org/sites/taxfoundation.org/files/docs/ff242.pdf.

22. Amendment V: Rights in criminal cases, to the Constitution of the United States of America.

23. Institute for Local Self Governance, [California] Municipal Finance Quick Reference, 2004. Found at www.californiacityfinance.com/ILSGquickRef.pdf.

24. Fisher, Glenn W., "History of Property Taxes in the United States." EH.Net Encyclopedia, edited by Robert Whaples, September 30, 2002. Found at http://eh.net/encyclopedia/history-of-property-taxes-in-theunited-states/.

25. Fisher, Glenn W., The Worst Tax? A History of the Property Tax in America, University of Kansas Press, Lawrence, KS (1996).

26. Hamilton, Alexander, James Madison, and John Jay, The Federalist Papers, with introduction, table of contents, and index of ideas by Clinton Rossiter, New American Library, Inc. (Mentor Books paperback edition), New York, NY (1961), pg. 91.

27. Ibid., pg. 93.

28. "No person shall be . . . subject for the same offense to be twice put in jeopardy of life or limb" (Amendment V, Constitution of the United States).

29. The author acknowledges the work of Christin Martinelli, one of his graduate students in real estate law, selected portions of whose final paper for the course "The PUD Process: Know the Rules, Roles, and the Right People," dated April 26, 2013 (Georgetown SCS, FREL 601–01, Spring 2013), have been adapted for this chapter and/or provided some of the legal research and analysis on which discussions in this chapter about the District of Columbia's land use approval processes are based. This feature box was excerpted from Ms. Martinelli's paper with minimal editing.

30. Olmsted, Jr., Frederick Law, "Landscape in Connection with Public Buildings in Washington," excerpted from Moore, Charles, Editor, Papers Relating to the Improvement of the City of Washington, Government Printing Office, Washington, DC (1901), pg. 34.

31. "History." National Capital Planning Commission, accessed April 10, 2013. Found at www.ncpc.gov/ncpc/Main(T2)/About_Us(tr2)/About_Us(tr3)/History.html.

32. Office of Planning, "District Elements." Comprehensive Plan Chapter 1 in Volume 1, (2007): 1–3.

33. Ibid., pgs. 1–7.

34. "Policy Guide on Smart Growth." American Planning Association, Policy Guide on Smart Growth, Chicago, IL, last modified April 15, 2002. Found at www.planning.org/policy/guides/adopted/smartgrowth.htm.

35. Martinelli, "The PUD Process."

36. "Administrative Process Study." District of Columbia Office of Zoning, last modified April 2013. Found at http://dcoz.dc.gov/services/zoning.

37. Martinelli, "The PUD Process."

38. Jennifer Steingasser, "Setdown Report for ZC #11–17 Adams Morgan Church Hotel Consolidated Planned Unit Development and Related Map Amendment." *District of Columbia Office of Planning*, November 4, 2011, p. 12.

39. Moravec, Alexandra Croft, "An Analysis of Planned Unit Development Regulations and Processes in Washington, DC: A Development Risk Management Case Study." University of North Carolina, Chapel Hill, Master of Regional Planning in the Department of City and Regional Planning Thesis Paper (2009), pg. 31.

40. District of Columbia, "Planned Unit Development Procedures," *Municipal Regulations Title 11 Chapter 24*, (2007): 24–25.

41. Moravec, "An Analysis of Planned Unit Development Regulations and Processes," pg. 31.

Zoning and land use regulations in action

The New York law, formulated by a group of technical experts, was based on purely practical considerations. Public safety was a primary concern; by limiting the bulk of a building, the number of occupants was limited; fewer people required access and egress; traffic on adjoining streets was lightened. The limitation in mass had also of course the effect of permitting more light and air into the streets as well as into the buildings themselves. The law as a whole was directed to securing an increase in public safety, convenience and health.[1]

Zoning and land use codes in use in the United States are a relatively new phenomenon, given how long civilizations have created centralized places where people could congregate to live, engage in trade, and form societal norms.[2] The "New York law" to which architect and renowned architectural illustrator Hugh Ferris refers in the passage just quoted from his landmark book, The Metropolis of Tomorrow, is the resolution, adopted on July 25, 1916, by the City of New York's Board of Estimate and Apportionment, titled "Building Zone Resolution," and hereinafter referred to as the New York City 1916 Zoning Resolution.[3]

Chapter outline

Chapter introduction
The evolution of skyscraper design and construction as a parable for the evolution of urban Land Use Controls
Dispelling the urban legends about the rationale for Washington, DC's Height of Buildings Acts of 1899 and 1910
The One Bad Building Rule and its corollary, the One Good Building Rule
Defending the value of light, air, and views: How Manhattan's 1915 Equitable Building served as the catalyst for the United States' comprehensive zoning laws
The impact of the International Style of architecture on the Manhattan skyline and New York City's 1960 Zoning Resolution
From "Edge City" to connected WalkUPs: How comprehensive master planning changed the character of Tysons Corner, Virginia
The rise of PUDs and form-based codes: How changes in Land Use Controls can encourage more WalkUPs

Chapter introduction

Before delving into the New York City 1916 Zoning Resolution, how it came about, and how it impacted real estate development in New York City thereafter, it is important to understand one, simple rule regarding Land Use and Zoning Law in its application: *Land use decision making is as much a political act as it is a legal act*, and some would argue that it is almost exclusively a political act. Generally, municipalities like real estate development. As discussed in Chapter 4, more municipalities rely on real estate taxes as their principal source of tax revenues than any other type of tax. Put as simply as possible: Real estate taxes fund local governments. Less real estate development means less tax revenue; means less local government; means someone's losing their job soon, perhaps someone high up on the food chain.

Conversely, existing residents and businesses in close proximity to a proposed project seeking necessary land use approvals from the local municipality may be impacted, to one extent or another, by a proposed project. As suggested in Chapter 4, the extent of vocalization of their concerns and their active engagement in the land use decision-making process are likely to be directly proportional to the extent to which such stakeholders *perceive* such a project will impact them. Consequently, elected officials may find themselves between the proverbial rock and a hard place, with their constituents opposing a project that the elected official would like to approve because it will contribute to the tax base, or, maybe, also because the developer has contributed to the elected officials' campaigns. Land use decision making is political, after all.

So, unlike most of the other substantive chapters in this textbook, which endeavor to convey to the student or the reader the frameworks and mechanics of how a particular discipline of law impacts The Development Process, this chapter seeks to convey a deeper understanding about the context within which land use issues arise, and how the solutions – in whatever form – shape the built environment, including the scope and extent of the next project. If such a "next project" is the Developer's, understanding the political as well as the land use regulatory context will be critical to the success of the Developer's Project.

It would be a mistake to consider zoning and land use regulation, also referred to elsewhere in this textbook, and sometimes hereinafter as "Land Use Controls," as a static set of rules and regulations only as they exist at this very moment in time, today. As stated in the Foreword to this textbook, "*Nothing occurs in a vacuum.*"

It is important to understand at the outset that Land Use Controls in the United States have been as much *events-driven* as they've been the result of some larger, objective planning effort. In fact, as suggested in a later section of this chapter, which takes up Sir Peter Hall's review of eighty years of land use planning in the United States looking back from the early 1990s, the planning profession has vacillated between the ends of the spectrum presented by two, related planning paradigms: One paradigm relates to *who and what planning is intended to benefit*; the other paradigm relates to *how planners go about their business* of shaping the built environment around them.[4] Before exploring these two planning paradigms, however, two examples are offered to illustrate how shifts within these two paradigms may be events-driven rather than the end product of some rational, deliberative process, providing the student and the reader alike with the proper context for understanding how Land Use Controls come about and how they are changed over time.

The evolution of skyscraper design and construction as a parable for the evolution of urban Land Use Controls

The New York City 1916 Zoning Resolution is considered the first comprehensive zoning ordinance in the United States. Among other things, it served as a model for the development and adoption by the U.S. Department of Commerce, under Secretary Herbert Hoover (serving under both Presidents Warren G. Harding and Calvin Coolidge, respectively), of model zoning enabling acts for both state and local governments, discussed at length in this chapter. Those enabling acts, in turn, were the genesis for state and municipal zoning codes enacted throughout the United States in the early 1920s and thereafter.

> The New York law of 1916 was the country's first comprehensive zoning legislation.[31] The law divided the city into districts which were regulated by use (business, residential, and industrial) and also placed restriction on the height and bulk of a building. Reacting to the rampant development in lower Manhattan where many buildings rose precipitously over virtually 100 percent of their lots, the framers of the legislation had invented the concept of the "zoning envelope."[5]

It is common in today's zoning and land use parlance to refer to a parcel's "FAR," which, depending on with whom one speaks, means its "Floor Area Ratio" or "Floorspace Area Ratio." A parcel's FAR is the ratio that the total floor area of the proposed building or buildings bears to the number of square feet comprising the parcel itself. For example, a building that is constructed to the edges of its parcel, with every floor being the same size as the base, and rising forty stories, would have an FAR of 40.

As discussed in some detail later, prior to the completion of the Equitable Building at 120 Broadway in Manhattan in 1915, no zoning code limited a building's FAR. The height and massing of any skyscraper were limited only by the ability of architects and engineers to design and of general contractors to build something that wouldn't fall. In this regard, the larger the base of the building, the better it could carry its load and the various forces to which it would be subjected by virtue of its height. Accordingly, the concept of a parcel's "building envelope," as well as its FAR, were both foreign in the heyday of skyscraper design and construction in the latter part of the nineteenth century and the early part of the twentieth. The same goes for "setbacks" from the public right-of-way. The Equitable Building became the poster child for what happens when the municipality – in this case, the City of New York – fails to place any limits on what can be built on a particular parcel of land. All of this changed, however – quite dramatically, in fact – after the completion of the Equitable Building and the strong reactions it evoked.

Bringing the discussion forward 100 years from the 1915 completion of the Equitable Building, major metropolitan cities generally, and New York City in particular, are encouraging and embracing ever more ambitious new projects – not only in terms of the ever grander scale of these projects, but also in terms of some of their individual buildings; new buildings recently completed, under construction, and proposed or envisioned are literally soaring to new heights in cities throughout the United States. It is accordingly, both timely and noteworthy, in the context of how Land Use Controls are developed, enacted, and applied, to consider the historical and legal contexts for how the United States got to this point in real estate development.

With the recent completion of One World Trade Center (recently renamed from its original moniker, "Freedom Tower," standing on the site of the Twin Towers), and its certification as the tallest commercial building in the United States, the same issues regarding light, shadow, air, and views are once again coming to the public fore, just as they had a century before,

---

31. *A more detailed discussion of the 1916 New York City zoning law, and especially its influence on theory and design, can be found in my article "Zoning and Zeitgeist: The Skyscraper City in the 1920s," Journal of the Society of Architectural Historians (March 1986).*[6]

following the completion of the Equitable Building. For example, One57, Extell Development's Mixed-Use "hyper-skyscraper" at 217 W. 57th St. in Manhattan, casts a shadow three-quarters of a mile long (~4,000 linear feet), according to shadow studies the Municipal Arts Society of New York City undertook in the fall of 2013.[7] Accordingly, a grassroots effort is growing in New York City to place more reasonable curbs on these hyper-skyscrapers to prevent large swaths of Manhattan from being submerged in the darkness of their collective shadow for large portions of the daylight hours. Similarly, the building height limitations in the District of Columbia, which have been in place since 1899 (but not for the reasons most people think), are once again being challenged. Ironically, in this particular instance, the challenger is not a marquee-name developer but the District of Columbia itself, seeking to lift the cap on building heights, which has also placed a cap on its commercial tax base.

WHY DOES THIS MATTER?

As with the two other components of the Holy Trinity of real estate law – Environmental Law (Chapter 6) and Contract Law (Chapter 7) – Zoning and Land Use Law is not an area into which the Developer is going to foray without competent and experienced counsel. This generally means, among other things, engaging a land use law firm that is very well versed in the zoning and land use regulations in the jurisdiction in which the Project is located, but someone who is also very well recognized and well-respected by the members of the various decision-making bodies involved. With this in mind, the student or reader might wonder: *"If I have to engage local land use counsel anyway, why do I need to understand the practical application of Land Use Controls to my Project?"* There are several compelling reasons:

- As has been suggested elsewhere in this textbook, *"All politics is local."* And no aspect of The Development Process is more affected by politics than Zoning and Land Use Law. A change in the composition of a city council or county board of supervisors can literally torpedo changes in the local Land Use Controls in the middle of their being revised to favor or support a project but before such changes have been finalized and adopted. An animated and motivated group of residents opposed to a particular project can have dramatic impacts on its scale, scope, and, consequently, profitability or even feasibility.
- While the Developer's land use counsel, if properly vetted and selected, can and will take charge of all of the technical aspects of Land Use and Zoning Law that affect the Project, requiring such land use counsel to hold the Developer's hand and educate the Developer's principals and staff about the fundamental nature of the land use decision-making process – including, most importantly, that it is *a process* – is an extremely expensive proposition – for the Developer. Having a partner in a land use law firm who charges $500 per hour, for example, to explain "how things work" can run up the bill pretty quickly. Any student or reader who considers carefully the lessons offered in Chapter 5 about how, what, and why things that are not fundamentally legal in nature may have a dramatic impact on any project will be much better prepared to embark on the particulars of the land use decision-making process almost anywhere in the country.
- One of the worst things a Developer can do in connection with the land use decision-making process is to publicly lose its collective patience or otherwise disrespect, in any detectable manner, the process itself or the players and stakeholders involved. Losing the respect of the local community as the result of a misstep at a community meeting or at a public hearing can easily delay the process by weeks or even months. Worse yet,

fomenting an atmosphere of mistrust can literally end the prospects of the Project ever getting approved. Having dozens or even hundreds of angry citizens – voting citizens who contribute to and volunteer for election and reelection campaigns – show up at a public hearing waving placards that read "XYZ Development Company CAN'T BE TRUSTED" can present an insurmountable obstacle for the Developer. And inasmuch as so much about the land use approvals process is discretionary and subjective, any elected official, or an appointed official appointed by an elected official, may find it nigh impossible to go against the will of a very vocal and impassioned constituency. One of the best ways for a Developer to learn not to derail its own Project is to understand the importance of context – including historical context – to the land use decision-making process.

- Some of the most ambitious and most successful real estate development projects around the country have evolved out of Developers participating actively in the process of revising and updating the local Land Use and Zoning Laws. While the Developer faces some risks in "getting in on the ground floor" of this process – primarily the risk of investing hundreds and possibly thousands of hours to professional staff time, as well as hundreds of thousands (and sometimes millions) of dollar and, in the end, not benefiting from what the process produces – there are a number of potential advantages:

  - Getting to help the deliberative land use decision-making bodies with the "Visioning Process";
  - Getting to work collaboratively, rather than adversarially, with deliberative advocacy and neighborhood organizations and bodies;
  - Having the opportunity to shape land use laws that are grounded in the economic realities of real estate development and finance, which, although it may help the entire development community, will at least make sure, for the benefit of the Developer, that new land use laws and procedures don't preclude the Developer from pursuing potential opportunities; and
  - Having a potential competitive advantage over other Developers by understanding the ins and outs, as well as the whys, of the new land use regulatory approval framework.

Dispelling the urban legends about the rationale for Washington, DC's Height of Buildings Acts of 1899 and 1910

Many visitors to the nation's capital are struck by its orderliness and visual appeal. It is often referred to as America's "most European" city, owing in large measure to the uniformity of the scale and massing of its monumental and urban cores; the hierarchy of streets, avenues, and boulevards; the relative architectural homogeneity of its public, institutional, and private-sector buildings; and its proliferation of squares, monuments, parks, museums, and other public spaces and their relationships to each other, as well as their relationship generally and specifically to the topography of the site.

Many of these seemingly laudable characteristics of the Federal City are *unduly* credited exclusively to Major Pierre Charles L'Enfant of the French Corps of Engineers, who was dispatched from France during the American–Indian Wars and remained in the colonies thereafter. L'Enfant was specifically commissioned to design the layout of the capital of the new country, and was also ultimately and prematurely dismissed by President George Washington, with whom L'Enfant had served.

Within less than a year of being commissioned by Washington, L'Enfant was fired for flagrantly disregarding the authority of the three commissioners Washington had appointed to oversee the surveying of the proposed new capital site along the Potomac River. In reality, the "L'Enfant Plan" was completed after L'Enfant's discharge by surveyor Major Andrew Ellicott (referred to as the "unofficial geographer general of the United States") and engineer Benjamin Banneker, the son of freed slaves who grew up in Baltimore, Maryland. Ellicott and Banneker had been hired by Washington, prior to L'Enfant's commission, to conduct the land surveying necessary for the creation of the District of Columbia, an area substantially larger than the portion L'Enfant planned for the Federal City. Ellicott and Banneker jointly completed L'Enfant's work, which was far from over at the time of L'Enfant's summary dismissal.

One hundred years after the creation of what came to be known as "the L'Enfant Plan," the MacMillan Plan made substantial revisions to the original L'Enfant Plan.[8] In fact, a number of different components have evolved following the completion of the L'Enfant Plan and the completion of the McMillan Plan that have collectively come to be known as the current master plan for the District of Columbia.[9] Some of the history of the plan of Washington, DC, is discussed in more detail in The Importance of a Comprehensive Plan: Land Use Planning in Washington, DC, in Chapter 4.

Not surprising, then, with all this attention to planning and the manifold details comprehensive planning requires, it is all-too-common lore in the District of Columbia and the surrounding Washington, DC, metropolitan area that the limit on the height of buildings within the District's boundaries was dictated by the height of the Capitol dome or by the need to preserve the visual prominence of the Washington Monument, consistent with L'Enfant's original vision for the nation's capital. However, nothing could be farther from the truth. Recalling the metaphor, from Chapter 3, of real estate law being like one's favorite cable television series, with fascinating characters telling an interesting story, in the following parable of Land Use Controls, the most interesting character is not a person but a building.

The original Height of Buildings Act of 1899, which was succeeded by the federal Height of Buildings Act of 1910, was initiated because of the visual irritant that was "The Cairo." Much like the completion of the Equitable Building in Manhattan twenty-one years later – the villain in the following vignette about how the nation's first comprehensive zoning law was passed – the completion of The Cairo in 1894 prompted an immediate outcry for greater Land Use Controls in the District of Columbia. And although the pretext for such greater Land Use Controls was limiting the height of buildings for public safety reasons, the undercurrent was that The Cairo was universally considered ugly.

> Contrary to popular belief, the structure that engendered the District of Columbia's first building height limitation was neither the Capitol nor the Washington Monument, but rather this bizarre, "Moorish" pile of bricks and limestone. At a height of more than 160 feet, the 12-story tower – the upper floors of which were beyond the reach of fire ladders available at the time – *so alarmed its neighbors* that they successfully lobbied the District's Board of Commissioners to enact restrictive zoning regulations in July 1894, before the building was even finished (the first federal legislative height restriction was enacted by Congress in 1899; the current law passed in 1910). In truth, the Cairo's opponents probably represented a strange alliance of architectural sophisticates appalled by its ungainly design and Luddites who feared that it was only a matter of time before such a "sky-scraper" would topple from sheer weight and hubris.[10]

The history of the Height of Buildings Act of 1910 may seem nothing more than a stroll down Memory Lane; a tangent in an otherwise dry and technical consideration of Land Use Controls. That might be a reasonable conclusion were it not for periodic efforts to revisit the merits of the District's overall height limitation imposed by the Height of Buildings Act of 1910, which constrains real estate development in *all* of the District's commercial corridors, including those geographically well removed from the city's Monumental Core. This tension also highlights one of the two planning paradigms offered at the outset of this chapter: *For whom and what is planning intended to benefit?* A recent joint examination, initiated by the U.S. Congress, of the Height of Buildings Act of 1910, by two planning organizations with completely different motivations in undertaking the review, demonstrates clearly this tension. This tension is fully on display in the preface each of these joint participants – the National Capital Planning Commission[11] and the Office of Planning of the District of Columbia[12] – provided in their respective reports.

The most recent reconsideration of the Height of Buildings Act of 1910 in Washington, DC, is only a few years old. It was an effort Congress initiated on October 3, 2012, to once again examine the impact of the Land Use Controls placing a cap on the overall height of buildings constructed within the boundaries of the District of Columbia.[13] Because of the unique nature of the governance of the District of Columbia, which has limited autonomy over its affairs because it also serves as the nation's capital, the requested review was undertaken jointly by the National Capital Planning Commission (NCPC) and the Office of Planning of the District of Columbia (the "Office of Planning"). Each delivered its own report to the House Committee on Oversight and Government Reform, which requested that the study be undertaken. Unsurprising, each took a different perspective on the potential impact of easing the height caps imposed under the Height of Buildings Act.

In its report, titled *Height Master Plan for Washington, DC: Federal Interest Report and Final Recommendations*, dated November 27, 2013 (hereinafter the "NCPC Federal Interest Report"), the NCPC took a very circumspect view of any potential future relaxation of the Height of Buildings Act:

> Over the long term, the Commission believes that there may be opportunities for strategic changes to the Height Act in areas outside of the L'Enfant City where there is less concentration of federal interests. However, the Commission recommends detailed and joint planning work through the Comprehensive Plan for the National Capital prior to proposing any changes to the law. *By contrast, the District recommends amending the law today* to allow for a process where targeted areas are identified and authorized to exceed the limits under the Height Act outside the L'Enfant City through the Comprehensive Plan.[14]

In its report, titled *Height Master Plan for the District of Columbia: FINAL EVALUATION & RECOMMENDATIONS*, dated November 20, 2013 (hereinafter the "DC Height Master Plan Recommendations"), the District of Columbia Office of Planning came to fundamentally different conclusions about the potential impact of the strategic relaxation of the Height of Buildings Act[15] and, accordingly, made fundamentally different recommendations, as alluded to in the previously quoted language from the NCPC Federal Interest Report:

> The District recommends retaining the Federal height limits outside the L'Enfant City *unless and until* the city amends the District Elements of its Comprehensive Plan to allow heights above 130 feet or otherwise above the current federal limits; that Comprehensive Plan is approved by the Council of the District of Columbia; the NCPC approves those amendments; and after submittal to Congress, that Comprehensive Plan is approved by Congress. The District also *recommends allowing some streets within the L'Enfant City to have additional height* in a manner that retains the characteristic relationship between street width and building height, ensuring light, air and a human-scaled city, but uncapped by 19th century fire safety constraints.[16]

The District of Columbia generally has autonomy over land use and zoning issues within its boundaries, other than on federal land, which comprises a substantial proportion of the District.[17] However, because the Height of Buildings Act of 1910 is a federal law, it will take an act of Congress – as the saying goes, but this time without the usual hyperbole – to make what would be the most dramatic change in the Land Use Controls of the District impacting commercial real estate development in one of the ten largest commercial real estate markets in the United States.

In its *Height Master Plan* recommendations, the District's Office of Planning presented very compelling modelling of the undeveloped areas of the District, relative to projected growth demand and considering several alternatives for expanding the aggregate building envelope for what constitutes the undeveloped areas of the District based on incremental expansions of the Height of Buildings Act. The Office of Planning report to the House Committee on Oversight and Government Reform suggests a difference of *285.6 million square feet* in the "Net Development Capacity" of the District of Columbia between the status quo and the most aggressive, maximum Net Development Capacity (by eliminating all height caps under the Height of Buildings Act). Assuming, for the purposes of establishing an order of magnitude for this analysis, an average value of only $200 per square foot of this available Net Development Capacity, this maximum increase translates to *$71.12 trillion in commercial real estate value*.[18] Anyone who, at this point, still questions the relevance and importance of Land Use and Zoning Law specifically, and land use planning in general, to the value proposition of real estate development should perhaps close this textbook and consider other career options.

Even a less aggressive relaxation of the building height caps, which leaves the status quo in place for the Federal City but raises building heights incrementally, depending on location, between 200 and 250 feet, yields 255.7 million square feet of Net Development Capacity, for an increase in the overall value of commercial real estate in the District, under the same assumptions as earlier, by *$51.14 trillion*. The potential fiscal benefits to the District of Columbia by increasing its commercial real estate tax base by more than $50 trillion cannot be overstated. Of course, the ripple effects on the District's economy from having an additional quarter billion square feet of commercial office space occupied – and the concomitant fiscal benefits to the District from the increases in tax revenue collections, beyond real estate taxes – could be transformative for the nation's capital.

THE POWER OF A STRONG VISION

Washington, DC, is, indeed, one of the world's most beautiful cities; at least the parts that most tourists, workers, and Washingtonians see on a regular basis. Like cities in every major metropolitan area, Washington, DC, has its areas of extreme poverty and severe distress of the built environment.

The beauty and powerful image of the nation's capital was by no means a foregone conclusion during the first 150 years of the city's evolution, however. Indeed, looking at some of the historical depictions and verbal accounts of the development of the Federal City, it's hard to fathom how the city turned out as well as it did.

As the city continues to evolve to meet the needs and demands of a modern, twenty-first-century city in a major metropolitan area, facing challenges such as those reflected in the tensions between the *Height Master Plan* reports between NCPC and the District's Office of Planning, it is worthwhile to take a moment to recognize and praise the power of formulating and articulating a strong vision for the Federal City, starting with Washington's decision to commission L'Enfant to draw up a plan. Granted, the L'Enfant Plan has had many valuable contributions made to its improvement over more than two centuries. However, the essence of what L'Enfant envisioned in 1792 is still very much intact in the second decade of the twenty-first century, having made a lasting impact on everything that has come after it. The strength of the vision L'Enfant articulated for the Federal City, and the dedication to that vision by hundreds of politicians, planners, architects, engineers, historians, artists, "technical experts" (to quote Hugh Ferris), and bureaucrats who worked with and followed L'Enfant, is proof positive of the power of a strong vision in shaping the built environment and in influencing real estate development and finance.

Naturally, the question arises from time to time: How far can that vision be pushed to comport with the demands of the contemporary world without being violated to the point where Washington, DC, loses its inherent qualities of organizational and aesthetic beauty?

To understand the broad implications of this blunt instrument of Land Use Control that is the Height of Buildings Act of 1910, and to consider the tensions between the NCPC and the DC Office of Planning *Height Master Plan* reports in a different context, try imagining the following parallel universe: What if, rather than evoking visual horror, The Cairo had *inspired* Washingtonians to emulate their New York City counterparts in embracing the skyscraper as the preferred form for commercial and residential building type, which building type is flourishing – and reaching new heights – once again throughout the United States. In the late nineteenth and early twentieth centuries, New York City was by no means alone in exploring the skyscraper as the epitome of efficiency and progress, and a proud symbol of America's unique inventiveness and audacity. Once could easily argue, in fact, that the skyscraper, starting out as a uniquely American invention, is as representative of what the United States represented at the turn of the nineteenth century as the Declaration of Independence was in 1776 (and that, accordingly, the skyscraper is just as valid a symbol of the country and its capital city as the Washington Monument or the halls of Congress).

Chicago was the early epicenter of skyscraper design and construction.[19] Many of the preeminent city planners and architects of the First Chicago School, the moniker given to a group of architects who pioneered the skyscraper, were also involved in the creation of a new vision for the United States through the World's Columbian Exposition of 1893, including Daniel H. Burnham and his partner, John Wellborn Root, of Burnham & Root; Dankmar Adler and Louis Sullivan of Adler & Sullivan; and landscape architect Frederick Law Olmstead. Many of these key figures also made their mark in New York City and Washington, DC.

Burnham, for example, designed Washington, DC's Union Station, as well as New York City's iconic Flatiron Building. Olmstead was involved in the creation of the MacMillan Plan for the Federal City in Washington, DC, on the 100th anniversary of the L'Enfant Plan. Burnham also designed a sixty-two-story skyscraper for the site of the Equitable Life Assurance Company's New York City headquarters, which was never built. However, shortly after Burnham's untimely death, a partner in his New York City architectural office, Ernest R. Graham, designed the building that eventually led to the enactment of the New York City Zoning Resolution of 1916. Clearly, then, the First Chicago School of architecture and its adherents had a tremendous impact on other parts of the country, as well as on the evolution of its early principal cities.

Closer to home, Baltimore[20] also enjoyed its share of late nineteenth-century and early twentieth-century skyscrapers, as did Philadelphia, a mere 120 miles north of the District. But for the District, The Cairo was – for all intents and purposes – the beginning *and the end* of Washington, DC's flirtation with this uniquely American building type.[21]

What if, instead of The Cairo, the District's first skyscraper had been designed by Daniel Burnham or Louis Sullivan? That one difference – a new, twelve-story building at which residents of the District marveled rather than from which they recoiled – might have altered dramatically the eventual skyline of the nation's capital. Such a dramatic change in the course of the evolution of the District's commercial core also would have generated an exponential increase in the aggregate size and value of the District's commercial properties into the twenty-first century, perhaps even well beyond what the District of Columbia's Office of Planning modeled and projected in its 2012 DC *Height Master Plan* recommendations.[22]

The One Bad Building Rule and its corollary, the One Good Building Rule

Students and readers, in considering the tremendous impact Land Use Controls may and often do have on The Development Process generally, should also be mindful of one of the great lessons to be learned from The Cairo: the "One Bad Building Rule." It takes only *one bad building or one bad project idea* to energize the public's involvement in the land use and zoning process, getting them fully engaged in *making sure that land use and zoning ordinances serve the entire community, and not just the Developer's "Idea."*[23] The One Bad Building Rule is also illustrated by the discussion that follows about New York City's Equitable Building, which served as the catalyst for the eventual adoption of comprehensive zoning-enabling legislation across the United States, as well as the adoption of comprehensive municipal zoning ordinances throughout the country, through the promulgation of national model enabling acts for states and municipalities, sparked by the adoption of New York City's 1916 Zoning Resolution.

As a corollary to the One Bad Building Rule, it is equally important to understand the "One Good Building Rule." All it takes is *the loss of one good building* to enrage and activate public sentiment and engagement about the built environment and the Land Use Controls that shape it. An excellent example of the One Good Building Rule follows.

New York City and its love affair with Pennsylvania Station. Robert Moses, New York City's revered and reviled "Master Builder," through a series of State of New York commissions and appointments, wielded almost unlimited power over planning and construction in the city. He became so brazen in his large-scale project plans throughout New York City, and elsewhere within the Empire State, that in the early 1960s he garnered growing criticism of his oftentimes heavy-handed urban renewal approach.

However, it was the proposed demolition of New York City's beloved Pennsylvania Station – that "One Good Building" – that galvanized growing opposition to Moses generally and his overall "urban removal" approach and tactics. Moses became the primary target of rising vocal criticism from fledgling urbanist Jane Jacobs, spawning a new movement promoting a more intimate urbanism advocating for the preservation of neighborhoods. In this respect, the proposed demolition of Penn Station and the controversy that surrounds it is emblematic of the second planning paradigm offered earlier in this chapter: how planners go about their business. Moses was the twentieth century's poster child for Project Planning, which in the second half of the twentieth century was most actively practiced during the period of the federal Urban Renewal Program; Jacobs, for her part, was the City's most vocal advocate for preserving neighborhoods and encouraging their organic growth. This is the same tension illuminated in Roberta Gratz Brandes' *Cities Back from the Edge*, which opens Chapter 3. Looking at the 100-year history of the professional practice of planning, and its impact on The Development Process, always seems to be a reflection of the prevailing wisdom of its time on whether planning should be more fine-grained, more organic, and more neighborhood-oriented, or whether it should be more visionary, citywide, or even regional in its potential impact, and a function of Project Planning.

The fight over the proposed demolition of New York's Penn Station also galvanized a growing movement for the preservation of New York City's historic buildings, which ultimately influenced a national, historic preservation movement in the United States. Although Robert Moses won his battle, and historic Penn Station was demolished to make way for the new Madison Square Garden, the grassroots effort to preserve Penn Station resulted in the passage of New York's Landmark Law of 1965, which in turn served as the model for the National Historic Preservation Act of 1966. The national historic preservation law has had a remarkable impact on the evolution of a majority of U.S. cities, particularly on the East Coast and in the Midwest, in terms of requiring the preservation of historic commercial buildings that today give those cities much of their enduring character. In this way, the demolition of New York's Penn Station, which derailed Moses' career while serving as the springboard for Jacobs', is a fitting example of the One Good Building Rule and its far-reaching implications.

As suggested earlier, and presented in greater detail in the discussion that follows, Manhattan's 1915 Equitable Building is an example of the One Bad Building Rule. One hundred years later, will Extell Development's One57, also discussed later, become the latest New York City skyscraper to earn the One Bad Building moniker, serving as the catalyst for another grassroots, land use planning movement, this time to seek limitations on the ambitions of hyper-skyscraper developers by lobbying the city's Planning Commission to make it more difficult to get them approved in Manhattan?

Defending the value of light, air, and views: how Manhattan's 1915 Equitable Building served as the catalyst for the United States' comprehensive zoning laws

It is a fundamental, underlying premise of this chapter that students and readers not only come to know, by way of a few, selected examples presented herein, how planning and zoning – the *process* of developing, enacting, and applying Land Use Controls – impact real estate development (and vice versa), but also come to a deeper understanding of the episodic – some would argue periodic or even cyclical – social and political forces that occur to reshape the prevailing Land Use Controls toward far different means and ends than the ones they replace. In this respect, this chapter presents, by intention, a series of history lessons on the evolution of city form, as well as the evolution of the planning profession. By understanding the interplay of such forces, and how that interplay results in changes in the regulatory environment and their impact on The Development Process, Developers may not only more effectively anticipate such changes but *participate actively in shaping such resulting regulations of land use*.

It has been argued, over the more than 100 years that professional planning has existed as a discipline in the United States, that not only do planning and land use shape real estate development but *real estate development shapes land use and planning*. These mirror-image axioms are perhaps no better illustrated than by the construction of the Equitable Building in New York City, which was completed in 1915, and the controversy that ensued over it.

Before beginning the journey toward understanding the significance of the relationship of the construction of the Equitable Building to the emergence of professional planning and the enactment of state and municipal zoning ordinances, it is important to set the stage historically regarding the form and evolution of cities in the United States up to the mid-nineteenth century, following the end of the Civil War but before the beginning of the next significant phase of urban development characterized by the "rise of the skyscraper."

Prior to adoption by the New York State Legislature of the Commissioners' Plan of 1811 for New York City, the location and construction of buildings in New York City, as well as the development of the city proper as a cohesive place, was relatively ad hoc, even chaotic, some would argue. There were no zoning ordinances or land use regulations to follow, as the concept had yet to be invented and would not come to fruition for more than 100 years. There was no regulating plan for how streets would be laid out or how the size of buildable parcels would be determined. Although there were a few "plans" for New York City streets prior to this time – the Taylor-Roberts Map of 1797, the Mangin-Goerck Plan of 1801, and the Bridges Plan of 1807, which were each commissioned but never adopted as legislative enactments – the Commissioners' Plan of 1811 was the first comprehensive street and plat plan organizing the entirety of what was then New York City proper, comprised on the island of Manhattan. Urban planners and real estate developers have described the Commissioners' Plan of 1811 as the most important document in the development of New York City because of its imposition of the "gridiron" – an orthogonal network of streets creating primarily rectangular lots – establishing buildable parcels. Absent the aggregation and merger of those lots into larger lots, building sizes were, for the most part, determined by the lot sizes of the Commissioners' Plan of 1811, without any zoning, land use, or building regulations to speak of trying to accomplish those same ends.

After the end of the Civil War, and just under sixty years after the adoption by the New York State Legislature of the Commissioners' Plan of 1811, the Equitable Life Assurance Society of the United States constructed its headquarters building, located at 120 Broadway in Manhattan. The Equitable Life Assurance Building, as it came to be known, was completed in May 1870 and served as the offices of numerous, well-established New York bankers and lawyers, in addition to the insurance company's headquarters. At 130 feet tall, it was the country's first "skyscraper," and the first commercial building served by hydraulic passenger elevators, which go hand in hand in order for skyscraper occupants to be able to comfortably reach the upper floors. In the early morning hours of January 9, 1912, a fire was accidentally started in a ground-floor café in the building and quickly spread to the upper floors through the building's elevator shafts and dumbwaiter systems, which essentially serve as airshafts during a fire, facilitating its rapid spread throughout a multistory building. Claims that, because of the construction materials used in building it, the Equitable Building was "fireproof" notwithstanding, within four hours of the start of the fire on the ground floor, the Equitable Building was a total loss. The fire claimed six lives. Ironically, the fact that fire ladders at the time could not reach the top floors of the Equitable Building, the fire, as well as the consequent loss of life – including Battalion Fire Chief William Walsh – important personal property, and the building itself, sparked a debate about the safety of this new building form, "the skyscraper." Perhaps this was a foreshadowing of the role the Equitable Life Assurance Company, and its penchant for creating unique, signature buildings, would have on the future of planning, zoning, and commercial building construction in New York City.

Ironically, even before the fire that destroyed the "fireproof" Equitable Building, the insurance company had decided to build a new, more modern headquarters on the same site, 120 Broadway, and commissioned Daniel H. Burnham to design the new building. At the time in New York City, life insurance companies had become a considerable force in the construction of skyscrapers, and engaged in a quiet competition through the architecture of their buildings. The CEO of the insurance company wanted a headquarters building that would rival and exceed the tallest among the New York City skyscrapers: The Singer Building, the Metropolitan Life Tower, and the Woolworth Building. Burnham's design for a sixty-two-story tower on the site at 120 Broadway was never realized, however. Having been commissioned and delivered prior to the fire that destroyed the original Equitable Building, Burnham's design was viewed as an overly ambitious and bold undertaking not suited to an insurance company that had just suffered a catastrophic loss of documents and lives. Accordingly, after the fire, the company's president vowed to never again engage in such an extravagant venture.

Instead, the Equitable Life Assurance Company decided to sell the property to a developer, the recently retired president of E.I. du Pont de Nemours & Company and a du Pont heir, who had expressed an interest in the site and had already invested in another New York City operating property. By the time the transaction was consummated, du Pont had enlisted two other partners, who would also be involved in the construction of the speculative office building on the site. In conveying the site at 120 Broadway to the developer, Equitable took back a mortgage, thereby providing the financing for the sale of its property instead of requiring that the three developers pay cash for the transaction.

Equitable agreed to become an anchor tenant in the new building, leasing three contiguous floors for a period of twenty years. Equitable also provided a substantial amount of the construction financing for the speculative office building in which its headquarters would be located, perhaps presaging a very long history of life insurance companies entering into financing and investment partnerships with developers, providing the permanent financing for and/or acquiring newly developed commercial real properties for their investment portfolios.[24]

Because Equitable was no longer in charge of the project and its president had decided not to pursue Burnham's sixty-two-story office tower design, the developers decided to give commission for the design of the Equitable Building to Ernest R. Graham, a principal architect in Burnham's New York City architectural office. Burnham had died in a car accident in Germany in 1912. Given the new client and new program, Graham's primary design motivation was to make the Equitable Building a successful speculative office building, emphasizing its efficiency and maximizing the amount of office space available for lease. Graham's design is considered a success in achieving these two design goals.[25]

In 1915, when the Equitable Building was completed, it stood at 545 feet in height.[26] While not the tallest commercial office building in the world at the time of its completion, the Equitable Building was the *largest* office building in the world in terms of its overall size, and it held that distinction for thirteen years. However, neither its height nor its total floor area is as remarkable as the furor the building caused because it occupied nearly the full "building envelope" represented by its buildable lot, a term that did not exist in the real estate community until after the building's completion.

Although it appears to be composed of two separate towers, the Equitable Building is actually H-shaped in plan: two towers connected by a wing approximately halfway between the back and front of each tower. This design increases the number of windows on the "inside" of each tower while allowing the floors of each tower to be connected. However, it also means that, unlike two separate towers, no light passes through the H-shaped design.

The Equitable Building was (and is) massive. It comprised 1.2 million square feet of leasable space and was capable of accommodating 16,000 occupants, which was the size of a large town or small city at the time. At 545 feet tall, the Equitable Building blocks out the sunlight, and the oppressive shadows it casts on neighboring buildings and the streets and sidewalks below caused a public outcry even before the two-year construction of the building commenced, merely based on the plans for the building.

> It was said that the Equitable blocked ventilation, dumped 13,000 users onto nearby sidewalks, choked the local transit facilities, and created potential problems for firemen. The Equitable's noon shadow, someone complained, enveloped six times its own area. Stretching almost a fifth of a mile, it cut off direct sunlight from the Broadway fronts of buildings as tall as 21 stories. The darkened area extended four blocks to the north. Most of the surrounding property owners claimed a loss of rental income because so much light and air had been deflected by the massive new building, and they filed for a reduction in the assessed valuations of their properties.[27]

No zoning and land use code existed at the time of the Equitable Building's design and construction – that is, there were no Land Use Controls – to keep the insurance company from building its new headquarters, or any other subsequently constructed commercial buildings in Manhattan, for that matter, built out to the boundaries of its lot (i.e., taking up 100% of the building envelope to the full height of the building).[28] At the time of its construction, critics of this bad precedent being set by the Equitable Building – having no setbacks from its front or side parcel boundaries – imagined that other landowners, desiring to maximize the returns realized from their buildings, would want to do the same, eventually creating block after block of opaque curtains of skyscrapers that would block out the sun and fresh air from the streets and sidewalks below, casting lesser buildings in complete shadow for most of the day. Imposing minimum setback requirements – such that as a building rises from its base its physical footprint becomes narrower than its base – would assure that no more buildings would be designed and built to emulate the Equitable Building. And so it was that, in reaction to this One Bad Building, things were set in motion to develop and enact New York City's, and the United States', first comprehensive zoning and land use code to make sure there would never be another skyscraper built in New York City like the Equitable Building.

Discussions about adopting some form of skyscraper-building regulation in New York City were taking place prior to the proposal to build the Graham-designed Equitable Building. In fact, the architect who designed the tallest, built skyscraper in New York City at the time – Ernest Flagg and the Singer Building (headquarters of the Singer Sewing Machine Company), respectively – was at the forefront of this effort.[29] However, the proposal for the construction of the Equitable Building, and the growing controversy about its combined height and massing without setbacks, accelerated and intensified the process. During the hearings held in 1915 by the Committee on the Limitation of Height and Area of the Building Code Revision Commission of New York City regarding the proposed adoption of zoning regulations for commercial buildings, the Equitable Building became the poster child for why the proposed zoning regulations were imperative. Serving as a veritable whipping boy for those testifying before the Commission, the hearings provided those offended by the Equitable Building's very existence a public opportunity to heap their scorn upon the building and its developers.

To say that the Report of the Height of Buildings Commission to the Committee on the Height, Size and Arrangement of Buildings of the Board of Estimate and Apportionment of the City of New York (hereinafter the "Height of Buildings Commission Report") was a substantial, well-researched, and thoughtfully considered document would be an unforgiveable understatement.[30] In its published form, as a bound volume, the Height of Buildings Commission Report is 295 pages long; its table of contents alone is four pages long, and not only details the substantive contents of the report itself but also lists numerous appendices, public statements, diagrams, and maps relating to the Commission's exhaustive work. Attempting a summary of the Height of Buildings Commission Report here could not possibly do it justice. However, the overall impact of the Height of Buildings Commission Report was clear: New York City needed to regulate its built environment and it needed to do so immediately. Although the Equitable Building has been identified as a culprit in the necessity of such zoning and land use regulation, Fifth Avenue is highlighted in the report as being particularly imperiled absent some immediate regulatory action by the city.

> The Commission finds conclusive evidence of the need of greater public control of building development. The present almost unrestricted power to build to any height, over any proportion of the lot, for any desired use and in any part of the city, has resulted in injury to real estate and business interests, and to the health, safety and general welfare of the city.[31]

The Height of Buildings Commission Report, for illustrative purposes, theoretically applies the Commission's proposed regulation of building areas and building heights (the latter being somewhat a function of the former) to eight commercial skyscrapers, including: 1) the Singer Building (which, as the reader may recall, was initially the "goalpost" that the Burnham design for 120 Broadway, and the insurance company's new headquarters, was expected to move past); 2) the Equitable Building as designed by Graham, which was, at the time of the Report's issuance, well under construction; and 3) what, over time, has become one of the most iconic commercial buildings in Manhattan, the Flatiron Building, also designed by Burnham. The theoretical application of the Commission's proposed regulations to two of these three buildings are depicted in Diagram 6 (Equitable Building), and Diagram 10 (the Flatiron Building, aka the Fuller Building); no diagram was produced for the Singer Building.

The section of the Height of Buildings Commission Report that discussed the application of the Commission's recommendations regarding the allowable heights and areas (i.e., aggregate square footage of all of the floors), including the drawings, appearing as a series of numbered Diagrams in the report, showing how those recommendations would impact existing or planned buildings, provides an excellent opportunity for students and readers to fully comprehend how Land Use Planning and Zoning Law affects The Development Process. This section of the Height of Buildings Commission Report is literally a before-and-after look at New York City's real estate development at the turn of the century, showing how each developer would treat a particular development opportunity *before* the city had enacted any significant Land Use Controls – because those developers had, in fact, done just that with those buildings featured in the report – and how those same buildings would look *after* the application of proposed Land Use Controls.

The Equitable Building, for its part, would be largely unrecognizable based on the application to the building, at that point under construction, of the Commission's recommendations for specific setbacks, floor-by-floor reductions in building volume, and "courtyards" on upper floors. Among other changes, at the twentieth floor, the recommended Land Use Control in the Height of Buildings Commission Report would have required that the two towers of the Equitable Building be merged into a single tower, because, at a specified height, a tower with floor areas no larger than 25% of the lot size were permitted. Clearly, no architect would design, from scratch, the building that would have emerged if the Equitable Building had merely "adapted" its current plan to the limitation of the Commission recommendations. Nonetheless, Diagram 6 in the report is very instructive in terms of understanding the impact of Land Use Controls on The Development Process and on real estate development projects. Selected excerpts from the 1916 Zoning Resolution, a discussion of the first model-enabling act for zoning at the state and local levels, and a brief history of professional planning practice in the United States are available on the companion website.

The impact of the International Style of architecture on the Manhattan skyline and New York City's 1960 Zoning Resolution

Reining in the unbridled exuberance of real estate developers. Although their goals were certainly laudable, and they approached their charge with rationality, diligence, and due seriousness, the Height of Buildings Commission and its Report recommendations once translated into the New York City Zoning Resolution of 1916, *changed the way skyscrapers had to be designed*. Fortunately for the development community, the prevalent styles of architecture at the time – the spare classicism frequently associated with the First Chicago School (the Equitable Building), the Beaux-Arts style (the Municipal Building), American Art Deco style (the Barclay-Vesey Building and, in 1930, the city's most iconic skyscraper, the Chrysler Building), and the Gothic style (the Woolworth Building) – largely relied on a tripartite composition or "classical order," consisting of 1) a well-defined base, 2) a middle comprising a substantial proportion of the building's volume, and 3) a cornice, entablature, or top. As suggested later, this facilitated an easy transition for developers and their architects in the implementation phase of the 1916 Zoning Resolution.

A natural fit between public goals and the desire to create "signature" buildings. Based on the architecture of ancient Greece, specifically the composition of each of three "classical Greek columns" – the Ionic, Doric, and Corinthian – and on the design of the Parthenon on the Acropolis in Athens, this approach to building composition or "form" has permeated construction and building design ever since.[32] Regardless of the actual style of the building being designed, the classical Greek form dovetailed extremely well with the 1916 Zoning Resolution prescriptions regarding formulaic setback, courtyards, and lot-coverage-ratio requirements. Accordingly, the 1916 Zoning Resolution did not have a profoundly negative impact on real estate development in the several decades immediately following its passage (although developers who favored the approach of maximizing yield epitomized by the Equitable Building would surely disagree), despite the fact that those buildings designed and constructed following its implementation took on more of a "wedding cake" form as a consequence of the setback requirements.

Meanwhile, in Post–World War I Europe . . . Toward the end of the second decade of the twentieth century, not long after the end of World War I (or the enactment of the 1916 Zoning Ordinance, for that matter), new ideas began to emerge in Europe, primarily in postwar Germany, but also in France and a few other countries, regarding the role of the arts, including architecture, in improving people's lives. By comparison, although the improvement of the health and general welfare of the public was most certainly a principal, motivating factor in the framing and enactment of the 1916 Zoning Ordinance, the committee charged with that task was *broadly composed*, including representatives from the real estate development and finance communities, respectively. By contrast, despite these emerging social and artistic movements in Europe, however, no such economic or otherwise pragmatic influences or filters were at play.

What would eventually coalesce from this new thinking came to be labelled, by the first director of the Museum of Modern Art in New York City, Albert Barr, as the "International Style," and it had a tremendous influence on architects in the Unites States and on the skylines of a number of the country's largest cities. Many of the pioneers of the International Style – Bruno Taut, Walter Gropius, Ludwig Mies Van de Rohe, Le Corbusier – either eventually emigrated to the United States and joined the faculty of prestigious architecture schools or designed or collaborated on new buildings in the International Style. Additionally, many domestically trained architects already practicing in the United States – Phillip Johnson, I. M. Pei, and Louis Kahn among them – embraced the International Style, and also became some of the most influential architects in the second half of the twentieth century in the United States.

Unintended, or at least unanticipated, consequences of the 1916 Zoning Ordinance. So, what does the 1916 Zoning Ordinance have to do with the skyline of Manhattan after World War II? William Lescaze's 1931 PSFS Building is considered to reflect the first application of the International Style in the world, and it is curious that such an application did not occur in the urban contexts of either the original epicenter of the building type, Chicago, or the largest collection of skyscrapers, New York. Raymond Hood's McGraw-Hill Building in New York City, completed in 1932, is also considered an early expression of the International Style, although it also has features consistent with both classical architecture, in terms of its composition (having a base, middle, and top, each being well-articulated), as well as with *Streamline Moderne*, reflecting the end of the Art Deco period (with the base and top of the McGraw-Hill Building reflecting its Art Deco influences for which Hood was best known). By contrast, the PSFS Building is more monolithic and unlike the McGraw-Hill Building, almost completely lacking in ornament and is, as such, a much better representation of the International Style. While the prevalent design forms for, and the architectural styles of, the skyscrapers designed and built in New York City prior to and immediately after enactment of the 1916 Zoning Resolution were easily reconciled to the new zoning law's requirements, there was nothing "wedding cake" about the International Style.

The International Style's primary introduction to New York was not, in fact, through the design and erection of a new building but, as referenced earlier, via the 1932 exhibition at New York's Museum of Modern Art (MOMA) titled *Modern Architecture – International Exhibition*. The exhibition was curated by architectural historian Henry-Russell Hitchcock and Harvard grad (Philosophy) Phillip Johnson, who later went on to his own remarkable career as a self-taught architect employing the International Style. Lescaze's PSFS Building was featured in the MOMA exhibition, as was Hood's McGraw-Hill Building. These were the only skyscrapers featured in the exhibition.

PUTTING THE EMPIRE STATE BUILDING INTO ITS HISTORIC AND REGULATORY CONTEXT

It would be bad form, as well as irresponsible, to entertain any discussion about the advent of the 1916 Zoning Ordinance in New York City and its impact on the Manhattan skyline without paying homage to New York's most iconic building: the Empire State Building. Completed in 1931, and in seemingly record time, it maintained its preeminence as the world's tallest building for more than forty years, from 1938 until 1972, when the first of the two World Trade Center towers was completed.

Interestingly, contrasting the form of these two buildings – the Empire State Building and the slightly taller of the fraternal twin World Trade Center towers – could perhaps serve as the Cliff Notes version of the evolution of the 1916 Zoning Resolution to New York City's 1961 Zoning Ordinance,[33] which remains in effect today (see following discussion of the 1961 Zoning Ordinance). The World Trade Center Twin Towers were very much a reflection of the International Style. By contrast, the Empire State Building may accurately be referred to as 1) the epitome of the building form or composition dictated by the setbacks, lot coverage ratios, and "courtyards" dictated by the 1916 Zoning Ordinance and 2) reflective of the transition of the architectural style of New York City skyscrapers from the more ornate styles that had dominated the Manhattan skyline – the First Chicago School (the Equitable Building), the Beaux-Arts style (Municipal Building), American Art Deco style (the Barclay-Vesey Building and, in 1930, the city's most iconic skyscraper, the Chrysler Building), and the Gothic style (the Woolworth Building) – to the International Style to come. Curiously, however, the Empire State Building was not included in the MOMA exhibition, *Modern Architecture – International Exhibition*, despite the fact that it is, arguably, more reflective of the International Style than Raymond Hood's McGraw-Hill Building, which was included in the exhibition.

At least three additional facets of the design, construction, and operation of the Empire State Building are worthy of note in the context of The Development Process.

- The Empire State Building was completed two years *after* the crash of the New York Stock Exchange, aka "Black Tuesday," which marks the official beginning of the Great Depression. This is in part a reflection of the long lead time between when the "Idea" is first conceived – the first Sub-Phase of the Project Conception Phase of The Development Process – and the contractual commitment to building the resultant Project or risk financial repercussions for breaches of contracts and claims for promised returns by lenders and investors.
- The sparseness of ornament of the completed Empire State Building that marks its position in the transition from all the skyscrapers that preceded it and the International Style buildings that followed is that this design approach may have been more a reflection of the developer's desire to have the Empire State Building constructed as efficiently, as quickly, and as inexpensively as possible. This offers an excellent example for students and readers of the intersection of design and financial feasibility.
- The long run of "The Empty State Building" is largely ignored except by more mature veterans of the Manhattan commercial real estate market. The Empire State Building could not have come "online" at a worse time in terms of the market cycle in New York City's commercial core. Vacancy rates were at historic highs, and that wasn't merely a reflection of those stock traders and investment bankers who vacated their Wall Street offices via the windows on Black Tuesday. To add insult to injury, the significantly reduced demand for commercial office space was greatly exacerbated by other skyscrapers coming online about the same time, such as the Chrysler Building, as well as existing skyscrapers, such as the Equitable Building (built as a spec office building and offering 1.2 million square feet). A glut of available office space combined with a precipitous decline in demand for office space in Manhattan meant that for many, many years after its completion, the Empire State Building was never fully occupied, earning it the moniker the "Empty State Building."

After its run in New York City, MOMA's *Modern Architecture – International Exhibition* traveled the United States for six years, making it the most widely exhibited art exhibition up to that point in time. Despite its impact on the thinking and vision of practicing architects and architecture students alike, and the inspiration the exhibition sparked throughout the nation, New York City did not see physical evidence of the International Style, in the form of new skyscrapers, until the early 1950s. Just as the United States was starting to come out of the Great Depression, it was confronted with growing domestic concerns about the run-up to the start of World War II, beginning with Adolph Hitler's election to the leadership of the Nazi Party in 1930, followed by the start of open hostilities in Czechoslovakia and Spain, respectively, in 1937. Upon the United States' decision to enter the war on December 8, 1941, the construction and manufacturing sectors of the U.S. economy fully focused on the war effort: Designing and building audacious skyscrapers was not at the forefront of the development community's mind.

A skyscraper for the modern world: Lever House, the Seagram Building, and the Time-Life Building. Following the end of World War II, the United States entered a period of great invention and productivity, with the manufacturing capacity built up during the war effort in the United States turning to domestic production of consumer, business, and industrial goods and products. This economic growth and prosperity led to the design and development of three landmark office buildings in the International Style: Lever House, the Seagram Building, and the Time-Life Building. These buildings were, however, dramatically different in composition and appearance than Manhattan's McGraw-Hill Building or Philadelphia's PSFS Building, both of which had previously been included in the MOMA exhibition as U.S. examples of the International Style. The collision in the early 1950s of Manhattan's building boom in the International Style with the 1916 Zoning Resolution proved a happy accident. The rule of the 1916 Zoning Resolution allowing only a tower form above a specified height, with a volume no larger than 25% of the lot area (intended to define the volume and form of a tower on top of the wedding cake of a building), found a completely different application in the austere and monolithic forms of the International Style, which used 75% of the lot area for grandiose public plazas of low-rise building elements that made their monolithic towers that much more impressive. Ironically, then, at least in this regard, the city's and the country's first zoning ordinance, intended of putting a cap on the heights of New York City's skyscrapers became the catalyst for an entirely new skyscraper form, pushing building heights ever skyward. However, as discussed in another section of this chapter (see Taking Urban Living to New Heights), even these dramatically new examples of the International Style the latest iteration of the Manhattan skyscraper, would less than a decade-and-a-half latter be completely dwarfed by the World Trade Center's Twin Towers (completed in 1972 and 1974, respectively), by One World Trade Center – which in 2015 replaced the Twin Towers (brought down by a terrorist attack on September 11, 2001) – and by Midtown's One57, located at 157 W. 57th Street.

By 1961, the City decided that the 1916 Zoning Resolution was no longer compatible with the new postwar era in commercial building in New York City, and replaced it with a new zoning code that was less prescriptive in the form that new buildings would be required to take; instead focusing on the relationship between the building envelope and the size of the lot on which it was to be built. As will be shown, the 1961 Zoning Resolution has, since its adoption, been challenged and amended in order to permit ever denser development, with buildings reaching dizzying heights once again.

From "Edge City" to connected WalkUPs: how comprehensive planning and updated Land Use Controls are changing the character of Tysons Corner, Virginia

In his groundbreaking 1991 book, *Edge Cities*, author Joel Garreau posited that the suburban sprawl that started with the proliferation of the bedroom communities that lured the white flight leaving America's cities had evolved into the country's next urban form. Garreau counts among the leading example of America's new Edge Cities Tysons Corner, just outside the Capital Beltway in northern Virginia. Garreau describes the advent of Edge Cities as follows:

> Edge Cities represent the third wave of our lives pushing into new frontiers in this half century. First, we moved our homes out past the traditional idea of what constituted a city. This was the suburbanization of America, especially after World War II.
>
> Then we wearied of returning downtown for the necessities of life, so we moved our marketplaces out to where we lived. This was the malling of America, especially in the 1960s and 1970s.

Today, we have moved our means of creating wealth, the essence of urbanism – our jobs – out to where most of us have lived and shopped for two generations. That has led to the rise of Edge City.[34]

Garreau offers, in *Edge City: Life on the New Frontier*, a five-part definition of what is an "Edge City," which he describes as a place:

1. That has *5 million square feet* or more of commercial office space.
2. That has *600,000 square feet* or more of retail space.
3. That has *more jobs than bedrooms*.
4. That is generally *perceived as a single "place."*
5. That has been *dramatically transformed* in the past thirty years or so.

In designating Tysons Corner, Virginia, as the quintessential Edge City, Garreau notes the Tysons Corner area's strategic geographic location between the Department of Defense's headquarters at the Pentagon, in Arlington County, Virginia, and Dulles International Airport, which brought direct international flights to the Washington, DC, area upon its completion in 1962. The thirteen-and-a-half-mile Dulles Access Road connected the international airport with the recently completed Capital Beltway, one interchange away from the first of two Tysons Corner interchanges on the Capital Beltway, making the Tysons area very accessible by car, and making the new airport very accessible from the Tysons Corner area. When the planned Interstate 66 was completed in 1983, the remaining two-and-a-half-mile stretch of the originally planned sixteen-mile Dulles Access Road was completed and connected with the new interstate.

Much of the suburban-style corporate campus development in the Tysons Corner area was initially undertaken by so-called Beltway Bandits, defense contractors having their principal business with various branches of the U.S. military, all headquartered at the Pentagon. Adding to the growing presence in Tysons Corner of the corporate campuses of defense contractors, in 1969 a partnership between two Washington-area developers – Isadore Gudelsky and Theodore Lerner – opened the Fashion Centre at Tysons Corner, a "super-regional," which at the time was billed as the United States' largest, fully enclosed, climate-controlled shopping mall. Comprised of 1.2 million square feet of retail space at the time, a subsequent renovation, adding a lower floor, increased the size of what was renamed "Tysons Corner Center" to 2.1 million square feet. When combined with the 800,000 square feet of high-end retail space at the Galleria at Tysons Corner, on the north side of Virginia State Route 123, a major arterial connecting northwest Washington, DC, with the northern Virginia suburbs, the Tysons area represents one of the largest retail areas in the country, with well over 3 million square feet of retail space within a one-half-mile radius of the intersection of Route 123 and Virginia State Route 7.

Contrary to the premise of Garreau's book, however, the Fairfax County government, and many landowners and business leaders located in the Tysons Corner area, believed that the area could become much more than the sum of its disparate and disconnected parts, Garreau's arguments in *Edge City* for how valuable they had nonetheless become notwithstanding. Subsequent to the decision by the Washington Metropolitan Transit Authority (WMATA), following the Commonwealth of Virginia Department of Transportation entering into a Comprehensive Agreement with the Dulles Transit Partnership to proceed with the construction of the Silver Line of the metro rail system connecting its West Falls Church metro station with Dulles International Airport, the Fairfax County government decided to pursue a long-range – forty-year – plan for the complete transformation of Tysons Corner from Garreau's archetypal Edge City to something more akin to one of Professor Leinberger's WalkUPs.[35]

Through increased tax revenues and reductions in traffic congestion, among others, the County believed its fiscal health and its residents would benefit from this comprehensive transformation of Tysons Corner. Local landowners and area real estate developers would also benefit from the grandiose development opportunities. And, last but certainly not least, the future occupants, residents, guests of, and visitors to the Tysons Corner area would all benefit from the convenience, walkability, connectedness, and diverse mix of uses the transformation would create. At completion, what Fairfax County has denominated "Urban Tysons Corner" will be comprised of more than 100,000 residents, 200,000 jobs, and approximately 113 million square feet of commercial development, including the redevelopment of existing properties at the time the Urban Tysons Corner Comprehensive Plan was adopted. Using 2000 census data by way of providing an order-of-magnitude reference, the projected 2050 employment in Urban Tysons Corner would make it the seventh largest central business district (CBD) in the country, just behind Philadelphia, Pennsylvania, with approximately 220,000 jobs in its CBD. The District of Columbia's CBD, according to the same 2000 census ranking, represented 382,400 jobs.

The impetus for considering what Tysons Corner might become if it were properly re-planned and redeveloped was the June 10, 2004, decision by the Commonwealth of Virginia's Department of Rail and Public Transportation (DRPT) to enter into a Comprehensive Agreement with the Dulles Transit Partnership (DTP) – the first agreement of its kind for a transit project by the Commonwealth of Virginia under the Public-Private Transportation Act (PPTA) of 1995 – for the creation of the Silver Line, extending the DC area's metro rail system farther west, from its West Falls Church station out to Dulles International Airport. Although funding for the Silver Line would need to come from a variety of sources, including the District of Columbia, the State of Maryland, and the federal government, among others, it would not have been possible absent the agreement between DRPT and DTP. This subject is revisited in Chapter 10.

The addition of the Silver Line will connect all three of the Washington, DC–Baltimore, MD region's three airports – two of which are international airports – to the mass transit system in Washington, DC.[36] As planned, the Silver Line will have a total of eleven stations, including the one at Dulles International Airport. The first five stations contained in Phase I of the Silver Line construction project – including the four metro stations located in Tysons Corner; the McLean, Tysons Corner, Greensboro Drive, and Spring Hill stations – were completed and opened for operations on July 26, 2014. Phase I of the Silver Line terminates at the Wiehle-Reston East Station. Tysons Corner and Reston are the largest and second-largest employment centers in the Commonwealth of Virginia.

The Tysons Comprehensive Plan creates four distinct neighborhoods around each of the four Tysons Corner Silver Line metro stations, with the highest-density buildings permitted within a one-eighth-mile radius of each station.

The rise of PUDs and form-based codes: how changes in Land Use Controls can encourage more WalkUPs

As suggested in the latter part of Chapter 4, Planned Unit Developments (PUDs) have gained popularity throughout the United States in the past twenty years, in order to encourage developers to submit Mixed-Use projects that are more responsive to market demands and trends than comprehensive master planning is capable of doing, despite their best intentions to see the future and invite its physical manifestation through the built environment.

Research on metropolitan D.C.'s WalkUPs is based upon the 2012 Brookings Institution report, mentioned above, that developed a methodology to define WalkUPs (geographically and by product mix) and to rank them using separate economic and social equity performance metrics. The Brookings research statistically defined regional significance as having a minimum of 1.4 million square feet of office space and/or a minimum of 340,000 square feet of retail space.[5] These metrics were used to rank the WalkUPs that emerged from the research and to create four levels of economic and social equity performance.[6]

Regionally significant and local serving WalkUPs are likely to be the major generators of real estate growth in the future. Although no fiscal impact analysis has yet been undertaken for the D.C.-area WalkUPs, their contribution to total government tax revenues in the region is expected to be many times the proportion of land they consume. In Arlington County, for example, the share of property tax assessments from the county's seven regionally significant WalkUPs is five times the amount of the land the WalkUPs occupy.[7] Fiscal impact studies throughout the country indicate that WalkUPs tend to produce a significant net surplus (tax revenues minus costs of service), subsidizing the local serving areas of the jurisdiction.[8,37]

6. *A fifth level – the lowest – of walkability and performance, made up of the regionally significant drivable suburban locations, such as the Dulles Corridor or the I-270 corridor, was not included in this ranking since it was not the focus of this research. In the "Walk This Way" methodological research, this fifth level had to be included to help define where WalkUPs began from walkability and size perspectives.*
7. *The seven Arlington WalkUPs occupy about 10 percent of the county's land and produce more than 50 percent of the county property tax assessment.*
8. *For example, the downtown and Golden Triangle in the District of Columbia generate a net fiscal surplus (revenues minus cost of services) of approximately $750 million annually, which is about the size of the total District's public school budget.*

Notes

1. Ferris, Hugh, *The Metropolis of Tomorrow*, Princeton Architectural Press, New York, NY (1986), *a reprint of the 1929 original by Ives Washburn, Publisher, with additional material added*, pg. 72.
2. According to Sir Peter Hall, Athens, Greece, is the first known "city," existing between 500 and 400 B.C. That means cities have existed for two millennia and five centuries, or 2,500 years. However, the early Mesopotamian settlements of Eridu and Uruk, in what are parts of modern-day Iraq, are considered by some man's first attempts to organize in an urban form. These ancient Sumerian cities date back to 4,500 B.C., 4,000 years before the ancient city of Athens. By this measure, having some form of comprehensive zoning for only the past 100 years of the 6,500-year history of the evolution of cities is, indeed, a de minimus amount of time. Hall, Sir Peter, *Cities in Civilization*, First Fromm International Edition, New York, NY (2001), pg. 24 (original copyright 1998), and LeGates, Richard T. and Frederic Stout, Editors, *The City Reader*, Second Edition, Routledge, New York, NY. (1996), pg. 295.
3. Board of Estimate and Apportionment, City of New York, "Building Zone Resolution." Adopted July 25, 1916. Found at www.nyc.gov/html/dcp/pdf/history_project/1916_zoning_resolution.pdf.
4. In his essay for the *Journal of Planning*, Hall describes ten distinct periods during the eighty years of planning practice since the very first conference of professional planners

occurred. The author has interpolated from this recitation of the history of American planning, and what has transpired after, two clear paradigms: Beneficiary-Based Planning, and Organic Planning versus Project-Based Planning.

5. Willis, Carol, "Drawing Toward Metropolis." Included as additional material to Ferris, *The Metropolis of Tomorrow*, pg. 157, footnote at pg. 181.

6. Ibid., pg. 181.

7. "Shadows from 217 W 57th St. will be 4000' long on September 21st at 4 pm – or ¾ of a mile long." Municipal Art Society of New York Report, *Accidental Skyline*, December 2013, pg. 6.

8. Gutheim, Frederick Albert, *The Federal City: Plans and Realities*, Smithsonian Institution Press, Washington, DC (1976).

9. Ibid., pg. 1:

> What is commonly referred to as "the L'Enfant Plan" embraces not only the initial design of the French Engineer, but its transposition by the surveyor Andrew Ellicott into the first official map of the city; the 1803 plats by the city surveyor Nicholas King; various building regulations, by George Washington and others, to implement the plan; and the various documents, particularly the "manuscript map," that were drawn by L'Enfant and illustrate his intentions, permitting more detailed interpretation of his basic design. This body of material should be regarded in its totality.

10. Moeller, Jr., G. Martin, *AIA Guide to the Architecture of Washington, D.C.*, Fifth Edition, The Johns Hopkins University Press, Baltimore, MD (2012), pg. 214. Emphasis added.

11. In the introduction to its report, the National Capital Planning Commission highlights what it deems the critical role the Height of Buildings Act has played in creating the capital, which presages its recommendations against making any major revisions to the Height of Buildings Act:

> As the capital of the United States, Washington is a unique place with its own authentic character and identity. For more than a century, the Height Act has played *a central role in shaping Washington's unmistakable and symbolic skyline*. The Height Act also fosters an open, pedestrian scale that is enjoyed by residents of the District of Columbia, the nation's citizens, and the millions of visitors who come here annually. *The form of the capital city is a national trust and a legacy for future generations.*
>
> Washington, DC is one of the great planned capital cities of the world. Since its founding, the *U.S. Congress has acted as the steward of the capital city's form*, including on matters related to building height. Through the Height Act, *Congress has ensured that the image and experience of the capital city reflects the preeminence of our democratic institutions, now and into the future*. These actions fulfill the early planning vision for a magnificent capital city, *as set forth by our nation's founding fathers*. [Emphasis added.]

The language that appears in italics in the above excerpt is intended by NCPC to highlight for the House Committee on Oversight and Government Reform that any relaxation of the Height of Building Act will betray the trust reposed in the committee's members to protect the sanctity of what the country's Founding Fathers intended. Some of those highlighted statements from NCPC are, indeed, hyperbolic, inasmuch as the Founding Fathers were concerned almost exclusively with shaping the organizational framework for governing the United States of America. Only two of those Founding

Fathers – President George Washington and Thomas Jefferson – were intimately involved in establishing the new capital of the young nation in the swampland that would eventually become Washington, DC. Additionally, and as already discussed earlier in this chapter, it was the horror of The Cairo, and how its appearance offended and angered its neighbors – and not some enlightened act of planning – that produced the original Height of Buildings Act of 1899 and its successor, the Height of Buildings Act of 1910. National Capital Planning Commission, *The Height Master Plan for Washington, D.C.: Federal Interest Report and Final Recommendations*, November 27, 2013, pg. i.

12. In the opening of its report, the Office of Planning makes clear the District's priorities in reexamining the Height of Buildings Act:

> Washington, DC, recognized around the world as this nation's capital and as a monumental city of great beauty, is also a city that *must provide services* to over 630,000 residents *as well as to hundreds of thousands of workers* and visitors every day. These services run the gamut from those typically provided by municipal governments like police and fire safety, to those normally funded by counties or states such as public schools, transit and housing finance. The District has to fund all of these responsibilities *from a tax base that excludes half of the District's land and is thus inordinately reliant on a small base of locally-generated property, income and sales taxes.* This means that to maintain fiscal stability the District must attract and retain many of the middle class residents that fled the city in the previous four decades, while also diversifying our economy and increasing jobs for District residents. For more than 100 years, the District has endeavored to achieve these goals under federal building height restrictions that apply citywide. For much of the first 100 years, these height limitations gave this city its unique horizontal character, giving particular prominence to nationally significant monuments and structures that reinforced the urban design principles of the L'Enfant Plan. However, over the next 100 years, the District is and will continue to face growing demand for space and services that are increasingly constrained under the current federal height limits. [Emphasis added.]

The language that appears in italics in the above excerpt is intended to highlight for the House Committee on Oversight and Government Reform those aspects of the day-to-day operations of the District of Columbia, as a somewhat self-governing municipality, that are peculiarly impacted by its dual role as the Nation's Capital. District of Columbia Office of Planning, *Height Master Plan for the District of Columbia: Final Evaluation & Recommendations*, November 20, 2013, pg. 1.

13. In a letter dated October 3, 2012, the chairman of the House Committee on Oversight and Government Reform sent a letter to the chairman of the National Capital Planning Commission and to the mayor of the District of Columbia requesting a joint study of the Height of Buildings Act of 1910, stating, in pertinent part:

> Any changes to the Height of Buildings Act that affect the historic L'Enfant City should be carefully studied to ensure that the iconic, horizontal skyline and the visual preeminence of the Capitol and related national monuments are retained.

National Capital Planning Commission, *Height Master Plan: Federal Interest Report and Final Recommendations*, November 27, 2013, *Appendix A: Key Correspondence.* House Committee Chairman Issa letter to NCPC Chairman Bryant & DC Mayor Gray (October 3, 2012).

14. National Capital Planning Commission report, *The Height Master Plan for Washington, DC*, pg. vi. The "L'Enfant City," as defined in the NCPC Report, refers to the original plan for the new capital city, which encompasses the federal core; it does not cover the entirety of the District of Columbia. Emphasis added.

15. Interesting, even in the case of an Edge City such as Tysons Corner, Virginia, which, through prolonged and comprehensive land use planning, is seeking to transform itself, over time, into a "walkable urban place," and that doesn't present the kind of severe aesthetic constraints of the nation's capital, concerns exist about building heights. See, generally, in this regard, the following section titled "From 'Edge City' to Connected, Walkable Urban Places," and the discussion therein about imposing artificial height limits in the highest-density zones within the Urban Tysons Corner Comprehensive Plan.

16. DC Office of Planning, *Height Master Plan for the District of Columbia*, pg. 2. Emphasis added.

17. Regarding the limitations on the District's ability to raise tax revenues needed to operate the city and to provide essential city services, the report states, in pertinent part:

> The District's revenue structure is a hybrid of state and city taxes. However, contrary to what any state can do, *the District cannot determine whom and what it taxes*, and unlike any other city, it *receives no state aid or compensation for the prevalence of tax-exempt property and organizations*. We have a narrow tax base because *nearly half our property and a significant portion of our sales are tax exempt*, and – especially – because we are *prohibited from taxing non-resident income*. Since income earned by non-residents, mostly commuters, accounts for about two-thirds of the income earned in the city, our inability to tax that income stream is a serious restriction of resources. Moreover, because a considerable proportion of the District's population has low incomes and lives in neighborhoods with high concentrations of poverty, *the need for public services is greater and the cost of delivering them is higher than in the average community*, where a broader state tax base can be tapped to address the proportionately higher city needs. For instance, the District of Columbia provides 42% of the region's subsidized housing units, although the city represents only 11% of the region's population.
>
> Ibid., pg. 39. [Emphasis added]

18. Ibid., *Development Capacity Under Current Scenarios & Modeling Study Scenarios*, pgs. 33–36.

19. For example, the Reliance Building, designed by the architecture firm Burnham and Company and completed in 1894, rose to a height of 200 feet, compared with The Cairo's height of 160 feet, which was completed the same year. Dupré, Judith, *Skyscrapers*, Black Dog & Leventhal Publishers, Inc., New York, NY (1996), pg. 23.

20. The Fidelity Building in Baltimore, also completed in 1894, reached a height of 220 feet, twenty feet taller than Chicago's Reliance Building and sixty feet taller than Washington, DC's The Cairo.

21. After the construction of the Sears Tower, later renamed Willis Tower, in Chicago in 1973, Chicago laid claim to the tallest building in the world for twenty-five years. At 108 stories and 1,451 feet high, it surpassed the original World Trade Center Twin Towers to become the world's tallest building. It is now the twelfth tallest building in the world.

22. DC Office of Planning, *Height Master Plan*, pgs. 33–36.

23. A project-based example of the One Bad Building Rule of relatively recent vintage may be found in The Walt Disney Company's failed proposal to build an historically themed amusement park, Disney's America, in the outskirts of Washington, DC, in very close proximity to an historic, Civil War landmark, the Manassas battlefield, where the Battle of Bull Run was waged. *New York Times* Editorial Board, "Disney Retreats at Bull Run," *New York Times*, September 30, 1994. Found at www.nytimes.com/1994/09/30/opinion/disney-retreats-at-bull-run.html. Noted the *New York Times*:

> More than the fate of the battlefields of Manassas, or Bull Run, was involved. "Disney's America" would have flooded one of America's most historic and scenic regions, including the nearby Shenandoah National Park, with traffic and tacky development. In response to the threat to these national treasures, *a large, articulate coalition defeated one of the country's richest corporations and its boosters in Virginia's Statehouse and Legislature*. [Emphasis added.]

24. Landmarks Preservation Commission of New York, record of decision of Landmark Designation of the Equitable Building, June 25, 1996, Designation List 273, LP-1935. The record noted as follows regarding the ownership of the Equitable Building, pg. 3:

> Though 120 Broadway continued to be the address of the Equitable Life Assurance Company's headquarters, the new building on the site was built not by Equitable, but by General Thomas Coleman Du Pont (1863–1930), who formed a complicated financial partnership with the Equitable company to sponsor a speculative venture.

25. Ibid., at pg. 4:

> Having no apparent need for or interest in a striking corporate symbol after the fire of 1912 destroyed the first Equitable building, Du Pont and Graham designed and built *the largest building that could be squeezed onto its site*. As an advanced, up-to-date office building, it featured many practical innovations: "The new Equitable building . . . was not constructed to create an architectural splurge or to stand as a monument to perpetuate any one's name. *The building was planned upon the idea of an ocean liner, to carry a maximum cargo with the highest degree of efficiency, comfort, and safety to its tenants at a minimum cost.*" [Emphasis added.]

26. Ibid, pg. 6:

> The Equitable Building occupies an entire block and extends approximately 168 feet on Broadway, 310 feet on Cedar Street, 152 feet on Nassau Street, and 305 feet on Pine Street. (Fig. 2) Rising 38 stories to setback two-story penthouses, it reaches a height of 545 feet.

27. Ibid., pg. 6.

28. Ibid., pg. 5:

> New York City had a variety of building codes prior to 1916, initially aimed at preventing fires, later extended to insuring the general safety of buildings. Various initiatives to reform tenement construction resulted in laws governing residential buildings. Until 1916, however, no municipal code regulated the height or shape of office buildings, in part because until the late 1800s there had been no compelling reason to do so. But as the new technology of steelcage construction and elevators combined with rising prices to push office buildings ever higher, demands grew for laws regulating their height and bulk.

29. Ibid., pg. 5:

   Discussions and proposals for skyscraper regulations predated the Equitable Building. Ernest Flagg, himself the architect of the Singer Building, holder of the title of "world's tallest building," began to campaign for such regulations in 1908. As chairman of building code committees for both the Society of Beaux-Arts Architects and the New York Chapter of the American Institute of Architects, he testified before the Committee on the Limitation of Height and Area of the Building Code Revision Commission of New York City, proposing regulations that would restrict the area of a plot on which a building could be constructed, but permit unlimited height on 25 percent of the plot – a model which would encourage the design of skyscrapers as towers, more or less like his own Singer Building. A competing proposal put forth by D. Knickerbacker Boyd, the president of the Philadelphia Chapter of the American Institute of Architects, focused on formulas that would mandate a series of set-backs the higher a building went, producing a "stepped facade." As finally adopted in 1916, the Building Zone Resolution combined aspects of both proposals, encouraging the construction of "stepped facade" towers.

30. Bassett, Edward M., chairman, *Report of the Height of Buildings Commission to the Committee on the Height, Size and Arrangement of Buildings of the Board of Estimate and Apportionment of the City of New York*, M. B. Brown Printing & Binding Company, New York, NY (December 23, 1913).

31. Ibid., pg. 6.

32. Dupré, *Skyscrapers*, pg. 11:

   The Classical Period witnessed the birth of the most perfect building in ancient Greece, the Parthenon (447–423 B.C.). Built of marble on the Acropolis as a temple to the goddess Athena, the Parthenon was conceived as a sculptural form, yet was based upon strict geometry and proportion. It embodied the Greeks' desire for orderly and symmetrical architecture and their abiding belief that these ideals reflected the dignity of the individual. They developed the Doric, Ionic, and Corinthian columns with articulated base, shaft, and capital (the Romans would later add a base to the Doric) – the orders that would inform the organization of classical structures from that time onward. So pervasive is the architectural legacy of the Classical Period that people today are probably as familiar with its design elements as the ancients themselves.

33. Zoning Resolution of the City of New York, enacted December 15, 1961, replacing the 1916 Zoning Resolution.

34. Garreau, Joel, *Edge City: Life on the New Frontier*, Anchor Books, New York, NY (1991), pg. 4.

35. Interestingly, what Urban Tysons Corner is anticipated to become by the year 2050 fits neatly into neither the suburban town center nor the greenfield WalkUPs categories described in Chapter 1. Accordingly, it may require its own definition, given the scale and complexity of transformation required to turn an Edge City into a walkable urban place.

36. Baltimore/Washington International Thurgood Marshall Airport (BWI) is served by the Maryland Department of Transportation's Maryland Area Regional Commuter (MARC) Train Service, which connects to the Washington, DC, metro rail service at Union Station on Capitol Hill.

37. Leinberger, Christopher B., *The WalkUP Wake-Up Call: D.C.*, Center for Real Estate and Urban Analysis, The George Washington University School of Business, Washington, DC (2012), pg. 7. Footnotes in the original text.

CHAPTER **6**

Environmental Law

Imagine for a moment a world where cities have become peaceful and serene because cars and buses are whisper quiet, vehicles exhaust only water vapor, and parks and greenways have replaced unneeded urban freeways. OPEC has ceased to function because the price of oil has fallen to five dollars a barrel, but there are few buyers for it because cheaper and better ways now exist to get the services people once turned to oil to provide. Living standards for all people have dramatically improved, particularly for the poor and those in developing countries. Involuntary unemployment no longer exists, and income taxes have largely been eliminated. Houses, even low-income housing units, can pay part of their mortgage costs by the energy they produce; there are few if any active landfills; worldwide forest cover is increasing; dams are being dismantled; atmospheric CO levels are decreasing for the first time in two hundred years; and effluent water leaving factories is cleaner than the water coming into them. Industrialized countries have reduced resource use by 80 percent while improving the quality of life. Among these technological changes, there are important social changes. The frayed social nets of Western countries have been repaired. With the explosion of family-wage jobs, welfare demand has fallen. A progressive and active union movement has taken the lead to work with business, environmentalists, and government to create "just transitions" for workers as society phases out coal, nuclear energy, and oil. In communities and towns, churches, corporations, and labor groups promote a new living-wage social contract as the least expensive way to ensure the growth and preservation of valuable social capital. Is this the vision of a utopia? In fact, the changes described here could come about in the decades to come as the result of economic and technological trends already in place.[1]

In following up on his groundbreaking book, *The Ecology of Commerce: A Declaration of Sustainability*, Paul Hawken enlisted the help of Amory and L. Hunter Lovins, of the Rocky Mountain Institute, to write *Natural Capitalism: Creating the Next Industrial Revolution*, from which the foregoing quote is excerpted. Although this chapter is titled simply Environmental Law, real estate development has seen a growing emphasis on sustainability that impacts everything from Site Selection to building design to land planning to project financing to property management and building operations. Because the practice of sustainability and its impact on The Development Process continue to expand and evolve, sustainability-specific materials and information are delivered through the companion website for this textbook, which better supports keeping students and readers up to date on what's happening in this aspect of Environmental Law.

To better appreciate how making sustainability a controlling principle in The Development Process, consider the following examples:

- On December 7, 2012, the District of Columbia published a Green Building Code, based on the 2012 International Green Construction Code. The District's Green Code seeks to[2] modify the international standards of sustainability while codifying green building best practices, tailoring them for enforceability within the District. DC's proposed Green Code was allowed a public comment period from its publication until February 22, 2013, with the intention to enact the Green Code in the spring of 2013, and a one-year enforcement grace period until the spring of 2014.

- Despite its status as the most iconic commercial building in the United States, as well as one of the best-known skyscrapers in the world, at the turn of the century the Empire State Building was worn and looking a little shabby. Its rent roll was dominated by smaller tenants of little fame or notoriety, and the building's energy efficiency, in a market where things like LEED certification have become effective marketing tools, was subpar. To paraphrase an old saying, it was a nice place for tourists to visit, but you wouldn't want your office there. As part of a $550 million makeover commenced in 2009, the owner of the Empire State Building made extensive energy efficiency improvements, such as replacing *all* of the building's windows with much more energy-efficient, custom-made replacements matching the design of the original windows; rebuilding the chillers in the basement; installing a new elevator system; and a host of other sustainability upgrades, eventually earning the building LEED-Gold status.[3]

- The impact of climate change on cities has increasingly become a priority in international efforts to develop "adaptability solutions" that can and should be adopted into the land use and zoning codes of all major cities throughout the world, including in North America. See for example in this regard, the Intergovernmental Panel on Climate Change (IPCC) Fifth Assessment Report (5AR), delivered at the Twelfth Session of Working Group I (WGI-12) to the IPCC at a conference held from September 23 through 26, 2013, in Stockholm, Sweden. These are referred to as adaptability solutions because numerous international scientific organizations had determined that climate change is real, is already present, and may take centuries to arrest, much less reverse, such that in the interim period, decision makers need to focus as much attention on adapting the built environment to the negative impacts of climate change as they spend on developing and implementing the strategies necessary to slow down the rate of climate change worldwide.[4]

- At the twenty-first meeting of the United Nations Climate Change Conference held in Paris, France, from November 30 through December 12, 2015, commonly known as COP 21 (or CMP 11), the conferees agreed to specific, although nonbinding, emissions limitations documented in what is now referred to as the "Paris Agreement." Efforts to meet these emissions limitations, including the commitment from the United States, will also require policy changes in how U.S. cities evolve and grow. Conferees will likely be expected to report back at the twenty-second meeting of the United Nations Climate Change Conference on their progress regarding efforts to meet the emissions limitations, and it is not unreasonable to expect that the United States and other nations will have policies in place, or at least proposed policies, regarding the future development of the built environments in urban areas generating the largest amount of carbon emissions as one strategy for meeting that conferee's carbon-reduction targets.

Having raised the dual issues of sustainability and sustainable urban development as having considerable importance to and potentially critical impacts on The Development Process, the chapter contents that follow are focused on giving the student or reader a comprehensive understanding of the Environmental Law framework in the United States and its potential impact on The Development Process through the hypothetical Hardrock Development Company Problem statement and solution presented at the end of this chapter.

Chapter outline

Chapter introduction[1]

As mentioned in Chapter 2, a critical step in the Project Conception Phase of The Development Process is the Land Use Analysis of the Subject Site. As contrasted with the Preliminary Infrastructure Assessment, the Land Use Analysis reviews and assesses a number of characteristics of a property. These may include but are not limited to site conditions such as slope, the presence of still or moving water, biological and cultural resources, known or reasonably predictable soils conditions (in lieu of actual soils testing, normally conducted during the Pre-Development Phase), access and egress issues, and any observable endangered species or endangered species habitats.

---

1 The author acknowledges, and greatly appreciates, the contributions of Thomas E. Hogan, Esquire, counsel to the Washington, DC, office of Baker Hostetler, for his various contributions to this chapter, including but not limited to serving as a reviewer of and providing substantive input to the author's initial draft of this chapter, as well as his contributions as a guest lecturer on Environmental Law in the author's graduate real estate law courses at Georgetown University and The George Washington University, respectively.

The Land Use Analysis is the first step in identifying what portions of the potential site may be developed and what portions will or should be restricted in terms of the construction of Improvements thereon. Some of these limitations on the development of the Subject Site will be the result of engineering concerns, the reconciliation of which either cannot be guaranteed or are cost-prohibitive. Engineering issues generally are more related to the laws of physics than real estate law. Conversely, other issues impeding or constraining the development of the Subject Site involve environmental issues, and these fall within the purview of one of the Holy Trinity of real estate law: Environmental Law.

For example, steep slopes present challenges for both the construction of improvements and managing water runoff on a property. Depending on the location, direction of pitch, and severity of the incline of a steep slope, normal grading techniques may not be sufficient, and building retaining walls may prove too costly a solution to create more buildable area. The presence of either still or moving water (e.g., a pond or lake or a stream or creek, respectively) may present both flooding and environmental issues. Either may also provide on its shoreline habitats for critical botanicals and/or endangered species, again raising Environmental Law issues. The Land Use Analysis is intended to provide the Developer with a threshold set of constraints on how the Subject Site may be developed with Improvements beyond any that may already be present on the property.

Understanding the legal framework of federal environmental regulation and protection

Basics of Environmental Law

Environmental Law is a sprawling, multifaceted, and complicated subject. Complying with environmental laws and managing environmental risk are complex endeavors, and even the wary can fall into traps. Failing to properly anticipate and fully address environmental issues may have severe consequences for the Developer, including:

Fines
Project delays
Operational shutdowns
Loss of project financing
Imprisonment for parties found liable

Environmental Law issues manifest themselves in a great variety of ways and take many forms. In the United States, environmental laws exist at the federal, state, and local levels. While federal law predominates, state environmental statutes and regulations, and even local environmental ordinances, may impose additional requirements over and above federal statutes and regulations. However, it is well beyond the scope of this textbook to cover the full range of state and local environmental regulations. Consequently, the focus of this chapter will be on the federal government, which has adopted and enforces a panoply of environmental regulations.

The federal framework of environmental laws and regulations is comprised of approximately twenty legislative enactments by the U.S. Congress, starting with the National Environmental Policy Act, signed into law by President Richard Nixon on January 1, 1970, and followed by his July 9, 1979, Executive Order creating the U.S. Environmental Protection Agency.

Seven of the most significant federal environmental laws from the perspective of real estate development are listed later and covered in detail in this chapter. These laws were enacted by Congress, but the details are in large measure found in a substantial body of federal regulations promulgated and administered by the Environmental Protection Agency (hereinafter the "EPA") under the EPA's Rulemaking Authority, as granted by the statutes that Congress enacted. In addition to the statutes and the regulations promulgated thereunder, there is also an almost equally comprehensive body of case law interpreting and enforcing the United States' environmental statutes and regulations. These three primary components – statutes, regulations, and case law – are referred to in this chapter and elsewhere in this textbook as Environmental Law.

Each federal enactment forming the foundation for Environmental Law, as it relates to real estate law and The Development Process, is covered in this chapter. These specific federal environmental laws are listed next, and each one is covered in detail in the chapter section titled "Environmental Laws Affecting Site Development," as well as in the Problem Statement presented at the end of this chapter:

- Comprehensive Environmental Response, Compensation, and Liability Act (CERCLA)
- Resource Conservation and Recovery Act (RCRA)
- Federal Water Pollution Control Act (aka Clean Water Act)
- Endangered Species Act
- Clean Air Act
- National Environmental Policy Act (NEPA)
- National Historic Preservation Act (NHPA)

As mentioned earlier, the U.S. Environmental Protection Agency (EPA) was created by President Nixon by Executive Order on July 9, 1970, as part of the administration's Reorganization Plan No. 3, to provide the administrative capacity and infrastructure necessary to implement the provisions of the National Environmental Policy Act of 1969 (NEPA, 42 U.S.C. §§ 4321–4347), which Congress passed in 1969 and enacted into law on January 1, 1970. Not until more than fourteen years later, when the EPA received congressional authorization as part of the Reorganization Acts Amendment (Public Law 98–614), was it signed into law, on November 8, 1984.

As depicted in **Figure 6.1**, the EPA is an independent agency. The administrator of the EPA is a non-Cabinet-level position within the administration, appointed by the president of the United States and approved by Congress. However, the EPA administrator is often invited to participate in Cabinet meetings. The EPA is comprised of ten regional offices, shown in **Figure 6.2**, responsible for the administration and enforcement of federal environmental laws in the states and territories comprising that region. For example, although the EPA is headquartered in Washington, DC, with all of the other federal agencies, Environmental Law issues arising at sites in the neighboring state of Maryland are typically handled by the EPA Region 3 Office in Philadelphia, Pennsylvania, and not by EPA headquarters. Within this network of regional offices, the EPA maintains a number of subject-matter offices, including Air and Radiation, Water, Solid Waste, and Emergency Response.

Through its Rulemaking Authority, the EPA promulgates and enacts regulations for the administration and enforcement of the wide range of environmental enactments by Congress comprising federal Environmental Law, which often provide only broad environmental policy guidance, leaving the details for implementation and enforcement to EPA regulations. In addition to voluminous environmental regulations, the EPA shapes environmental policy through other actions, including but not limited to issuing policy and guidance documents;

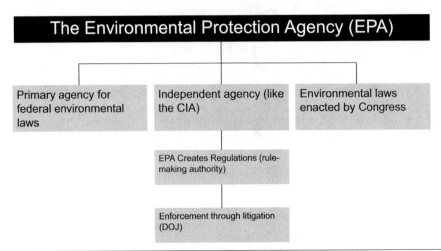

Figure 6.1 Understanding the Environmental Protection Agency within the structure of the executive branch of the federal government. Unlike the major departments of the executive branch, such as the U.S. Treasury (Treasury) and the U.S. Department of Housing and Urban Development (HUD), the EPA is an independent agency with an administrator instead of a cabinet secretary, and enforcement actions are handled by the U.S. Department of Justice

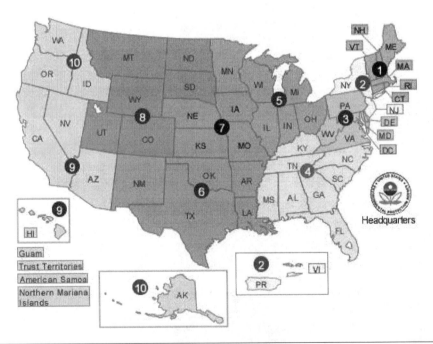

Figure 6.2 Map of the EPA's ten regional offices. U.S. environmental laws, and regulations promulgated by the EPA thereunder, are administered through ten regional offices. For example, even though the EPA headquarters office is in Washington, DC, the District of Columbia is included in EPA Region 3, which is located in Philadelphia, PA

entering into Settlement Agreements resolving claims prior to the initiation or conclusion of enforcement litigation; issuing Records of Decision providing the Agency's rationale for specific remedial action to be taken at designated Superfund clean-up sites under the Comprehensive Environmental Response, Compensation, and Liability Act (CERCLA); and entering into Memoranda of Understanding (MOUs) governing a variety of arrangements with other federal or state government entities.

As stated in Chapter 2, while real estate developers may be romantically portrayed as risk takers, Developers are, in fact, risk averse. The most successful Developers are adept at identifying and mitigating or at least managing the risks associated with The Development Process. Therefore, it may not be at all surprising that most Developers seek to avoid sites that present significant environmental risks. Some environmental issues may be relatively easy to predict, based on the location of a particular site or known and well-documented environmental issues in the area. Additionally, a previously marketed site may have due diligence materials available through the Seller, such as Phase I and Phase II Environmental Assessment reports, which may be available to an interested Developer merely by making an inquiry of the Seller regarding the existence of these documents.

However, not all Developers are risk averse when it comes to potential environmental risks and the Site Selection process (the first listed Sub-Phase of the Project Conception Phase of The Development Process). In fact, some Developers seek out sites with known environmental hazards, commonly referred to as "Brownfields Sites"). Why would a Developer knowingly and intentionally take on environmental liabilities? For one reason, because the vast majority of Developers intentionally avoid Brownfields Sites, a potential site may be the "the hole in the donut," because it has been left out of the path of development or redevelopment of an area. Consequently, the Subject Site is ideally located. Additionally, Brownfields Sites tend to be deeply discounted because of extremely low demand in light of the high costs and uncertainties of environmental remediation. Finally, a Developer may intentionally seek out Brownfields Sites because of the availability of OPM (Other People's Money) to fund a portion of the Development Budget, which in the case of remediating the environmental hazards of a Brownfields Site could include both federal and state grant funds specifically available for clean-up.

Environmental laws affecting site acquisition

State property transfer laws triggering disclosure/remediation

Even before a Developer has consummated the acquisition of its Subject Site (aka "Closing"), the laws of the state in which the Subject Site is located may impose certain disclosure obligations on the Seller. The Developer and its real estate lawyer need to be familiar with any state environmental laws impacting the rights and duties of the respective parties under the Purchase and Sale Agreement, inasmuch as a Seller's failure to comply with state environmental laws may not automatically give rise to a private right of action to overturn the PSA and seek remedies against the Seller for such violation(s).

To that end, the Purchase and Sale Agreement may benefit from including a Seller's Representations and Warranties provision or clause asserting the Seller's affirmative compliance with all state environmental laws impacting or involving the Subject Site. Such provision or clause may include, but would certainly not be limited to, state environmental laws regarding triggering disclosure and remediation of environmental hazards upon a transfer of title to real property.

For example, Connecticut requires disclosure of specific environmental conditions found or that may be found in "Areas of Concern" when the ownership of certain properties and/or operating facilities is transferred. When an establishment is transferred, one of eight Property Transfer Forms must be executed, and a copy of the form must be filed with the Department of Energy & Environmental Protection. When transferring an establishment where there has been a release of a hazardous waste or substance, the parties negotiate who will sign the Property Transfer Form as the Certifying Party to investigate the parcel and remediate pollution caused by any such release.

It should be noted that there is much variation among the states in whether and to what extent they require reporting of environmental conditions in connection with property transfers. In addition, a given state's law may change from time to time. For example, in 2014, Indiana repealed Indiana's Responsible Property Transfer Law, which had required the transferor of property to disclose information relevant to the environmental conditions at the subject property to the buyer and the state under certain conditions.

The Small Business Liability Relief and Brownfields Revitalization Act

Under the Small Business Liability Relief and Brownfields Revitalization Act of 2002, one who purchases contaminated property may be relieved of liability for cleanup costs under CERCLA if the purchaser meets the requirements of a "bona fide prospective purchaser" (BFPP). The intent of the Act is clear: to incentivize developers to revitalize properties with known contamination that would be attractive but for the threat of liability under CERCLA. To qualify as a BFPP, the purchaser must meet the following requirements:

1. Conduct appropriate pre-purchase due diligence, such a Phase I Environmental Assessment;
2. Take appropriate care with respect to the prior releases of hazardous substances at the site;
3. Cooperate with EPA and those undertaking any remediation at the site;
4. Comply with any land use restrictions;
5. Comply with any requests from EPA for information regarding the site;
6. Provide any notices required by law regarding hazardous materials at the site; and
7. Have no affiliation with any person who is liable for the contamination at the site.

The EPA will not typically grant requests to confirm a purchaser's status as a BFPP, so it is up to the purchaser to become familiar with EPA's requirements, make sure it is meeting all requirements, and be prepared to demonstrate that it qualifies as a BFPP if it is threatened with liability for clean-up costs. Additionally, a 50-State Survey of Protections Available for Purchasers of Contaminated Property, as of May 9, 2013, presented by the Environmental Litigation Committee of the American Bar Association in January 2014, is provided among the Supplementary Materials on Environmental Law available on the companion website for this textbook.

State law may also provide important protections to prospective purchasers of contaminated property. For example, state law may establish a voluntary clean-up program pursuant to which a prospective purchaser can agree up front to perform certain clean-up actions in exchange for confirmation that the state will not sue the purchaser in connection with the contamination at the site.

Implications of regional, state, and local environmental requirements

While federal Environmental Law is extensive, the states and local governments also enact their own environmental laws, which are enforced by the state or county environmental regulatory agencies and not by the federal government. State and local laws may address subjects that are also addressed by federal law provided that the state or local laws are more stringent than the federal law and that the federal law does not preempt the state or local laws (i.e., prohibit the state or local governments from enacting a law on the subject). State and local governments may also enact laws that address subjects that are not covered by federal law, such as project siting requirements, zoning, and land use regulations.

In addition to enacting and enforcing their own laws, states are delegated authority from the federal government to administer and enforce some programs established under federal environmental laws. These include programs under the Clean Air and Water Acts and RCRA. Thus, even when dealing with federal law environmental programs, the developer may be interfacing with a state regulator. In these circumstances, the EPA will usually defer to the state regulators, but the EPA often retains final authority to take enforcement action or object to the issuance of a permit.

Environmental laws affecting site development

Known Knowns, Known Unknowns, and Unknown Unknowns. A Developer's awareness of the environmental risks associated with a Subject Site may be characterized in three ways, more than one of which may apply in a given scenario:

1. **First, there may be some environmental risks that the Developer knows about with a reasonable degree of certainty before Closing on the Subject Site.** An example of this scenario would be a Developer who acquires a property with known environmental risks, such as a designated Brownfields Site, the development of which may be a fundamental part of the Developer's business model.
2. **Second, there may be some environmental risks about which the Developer should have known before Closing on the Subject Site but that were not investigated.** An example of this scenario would be the Developer who, overly focused on other fundamentals – such as location or price – of its Site Selection process, acquires a property with unknown environmental risks, such as soils contamination or asbestos-containing materials incorporated into existing improvements on the Subject Site, because the Developer did not perform prudent due diligence measures as part of the Developer's Site Selection process.
3. **Third, there may be some environmental risks about which even a reasonably prudent developer would not have known until after Closing on the Subject Site, usually once site work or other activity disturbing existing conditions has commenced.** An example of this scenario would be the Developer who acquires a property with unknown environmental risks, such as subsurface conditions, that even prudent due diligence measures during the Site Selection process and pre-Closing requirements prior to acquiring title to the Subject Site were unable to reveal. For example, a clean Phase I Environmental Assessment might have identified no historical uses of hazardous substances at the site or at nearby sites, but it turns out that when buildings are constructed on the site they are affected by the intrusion of vapors from an undiscovered contaminated groundwater plume caused by historical releases at a distant up-gradient site.

Washington, DC, environmental lawyer Thomas E. Hogan, the original author of the *Hardrock Development Problem Statement* at the end of this chapter, paraphrasing former U.S.

Secretary of Defense Donald Rumsfeld, refers to these three scenarios as "Known Knowns," "Known Unknowns," and "Unknown Unknowns."

While it is well beyond the scope of this chapter, and perhaps more fitting for a textbook devoted exclusively to Environmental Law, to delve into all of the possible areas of potential environmental liability involved in Site Development, the following excerpt from the table of contents of the EPA's 2005 report, *Managing Your Environmental Responsibilities: Guide for Construction and Development*, is illuminating if not instructive:

II. List of Questions for Owners and Contractors

A. Storm water Permits
B. Dredge and Fill Wetlands (Section 404) Permit Requirements
C. Oil Spill Prevention Requirements
D. Hazardous and Non-Hazardous Solid Waste Requirements
E. Hazardous Substances (Superfund Liability) Requirements
F. Polychlorinated Biphenyl (PCB) Waste Requirements
G. Air Quality Requirements
H. Asbestos Requirements
I.   Endangered Species Act (ESA) Requirements

The following paragraphs cover functional environmental risks and their attendant environmental liabilities associated with Site Development.

Contamination – Comprehensive Environmental Response, Compensation, and Liability Act

The Comprehensive Environmental Response, Compensation, and Liability Act (CERCLA), commonly referred to as Superfund, gives the EPA broad powers to force owners of property with evidence of hazardous materials or other contaminants or pollutants to remediate their property and/or property contaminated by releases from their property or face the prospect of having the property remediated under the direction of the EPA and having to pay for it. The cleanup of a Superfund Site generally must meet all relevant or applicable requirements, such as state regulations and regulations issued in connection with other environmental laws. In the absence of other, existing regulations specifying the scope and extent of the remediation necessary, the EPA may establish site-specific clean-up requirements. Clean-up requirements depend, of course on the nature of the hazardous material(s) and/or other contaminants or pollutants, as well as on the scope and extent of the contamination of the property.

As suggested in the three scenarios posited earlier – the Known Knowns, Known Unknowns, and Unknown Unknowns – sometimes site contamination exists and is readily susceptible to testing but the Purchaser of the Subject Site does not exercise due care in determining whether any such hazardous condition exists. This intentional disregard for the existence of hazardous site conditions is increasingly unlikely where a third party is providing equity and/or debt financing for the acquisition transaction, since some level of environmental due diligence is normally a condition precedent to securing funding for the acquisition.

A clean Phase I Environmental Assessment is usually the minimum threshold requirement to assure equity investors and lenders of the absence of environmental contamination. However, subsurface contamination, which in most cases will not be evident from a Phase I Environmental Assessment, may not be discovered until site preparation activities, such as excavating and grading. Generally speaking, a Developer will not agree to undertake, and an equity investor or lender will not require, a Phase II Environmental Assessment unless the Phase I Environmental Assessment indicates it is warranted. Accordingly, a Developer may find, after the fact, that it has become a "Responsible Owner" under CERCLA until long after title to the property has changed hands from the Seller to the Developer.

Under CERCLA, the EPA, a state, or a Native American tribal organization may recover the costs they incur to effect a cleanup, also known as "remediation," of the hazardous substances at a site from the current property owner or other Potentially Responsible Parties (PRPs). Or, the EPA may issue an order requiring the property owner or other PRPs to remediate the affected site. The EPA, a state, or a Native American tribal organization may also recover money for natural resource damages caused by the contamination. CERCLA also authorizes suits by private parties who incurred costs to remediate contamination against other PRPs who did not contribute their fair share to the clean-up effort.

Clean-up activities may involve Removal and/or Remedial actions. A Removal action is a short-term action intended to address localized risks and mitigate or limit further risks of exposure. For example, the immediate removal of an underground storage tank (UST) leaking a hazardous substance will end the ongoing contamination but will not fully address all contamination. Remediation, on the other hand, is a longer-term action or set of actions intended to more fully address the contamination resulting from the release of hazardous substances. For example, in the preceding example of the leaking UST, all of the contaminated soils may need to be excavated and treated prior to disposal.

Identifying Potentially Responsible Parties (PRPs). Four classes of persons may be held liable under CERCLA:

1. Any current owner or operator of the facility;
2. Any owner or operator of the facility at the time a release of a hazardous substance occurred;
3. Any person who arranged for the disposal of a hazardous substance at the facility; and
4. Any person who transported the hazardous substance to the facility where it was disposed.

Waste storage and disposal – Resource Conservation and Recovery Act (RCRA)

The introduction of the Resource Conservation and Recovery Act (RCRA) in 1976 gave the EPA comprehensive authority to control the creation, transportation, treatment, storage, and/or disposal of a material or product determined to be "hazardous waste material" as defined by the authorizing legislation and regulations promulgated under the EPA's Rulemaking Authority. Whereas CERCLA is generally used to address historic contamination at non-operating sites, RCRA generally addresses facilities that continue to operate.

Storm water – Clean Water Act

Storm water is runoff from any surface (e.g., vegetative areas, parking lots, rooftops). Storm water runoff affects water quality because it picks up pollutants as it travels and deposits those pollutants in streams, rivers, tributaries, ponds, lakes, bays, and oceans.

Storm water discharges from construction sites are regulated under the Clean Water Act. If the runoff flows to "waters of the United States or a municipal storm water system," then the EPA has jurisdiction over that storm water discharge. The EPA program to regulate storm water runoff is called the National Pollutant Discharge Elimination System (NPDES).

If a Developer or its General Contractor is an operator of a project that is larger than one acre, the operation of that project must meet the requirements of the EPA's Construction

General Permit, state-specific general storm water permits, and/or site-specific storm water permits. Most states administer the permit program, but in Washington, DC, and a few states a Storm Water Discharge Permit must be secured from the EPA.

In order to apply for a Storm Water Discharge Permit, the Applicant must prepare and submit a Storm Water Pollution Prevention Plan, demonstrating how the Developer or General Contractor in charge of the Subject Site will control storm water flow and ongoing assessment of impacts on species and habitat. The penalties for failing to secure a Storm Water Discharge Permit are substantial. Administrative penalties imposed by the EPA may be up to $16,000 per day, up to a maximum of $177,500, and judicially imposed penalties may be up to $37,500 *per penalty, per day, with no maximum*. Also, an EPA determination that a Subject Site is discharging storm water runoff without the required permit(s) increases the risk of private lawsuits and increased scrutiny over future projects. For example, in 2004, Wal-Mart paid a $3.1 million civil penalty to settle storm water violations at store construction sites.

Wetland conservation – Clean Water Act

If a Subject Site and/or a project thereon involves work in "waters or wetlands" of the United States, a Clean Water Act Section 404 Permit is most likely required. A Section 404 Permit covers the discharge of dredged (i.e., excavated) material, as well as the discharge of fill material (e.g., replacing waters with dry land). Issued by the local district office of the Army Corps of Engineers with jurisdiction over the Subject Site, a Section 404 Permit is required before construction begins. The application process from start to issuance of the Section 404 Permit takes approximately three months and requires public notice and comment, unless the Subject Site/project falls within an existing nationwide permit.

Typically, the Owner, Developer, General Contractor, or architect will obtain the Section 404 Permit. However, it is usually the Owner/Developer who will be responsible for determining whether a permit is required. Courts have found both General Contractors and Owners liable for unpermitted discharges – the General Contractor for engaging in the discharge activity and the Owner as the party with control over the project/Subject Site.

Penalties for engaging in activities covered by a Section 404 Permit without obtaining one in advance are the same as for storm water violations: administrative penalties imposed by the EPA may be up to $16,000 per day, up to a maximum of $177,500, and judicially imposed penalties may be up to $37,500 *per penalty, per day, with no maximum*.

Whether a project and/or Subject Site "involves" waters of the United States can be complicated to determine. Developers are strongly encouraged to secure professional assistance to identify and delineate any "waters of the United States" relating to the Subject Site and project. The EPA has promulgated and administers complex regulations, which have been clarified but made much more complicated by the 2006 U.S. Supreme Court decision in *Rapanos v. U.S.* and *Carabell v. U.S.* (clarifying when "adjacent wetlands" qualify for protection). The EPA has issued guidance in effort to further clarify this complicated area, but this guidance has itself become the subject of controversy and dispute. This area of law is very much in flux.

Habitat conservation – Endangered Species Act

Under the Endangered Species Act, if a development project requires any federal permits (e.g., a Section 404 Permit from the U.S. Army Corps of Engineers to impact wetlands or a storm water construction general permit), then an Endangered Species Act evaluation will typically be required. The first step in this process is to determine whether protected species or habitats live in the area. If there is a likelihood of species or habitat protected under the Endangered Species Act, either a confirmatory visual inspection (for small sites) or formal biological survey (for larger sites) will be required. The second step is to assess the potential impacts of the planned activity on the protected species or habitat. The third step is to evaluate ways to avoid those impacts. Finally, either the U.S. Fish and Wildlife Service will issue a "no jeopardy opinion" or a permit will be required to authorize incidental take (i.e., harass, harm, or kill) of the protected species of habitat. Incidental take without a permit carries potentially steep civil penalties and is a federal crime, even if a project does not have a federal component.

Air quality – Clean Air Act

The Clean Air Act requires states to adopt State Implementation Plans (SIPs) to achieve certain clean air goals established under the Act. Under these SIPs, states may require permits for construction-related emissions. Sources of such emissions may include, for example, burning debris, dust generation from vehicle traffic, nitrogen oxides from diesel engines, oil-fired heaters, release of chlorofluocarbons, visible stack emissions from off-road equipment, and volatile organic compounds from paints and solvents. Any such permitting requirements will vary by state, but will include record-keeping and air-monitoring requirements. Failure to obtain a required permit may carry civil and criminal penalties. Separate from the Clean Air Act, but related to air quality, OSHA and its state law counterparts also impose requirements on the quality of indoor air to protect workers' health. Thus, a development's impacts on indoor and outdoor air need to be considered for compliance with environmental laws.

Oil spill prevention – the EPA's Spill Prevention Control and Countermeasures Plan (SPCC Plan) under the Clean Water Act

If a project involves using, consuming, storing, transferring, or handling oils kept in storage tanks, the Developer and/or General Contractor will need to follow the EPA's Spill Prevention Control and Countermeasures Plan (SPCC Plan), developed under the Clean Water Act. Oil is almost anything oily (e.g., petroleum, fuel, fats, greases, even vegetable oils). Generally, these requirements involve demonstrating adequate containment, drainage, inspection, and security plans. The SPCC Plan requires the Developer to secure the certification of a petroleum engineer to have its compliance measures deemed satisfactory. However, the requirements of the SPCC Plan apply only if there is a reasonable expectation that spills on the Developer's property or Subject Site could impact "waters of the United States." See discussion in the subsection titled "Wetland Conservation – Clean Water Act."

Penalties are similar as for other Clean Water Act violations, but failure to give notice of a spill can result in criminal fines up to $500,000 and five years in prison *per violation*, up to fifteen years. There are specific requirements regarding who is entitled to notification of what, and by when.

Federally funded or permitted projects – the National Environmental Policy Act and the National Historic Preservation Act

The National Environmental Policy Act (NEPA) requires the federal agency with primary responsibility for approving a project to prepare an environmental impact statement (EIS) if the project has potential to significantly affect the quality of the human environment. This requirement is procedural and not substantive, and there is no affirmative, federal obligation under the act requiring that the responsible party avoid environmental harm; only that such potential environmental harm be discovered and disclosed through the required EIS, which must identify the risks and consider the alternatives. The requirement that the responsible party commission and submit an EIS is heavily litigated and the preparation of the EIS itself and litigation over its requirement often leads to substantial delays in the proposed project's timeline. NEPA's requirements apply even if the project is a private-sector development receiving substantial private funding, provided the federal government plays a major role in the project, such as opening up federal lands for development.

The National Historic Preservation Act (NHPA) is purely procedural in nature; it does not independently impose any substantive requirements to preserve historic/cultural resources. Under the NHPA, the owner is required to:

- Identify properties
- Consult with affected parties
- Take effects into account/evaluate mitigation

Environmental laws affecting property ownership and management

Where the Developer will continue to own and/or operate a site after construction is complete, it will need to be mindful of the environmental laws affecting property ownership and management. All of the laws discussed earlier are potentially applicable during this Phase as well. A key difference, however, is that once a property is operable, it presumably has tenants. As a general matter, the tenants are primarily responsible for compliance with environmental laws implicated by their operations, including securing necessary permits for their operations. However, if the owner exercises control over its tenants' operations, the owner, too, may have responsibilities and potential liability under those environmental laws. Thus, the owner should know its tenants' businesses, be clear about who has responsibility for regulatory compliance, and actively evaluate how best to manage its potential environmental responsibilities and liability under the circumstances.

How the legal framework of environmental regulation and protection applies to The Development Process

Problem statement: Hardrock Development Company

The application of the federal regulatory framework of environmental regulation and its implications for real estate development and finance may best be demonstrated through a complex hypothetical. Offering students and readers alike the opportunity to understand how a real estate development project may be required to navigate such legal requirements.

Environmental Law problem statement[2]
I. The Hardrock property
Hardrock Development Company, a wholly owned subsidiary of Hardrock Holdings, Inc., has acquired 200 acres from Integrated Defense Machines (IDM), an aircraft manufacturer, along

2. *The Environmental Law Problem Statement was adapted from a Hypothetical Problem Statement initially created by Thomas E. Hogan for the author's "Fundamentals of Real Estate Law" course in Georgetown University's School of Continuing Studies Master's in Real Estate Program (MPRE) in the spring 2013 semester. Although the author made substantial revisions to the hypothetical for the course, in the form presented in this chapter, he is grateful for Mr. Hogan's contribution to both the course and the textbook in this regard.*

the coast of a bay in the fictional state of Hometown (alternatively referred to as "the property," the "Subject Site," or simply the "Site"). IDM acquired the property from the U.S. Navy in 1960. In the northwest quadrant of the property, on approximately fifty acres, is a 100-bed hospital that was built in 1950 and operated by the Navy until 1960 (hereinafter referred to as "the Hospital Building"). After IDM acquired the property in 1960, it leased the Hospital Building to a nonprofit healthcare organization and used the remaining 150 acres as a staging ground to test fly prototype helicopters over the ocean. The fifty-year lease with the nonprofit expired in 2010 and the Hospital Building has been vacant since. The remainder of the property appears as undeveloped land.

II. The development plans
A. Medical Center

HealthyCare, a large healthcare company, has signed a fifty-year lease with Hardrock to operate a 500-bed regional medical center to be constructed on 100 acres of the property (the northwest and southwest quadrants of the Site).

Hardrock plans to refurbish the Hospital Building and convert it into a wing of a new 500-bed medical center to be constructed by Hardrock, for which it will be compensated through the fifty-year lease.

B. The Wind Farm

Hardrock has leased the remaining 100 acres to CleanEnergy Corp., a newly formed subsidiary of Hardrock Holdings, Inc., Hardrock's parent company. CleanEnergy plans to use the property as a staging ground to construct an off-shore wind farm (in federal waters) and to construct an on-shore transformer and transmission facility to connect the wind farm to the energy grid.

III. Impediments to development discovered after closing on the acquisition of the site
Hardrock made the following findings after completing the acquisition of the Site (hereinafter referred to individually as a "Post-Closing Discovery" and collectively as the "Post-Closing Discoveries"):

1. The existing hospital building has asbestos-containing material.
2. The hospital historically operated boilers and emergency generators, which will need to be increased to meet the needs of the expanded facility.
3. The groundwater is contaminated with solvents from an undetermined source.
4. During excavation for the foundation of the new Hospital Building a disposal pit containing degraded drums and an abandoned underground storage tank were uncovered.
5. Storm water is channeled through a series of unlined ditches into a stream that runs through the property. The stream and its banks are contaminated with mining tailings from a former mine located far upstream. The stream empties into the ocean.
6. Clover growing on the site has become part of the larger habitat for a bee that has been designated as an endangered species.
7. The plans for the expanded medical campus partially extend into a wetlands portion of the property that is adjacent to off-site, non-navigable seasonal tributaries.
8. The planned location for the new parking garage is currently a large, paved parking lot. The parking lot was constructed over a substantial amount of fill material that was brought

onto the site in the 1930s from a gaslight mantle manufacture. That manufacturer, which has no known successor, refined radioactive thorium ore to make incandescent gaslight mantles for home and street lighting. The ore-refining process created a radioactive sandy material that made for useful fill material with good compaction. The material is known to have been used for fill throughout the state.

9. During shallow excavation for an access road on the 100-acre site to be dedicated to the operation of the wind farm, cannons dating to the early nineteenth century were uncovered. In addition, the Keeper of the National Register of Historic Places is considering designating the entire bay as a Traditional Cultural Property based on its historical cultural significance to a local Native American tribe, although the land is not tribal land.

IV. Problem statement

You have just been hired as Hardrock's new vice president of real estate development and facilities management shortly after the summary termination of your predecessor, who was escorted from Hardrock's headquarters after the third of the nine Post-Closing Discoveries came to light. Also undisclosed to you at the time you were hired was the existence of the nine Post-Closing Discoveries threatening Hardrock's development plans for the property.

The CEO, to whom you report directly, has advised you that his job is on the line and, therefore, so is yours (the fact that you were just hired, with no previous knowledge about the Post-Closing Discoveries, notwithstanding), with regard to how Hardrock is going to extricate itself from its Environmental Law entanglements. The Board of Directors has ordered the CEO to fully apprise the Board of the full scope, extent, and nature of all Post-Closing Discoveries and the potential liabilities associated with each one, as well as to offer a mitigation plan that would permit development to proceed on the two proposed projects on the Site (the HealthyCare long-term facility lease and the CleanEnergy Corp. wind farm project).

In this regard, the CEO has instructed you to prepare a report, which must be at least twenty-five pages in length but not more than forty pages (excluding any exhibits or attachments thereto, except as expressly noted later), fully briefing the Board of Directors on each of the nine Post-Closing Discoveries.

Specifically, the CEO has determined that your report to the Board must contain the following substantive sections:

1. Identification of any additional potential environmental liabilities not included among the Post-Closing Discoveries. This section should not exceed two pages in length.
2. Provide a comprehensive outline for the Board, not to exceed ten pages in length, of the federal Environmental Law violations presented by each Post- Closing Discovery.
3. Select three of the nine Post-Closing Discoveries, and brief the Board in detail about the legal issues each presents, including the potential liabilities posed and mitigation strategies necessary to proceed with development. For each of these three issues, your report to the Board must identify and summarize or brief at least one foundational legal precedent – a statute, regulation, or court opinion – on which your analysis and recommendations rely. These case summaries or briefs, as the case may be, are to be attached to your report as appendices, and will be counted in the total number of pages of your report.

Sample Legal Memorandum from Joseph Brennan, V.P. of Real Estate Development & Facilities Management, Hardrock Development Company, Responding to Hardrock Problem Statement.[5]

BRIEFING MEMORANDUM[6]

To: The Board of Directors of Hardrock Holdings, Inc.
Through: CEO, Hardrock Development Company
From: Joseph Brennan, Vice President of Real Estate Development and Facilities Management
RE: Post-Closing Discoveries Impacting Development of the IDM Site

INTRODUCTION

The purpose of this Memorandum is to apprise the Board of Directors of the parent corporation of Hardrock Development Company (Hardrock), Hardrock Holdings, Inc. (Hardrock Holdings), of material concerns about the ability of Hardrock to develop its 200-acre property acquired from Integrated Defense Machines (IDM), an aircraft manufacturer, which property is commonly referred to as the "Bay View Property," located in the Commonwealth of Hometown, arising out of nine separate Post-Closing discoveries of material facts (individually a "Post-Closing Discovery" and, collectively, the "Post-Closing Discoveries") potentially giving rise to various civil, and possibly criminal, liabilities under various environmental laws of the United States (collectively referred to as the "Environmental Laws").

Hardrock purchased the Subject Site from the well-known aircraft manufacturer Integrated Defense Machines (IDM) in 2011, and has been marketing the project for lease during the past two years. After the commencement of initial construction, Hardrock's Development Team discovered nine separate environmental concerns regarding the Subject Site, collectively referred to as the "Post-Closing Discoveries." Each Post-Closing Discovery has a material negative impact on the value of the Subject Site and on Hardrock's ability to develop the Subject Site as a way to extract value from it, and portends significant potential federal environmental liabilities.

Had a Phase I Environmental Assessment been prepared during the Site Selection process, or even during the Due Diligence Period under the Purchase and Sales Agreement, while Hardrock's obligation to purchase the IDM property was still contingent, either Hardrock would have walked away from the proposed transaction or it would have factored into the Purchase Price, as well as the Seller's Warranties and Representations and the Seller's Indemnification of Buyer deliverables at Closing, the economic consequences of the environmental liabilities with which Hardrock is now faced as the Owner of the Subject. Now that Hardrock is the owner of record of the Subject Site, however, there is no option to simply "walk away" from the property.

PREVIOUS CHAIN OF OWNERSHIP

As background, IDM purchased the site from the U.S. Navy in 1960 and used the facility to test and service prototype helicopters. IDM also leased 25% of the site to a local healthcare company who operated a 100-bed hospital on the northwest corner. These two operations were conducted on the property for approximately fifty years before we owned it and should have been cause for serious environmental concerns by our acquisitions team prior to our purchase of the site.

The site was acquired by IDM from the U.S. government in the first Department of Defense Base Realignment and Closure (BRAC) round in 1960. The U.S. Department of Defense (DOD) successfully uses the program to realign its missions and, as in the case of the BAY VIEW property, shed nonessential real estate holdings. BRAC disposal is a usual course of business for the U.S. military. It is also critical to note that the U.S. Navy operated a military base on the site for more than 100 years before the IDM purchase, again another use that should have caused the acquisition team real concern.

The BAY VIEW site sits on a spectacular bluff overlooking the beautiful and historic FISHING BAY that provides protected and direct access to the Atlantic Ocean. At first impression, the site looks pristine with only the quaint 35,000 sf hospital building providing any visible signs of past development activity on the 200-acre property. In the past year our Hardrock Development subsidiary has signed two long-term leases for the property. The initial economic terms appeared to be favorable and were with strong credit tenants. On the surface, the uses appear compatible with the site and with our corporate goals BUT upon the commencement of the initial phases of construction due diligence, soils testing and actual discovery has revealed material environmental exposure to both Hardrock Holdings and Hardrock Development exists and this exposure needs to be addressed immediately.

CLEANENERGY AND HEALTHYCARE EXECUTED LEASES AND DEVELOPMENT AGREEMENTS THAT ARE HIGH-VALUE WINS BUT MAY COMPOUND THE PROBLEM AND INCREASE OUR EXPOSURE.

The first lease is a fifty-year lease commitment for 100 acres with the multinational healthcare provider HealthyCare. The tenant plans to renovate and expand the existing sixty-year-old 100-bed hospital and develop a 500-bed world class regional medical center. Hardrock Development is the "at risk" developer for this job. The Commonwealth of Homeland is ecstatic about the proposed use. The governor and Commonwealth's Economic Development Authority were all very involved in the pursuit of the HealthyCare regional medical center. The Commonwealth has committed to promote the HealthyCare effort on various levels including providing material economic assistance, which was central to Hardrock and the Commonwealths' efforts in winning the multistate competition for this prestigious tenant.

The 100-acre balance of the property is now under a long-term lease to CleanEnergy Corp (CEC). CEC is a Hardrock Corporation subsidiary. CleanEnergy plans to construct and operate a state-of-the-art wind farm facility on the property. Hardrock is also the at-risk developer for the facility. The fully integrated facility is planned to be the "on-shore" central plant of the power generation facility. During stage one the site will be used to receive (via truck) the components of every element of the plant: windmill components, conduit, cable, transformers, and all operations equipment. During stage two, CleanEnergy plans to build an operations facility and assemble all of the components and buildings for the generation, operation, and distribution of the massive wind farm which will be located directly offshore in U.S. federal waters.

CleanEnergy plans to receive components via truck and has constructed an access road along the northwest corner of the site. They plan to ship components and stage all off-shore construction from a substantial (to be constructed) dock located on the eastern edge of the BAY VIEW property located directly on FISHING BAY. During the third stage CleanEnergy plans to operate and maintain a complex electric power generation plant that stretches east to federal waters and distributes power to the utility grid. The BAY VIEW site is obviously only one component of many complex variables for the CleanEnergy plant, but all other components and agreements assume this lease and substantial investment is the base for the entire operation.

On the surface, this appears to be another great development success for our firm; to be crystal clear, at present it is not. We have discovered numerous "Post-Closing Discoveries" that pose material risks and great exposure to federal environmental laws to the firm. Presently we have identified nine environmental impediments to the development of the site that will directly impact our ownership rights and our obligations to our tenants and expose the firm to damages well in excess of the value of the property. We have exposure to the site's potential creation and migration of ongoing pollution, to remediation requirements, to reimbursements of third parties, as well as to federal and state fines and penalties.

INITIAL STEP

The very first thing we must do is to quantify our exposure. Now that we are aware of the environmental problems at BAY VIEW, we must stop the construction on the site immediately. Disturbing the existing conditions increases our liability and exposure. I have ordered all construction on the site to cease. We must immediately assemble a team of:

1) Environmental experts – including a top environmental attorney
2) Litigation experts – to research the previous chain of ownership and other persons potentially liable for contamination at the site
3) A communications team skilled in crisis management.

Next, we need to prepare for our initial contact with the Commonwealth of Homeland as well as the Environmental Protection Agency (EPA). Managing our initial communications will be critical. The Commonwealth may be our one ally, and the EPA will be a formidable opponent.

We are not the creator or the generator of the environmental issues and contamination on the site, but have owned this site for more than two years and we are (and will be judged as) a sophisticated organization and owner of real estate and we must react accordingly; ignorance will not be tolerated as a defense.

I am your vice president of development; I am *not* your lawyer, but my research indicates that the BAY VIEW site contamination and violations expose Hardrock to numerous federal acts and laws. We will need legal, engineering, and political assistance to recover from the development impediments present on the site. The Federal Water Pollution Control Act, Clean Air Act, Solid Waste Disposal Act, Water Quality Act, Occupational Safety and Health Act, Clean Water Act, Endangered Species Act, Safe Drinking Water Act, Hazardous Materials Transportation Act, Toxic Substances Control Act, and CERCLA (Superfund) are all points of major federal legislation that we have potentially violated.[7]

We own this site and have for a material period of time, and our options, short of assuming all of the required cleanup on the site, are very limited. In addition to assembling a top environmental team we will also assemble a top team of litigators. All of the parties associated with the acquisition of this site in 2006 need to be vetted. A full effort will be immediately initiated into understanding all of the decisions and due diligence associated with the BAY VIEW site acquisition. The brokers, the lenders, the engineers, the architects, and the lawyers on both sides of this transaction will be assessed for liability. All of the previous owners of the site will be assessed for their contribution to the contamination and their liability.

A skilled public relations team will be essential in salvaging success at BAY VIEW. The Commonwealth should be viewed as our ally. They desire the construction jobs, the real estate taxes, and the long-term employment provided by the HealthyCare and CleanEnergy corporations. The hospital and the clean energy plant are viewed as economically and politically valuable to all of the stakeholders. We will have one opportunity to rally our stakeholders with the Commonwealth as the most critical advocate.

Environmental Law is complex. A major goal of U.S. environmental laws is to ensure that the "polluter pays."[8] This goal is noble, but in practice the central piece of legislation, the Comprehensive Environmental Response, Compensation and Liability Act (CERCLA), also known as SUPERFUND, has six "strict liability provisions that have become a scourge to countless owners and operators of contaminated properties. As explained by one court, CERCLA has become a 'black hole that indiscriminately devours all who come near it.'"[9] We own the BAY VIEW site and we must mount a serious effort to manage our financial, political, legal, and personal exposure.

THE ENVIRONMENTAL PROTECTION AGENCY (EPA)

The BAY VIEW site has numerous environmental, historic, and endangered species issues embedded on and around the site. The Environmental Protection Agency will be the primary federal government agency with jurisdiction over the environmental discoveries on the site. The development team should also expect The Commonwealth of Homeland to be active in all environmental discussions. The mission of the EPA is to "protect human health and the environment." The EPA develops and enforces federal environmental regulations and is a very powerful federal agency; its power is particularly magnified in commercial real estate development. The EPA is an independent agency; it does not serve under a traditional Cabinet post, though it is often treated as such. Central to the nature of the development business is to efficiently meet market demand in a timely fashion. Successfully meeting the demands of any market takes great skill in the best of circumstances, and the discovery of contamination on BAY VIEW Post-Closing is a huge impediment to our development plans. The EPA has the power to stop the development of BAY VIEW, but it also has the power to impose civil and criminal penalties well in excess of our investment in the site. The EPA has the power to compel ownership to remediate any site contamination and impose day-for-day fines until the site has been cleaned up. We will need to skillfully deal with the EPA.

Many of the elements that make BAY VIEW valuable to us are also the elements that are central to the EPA's mission of protection and enforcement. We are a coastal site with wetlands and streams on the property. The EPA concerns itself with almost all things dealing with water: wetlands, groundwater, drinking water, navigable waterways, and wildlife living in and depending on water on and adjacent to the site. Storm water issues of all kinds will be a concern to the EPA: erosion, flow into the Bay, flow onto the site, flow from our site onto adjacent sites and of course storm water dispersing contamination anywhere.

The EPA concerns itself with almost all things dealing with air pollution. The boilers and generators associated with the old and the new hospital will have clean air implications.

SUPERFUND DEFENSES

The following flow chart is a description of the path for Superfund defenses related to contaminated sites and landowners' responsibilities and obligations. Superfund is a powerful piece of legislation that allows the EPA to, in effect, perform self-help on contaminated sites. The U.S. government, through the EPA and Superfund legislation, has the ability to compel polluters and landowners to remediate contamination. The process of identification, extraction, and disposal of toxic waste is described in specific detail and process in the Superfund legislation. This is a process to avoid at all costs. The time and financial exposure to ownership is open-ended. The EPA has the right to prefect every element of site remediation, including long-term monitoring. Upon conclusion of the physical remediation, the EPA also has the latitude to assign liability and impose fines and penalties depending on the scope of the pollution.

THE U.S. ARMY CORPS OF ENGINEERS, FISH AND WILDLIFE, DEPARTMENT OF ENERGY, OFFICE OF ENVIRONMENTAL MANAGEMENT

We will potentially be dealing with other federal agencies that often have overlapping concerns and missions intertwined with the EPA. BAY VIEW has potential issues with habitats serving endangered species. The U.S. Fish and Wildlife Agency will be the agency with jurisdiction.

The BAY VIEW site has potential issues with fill dirt believed to have some low-level radioactive contamination. Thorium is believed to have been used as fill on the site, and the removal, transportation, and disposal of the substance will require the involvement of the Department of Energy and the Office of Environmental Management, in addition to the EPA.

The initial commercial use for the site was as a U.S. Navy base constructed prior to the U.S. Civil War. The strategic location of the base at the entrance to FISHING BAY may have material historic significance, and, as we have now discovered, was the site for a battery of cannons during the War Between the States. The Keeper of the National Register of Historic Places already has some interest in the site due to the cultural significance of FISHING BAY, primarily to Native Americans. We will explore NEPA for solutions relating to any DOD liability.

HEALTHYCARE AND CLEANENERGY CORPORATION LEASES AND DEVELOPMENT AGREEMENTS ARE VERY VALUABLE BUT MAY CREATE ADDITIONAL EXPOSURE.

The leases for the site are extremely valuable. The HealthyCare 400-bed regional hospital is highly desired by the local community and a substantial development for Hardrock Corporation. The CleanEnergy generation facility is a state-of-the-art clean energy operation with local support and U.S. Department of Energy federal funding. All of the stakeholders involved want those uses to succeed.

There are also numerous unresolved issues associated with our tenants for the site:

1. CleanEnergy will need a dock and will need to navigate the waters adjacent to BAY VIEW. The U.S. Army Corps of Engineers will need to be involved. The permitting multiple elements of the wind energy facility with concerns of: noise, land use, birds and other biological resources, visual resources, soil erosion and water quality, public health and safety, cultural and paleontological resources, socioeconomic/public service/infrastructure, solid and hazardous wastes, and air quality and climate change.[10]
2. HealthyCare use is much more regular but will also have issues common in the healthcare industry like the collection, storage, and disposal of hazardous waste. These are issues more dependent on the tenant's specific use for the site and will need to be addressed prior to the commencement of any operations. These issues are not central to the

concerns of this report, but they are important. Should we resolve the Post-Closing impediments to the development of the BAY VIEW property? These serious concerns need to be immediately addressed if the tenants are to be able to conduct and operate their business. If the tenants cannot profitably operate, they are of little use to us as tenants.

THE FEDERAL PERSPECTIVE

The BAY VIEW site will attract significant attention by the federal government not as an economic engine but as a contaminated site that needs remediation and not as a great investment for Hardrock but first as an historic site that needs to be vetted. The government, through the EPA, is in the business of cleaning up contaminated sites and assigning the liability and the expense to owners and polluters after the fact. We are exposed, and this report is a first step in defining and qualifying our exposure. Secondarily, this report will develop initial recommendations regarding when and if our investment can be salvaged and, if not, what we can do to mitigate our exposure in excess of our initial investment in the site.

THE COMMONWEALTH OF HOMELAND PERSPECTIVE

The Commonwealth has the ability to assist our development efforts at BAY VIEW and to mitigate the expense and exposure associated with the environmental problems on the site. The Commonwealth views the economic development at BAY VIEW as significant. Each construction project is valued in excess of $100 million and represents significant short-term employment as well as long-term services and employment. The governor and the director of economic development were both intimately involved in the pursuit of HealthyCare and CleanEnergy and we can expect their assistance in dealing with the new environmental exposure.

WE DID NOT KNOW ABOUT THE CONTAMINATION, BUT WE ARE RESPONSIBLE TO DEFEND OUR POSITION.

Our goal is not only to uncover problems but to seek solutions; our preliminary defense strategies are not promising. The CERCLA Brownfields Amendments provide for three landowner liability exemptions:[11]

1. Innocent landowner
2. Bona fide purchasers
3. Contiguous property owners

"Innocent landowners" have three tests to qualify for the liability exemption:

1. They did not cause or contribute to the hazardous substances.
2. The property was acquired by inheritance or bequest.
3. After completing all appropriate studies did not know and had no reason to know of "release or threatened release" at the time of acquisition.

The BAY VIEW acquisition was a real estate transaction between a sophisticated buyer and seller. The transaction was not an inheritance or bequest. If a competent phase 1 analysis had been completed, a phase 2 would have surely followed and discovered the multiple problems with the site. My sense is we will not qualify as an innocent landowner.

A "bona fide purchaser" has six tests to qualify for the liability exemption:[12]

1. Acquired ownership after 1/06.
2. Hazardous substances released before the purchase.
3. No potential liability or connection with the Potentially Responsible Party other than the purchase agreement.
4. Rigorously completes ALL APPROPRIATE INQUIRIES (Phase 1 and Phase 2 studies).
5. Appropriate care in dealing with hazardous substances.
6. Cooperates with regulatory agencies mandated remedial work, contractors, etc.

The bona fide purchaser exemption assumes that the buyer knew the site was contaminated prior to the purchase and that the buyer had performed a comprehensive due diligence effort on the site and into the previous owners. As an example, U.S. military facilities are universally considered to contain hazardous soils and water. BAY VIEW is a coastal site that was operated by the Navy for more than 100 years and was commissioned prior to the Civil War. Hazardous waste, historic significance, and costal impact should all have been revealed in an initial phase 1 analysis. My initial evaluation is we will have a very difficult time seeking liability protection under the bona fide purchaser exemption.

The "Contiguous landowner" exemption has four tests for liability exemptions:[13]

1. An adjacent property owner.
2. Did not cause, contribute, or consent to release or threatened release.
3. After completing ALL APPROPRIATE INQUIRIES (phase 1 and phase 2) did not know and had no reason to know of "release or threatened release" at the time of purchase.
4. No potential liability or connection with neighboring Potential Party.

BAY VIEW may have potential partial liability mitigation associated with the contiguous landowner exemption associated with some of the mine tailings detected in one of the creeks and some of the common wetlands shared with an adjacent landowner (located near the southwest corner of the property), but I do not expect it to be material.

Another issue we must evaluate is the potential exposure to our subsidiary and tenant CleanEnergy Corp. as they are most certainly connected to Hardrock Corporation. I believe the protections available to us through the contiguous landowner exemption are minimal.

A Chapter 11 filing must also be considered to escape the potential material environmental liability, but that path is also filled with "muddled case law" and does not appear to be a sound solution for the BAY VIEW effort at this time.[14]

A "Transfer of Environmental Liability" (TEL) structure will also be evaluated and may be a valid approach to the environmental liability associated with BAY VIEW. As we continue to evaluate the exposure to the development company and to Hardrock Corporation, a TEL structure becomes more attractive as the amount of the potential liability approaches the investment potential of the property. This structure is further explained as a potential solution in the conclusion.[15]

WHAT IS THE CONDITION OF THE BAY VIEW SITE TODAY?

We must first determine where we are today, we need to stop and evaluate the scope of the problem at BAY VIEW, and it is imperative we not create more damage than exists today. At a minimum, we must "do no [more] harm." The purpose of this report has precisely that scope. All other efforts depend on first defining the extent of the problems and exposure at BAY VIEW. The findings in this report will initiate and shape our efforts with our environmental team, our litigation team, and our communications effort.

The following sections will:

1. Identify any additional potential environmental liabilities over and above the nine we are sure of today.
2. Provide a comprehensive outline of the federal environmental law violations presented in the Post-Closing Discoveries we have uncovered.
3. Provide expanded briefs on three of the Post-Closing Discoveries that will include potential liabilities and mitigation strategies.

The goals of these sections will be to:

1. Define the extent and nature of the Post-Closing Discoveries.
2. Determine the potential liabilities associated with each of the Discoveries.
3. Explore how to extricate Hardrock from the environmental entanglements associated with the BAY VIEW site and offer a plan that would permit development to proceed with HealthyCare and CleanEnergy Corporation.

In an effort to establish a new baseline position, I would like to:

1. Outline ten environmental impediments.
2. Initiate a new Phase I and Phase II Environmental Assessment for the BAY VIEW site.

It is critical we qualify our new baseline position.

TEN ADDITIONAL POST-CLOSING IMPEDIMENTS TO THE DEVELOPMENT OF BAY VIEW HAVE BEEN IDENTIFIED AND ARE LISTED NEXT:

The history of the past owners and past uses on the site indicates more environmental impediments will likely be found. I offer possible additional environmental impediments and cite some of the laws that could affect the development of the BAY VIEW site:

1. The original use for the site was a U.S. Navy base. The site was a key position for the protection of FISHING BAY during the U.S. Civil War.

    • No exploration of the immediate shore line or adjacent waterways appears to have been performed.
    • Historic U.S. Navy shipwrecks, piers, and infrastructure potentially exist.
    • Unexploded ordnance as well as lead, mercury, and asbestos contamination is common on decommissioned military facilities.

2. Cemeteries, limb yards, and field hospitals are often elements of historic military facilities and will generate interest and implications with the government. Relevant laws: contamination – Comprehensive Environmental Response, Compensation, and Liability Act (CERCLA), historic structures and functions – National Historic Preservation Act (NHPA).

3. The site is not located on tribal land today, but appears to be located in an area that was inhabited by Native Americans. Archeological research and excavation does not appear to have been performed on the site, but FISHING BAY appears to be significant to the Keeper of the National Register of Historic Places. Relevant laws: National Historic Preservation Act (NHPA).

4. Helicopter prototype testing by IDM would indicate a potential for numerous environmental issues.
   - Failures resulting in crashes both on land and in the water. Crashes could result in environmental contamination fuel, oil, and munitions.
   - A helicopter testing facility could also have historic implications – test pilots who died, historic/important designs or prototypes.
   - A helicopter servicing facility would raise environmental concerns regarding paint, oil, and solvents. Relevant laws: CERCLA, NHPA.

5. Older hospitals commonly have cleaning and disposal practices that contaminate many sites; these need to be explored.
   - Cemeteries are often an element associated with hospitals that need to be considered.
   - Waste pits and underground storage facilities should be expected. Relevant laws: CERCLA.

6. CleanEnergy requires a substantial pier for the transportation of construction materials to federal waters. The U.S. Army Corps of Engineers will need to approve the facility.

7. The off shore turbines will be visible from the shore. Have the environmental impacts regarding wind, waterfowl, and noise been explored?

8. The expansion of the boilers and emergency generators needs to be increased . . . increased power generation also increases impacts on:
   - Air quality
   - Noise

9. The increase of the hospital population by five times will impact the adequate public facilities. Has the scope of the impact been calculated and priced?

10. The groundwater contamination may not only affect our site; contaminated water may have leached to:
   - Surrounding sites
   - Into FISHING BAY
   - Into the wetlands on the southwest corner of the site

11. Stream contamination will have impacted FISHING BAY and Atlantic Ocean U.S. waters.

The nine Post-Closing impediments to development we are aware of are listed and evaluated next:

1. Asbestos detected in the old hospital building.

   The 35,000 sf BAY VIEW hospital building was constructed in 1950 and is most certainly filled with asbestos. After World War II, asbestos was widely used in thousands of institutional buildings all over the country. I anticipate the existing hospital building on BAY VIEW is no exception. Asbestos is a mineral that is extracted via mining. The material is strong, flexible, and will not burn, and it is estimated that asbestos is contained in more than 3,000 different commercial products.[16] We should anticipate existing hospital building to be riddled with the carcinogen. Exposure to employees, patients, and contractors is a material concern, particularly if it is determined that the asbestos in the building was disturbed or was "friable," a condition that allows the substance to easily be inhaled or ingested.

Asbestos was used to insulate fireproof, soundproof, and decorate thousands of institutional buildings, and I anticipate we will find asbestos contamination in the roof, insulation, ceiling tiles, floor tiles, and in the mastic on all glued surfaces of the old hospital building. Asbestos is linked to cancers like lung cancer and mesothelioma. It is also linked to other respiratory diseases like Asbestosis. Asbestos contamination is a serious problem. The EPA and the Occupational Safety and Health Administration (OSHA) are the primary organizations responsible for the regulation of environmental exposure and the protection of workers exposed to asbestos.[17] The EPA's key regulations governing asbestos are:[18]

1. The Toxic Substance Control Act (TSCA) began in 1979 and was founded with the goal of providing technical assistance to building owners for the proper handling of asbestos abatement.
2. The Asbestos Hazard Emergency Response Act (AHERA)
3. The Asbestos Information Act
4. The Clean Air Act
5. The Safe Drinking Water Act

Our liability associated with the asbestos in the old hospital building is unclear at the moment. A specific understanding of our role in the fundamental differences between owning the property and operating the property/development is essential. Passive ownership of a building containing asbestos is a relatively minor problem.[19] My concern is we have unknowingly expanded our role on the property from owner to operator. As an operator/developer, improperly disturbing or removing of asbestos from the building is a material problem on numerous levels: 1) we are in potential violation of all of the laws listed earlier. We own this property under an LLC (Limited Liability Corporation), and the protections allowed a passive owner are not those protections afforded an operator who is viewed as a contributor to spreading contamination. Regulations regarding removal, transportation, and disposal of asbestos are precise and require certified professionals to execute each phase.

If our team on the ground has done nothing to disturb the asbestos in the building, that is certainly positive, but we still need to evaluate the additional costs and lost time associated with professional remediation of the building, as it is central to our lease with HealthyCare. The discovery of asbestos in the old hospital building remains a Post-Closing discovery and represents a material impediment to the development of the BAY VIEW site and an additional and unanticipated cost to the project.

If our on-site team has begun to remove and dispose of the asbestos in the building, our exposure is material in every phase of the effort. Expanding the contamination on the site into the air and water and exposing unprotected workers to friable asbestos are federal crimes and expose Hardrock Development Company and Hardrock

Corporation to much more than simple development risk. A clear assessment of our exposure to asbestos litigation will be at the top of our legal teams' assessment.

2) Commercial boilers

Commercial Boilers are used to generate energy in the form of steam heat. They are traditionally fired by fossil fuels; the existing boilers on BAY VIEW are oil fired and are more than fifty years old. Emergency electrical generators are critical to the operation of healthcare facilities. The service and capacity of generators vary widely from supporting emergency lighting to creating an uninterruptable power supply for communications, computer and healthcare technology. The existing generators are diesel and have been in service for more than thirty years. The existing boilers and generators have substantial underground storage tanks for fuel and both boilers and generators have been dormant since 2010.[20]

The EPA considers the existing boilers "major area source boilers," and the boilers are therefore subject to new (12/20/12) EPA Clean Air Act standards. The EPA has concluded that, of the 1.5 million boilers in the United States, less than 1% will meet the new numerical emission standards (1). Emissions concerns are in the form of mercury, lead, arsenic, cadmium, chromium, manganese, nickel, ethylene dioxide, and PCBs. The fifty-year-old boilers at BAY VIEW are sure to meet none of the modern standards. The larger concerns for the existing boilers are the underground fuel tanks. The two 10,000-gallon tanks were not discovered until after Closing, and we should expect leaks and soils contamination. The project does not have the required insurance, and we will need to support our financial strength (a central goal of the U.S. Congress and the EPA) should we need to remediate a spill.[21]

The emergency electrical generators fall into the same category. The EPA Clean AIR Act will need compliance, but the fifty-year-old underground fuel tanks will be a problem. The fact that both sets of tanks are old, were abandoned, and were not discovered in the acquisition due diligence is a serious setback for both the projects. Our position as passive owner will be an important distinction as it relates to the fuel tanks. If we were servicing and/or operating the boilers and generators after Closing, our liability and exposure is significantly increased.

3) Groundwater contamination from solvents of an unknown source

BAY VIEW was originally a substantial navy base. IDM operated a prototype helicopter-testing facility and a 100-bed hospital operated on the site for sixty years – which means the groundwater being contaminated with solvents should be no surprise to anyone.

Military facilities are generally (by design) self-contained communities that can function as a military facility and operate independently from the outside community; the prolific use of solvents in multiple functions is to be expected on navy bases. The IDM testing facility should be expected to have a substantial use of solvents for the maintenance of the parts and facilities associated with helicopter maintenance and testing. Hospitals are notorious producers of hazardous waste and the use of solvents in hospitals is also prolific.

The chain of generators of the contamination is now obvious; the challenge will be to connect them with the specific contamination and successfully and practically attach any liability claims to them.

"Half of all Americans and more than 95% of rural Americans get their household water
supplies from underground sources of water, or groundwater. Groundwater also
is used for about half of the nation's agricultural irrigation and nearly one third of
the industrial water needs. This makes it a vitally important national resource."[22]
"Groundwater is rain water or water from surface water bodies, like lakes or streams,
which soaks into the soil and bedrock and is stored underground in the tiny spaces
between rocks and particles of soil. Groundwater pollution occurs when hazardous
substances come into contact and dissolve in the water that has soaked into
the soil."[23] Once the groundwater is contaminated, it is very difficult and costly to
remediate, and often the general solution is to carefully monitor the condition with the
hope it remains contained underground as the real issue is if the contaminated water
reaches the surface and can harm plants, animals, and people.

BAY VIEW has two major problems with contaminated groundwater:

1) The site is in a relatively remote location and has always used ground/well water to serve
the site's need for water.
2) The BAY VIEW property is a coastal location, and the potential for contaminated
groundwater to migrate into FISHING BAY is high.

Groundwater contamination is a huge problem at BAY VIEW, and remediation options are
limited:[24]

1) Contain the contaminants to prevent migration.
2) Withdraw the pollutants from the aquifer.
3) Treat the groundwater where it is withdrawn or at its point of use.
4) Rehabilitate the aquifer by either immobilizing or detoxifying the contaminants while they
are still in the aquifer.
5) Abandon the use of the aquifer and find alternative sources of water.

The EPA is responsible for the protection of groundwater through – the Safe Drinking
Water Act, the Resource Conservation and Recovery Act, the Comprehensive
Environmental Response, Compensation, and Liability Act (CERCLA/Superfund), the
Federal Insecticide, Fungicide, and Rodenticide Act, the Toxic Substances Control
Act, and the Clean Water Act. The Commonwealth of Homeland will be a player in
any groundwater issues as well.

The BAY VIEW development has major exposure to financial and governmental risk due
to groundwater contamination. It is the primary source of water on the site, it will need
to be remediated, and we are in violation of multiple federal laws. Prior to sale, a
competent phase 1 would have indicated the need for testing, and the testing required
under a phase 2 would have revealed this contamination and the purchase of this
property could have been properly evaluated. The extensive groundwater contamination
at BAY VIEW will have a huge negative impact on the value of the development.

4) A disposal pit, degraded drums, and an abandoned underground storage tank were
uncovered while digging the foundation for the New Hospital.

The new HealthyCare hospital will add a 400-bed wing to the existing 100-bed old
hospital building, and initial horizontal construction (foundations, utilities, roads,

curb, gutter, etc.) started last month. Hardrock Development Company is the "at-risk" developer for the job, and central to compliance with the lease terms is a rigid development schedule with specific goals and target completion dates.

On the first day of excavation for the foundation of the new hospital wing, a disposal pit was uncovered; the age and specific use of the pit are unclear at the moment, but the discovery of this undocumented and unexpected dump is an indication of a very serious problem at BAY VIEW. Immediately it was evident to the construction team that degraded drums and an underground storage tank were in and adjacent to the pit and had been disturbed. We now know all of the previous owners and occupants used and stored various liquid and solid hazardous wastes and did so over a very long period of time. The presence of an undocumented and uncontrolled disposal pit and the obvious signs of contamination require immediate action in order to mitigate our exposure. Pits like this and on sites of this age and use should be expected to contain: paint, lead, asbestos, solvents, oil, sludge and ash, PCBs, arsenic, mercury, barium, zinc, and so on.[25]

Disposal pits on old industrial sites like this were just that; they were the dump. As an example, a similar 3.5-acre pit was discovered at a Wisconsin site called the Wheeler Pit.[26] The twenty-year cleanup forced the site to be fenced off, monitored for years, and capped, not exactly ideal for a development in progress with a rigid schedule.

Our construction and development risk is material and may be fatal to the HealthyCare project, but our risk as an operator is another very real additional problem for the development company and for Hardrock Corporation. Ignorance is not a defense in Environmental Law.[27] Sadly, we can't claim that ground in this development. The penalties associated with oil spills (from the UST and potentially the barrels) begin with the responsibility to clean up the site. At this point, we do not know the scope of the problem, but we should assume that oil and solvents (already discovered in the groundwater) will be present in the disposal pit and in the adjacent soils and groundwater. Administrative penalties can reach $157,500 and civil penalties can reach $32,000 per violation per day or $1,100 per barrel of oil spilled if the spill reaches waters of the United States (like FISHING BAY). The fine for not notifying the appropriate federal agency can reach $250,000 for an individual or $500,000 for an organization. The maximum prison fine is five years. Should the violations turn criminal in nature, the fines can be up to $250,000 and fifteen years in prison.[28]

Numerous state and federal agencies need to be notified, starting with the EPA's National Response Center. We did not have a Spill Prevention Control and Counter Measures (SPCC) plan in place, and we are in clear violation of the Clean Water Act and the Resource Conservation and Recovery Act (RCRA) and can expect EPA enforcement of both violations.[29]

5) Storm water – channeled through unlined ditches and mining tailings – empties into the bay/ocean

A key element of any major construction project is the management of storm water discharges flowing from and through a development site. The BAY VIEW site is a 200-acre coastal site that we have now determined has substantial storm water runoff traveling from and through the site, and the water is being discharged into the public waters of FISHING BAY and the Atlantic Ocean. The current storm water flow is not a result of any of our construction, but it is an existing condition on the site. Storm water is generated from snow/rainfall, and the flow is dramatically increased from the presence of impervious surfaces like roads, parking lots, and roofs. Storm water discharge often carries pollutants and causes erosion and is viewed by the EPA as a critical item to be controlled on any site, particularly a coastal property.

Compounding our problems at BAY VIEW, we have detected the unlined ditches present on the site are contaminated with mining tailings. The source of this contamination is unclear at the moment, and there is no active mine upstream from the BAY VIEW property. The lack of an obvious source of the contamination is a cause for an investigation to determine if the polluter is still in existence and can be viewed as a potential contributor to the remediation that the EPA and the Commonwealth of Homeland will require.

The Goal of the Clean Water Act (CWA) is to "restore and maintain the chemical, physical and biological integrity of the nation's waters," and the EPA is very clear on the requirements for Storm Water Construction Permit requirements and BAY VIEW will require a Storm Water Permit and Storm Water Pollution Prevention Plan. First, we must resolve the existing conditions and contamination on the site.[30]

We are exposed to numerous storm water violations at BAY VIEW; as an example, the CWA explicitly prohibits pollution flowing from any source into the waters of the United States; FISHING BAY is clearly a water of the United States. The EPA has the power to impose administrative, civil, and criminal sanctions on a property owner and or contractor who fails to comply with the CWA. Administrative penalties can be as high as $157,500 and civil penalties can reach $32,000 per violation per day. We know the property is currently in violation of the CWA, and if our development is to proceed we need to stabilize the problem, resolve any issues with the EPA, and then apply for construction permits with both the EPA and with the Commonwealth of Homeland.[31]

6) Endangered Species Act – clover habitat for endangered bee

"Before beginning any construction project, you should consider the impact of your construction activities on species listed or proposed under the Endangered Species Act (ESA) as threatened or endangered ('listed species'), and the habitat of listed species. You should assess the impacts on listed species as early as possible in the construction process to avoid delays in your project."[32]

"CRITICAL HABITAT – The specific areas within the geographic area currently occupied by a species, at the time it is listed in accordance with the ESA, on which are found those physical or biological features essential to the conservation of the species and that may require special management considerations, and specific areas outside the geographic area occupied by a species at the time it is listed upon determination by the Secretary that such areas are essential for the conservation of the species (defined at section 3(5) of the federal ESA)."[33]

"Harass – Actions taken that create the likelihood of injury to listed species to such an extent as to significantly disrupt normal behavior patterns which include but may not be limited to breeding, feeding, or sheltering."[34]

"Harm – An act that actually kills or injures wildlife. Such an act may include significant habitat modification or degradation where it actually kills or injures wildlife by significantly impairing essential behavior patterns, including breeding, feeding, or sheltering."[35]

These quotes are from the first lines of chapter XI of the EPA's Planning Guide for Construction and Development. The chapter is entitled Endangered Species Act (ESA) Requirements for Construction Activities. The BAY VIEW site contains a specific clover growing on the site that has become part of the larger habitat for a bee that has been designated as an endangered species. The northern portion of the site has the primary population of the clover and was discovered during the application for our Storm Water General Construction Permit. The access road for the CleanEnergy site and dock happened to cut through the middle of the habitat. None of the proper procedures or notifications was followed on the BAY VIEW site and our exposure is significant. At a minimum our Storm Water Permit for the site is delayed and at grave risk. At the extreme the U.S. Fish and Wildlife Service may impose civil and criminal sanctions for failure to comply with the ESA. Civil penalties can reach $27,000 per day per violation; it appears we have three violations. Criminal violations can be imposed by the courts for negligent or knowing violations of $50,000 per day and three years' imprisonment or both. The extreme is a $250,000 fine and as much as fifteen years in jail.[36]

We are exposed to the ESA at BAY VIEW due to the lack of due diligence of our acquisition team. The extent of our exposure is not yet determined, but it appears we have Critical Habitat and we have Harassed and Harmed an endangered species. The ESA violations will have unexpected impact on our time table and costs at BAYVIEW.

7) Unexpected wetlands located on a portion of the site for the new hospital, adjacent to/will impact adjacent non-navigable seasonal tributaries

Another unexpected pleasure at BAY VIEW – our development team's plan for the 400-bed expansion of the hospital has encountered a material setback. A section of the southernmost portion of the building has now been found to be sited on wetlands. Should we wish to proceed with the existing design, the development company will need to: file for a Clean Water Act Section 404 Permit with the U.S. Army Corps of Engineers and submit to a federal and public process to obtain a permit. At a minimum this will stop our efforts on the new wing for at least three months assuming the permit is approved and we do not encounter any objections from the public process or from the adjacent landowner.[37]

The wetlands on the BAY VIEW property are adjacent and assumed to be linked with non-navigable seasonable tributaries on an adjacent parcel. Our construction efforts have the potential to impact the flow and water quality on the adjoining parcel. We should expect some opposition or at least some indemnification or compensation required by the adjacent landowner. We will also need to enlist additional civil engineering help to determine if the wetlands have the potential to be considered U.S. waters; if they do, it will increase the exposure to federal law and decrease the likelihood of obtaining a permit from the Army Corps.[38] An additional problem is that the development team has begun construction on the site; it has started the foundation of the new hospital wing. The EPA and the Army Corps require permit application and issuance prior to the commencement of construction; regardless of our course of action (seek a permit or redesign the wing) our construction effort must cease.

The penalties for working without a permit are consistent with other EPA violations. Administrative penalties may reach $157,500 and civil penalties may reach $32,500 per violation per day; this, of course, does not consider legal fees, project delays, and impacts to the development and leasing agreement with HealthyCare.[39] This wetlands discovery is a material setback for the BAY VIEW development and will have considerable negative impacts to our budget and schedule for the project.

8) Thorium ore fill below the existing surface lot

The existing 100-bed hospital building was built by the U.S. Navy in 1950 and the Navy operated the facility for ten years. The facility was then operated for the next fifty years by a nonprofit hospital and it was vacated and essentially abandoned in 2011. During the construction of the one-acre surface lot in 1950 the government's contractor used thorium ore as fill to facilitate the stabilization of the lot. Thorium had been present on the site since 1930 and was brought to the site by the Navy from a gaslight manufacturer that is no longer in existence. Thorium is a radioactive material that once was deemed a sound product for site work fill material; today it is viewed as serious radioactive contamination. The contamination has been on the site for more than seventy years; much of it is under the hospital surface lot, and the location of the balance of the material is not clear, but it should be expected to have contaminated the majority of the site after more than seventy years of seepage into the groundwater, distribution by storm water runoff, distribution from the wind and from the various construction projects over the years.

Hardrock Corporation, Hardrock Development Company, and BAY VIEW LLC (owner) are not the generators of this pollution; it was on the site when we bought it. The problem lies in the fact that we did not know it existed until two years after we owned the site. It should be expected that storm water has continued to distribute the radioactive thorium throughout the site and into FISHING BAY.

The sixty-year-old parking lot that has the most concentrated portion of the fill is cracked and in general ill repair and is most certainly allowing thorium to seep into the groundwater and the extent of that contamination should be expected to be material. Not only did we own the site but we leased it to third parties and we commenced construction; we are clearly operators on the BAY VIEW property, and our corporate exposure is increased in the role of operator and potential to our tenants and contractors.

The thorium manufacturer, the U.S. Navy, IDM, the Navy's contractor, are all in the chain of contributors to this pollution. The problem is we have identified this contamination a full two years after we bought the site. The EPA will require full remediation, and today we are at a minimum in violation of the Clean Water Act, the Clean Air Act, and the Resource Conservation and Recovery Act. Our exposure related to this contamination is substantial and puts the BAY VIEW development in real jeopardy. Our largest exposure lies in the interpretation of the ongoing distribution of thorium on the site and if it could be viewed as improper disposal of hazardous waste. The EPA has the latitude to impose civil penalties of $32,000 per day per violation and criminal penalties of $50,000 per day and up to five years in jail and, ultimately, if we are convicted of endangering others, $250,000 to $1,000,000 in fines and fifteen years in prison.[40]

The thorium contamination will require remediation and substantial and unexpected time and capital from ownership. Capturing others in the chain of ownership responsible for the creation of the contamination (in an effort to mitigate the liability) will be considered. Simply acquiring the noble high ground is good, but may not be relevant to salvaging the BAY VIEW development. A rigorous attempt to spread the liability may be a necessary investment should the veil of protections offered by our LLC ownership structure be pierced.

Thorium case analysis

ISSUE

The BAY VIEW property owned by BAY VIEW LLC is located in the Commonwealth of HOMELAND and is contaminated with high concentrations of radioactive thorium ore. The toxic substance was transported to the site in 1930 by a now defunct gaslight manufacturer when the U.S. federal government owned the site as a U.S. Navy base. The Navy used the manufacturing byproduct as landfill.

Throughout the 200-acre property and in the highest concentration detected to date is under an existing one-acre surface parking lot constructed in 1950. BAY VIEW LLC purchased the property in 2011 from Integrated Defense Machines (IDM). IDM purchased the property from the Navy in 1960. BAY VIEW LLC was unaware of the presence of thorium until the first quarter of 2013 and discovered the contaminant on the development site upon the commencement of the demolition of the one-acre parking lot.

Thorium is a hazardous material that has a radioactive half-life of 14 billion years and the EPA and the Commonwealth of HOMELAND will require its removal from the site before the intended BAY VIEW development can continue. Who is responsible for the cost of removal and environmental liability of the thorium contamination?

RULE OF LAW

The EPA is the primary regulator and enforcer of radioactive hazardous contamination. Thorium contamination is a violation of multiple federal laws:

- The Clean Air Act – thorium contamination can be wind borne
- The Clean Water Act – Thorium contamination at BAY VIEW could reach U.S. waters via multiple sources. The mine/mill tailings have been detected in storm water on the BAY VIEW site.
- Comprehensive Environmental Response, Compensation, and Liability Act (CERCLA or Superfund) – BAY VIEW is expected to qualify as a Superfund site. The EPA will compel remediation, and if ownership does not move to remediate, the EPA should be expected to initiate and complete cleanup, and it then will assess liability and financial liability at the conclusion of the effort.
- Nuclear Waste Policy Act – their primary concern will be with disposal of the thorium
- Occupational Safety and Health (OSHA) – safety of workforce laws
- National Environmental Policy Act (NEPA) – Navy sold the site in 1960, NEPA enacted in 1970, may not apply
- Safe Drinking Water Act – thorium contamination of groundwater
- Shore Protection Act – should thorium be removed via ship

Application of the relevant rule of law

The federal government is in the business of and has the latitude to compel polluters to remediate contaminated sites. Environmental Law provides the EPA with wide latitude to exact remediation for the site, including the ability through Superfund to perform the work and assign liability and costs after the fact. BAY VIEW LLC has owned the property since Q/1 of 2011 and did not perform adequate due diligence when it bought the property to discover the thorium contamination. BAY VIEW LLC and the Hardrock Development operating company own the site and have operated a development on the site for more than two years.

Conclusion

BAY VIEW LLC is the owner of the property. Hardrock Development Company has marketed and committed to two major leases on the property. Hardrock Development Company has begun to construct two major facilities on the property and has caused contained thorium to be disturbed. BAY VIEW LLC is an investment of Hardrock Development Company, and the development company is a wholly owned subsidiary of Hardrock Corporation; all are sophisticated owners and developers of real estate and should have been aware of the thorium contamination and the increases in the risks and liability of negligently operating a development on the site without the proper due diligence. BAY VIEW LLC and Hardrock Development Company will be viewed as liable as both an owner and an operator.

9) National Historic Preservation Act

During the construction of an access road for the CleanEnergy site, we uncovered what appear to be pre-nineteenth-century military cannons. After some basic research, we determined that the first "commercial" use for the site was as an important naval base for Union forces, guarding access to FISHING BAY and ultimately the capital city of the Commonwealth of Homeland. The site will be of significant interest to the Commonwealth and to the federal government.

Fort Smirniotopoulos not only was strategic as a battery, but was also an important, well-protected port with unimpeded access to the Atlantic Ocean. Additional research has uncovered the Fort was involved in multiple important military conflicts over its 100-year history. We should expect both state and federal interest in the waters adjacent to the site with research and archeological efforts impacting our shore and access to the bay and the ocean.

The requirements of the National Historic Preservation Act should have been considered upon the initial sale of the site from the U.S. Navy to IDM; this appears not to have happened. A competent phase 1 environmental study would have uncovered multiple clues to the significant historical value of the site and would have had material impact on the commercial value of the BAY VIEW property.

The National Park Service will be the primary federal agency with interest in the historic find on the site, but we should also expect the Commonwealth to involve the State Historic Preservation Officer. In addition, we will need to allow the Advisory Council on Historic Properties (ACHP) a reasonable amount of time to evaluate the find and to determine a course of action.[41] Today the property is not designated as a National Historic Landmark, but it could be, and the manner in which the site and cannon were discovered certainly damaged the historic site. Our total exposure is at this stage unclear, but it is certain that our development will be substantially delayed as the Commonwealth and the Park Service initiate and complete their evaluations.

Another compounding problem for our development plans has now surfaced. The Keeper of the National Register of Historic Places is considering designating FISHING BAY as a Traditional Cultural Property. The BAY VIEW site is not tribal land, but the Bay appears to have important historical and cultural significance as an early hunting and fishing ground to Native Americans. Currently we should view this problem as one that is yet to evolve but should not be ignored, particularly if we are required to seek independent decisions from multiple federal agencies.

Once again this Post-Closing Discovery is a material impediment to our development plans. The lack of competent due diligence has given our development company a false sense of security and has caused it to compound our exposure by initiating construction. The commencement of our development and construction operations on the site and their efforts has only made our position and exposure worse.

CONCLUSION: IS THIS A LEGAL PROBLEM OR A DEVELOPMENT PROBLEM?

If we had known about the Post-Closing impediments to the development at the BAY VIEW site, to be sure – WE WOULD NOT HAVE BOUGHT THE PROPERTY – So the answer to the question is both.

LEGAL EXPOSURE

We will continue to uncover the balance of our exposure at BAY VIEW, and my sense is we will continue to find more legal exposure. At a minimum our lessons learned are gigantic and will never be repeated again, but this is a legal fight that will be a loser for us no matter what the outcome. The lack of due diligence by the acquisition team in 2011 is a mystery that needs to be understood and perhaps may also allow us to shed some of the BAY VIEW liability. Our litigation team is being assembled, and we will vet all of the individuals and disciplines involved with this acquisition on both sides of the ledger, BUT, to be clear, no matter what we uncover, we have lost a great deal due to negligent execution by our acquisitions team.

Should the environmental problems uncovered at BAY VIEW increase to the point that our investment is a failure, we will lose substantial time, money, and influence in the Commonwealth of Homeland. We will lose an important relationship with our lender, and this deal will hurt our reputation in the market. We will also be subject to legal action from our tenants for violating our lease and development agreement. In addition, we have allowed our contractors employees to be exposed to toxic wastes.

Our BAY VIEW development is a potential business failure and we may be lucky to walk away with only the loss of our investment in the property (I do not expect to be that fortunate). I also believe our legal battles with this site may be just beginning. We now have numerous stakeholders at BAY VIEW that will be damaged by our failures, and they all will come to us for relief and first in line will be the EPA. This is a potential disaster that should never have happened and will infect our entire company. My team will do everything in our power to continue to fight and win the legal battles arising from BAY VIEW but I expect it to be long and expensive.

DEVELOPMENT EXPOSURE

The development business is all about balancing of risk. The risks in any development deal are numerous and they are most often intertwined. Interest rate risk, construction risk, performance risk, insurance risk, market supply and demand risk, leasing risk, Acts of God and yes – ENVIRONMENTAL RISKS. We are in the business of managing all of these, but the key is to manage most of them before you own the property. Somehow, we lost our advantage as a buyer and assumed 100 years of environmental risk at BAY VIEW on a site we did not pollute! We then compounded that mistake and started development and construction on a property littered with risk and have probably crossed the line from owner to operator, placing the development company and the parent, Hardrock Corporation at material risk. We have a great deal of important work ahead.

TWO POTENTIAL SOLUTIONS

Evaluate a transfer of environmental liability (TEL). The oil and gas industry has been the leader in an effort to transfer environmental liabilities to organizations that are primarily in the business of remediating brownfields.[42] I believe BAY VIEW is a good candidate for this type of deal structure. Environmental liability buyouts are primarily driven by the need of a corporation to get environmental liability off of its balance sheet, and a market has been created to deal with this problem.

The seller of a contaminated property conveys the ground to a traditional remediation company as a buyer with the delta between the "clean" market value and the expected clean-up cost as the price. The seller sheds all liability and often pays a fee to the buyer to take the property. The categories of owners/buyers in this space are well capitalized, in the business of remediation and experienced in all of the insurance and federal nuances associated with brownfields.[43] Many of them are recognized firms that have been veterans in the business of remediating U.S. military facilities.[44] This has been a proven successful structure for many major U.S. corporations. In these transactions the project equity is almost certainly lost, but the exposure will be defined and limited. I recommend we explore this avenue thoroughly.

Ask the Commonwealth of Homeland for assistance. The Commonwealth has resources and influence that could mitigate our exposure and allow the BAY VIEW development to proceed. We need to enlist its help and explore solutions with it as our advocate.

We are owners of the BAY VIEW property. We have identified substantial problems that need to be resolved. The EPA will be a material challenge, but the Commonwealth of Homeland could help us resolve many of the issues we face.

I will keep the board and the officers informed of our progress as it develops.

Notes

1. Hawken, Paul, L. Hunter Lovins, and Amory Lovins, (October 15, 2007). *Natural Capitalism*, U.S. Green Building Council, First Edition, Washington, DC (October 12, 2000); Hachette Book Group. Kindle Edition, October 10, 2007, at Kindle Locations 270–272.
2. See Environmental Law, "The District of Columbia's Green Building Code," on the companion website for this textbook.
3. See Environmental Law, "The Empire State Building's LEED Makeover," on the companion website for this textbook.
4. See Environmental Law, "How Are U.S. Cities Responding to the Intergovernmental Panel on Climate Change (IPCC) Fifth Assessment Report (5AR), from The Twelfth Session of the IPCC Working Group I (WGI-12)?" on the companion website for this textbook.
5. Brennan, Joseph, "Hardrock Development Corporations 200 Acre Bay View Development – a New Direction?" April 3, 2013, submitted as a final project paper in the

author's graduate course, "Foundations of Real Estate Law," in the Master's in Real Estate Program at Georgetown University (MPRE-690, MPRE-601–01, Spring 2013).

6. For a complete listing of research resources Joseph Brennan developed in researching and writing his legal memorandum, see the companion website for this textbook, under Environmental Law.

7. "Laws and Executive Orders." *United States Environmental Protection Agency*. March 28, 2013. Found at www.epa.gov/lawsregs/laws/.

8. Skanchy, Andrew, "Brownfields and the Bona Fide Perspective Purchaser Defense: Navigating CERLA's Web of Liability." *California Real Property Journal* 29.4 (2011). March 27, 2013. Found at www.downeybrand.com/publications/articles/120321_CaRealPropertyJournal.php.

9. Ibid.

10. "Permitting of Wind Energy Facilities." *National Wind Coordinating Committee: A Handbook Revised 2002*. 2002.

11. Gilberg, Elliott, "United States. Environmental Protection Agency." *Enforcement Discretion Guidance Regarding the Affiliation Language of CERCLA's Bona Fide Prospective Purchaser and Contiguous Property Owner Liability Protections*. 2011.

12. United States, "Environmental Protection Agency." *Interim Guidance Regarding Criteria Landowners Must Meet in Order to Qualify for Bona Fide Prospective Purchaser, Contiguous Property Owner, or Innocent Landowner Limitations on CERCLA Liability*. 2003.

13. "CERCLA Liability Limits." *Harris & Lee Environmental Sciences, LLC*. March 27, 2013. Found at www.hlenv.com/CERCLA_landowner_liability_limits.htm.

14. Nashelsky, Larren, Robert Falk, Miles Imwalle, and Kristin Hiensch, "Contemplating Chapter 11 as a 'Fresh Start'? Consider Recent Developments in Environmental Claims Liability." *Lexology*. April 26, 2011. Found at www.lexology.com/library/detail.aspx?g=23851ef6-a1ee-47e2–9d00–78b0923d9e17.

15. Bloom, Joshua, "Environmental Liability Buyouts: How to Know When It's the Real Thing." *Natural Resources & Environment* 20.3 (2006): n. pg.

16. United States, "Environmental Protection Agency." *The Asbestos Informer*. Found at www.epa.gov/region04/air/asbestos/inform.htm.

17. Ibid.

18. Ibid.

19. Ibid.

20. "Fact Sheet: Adjustments for Major and Area Source Boilers and Certain Incinerators." *United States Environmental Protection Agency*, pgs. 1–4.

21. Ibid.

22. "Citizen's Guide to Ground-Water Protection." *Office of Ground-Water Protection*. US Environmental Protection Agency. April 2, 2013.

23. Ibid.

24. Ibid.

25. "Waste, Chemical, and Cleanup Enforcement." *Enforcement. United States Environmental Protection Agency*, December 4, 2012. March 28, 2013. Found at www.epa.gov/enforcement/waste/index.html.

26. "Wheeler Pit." *United States Environmental Protection Agency*. 2013. March 28, 2013. Found at www.epa.gov/region05/cleanup/wheelerpit/.

27. "Financial Responsibility Requirements for Underground Storage Tanks." *EPA: Dollars and Sense*. July 1995, pgs. 1–14.

28. Hogan, Thomas, "Introduction to Environmental Law." *Class No. 4: Environmental Law*. Georgetown University. Washington, DC. February 5, 2013.

29. Ibid.

30. "Managing Your Environmental Responsibilities: A Planning Guide for Construction and Development." *EPA Office of Compliance*. U.S. Environmental Protection Agency. March 28, 2013. Found at www.cicacenter.org/links.

31. Ibid.

32. Ibid.

33. Ibid.

34. Ibid.

35. Ibid.

36. Ibid.

37. Ibid.

38. Ibid.

39. Ibid.

40. Ibid.

41. Ibid.

42. "Transfer of Environmental Liabilities – a Formula for Successful Divesture in the Oil & Gas Industry." *White Paper by WSP Environment & Energy*. WSP. April 1, 2013.

43. Bloom, "Environmental-Liability Buyouts."

44. "About ELT." *Environmental Liability Transfer*. N.p. April 2, 2013. Found at www.eltransfer.com/about-elt.html.

CHAPTER 7

Contract Law

We are told that Contract, like God, is dead. And so it is. Indeed the point is hardly worth arguing anymore. The leaders of the Contract is Dead movement go on to say that Contract, being dead, is no longer a fit or worthwhile subject of study. Law students should be dispensed from the accomplishment of antiquarian exercises in and about the theory of consideration. Legal scholars should, the fact of death having been recorded, turn their attention elsewhere. They should, it is said, observe the current scene and write down a description of what they see. They should engage in sociological analysis rather than in historical or philosophical synthesis. It is at this point that I find myself not so much in disagreement with their aims as completely uninterested in what they are doing.

Describing what you see is undoubtedly a useful exercise. . . . However, when you have finished describing something, all you really have is a list. In itself the list is meaningless. . . . The list takes on meaning only as it is related to other lists. . . . The most lovingly detailed knowledge of the present state of things . . . begins to become useful to us only when we are in a position to compare it with what we know about what was going on last year and the year before that and so on back through the floating mists of time. . . . We are not scientists – not even social scientists – nor were we meant to be. Let us not be overly depressed at that not altogether depressing thought.[1]

Professor Grant Gilmore published *The Death of Contract* the same year I graduated from high school. By the time I entered my first year at the Georgetown University Law Center, in 1978, *The Death of Contract* had stirred considerable controversy among Contract Law professors and legal scholars alike – oftentimes one and the same – a development in the pedagogy of law school not lost on Professor Dennis Hutchinson, my Contract Law professor at Georgetown.

As explained in greater detail in the essay titled "The Death of Formalism in Contract Law," on this textbook's companion website, Professor Gilmore's book thumbed its nose at the approach to teaching Contract Law reflected in our Contracts textbook, essentially saying, "everything you've just read is a lie." While that summary is, by intention, hyperbolic, by contrasting our traditional Contract Law textbook with Professor Gilmore's contrarian views on the subject, Professor Hutchinson sought to not only teach our first-year Contracts class the essential elements of common law contracts, but also to challenge the historicist perspective of the law's evolution. In so doing, he insisted, we become more critical thinkers in the process.

It took the author of this textbook a while – almost thirty-seven years, to be precise – and the commitment to take on this Herculean task, for those subtle messages to sink in. Interestingly, however, the import of Professor Gilmore's 1974 book has lost none of its relevance to the discipline of Contract Law in the more than forty years since its publication. *The Death of*

Contract has been the subject of periodic law review articles in some of the most prestigious academic law journals in the United States since that time, as recently as 2011.[2]

The arguments Professor Gilmore put forth in *The Death of Contract* are particularly relevant to Contract Law as it's presented in this and other chapters of this textbook. One of the foundational concepts of this textbook is its emphasis on the "Holy Trinity of Real Estate Law," which is comprised of Land Use Law, Contract Law, and Environmental Law. However, each of these disciplines of real estate law is fundamentally different in the methodology of its application from the other two. Environmental Law, for instance, is a subset of the broader category of Administrative Law: it is focused primarily on compliance with and avoiding violations of what are primarily federal environmental laws and regulations. Success in Land Use Law, on the other hand, is a subset of Local Government Law: it is primarily defined by navigating the land use approvals process in the particular jurisdiction in which the Subject Site is located, which in some cases may also involve actively participating in long-range community planning and "visioning" processes to help shape the land use policies of the local jurisdiction, including the "evolution" of its local Land Use Control ordinances.

The relevance of the textbook's approach to Contract Law, as it relates specifically to real estate development and financing, is not so much a function of understanding and complying with the common law of contracts, as interpreted by the courts having jurisdiction over the Subject Site and/or the parties involved, as it is on addressing the memorialization, *in legally enforceable agreements*, the various rights, duties, liabilities, and responsibilities of the parties involved in various aspects of The Development Process (as well as on the built-in mechanisms for enforcement, by one party against the other, in the event there's a claimed breach of any such rights, duties, liabilities, and responsibilities). In this regard, Professor Gilmore's prescience, articulated in his groundbreaking 1974 book, and Professor Hutchinson's insightful use of *The Death of Contract* in my 1978 Contract Law course prevail to this day.

Chapter outline
Chapter introduction
Understanding Contract Law
Selected, common law elements of contracts
Offer and acceptance
Due consideration
Enforceability of the agreement
Contracts against public policy
Statute of Frauds
Contracts commonly used during the Project Conception Phase
Contracts for professional services
Letters of intent
Options contracts
Selected Purchase and Sale Agreement clauses

Chapter introduction: understanding Contract Law

In teaching various courses related to real estate development, finance, and investing at the graduate and undergraduate levels, one of my favorite and most-used phrases is a parody of one of the most successful marketing slogans ever devised: *"What Happens in Vegas Stays in Vegas."* The parody version of this successful marketing slogan that I've adopted as a cautionary axiom for students is: *What happens in vagueness stays in vagueness*. The fundamental purpose served by Contract Law, in the context of The Development Process, is *to favor clarity and certitude over ambiguity and uncertainty*. Period.

This is a very important point, because not everything that falls into the category of "real estate law" involves compliance with or challenging an alleged violation of a federal law, state statute or local ordinance, or a dispute among parties requiring resolution by a court. In fact, *avoiding ambiguity in legal agreements is one of the principal strategies for avoiding one party or another having to turn to a court or some alternative form of dispute resolution to interpret their respective and various rights, duties, liabilities, and responsibilities* or, equally important, their intentions with respect thereto (which becomes a legitimate area of judicial inquiry in the event the various rights, duties, liabilities, and responsibilities of the parties are, in whole or in part, ambiguous).[3]

The vast majority of "things" comprising real estate law involve legal relationships or arrangements that must or should be reduced to an enforceable, written document, such as:

- a contract for professional services,
- a limited partnership agreement used to raise equity for the enterprise,
- a promissory note evidencing debt incurred as part of the financing of a project,
- a deed of trust or mortgage allowing the property to serve as collateral for debt, or
- an agreement of lease between the property owner and a prospective tenant that will contribute to the project's long-term cash flow.

Even without the benefit of a law degree (plus the legal training allowing someone to refer to her or himself as "a real estate lawyer"), the student or reader should benefit greatly from gaining an understanding of the principal components of the typical arrangements of parties involved throughout The Development Process, and the respective relationships and business transactions in which they engage, in order to take "the Idea" from conception to successful completion.

Without the benefit of a law degree and years of practice as a real estate lawyer, the student or reader may, nonetheless, develop a working understanding of many if not all of the components and of the essential contracts that arise throughout and in furtherance of The Development Process by making intellectual inquiries in each Phase, Sub-Phase, Task, and Sub-Task in The Development Process as follows:

1. What is the Purpose?
2. What are the Goals supporting that Purpose?
3. Who or what are the Parties?
4. What are the relevant Definitions?
5. What is or are the Relationships of the Parties?
6. What Duties does one Party owe to another Party or multiple Parties?
7. What are the respective Rights and Responsibilities of the Parties to each other?
8. What are the details necessary to describe and define all of the foregoing?

The student or reader should keep this inquiry in mind throughout this textbook, as a layperson's approach to understanding and assessing real estate law within the framework of The Development Process, but this approach is particularly relevant to this chapter on Contract Law.

Purpose. Every relationship and related transaction that occurs during The Development Process has a *fundamental, underlying purpose*. The fundamental purpose of a Purchase and Sale Agreement involving real property, whether improved or not, is *to affect the conveyance* *of title* to that property in a manner that is not susceptible to challenge, from the Owner and Seller of that property to its Buyer (also sometimes referred to in such documents as the "Purchaser"), at *"a price certain."* Similarly, the underlying purpose of a Lease Agreement is to grant the Tenant sufficient legal rights to the occupancy and "quiet enjoyment" of a specific physical location (the "Premises") for a finite period of time, for a specified monthly rent (which oftentimes has various components in its calculation, each of which must be precisely defined). By way of final example, a Loan Agreement together with a Deed of Trust or Mortgage, guarantees a Lender certain rights to collateral in the event the Borrower does not repay its loan in accordance with its terms or otherwise fails to honor specific terms and conditions of that loan. Understanding the underlying Purpose of each relationship or transaction that is part of The Development Process helps make sense of everything else characterizing that relationship or transaction.

"THE ROLE OF EXCHANGE": HOW CONTRACT LAW EVOLVED TO SUPPORT COMMERCE

Books on the law of contracts usually begin by explaining what lawyers mean by the word *contract*. Sometimes lawyers use the word [to refer to written agreements]. But they often use the word in a more technical sense to mean *a promise* or a set of promises that the law will *enforce* or at least recognize in some way.[1]

1 Restatement Second § 1 defines a *contract* as "a promise or a set of promises for the breach of which the law gives a remedy, or the performance of which the law in some way recognizes as a duty." As we see later, a promise that is not directly enforceable may nevertheless indirectly receive legal recognition. See the discussions of the meaning of *unenforceable* and of other effects in § 6.10 *infra* in connection with the Statute of Frauds.[4]

In his highly regarded treatise on Contracts, Columbia University Law Professor Allan Farnsworth offers that one of the principal purposes of Contract Law is to support a society's economy by promoting "The Role of Exchange" in commerce.

§1.2. The Role of Exchange. Exchange is the mainspring of any economic system that relies as heavily on free enterprise as does ours. Such a system allocates resources largely by direct bilateral exchanges arranged by bargaining between individuals. In these exchanges each gives something to the other and receives in return something from the other.[15]

1/ See *Johnson v. Scandia Assocs.*, 717 N.E.2nd 24 (Ind. 1999) (quoting this section of this treatise).

Professor Farnsworth goes on to quote from economist Adam Smith's *An Inquiry into the Nature and Causes of the Wealth of Nations*, to suggest that in an economy that "relies on direct bilateral exchanges between individuals and business entities," two unrelated, self-interested parties, through bargaining, should be able to arrive at the terms of their exchange such that at least one of those parties is better off than he was before as a result of that bargain, while doing harm to neither.[6] Professor Farnsworth concludes his discussion about the role of exchange by enumerating three different types of exchanges: primitive barter, a present sale for money, and exchanges involving future promises. He argues that it is this third type of exchange – those involving future promises – that required a body of Contract Law for its efficacy. The relationship between the evolution of the common law of contracts and exchanges involving future promises is explored in a separate feature box in this chapter. See also the excerpt from The Restatement (Second) of Contracts.

Goals. Goals are the means by which the Purpose of a relationship or transaction is affected. For example, one of the Goals of the Purchase and Sale Agreement is to assure the Buyer that the Seller will have "good and merchantable title" in and to the property to be conveyed, such that the Buyer will be free to pursue whatever endeavors it chooses in acquiring the property in the first place. In the context of the Lease Agreement, one of the Goals is to accurately and precisely define "the Premises" the Tenant seeks to occupy.

Parties. Every relationship or transaction in The Development Process must have more than one Party. More often than not, each relationship or transaction that is part of The Development Process has multiple parties (i.e., more than two). In fact, two of the aspects of The Development Process that make it analogous to all of those great cable series enumerated earlier in this textbook is (i) the multiplicity of parties involved and (ii) the extent to which the interests of each of these parties diverge from and need to be reconciled with the conflicting interests of other Parties to the overall subject matter of The Development Process. Take, for example, the parties to a construction loan agreement funding a Project.

The Construction Lender wants the Developer and the Development Entity to succeed: Otherwise, the Construction Lender may never see the return of the full amount loaned through, much less all of the accrued but unpaid interest on, the Construction Loan. On the other hand, the Construction Lender benefits from exhibiting a healthy level of distrust in order to protect its financial interests in the transaction. In this respect, the Lender's perspective in negotiating the Loan Documents may best be analogized to a nation negotiating a nuclear arms reduction agreement with another nation: "Trust but Verify" must be the governing axiom.

Additionally, although the Construction Lender and the General Contractor do not have "privity of contract," because neither is party to the other's contracts, their fates are nonetheless inextricably tied. The same goes for the General Contractor's subcontractors, who must rely on the GC's relationships with the Development Entity, and the Development Entity's relationship with the Construction Lender, in order to enjoy timely payment of their invoices to the GC. Finally, the Construction Lender has relied on the Development Entity's relationship with the provider of its Take-Out Financing, which had to issue a Financing Commitment prior to the Construction Lender's issuance of a Financing Commitment for the Construction Loan (on which the General Contractor must have relied in bidding on the Project in the first place).

The General Contractor won't receive the payments to which it may be entitled under the Construction Contract unless the Construction Lender is satisfied with the accuracy and quality of the former's Draw Requests (see Supplementary Materials on the companion website, under Construction Phase Issues, The Draw Request Process, for more details on all aspects of the Construction Loan, including the importance of and procedures involved in Draw Requests). The Lender is less likely to be made whole on the outstanding principal amount of its Construction Loan, plus any and all accrued but unpaid interest thereon, unless the General Contractor completes the Project on time and on budget. As such, these two Parties in The Development Process are not Parties to the same contracts. In legal parlance, there is no "privity of contract" between and among them. As a consequence, they have no rights to proceed in court in the event one of these Parties fails one or more of *its* contractual commitments to other parties, such as the Development Entity, with which they have direct contractual relationships. This technicality exists despite the fact that all such contracts, regardless of the specific Parties thereto, may negatively and critically impact the outcomes relating to the Project.

Definitions. Creating relationships and effecting transactions, which are accomplished primarily through written agreements – although some relationships and transactions may be effected by either oral agreements or even merely by the conduct of the Parties – almost always involve creating a set of Definitions to which the Parties must agree as well. In a

Purchase and Sale Agreement, for example, the "Definitions" or "Defined Terms" section may run several pages. Using Definitions or Defined Terms makes the drafting of legal agreements much easier because specific language relating to a definition or a Defined Term does not have to be repeated throughout the document. Additionally, Definitions or Defined Terms provide substantive meaning and are not relegated to merely serving convenience.

Relationships. One of the key questions in understanding and evaluating each component of The Development Process is, in any given instance, "What are the Relationships of the Parties?" Legal Relationships by and between specific Parties may be imputed, under Common Law, by the conduct of the specific Parties and/or oral agreements, or may be specifically defined in written contracts. As one might imagine, relying on oral agreements or, worse yet, the conduct of one Party or another, increases the likelihood that there will be ambiguity. Accordingly, use of written contracts, whenever possible, is by far the most common method within The Development Process for defining the Relationships among the Parties to such written agreements. That is why Contract Law is a principal component of the Holy Trinity of real estate law (i.e., Land Use, Environmental, and Contract Law), as discussed earlier and elsewhere in the textbook. Understanding the nature of the Relationships by, among, and between the Parties is an essential element in navigating The Development Process.

Duties. A "Duty" is a legal obligation one Party owes to another Party or to multiple Parties, as the case may be. For example, under Common Law (although much of the Common Law in this area has since been codified under state statutes), Duties agents owe their principals specific duties. For more on this, see the section on the Law of Principal and Agent in Chapter 11. For purposes of this framework for understanding the law generally, a Duty may be distinguished from a Responsibility because the former exists independently of any other action on the part of another Party while the latter is usually predicated on some other obligation on the part of another Party or is directly tied to a benefit being received or conferred upon the Party that owes the Responsibility.

THE CONCEPT OF "DUTY" AND ITS RELATIONSHIP TO RIGHTS UNDER CONTRACT LAW

In his Contracts treatise, Professor Farnsworth draws a distinction between a "duty" and a liability or obligation, in that the former has a concomitant right attached to it, such that the failure of such right may excuse nonperformance of the duty:

> Traditional analysis has it that in a bilateral contract[7] there are promises on both sides (the buyer's promise to pay and the seller's promise to deliver); there are *duties* on both sides (the buyer's duty to pay and the seller's duty to deliver) and *rights* on both sides (the seller's right to payment and the buyer's right to delivery). In a unilateral contract, however, there is a promise on only one side (the buyer's promise to pay); there is a duty on only one side (the buyer's duty to pay) and a right on the other side (the seller's right to payment).[8]

Under traditional Contract Law analysis, this was an important distinction when it comes to the parties' performance of their respective duties and the expectations of those same parties as to their rights under a contract. However, in contemporary legal analysis of the rights and duties of parties to a contract, the traditional formulations of "bilateral" versus "unilateral" agreements seem to have lost their significance.

> The Restatement Second abandons the use of the terms because of "doubt as to the utility of the distinction," which causes "confusion in cases where performance is complete on one side except for an incidental or collateral promise, as where an offer to buy goods is accepted by shipment and a warranty is implied."[9]

> The breach of a right under contract may give rise to the party whose right was breached to refuse to perform its correlative duty to the breaching party. Similarly, failure of a party to perform a duty established by contract may negate the non breaching party's duty to the breaching party grounded in such correlative right.[10]

Rights and Responsibilities. As suggested in the preceding paragraph, there is a mutuality implied by Rights and Responsibilities, although arguably this might be more accurately referred to as "Rights and Duties," if Professor Farnsworth were to have his way (see "The Concept of 'Duty' and Its Relationship to Rights under Contract Law" feature box in this regard). For example, a Party may have an obligation of "fair dealing" with another Party but may have a concomitant expectation of "fair dealing" from that other Party.

Details. As helpful as it should be to the student or reader to understand these fundamental components of contractual relationships, this construct should not overshadow the fact that contracts should and must convey all of the essential details of the transaction they're intended to document and memorialize.

> If you're not interested in *paying attention to a plethora of small but important details*, in getting your hands dirty, in mixing it up with a wide range of people, then real estate is almost certainly not for you.[11]
> Professor William Poorvu, *The Real Estate Game*

Avoiding ambiguity means not only paying attention to the details but putting as many of the details as possible relating to agreements between parties into the contracts that memorialize those agreements. If what happens in vagueness stays in vagueness, then the extent of the vagueness is often inversely proportional to the level of details expressed in a contract. Although not always, or even often, expressed in these terms, contracts involving real estate transactions oftentimes require expressing a very specific Scope of Work. A Scope of Work is a narrative description of the actions to be taken or performed by one of the parties to an agreement. In a contract for professional services, the Scope of Work expressly defines the work the professional services firm will perform in exchange for the compensation that firm expects to receive in consideration of those services. Without a detailed Scope of Work, there is no reasonable way for the party receiving, benefiting from, and paying for such services to know whether the services being delivered warrant the payment of the agreed-upon compensation. Additionally, the party for whom the services are being performed has no way of knowing whether the services to be performed will adequately serve the receiving party's needs; whether they will serve the Purpose of the contract. The same observations can be made regarding much more complex contracts, such as for the construction of improvements to real property. A Construction Contract may not employ the specific term "Scope of Work." However, the ability of the General Contractor to properly perform the work described in the Construction Contract, as well as the ability of the Owner and of the Construction Lender to evaluate the proper and timely performance of the work, all depends on a comprehensive and accurate description of what, how, and when the General Contractor will be constructing the work as defined and described in the Construction Contract.

"THE ROLE OF EXCHANGE": EXCHANGES INVOLVING FUTURE PROMISES

As set forth in the feature box titled "The Role of Exchange": How Contract Law Evolved to Support Commerce," the introduction of exchanges involving future promises required the development of a body of Contract Law for its efficacy. The relationship between the evolution of the common law of contracts and exchanges involving future promises is explored in this section.

In his Contracts treatise, Professor Farnsworth goes as far back as the law of ancient Rome to find the antecedents of the body of Contract Law supporting the exchange of future promises. In introducing the subject, Professor Farnsworth offers the following:

> §1.3. The Role of Promise. The germ of promise was credit. The simplest form of credit transaction is the loan of money. From the loan it was but a short step to the sale on credit, in which performance on one side is deferred, the buyer merely promising to pay while the seller immediately performs. A seller delivers apples to a buyer, and, in return, the buyer promises to pay the seller at the end of the month. Credit became even more significant when a specialization of labor generated demand for services. Services usually take time to perform, so an exchange of services for payment cannot be simultaneous – an extension of credit by one of the parties is inevitable. If a builder is to put a new roof on an owner's house, either the builder must work in reliance on the owner's promise to pay or the owner must pay in reliance on the builder's promise to do the work.[1]
>
> §1.3 1 The extension of credit is often minimized by providing for "progress payments" to be made by the owner as the work progresses.[12]

In this regard, the execution of specific provisions in the Purchase and Sale Agreement may include the exchange of a number of pre-Closing promises (e.g., the Seller's commitment to deliver to Purchaser, during the Due Diligence Period under the contract, essential documents for the Purchaser's or its designees' review and approval), the fulfillment of which are conditions precedent to Closing. See the following excerpt from a sample Purchase and Sale Agreement, regarding the Seller's obligation to deliver the "Due Diligence Materials" to the Purchaser. The ultimate exchange contemplated under a Purchase and Sale Agreement, however, is a simultaneous exchange at Closing of good title to the Property, passing from Seller to Purchaser, on one hand, in exchange for payment of the Purchase Price, from Purchaser to Seller, on the other hand, to which the parties agreed in the PSA. The PSA is an excellent example of "the executory exchange of promises" for which Professor Farnsworth argues the credit transactions he describes are a less-than-perfect analog.[13]

Contrast the PSA, on one hand, with the standard Construction Contract, on the other. As Professor Farnsworth suggested in the footnote to the excerpted language from his Contracts treatise, the parties to the Construction Contract agree to a system of Progress Payments, the release of which, from the Construction Loan, is controlled by the Construction Lender's procedures for Draw Requests to be submitted by the General Contractor, as set forth in the Owner's Construction Loan Agreement. See, in this regard, Chapters 9 and the Supplementary Materials on the companion website, under Construction Phase Issues, The Draw Request Process, respectively.

Selected, common law elements of contracts

In its most basic form, a contract is nothing more than an agreement between two parties to which they intend to be bound,[14] and which may be enforced in a court of law should one of those parties renege on any critical aspect or component of that agreement. In the event of a nonperformance by one party to the agreement, an issue is sometimes raised, as an affirmative defense to that nonperformance, as to whether the two parties had a "meeting of the minds" regarding the substance and/or details of their agreement. Contracts involving real estate transactions run the gamut from very straightforward – a contract for the purchase and sale of a single-family residence – to the exceedingly complex, engaging and binding multiple parties through a variety of transactions and their related contracts, yet all relating to the same Project. Getting the details right, in each instance, and making sure the respective parties' rights, responsibilities, duties, and obligations are clearly, comprehensively, and accurately stated (and that they are enforceable in a court of law having competent jurisdiction over the parties and the subject matter of their dispute) is paramount to the successful completion of every transaction involving real estate.

For a contract to be formed at common law, there must be an offer and an acceptance, as well as due consideration supporting the formation of the contract. These essential elements of a contract at common law are described later. However, consider first the following simple example.

As Popeye's friend, J. Wellington Wimpy, famously (and frequently) offered, *"I'll gladly pay you Tuesday for a hamburger today."* This appears to be as straightforward a transaction as to which two parties might engage (although one might wonder whether Wimpy's request would be more accurately described as seeking an unsecured loan, which would still constitute a contract, if all of the requisite elements are present).

Accepting Wimpy's offer by purchasing a hamburger for him, and then handing him that hamburger, presumably constitutes entering into a binding contract in accordance with which Wimpy is legally required to pay the other party the cost of that hamburger. However, this seemingly simple "agreement between two parties" raises some questions about whether Wimpy's offer was clear.

Did Wimpy's offer mean the cost of the hamburger would be repaid, in full, *on the Tuesday next following*, or merely on *any Tuesday of Wimpy's choosing*, or perhaps the *next Tuesday on which Wimpy has on his person sufficient funds* to make good on his promise?

What if the payment of sales tax was involved in the purchase of the hamburger that is the subject of Wimpy's offer? Will the law conclude that the repayment of the sales tax assessed at the purchase of the hamburger is implied by Wimpy's offer and, consequently, should be included as part of Wimpy's contractual commitment to pay for the hamburger, even if that was not explicitly stated in his offer?

As a well-known person of impecunity (these are, after all, Wimpy's most frequently uttered words), what if Wimpy has a history, known to the other party, of making such offers but *never* living up to his end of the bargain, such that his offer is truly a request that someone engage in the gratuitous act of buying him a hamburger, because he's hungry but has no money? Even if Wimpy's words are clear, may the other party rely on those words knowing Wimpy's intent is not accurately reflected therein? By the way, if this simple offer-and-acceptance hypothetical has made you hungry, please feel free to take a food break before returning to complete this chapter.

Offer and acceptance

In common law, in order for an enforceable "agreement" to be made or entered into between two parties, one party must (i) offer to convey a "thing," which may include money, or (ii) engage in some affirmative act benefiting the other party, or (iii) refrain from engaging in an affirmative act the offeror may have a right to otherwise perform, also to the benefit of the other offeree. The other party (i.e., the "offeree"), in turn, must accept whatever it is the first party is offering. If, in response to the offer, the offeree offers something even only slightly different from what the offeror has offered – what is commonly referred to as "negotiation" – that constitutes a rejection of the original offer and the submission of a new offer. This is often recognized under common law as a "counteroffer." Offer and acceptance is the *sine qua non* of the formation of a valid contract.

Due consideration

In addition to offer and acceptance, to be valid there must be due consideration passing from one party to the other party, an exchange of value supporting the making of a contract. While money is the most common form of consideration, consideration may take other forms, including the performance of an affirmative act or the forbearance from an act (i.e., an agreement not to do something the forbearing party has the right to otherwise do).

The issue of whether there is due consideration to support the existence of a contract is usually only presented where one party claims the formation and existence of a valid and binding contract based on the parties' respective conduct, rather than from any express, written manifestation of the existence of an agreement between the parties. For example, a land broker who has been sending a developer emails with leads on properties not yet listed for sale but that might, nonetheless, be available for sale might claim that an implied agreement exists between the broker and the developer that the former will be compensated as the latter's broker, entitled to a commission on the sales transaction, in the event the developer purchases a property the broker shared with the developer. Such a claim may be made even if that specific email was not how the developer was introduced to the seller, the putative broker claiming that an agency relationship has been formed based on the parties' conduct vis-à-vis one another. In such a situation, the broker might claim that, in establishing the agency relationship with the developer, the broker refrained from sharing the leads contained in those emails with other clients (an act of forbearance serving as consideration) in order to give the developer the first opportunity among the broker's other clients to pursue them. In such a factual scenario, the offer and acceptance may be implied from the parties' course of conduct with each other and with the outside world.

On the other hand, modern, written contracts generally do not suffer from issues such as whether there was an offer and acceptance or due consideration exchanged by the parties, as the vast majority of real estate–related arrangements and agreements among various parties, emanating from The Development Process, will be reflected in carefully and diligently drafted contractual documents prepared by the parties' respective legal counsel. In particular, modern contracts generally contain boilerplate language confirming that the parties agree the contract is sufficiently supported by consideration and that a valid "exchange" has occurred, as evidenced by the contract. Such contract boilerplate regarding due consideration commonly provides: *"For due and valuable consideration, the receipt and sufficiency of which are hereby acknowledged by the parties. . ."* This language has supplanted similar language which, in a nod to the common law requirements, stated: *"For the sum of Ten Dollars ($10.00),* *and such other due and valuable consideration exchanged by the parties hereto, the receipt and sufficiency of which are hereby acknowledged by the parties. . ."* So long as the parties concur that the value of the consideration supporting the contract is "sufficient," courts are very reluctant to interject their own value judgment regarding the sufficiency of the consideration, unless other relevant facts support a contrary conclusion, such as fraud or mistake.

Enforceability of the agreement

Protecting Parties from "Unfairness". There is a range of cases in which the courts have demonstrated an obligation and willingness to "police" the conduct of parties to a contract, coming to the aid and assistance of one party who is deemed to have been wronged by the conduct of another party. This line of cases reflecting the courts policing the conduct of the parties includes the following circumstances.

    Fraud in the Inducement versus Fraud in the Execution (aka "fraud in the *factum*"). Whether there has been material misrepresentation in the making of a contract or a misrepresentation in the execution of the contract will determine the remedies to which the aggrieved party may resort:

> In the typical case, as when a seller misrepresents the *quality* of goods, the misrepresentation is said to go to the "inducement." The effect of such a misrepresentation is to make the contract voidable at the instance of the recipient. In rare cases, however, the misrepresentation is regarded as going to the very character of the proposed contract itself, as when one party induces the other to sign a document by falsely stating that "it has no legal effect." Such a misrepresentation is said to go to the "execution" (or the "factum"). If the other party neither knows nor has reason to know of the character of the proposed agreement, the effect of such misrepresentation is that there is no contract at all.[15]

    In the case of the hundreds of thousands of borrowers who arguably were misled by commercial banks and loan originators into taking out subprime mortgages, both fraud in the inducement and fraud in the execution defenses to the enforcement of those mortgages were available. The massive defaults on billions of dollars in subprime mortgages, which contributed significantly to the financial and real estate market collapses in 2008 in the United States and resulted in the Great Recession of 2008, were inevitable because the risks inherent in those subprime mortgage loans were intentionally obfuscated in the loan origination process.

    In the case of the fraud in the execution defense, the argument goes that based on the subprime borrower's annual income and net worth, that borrower could not possibly repay the loan secured by that mortgage, and the financial institution or loan originator knew that to be the case at the time the loan was made. Accordingly, the argument can be made that the contracts comprising the loan documents should be deemed not to exist because of misrepresentation in the execution (i.e., fraud in the *factum*).

    In the period immediately before the Great Recession of 2008 – as a few prescient observers and market participants began to predict the pending market collapses – and for some time thereafter, a number of scholarly and professional articles were published recounting or foretelling various legal challenges to the subprime loans and their related mortgages or deeds of trust (the precise form of the security instrument for these loans depends on state law). These challenges to the validity of the mortgages and their underlying subprime loans were quickly eclipsed by a flood of scholarly and/or legal analyses of the securities fraud aspects of subprime mortgage bonds and various derivatives thereof.

However, a sampling of the articles focused on the Contract Law aspects of the contracts comprising a subprime mortgage loan may be instructive for students and readers alike:

If the recent (and anticipated) wave of litigation is any indication, no one involved in this scenario is immune from litigation. Lenders currently face the largest volume of litigation including, most prominently, lawsuits filed by borrowers trying to get out of their loans.[16]

The earliest cases in this area were brought by individual borrowers facing foreclosure who claimed, based largely on state law, that mortgage lenders and their agents had deceived them, resulting in borrowers taking on payment obligations they were unable to satisfy, particularly in the context of depreciating home prices.[17]

Erroneous allocation of the risk of emotion in the mortgage contract. The risk allocation model assumes that the lender has no incentive to manipulate borrower emotion but, rather, has a strong stake in carefully assessing the borrower's underlying resources and repayment prospects. Any other strategy by the lender would generate borrower default and financial loss in the lender. In short, the law regards the lender as a rational, self-interested gatekeeper, assessing borrowers and reining [SIC] their loan expectations as necessary. The law also concludes that, even if incentives somehow emerged whereby the lender played upon borrower emotion, borrowers are their own best and last line of defense. If a naive borrower chooses to be "emotional" or unrealistic as to what the borrower can afford, the borrower will receive the adverse economic consequences that Contract Law concludes the borrower so richly deserves. In this way, the law punishes emotion even when it leads to an utterly ruinous contract.[18]

As the foregoing discussion and article excerpts make clear, neither of these common law defenses – fraud in the inducement and fraud in the execution – has lost its import in a court's available arsenal to protect parties from "unfairness."

False Manifestations of Assent: Duress and Undue Influence. In many respects, "Duress" and "Undue Influence" are two sides of the same coin, both going to differentiating physical manifestation of "assent" (i.e., a party's signature on a written contract from actual assent as the signatory's free act and deed). In order for parties to have reached a binding agreement – a "meeting of the minds" with each party's assent evidenced by her or his signature – the parties to a contract must have acted of their own "free will" in entering into such agreement, intending to be bound by an enforceable contract. The defense of Duress and Undue Influence that follow are grounded in whether a party to a written contract freely executed that written manifestation of the parties' agreement. In the case of duress, the aggrieved party claims that her signature was somehow coerced, through physical or nonphysical threats. Alternatively, in the case of undue influence the aggrieved, weaker, or susceptible party claims that the superior or dominant party used their "special relationship" with the susceptible party to that party's disadvantage in signing the contract.

Duress. Duress occurs in situations where one party exercises some form of physical compulsion, or threatens that such physical compulsion will be forthcoming, in order to coerce the other party to sign a contract. As Professor Farnsworth stated:

Under the general principles of contract laws relating to assent, if a victim acts under physical compulsion, for instance, by signing a writing under such force that the victim is "a mere mechanical instrument," the victim's actions are not effective to manifest assent. Such duress by physical compulsion results in no contract at all or in what is sometimes anomalously described as a "void contract."[19]

A party being physically forced to sign a document constitutes a clear case of duress. But what if that party is merely *threated* with physical coercion? The defense of duress still applies but its availability is more complicated to demonstrate. In the case of a threat of coercion, four elements must be demonstrated for a court to determine there is no contract:

1. *Is there a threat?* Professor Farnsworth describes a threat as "a manifestation of an intent to inflict some loss or harm on another."[20] It should be distinguished from "a mere prediction of the probable consequences of a course of action."[21]

2. *Is the threat improper?* The Latin axiom *res ipsa loquitur* – the thing speaks for itself – helps to explain when a threat is improper. A threat that is made solely for the purpose of inducing a party's signature where that party's assent to the transaction or agreement is otherwise lacking is, by definition, an improper threat under the four elements of duress by threat of physical coercion. However, that's a tautological definition that offers little in the way of helping students and readers fully comprehend the element of propriety. Since its inception, the doctrine of duress by threat of physical coercion has expanded well beyond the threat of actions that, if carried out, would themselves constitute crimes of actionable torts.[22] Threats of criminal prosecution, civil action, or to break the contract at issue have all been deemed, under specific circumstances, to constitute improper threats for purposes of proving duress by threat of coercion.[23]

3. *Did the threat induce the manifestation of assent?* In order to prove a party's signature on a written contract was secured through duress grounded in the threat of coercion, the aggrieved party must show causality. For example, if the plaintiff seeking to have the alleged contract to, as a matter of law, not exist, that party cannot have signed that contract for other, legitimate reasons, and later seek to have it deemed void by a court merely because of buyer's remorse, the fact that there was an improper threat of coercion notwithstanding.

4. *Was the threat itself sufficient to secure a coerced signature?* Since the inception of the defense of duress, courts have increasingly liberalized the range of threats rising to the level of being sufficient to induce the signature of a party otherwise not desiring to be bound. The standard of sufficiency has been expanded well beyond various types of physical harm, including loss of life, to a variety of perceived economic harms that might befall the recalcitrant party, leading to doctrines such as "economic duress" and "business compulsion."[24]

Undue Influence. As stated in the introduction to this subsection, as with duress, the defense of undue influence goes to whether a party's signature on a contract evidences that party's assent to the terms and conditions of the agreement. Rather than relying on a claim that some form of coercion was involved in securing the aggrieved party's signature, as is the case with duress, the defense of undue influence is grounded in a weaker or susceptible party succumbing to the improper influence of a stronger or dominant party, in cases where there is a special relationship between the two parties, and they are both parties to the same contract. As with duress, a court's finding of undue influence renders the purported contract null and void, as if it never existed in the first place. Finally, as with the defense of duress, specific elements must be proved to make out a defense of undue influence.

1. *Special Relationship.* As Professor Farnsworth stated, a ruling of undue influence "require[s] a special relationship between the parties that makes one of them peculiarly susceptible to persuasion by the other."[25] It is fundamental to the defense of undue persuasion that the special relationship is characterized by the weaker or susceptible party reasonably relying on the assumption that the stronger or dominant party will always look out for the former's best interests, such as is the case in the relationship between a parent and a child or a doctor and a patient. In presenting the defense of undue influence, the burden is on the aggrieved party to demonstrate

that a special relationship existed between the two parties to the contract the aggrieved party is seeking to have set aside.

2. *Improper Persuasion.* The existence of a special relationship, in the context of a signed contract between the parties in that relationship, in and of itself is not sufficient to make an effective defense of undue influence. In addition, the aggrieved party must show that the stronger or dominant party in the relationship used improper persuasion. As the defense of undue influence has evolved, some courts have determined that once the aggrieved party had demonstrated the existence of a special relationship, the burden of proof regarding improper persuasion shifts to the stronger or dominant party to demonstrate that undue influence was not used in securing the aggrieved party's signature of the contract that is the subject of the dispute. In terms of what constitutes "unfair influence," Professor Farnsworth offers the following explanation: "The degree of persuasion that will be characterized as 'unfair' depends on a variety of circumstances, but the ultimate question is whether the result was produced by means that seriously impaired the free and competent exercise of judgement."[26]

Generally speaking, the less opportunity the aggrieved party was allowed to thoughtfully contemplate the benefits and burdens of the contract in question, and the greater the effort by the superior or dominant party to "persuade" the aggrieved party to sign the document – including but not limited to using the special relationship to create a sense of urgency on the part of the aggrieved party to make a hasty decision – the greater the likelihood a court will find the superior or dominant party to have exercised undue influence in securing the aggrieved party's signature. Clearly, as with most disputes between parties the resolution of which are left to a court, the ultimate outcome will depend on the specific facts and circumstances in each case.

Lack of Capacity. Lack of capacity may come into play in a number of different situations, ranging from whether a signatory to a contract has the mental capacity to comprehend the consequences of a particular transaction to whether a signatory has the legal capacity to be bound to the subject matter or has organizational or corporate authority to enter in such a transaction, thereby binding that entity. For a broader discussion of the subject of delegation of authority, see the discussion in Chapter 11, in the section titled "Principal and Agent."

With regard to an individual's capacity to be bound contractually, as succinctly stated by Professor Farnsworth:

> Even though individuals differ markedly in their ability to represent their own interests in the bargaining process, one is generally assumed to have full power to bind oneself contractually. Only in extreme circumstances is one's power regarded as impaired because of an inability to participate meaningfully in the bargaining process.[27]

The defense of lack of capacity is not limited to proving that the party in question has been medically determined to suffer from a recognized mental disorder. In fact, the defense of lack of mental capacity may arise from a variety of causes, including age-related disorders, such as Alzheimer's disease or mental impairment due to drugs and/or alcohol.

Such impairments of individual capacity to be contractually bound include two broad areas of inquiry by the courts: Did the party in question have the maturity to enter into the contract, and did the party have the mental capacity to be bound? With the exception of the execution of leases for real property, the issue of whether a party has the maturity to enter into a contract is unlikely to arise in the course of contracts executed as part of The Development Process. Accordingly, a more expansive discussion of this test of a party's capacity is not provided in this subsection.[28]

With regard to whether a party possesses the mental capacity to enter into a contract, there is a broad range of cases and statutes at variance with one other as to how a court should determine the defense of incapacity. Generally, there is a dichotomy between two competing schools of thought, as represented by these conflicting cases, in making the determination of the incapacity of the party in question: the Cognitive Test and the Volitional Test. In the Cognitive Test, the question is whether the party in question had the requisite mental capacity to understand the burdens and consequences of entering into the contract. As Professor Farnsworth noted:

> The traditional test is a "cognitive" one. Did the party lack the capacity to understand the nature and consequences of the transaction in question? Was the party unable to know what he or she was doing and to appreciate its effects?[29]

The Cognitive Test has been subject to considerable criticism from legal scholars and courts as overly subjective, ambiguous, and "unscientific." These criticisms may be particularly meritorious, inasmuch as, under the Cognitive Test, the other party's knowledge of the incapacity of the party in question does not need to be alleged, much less proven, for the defense to hold sway with the court.

In response to instances in which a party may episodically lack the requisite mental capacity to be contractually bound – as might be the case with someone suffering from manic depression or bipolar disorder – the Volitional Test has evolved out of the court cases in which a party's "temporary lack of capacity" has been claimed. As Professor Farnsworth explained:

> The principal challenges to the cognitive test have come from instances in which mentally infirm persons understand the nature and consequences of their actions, but nevertheless lack effective control of them, a situation characteristic of manic-depressives. . . . In a seminal lower court New York case,[30] a previously frugal and cautious businessman passed from depressed to the manic phase of a manic-depression psychosis and . . . went on a buying spree, and embarked on ambitious construction projects. As part of one of these projects he contracted, against his lawyer's advice, to buy land for $51,500. Two weeks later he was sent to a mental hospital, and he later sued to rescind the contract.[31]

In an effort to reconcile conflicts between the Cognitive Test and the Volitional Test, the Restatement Second attempts a Solomon-like approach by adding a "reasonableness" test to the Cognitive Test. However, this compromise also requires that the other party to the transaction *have knowledge about the condition* of the party challenging the validity of the contract at the time that party enters into it.[32] This approach has not, however, been uniformly embraced by the courts and, consequently, the appropriate application of the Lack of Capacity defense remains both an open question and very much subject to the statutes and dispositive cases on the matter in the jurisdiction in which the defense has been raised and is being challenged, respectively.

As mentioned in the introduction of this subsection, there are also what are essentially "Lack of Capacity" challenges to the existence or enforceability of signed contracts relating to the authority – whether actual or implied – of the party signing a contract on behalf of a corporation, business organization, nonprofit, or other entity type. For more information on the authority of agents to enter into contracts binding their principals, See the section on "Principal and Agent" in Chapter 11. With regard to the broader question of "Corporate Authority" (or, as it's more aptly described, corporate liability for contracts signed with individuals who may or may not have actual authority to enter into such contracts), see the companion website.

Impossibility of Performance. As a general rule, courts will not enforce a contract that cannot possibly be performed, and for obvious reasons. The doctrine of "impossibility of performance" is also referred to as "impracticability" of performance.

> The common law is slow to give effect to the maxim *impossibilium nulla obligation est* ("there is no obligation to do the impossible"). Courts were less receptive to claims of excuse based on events

occurring after the making of the contract than they were to claims of excuse based on facts that existed at the time of the agreement.[33]

While the general rule that impossibility of performance is no excuse for nonperformance, many of the earliest English common law cases related to impossibility of performance recognized specific exceptions for "supervening" causes, such as the death of the party for whom performance was to be rendered under the contract or the destruction of the subject building a party was obligated under contract to maintain, repair, or modify. Additionally, a change in the laws rendering performance of a party's duties under contract illegal was recognized as a supervening cause constituting an exception to the general rule that impossibility of performance would not relieve a party of its obligation under contract.[34]

Contemporary common law cases in the United States involving impossibility of performance as related to property, personal or real (e.g., crops or goods) have generally focused on the precise moment at which ownership of the real property occurred in assessing who bears the risk of loss should such property be damaged or destroyed before actual possession or title to the property, as the case may be, was actually conveyed to the other party. Such cases have involved events outside of the control of either party, as when a building under construction was destroyed by fire or goods on their way to the buyer were destroyed in transit. Many of these issues of common law have been subsequently resolved by the advent of the Uniform Commercial Code (UCC) (discussed in the following paragraph after the excerpt from Farnsworth).

> Whether a particular thing is necessary for performance is a question much like whether a particular person is necessary for performance, and the answer depends on all the circumstances. A clear case is dealt with in the Uniform Commercial Code, which excuses the seller from its duty to deliver if "the contract requires for its performance goods identified before the contract is made, and the goods suffer casualty without fault of either party before the risk of loss passes to the buyer." More interesting questions are raised by the repair cases and the crop-failure cases.[35]

§2–615 of the Uniform Commercial Code sought to synthesize and modernize the common law cases that preceded it regarding the defense of impossibility of performance, which the UCC re-cast as *Excuse by Failure of Presupposed Conditions.*[36] Although the UCC does not apply to transactions in real property, UCC 2–615 has been largely adopted in the Restatement Second, which applies to contracts generally. UCC 2–615 sets forth four conditions that must be met in order for any performance to be excused by virtue of the modern-day version of "impossibility of performance":

1. **Performance "as agreed" has been rendered impossible.** In reality, there are two, separate elements to this component of UCC 6–215: a) what was the "agreed-upon performance" and b) what was the "event" precluding that performance.
2. **The parties assumed that the event making performance impossible would not occur.** It is a critical component of UCC 6–215 that both parties entering into a contract assumed that the event, which eventually precludes one party's performance under the contract, would *not* ever occur. Whether it be a plague of locusts decimating crops promised for delivery by a certain time at a specific price, a mischievous fire at a construction site that burns to the ground a structure prior to its completion and delivery to the other party, or a sudden change in governmental policies making illegal the delivery of a technological innovation in one country to the buyer in another country, the event to which the nonperforming party points in seeking to be held harmless for its nonperformance of a contract must be one that neither party contemplated occurring at the time they entered into the contract.

3. **The party seeking to have its performance excused did not bring about the event**. If, in the example of a fire burning to the ground a structure the completion and delivery of which one party promised to another in a construction contract, instead of being caused by juvenile delinquents, the conflagration was caused by an arsonist paid by the builder, excuse under UCC 2–615 would not be allowed: For the protections of this section of the Uniform Commercial Code to be effective, the supervening event must have been out of the control of the party seeking relief from its contractual obligations.

4. **The party seeking to have its performance excused did not assume a greater obligation.** There are instances in which the event serving as potential grounds for the excuse of performance by the party seeking relief under UCC 2–615 was foreseeable at the time the contract was made or that, alternatively, that party assumed obligations beyond that from which UCC 2–615 may offer relief, as in the case where that party makes an unqualified promise of completion. Such circumstances and contract language must be absent in order for this fourth requirement to be met.

As mentioned in the preceding paragraph, the analytical framework provided in UCC 2–615, which itself "synthesized," to use Professor Farnsworth's terminology, the common law of impossibility of performance, was largely embraced in the drafting of the Restatement Second. In the words of Professor Farnsworth:

> The [Uniform Commercial Code's] synthesis, designed for the sale of goods, has already had a substantial influence on the law of contract generally and has been adapted by the Statement Second.[37]

Restatement Second §261 provides as follows:

§261. Discharge by Supervening Impracticability

> Where, after a contract is made, a party's performance is made impracticable without his fault by the occurrence of an event the non-occurrence of which was a basic assumption on which the contract was made, his duty to render that performance is discharged, unless the language or the circumstances indicate the contrary.[38]

The Commentary provided in Restatement Second §261 expressly identifies areas in which the section and its application follow or parallel UCC 2–615, as well as those areas or instances in which the two diverge. For example, the Commentary to §261 provides, in pertinent part, as follows:

> like Uniform Commercial Code § 2–615 (a), this Section states a principle broadly applicable to all types of impracticability and it "deliberately refrains from any effort at an exhaustive expression of contingencies" (Comment 2 to Uniform Commercial Code § 2–615).[39]

Because it does not serve the same purpose as the Uniform Commercial Code (inasmuch as it is intended to address Contract Law generally and not exclusively as it impacts business transactions), and because the Restatement of Contracts predates the advent of the UCC by a very significant period of time, the Restatement Second does not address the elements of the impracticability of a party's obligation to perform in accordance with a contract in precisely the same order or manner as UCC 2–615. Yet, as Professor Farnsworth pointed out, in reading the Restatement Second, Sections 261 through 272 (which, collectively, address the general issue of impracticability), it is clear that UCC 2–615 was given considerable deference in the crafting of these sections.

In addressing the general statement about impracticability set forth in §261 of the Restatement Second, the three substantive sections that follow address the three categories of scenarios in which a party may be excused from its duty to perform as the result of the impracticability of that performance:

> This Section states the general principle under which a party's duty may be [discharged by the occurrence of a supervening event]. The following three sections deal with the three categories of cases where this general principle has traditionally been applied: supervening death or incapacity of a person necessary for performance (§262), supervening destruction of a specific thing necessary for performance (§263), and supervening prohibition or prevention by law (§264).[40]

Relevant cases in which impossibility or impracticability is claimed as a defense to the nonperformance of construction contracts are taken up in the Supplementary Materials on the companion website, under Construction Phase Issues. Relevant cases in which impossibility or impracticability are claimed as a defense to the nonperformance of leases of real property are taken up in Chapter 11.

Contrary to public policy

Courts, as a general rule, will not enforce contracts between private parties the substance of which is against public policy. Professor Farnsworth offers a succinct explanation of the principle of the unenforceability of contracts contravening public policy:

> The principle of freedom of contract rests on the premise that it is in the public interest to accord individuals broad powers to order their affairs through legally enforceable agreements. In general, therefore, parties are free to make such agreements as they wish, and courts will enforce them without passing on their substance. Occasionally, however, a court will decide that this interest in party autonomy is outweighed by some other interest and will refuse to enforce the agreement or some part of it.[41]

This inherent tension between the courts' willingness to uphold the rights of private parties to contract with each other as they please, and the courts' protection of the general population by disfavoring contracts running counter to public policy can be traced back to at least 1875, in the opinion of the English common law case of *Printing & Numerical Registration Co. v. Sampson*:

> It must not be forgotten that you are not to extend arbitrarily these rules which say that a given contract is void as being against public policy, because if there is one thing which more than another public policy requires it is that men of full age and competent understanding shall have the utmost liberty of contracting, and that their contracts when entered into freely and voluntarily shall be held sacred and shall be enforced by course of justice.[42]

Broadly, there are two areas in which a court may find it appropriate to overturn the substance of an agreement between two private parties by virtue of the fact that their agreement contravenes public policy. First are those cases in which the court views the substance of the agreement as requiring, encouraging, allowing, or supporting "undesirable conduct" by those parties, such as an agreement constituting commercial bribery.[43] Second are those cases in which sought-after enforcement of such contracts is seen as an "inappropriate use of the judicial process to uphold an unsavory agreement."[44]

Statute of Frauds

This is an appropriate moment at which to repeat the maxim *"What Happens in Vagueness Stays in Vagueness."* There is no general rule that all contracts *must* be in writing and signed by the parties to be enforceable. To be clear, the extent to which all of the details of the parties' mutual agreement is in an unambiguous writing will determine the ease with which a court of competent jurisdiction over those parties can resolve any disputes between them as to what that "unambiguous writing" actually means in terms of the rights, obligations, and liabilities of each party. In other words, a signed, written contract may resolve, by its very existence and explicit language, matters of proof of the existence and interpretation of the particulars of the agreement between the parties. However, it is *not* a condition precedent of the enforceability of that agreement or for an enforceable contract to be found.

Having stated this general rule, there are categories or classes of contracts that, *in order to be enforceable, must* be in writing. Conveyances of interests in real property – including but not limited to sales of real property and leases of improvements on real property – are among such contracts. This is one of the principal tenets of the Statute of Frauds.

In the common law, this requirement was introduced in the Statute of Frauds in England, which dates back almost four and a half centuries (1677).

§6.1. History and Functions of the Statute [of Frauds]. It would be difficult to imagine a question more important to a person expecting to make agreements in an unfamiliar legal system than this: When is a writing needed for an enforceable agreement? The answer will determine both one's willingness to give unwritten assurances and one's insistence that the other party put its undertaking in writing.[45]

The English Statute of Frauds[46] serving as the antecedent to the doctrine as applied by courts in the United States has in many instances long since been replaced by specific statutes in each of the fifty states regarding what classes of contracts must be in writing to be enforceable. Each state's statute of frauds has its own set of specific requirements regarding what types and kinds of contracts conveying interests in land must be in writing to be enforceable.

Some of these statutes also provide that, to be enforceable, specific contracts for conveyance of certain types of interests in land must not only be in a writing signed by the parties but *must also be recorded* in the land records in the jurisdiction wherein the land that is the subject matter of the contract is located. Further specifics in these state statutes provide that the parties may record a memorandum disclosing only required details regarding that conveyance, such that the parties need not record the entire written contract for it to be enforceable. This is the case, for example, in those states where the statute of frauds requires that commercial lease agreements must be recorded to be enforceable, but a Memorandum of Lease signed by the parties can be recorded in lieu of the complete lease agreement itself.

The Restatement Second provides guidance regarding contracts that must be in writing to be enforceable in the absence of an applicable state statute providing to the contrary or in the case of interpreting such state statutes where their application may be ambiguous.

§125. Contract to Transfer, Buy, or Pay for an Interest in Land

(1) A promise to transfer to any person any interest in land is within the Statute of Frauds.

(2) A promise to buy any interest in land is within the Statute of Frauds, irrespective of the person to whom the transfer is to be made.

(3) When a transfer of an interest in land has been made, a promise to pay the price, if originally within the Statute of Frauds, ceases to be within it unless the promised price is itself in whole or in part an interest in land.

(4) Statutes in most states except from the land contract and one-year provisions of the Statute of Frauds short-term leases and contracts to lease, usually for a term not longer than one year.

Comment:

a. Conveyance of land. The English Statute of Frauds in §§1 and 3 required a writing for the creation, transfer, or surrender of an interest in land. The words "contract or sale" in §4, therefore, have been read as "contract for sale" and not applied to present conveyances. American statutes modeled on §4 commonly use such phrases as "any agreement for the sale of real estate or any interest in or concerning it," and are similarly read to exclude present conveyances. The formal requisites of a conveyance of land are beyond the scope of this Restatement. See §1 Restatement of Property §§467, 522. What is an interest in land is the subject of §127.[47]

Contracts commonly used during the Project Conception Phase

Contracts for Professional Services

As introduced in Chapter 2, very early in the Project Conception Phase of The Development Process, the Developer will need to identify, engage, and assemble into a Development Team various professional services providers, including lawyers, land planners, architects, civil engineers, market analysts, and communications and marketing experts, to assist the Developer in the process of testing and refining "the Idea" into a viable Project concept. This means the Developer will need to enter into Professional Services Agreements with each of these service providers. These Professional Services Agreements will define the Scope of Work of the professional services to be provided and the compensation the Developer will owe each service provider in exchange for their respective Scope of Work.

In addition to the amount and terms of payment for each discrete set of services to be provided, the Professional Services Agreement will address any agreement between the Developer and the professional services provider regarding future work on the Project, should the Developer decide to proceed past the Project Conception Phase of The Development Process, including what role, if any, such service provider will continue to play on the Development Team. Any promise of future work contained in the initial agreement covering the professional service provider's services to be performed only during the Project Conception Phase must be carefully crafted, as the terms and conditions regarding such future services will need to be negotiated between the parties, as will the specific Scope of Work for all subsequent phases of The Development Process. Oftentimes, the primary incentive for professional services providers to become active members of the Development Team early in the Project Conception Phase is to secure the opportunity, or at least a competitive advantage, in being more formally engaged on the Project in the subsequent phases.

Finally, to the extent that any such professional services provider is providing its services on a discounted basis during the Project Conception Phase, any concomitant diminution in the service provider's exposure to professional liability allowed the provider in exchange for providing its services on a discounted basis should be spelled out, in detail, in the Professional Services Agreement. For example, design professionals such as architects and land planners may not, as a matter of law, incur professional liability to the extent their services are limited to schematic designs, from which nothing may be built because of the conceptual and preliminary nature of the designs and concepts. The same limitation of professional liability may be achievable by civil engineering firms, to the extent the scope of the services performed is preliminary and exploratory, such that neither the Developer nor any third party working on the Developer's behalf could move forward with the Project without the engineering firm providing additional work. Once the Scope of Work of a professional services provider is such that professional liability may attach to the work performed or work product being delivered, the compensation arrangement between the Developer and the professional services provider will need to address such accrual of professional liability for participating on the Development Team.

UNDERSTANDING THE IMPORTANCE OF THE SCOPE OF WORK

Parties to a real estate transaction, and their respective real estate counsel, often talk about the "boilerplate" of a contract. The term refers to specific provisions in a contract that may be the same from contract to contract, as distinguished from specifics addressing the services or tasks to be performed, or the physical materials and/or completed structures (i.e., "Improvements" to real property) to be completed and delivered.

By way of example, contract "boilerplate" may include the mechanics, timing, and methods of payment (but not the price, which must be added to customize the contract); the acceptable method(s) for one party to give formal "notice" to the other party (but not the identities of both parties, which also must be added to the contract); the parties' agreement to the jurisdiction in which interpretation and other enforcement actions may be brought; and any provisions for alternative dispute resolution (e.g., binding or nonbinding arbitration as an interim or final process through which any and all disputes may be determined by one party to the contract claiming to be aggrieved by the other party).

However, particularly in the case of professional services agreements, the parameters of the legal rights, obligations, and duties of the parties to a contract will be described, in detail, in the Scope of Work. The more detailed the Scope of Work, the less likely there will be disagreements between the parties about the nature of *what* one party promised to the other, in exchange for payment at an agreed-upon amount and on an agreed-upon schedule. The disputes between the parties, then, may be based on a factual determination, by a judge, jury, or some other finder of fact (as would be the case with an arbitrator in disputes over contracts containing arbitration clauses), as to whether the party providing the services has successfully completed each component of the contract as described in and defined by the Scope of Work. The companion website for this textbook provides several sample Scope of Works for different types of professional services providers typical of The Development Process.

Letters of Intent

Letters of Intent are used to facilitate a broad range of business transactions, including, in the context of The Development Process, Purchase and Sale Agreements, future capital formations, Lease Agreements, and the like. The underlying purpose of a Letter of Intent is to describe, generally, the business intent of two parties to a potential real estate–related transaction, without getting bogged down in all of the details needed to memorialize the transaction. Generally speaking, courts have interpreted Letters of Intent as an agreement by the parties to agree in the future. This is fundamentally different from Professor Farnsworth's formulation concerning the evolution of exchange contracts intended to support the enforceability of future promises.

As the document name implies, Letters of Intent are not intended by the parties to be enforceable. As the argument goes, if the parties to a Letter of Intent truly intended to be bound, they would negotiate the contract document the Letter of Intent states they will enter into at a later date. As such, the main purposes of the Letter of Intent are to (i) frame the basic terms and conditions of a written agreement that the parties would like to enter into in the future and (ii) to lay the foundation for the further negotiations needed to craft a binding contract relating to the subject matter of the Letter of Intent.

In reality, the more complicated a real estate transaction, the greater the imperative among the parties to describe the essential elements of the business terms in a Letter of Intent, if for no other reason than because the actual contract necessary to fully document a complicated transaction is likely to be very lengthy and time-consuming to negotiate, working out all of the details not addressed in the Letter of Intent. During such contract negotiations, the intent of the parties set forth in the Letter of Intent will likely be invoked repeatedly by one side against the other, in order to steer the drafting of the actual contract in a consistent direction.

A Letter of Intent for a commercial office lease might contain essential details regarding the following key lease terms:

1. Property or building address
2. Tenant
3. Premises
4. Lease term
5. Lease commencement date
6. Base rent
7. Escalation
8. Operating expenses and real estate taxes
9. Tenant improvement allowance of TI budget
10. Maintenance
11. Parking
12. Building signage
13. Brokerage commission
14. Security deposit
15. Right to terminate
16. Liability
17. Renewal option(s)
18. Due authority

The process of getting to the finalization and due execution of the critical, binding agreements defining milestones in The Development Process, as well as understanding fully the relationship between a Letter of Intent on one hand, and a written contract memorializing a complex transaction such as the sale and purchase of real property (e.g., a Purchase and Sale Agreement), are well described in Professor Farnsworth's discussion of "the Bargaining Process" in Chapter 3 of his treatise:

> Traditional analysis, in terms of an offer followed by an acceptance, may adequately describe the agreement process in simple transactions in which, for example, one party presents a printed form for the other to sign or both exchange letters or facsimiles. But it is difficult to accept this model as representative of the complex negotiations typical of substantial transactions – of "deals" for the long-term supply of energy, *for the development of a shopping center*, for the friendly takeover of a corporation, of the signing of a first-round draft choice.[48]

Professor Farnsworth contrasts the laborious and time-consuming process of negotiating the complex documents the parties will be executing and exchanging at a Closing with the common law Contract Law principles of "offer and acceptance," with initial negotiations taking place very early in the process by the principals of the parties to these business arrangements, framing the essential elements of their "business deal," which is eventually transcended by the respective legal counsel representing those parties, negotiating, and finalizing detailed contracts.

> Major contractual commitments are typically set out in a lengthy document, or in a set of documents, signed by the parties in multiple copies and exchanged more or less simultaneously at a closing. The terms are reached by negotiations, usually face-to-face over a considerable period of time and often involving corporate officers, bankers, engineers, accountants, lawyers, and others. *The negotiations are a far cry from the simple bargaining envisioned by the classic rules of offer and acceptance,* which evoke an image of a single-issue, adversarial, zero-sum bargaining as opposed to multi-issue, problem-solving, gain-maximizing negotiation.[49]

Contrary to the common law principles of "offer" and "counteroffer," without a contract being formed unless and until the final counteroffer is accepted by its recipient, the negotiation of the kind of multi-issue, complex documents Professor Farnsworth described are the product of a bargaining and negotiating "process," the intended outcome of which is a complete set of written agreements to which each of the respective, critical parties have manifested their assent by executing and exchanging counterpart originals of a set of interrelated contracts to exchange at Closing.

> During the negotiation of such deals there is often no offer or counteroffer for either party to accept, but rather *a gradual process in which agreements are reached piecemeal in several "rounds" with a succession of drafts.* There may first be an exchange of information and an identification of the parties' interests and differences, then a series of compromises with tentative agreement on major points, and finally a refining of contract terms. The negotiators may refrain from making offers because they want the terms of any binding commitment to be worked out by their lawyers, to whom things will be turned over once the original negotiators decide that they have settled those matters that they regard as important.[50]

Although he does not express it as such, Professor Farnsworth's reference to business principals not wanting to enter into *"any binding commitment"* while nonetheless wanting to feel that they have "settled those matters that they regard as important" describes succinctly the *raison d'etre* of the Letter of Intent as the document that commences the "negotiating process" through which complex business arrangements – such as the sale and purchase of real property for development – are reduced to a series of complex, lengthy, and excruciatingly detailed interrelated documents.

If students and readers of this textbook accept the contention that, because of what has become the custom and practice of real estate executives and entrepreneurs, and their lawyers, common law contract principles of "offer and acceptance" have been replaced, in whole, by a "bargaining process" represented by some mutual assent by the business principals of a limited number of deal points to be expanded and expounded into complex and lengthy contracts, they might ask, "then why study common law principles of Contract Law at all?" One answer is that, when parties' respective efforts to reach agreement fail or when one party feels it has been aggrieved by another, such disappointed or aggrieved parties inevitably turn to the courts for redress. And the courts, more often than not, turn to common law principles of contract to asses who is liable for what.

> If the parties sign at a closing, there is no question that they have given their assent to a contract, and there is therefore scant occasion to apply the classic rules of offer and acceptance. *But if the negotiations fail and nothing is signed, a number of questions may arise that the classic rules of offer and acceptance do not address:* May a disappointed party have a claim against the other party for having failed to conform to a standard of fair dealing? If so, what is the meaning of fair dealing in this context? And may the disappointed party get restitution? Be reimbursed for out-of-pocket expenses? Recover the lost opportunities? As deals have become larger and more complex [and] negotiations have become more complicated and prolonged, these questions have reached courts in increasing numbers, calling on courts for imaginative application of traditional contract doctrines.[51]

In being asked to answer such questions as those posed, hypothetically, by Professor Farnsworth, courts may, indeed, consider what the principals of a failed "bargaining process" intended, by looking to the Letter of Intent that may constitute the only objective evidence of what the parties intended from the start. Several selected examples of cases in which Letters of Intent serve as the court's point of reference for resolving disputes in which pre-contractual liabilities are sought to be imposed by one party on the other are taken up on the companion website for this textbook.

Option Contracts

As discussed in Chapter 2, the Project Conception Phase of The Development Process will end in one of two ways: Either the Developer will abandon "the Idea" and move on to another opportunity, or the Developer will secure Site Control. Securing Site Control will most likely be achieved by the Developer and the Property Owner entering into one of two agreements: an Option Contract or a Purchase and Sale Agreement. There are, however, a few less common ways for the Developer to secure Site Control, including but not limited to entering into a Joint Venture Agreement with the Property Owner, through which the Property Owner contributes the Subject Site to the Joint Venture in exchange for a specific percentage interest in the Project going forward.

Under an Option Contract, the Option Purchaser pays a fee to the Property Owner, usually expressed as a fixed percentage of the Purchase Price for the Subject Site specified in the Option Contract, in exchange for which the Property Owner grants the Option Purchaser the right to purchase the Subject Site, within a specified period of time (the "Option Period"), for the Purchase Price specified in the Option Contract. If the Option Purchaser consummates the purchase of the Subject Site by exercising the Option Contract during the Option Period, the Option Payment is generally credited toward the Purchase Price. If the Option Purchaser fails to exercise the Option Contract during the Option Period, however, the Property Owner gets to retain the Option Payment as compensation for having granted the Option Contract and being ready, willing, and able to perform the Option Contract at any time during the Option Period. The disposition of the Option Payment stands in stark contrast with the good faith deposit given by the Purchaser to the Seller under the Purchase and Sale Agreement, as explained in greater length in the section that follows.

The Purchase and Sale Agreement (PSA). As suggested in the subsection of this chapter on Letters of Intent, Purchase and Sale Agreements tend to be fairly complex and technical documents. They can run twenty, forty, sixty pages or more, not including exhibits, which themselves can be voluminous.[52] They often have "Defined Terms" or "Definitions" sections requiring more than just a few pages. Depending on the length of the Due Diligence Period and the provisions of the agreement regarding securing all necessary land use approvals, each of which is discussed later, and any unilateral or bilateral extensions thereof permitted in accordance with the terms and conditions of the PSA, the duration of the PSA may be as short as three to six months or as long as several years. Also as suggested in the foregoing discussion, the PSA is generally comprised of a series of executory promises, the satisfactory completion of which may be conditions precedent to the Purchaser's obligations due at the Closing.

Selected Purchase and Sale Agreement clauses

The Property. In a PSA for an operating commercial building, for example, there are a number of specific components that comprise "the Property" and that the Seller is conveying to the Purchaser; the "Land" or "real property" is only one such component. To better explain the bundle of real, personal, and other property rights potentially making up "the Property" that is the subject of the PSA, a sample clause from a form of commercial property PSA is provided next:

1. The Property

    1.1 Description:

    Subject to the terms and conditions of this Agreement, and for good and valuable consideration herein set forth herein, the receipt and sufficiency of which are hereby acknowledged by the parties to the Agreement, Seller agrees to sell and transfer, and Purchaser agrees to purchase and take ownership and title to, all of the following (collectively referred to herein as the "Property"):

    1.1.1 That certain land (the "Land") located in the [INSERT NAME OF JURISDICTION] and more specifically described in Exhibit 1.1.1 attached hereto and incorporated herein by reference, together with all of Seller's right, title and interest, if any, in and to any appurtenances, licenses, privileges and other similar property interests belonging or appurtenant to said Land, and any roads, streets and ways, public and private, serving the Land (including, without limitation, all rights to develop the Land granted by governmental entities having jurisdiction over the Land), and any mineral, oil and gas rights, water rights, sewer rights and other utility rights, and any transferrable development rights ("TDRs") and air rights allocated to, attendant, and/or associated with the Land;

    1.1.2 The buildings, parking areas, improvements, and fixtures now or hereafter situated on the Land (the "Improvements");

    1.1.3 All of the furniture, personal property, machinery, apparatus, and equipment described on Exhibit 1.1.3 attached hereto and incorporated herein by reference (collectively, the "Personal Property"), currently owned by Seller and located on or in and/or used in the operation, repair, and/or maintenance of the Land or the Improvements. The Personal Property to be conveyed is subject to reasonable depletions, replacements (with Personal Property of reasonably equivalent or greater value), and additions in the ordinary course of Seller's business;

    1.1.4 All of Seller's right, title and interest in and to the easements, hereditaments, and appurtenances belonging to or inuring to the benefit of Seller and pertaining to the Land, if any;

    1.1.5 The leases, licenses or occupancy agreements, including those in effect on the date of this Agreement which are identified on the Schedule of Leases, Licenses and Security Deposits as Exhibit 1.1.5 attached hereto and incorporated herein by reference, and any new leases or licenses entered into which as of the Closing (as hereinafter defined) affect all or any portion of the Land or the Improvements (collectively, the "**Leases**"), and any security deposits actually held by Seller or on Seller's behalf by an escrow agent, trustee, finan-cial institution, depository institution, or commercial bank, with respect to any such Leases;

1.1.6 All Contracts (defined in Section 3.4 below) assumed by Purchaser on and as of the Date of Closing (as defined below) pursuant to Sections 3.4 and 4.3 below;

1.1.7 All assignable warranties and guaranties issued in connection with the Improve-ments or the Personal Property;

1.1.8 All transferable consents, authorizations, variances or waivers, licenses, permits, and approvals from any governmental or quasi-governmental agency, depart-ment, board, commission, bureau, or other entity or instrumentality solely in respect of the Land or the Improvements ("Permits"); and

1.1.9 All of Seller's right, title, and interest in and to the intangible property owned by Seller and affecting or relating to the Land or Improvements including, without limitation, all refundable deposit, and any accrued but unpaid interest thereon as of the Effective Date of the Agreement and thereafter; all transferable licenses, permits, accounts, authorizations, approvals, certificates of occupancy, and other consents and approvals necessary for the current use and operation of the Property; and all right, title, and interest of Seller in all transferable warranties, telephone exchange numbers for the Building, trade names, plans and specifi-cations, and development rights related to any of the foregoing (collectively, the "Intangible Personal Property").

It should be evident from a careful reading of this description of the Property that the Purchaser intends to acquire and the Seller intends to convey, through the PSA, all of the real, personal, and other property rights, tangible and intangible, relating to the Seller's operation of the Property. Accordingly, the Property clause in a PSA must be both specific and comprehensive in its identification and description of all such components of "the Property."

Purchase price and payment terms, including the good faith deposit. One of the essential elements of the PSA is the declaration of the Purchase Price. That is not to say, however, that the Purchase Price stated in a duly executed and enforceable PSA is never subject to renegotiation prior to Closing. In fact, should some infirmity in the transaction be discovered during the Purchaser's Due Diligence Period, it is just as likely that the parties will agree to a concomitant adjustment to the Purchase Price as that the Purchaser will terminate the PSA and walk away from the transaction (assuming, of course, that such an infirmity is not fatal to the Purchaser's plans for the Property). To better understand how payments under the PSA are structured, and the Purchaser's obligation to honor the stated Purchase Price at Closing in a commercial property PSA, a sample clause is provided next:

2. Price and Payment

    2.1 Purchase Price

    The purchase price for the Property (the "Purchase Price") is _____ and __/100 Dollars (\$_____).

    2.2 Payment

    Payment of the Purchase Price is to be made in cash as follows:

    2.2.1 Within two (2) business days after the Effective Date, Purchaser shall make an earnest money deposit of _____ and __/100 Dollars (\$_____) (the "First Deposit").

2.2.2 If the Purchaser does not elect to terminate this Agreement on or before the Approval Date (as defined in Section 3.6 below), then Purchaser shall make a second deposit of _____ and__/100 Dollars ($_____) (the "Second Deposit") on the Approval Date. If Purchaser shall fail to make the Second Deposit before 5:00 p.m., Washington, D.C. time on the Approval Date, Purchaser will be deemed to have elected to terminate this Agreement in accordance with Section 3.6 below, in which event the First Deposit and all interest earned thereon shall be returned to Purchaser by Escrow Agent and neither party shall have any further rights, obligations, or liability hereunder, except as expressly set forth herein.

2.2.3 The First Deposit, the Second Deposit, and if posted by Purchaser in accordance with Section 2.3 below, the Additional Deposit (defined below) (collectively, the "Deposit"), when paid, will be placed and held in escrow by _____ ("Escrow Agent") in an interest bearing account at a mutually acceptable banking institution pursuant to the terms of this Agreement and the Escrow Agreement attached hereto as Exhibit 2.2.1. Any interest earned by the Deposit shall be considered as part of the Deposit. Except as otherwise provided in this Agreement, the Deposit will be applied to the Purchase Price at the Closing.

2.2.4 At the Closing, Purchaser shall deliver to the Escrow Agent for payment to Seller the Purchase Price, inclusive of the Deposit and subject to adjustment for the prorations as provided herein (and, in the event Purchaser assumes the Bank Loan (as defined below), less the outstanding amount of the Bank Loan on the Date of Closing (defined below) via wire transfer in immediately available funds).

Due Diligence. The Purchaser of the Subject Property does not want to invest the time, effort, and cost involved in conducting its due diligence about the Property without first having a binding commitment from the Seller to convey the property at the agreed-upon Purchase Price; the Purchaser's Due Diligence is intentionally deferred until after the PSA has been negotiated and executed by the parties but well before the Closing Date. Accordingly, the Seller's promise to deliver all Due Diligence Materials to the Purchaser, within a specified period of time following the due execution of the parties of the final version of the PSA, is one of the Seller's executory promises that constitute a condition precedent to the Closing. To better explain what constitutes the Due Diligence Materials in a commercial property PSA, a sample clause is provided next:

3.2   Due Diligence Materials

Within seven (7) business days following the Effective Date, Seller shall deliver to Purchaser a true, complete and accurate copy of each of the following documents to the extent in Seller's possession or control, (all of which constitute the "Due Diligence Materials"):

3.2.1 The three (3) most recent real estate and personal property tax bills (including the current year, or estimates thereof if such tax bill is not yet available), together with copies of all tax assessment notices for the three (3) years immediately preceding the Effective Date.

3.2.2 To the extent presently in force or effect, all insurance policies (together with certificates of insurance and paid receipts therefore), warranty agreements, brokerage, management, leasing, consulting, service, supply and maintenance contracts and agreements (including, without limitation, any warranties or service contracts relating to termite damage or infestation), and to the extent presently in force and effect, any other, license, option, contract or agreement affecting or relating to the Property.

3.2.3   All plans, specifications, soil reports, site plans, surveys, environmental reports and audits, flood plain studies, easements, licenses, and all engineering, and inspection reports (including, but not limited to **Building Inspection** reports for calendar years 1999, 2000, and 2001 and a current year-to-date report) that were prepared by or for Seller or are in Seller's possession or reasonably obtainable by Seller.

3.2.4   All licenses, permits, zoning variances, special permits, special exceptions, or similar zoning approvals (and all pending applications therefore, if any), certificates of occupancy, authorizations, consents, easements, and other approvals or instruments required in connection with the construction, use, or operation of the Property (including any appurtenant parking uses), and all applications or requests submitted in connection therewith.

3.2.5   All Occupancy Leases and subleases and other occupancy agreements affecting the Property, and all agreements relating to leasing commissions or other fees due with respect to the Occupancy Leases or other tenancies.

3.2.6   Operating statements and management reports relating to the income and expenses of the Property, for the current year to date and for full operating years since 1999. Specifically, actual expenses for the year and actual expenses for all years that are base years under the Occupancy Leases and copies of estimated operating expense statements given to the tenants for the current year. In addition, subject to 3.4 below, Seller shall make all of its books and records, excluding any market and feasibility studies pertaining to the Property, available for review and/or review and copying by Purchaser and its agents and consultants.

3.2.7   A detailed list of capitalized expenditures made since _____.

3.2.8   All documents filed or prepared with respect to any pending or threatened suit, action, arbitration, or legal, administrative, or other proceeding relating to or involving the Property and any correspondence relating thereto.

3.2.9   All title policies, surveys and all documents creating any exceptions to title

Purchaser's Right to Secure All Necessary Land Use Approvals. In addition to providing a Due Diligence Period during which the Purchaser has the opportunity to fully and thoroughly review and analyze the Due Diligence Materials the Buyer is required under the PSA to deliver to the Purchaser – the Purchaser's satisfaction with which will be a condition precedent to Closing – in cases in which the Purchaser's intended use of the Property will require land use approvals that have yet to be secured relative to the Property, the PSA will contain a land use approvals contingency clause. By securing site control through the PSA, the Purchaser will have legal standing in the jurisdiction in which the Property is located to seek such expanded land use approvals.

While the Purchaser will be required to assume the full cost of seeking and securing changes to the Land Use Controls impacting the development or redevelopment of the Property, in the event the Purchaser fails in such efforts, it may have the unfettered right to terminate the PSA, without further liability or the loss of its good faith deposit under the PSA, in accordance with the land use approvals contingency clause in the PSA.

Unlike other PSA sections and subsections provided by way of example in other sections of this chapter, which are taken from an intentionally generic form of PSA, land use approval contingency clauses need to be drafted as specifically as possible to (i) the specifics of the Purchaser's proposed Project for the Property; (ii) the specific land use approvals process through which Purchaser has the best chance of securing the necessary land use approvals to make the Project permissible in the jurisdiction, and (iii) the Purchaser's and the Seller's respective understandings of the process described in clause (ii) of this sentence. Accordingly, and to help students and readers better understand how the land use approvals contingency clause works in a commercial property PSA, a Land Use Approvals Contingency clause excerpted from a PSA from a completed transaction, and in which the local land use approvals process involves a two-step process before the land use application is filed, has been redacted and revised to adapt it for illustrative purposes and is reproduced next:

X.3 Development Approval Covenants.

X.3.1 Development-Related Definitions.

(a) The term "City" means [INSERT NAME OF JURISDICTION].
(b) The term "City Approval of the Land Use Application" shall mean the affirmative vote of the necessary majority of [INSERT NAME OF EACH DELIBERATIVE BODY, IN HIERARCHICAL ORDER, WITH RECOMMENDATION OR DECISION-MAKING AUTHORITY, AND NAME OF GOVERNING BODY] of the City to approve the Land Use Application.
(c) The term "Contemplated Development" shall mean [INSERT SUMMARY DESCRIPTION OF THE PROJECT] as depicted in the illustrative documents attached as Exhibit [TBD] and incorporated herein by reference (hereinafter referred to as the "Illustrative Documents").
(d) The term "Land Use Application" shall mean a full application for [INSERT FORMAL NAME OF THE TYPE OF APPLICATION BEING SUBMITTED IN ACCORDANCE WITH THE JURISDICTION'S LAND USE PLANNING APPROVAL PROCESS] in accordance with all applicable law; however, Purchaser has notified Seller that Purchaser elects to pursue [INSERT NAME OR DESCRIPTION OF ALTERNATIVE LAND USE APPROVAL APPLICATION PROCESS, IF ONE IS AVAILABLE AND VIABLE FOR THE PROJECT] in accordance with all applicable law.
(e) The term "Phase I Submission" shall have the meaning given such term in the [INSERT NAME OF LAND USE APPROVAL DOCUMENT PURSUANT TO WHICH APPROVAL IS BEING SOUGHT] promulgated by the City in accordance with all applicable law.
(f) The term "Phase II Submission" shall have the meaning given such term in the [INSERT NAME OF LAND USE APPROVAL DOCUMENT PURSUANT TO WHICH APPROVAL IS BEING SOUGHT] promulgated by the City in accordance with all applicable law.

X.3.2 Purchaser's Development of Concept Plan to Be Approved by Seller.

(a) No later than [INSERT NUMBER OF] days prior to the expiration of the Study Period, Purchaser, at its sole expense, shall prepare and deliver to Seller all narratives, plans, and other materials necessary to constitute a concept plan for the Project (the "Proposed Concept Plan") for the Project that is sufficient to schedule a pre-development conference with the relevant governmental subdivision(s) of the City.
(b) Following Purchaser's delivery of the Proposed Concept Plan to Seller, Purchaser, at Seller's request from time to time, shall meet with Seller to discuss the Proposed Concept Plan and Seller's comments and questions relating thereto. If, prior to the expiration of the Study Period, Seller and Purchaser, each acting in its sole and absolute discretion, agree upon all narratives, plans, and other materials necessary to constitute a concept plan for the Project that is sufficient to schedule a predevelopment conference with the City, then such agreed-upon conceptual plan shall constitute the "Approved Concept Plan."

(c) If Seller and Purchaser have not agreed upon an Approved Concept Plan by the end of the Study Period, then this Agreement shall terminate upon the expiration of the Study Period as if Purchaser had terminated this Agreement pursuant to [INSERT CROSS-REFERENCE TO SECTION OF THE PSA PROVIDING FOR THE FULL RETURN OF THE GOOD FAITH DEPOSIT], above.

(d) If Seller and Purchaser have agreed upon an Approved Concept Plan by the end of the Study Period, then, not later than thirty (30) days after Seller and Purchaser agree on the Approved Concept Plan, Purchaser, at its sole expense, shall submit that Approved Concept Plan to the City and meet with representatives of the [INSERT NAME OR NAMES OF CITY DEPARTMENTS WITH WHICH DEVELOPER IS REQUIRED OR OTHERWISE SHOULD MEET AS A PREDICATE TO FORMAL COMMENCEMENT OF ANY LAND USE APPROVALS PROCESS] to discuss such plan.

X.3.3 Development of Phase I Concept Plan. Not later than [INSERT PERIOD OF TIME] days after first meeting with representatives of the City departments as referenced, above, to discuss the Approved Concept Plan, Purchaser shall, at its expense, submit a Phase I Concept Plan submission to the City. Purchaser shall not submit a Phase I Concept Plan submission prior to obtaining Seller's approval thereof, which approval may not be unreasonably withheld, conditioned, or delayed. In addition, Purchaser shall obtain Seller's written approval (which also shall not be unreasonably withheld, conditioned, or delayed) of any modifications to the Phase I Concept Plan submission before submitting and/or agreeing to the same. Without limiting the generality of the foregoing, it is specifically agreed that it shall be reasonable for Seller to withhold its approval to any proposed Phase I Concept Plan submission (or modification thereto) that differs from the Approved Concept Plan in any material respect or includes any Binding Undertaking; similarly, it shall not be reasonable for Seller to withhold its approval to any proposed Phase I Concept Plan submission (or modification thereto) to the extent that any objections of Seller to the same would require any changes to the Approved Concept Plan and the same includes no Binding Undertaking. Within one (1) business day after the City approves the Phase I Concept Plan submission, Purchaser shall notify Seller in writing of such City approval.

X.3.4 Development of Phase II Concept Plan. Not later than [INSERT NUMBER OF] days after submitting the Phase I Concept Plan submission to the City, Purchaser shall, at its expense, submit a Phase II Concept Plan submission to the City. Purchaser shall not submit a Phase II Concept Plan submission prior to obtaining Seller's approval thereof, which approval shall not be unreasonably withheld, conditioned, or delayed. In addition, Purchaser shall obtain Seller's written approval (which written approval shall not be unreasonably withheld, conditioned, or delayed) of any modifications to the Phase II Concept Plan submission before submitting and/or agreeing to the same. Without limiting the generality of the foregoing, it is specifically agreed that it shall be reasonable for Seller to withhold its approval to any proposed Phase II Concept Plan submission (or modification thereto) that differs from the Approved Concept Plan (as the same may have been modified by the Phase I Concept Plan submission) in any material respect; similarly, it shall not be reasonable for Seller to withhold its approval to any proposed Phase II Concept Plan submission (or modification thereto) to the extent that any objections of Seller to the same would require any changes to the previously approved Concept Plan (as the same may have been modified by the Seller-approved Phase I Concept Plan submission) and the same includes no Binding Undertaking.

Within one (1) business day after the City approves the Phase II Concept Plan submission, Purchaser shall notify Seller in writing of such City approval.

X.3.5 Development and Finalization of Land Use Application.

(a) Not later than [INSERT NUMBER OF] days after submitting the Phase II Concept Plan submission to the City, Purchaser shall, at its expense, submit a Land Use Application to the City.

(b) Not later than [INSERT NUMBER OF] days after submitting the initial Land Use Application to the City, Purchaser shall, at its expense, revise, finalize, and submit a final Land Use Application to the City and take all such other steps as may be necessary or appropriate to prepare for the required public hearings attendant or otherwise supportive of Purchaser's efforts to seek and secure City Approval of Purchaser's Land Use Application.

(c) Purchaser shall not submit a Land Use Application (whether pursuant to clause (a) above, clause (b) above or otherwise) prior to obtaining Seller's approval thereof, which approval shall not be unreasonably withheld, conditioned, or delayed. In addition, Purchaser shall obtain Seller's written approval (which written approval shall not be unreasonably withheld, conditioned or delayed) of any modifications to the Land Use Application before submitting and/or agreeing to the same. Without limiting the generality of the foregoing, it is specifically agreed that it shall be reasonable for Seller to withhold its approval to any proposed Land Use Application (or modification thereto) that differs from the Party-Approved Conceptual Plan (as the same may have been modified by the Stage II Concept Submission) in any material respect or includes any Binding Undertaking; similarly, it shall not be reasonable for Seller to withhold its approval to any proposed Land Use Application (or modification thereto) the extent that any objections of Seller to the same would require any changes to the previously approved Party Approved Conceptual Plan (as the same may have been modified by the Seller-approved Stage II Concept Submission) and the same includes no Binding Undertaking. Within one (1) business day after the City approves the Land Use Application, Purchaser shall notify Seller in writing thereof.

X.3.6 Pursuit of Approvals; Updates.

(a) Purchaser shall diligently and in good faith pursue approval of the Phase I Concept Plan submission, the Phase II Concept Plan submission, and the Land Use Application and any other applications necessary to develop the Project. Without limiting the generality of the foregoing sentence or the other requirements of this Article, Purchaser shall diligently and in good faith use reasonable efforts to comply with the development schedule attached hereto as Exhibit TBP (or, as applicable, any development schedule substituted therefore pursuant to this Section X.3.6). To the extent Purchaser does not satisfy any "Required Action" item set forth on the then-applicable development schedule by the applicable "Month from Contract Execution" date set forth thereon, Purchaser shall, within five (5) business days thereafter, deliver to Seller a substitute development schedule that replaces the "Month from Contract Execution" column with a "Revised Target Date" column (using fixed calendar dates) that represents Purchaser's good faith estimate of the date on which the outstanding "Required Action" items could reasonably be satisfied using good faith reasonable efforts.

(b) On the first day of each calendar month from and after the expiration of the Study Period, Purchaser shall provide written notification setting forth in reasonable detail the status of the approvals contemplated by this Section X.3 and all approval related developments since the last such notice. In addition, Purchaser shall cause its attorneys and other representatives promptly to respond in good faith to inquiries from time to time from Seller's attorneys and other representatives. Purchaser shall provide Seller with reasonable notice of, and an opportunity to attend and participate in all hearings and other meetings (whether in-person, telephonic or otherwise) relating to all approvals contemplated by this Section X.3, whether with the City, community groups, Purchaser's consultants, or otherwise (including, without limitation, the pre-development conference with the City and the public hearing following review of the Land Use Application by the City's [INSERT NAME OF APPLICABLE REVIEW AND/OR APPROVAL BODY]).

(c) Notwithstanding anything to the contrary contained in this Agreement, Purchaser shall not have the power or authority to, and shall not, make any commitments to any governmental authority, community group, or any other organization, group, or individual, relating to the Property which would impose any obligations upon Seller or its successors or assigns, or be binding on the Property, prior to Closing or if Closing did not occur.

(d) Seller shall cooperate with Purchaser, at no cost to Seller, in such manner as Purchaser may reasonably request in connection with processing with the City the land use submissions and requests for approval described in this Section X.3.

X.3.7 Approvals Default. An "Approvals Default" shall have occurred if Purchaser breaches any of the covenants or obligations to be performed by Purchaser under any one or more of Sections X.3.3, X.3.4, and X.3.5 above, and, within five (5) business days thereafter fails to deliver to Seller a substitute development schedule (in the manner set forth in Section X.3.6(a) above) that (a) demonstrates to Seller's reasonable satisfaction that Purchaser can reasonably be expected to obtain City Approval of the Land Use Application on or before the eighteenth (18th) monthly anniversary of the Effective Date (or such later date as Closing may be permitted to occur hereunder) and (b) is otherwise reasonably acceptable to Seller.

X.3.8 Seller Approval. Seller shall respond to all written requests for approval of a proposed Phase I Concept Plan submission, a proposed Phase II Concept Plan submission, or a proposed Land Use Application (or a modification to any of them) within five (5) business days after Seller's receipt thereof; failure timely to respond shall be a deemed approval of such submission in the form provided by Purchaser to Seller with such request, if and only if: (a) Seller continues to fail to respond within five (5) business days after Seller's receipt of a second written request for approval of such submission, (b) each such written request for approval prominently specifies such time for response and prominently states that Seller's failure to respond within that time shall be a deemed approval under this section, and (c) such submission includes no Binding Undertaking. In no event shall any Binding Undertaking be deemed approved by Seller.

Clearly, then, Land Use Approval Contingency clauses are critically important to the Developer whose plan, in making a contract for the purchase of real property, contemplates the construction of improvements or the substantial alteration of existing improvements, to be provided an adequate amount of time to seek and secure the necessary land use approvals without having the Developer's good faith deposit at risk or be required to proceed to Closing on a Property for which the intended, future use cannot be achieved because it will not be allowed.

Permitted Exceptions. The Due Diligence Period in the PSA benefiting the Purchaser and the Seller's related obligation under the PSA to deliver or otherwise make the Due Diligence Materials available to Purchaser in accordance with the terms and conditions of the PSA provides the practical foundations of the Purchaser's assumption of liability under the PSA for any problems arising out of its due diligence of which the Purchaser does not duly notify and apprise the Seller in accordance with the PSA. In essence, the Permitted Exceptions clause of the PSA shifts to the Purchaser the burden of accepting the Property subject to whatever exceptions as to which the Seller is not notified by the Purchaser. In other words, the Due Diligence Period and Due Diligence Materials clauses of the PSA put the Purchaser in the position of identifying any infirmities in the particulars of the Property as to which Purchaser was unaware as of the Effective Date of the PSA. However, in order for the Seller to be able to address any such discovered infirmities, the Seller must be duly apprised of their existence by the Purchaser. Failure to duly notify the Seller of such infirmities makes them the Purchaser's, and not the Seller's, responsibility at Closing. To better explain how the Permitted Exceptions Clause works in a commercial property PSA, a sample clause is provided next:

3.5 Permitted Exceptions

Purchaser shall be deemed to have approved and to have agreed to purchase the Property subject to the following (hereinafter the "Permitted Exceptions"):

3.5.1 All matters of title set forth in Exhibit 3.3 attached hereto;

3.5.2 Any Title Objections, Survey Objections, and any defects in or to title to the Property or other matters affecting or relating to the title to, or the survey of, the Property existing as of the effective date of Purchaser's title insurance commitment and not included in a Title Notice given by Purchaser prior to the Interim Date and/or which Purchaser has otherwise approved or is deemed to have approved pursuant to Section 3.3 hereof;

3.5.3 To the extent accurately disclosed to Purchaser by Seller, all Contracts remaining in effect as of the Date of Closing which Purchaser has elected to assume, or is required to assume, in accordance with the provisions of Section 3.4 and 4.5 hereof;

3.5.4 All Leases in effect as of the Effective Date and all Leases which Purchaser has approved or is deemed to have approved pursuant to Section 4.4 hereof;

3.5.5 The lien of non-delinquent real and personal property taxes and assessments;

3.5.6 Discrepancies, conflicts in boundary lines, shortages in area, encroachments, and any state of facts which an inspection of the premises would disclose and which are not shown by the public records;

3.5.7 Subject to the proration provisions hereof, charges for sewer, water, electricity, telephone, cable television, or gas; and

3.5.8 Security interests on personal property installed upon the Property by tenants and rights of tenants to remove trade fixtures at the expiration of the term of the Leases as contained in the Leases.

3.5.9 Notwithstanding anything contained in this Section 3.5 to the contrary, Permitted Exceptions shall expressly exclude Must-Cure Objections. The provisions of this Section 3.5 shall survive Closing.

Purchaser's Right to Terminate the Contract. As stated in this section, and alluded to elsewhere in this chapter, the nature of acquisition transactions in the context of commercial property tends to be extremely detail-oriented and complex, necessitating that the parties be bound to a PSA before the Property has been fully vetted by the Purchaser for the purposes for which it intends (which purposes may not necessarily be fully disclosed to the Seller at the time of the parties' negotiations or through anything contained in the PSA). It is endemic to the nature of commercial real estate transactions that if the Purchaser's true intentions regarding a Subject Property are fully disclosed to the Owner of that property, the Purchaser may not be able to acquire the Subject Property at the most advantageous Purchase Price. Accordingly, the Purchaser needs the Seller to be bound by certain duties, such as delivering all Due Diligence Materials (see sample PSA clause) in order for the Purchaser to make a determination about the suitability of the Property for what the Purchaser has planned for the Property. Moreover, the Purchaser must have the unfettered right to terminate the PSA should it determine that the Property is not, in fact, suitable for the purpose or purposes for which the Purchaser intends for the Property. It is the Purchaser's Right to Terminate the PSA that provides the principal leverage for the Purchaser, should a decision be made to renegotiate the Purchase Price rather than exercising the Purchaser's ultimate remedy of contract termination. To better explain the Purchaser's Right to Terminate a commercial property PSA, a sample clause is provided next:

3.6 Purchaser's Right to Terminate

> Purchaser shall have the right to terminate this Agreement, for any or no reason whatsoever, by giving Seller written notice of such termination (the "Termination Notice") on or before 5:00 p.m. Eastern Time, on the date which is thirty (30) days after the Effective Date, (the "Approval Date") to terminate its obligation to purchase the Property. Notwithstanding the foregoing, in the event Seller shall give Purchaser notice of any new Leases as required under Section 4.4 below during the last five (5) business days of the aforesaid thirty (30) days period, the Approval Date shall be deemed further extended to the fifth business day following Purchaser's receipt of Seller's notice of such additional Lease. If the Termination Notice is timely given or Purchaser is otherwise deemed to have terminated this Agreement pursuant to Section 2.2.2 above, Escrow Agent shall promptly return the First Deposit to Purchaser and neither party shall have any further obligations or liability hereunder except the Purchaser's Indemnity Obligations set forth in Section 3.1.2 hereof, the Confidentiality Obligations set forth in Section 3.7 hereof and the Broker Obligations set forth in Section 6.3 hereof. If the Termination Notice is not timely given and Purchaser is not otherwise deemed to have terminated this Agreement pursuant to Section 2.2.2 above: (a) Purchaser shall tender the Second Deposit to the Title Company, in immediately available funds, prior to 5:00 p.m. Eastern Time on the Approval Date; (b) the Deposit shall be nonrefundable, except as may be expressly provided in this Agreement; and (c) Purchaser shall have no further rights to the Deposit, and no further right to terminate this Agreement, except as may be expressly provided in this Agreement.

Seller's Obligation to Operate the Subject Property in the Ordinary Course, through and until Closing. As suggested elsewhere in this section, the period of time between when the Seller and Purchaser complete their negotiations of the PSA and duly execute the contract, and when they consummate that transaction at Closing, may range between thirty to sixty days on the short end, to several years on the long end, in cases where a dramatic change in the Land Use Controls impacting the development or redevelopment of the Property are a condition precedent to the Purchaser's obligation to proceed to Closing.

In the case of a PSA for an operating commercial property, there are far more "knowns" than there are "unknowns," and the Purchaser's due diligence undertakings constitute a discrete set of tasks and, therefore, a brief period of time after the Effective Date of the PSA. However, regardless of how short or long the time period between the due execution of the PSA and the Closing, the Seller must be legally bound to continue to operate the Property in the ordinary course, while simultaneously committing to not create any new contractual commitments, including entering into new leases, without the Purchaser's advance written consent or unfettered right to cancel any such contracts shortly after Closing if they do not suit the Purchaser. To better explain the breadth of the Seller's legal duties, under the PSA, to operate the Property in the ordinary course, a sample clause covering Seller's Pre-Closing obligations is provided next:

4. SELLER'S OBLIGATIONS PRIOR TO CLOSING

Until the Closing, Seller and/or Seller's agent:

4.1 Shall keep the Property insured against fire and other hazards covered by extended coverage endorsement and comprehensive public liability insurance against claims for bodily injury, death and property damage occurring in, on or about the Property.

4.2 Shall operate and maintain the Property in a businesslike manner and substantially in accordance with Seller's past practices with respect to the Property, and make any and all repairs and replacements reasonably required to deliver the Property to Purchaser at the Closing in its present condition, normal wear and tear excepted, provided that in the event of any loss or damage to the Property as described in Section 5, Seller shall have an obligation to Purchaser to repair the Property only if Seller so elects and then shall be obligated only to the extent of available insurance proceeds.

4.3 Shall enter into only those new third party contracts which are necessary to carry out its obligations under Section 4.2 and which shall be cancelable on not more than thirty (30) days written notice. If Seller enters into any such contract, it shall promptly provide written notice thereof and a copy of such contract to Purchaser and unless Purchaser, within seven (7) days thereafter, notifies Seller in writing of its intention not to assume such contract, it shall be treated as a contract assumed by Purchaser under Section 3.4 hereof.

4.4 Between the Approval Date and the Date of Closing, Seller will not execute any new Leases or amend in any material respect, terminate (except upon a default by the tenant thereunder), or accept the surrender of any existing tenancies or approve any subleases without the prior consent of Purchaser, which consent shall not be unreasonably withheld in the case of any subleases but may be granted or withheld by Purchaser in its sole discretion in the case of any proposed new leases or amendments thereto or termination or acceptance of surrender under any existing Leases; provided however that Seller is authorized to accept the termination of Leases at the end of their existing terms and to expand, extend, or renew any Leases pursuant to expansion, extension, or renewal options contained therein. With respect to both (i) all Leases entered into after the date of this Agreement but prior to the Approval Date and which have been disclosed to Purchaser prior to the Approval Date and (ii) all Leases executed after the Approval Date which Purchaser has approved or shall be deemed to have approved pursuant to this Section 4.4 (such Leases in both (i) and (ii) herein being collectively referred to as the "Supplemental Leases"), which Supplemental Leases require the construction of tenant improvements, the payment of leasing or brokerage commission(s) and/or the payment of tenant improvement allowances, moving allowances, or other concessions by Landlord, including without limitation brokerage commissions upon the exercise by the tenant thereunder of an expansion, extension, or renewal option contained in such tenant's Lease, to the extent such improvements, commissions or allowances have been disclosed by Seller to Purchaser in Seller's notice to Purchaser of such Supplemental Lease, Purchaser shall: (a) pay, and/or reimburse Seller at Closing for the paid portion of, the cost of such improvements, such leasing or brokerage commission(s), such tenant improvement allowances, moving allowances, concessions, and any other costs associated with such Lease; and (b) assume in writing at Closing all of Seller's obligations as Landlord thereunder with respect to the construction of tenant improvements and the payment of leasing or brokerage commissions, tenant improvement allowances, moving allowances, concession and other costs associated with such Lease after Closing. In the event any such Supplemental Lease shall have commenced prior to the Closing, then the improvements, commissions or allowances shall be prorated as of the Date of Closing. Failure of Purchaser to consent, or to expressly withhold its consent in writing stating with specificity the reasonable basis of its objection, within three (3) business days after its receipt of written request by Seller for such consent accompanied by a copy of the proposed Lease and disclosure of commissions, allowances, or improvements, to any Supplemental Lease, Lease amendment, or sublease submitted by Seller to Purchaser after the Approval Date, shall be deemed to constitute consent. Seller shall, promptly upon Seller's delivery or receipt thereof, provide Purchaser a copy of any notice of default either sent or received by Seller or its management agent under any Lease or Supplemental Lease.

4.5 From and after the Effective Date, and except as expressly provided herein, Seller will not mortgage, pledge, encumber, lien, transfer or dispose of, or enter into any agreement or instrument which would survive Closing and be binding on Purchaser or modify any of the Contracts in any material manner which would be binding on Purchaser. Seller shall continue to comply with all of its obligations under the terms of the Bank Loan through Closing.

4.6 Promptly upon Seller's receipt thereof, Seller shall provide to Purchaser a copy of any written notice alleging a violation by the Property of any law, statute, rule, regulation, ordinance, or order applicable to the Property or the operation thereof received by any governmental or quasi-governmental authority asserting jurisdiction over the Property. Seller shall have the right, but not the obligation or duty, to take such actions as may be required to cure or attempt to cure the violation of law noted or alleged in such notice. Without in any manner limiting Purchaser's rights in the event of a failure of condition as set forth in Section 10 below, the parties expressly agree that the cure by Seller of such violation or alleged violation shall not be a condition precedent to Purchaser's obligations under this Agreement; provided that Seller shall be required to cure any violations arising after the Effective Date hereof caused by the willful or negligent action of Seller or any agent, employee or contractor of Seller.

4.7 From and after the Effective Date, Seller shall not take any action, or omit to take any action, which action or omission would have the effect of violating or rendering untrue any of its representations, warranties, covenants, and agreements contained herein in any materially adverse manner.

4.8 From and after the Effective Date, Seller shall comply with its obligations under the Leases and Contracts.

4.9 Seller will not apply any part of a security deposit of a tenant except (a) if the tenant has vacated the Premises, or (b) as reimbursement for money spent for repairing damage, or for paying operating expenses, for which the tenant is responsible. Seller will promptly notify Purchaser of any adjustments in any security deposits and will freely cooperate with Purchaser in order to transfer any letters of credit held by Seller as a security deposit at Closing without cost or expense to Purchaser, which obligation shall expressly survive Closing.

Seller's Representations and Warranties. The Purchaser can only learn so much from its careful review and analysis of the Due Diligence Materials Seller is bound to deliver or make available to Purchaser in accordance with the PSA. Accordingly, Purchaser must also be able to demand and to rely on a series of Representations and Warranties made by the Seller to the Purchaser in a separate section of the PSA. The Seller's Representations and Warranties are an essential element of the integrity of the purchase and sale transaction, and their veracity at the time made and as of the Closing generally is expected to survive the Closing; in other words, the consummation of the transaction at Closing neither relieves the Seller of its responsibility for the veracity of those Representations and Warranties nor precludes the Seller's Post-Closing liabilities should any such Representation or Warranty subsequently prove false. To better explain the breadth of Seller's Representations and Warranties contained in the PSA, a sample clause is provided next:

6. Representations and Warranties.

  6.1   By Seller

      Seller represents and warrants to Purchaser that:

      6.1.1 Seller is a _____ duly organized, validly existing and in good standing under the laws of the _____, has duly authorized the execution and performance of this Agreement, and such execution and performance will not violate any term of its articles of organization, operating agreement, or other document by which Seller is bound. All consents, approvals, and authorizations from any person, entity, governmental, or quasi-governmental authority required with respect to this Agreement (including, but not limited to, any partner in or shareholder of Seller whose consent may be necessary) have been obtained.

      6.1.2 Neither the entering into of this Agreement nor the consummation of the transaction contemplated hereby will constitute or result in a violation, breach, or default by Seller of, nor conflict with, any contract, organizational document or other instrument to which it is a party, or to which it is subject, or by which it or any of its assets or properties may be bound.

      6.1.3 Seller will, prior to the Closing, operate and maintain the Property in a businesslike manner and substantially in accordance with Seller's past practices with respect to the Property.

      6.1.4 There is no litigation pending or threatened in writing against the Property or Seller which would affect the Property. No petition in bankruptcy (voluntary or otherwise), assignment for the benefit of creditors, or petition seeking reorganization or arrangement or other action under Federal or state bankruptcy or insolvency law is pending against or contemplated by Seller.

      6.1.5 There are no existing condemnation proceedings affecting the Property (or any portion thereof) and Seller has received no written notice of the threatened commencement of any such action affecting the Property (or any portion thereof). There are no proceedings pending or to the best of Seller's knowledge, threatened to change or down-zone the existing zoning classification as to any portion of the Property. To the best of Seller's knowledge there are no proffers, development agreements or other restrictions affecting the use or development of the Property.

6.1.6 The Schedule of Leases, Licenses, and Security Deposits attached hereto as Exhibit 1.1.5 is a true, accurate, and complete list of all leases, subleases, licenses, or other rental or occupancy agreements with respect to or affecting the Property as of the Effective Date. Such Schedule of Leases, Licenses and Security Deposits sets forth in respect of each Tenant space: (i) the number identifying such space and the amount of rentable area thereof (ii) the name of the Tenant occupying such space, (iii) the current base monthly rental payable under the Lease to Landlord for such space, (iv) the amount of the security deposit required under such Lease and the amount of the security deposit received by Landlord from such Tenant, less amounts previously applied or returned to such Tenant, (v) the commencement and expiration dates of the term of such Lease, and whether there are any renewal terms thereunder (vi) whether any rents or other charges are in arrears or prepaid and the period to which such arrearages or prepayments relate, and (vii) the date of such Lease and all amendments thereof. The copies of the Leases and other agreements with the Tenants under the Leases (the "Tenants") delivered to Purchaser are true, correct, and complete copies and are in full force and effect. In addition, the Leases provided to Purchaser constitute the entire agreements with such Tenants relating to the Property and have not been amended, modified or supplemented, except for any amendments, modifications, and supplements previously delivered to Purchaser and listed on the Schedule, and there are no other leases or tenancy agreements affecting the Property; and to the actual knowledge of Seller, are without default by any party and without any right of setoff.

6.1.7 The Schedule of Contracts attached hereto as Exhibit 3.4 is a true, accurate, and complete list of all of the Contracts and all amendments, supplements, and modifications thereof, affecting the Property as of the Effective Date.

6.1.8 Seller shall pay on or before the Closing the full cost of all tenant improvements, leasing or brokerage commission(s) and/or tenant improvement allowances, moving allowances, or other concessions required under the Leases designated on the Schedule of Leases, and except as expressly stated in Exhibit 6.1.8, there is no requirement to pay any brokerage commissions upon the exercise by the Tenant thereunder of an expansion, extension or renewal option contained in such Tenant's Lease.

6.1.9 Seller has received no written notice and has no actual knowledge that there are violations of any laws, ordinances, orders, regulations, or requirements of any federal, state, county or municipal authority or any insurance carrier ("Laws") affecting the Property or any portion thereof (including, without limitation, Comprehensive Environmental Response, Compensation and Liability Act of 1980 (CERCLA), 42 U.S.C. 9601(14), pollutants or contaminants as defined in CERCLA, 42 U.S.C. 9601(33), or hazardous waste as defined by the Resource Conservation and Recovery Act, 42 U.S.C. 6903(5), or other similar applicable federal or state Laws (collectively the "Environmental Laws") and the Americans with Disabilities Act). To the best of Seller's actual knowledge, no Hazardous

Substances and no Hazardous Wastes are present on the Property except as may have been disclosed in the reports provided by Seller as part of the Due Diligence Materials or which are typically maintained in commercial offices by tenants such as copier fluids, toners, and similar items.

6.1.10 To the best of Seller's knowledge, no work has been performed at the Property, and no materials have been furnished to the Property, which though not presently the subject of a lien might give rise to mechanics', materialmen's or other liens against Seller's interest in the Property or any portion thereof.

6.1.11 No litigation, proceeding, or action is pending or to the actual knowledge of Seller, is threatened against or relating to the Property or Seller, that could materially adversely affect the Property or its ownership or operation by Purchaser.

6.1.12 Seller is not, and as of the Closing will not be, a party to any agreement or undertaking of any kind whatsoever, written or verbal, which will be binding upon the Purchaser from and after the Closing or which will adversely affect the Property, other than those furnished to Purchaser pursuant to Article 3 or approved by Purchaser in writing.

6.1.13 To the best of Seller's knowledge, all of the Permits have been obtained and remain in full force and effect. To the best of Seller's knowledge, the financial statements delivered to Purchaser as part of the Due Diligence Materials present fairly the financial condition of the Property at such date and the result of its operations for the period then ended.

6.1.14 To the best of Seller's actual knowledge, without independent investigation or inquiry, Seller has no knowledge of any facts that would render the Due Diligence Materials provided to Purchaser materially untrue or incomplete.

The above-stated representations and warranties of Seller shall survive Closing for a period of one (1) year with the exception that the representations under Section 6.1.8 shall survive Closing without limitation.

Overview of common contracts developed and/or negotiated in Pre-Development
The Purchase and Sale Agreement (PSA)

Professional services contracts (See Supplementary Materials on the companion website, under Construction Phase Issues, The Draw Request Process.)
Architectural services contracts
Engineering services contracts
Value engineering services contracts

Construction contracts (See Supplementary Materials on the companion website, under Construction Phase Issues, The Draw Request Process.)
Horizontal construction
Vertical construction
Contract for general contractor
Contracts for subcontractors
Construction management relationships and contracts
Construction manager (professional services contract)
Construction manager at-risk
Marketing and pre-leasing/pre-sales contracts (See Chapter 11.)
Construction loan documents (See Chapter 9.)
Permanent financing documents (See Chapter 9.)
Owner's/landlord's standard form of lease (See Chapter 11.)

Notes

1. Gilmore, Grant, *The Death of Contract*, Ohio State University Press, Columbus, OH (1974).

2. Gordon, Robert W., "Book Review: The Death of Contract." *Yale Law School, Faculty Scholarship Series* (1974). Paper 1376; Dalton, Clare, "Book Review: The Death of Contract." *The American University Law Review* 42 (1975), pg. 1372; Farber, Daniel, "Ages of American Formalism." *Northwestern University Law Review* 90 (1995), pg. 89; Hillman, Robert A., "The Triumph of Gilmore's the Death of Contract." *Cornell Law Faculty Publications* (1996), Paper 922; Hakes, Russell A., "Focusing on the Realities of the Contracting Process – An Essential Step to Achieve Justice in Contract Enforcement." *Delaware Law Review, University of Delaware* 12.2 (2011), pgs. 95–119, at pgs. 96–97.

3. Professor Farnsworth, in addressing whose "meaning" in contract language should prevail when a dispute arises between two meanings, offers the following:

   §7.9. The Choice of Meaning. In a dispute over contract interpretation, each party claims that the language should be given the meaning that that party attaches to it at the time of the dispute. However, the resolution of the dispute begins, not with these meanings, but with the meanings attached by each party at the time the contract was made.Farnsworth, E. Allan, *Contracts*, Fourth Edition, Aspen Publishers, New York, NY (2004), pg. 445.

4. Ibid., pg. 3. Footnote in the original text.

5. Ibid., pg. 5. Footnote in the original text.

6. Ibid., pg. 6.

7. Professor Farnsworth puts the dichotomy between bilateral and unilateral contracts into perspective in the context of the bargaining process as follows:

   Traditional analysis of the bargaining process developed a dichotomy between "bilateral" and "unilateral" contracts. In forming a bilateral contract each party makes a promise: the offeror makes the promise contained in the offer, and the offeree makes a promise in return as acceptance. . . . In forming a unilateral contract only one party makes a promise: the offeror makes the promise contained in the offer, and the offeree renders some performance as acceptance. [Footnotes in the original omitted.]

   Farnsworth, *Contracts*, pg. 111.

8. Ibid., pg. 112. Emphasis in the original; footnotes in the original omitted.

9. Ibid., pg. 112. Footnotes in the original omitted.

10. This is not the same as Professor Wesley Newcomb Hohfeld's formulation of Party B's duty to perform and Party A's right to enforce Party B's duty, as set forth in Farnsworth, at pg. 112, footnote 3, providing, in pertinent part in this regard, as follows:

    A is said to have a *right* that B shall do an act when, if B does not do the act, A can initiate legal proceedings that will result in coercing B. B in such situation is said to have a *duty* to do the act. *Right* and *duty* are therefore correlatives, since in this sense there can never be a duty without a right.

11. Poorvu, William with Jeffrey L. Cruikshank, *The Real Estate Game: The Intelligent Guide to Decision-Making and Investment*, The Free Press, a Division of Simon & Schuster, Inc., New York, NY (1999), pg. ix. Emphasis added.

12. Farnsworth, *Contracts*, pg. 7. Footnote in the original text.

13. Ibid., pg. 8.

14. The manner in which the parties manifest their "intent to be bound" has been the subject of considerable debate among legal scholars and in the interpretations of contracts, or alleged contracts, in the courts. The dispute in interpretation of whether and how parties manifest their intent is reflected in the contrasting approaches of the Subjective Theory of Assent and the Objective Theory of Assent, respectively. For more on this dichotomy of approaches, see Farnsworth, §3.6 through §3.9, pgs. 114–129.

15. Farnsworth, *Contracts*, pg. 236. Emphasis in the original; footnote in the original omitted.

16. Sarachan, Ronald A. and Daniel J. T. McKenna, "Litigation, Subprime Lending, and the Financial Crisis." *The Philadelphia Lawyer* (Winter 2009), pgs. 27–31.

17. Massey, Kathleen N., "Securities Litigation Arising out of the Financial Crisis: A Survey of Relevant Decisions and Their Implications." *The Investment Lawyer* Vol. 16, No. 5, May 2009 (May 2009) (Aspen Publishers), pgs. 1–5. Footnote in the original omitted.

18. Cohen, Ronnie and Shannon O'Byrne, "Law, Emotion, and the Subprime Mortgage Crisis." *SOLOGP Magazine* 29.1 (January/February 2012), ABA Solo, Small Firm, and General Practice Division. Emphasis in the original.

19. Farnsworth, *Contracts*, pg. 255. Footnotes in original omitted.

20. Ibid., pg. 256.

21. Ibid.

22. Ibid., §4.17, footnotes 1–4, pg. 257.

23. Ibid., pg. 258.

24. Ibid., pg. 259.

25. Ibid., pg. 264.

26. Ibid., pg. 266.

27. Ibid., pg. 219. Emphasis added; footnote in the original omitted.

28. However, for such an expansive treatment of the role of maturity in contracts where the capacity of a party to a contract is an issue, see Farnsworth, *§4.3. The Test of Maturity; §4.4. Effects of Minority; and §4.5. Restitution on Minor's Avoidance*, pgs. 220–228.

29. Farnsworth, *Contracts*, pg. 229.

30. In the State of New York, the court of first impression or trial court is the Supreme Court of the State of New York or, simply, the New York Supreme Court, established in 1691. It is aptly named, distinguishing it from local courts within the state, but the name confuses most laypeople as well as many lawyers who are unfamiliar with practice in the state, assuming its name refers to the court of final impression in the state, hearing only appeals from the state's trial courts.

31. Farnsworth, *Contracts*, pg. 229, citing *Faber v. Sweet Style Mfg. Corp.*, 242 N.Y.S.2nd 763, 767, 768 (Sup. Ct. 1963).

32. Farnsworth, *Contracts*, pg. 230, citing Restatement Second §15(1).

33. Farnsworth, *Contracts*, pg. 619.

34. Ibid., pg. 620, citing a 1536 case before the Court of King's Bench, *Abbot of Westminster v. Clerke*, 73 Eng. Rep. 59, 63 (K.B. 1536):

> When the party by his own contract creates a duty or charge upon himself, he is bound to make it good, if he may, notwithstanding any accident by inevitable necessity, because he might have provided against it by his contract. And therefore if

the lessee covenant to repair a house, though it be burnt by lightning, or thrown down by enemies, yet he ought to repair it.

35 Farnsworth, *Contracts*, pg. 62. Footnote omitted.

36 UCC 2–615.

37 Farnsworth, *Contracts*, pgs. 624–625. Footnote omitted, referring to Restatement Second §261.

38 American Law Institute (2013–08–22). Restatement (Second) of Contracts (Kindle Locations 10515–10518). American Law Institute. Kindle Edition.

39 American Law Institute (2013–08–22). Restatement (Second) of Contracts (Kindle Locations 10523–10525). American Law Institute. Kindle Edition.

40 American Law Institute (2013–08–22). Restatement (Second) of Contracts (Kindle Locations 10520–10523). American Law Institute. Kindle Edition.

41 Farnsworth, *Contracts*, pg. 313. Footnotes in the original omitted.

42 *Printing & Numerical Registration Co. v. Sampson*, L.R. 19 Eq. 462 (1875).

43 *Sirkin v. Fourteenth St. Store*, 108 N.Y.S. 830 (App. Div. 1908.)

44 Farnsworth, *Contracts*, pg. 314, citing *Bank of the United States v. Owens*, 27 U.S. (2 Pet.) 527 (1829), quoting from the Court's decision: "No court of justice can in its nature be made the handmaid of iniquity."

45 Farnsworth, *Contracts*, pg. 353.

46 The Restatement Second provides, in pertinent part, as follows:

> a. Classes of contracts. The five classes of contracts listed in Subsection (1) were included in different language in §4 of the English Statute of Frauds, enacted in 1677. The English Statute was repealed in 1954 except for the suretyship and land contract provisions. Subsections (2) and (3) refer to four separate Statute of Frauds sections found in the Uniform Commercial Code, which displace §4 of the Uniform Sales Act and §17 of the English statute. The Code sections are not elaborated in this Restatement. Subsection (4) is a statement of a provision of Lord Tenterden's Act, 1828, which has been widely copied in the United States. As to the extent of enactment of these and other similar statutes, see the Statutory Note preceding this Section. The formal contracts referred to in §6 of this Restatement are not affected by the Statute of Frauds, but in some cases are subject to separate statutes containing formal requirements.American Law Institute (2013–08–22). Restatement (Second) of Contracts (Kindle Locations 3717–3723). American Law Institute. Kindle Edition.

47 American Law Institute (2013–08–22). Restatement (Second) of Contracts (Kindle Locations 4008–4018). American Law Institute. Kindle Edition.

48 Farnsworth, *Contracts*, pg. 113. Emphasis added.

49 Ibid., pg. 113. Emphasis added; footnotes in the original text omitted.

50 Ibid., pg. 113.

51 Ibid., pg. 114. Emphasis added; footnotes in the original text omitted.

52 The substantive provisions of the Form of Purchase and Sale Agreement from which excerpts are included in this section, for example, run twenty-six pages in length, excluding the cover page, table of contents, List of Exhibits, Term Sheet, signature page, and exhibits.

CHAPTER 8

Tax considerations of real estate transactions

"Price feedback is inherently well integrated," said Hiram. "It's not sloppy, not ambiguous. As [Adam] Smith perceived, the data carry meaningful information on imbalances of supply and demand and they do automatically trigger corrective responses. So data and its purport and responses are all of a piece. But – and this is a very big but – the data themselves, prices, can be false, and of course that makes the inherent integrity count for nothing – go haywire."

"Cost are a major ingredient of prices," Murray put in. "Costs can be falsifies, and if so, then prices will be falsified too."

"Yes, subsidies falsify both costs and prices," said Hiram. "And as I indicated in passing earlier, lies of that sort warp development."

"As if printing was an economic failure because hand-copied manuscripts were too heavily subsidized by monasteries," said Hortense. "I suppose that's an idiotic suggestion."

"Not idiotic in principle," said Hiram. "In addition to subsidies, there are many other ways to falsify costs and prices. Taxes are significant costs, and tax policies can favor some types of investment and production and penalize others. Tariffs falsify prices; that's their purpose. Speculative bubbles falsify prices by injecting wishful thinking, which is why bubble prices collapse when more solid realities eventually catch up with them. Kickbacks and bribes falsify honest costs."[1]

In this excerpt from Jane Jacobs' dialectic *The Nature of Economies*, Hiram, Murray, and Hortense discuss the impact of taxes – and, specifically, tax subsidies – on development, with Hiram suggesting that subsidies distort values. A cynical person, someone with extensive experience in structuring real estate transactions over the past thirty years, might interject into Hiram, Murray, and Hortense's fictitious conversation that such distortions in the value of subsidized transactions distort the behaviors of actors interested or involved in such transactions, and that such distorted values are, indeed, an intentional consequence sought by those who promote and advocate for the enactment of such tax subsidies. Anyone who worked their way through the detritus of the S&L Crisis in the United States in the late 1980s will find this discussion about "bubble prices" resonates with the vibration of personal experience.

Chapter introduction

The Internal Revenue Code of 1986 is a labyrinth of tax subsidies – provisions favoring specific types and methods for the development of real estate in the United States, intended to alter the values of developers and projects benefiting from those provisions – and this is a function of the legislative structure within which the tax code is enacted and amended by the U.S. Congress. From the mortgage interest deduction for qualifying indebtedness on a taxpayer's personal residences to the carried interest rule favoring real estate investment trusts and private equity funds to the Low-Income Housing Tax Credit, Historic Rehabilitation Tax Credit, and New Markets Tax Credit programs, plenty of incentives have been built into the tax code over the past half century to make real estate a more attractive investment than other asset classifications.

Some of these provisions in the tax code were the brainchild of members of the Senate Finance Committee and others on Capitol Hill genuinely interested in creating broad-based programs to incentivize real estate development as a means of stimulating the economy of the United States, although undoubtedly there were lobbyists whispering these ideas in the ears of the sponsors of such bills. More often than not, however, such provisions were inserted in other legislation not specifically intended to address the tax code, at the behest of specific taxpayers seeking very specific treatment of their real estate business operations and transactions.

The Byzantine complexity of the Internal Revenue Code, and its disparate treatment of taxpayers seeming to be similarly situated, has made genuine tax reform the cause célèbre from time to time over at least the past three decades. As recently as the issuance of the President's National Commission on Fiscal Responsibility and Reform on December 1, 2010, and as far back as 1986, with the enactment of the last major reform legislation focused on the tax code, the Tax Reform Act of 1986 (Public Law 99–514), there have been efforts to make fundamental changes to the structure of the tax code and its impact on specific types of taxation, including the federal taxation of real property and real property transactions, with only very limited success.[2]

As a general proposition, Developers, in consultation with their tax lawyers and/or accountants, endeavor to minimize the impacts of federal taxes on their operations. This chapter is intended to highlight and provide an analytical framework for understanding how the potential impacts of federal tax laws shape The Development Process, without readers feeling compelled to try and become their own tax lawyers or accountants.

As suggested in Chapter 2, the Developer may and probably should be thinking about the federal tax implications for The Development Process at the very outset of the Project Conception Phase. As introduced in Chapter 2, The Development Process is both linear and iterative. One of the most consistent themes reinforcing the linear aspect of The Development Process is how money *comes into* and *flows out of* the Development Entity, first introduced in Chapter 2 and then discussed in greater detail in Chapter 3. Also introduced in Chapter 3 is the critical importance of starting The Development Process out with a clear Exit Strategy, or what I've affectionately referred to as "the Ronin Principle". (See the section on Real Estate Development 101: A Few Basic Principles in Chapter 3.)

The specific structure of the Development Entity is going to impact the following critical legal attributes of the Project and its principal stakeholders:

- How the *liabilities* of the Development Entity will be *assessed*, as in cases where:
    - The Development Entity's liquid assets are unable to cover its short-term obligations.
    - The Development Entity's operating liabilities exceed the value of its assets.
    - An event occurs on the Subject Site giving rise to additional liabilities that exceed the Development Entity's insurance coverage limits plus its aggregate net assets.
- The *rights* of various parties providing monetary support to the Project to various *proceeds* generated by the Project once it's operational, including without limitation:
    - The rights and priorities of Lenders to the Project
    - The rights and priorities of Investors in the Project
    - The rights and priorities of the Developer, in whatever shape the Developer's interests have taken in the Development Entity.
- The *legal liabilities of various parties* having ownership interests in the Development Entity with respect to the legal *allocation of all "tax attributes"* of the Development Entity, including but not limited to:
    - Distributions of non-taxable income
    - Distributions of taxable income
    - Allocations of tax attributes that are taxable regardless of whether accompanied by distributions of cash
    - Allocations of deductions from income, such as for interest paid and depreciation incurred by the Development Entity.

- The *legal rights* of various parties to the Development Entity and/or to the transaction, in the *event of a termination* of the Project, to:
  - A recovery of the outstanding principal and unpaid interest on any debt the Development Entity owes
  - A recovery by equity investors of any outstanding, undistributed value in the Development Entity represented by their ownership interests in the Development Entity
  - A recovery by the Developer and its principals of their respective shares of the remaining value of the Development Entity once all priority claims have been satisfactorily resolved.

Taxation of transactions involving, and investments in, real estate

As the subtitle of this section of Chapter 8 suggests, the textbook asserts and relies on a dichotomy between the intentional tax treatment of a Project through its structure developed through The Development Process, on one hand, and how an investment in another entity's real estate project or portfolio, such as the purchase of shares in a Real Estate Investment Trust or REIT, will be taxed in the hands of the owner of those REIT shares. The space in between these two ends of the spectrum – for example what happens when, early in the Project Conception Phase of The Development Process, the Developer's endeavors attract the attention of a REIT, which would like to serve as the take-out financing for the Developer's Project – is explored within the context of this dichotomy.

How and when "deal-structuring" comes into play during The Development Process is a subject of some intellectual and theoretical debate. In developing and teaching graduate students using The Development Process as the theoretical framework for learning about real estate law, I have offered several intentionally conflicting scenarios in The Development Process as to how and when the Developer will start to contemplate the optimal deal structure for the development and financing of "the Idea." This is done, in large part, because it allows and enables students to start to gain a better baseline understanding of how many moving parts there are in The Development Process and how a decision about or change in one part or component manifests changes in other parts or components. This, of course, reinforces the axiom from Chapters 2 and 3, respectively, that The Development Process is *both linear and iterative*.

In some scenarios, the Developer's hand regarding deal-structuring may be forced by circumstances. For example, an initial source of Acquisition and Development (A&D) Financing, discussed in greater detail in Chapter 9, evaporates at a very inopportune moment in The Development Process, and the Developer is forced to scramble to find a replacement or risk losing the development opportunity being actively pursued at the time. Not only is this not a remote possibility but, during the early period prior to the full onset of the Great Recession of 2008 and for quite some time thereafter, this occurred with some considerable frequency as savvy investors started reading the tea leaves and pulling out of informal and formal commitments to fund real estate development projects in various stages of gestation, on the assumption that the Developer's previously promised return projections, as well as its assurances regarding the risks the Project presented, no longer could be relied on in reconsidering the previously made funding commitment.

As discussed in greater detail in Chapter 9, and as also introduced in Chapter 2 and discussed in greater detail in Chapter 3, different types of funding, with different risk and return expectations, need to come into the transaction at different points during The Development Process. The timing of closing on each stage of Project Financing is critical to moving from one phase of The Development Process to the next.

For example, the Project – or, more accurately at this stage, the proposed Project – cannot advance from the Project Conception Phase to the Pre-Development Phase without the funds necessary to do the following:

- Provide transaction-specific funding essential to the Developer's securing Site Control, in the form of either:
  - A good faith deposit required by the Purchase and Sale Agreement (PSA) (see Chapter 7), or
  - Payment of the Option Price for an Option Contract to acquire the Subject Site, also discussed in Chapter 7.
- Pay various members of the Development Team the compensation to which the parties agreed for their respective participation on the Development Team, which the Developer committed to as an inducement to secure their professional services during the Project Conception Phase.
- Provide the funding necessary to take the Project through to the next funding milestone, which occurs during the Pre-Development Phase, that is, acquisition of the Subject Site, comprised primarily of essential professional fees not susceptible to being deferred to the Construction Funding.

Securing Site Control, which is a specific, defined term in The Development Process, is the first Financing Milestone in the process, and only one of two ways that the Developer may complete the Project Conception Phase; the other is termination of the undertaking altogether, and absorbing all of the costs incurred in getting to a Go/No Go decision. The next Financing Milestone, which is arguably the most substantial and quantifies the greatest amount of risk for the Developer, occurs less than halfway through the Pre-Development Phase: Closing on the Subject Site (aka "the Property"). This Closing takes place as a condition precedent to the next Pre-Development Phase Financing Milestone: Closing on the Construction Financing.

In the interim period between Closing on the Subject Site – essentially converting Site Control to actual ownership of the Property, taking full, legal, recorded title to the property in the name of the Development Entity or an affiliate thereof – and Closing on the Construction Financing, the Developer will, among many other things, negotiate simultaneously with potential Construction Lenders and potential providers of Take-Out Financing, aka Permanent Financing (the term "Take-Out Financing" refers to the fact that this financing pays back the outstanding principal balance of the Construction Loan, plus any accrued but unpaid interest thereon, plus resolving any outstanding Construction Liens against the Property so that the provider of the Take-Out Financing is assured a security interest in clean, unencumbered, and unrestricted title to the Property plus all Improvements thereon).

The Construction Financing and the Permanent Financing may be provided by a single Lender, or even a consortium of Lenders, with the Construction Loan rolling into the Take-Out Financing, which may be true, permanent financing, with a term of seven or ten years or longer, or in the form of mortgage debt with a shorter time to maturity, commonly referred to as a "Mini-Perm" loan, with a term of anywhere between three and seven years, with the Developer's intention of refinancing that Mini-Perm at the most advantageous time during the term of the Mini-Perm. Whatever the specific terms of this form of Take-Out Financing, it is 100% debt (hereinafter referred to as an "All-Debt Take-Out Financing"), which poses a specific set of conditions, constraints, limitations, and opportunities for the structure of the transaction that the Developer should have figured out fairly early on The Development Process.

Alternatively, the Take-Out Financing could be provided by a Real Estate Fund, such as a REIT or Private Equity (PE) Fund, or by an Institutional Investor, such as an insurance company or a pension fund (collectively hereinafter referred to as an "Equity Investor" or "Equity Investors," as the case may be), committing to purchase an interest in the Development Entity (also known as "making an Equity Investment in the Project"), the proceeds from the sale of which purchased interest will be sufficient to discharge the Construction Loan in full (see the components thereof described in the preceding paragraph) or *providing, participating in, or permitting* a First Deed-of-Trust Mortgage to cover any balance of the Construction Loan not covered by the proceeds of the Equity Investment in the Development Entity. Assuming this form of Permanent Financing involves some combination of Equity Investment plus Permanent Financing covering any residual debt from the Construction Loan left over after applying the proceeds from the Equity Investment (hereinafter referred to as "Equity-Plus-Debt Take-Out Financing" or, in the case of the principal amount of the Permanent Financing exceeding the dollar amount of the Equity Investment, including all Staged Payments if applicable, referred to as "Debt-Plus-Equity Take-Out Financing"), with yet a different, specific set of conditions, constraints, limitations, and opportunities for the structure of the transaction. As with the All-Debt Take-Out Financing scenario, the Developer will have hopefully figured all of this out fairly early on The Development Process and made the necessary accommodations in structuring the Development Entity and the overall transaction.

Alternatively, a third Take-Out Financing scenario involves one or more Equity Investors purchasing the project, or purchasing all of the interests in the Development Entity, which transaction may or may not have its own debt component, the proceeds which sale will be sufficient to discharge fully the Construction Loan in full (see the components thereof described in the preceding paragraph) as well as providing the Developer the return it was projecting it would realize when "the Idea" was first conceptualized or, at least, shortly thereafter (hereinafter referred to as a "Sale" or "Other Disposition"). It is important to note, at this juncture – recall, we're just trying to get to a baseline understanding of the timing of how money comes in and flows out of the transaction for purposes of understanding how tax consequences come into play in structuring the transaction during The Development Process – that, as contrasted with the All-Debt Take-Out Financing scenario and the Equity-Plus-Debt or Debt-Plus-Equity Take-Out Financing scenario, the Sale or Other Disposition scenario terminates the Developer's interest in, and rights to receive distributable revenues or profits from, the Project, with the exception, of course, of the Developer or an affiliate thereof having a Management Agreement for the Property Management of the Property during the Ownership and Property Management Phase of The Development Process.

At this point, when the reader's head stops spinning, the question may rightfully be asked: What does all of this have to do with the *Taxation of Transactions Involving, and Investments in, Real Estate* (which, coincidentally, is the name of the this subsection of Chapter 8)? In each of these scenarios there may be multiple players with not only differing return expectations and tolerance for risk but also with differing tax situations; sometimes vastly differing. Funds coming into the transaction, depending on how, why, and when, may or may not trigger a Taxable Event for any of the principals involved in or providing financing to the Development Entity. However, how these parties will be taxed, if at all, as, when, and if funds flow back out of the Development Entity, or interests change hands in the Development Entity, will have been determined by how funds originally came into the transaction.

Formation or "choice of entity": structuring ownership interests in and financing for real estate projects

Taking by far the simplest situation – the All-Debt Take-Out Financing scenario – the Development Entity does not incur a Taxable Event when the Lender funds the Take-Out Financing and, similarly, the Lender does not incur a Taxable Event upon its receipt of that portion of periodic loan payments that represent the repayment of the principal outstanding balance of the loan. The Lender is taxed only on the origination fees received at Closing and on interest paid over the life of the loan, while the Development Entity is allowed deductions for all such payments, which deductions will "pass through" to individuals having ownership interests in the Development Entity if it was created using certain entity structures recognized under the tax code.

The inquiry regarding "Choice of Entity" becomes much more involved when the entire life-cycle of the Development Entity is considered, however. Referring again to material covered in greater detail in Chapters 2 and 3, respectively, regarding The Development Process, and Chapter 9, several "decision points" occur throughout The Development Process at which aspects of the Choice of Entity analysis will need to have been completed. For example, the first time the Developer is negotiating to secure Site Control over the Subject Site, the property owner or "Seller" will need and expect to know with whom or what the Seller is negotiating, and to whom or what the Seller will ultimately be conveying the Subject Site. Even at this point – which is a condition precedent to the culmination of the Project Conception Phase of The Development Process, securing Site Control – the Seller may be satisfied to know it is dealing directly with the Developer, and that the Developer's intention is to convey the Purchase and Sale Agreement of the Option Contract to an entity to be created by the Developer solely for the purpose of undertaking the Project. Such an entity is commonly referred to as a "Single-Purpose Entity," "Special-Purpose Entity," or simply an "SPE." Depending on the Terms and Conditions of the PSA or option, the Seller may want or need certain assurance of (i) the continued involvement of the Developer with the SPE to be created going into the Pre-Development Phase of The Development Process and/or (ii) the capital structure of the SPE. In other words, assuming the Developer is a well-known and well-capitalized individual or entity, assurances given and contractually binding promises made by the Developer could be rendered meaningless if the Developer is allowed to enter into a PSA or Option Contract with the Seller but later transfer 100% of the Developer's interests in and obligations and liabilities under such contractual agreement to a shell entity, cutting off all recourse against the Developer after the transfer has been made to that shell entity. The various types of Development Entities, and their tax treatment and implications for principals, other equity holders, and lenders, respectively, is addressed in the next subsection of this chapter.

Based on the foregoing scenario, the Developer would seemingly be okay not having given much *or even any* consideration about Choice of Entity during the Project Conception Phase of The Development Process, almost up to and including securing Site Control, which will transition the Developer and the Project into the Pre-Development Phase. However, this represents only part of the complete picture regarding Choice of Entity during the Project Conception Phase. This scenario, which is encompassed in the final Project Conception Phase component, is immediately preceded in the Project Conception Phase by the Negotiate Acquisition and Development (A&D) Financing Commitment component. Clearly whomever or whatever entity is considering funding what is perhaps the riskiest type of funding for the Developer's "Idea" will have very specific return requirements and hedges against the risk of loss of its funds. Although historically the banking community was willing to provide A&D Financing for Projects, particularly to Developers with whom a Lender had a positive prior lending experiences, following the S&L Crisis starting in the late 1980s and continuing into the early 1990s[3] and the subsequent enactment by the U.S. Congress of the Financial Institutions Reform, Recovery and Enforcement Act of 1989, commonly referred to as "FIRREA" (pronounced "fye-ree-ah"), and the creation of the Resolution Trust Corporation or RTC, charged with responsibility, many of the savings and loans that commonly made A&D loans, as well as the practice itself, largely disappeared.

This historical aspect of the evolution of early stage, essentially exploratory funding for real estate development projects is relevant here for the same reason that the All-Debt Take-Out Financing scenario is relevant to an understanding about Choice of Entity. As long as this early stage funding came in the form of loans, even if they had to be guaranteed by the Developer and/or its individual principals, these loans did not present serious entity structuring issues for tax purposes because the tax treatment of loans, as discussed earlier, is very straightforward. However, once early stage Project Conception Phase lending went away in the wake of FIRREA following the S&L Crisis, pure equity investments or debt plus equity investments, looking more like start-up venture capital than like the A&D loans of old, became the only game in town. And introducing equity concepts changes the dynamics of Choice of Entity significantly.

Equity vs. debt: an overview of structuring options for the development entity[4]

Once again, because The Development Process is *both linear and iterative*, there's an inherent tautology in teaching real estate law through the framework of The Development Process. The student and/or reader can't fully understand the tax considerations of real estate development and financing transactions without understanding the Choice of Entity issues inherent in forming the Development Entity; Choice of Entity issues cannot themselves be understood without first understanding the fundamental definitions of and differences between debt and equity, *and everything in between*, and these are concepts much more appropriately taken up in Chapter 9. Rather than merely referring readers to Chapter 9, forcing readers to jump ahead, and then jump back, in order to explain how the Choice of Entity analysis may come up much earlier in the Project Conception Phase than it otherwise would in the pre–S&L Crisis days, this very brief overview is offered.

Equity. Essentially, "equity" is an ownership interest in a legal entity. That "legal entity" could be any one among a growing array of legal constructs recognized under the Internal Revenue Code and codified in state legislation – C Corporations, **S Corporations**, general partnerships (GPs), limited partnerships (LPs), limited liability companies (LLCs), and the like – in which ownership interests may be conveyed. Depending on the type of legal entity, a General Partnership versus an Limited Partnership, for example, the owner's liability attendant such ownership interest may be unlimited or, alternatively, may be capped at the value of the interest purchased and owned (i.e., the liability or exposure to loss of the owner of such limited ownership interest, such as a Limited Partner in a Limited Partnership, is limited to the money invested in purchasing such Limited Partnership Interest, and does not expose the other assets of the Limited Partner to losses suffered or liabilities incurred by the Limited Partnership.,

Debt. Debt, on the other hand, is nothing more than something of value loaned by one party (the "Lender") to another party (the "Borrower") with a legally binding promise of repayment, plus interest on the value of the principal amount of the value loaned for as long as all or some portion of that principal amount is outstanding, and generally some form of "security" to assure repayment of the debt in accordance with its terms.[5] Debt does not convey any ownership interest in the Borrower, although the Lender's rights could, eventually, be exercised in a manner in which the Lender becomes the owner of all or some portion of Borrower entity and/or all or some portion of the assets the Borrower entity owns. Except as stated in the Loan Documents evidencing the Debt, the Lender does not have any rights in the decision-making authority of the Borrower entity (although, once again, the enforcement of Events of Default under the Loan Documents evidencing the Debt may speak to such matters).

And Everything In Between. As suggested in the introductory paragraph to this subsection, "*Choice of Entity issues cannot themselves be understood without first understanding the fundamental definitions of and differences between debt and equity, and everything in between.*" And it is in the "and everything in between" part of that quote where things have gotten very interesting over the past quarter century or so, as real estate development and financing have gotten more sophisticated and more complex, and the Projects have grown increasingly larger and reflective of a broader mix of uses. As with Wall Street investment banks generally – introducing increasingly sophisticated and sometimes opaque and cryptic investment vehicles such as Collateralized Debt Obligations (CDOs) and highly segmented Commercial Mortgage-Backed Securities (CMBSs) – the specific investment vehicles for structured financing supporting real estate development projects have also become increasingly customized and customizable. As one of the contributors to this textbook has suggested, if the parties can decide and agree upon what their respective roles should be in the Development Entity, and what they should receive or be entitled to as compensation for such roles, there's probably a way to structure their relationships in a manner that will be recognized under state law and by the Internal Revenue Service.[6]

Given that potentially infinite variety of what the "and everything in between" might look like when crafting ownership structures and specific transactions as part of The Development Process and in the creation of the Development Entity, the following serve merely as examples of what can be created in the interstitial space between equity and debt.

Convertible debt aka "mezzanine financing". Because of the inherently high risk in providing A&D Financing for a new real estate development enterprise, in addition to charging an interest rate with an appropriate risk-premium built into the annual percentage rate of the loan, the A&D Investor may also require that this early stage financing provide that, should the Developer or the Development Entity fail to meet specific covenants or conditions of the loan, the loan may be converted, in whole or in part, into an ownership interest in the Developer or the Development Entity, depending on to which entity the convertible debt is issued.

Debt with an "equity kicker". In the Convertible Debt scenario, the conversion right is a stick, threatening the Borrower with a dilution of its ownership interest, and control over The Development Process and the Project it is intended to produce, should the Developer or its Development Entity not perform under the terms of the loan. In the "Debt with an Equity Kicker" scenario, the debt and the equity are two unrelated components. The A&D Investor will have an array of remedies should the loan suffer an Event of Default, but even if the loan is serviced and repaid in full and in accordance with all of its terms and conditions, the investor will nonetheless receive some participation in the future success of the enterprise through an equity stake in the Development Entity or in the Developer itself.

Direct Participation in the Developer. In this scenario, the A&D Investor is making its investment "upstream" from The Development Process, the Development Entity, and the Project the Developer, through the Development Entity, will be pursuing. Depending on how the Developer is organized and capitalized, the investor's participation may be more directly tied to the success of the Project primarily or exclusively or may enjoy the broader successes and returns from the Developer's entire portfolio.

A distinction with a difference: understanding "legal entities" vs. "taxable entities"

Although a "Taxable Entity" and a "Legal Entity" may, in fact, be one and the same, the laws creating legal artifices, such as corporations and limited partnerships (general partnerships, also known simply as "partnerships," have been recognized in common law for centuries and, therefore, do not require a statutory authority for their existence), are fundamentally different from the body of law determining the tax status of, for federal income tax purposes, and tax consequences of transactions undertaken by, such "Legal Entity."

Legal Entity status is a matter of state law. And while the vast majority of states have enacted laws regarding the formation and operations of limited partnerships (LPs) and limited liability companies (LLCs) based on uniform statutes and model codes, the specific provisions of a particular state's statute governing LPs, and not the Uniform Limited Partnership Act (ULPA), for example, are dispositive of whether a valid LP exists.

However, whether an LP constitutes a "Taxable Entity" under the partnership provisions of the Internal Revenue Code and how the owners of interests in that LP will be taxed for federal income tax and estate tax purposes are determined by the Internal Revenue Code and not by the state statutes under which that LP was formed and operates.

For example, an LP that for all intents and purposes is organized and operated as a limited partnership, but that was not properly organized under the limited partnership statute will have the Taxable Entity status of a general partnership under the tax code. The following section of the Internal Revenue Code addresses how the Internal Revenue Service defines, and characterizes for federal tax purposes, different types of organizations formed under state law:

§ 301.7701–1 Classification of organizations for federal tax purposes.

(a) Organizations for federal tax purposes –

   (1) In general. The Internal Revenue Code prescribes the classification of various organizations for federal tax purposes. Whether an organization is an entity separate from its owners for federal tax purposes is a matter of federal tax law and does not depend on whether the organization is recognized as an entity under local law.

   (2) Certain joint undertakings give rise to entities for federal tax purposes. A joint venture or other contractual arrangement may create a separate entity for federal tax purposes if the participants carry on a trade, business, financial operation, or venture and divide the profits therefrom. For example, a separate entity exists for federal tax purposes if co- owners of an apartment building lease space and in addition provide services to the occupants either directly or through an agent. Nevertheless, a joint undertaking merely to share expenses does not create a separate entity for federal tax purposes. For example, if two or more persons jointly construct a ditch merely to drain surface water from their properties, they have not created a separate entity for federal tax purposes. Similarly, mere co-ownership of property that is maintained, kept in repair, and rented or leased does not constitute a separate entity for federal tax purposes. For example, if an individual owner, or tenants in common, of farm property lease it to a farmer for a cash rental or a share of the crops, they do not necessarily create a separate entity for federal tax purposes.

(3) **Certain local law entities not recognized.** An entity formed under local law is not always recognized as a separate entity for federal tax purposes. For example, an organization wholly owned by a State is not recognized as a separate entity for federal tax purposes if it is an integral part of the State. Similarly, tribes incorporated under section 17 of the Indian Reorganization Act of 1934, as amended, 25 U.S.C. 477, or under section 3 of the Oklahoma Indian Welfare Act, as amended, 25 U.S.C. 503, are not recognized as separate entities for federal tax purposes.

(4) **Single owner organizations.** Under §§ 301.7701–2 and 301.7701–3, certain organizations that have a single owner can choose to be recognized or disregarded as entities separate from their owners.

(b) **Classification of organizations.** The classification of organizations that are recognized as separate entities is determined under §§ 301.7701–2, 301.7701–3, and 301.7701–4 unless a provision of the Internal Revenue Code [such as section 860A addressing Real Estate Mortgage Investment Conduits (REMICs)] provides for special treatment of that organization. For the classification of organizations as trusts, see § 301.7701–4. That section provides that trusts generally do not have associates or an objective to carry on business for profit. Sections 301.7701–2 and 301.7701–3 provide rules for classifying organizations that are not classified as trusts.

(c) **Cost sharing arrangements.** A cost sharing arrangement that is described in § 1.482–7 of this chapter, including any arrangement that the Commissioner treats as a CSA under § 1.482–7(b)(5) of this chapter, is not recognized as a separate entity for purposes of the Internal Revenue Code. See § 1.482–7 of this chapter for the rules regarding CSAs.

(d) **Domestic and foreign business entities.** See § 301.7701–5 for the rules that determine whether a business entity is domestic or foreign.

(e) **State.** For purposes of this section and § 301.7701–2, the term State includes the District of Columbia.

(f) **Effective/applicability dates.** Except as provided in the following sentence, the rules of this section are applicable as of January 1, 1997. The rules of paragraph (c) of this section are applicable on January 5, 2009.

Liability/management issues in structuring ownership

Corporations

A corporation is a legal entity[7]:

- formed under state law, generally through the filing of Articles of Incorporation with the state's corporation commission
- that has perpetual existence, unless expressly stated in its Articles of Incorporation

- owned by its shareholders
- operated:
  - by the corporation's duly elected officers and other management personnel
  - in accordance with the corporation's By-Laws
  - without the participation or input of its shareholders, except on those matters with regard to which they are specifically allowed to vote, such as the annual election of officers
- with a principal office and a registered agent in the state of incorporation
- and a Taxable Entity under both federal and state law.

Although formed in one state, corporations are generally allowed to conduct business operations in other states provided the corporations register as "foreign corporations" in any state in which they conduct business operations. Naturally, this is not true of every kind of corporation and every type of business corporations conduct. For example, a corporation the principal business of which is gambling, may not, simply by virtue of registering in another state as a foreign corporation, engage in its principal business if the laws of that other state prohibit gambling. The same principles would apply in the case of a company that engages in hydraulic fracturing as a technique for extracting oil and natural gas from beneath the earth's surface (aka "fracking") if such activities are not permitted under or are actually banned by the laws of another state in which such a fracking company is registered to do business. In summary, a corporation legally organized and operated under and in accordance with the laws of State A must, nonetheless, operate its business interests in State B in accordance with the laws of State B. It is well-established law that this requirement that multi-state businesses, in whatever manner organized and operated, comply with the laws of each state in which they operate, regardless of the laws of the state in which they organized and are headquartered, does not violate the Interstate Commerce Clause of the U.S. Constitution.[8]

The "purposes" section of New York's Business Corporation Law is instructive as to how much flexibility most state statutes afford in terms of the businesses permitted to be organized in corporate form in the state:

> § 201. Purposes.
> (a) A corporation may be formed under this chapter for any lawful business purpose or purposes except to do in this state any business for which formation is permitted under any other statute of this state unless such statute permits formation under this chapter. If, immediately prior to the effective date of this chapter, a statute of this state permitted the formation of a.corporation under the stock corporation law for a purpose or purposes specified in such other statute, such statute shall be deemed and construed to permit formation of such corporation under this chapter, and any conditions, limitations or restrictions in such other statute upon the formation of such corporation under the stock corporation law shall apply to the formation thereof under this chapter.

However, not all corporations are treated equally under New York's Business Corporations Law, to wit, unions, childcare facilities, and hospitals must meet separate requirements to organize under New York law:

> (b) The approval of the industrial board of appeals is required for the filing with the department of state of any certificate of incorporation, certificate of merger or consolidation or application of a foreign corporation for authority to do business in this state which states

as the purpose or one of the purposes of the corporation the formation of an organization of groups of working men or women or wage earners, or the performance, rendition or sale of services as labor consultant or as advisor on labor–management relations or as arbitrator or negotiator in labor-management disputes.

(c) In time of war or other national emergency, a corporation may do any lawful business in aid thereof, notwithstanding the purpose or purposes set forth in its certificate of incorporation, at the request or direction of any competent governmental authority.

(d) A corporation whose statement of purposes specifically includes the establishment or operation of a child day care center, as that term is defined in section three hundred ninety of the social services law, shall provide a certified copy of the certificate of incorporation, each amendment thereto, and any certificate of merger, consolidation or dissolution involving such corporation to the office of children and family services within thirty days after the filing of such certificate, amendment, merger, consolidation, or dissolution with the department of state. This requirement shall also apply to any foreign corporation filing an application for authority under article thirteen of this chapter, any amendments thereto, and any surrender of authority or termination of authority in this state of such corporation.

(e) A corporation may not include as its purpose or among its purposes the establishment or maintenance of a hospital or facility providing health related services, as those terms are defined in article twenty-eight of the public health law unless its certificate of incorporation shall so state and such certificate shall have annexed thereto the approval of the public health council.

Beyond setting the rules for how individuals may organize their affairs, and the affairs of others, in various legal entities for purposes of conducting their business, each state determines under its tax code how corporations organized in that state, as well as foreign corporations, will be taxed. Federal income and other taxes levied on and collected from corporations are determined by the United States Code, which includes the Internal Revenue Code, which is Title 26 of the United States Code.

C Corporations. The term "C Corporation" is reminiscent of the old joke "What do they call Chinese food in China?: Food." The main reason for using the term "C Corporation" is to distinguish it for federal tax purposes, under the Internal Revenue Code, from an S Corporation, described later, which has the "Legal Entity" status of a corporation but is treated like a partnership for federal income tax purposes. The definition of a "C Corporation," other than for federal tax purposes, is the same as for a "corporation" as defined at the outset of this section.

A C Corporation is managed by its officers and other management staff. The corporation law of the state in which the C Corporation is incorporated, along with the C Corporation's duly adopted By-Laws (which cannot run counter to the state's corporations statute), establish what corporate officers a C Corporation must have. A C Corporation may have whatever other officers or company management it chooses.

Other than through voting for corporate officers, and the exercise of any other voting rights under the state's corporation statute and/or the entity's By-Laws, a shareholder in a C Corporation does not participate actively in the management of the company solely by virtue of owning shares. A duly elected C Corporation office or other management staff employed by the company may also own shares in the company, however. Shareholders may have voting rights under state law with respect to extraordinary management decisions (i.e., not associated with normal, day-to-day company operations) such as increasing the capital structure of the corporation, which has a dilutive impact on existing shareholders, or mergers, acquisitions, and the sale of operating assets.[9]

S Corporations. An "S Corporation" is not a creature of state statute. In other words, state codes include no provision to form an "S Corporation": It is a creature of the Internal Revenue Code that starts out as a C Corporation. In other words, an "S Corporation" is a C Corporation that meets specific requirements set forth in the Internal Revenue Code, and that makes a specific election to be treated under Subchapter S of the Internal Revenue Code as an "S Corporation." Until the advent of a number of relatively new organizational structures that facilitate capital formations and distributions of profits – such as LPs, LLCs, and LLLPs, described later – S Corporations were the preferred organizational structure for limiting the personal liability for equity participants in an enterprise while also allowing *all* of the tax attributes of that enterprise to "pass through" to those equity participants.

Limited Liability Corporations (LLCs). The State of Wyoming passed the United States' first Limited Liability Company Act in 1977. More than ten years after its passage in Wyoming, the Internal Revenue Service finally announced that an LLC formed under Wyoming Limited Liability Company Act would be taxed like a partnership. Moreover, it was not until 1996, almost twenty years later, that the National Conference of Commissioners on Uniform State Laws would complete drafting of the country's first model act, the Uniform Limited Liability Company Act (1996). In essence, limited liability companies or "LLCs" are corporations that act like limited partnerships with one major exception: None of the LLC members, including the Managing Member, assume any personal liability for the debts, obligations, and liabilities of the LLC, as partners normally do in a general partnership.

The Massachusetts Limited Liability Company Act, for example, provides in pertinent part, as follows:

> Section 22. Except as otherwise provided by this chapter, the debts, obligations and liabilities of a limited liability company, whether arising in contract, tort or otherwise, shall be solely the debts, obligations, and liabilities of the limited liability company; *and no member or manager of a limited liability company shall be personally liable, directly or indirectly, including, without limitation, by way of indemnification, contribution, assessment, or otherwise*, for any such debt, obligation, or liability of the limited liability company solely by reason of being a member or acting as a manager of the limited liability company.[10]

Partnerships and partnership-like entities

General Partnerships. A general partnership may be formed by two or more people, with or without an agreement between them, arising out of their conduct vis-à-vis each other and any third party. As a matter of real property law, Tenants in Common (see Chapter 1, "Ownership" of Real Estate: Estates in Real Property Section, Tenants in Common Subsection) are operating as a general partnership.

General partners have "joint and several liability" under common law for "the debts, obligations, and liabilities" of the general partnership, to borrow that phrase from the Massachusetts Limited Liability Company Act. That means that *any* liability, of whatever nature, created by one partner in the name or even under the guise of the general partnership automatically become the liability, in the full amount, of each general partner. In other words, not only does this liability attach automatically to a general partner, the amount of the liability is not ratably apportioned among the general partners. A creditor owed a debt by a general partnership may legally pursue just one of the general partners for the full amount of that debt – this is usually the general partner who is either the easiest over whom to secure the jurisdiction of the court, the general partner with "the deepest pockets" (i.e., the greatest amount of assets that may be the easiest to attach through a court order), or both – leaving it to such general partner to seek the ratable contribution of the other general partner(s) to share in the repayment of that debt.[11]

Because each of the partners in a General Partnership is jointly and severally liable for all of the debts, obligations, and liabilities of the General Partnership, regardless of how or by whom incurred (since each general partner is deemed to have authority to speak on behalf of and bind the General Partnership), third parties doing business with a General Partnership will generally look to the net worth and financial wherewithal of individual general partners with substantial net worth or to the collective net worth of all of the general partners, in deciding whether to enter into agreements with the General Partnership, such as a Purchase and Sale Agreement for the sale of land (See Chapters 2, 3, and 7 regarding more detailed information about the use of, and general terms and conditions provided in, Purchase and Sale Agreements or "PSAs"). Even if a General Partnership can deliver the required good faith deposit as a condition to the effectiveness of a duly executed PSA, the ability of the General Partnership to secure the financing, whether equity, debt, or some combination thereof, necessary to go to Closing on the purchase of the Subject Site will depend on the collective net worth of the general partners or the substantial net worth of only one or more of those partners. This is an important concept to grasp in understanding limited partnerships, introduced next, as well as the evolution of both general partnerships and limited partnerships into Limited Liability Partnerships and Limited Liability Limited Partnerships, respectively (also introduced next).

As suggested earlier, consistent with the theory of "joint and several liability" of general partners, each general partner is assumed to speak on behalf of the general partnership.[12]

A general partnership is *not* a "Taxable Entity."[13] It is merely a business arrangement among individuals who bear responsibility for paying the taxes on any income earned by the general partnership. General partnerships do not file tax returns and do not have to be registered in the state of their principal place of business or in any other state in which they do business in order to incur liabilities. The mere actions of a general partner in a general partnership are sufficient to incur the joint and several liability of each general partner.

By virtue of having an ownership interest, however such interest may be defined by the general partnership, in a "pass-through" entity that does not file tax returns, general partners in a general partnership may incur federal income tax liability regardless of whether there are concomitant distributions of cash from the general partnership that can be used to off-set the obligation to pays taxes on the tax attributes of the general partnership in a particular tax year.

Limited Partnerships. A limited partnership is a creature of state statute and has characteristics of both a general partnership and a corporation. The similarities to the latter include the fact that a Limited Partner's exposure to liability in a Limited Partnership does not extend beyond the potential loss of that Limited Partnership's investment in the Limited Partnership interest owned, although this liability would extend to any promissory notes given as part of the purchase price for such interest. Regarding the former, a Limited Partnership interest is similar to that of a general partner in that a Limited Partnership is a pass-through entity. All of the tax attributes of the Limited Partnership are "passed through" to its Limited and General Partners. These tax attributes are allocated each operating year of the Limited Partnership in accordance with the pro rata interests of 100% of the Limited and General Partners in the Limited Partnership.

State statutes regarding the formation and operation of Limited Partnerships tend to be relatively consistent because they all have the same antecedent: the Uniform Limited Partnership Act (1916), and subsequent amendments thereto (collectively, the ULPA), made by its governing body, the National Conference of Commissioners on Uniform State Laws (NCCUSL), also known as the Uniform Laws Commission or ULC. The ULP, like most uniform laws or codes, has been made available to state legislatures to consider for adoption. In order to afford some uniformity to commercial transactions from state to state, state legislatures tend to adopt the majority of provisions contained in the ULPA, which has been amended numerous times since the first one was adopted in 1916. However, the ULPA is not dispositive; it is only proposed as a template for state legislatures to consider. Consequently, each Limited Partnership is a creature of the state in which it is formed and is governed by that state's limited partnership laws and the cases interpreting those laws.

Limited Partners in a Limited Partnership, like shareholders in a C Corporation, do *not* participate actively in the management of the Limited Partnership. The management of the Limited Partnership is left up to the General Partner or the Managing General Partner, if there is one in the Limited Partnership structure. The General Partner or Managing General Partner, as the case may be, is responsible for the management of the Limited Partnership, and may be entitled to receive a management fee for its services.

The Limited Partnership was created as a legal construct to facilitate the formation of capital for various enterprises without imposing upon all investors the same, broad, joint-and-several liability of general partners in a General Partnership, while still providing the Limited Partners the benefits of the pass-through of all tax attributes, particularly early years' losses. Because a Limited Partnership is required to have one or more General Partners who manage the Limited Partnership, in order to avoid the individual exposure to liability for all of the Limited Partnership's debts, obligations, and liabilities beyond the assets of the Limited Partnership, individuals who would normally serve in the capacity of General Partners created Single-Purpose Entities (also sometimes referred to as Special-Purpose Entities or "SPEs"), to serve as the General Partner in a Limited Partnership. Such individual or individuals would own 100% of, and therefore control, such SPEs. Initially these SPEs were C Corporations. After the creation of Limited Liability Corporations, LLCs became a popular organizational form to serve as General Partners in Limited Partnerships. As real estate development Projects and transactions became increasingly complex and sophisticated, the real estate bar serving Developers and their Projects created new organizational forms – particularly the Limited Liability Partnership (LLP) and the Limited Liability Limited Partnership (LLLP) – allowing individuals to participate as General Partners in General Partnerships and Limited Partnerships, respectively, without needing to create C Corporations or LLCs to shield themselves from joint and several liability.

Limited Liability Partnerships (LLPs). A relatively recent creation, a Limited Liability Partnership (LLP) is essentially a general partnership without the problem of joint and several liability among the general partners. Put another way, it's an organization of general partners but they each have the insulation from liabilities as if they were limited partners. For example, the Official Georgia Code Annotated provides as follows:

> (6.1) "Limited liability partnership" means any partnership governed by this chapter [Chapter 8 – Partnerships], and any limited partnership that either is organized under Chapter 9 [Georgia's Uniform Limited Partnership Act] of this title [14. CORPORATIONS, PARTNERSHIPS, AND ASSOCIATIONS] or has elected to be subject to the provisions of Chapter 9 of this title pursuant to subsection (b) of Code Section 14–9–1201, that has become a limited liability partnership under Code Section 14–8–62 and that complies with Code Section 14–8–63.[14]

Section 14–8–62 of the Official Georgia Code Annotated, in turn, provides as follows:

> § 14–8–62. Limited liability partnership election; recording; fees; contents; procedures and effect; cancellation; dissolution of partnership; amendment of certificate to comply with name requirements.
>
> (a) To become and to continue as a limited liability partnership, a partnership shall record in the office of the clerk of the superior court of any county in which the partnership has an office a limited liability partnership election. Such election shall be recorded by such clerk in a book to be kept for

that purpose, which may be the book in which are recorded statements of partnership recorded pursuant to Code Section 14–8–10.1, and open to public inspection. As a prerequisite to such filing, the clerk of each such registry may collect a fee in the amount of the fee then allowed for the filing of statements of partnership. A limited liability partnership election shall state:

(1) The name of the partnership, which must comply with Code Section 14–8–63;
(2) The business, profession, or other activity in which the partnership engages;
(3) That the partnership thereby elects to be a limited liability partnership;
(4) That such election has been duly authorized; and
(5) Any other matters the partnership determines to include therein.

(b) Subject to any contrary agreement among the partners, the election shall be executed by a majority of the partners or by one or more partners authorized to execute an election.

(c) A partnership becomes a limited liability partnership at the time of the recording of the election or at such later date or time, if any, as is stated in the election and continues to be a limited liability partnership until a cancellation of limited liability partnership election, which states that it has been duly authorized, is:

(1) Subject to any contrary agreement among the partners, executed by a majority of the partners or by one or more partners authorized to execute such a cancellation; and
(2) Recorded in the office of the clerk of the superior court of each county in which the partnership recorded a limited liability partnership election.

(d) The status of a partnership as a limited liability partnership shall not be affected by changes, after the recording of a limited liability partnership election, in the information stated in the election.

(e) The fact that a limited liability partnership election has been recorded as required by this Code section is notice that the partnership is a limited liability partnership.

(f) If a limited liability partnership is dissolved and its business continued without liquidation of the partnership's affairs, the new partnership shall succeed to the old partnership's election to become a limited liability partnership and shall continue to be a limited liability partnership until cancellation of such election.

(g) A limited partnership organizing under or subject to Chapter 9 of this title may become and continue as a limited liability partnership if its certificate of limited partnership specifies a name which complies with subsection (b) of Code Section 14–8–63 and otherwise complies with the name requirements of Code Section 14–9–102 and includes in its certificate of limited partnership a statement that the limited partnership is a limited liability partnership. Subject to any contrary agreement among the partners, an amendment to become a limited liability partnership by an existing limited partnership shall be approved by all of the partners. A limited partnership becomes a limited liability partnership at the time its certificate which complies with the foregoing provisions of this subsection becomes effective and continues to be a limited liability partnership until its certificate of limited partnership is amended to remove the statement that such limited partnership is a limited liability partnership and so that its name no longer contains the words "limited liability limited partnership," or the abbreviation "L.L.L.P.," or the designation "LLLP." The fact that the certificate of limited partnership of a limited partnership has been amended as set forth in this subsection is notice that the limited partnership is a limited liability partnership. If a limited partnership that is a limited liability partnership is dissolved and its business continued without liquidation of the limited partnership's affairs, the new limited partnership shall continue to be a limited liability partnership until its certificate of limited partnership is amended as provided in this subsection. A limited partnership that becomes a limited liability partnership pursuant to this subsection shall otherwise remain subject to Chapter 9 of this title, including, without limitation, the annual registration provisions of Code Section 14–9–206.5.

HISTORY: Code 1981, § 14–8–62, enacted by Ga. L. 1995, p. 470, § 11; Ga. L. 1996, p. 787, § 3; Ga. L. 1997, p. 1380, § 1.

Limited liability limited partnership (LLLPs)

Just as a Limited Liability Partnership is a general partnership (aka a partnership), in which each of what would otherwise be general partners, having joint and several liability for all of the partnership's debts, obligations, and liabilities, are treated the same as if they were limited partners in a limited partnership, the general partners in a Limited Liability Limited Partnership or LLLP also have the same limitations on their liabilities as if they were limited partners.

A portion of the Comment section to Section 101 – Definitions, of the Uniform Partnership Act (1997), offers insight into the role and responsibility of a "general partner" in various partnership scenarios, from a General Partnership to a Limited Liability Limited Partnership (LLLP). Because both the Uniform Partnership Act (UPA) and the Uniform Limited Partnership Act (ULPA) are drafted by the same body, the comments to the UPA cut across both uniform acts, providing a more comprehensive and cohesive understanding of all four types of partnership entities: General Partnerships, Limited Partnerships, Limited Liability Partnerships, and Limited Liability Limited Partnerships.

Partner liability deserves special mention. RULPA Section 403(b) provides that a general partner of a limited partnership "has the liabilities of a partner in a partnership without limited partners." Thus limited partnership law expressly references general partnership law for general partner liability and does not separately consider the liability of such partners. The liability of a general partner of a limited partnership that becomes a LLLP would therefore be the liability of a general partner in an LLP and would be governed by Section 306. The liability of a limited partner in a LLLP is a more complicated matter. RULPA Section 303(a) separately considers the liability of a limited partner. Unless also a general partner, a limited partner is not liable for the obligations of a limited partnership unless the partner participates in the control of the business and then only to persons reasonably believing the limited partner is a general partner. Therefore, arguably limited partners in a LLLP will have the specific RULPA Section 303(c) liability shield while general partners will have a superior Section 306(c) liability shield. In order to clarify limited partner liability and other linkage issues, States that have adopted RULPA, these limited liability partnership rules, and RULPA may wish to consider an amendment to RULPA. A suggested form of such an amendment is:

SECTION 1107. LIMITED LIABILITY LIMITED PARTNERSHIP.
  (a) A limited partnership may become a limited liability partnership by:
      (1) obtaining approval of the terms and conditions of the limited partnership becoming a limited liability limited partnership by the vote necessary to amend the limited partnership agreement except, in the case of a limited partnership agreement that expressly considers contribution obligations, the vote necessary to amend those provisions;
      (2) filing a statement of qualification under Section 1001(c) of the Uniform Partnership Act (1994); and
      (3) complying with the name requirements of Section 1002 of the Uniform Partnership Act (1994).
  (b) A limited liability limited partnership continues to be the same entity that existed before the filing of a statement of qualification under Section 1001(c) of the Uniform Partnership Act (1994).
  (c) Sections 306(c) and 307(b) of the Uniform Partnership Act (1994) apply to both general and limited partners of a limited liability limited partnership.[15]

Tax issues in structuring ownership

C Corporations

Double taxation. One of the main disadvantages of using a C Corporation as the Development Entity, a component of the Development Entity (e.g., where the C Corporation is the General Partner of a Limited Partnership) or in any other aspect of the deal structure as part of The Development Process, is that C Corporations are subject to "double taxation." This refers to the fact that C Corporations are taxed on their adjusted gross income, without regard to the distribution of profits in the form of dividends paid to shareholders, and then those shareholders are taxed on their respective tax returns when they include dividends received from the C Corporation as part of the investment income required to be reported to the IRS. This is contrasted with the treatment of a Limited Liability Partnership, which is not a Taxable Entity for IRS purposes and, therefore does not file tax returns or pay taxes on the partnership's adjusted gross income, as all tax attributes are passed through to the partners, who report those tax attributes on their own, respective federal tax returns.

No shareholders liabilities. The liability of a shareholder in a C Corporation is limited to the value of their investment in the number of shares they have purchased and own. Shareholders in a C Corporation do not assume liability for the debts, obligations, and liabilities of the C Corporations in which they own shares of stock.

No Phantom Income. As discussed later, because partnerships are pass-through organizations and are not Taxable Entities, partners in a partnership may be taxed on "phantom income," which refers to a partner in a partnership receiving an allocation of taxable income in that partner's share of allocable tax attributes to all partners, without receiving a concomitant distribution of cash with which to pay the tax liability created by the allocation of taxable income. If, for example, a partner in a partnership is attributed, through the annual allocation of the tax attributes of the partnership to its partners, with $100,000 of income but does not, in that same tax year, receive a distribution of partnership distributable cash, that partner will have to use her own, personal resources to pay the tax liability, at the individual level, on that $100,000 of income.

New Medicare Tax. For information regarding the new Medicare tax on C Corporations, see the companion website for this textbook.

S Corporations

S Corporations are treated like partnerships, In that they are pass-through entities for federal tax purposes, much like partnerships. S Corporations do not file tax returns because all of their tax attributes are reported out to their shareholders, who then claim those tax attributes on their own federal tax returns.

Limitations on types of shareholders

In order to qualify as an S Corporation under Subchapter S of the Internal Revenue Code, the corporation filing a S Corporation election must also meet certain requirements:

Limitations on the Total Number of S Corporation Shareholders. An S. Corporation may not have more than 100 shareholders. This specific requirement has generally not been a significant obstacle to using an S Corporation for structuring a Development Entity or a real estate transaction within The Development Process. However, with the advent of crowdfunding (see the Crowdfunding Feature Box in Chapter 9), a limitation on the number of shareholders allowed in an

S Corporation could eliminate the use of S Corporations in structuring some real estate development and financing transactions.

Limitations on the Types of S Corporation Shareholders. Only individuals may own shares in an S Corporation. An S Corporation's shares may not be owned by a corporation (C or S Corporations) or by trusts.

Property distributions are taxable. Unlike partnerships, the property distributions from which are not taxable to the partners receiving such property distributions, property distributions from S Corporations to their shareholders are taxable.

Estate tax issues. For a limited discussion about estate tax issues relating to S Corporations, see related materials on the companion website for this textbook.

Partnerships (including LLCs, limited partnerships, general partnerships, LLPs, and LLLPs)

Pass-Through Taxation. Unlike C Corporations, partnerships are not Taxable Entities. All tax attributes generated by a partnership, regardless of whether it is a General Partnership, Limited Partnership, Limited Liability Partnership (a form of General Partnership), or a Limited Liability Limited Partnership (a form of Limited Partnership), are "passed-through" to the partners in accordance with whatever arrangements the partners have agreed to for the allocation of the partnership's tax attributes. The allocation of tax attributes, as well as distributions of distributable cash to partners, are made in accordance with each partners contributions to the partnership relative to the aggregate contributions of all partners to the partnership (i.e., tax attributes and distributable cash are allocated ratably to each partner). However, the partners in a partnership may agree to "Special Allocations," with regard to which the Internal Revenue Code imposes a number of rules in order for such Special Allocations to be honored in the event of an audit. See following discussion regarding Special Allocations.

IRC §704(b) and Special Allocations. As noted in this excerpt from Internal Revenue Bulletin (IRB) 200824, dated June 16, 2008, "providing rules for testing whether the economic effect of an allocation is substantial within the meaning of section 704(b) where partners are look-through entities or members of a consolidated group," although partners in a partnership are relatively free to arrange their respective affairs regarding partnership contributions and distributions, the Internal Revenue Service is similarly free to disregard such arrangements when they lack "substantial economic effect." Specifically, the IRS's 704(b) regulations provide, in pertinent part, as follows:

> Section 704(a) provides that a partner's distributive share of partnership income, gain, loss, deduction, or credit shall, except as otherwise provided, be determined by the partnership agreement. Section 704(b) provides that a partner's distributive share of income, gain, loss, deduction, or credit (or item thereof) shall be determined in accordance with the partner's interest in the partnership (determined by taking into account all facts and circumstances) if the allocation to the partner under the partnership agreement of income, gain, loss, deduction, or credit (or item thereof) does not have substantial economic effect.
> *In order for an allocation to have substantial economic effect, it must have economic effect and such economic effect must be substantial. For an allocation to have economic effect, it must be consistent with the underlying economic arrangement of the partners. This means that, in the event there is an economic benefit or burden that corresponds to the allocation, the partner to*

whom the allocation is made must receive the economic benefit or bear such economic burden. See §1.7041(b)(2)(ii).

The 704(b) Regulations go on to provide that:[16]

Allocations to a partner will have economic effect if, and only if, throughout the full term of the partnership, the partnership agreement provides for: (i) the proper maintenance of the partners' capital accounts, (ii) upon liquidation of the partnership (or any partner's interest in the partnership) liquidating distributions are required to be made in accordance with the positive capital account balances of the partners, as determined after taking into account all necessary adjustments for the partnership's taxable year during which the liquidation occurs, by the end of such taxable year, or if later, 90 days after the date of such liquidation, and (iii) if such partner has a deficit balance in the partner's capital account following the liquidation of the interest after taking into account all necessary adjustments for the partnership taxable year during which the liquidation occurs, the partner is unconditionally obligated to restore the deficit balance by the end of such taxable year (or, if later, within 90 days after the date of the liquidation), which amount is paid to the partnership's creditors or distributed to the other partners in accordance with their positive capital account balances. See §1.7041(b)(2)(ii)(b).

Even if the partnership agreement does not require an unlimited deficit restoration obligation of a partner, the allocation may still have economic effect to the extent such allocation does not cause or increase a deficit balance in the partner's capital account (in excess of any limited dollar amount of such partner's deficit restoration obligation) if requirements (1) and (2) of §1.7041(b)(2)(ii)(b) are satisfied and the partnership agreement contains a "qualified income offset." Section 1.7041(b)(2)(ii)(d). Finally, allocations that do not otherwise have economic effect under the foregoing rules shall be deemed to have economic effect if at the end of each partnership taxable year a liquidation of the partnership at the end of such year or at the end of any future year would produce the same economic results to the partners if such rules had been satisfied regardless of the economic performance of the partnership. Section 1.7041(b)(2)(ii)(i).

As a general rule, the economic effect of an allocation (or allocations) is substantial if there is a reasonable possibility that the allocation (or allocations) will affect substantially the dollar amounts to be received by the partners from the partnership, independent of tax consequences. See §1.7041(b)(2)(iii). Even if the allocation affects substantially the dollar amounts to be received by the partners from the partnership, the economic effect of the allocation (or allocations) is not substantial if, at the time the allocation (or allocations) becomes part of the partnership agreement, (1) the aftertax economic consequences of at least one partner may, in present value terms, be enhanced compared to such consequences if the allocation (or allocations) were not contained in the partnership agreement, and (2) there is a strong likelihood that the aftertax economic consequences of no partner will, in present value terms, be substantially diminished compared to such consequences if the allocation (or allocations) were not contained in the partnership agreement. See §1.7041(b)(2)(iii). This test is commonly referred to as the aftertax test. In determining the aftertax economic benefit or detriment of an allocation to a partner, the tax consequences that result from the interaction of the allocation with such partner's tax attributes that are unrelated to the partnership will be taken into account. Finally, the economic effect of an allocation is not substantial in two situations described in 1.7041(b)(2)(iii)(b) and (b)(2)(iii)(c). The latter two situations are generally described as shifting" and "transitory" allocations, respectively.

If the partnership agreement provides for an allocation of income, gain, loss, deduction, or credit (or item thereof) to a partner that does not have substantial economic effect, then the partner's distributive share of the income, gain, loss, deduction, or credit (or item thereof) is determined in accordance with the partner's interest in the partnership. References in section 704(b) or §1.7041 to a partner's interest in the partnership, or to the partners' interests in the partnership, signify the manner in which the partners have agreed to share the economic benefit or burden (if any) corresponding to the income, gain, loss, deduction.

Phantom Income. As mentioned in the discussion about C Corporations because partnerships are pass-through organizations and are not Taxable Entities, partners in a partnership may be subject to "phantom income." Phantom income refers to the scenario in which a partner in a partnership receives an allocation of taxable income in that partner's share of allocable tax attributes from the partnership *but does not receive* a concomitant distribution of distributable partnership cash with which to pay the tax liability. For example, if a partner in a partnership receives a K-1 with an allocation of the tax attributes from the partnership that includes $100,000 of income but, in that same tax year, there have been no distributions to partners of partnership distributable cash, *that partner will have to use her own personal resources to pay the tax liability, at the individual level, on that $100,000 of income.*

The Tax Reform Act of 1986's Passive Activity Loss Rules. Congress's perceived need to include the Passive Activity Loss Rules in the Tax Reform Act of 1986 was arguably caused by the confluence of (i) relatively favorable tax treatment for real estate development transactions and operations; (ii) a high marginal rate of tax on high-income earners, making the "sheltering" of income through other, loss-generating investments highly attractive; (iii) partnership provisions and regulations in the Internal Revenue Code allowing a partner's account to be credited with the full amount of future payments represented by promissory notes falling due in future years; and (iv) the promulgation of Regulation D by the U.S. Securities and Exchange Commission (SEC), allowing certain types of private offerings of securities without the issuer having to register as a "public company" under the Securities Act of 1933 or produce public offering documents in accordance with the requirements imposed upon public companies by the Securities and Exchange Act of 1934. These four, seemingly unrelated components of the United States' federal tax and securities regulatory systems led to a tidal wave of tax shelter transactions, allowing millions of high-income earners to avoid the payment of federal taxes in years they would otherwise be required to do so.[17]

Non-rental Real Estate Investments: Participation on a "regular, continuous, and substantial basis." With the exception of business activities involving the ownership and rental of real property, for which the passive activity rules are even stricter, a taxpayer is considered to have "materially participated" in a trade or business activity if the taxpayer is involved *"on a regular, continuous, and substantial basis."* The IRS offers "safe-harbor" rules for material participation, provided the taxpayer meets any of the following criteria during the tax year, although there are exceptions to these safe-harbor rules:

1. The taxpayer participated in the activity for *more than 500 hours.*
2. The taxpayer's participation was substantially all the participation in the activity taking into consideration the participation of everybody else, including those that did not own any interest in the trade or business, such as a third-party management company.
3. The taxpayer participated in the activity for more than 100 hours and also participated at least as much as anybody else (including those that did not own any interest in the trade or business).
4. The activity is a significant participation activity, and the taxpayer participated in all significant participation activities for more than 500 hours. A significant participation activity is any trade or business activity in which the taxpayer participated for more than 100 hours during the year and in which the taxpayer did not materially participate under any of the material participation tests, other than this test.
5. The taxpayer materially participated in the activity for any five of the ten immediately preceding tax years.

7. The activity is a personal service activity in which the taxpayer materially participated for any three preceding tax years. An activity is a personal service activity if it involves the performance of personal services in areas like health, law, engineering, architecture, accounting, actuarial science, performing arts, and consulting.

8. And the catch all: Based on all the facts and circumstances, the taxpayer participated in the activity on a regular, continuous, and substantial basis during the year.

Fortunately, this is one area where attribution rules work in your favor. For purposes of these criteria, your participation in an activity includes your spouse's participation. This is true even if your spouse did not own any interest in the activity and you and your spouse do not file a joint return.

Under the passive activity rules, the rental of real property is considered a de facto passive activity, even if the taxpayer otherwise meets one or more of the safe-harbor rules demonstrating *material* participation. Unless the taxpayer is deemed a "real estate professional" or "*actively* participates," and not just "materially" participates, the losses generated cannot be used to offset other income.

The passive activity loss rules essentially ended the practice of taxpayers buying losses from real estate limited partnerships with the primary purpose of generating substantial losses in the partnership's early years of operation to use those losses to offset other income on which the taxpayer would otherwise be subject to federal taxes at the highest marginal rates. With the Tax Reform Act of 1986 requiring rental real estate activities that the taxpayer claiming partnership losses either be a "real estate professional" or "actively participate" in the partnership's activities, the losses would be disallowed in the tax year claimed. Excess losses disallowed under the passive activity loss rules could be carried forward provided, in the carry forward years, they do not create a loss that could be used to shelter other income. By definition, a Limited Partner in a Limited Partnership is a "passive investor," since Limited Partners do not participate in the management of the business activities of the Limited Partnership.[18]

Property distributions are generally not taxable. The distribution of partnership property from the partnership to a partner is generally not taxable but does affect the partner's basis in her partnership interest. Internal Revenue Service Publication 541 (December 2013) provides, in pertinent part, as follows regarding the tax impact of a partnership's distribution of property to a partner:

Partnership distributions

Partnership distributions include the following:
- A withdrawal by a partner in anticipation of the current year's earnings.
- A distribution of the current year's or prior years' earnings not needed for working capital.
- A complete or partial liquidation of a partner's interest.
- A distribution to all partners in a complete liquidation of the partnership.

A partnership distribution is not taken into account in determining the partner's distributive share of partnership income or loss. If any gain or loss from the distribution is recognized by the partner, it must be reported on his or her return for the tax year in which the distribution is received. Money or property withdrawn by a partner in anticipation of the current year's earnings is treated as a distribution received on the last day of the partnership's tax year.

Effect on partner's basis. A partner's adjusted basis in his or her partnership interest is decreased (but not below zero) by the money and adjusted basis of property distributed to the partner. See Adjusted Basis under Basis of Partner's Interest, later.

Effect on partnership. A partnership generally does not recognize any gain or loss because of distributions it makes to partners. The partnership may be able to elect to adjust the basis of its undistributed property.

Estate tax basis step-up. On the death of an owner of a partnership interest or the death of an individual whose partnership interest is owned in his/ her revocable living trust, *the interest in the partnership interest takes a basis equal to the fair market value of the interest on the date of death or alternative valuation date*. Absent a Section 754 election, the basis of the assets inside the partnership are not changed.

A Section 754 election, if desired, is made with the timely filed tax return of the partnership in the year of the transaction or event that causes a basis step up of the partnership interest. Such events include the death of a partner or a sale of a partnership interest. If the election is late, Treas. Reg. Sec. 301.9100–2 provides an automatic extension to file for twelve months from the due date of the partnership tax return including extensions. The filing must include a notation at the top saying "Filed pursuant to §301.9100–2."

If the partnership already had a Section 754 election in place before death, the election remains in effect and applies to the basis on death. No additional election need be made but if the election is not desired, a revocation of the election is only available with the permission of the Secretary, which permission is not easily obtained.

The election if made and if the basis of the assets inside the partnership are stepped up, creates a separate basis for the asset inside the partnership, the basis of which and deductions generated from which, are allocated to the partner whose basis changed as a result of the event allowing the election. The basis alteration is allocated amongst the capital assets or § 1231(b) property inside the partnership per § 1.755–1(c)(1)(iii) in proportion to the gains in basis of each of these assets.[19]

Disregarded entity/SPEs. A minimum of two partners is required in order for the formation of a partnership. However, the same requirement is not the case for a Limited Liability Company or LLC, as an LLC can be wholly owned by a single, individual member or corporation. As mentioned earlier, the creation and use of an LLC to serve as the General Partner or Managing General Partner of a Limited Partnership was a common structuring technique for Developer's creating Limited Partnerships to facilitate capital formations for real estate development transactions, including the use Limited Partnerships as Development Entities.

The sole member of an LLC may file an election with the Internal Revenue Service to have the LLC entity disregarded, essentially having its business operations treated like a sole proprietorship of the LLC's sole member. Making this election does not, however, change either the legal status of the LLC or the sole shareholder's.

§301.7701–3 Classification of certain business entities.

(a) In general. A business entity that is not classified as a corporation under § 301.7701–2(b) (1), (3), (4), (5), (6), (7), or (8) (an eligible entity) can elect its classification for federal tax purposes as provided in this section. An eligible entity with at least two members can elect to be classified as either an association [and thus a corporation under §301.7701–2(b)(2)] or a partnership, and *an eligible entity with a single owner can elect to be classified as an association or to be disregarded as an entity separate from its owner.* Paragraph (b) of this section provides a default classification for an eligible entity that does not make an election. Thus, elections are necessary only when an eligible entity chooses to be classified initially as other than the default classification or when an eligible entity chooses to change its classification. An entity whose classification is determined under the default classification retains that classification (regardless of any changes in the members' liability that occur at any time during the time that the entity's classification is relevant as defined in paragraph (d) of this section) until the entity makes an election to change that classification under paragraph (c)(1) of this section. Paragraph (c) of this section provides rules for making express elections. Paragraph (d) of this section provides special rules for foreign eligible entities. Paragraph (e) of this section provides special rules for classifying entities resulting from partnership terminations and divisions under section 708(b). Paragraph (f) of this section sets forth the effective date of this section and a special rule relating to prior periods.[Emphasis added.]

  (b) Classification of eligible entities that do not file an election – (1) Domestic eligible entities. Except as provided in paragraph (b)(3) of this section, unless the entity elects otherwise, a domestic eligible entity is –

  (i) A partnership if it has two or more members; or

  (ii) Disregarded as an entity separate from its owner if it has a single owner.[20]

REITs.[21] The Real Estate Investment Trust is an investment structure originally created in the United States in 1960 to permit multiple investors to participate in the ownership of income-producing real estate assets. Since that time, REITs have expanded globally, in complexity, and to broadly reflect the full range of real estate investment opportunities through a centrally managed portfolio of assets, some of which are highly specialized geographically, by product type, or both. The "Trust" part of the REIT acronym is somewhat of a misnomer, since REITs are corporations the tax treatment of which most closely approximates how partners in partnerships are taxed. To understand the overall impact REITs have had on real estate investing, as of June 2014, the FTSE EPRA/NAREIT Global Real Estate Index Series included 456 stock exchange listed real estate companies from thirty-seven countries representing an *equity market capitalization of about $2 trillion*, almost 80% of which total valuation represents REIT holdings.[22] As of May 29, 2015, the FTSE EPRA/NAREIT United States Index had a market capitalization of $658,845MM.[23]

  An entity seeking to qualify as a Real Estate Investment Trust for federal tax purposes under the Internal Revenue Code must meet the following requirements or restrictions, as the case may be:

- Centralized management;[24]
- Transferable shares;[25]
- Taxable as a domestic corporation for federal tax purposes, even if it is an unincorporated association;[26]
- Not be a financial institution or insurance company;[27]
- Shares beneficially owned by at least 100 persons;[28]
- Not be "closely held";[29]
- Meet annual income and assets tests;[30]
- Meet distribution, earnings, and profits requirements;[31]
- REIT election[32]; and
- Calendar Year as its Tax Year.[33]

Quasi pass-through taxation. Unlike partnerships, REITs are Taxable Entities, and do not pass through all of their tax attributes to shareholders. However, unlike C Corporations, and more like partnerships, REITs can deduct distributions to shareholders from their gross income, whereas C Corporations are taxed on their adjusted gross income without regard to or being allowed deduction or offset for dividend distributions to shareholders. And since REITs are required to distribute each year 95% of their taxable earnings, not much is left for taxation at the REIT level.[34]

Limitations on ownership, types of income. Section 856(c)(2) of the Internal Revenue Code provides the following limitations and requirements on the type of income REITs may generate and continue to qualify for treatment as a REIT under the Code:

(2) at least 95 percent (90 percent for taxable years beginning before January 1, 1980) of its gross income (excluding gross income from prohibited transactions) is derived from –

(A) dividends?

(B) interest?

(C) rents from real property?

(D) gain from the sale or other disposition of stock, securities, and real property (including interests in real property and interests in mortgages on real property) which is not property described in section 1221(a)(1)?

(E) abatements and refunds of taxes on real property?

(F) income and gain derived from foreclosure property [as defined in subsection (e)]?

(G) amounts (other than amounts the determination of which depends in whole or in part on the income or profits of any person) received or accrued as consideration for entering into agreements

(i) to make loans secured by mortgages on real property or on interests in real property or

(ii) to purchase or lease real property (including interests in real property and interests in mortgages on real property)?

(H) gain from the sale or other disposition of a real estate asset which is not a prohibited transaction solely by reason of section 857(b)(6)? and

(I) mineral royalty income earned in the first taxable year beginning after the date of the enactment of this subparagraph from real property owned by a timber real estate investment trust and held, or once held, in connection with the trade or business of producing timber by such real estate investment trust.

Tax-exempt entities

Unrelated trade or business. A tax-exempt organization, including but not limited to nonprofit organizations qualified under Internal Revenue Code §501(c)(3) – often referred to as "501(c)(3) organizations" or, generically, as "nonprofits" – are limited in the amount they are allowed to receive of and be taxed on in their Unrelated Business Taxable Income (UBTI).[35] As long as the amount of UBTI received by a 501(c)(3) organization in a given tax year is both nominal and directly related to the organizations mission upon which its 501(c)(3) tax-exempt status is premised (in other words, the 501(c)(3) organization is not generating gross income unrelated to its mission, for the purpose of avoiding paying taxes thereon by virtue of its tax-exempt status), and properly declares and pays taxes on its UBTI, the receipt of UBTI will not jeopardize its tax-exempt status under IRC § 501(c)(3). However, under certain circumstances, a 501(c)(3) organization may have its tax-exempt status under IRC § 501(c)(3) revoked by the Internal Revenue Service.

How income from investments – either direct or indirect – in real estate is taxed in the hands of tax-exempt organizations may have a considerable negative impact on employee pension funds, which are required to be set up and operated as tax-exempt entities.[36] As a matter of balancing their investment portfolios on behalf of their beneficiaries, pension trust funds tend to invest anywhere between 10 and 20% of their asset value in real estate investments. It is not uncommon, in this regard, for a pension fund, such as TIAA-CREF, to participate directly in the financing of a Project at some critical stage during The Development Process.[37]

The provisions in the Internal Revenue Code regarding the taxation of tax-exempt organizations include a separate section – IRC § 514 – impacting the receipt of a tax-exempt organization of debt-financed income, which would include income from real property financed, in whole or in part, through indebtedness, by treating such "debt-financed income" as UBTI in the hands of the tax-exempt organization. This tax treatment includes, among other things, a tax-exempt organization's receipt of income on an interest it owns in another entity, such as a Development Entity or an investment fund that owns interests in a Development Entity.

Debt-financed income. IRC § 514 provides that all or a portion of a tax-exempt organization's income with respect to "debt-financed property" generally will be treated as unrelated business taxable income (UBTI), subject to federal income tax, based on the ratio of the average acquisition indebtedness with respect to the property over the average adjusted basis of the property for the relevant taxable year. This means that, among other things,

Section 511(a) imposes tax on the UBTI of certain tax-exempt organizations. Under section 512(c)(1), when a tax-exempt organization is a partner in a partnership that conducts a trade or business unrelated to the purpose justifying the tax-exempt status of the organization, the tax-exempt organization must include in calculating its UBTI its share of the gross income of the partnership from the unrelated trade or business and its share of partnership deductions directly connected with such gross income.

Certain types of income, such as interest, dividends, rents from real property, and gains from the sale or exchange of property that is not "dealer" property generally are excluded from UBTI.7 Income that is otherwise excepted from UBTI, however, may still be classified as UBTI under section 514 if the property generating the income is "debt financed." Section 514(b)(1) generally defines "debt-financed property" as property that is held to produce income and with respect to which there is "acquisition indebtedness" at any time during the taxable year (or, if the property was disposed of during the taxable year, with respect to which there was an "acquisition indebtedness" at any time during the 12-month period ending with the date of such disposition).

Although section 514 provides that a tax-exempt organization generally will earn UBTI with respect to "debt-financed property," section 514(c)(9) provides that real property subject to "acquisition indebtedness" will not be subject to these rules in certain circumstances. This favorable rule for real property applies only with respect to tax-exempt entities that are Qualified Organizations. Section 514(c)(9)(C) defines a "Qualified Organization" as: (1) a charitable organization described in section 170(b)(1)(A)(ii) and affiliated support organizations; (2) a pension trust described in section 401; (3) a title-holding company under section 501(c)(25); and (4) a retirement income account under section 403(b)(9).[38]

Fractions rule. Partnership Allocations Permitted Under Section 514(c)(9)(E).

Internal Revenue Regulation § 1.514(c)2 — Permitted allocations under section 514(c)(9)(E) – provides, in pertinent part, as follows:

(b) Application of section 514(c)(9)(E), relating to debt-financed real property held by partnerships

(1) In general. This § 1.514(c)2 provides rules governing the application of section 514(c)(9)(E). To comply with section 514(c)(9)(E), the following two requirements must be met:

(i) The fractions rule. The allocation of items to a partner that is a qualified organization cannot result in that partner having a percentage share of overall partnership income for any partnership taxable year greater than that partner's fractions rule percentage (as defined in paragraph (c)(2) of this section).

(ii) Substantial economic effect. Each partnership allocation must have substantial economic effect. However, allocations that cannot have economic effect must be deemed to be in accordance with the partners' interests in the partnership pursuant to § 1.7041(b)(4) does not provide a method for deeming the allocations to be in accordance with the partners' interests in the partnership) must otherwise comply with the requirements of § 1.7041(b)(4). Allocations attributable to nonrecourse liabilities or partner nonrecourse debt must comply with the requirements of § 1.7042.

Section 514(c)(9), however, provides an exception in the case of real property held by certain tax-exempt organizations ("Qualified Organizations") if several requirements are met. When a partnership in which the tax-exempt organization is a partner holds the real property, generally the exception will be available only if the partnership's allocations have substantial economic effect under section 704(b) and also satisfy the so-called "fractions rule" contained in section 514(c)(9)(E).

Under the fractions rule, a partnership's allocation of items to a partner that is a Qualified Organization cannot result in that partner having an overall share of partnership income for any partnership taxable year greater than such partner's percentage share of overall loss for the partnership taxable year in which the partner's percentage share of overall loss will be the smallest.[39]

The ABA Committee on Taxation, in its comment letter to the Internal Revenue Service regarding the fractions rule, has argued that the rule "often thwarts legitimate business arrangements." The Committee on Taxation's comment letter goes on to state:

> Although we believe that the general approach taken by the fractions rule is not well suited to address the perceived abuse at which the rule is aimed, these Comments do not address the general approach embodied by the fractions rule. Past commentators have stated the case against application of the fractions rule generally.[40]

Operational tax issues

Introduction to operational tax issues

Indicia of Activities as a Taxable Entity. Throughout The Development Process the "Developer" is taking a variety of steps, detailed in each of the five Phases of The Development Process, some of which may give rise to tax attributes. For example, even in the very early stages of the Project Conception Phase, the Developer may be incurring expenses, albeit very modest ones if the 80/2 Rule is being followed. Nonetheless, the act of incurring expenses gives rise to the query: Whose expenses are they?

Putting aside the question whether, at such an early stage in The Development Process the Developer should be concerned about issues of liability, such that these early stage activities should be undertaken by a Special Purpose Entity to shield the Developer from potential liabilities, should the developer be concerned about how deductions for the expenses incurred and by whom or what? The query here will be whether the IRS will allow the expenses incurred as legitimate deductions from income by the taxpayer at the time they're incurred. The reader should bear in mind that this is an issue separate and apart from the issue of at what point should the Developer discontinue proceeding with activities in The Development Process in its own name and proceed, instead, under the guise of a Development Entity created for that purpose, in order to avoid the assumption of imposition of the Developer of liabilities it does not want to have to satisfy with its own assets.[41]

Methods of Accounting. Every federal taxpayer must, among other things, have a Tax Year and a Method of Accounting that are consistently applied and honored from tax year to tax year. The average individual taxpayer uses a calendar year Tax Year – January 1 through December 31 – and the cash method of accounting. Most corporations, on the other hand, adopt a Fiscal Year that makes sense based on the industry in which their primary business is engaged, and the Accrual Method of Accounting, primarily because of the requirements for producing Audited Financial Statements.

Accounting for real estate transactions occupies its own area of discipline and is beyond the scope of this textbook. However, there are a few operational issues regarding the taxation of real estate transactions that bear mentioning here.

Cash and Accrual Methods of Accounting. Under the Accrual Method of Accounting, income is "recognized" when it is earned rather than when it is received. The same goes for expenses: Expenses are recognized when they are incurred, as opposed to when they are paid. The Accrual Method of Accounting is considered a more accurate reflection of an entity's income and expenses and, therefore, that entity's financial position and performance, because the impact of transactions cannot be manipulated by the timing of when payments are made (expenses) and payments are received (income).

Most real estate investments and other transactions are maintained on the Cash Basis of Accounting. However, General Contractors that are prohibited, under IRS rules, from using the Cash Method of Accounting, may use one of several Long-Term Methods of Accounting, which is a hybrid of the Cash and Accrual Accounting Methods.

Long-Term Contract Method of Accounting. Because construction contracts are generally performed over multiple years and have percentage-of-completion provisions allowing construction draws only after the General Contractor of "GC" has demonstrated that a specific percentage of the overall construction contract has been performed, the IRS allows special Accrual Method of Accounting rules for how GC's account for payments received during a Tax Year from multi-year construction contracts made in accordance with a draw schedule.

Deductions. As a general principle of the tax code, a taxpayer is allowed to deduct from gross income all expenses incurred in generating that gross income. However, in addition to general rules applying to the timing and recognition of business expenses, specific provisions in the tax code govern certain types of deductions. The most common deductions arising in the course of The Development Process are addressed next.

Depreciation and Amortization/*Crane* Rule. The allowance and timing of deductions for business expenses depend, in part, on the nature of the expenditure.[42] Just because a taxpayer incurs what is otherwise an allowable expense does not mean the full amount of that expenditure may be used to offset gross income in that same Tax Year. The development or purchase of Capital Assets, and expenditures for other long-lived assets, both intangible and tangible, *the benefits of which are expected to extend beyond a twelve-month period*, are subject to specific rules intended to match up the expenditure over the "life" of the asset acquired through such expenditure.[43]

Depreciation and amortization are two somewhat similar approaches to matching up the recovery of costs for long-lived assets in order to better match the costs up with the income those assets generate. It is important to note, however, that the "cost recovery systems" – of which depreciation and amortization are component parts – mandated under the Internal Revenue Code are not the same as cost recovery approaches mandated by Generally Accepted Accounting Principles (GAAP) mandated either for purposes of generating audited financial statements and/or for meeting the financial disclosure requirements imposed under the Securities and Exchange Act of 1934, to which public companies such as publicly traded REITs are subject. Accordingly, many real estate investment entities must employ two, separate methods for cost recovery purposes in order to comply with both IRS and GAAP requirements.

Because land does not have a limit to its useful life, its fee simple ownership is not subject to depreciation of amortization. Accordingly, in a Purchase and Sale Agreement for real property including Improvements, the parties will be required to make an allocation between that portion of the Purchase Price representing the value of the land, and the portion representing the value of the Improvements. In this regard, it should be noted that the existence of Improvements on real property being acquired by the Developer may not have value in the Developer's plans for the property. In other words, even though Improvements on real property may have a determinable fair market value, if the Developer's plans include demolishing those Improvements to make way for something else, the cost of such demolition and removal of existing Improvements may be added to the Developer's tax basis in the property prior to commencing construction.

Finally, not all occupancies of real estate for the development, and ownership and operation, of Improvements thereon take place on real property owned in fee simple. Periodic ground lease or ground-rent payments are allowed to be expensed in the Tax Year they are paid, assuming they are reflected in monthly or annual payments required to be made over the life of the ground lease.[44] If, however, the Developer, in acquiring a long-term leasehold in real property is required to make a large, lump-sum payment upon execution of the ground lease document, and also make periodic (monthly or annual) ground lease payments to the ground lessor, the lump-sum payment will be required to be capitalized, and amortized over the term of the ground lease.

Depreciation. Capital assets are required to be depreciated, generally ratably, over their "useful life," less salvage value, beginning when the asset is "placed in service." Certain expenditures relating to the acquisition or creation of a capital asset may be required to be capitalized (i.e., added to the asset's tax basis) and, therefore, recognized as a Tax Year expense through depreciation; others may be expensed in the same Tax Year as when incurred.

The U.S. Congress has, from time to time, lengthened or shortened the depreciation rules for "improvements to real property."

Selected schedules for depreciation of specific real estate assets, including certain equipment that may need to be incorporated into buildings such as fixtures where the useful life allowed for such equipment is shorter than the useful life of the building in which the equipment is incorporated, are included as part of the additional material provided on the companion website for the textbook.

Amortization. Similar to the treatment of a physical capital asset, certain intangibles with a useful life of more than twelve months are required to be capitalized and amortized over that useful life, rather than being allowed to be expensed in the Tax Year incurred.

Basis of Property and "the *Crane* Rule." A separate discussion of the Crane Rule is provided on the companion website for this textbook.

Interest. Investment interest is only available as a deduction to the extent of off-setting investment income. Suppose two people form a partnership by making capital contributions of $500,000 each. However, neither makes their capital contribution 100% in cash. In fact, each partner contributes $100,000 in cash and takes out a promissory note with the partnership for the remaining $400,000 of the promised capital contribution. The newly formed partnership then has $200,000 in cash and $800,000 in the two promissory notes of $400,000 each. In order to make sure their capital contribution transaction with the partnership has "economic substance," each promissory note bears interest at the prevailing market rate of interest for loans of this nature.

In this scenario, each partner may only deduct their interest expense paid on the promissory note up to and including the amount of any interest income received by the partnership. Accordingly, if Partner A pays $40,000 in interest on its promissory note to the partnership, and has investment interest exceeding $40,000 in investment income, then the $40,000 in interest paid to the partnership will be fully deductible. If Partner B, however, has no investment interest income in the tax year in which the $40,000 is paid to the partnership on the capital contribution promissory note, then the full amount of the $40,000 in investment interest expense will have to be carried forward to a tax year in which Partner B has off-setting investment interest income.

Management fees. When a partner in a partnership claims to be performing services for the partnership, for which the partnership pays that partner a fee, the question arises whether the transaction has economic substance, such that the fee received should be treated as regular income in the hands of the partner receiving the fee, and as a deductible business expense of the partnership, versus whether the transaction is merely a disguised distribution to that partner and, consequently, charged against that partner's basis in the partnership, which does not give rise to a business deduction because it is essentially in the form of a return of capital to the partner receiving that fee. In the case of a partner who is paid a management fee that is based on gross revenues received by the partnership on its income-producing properties, which that partner is, in fact, actively managed, the fact that the compensation arrangement is a fixed percentage of a variable number (i.e., the annual gross rental receipts from income-producing properties) does not make them guaranteed payments under IRC §704(c) and, consequently, subject to taxation under IRC §707(c). The characterization and tax treatment of "guaranteed payments," as defined under IRC §704(c), is discussed in the immediately following subsection.

704(c) guaranteed payments. Sometimes fees are paid to partners in exchange for services that might otherwise be provided, for compensation, by a third-party. In the example, above, describing an arrangement between a partnership and one of its partners for the provision of property management services to the partnership, the fact that the management fee is based on a percentage of annual gross income, where the percentage of the fee is fixed but the amount to which it is applied periodically is variable from period-to-period and tied, at least in part, to the job performance of the partner undertaking the property management, this is the most commonplace practice in the marketplace for property management services. However, sometimes, in order to attract capital in the form of partnership contributions, a partnership may offer to a specific partner or class of partners a guaranteed return on their capital contribution to the partnership regardless of and not tied to the economic performance of the partnership's income-producing properties. Such an arrangement – where the partner is receiving or entitled to a guaranteed payment not tied to the partnership's economic performance, is a "guaranteed payment" under IRC §704(c). The fundamental issue that remains somewhat up in the air is, assuming that the partner is receiving a "guaranteed payment" under IRC § 704(c), should that payment be treated as ordinary income to the partner or as a distributive share of capital (each of which treatments results in different tax treatments in the hands of the partnership).

Carried Interest Rule. The impact of the carried interest rule – particularly the manner in which it allows hedge fund managers to take capital distributions in a manner more closely resembling management fees but nonetheless taking them at much more advantageous capital gains rates – have been the subject of some considerable political and policy debates since the run-up to the 2012 presidential election. Given that this is a fluid issue and there is some likelihood, accordingly, that the favorable tax treatment afforded carried interest distributions may be subject to dramatic changes in the near future (possibly between when this textbook is completed but before its release date), the carried interest rule is covered in some detail on the companion website for this textbook.

Limitations on deductions

Partnership Basis. For purposes of this discussion, the term "partnership basis" relates both to a partnership's basis in property it acquires and to a partner's basis in her partnership interest.

Partnership's basis in acquired property. A real estate investment partnership that pays an unrelated party, in an arms-length transaction, for an operating property, the partnership's basis in the acquired property is the purchase price. However, the same partnership may not artificially inflate its basis in property it has acquired by paying more than the fair market value of the property to a related party. Among other things, such artificial boosting of the asset's basis would run afoul of the Sham-Transaction Doctrine, as well as the subsequent codification in the tax code of the Economic Substance Doctrine. These are two, very well-established doctrines of federal tax law. The Sham-Transaction Doctrine essentially holds that a taxpayer's transaction, and its asserted, attendant tax treatment of that transaction, will not be honored by the Internal Revenue Service if the underlying purpose of that transaction is the avoidance of taxation. The Economic Substance Doctrine holds that, in order for the taxpayer's asserted tax treatment of a specific transaction to be honored, that transaction must have "economic substance" independent of its tax consequences for the taxpayer.

Passive losses/tax shelters. See previous discussion under "*The Tax Reform Act of 1986's Passive Activity Loss Rules*," in the subsection titled Partnerships (including LLC's, limited partnerships, general partnerships, LLP's, and LLLPs), of the Liability/Management Issues in Structuring Ownership section of this chapter.

Investment interest. See subsection, above, titled *"Interest,"* in the section titled Deductions, regarding limitations on the deduction of investment interest.

Cancellation of debt income. Cancellation of indebtedness income is addressed on the companion website for this textbook. Generally speaking, however, the Internal Revenue Service treats the cancellation of a debt as if the debtor had earned the money that paid off the debt, treating the financial impact of the cancelation as "earned income."

Allocations of income

Promotes. See discussion on the companion website about *"Carried Interest Rule,"* referenced in the section of this chapter titled Deductions.

Sale issues
Long-term Capital Gains (IRC §1221 and §1231). Long-term capital gains – that is, the gain from the sale of a capital asset held for more than twelve months – are taxed at a lower rate (20% since 2013, after enactment of the American Taxpayer Relief Act of 2013 plus the addition of the 3.8% Medicare Tax) See the following discussion titled "3.8% Medicare Tax" regarding both the long-term capital gain rate increase from 15% to 20% for taxpayers in the top tax bracket, and the introduction of the new Medicare Tax. Even with the changes ushered in in 2013, the tax treatment of long-term capital gain is much more favorable than the marginal tax rate on "ordinary income," which at the top marginal tax rate is 39.5% on all Adjusted Taxable Income *over $464,850*, even before taking into account the application of the Alternative Minimum Tax. Because a partnership is a pass-through entity, a sale of a partnership's long-term capital assets is treated, in the hands of its partners, as if each partner sold its allocable share of the partnership's capital asset.

Rate differential. As mentioned earlier, long-term capital gains are taxed at a preferential rate compared with the gain from the sale of short-term capital assets or the taxation of ordinary income. While the raw number representing the difference in the tax treatment between long-term and short-term capital gain has diminished, the rate differential continues to favor the former treatment.

3.8% Medicare Tax. Under the American Taxpayer Relief Act of 2012, the top capital gain tax rate has been permanently increased to 20% (up from 15%) for single filers with incomes above $400,000 and married couples filing jointly with incomes exceeding $450,000. In addition, the new IRC Section 1411 imposes a 3.8% Medicare surtax on net investment income, which includes capital gains, results in an overall rate for higher-income taxpayers of 23.8%. The combination of the long-term capital gain rate increase from 15% to 20%, plus the impact of the 3.8% Medicare surtax, increases the net effective rate of taxation on long-term capital gains from its treatment in 2012 approximately 58%. Section 1402(a)(1) of the Health Care and Education Reconciliation Act of 2010 (Pub. L. 111–152, 124 Stat. 1029) added section 1411 to a new chapter 2A of Subtitle A (Income Taxes) of the Internal Revenue Code effective for taxable years beginning on or after January 1, 2013. Section 1411 imposes the 3.8% surtax on certain individuals, estates, and trusts. See sections 1411(a)(1) and (a)(2).

Recapture. The sale or disposition of a partnership asset may trigger certain events of recapture, essentially reversing favorable tax treatment of the asset while it was held by the partnership. Section 1245 of the Internal Revenue Code provides as follows:

(a) General rule

    (1) Ordinary income
        Except as otherwise provided in this section, if section 1245 property is disposed of the amount by which the lower of –

        (A) the recomputed basis of the property, or
        (B)

                (i) in the case of a sale, exchange, or involuntary conversion, the amount realized, or
                (ii) in the case of any other disposition, the fair market value of such property, exceeds the adjusted basis of such property shall be treated as ordinary income. Such gain shall be recognized notwithstanding any other provision of this subtitle.

    (2) Recomputed basis
        For purposes of this section –

        (A) In general
            The term "recomputed basis" means, with respect to any property, its adjusted basis recomputed by adding thereto all adjustments reflected in such adjusted basis on account of deductions (whether in respect of the same or other property) allowed or allowable to the taxpayer or to any other person for depreciation or amortization.
        (B) Taxpayer may establish amount allowed
            For purposes of subparagraph (A), if the taxpayer can establish by adequate records or other sufficient evidence that the amount allowed for depreciation or amortization for any period was less than the amount allowable, the amount added for such period shall be the amount allowed.
        (C) Certain deductions treated as amortization
            Any deduction allowable under section 179, 179A, 179B, 179C, 179D, 179E, 181, 190, 193, or 194 shall be treated as if it were a deduction allowable for amortization.

The Internal Revenue Service's *Audit Technique Manual* provides, in pertinent part, the following regarding the audit of a tax return where the taxpayer is reporting gain and/or other tax attributes from the partnership's disposition of a partnership asset:

Depreciation recaptured under IRC section 1245 or IRC section 1250 is probably the most common example of recapture treated as an unrealized receivable under IRC section 751(c). Other items of ordinary income recapture should be considered in evaluating the presence of unrealized receivables. Some examples include:

Amortization recapture on a disposition of an intangible asset. IRC section 197(f)(7).

Recapture resulting from a reduction in basis elected by a partner under the qualified real property indebtedness rules. IRC section 108(c).

Soil and water conservation expenditures recapture. IRC section 1252.

Ordinary gain recognized on the transfer of a franchise, trademark, or trade name. IRC section 1253.

Recapture of depletion, intangible drilling and development costs, and mining exploration costs. IRC sections 617 and 1254.

Accumulated earnings and profits recapture of certain controlled foreign corporations. IRC section 1248.

Ordinary income realized on a sale of market discount bonds or short term obligations. IRC sections 1278 and 1283.

Recapture of rental income accrued but deferred. IRC section 467.

The general rule is that any ordinary gain or loss that would be recognized by the partnership upon disposition of its property should be considered when determining the ordinary income component inherent in a sale of the partnership interest.

Dealer issues. The tax treatment of an entity deemed a "dealer" in real property disposing of a long-term capital asset will be different from the tax treatment of an entity that is not deemed to be a dealer.

Potential legislation. See the Supplemental Materials on the companion website to the textbook regarding any potential or pending legislation regarding Long-term capital gains (1221 and 1231).

Deferral of gain

Capital contributions. The transfer of real property into a partnership in exchange for a partnership interest does not, by itself, trigger the recognition of gain from the transfer by the transferee. Under Internal Revenue Code §721(a). Internal Revenue Code §722 provides that the transferee of such real property to a partnership takes as his basis in the partnership interest received in exchange of such real property his adjusted basis in such property plus the value of any cash also contributed with the real property. This means that the gain such transferee would have recognized had he sold that property for an amount exceeding his adjusted basis in the real property at the time of the sale will be deferred until such time as the transferee disposes of his partnership interest for an amount exceeding his adjusted basis there at the time of the partnership interest's disposition.

Like-kind exchanges. Internal Revenue Code §1031 provides rules deferring taxation on the disposition of a capital asset in what would otherwise constitute a Taxable Event in scenarios where the taxpayer exchanges "like-kind" property. Over time the rules governing the definition of what constitutes a qualifying like-kind exchange have been substantially relaxed. Among other things, current rules under § 1031 no longer require that the like-kind exchange occur simultaneously (following codification in the tax code of what is known as "the Starker rule") and also allowing tri-party like-kind exchanges, which has broadened the marketplace for § 1031 exchanges. In a § 1031 exchange, each taxpayer keeps their tax basis in the property being exchanged. However, inasmuch as it is extremely rare for the parties to a § 1031 exchange to value their respective exchange properties to be of precisely the same value, there is usually a contribution of cash by one party to the other, to even up the values being exchanged. The receipt of cash in a § 1031 exchange is taxable and is added to the basis of the property acquired by the party making the cash payment. A § 1031 exchange may have one additional advantage: Deferral of the imposition of the 3.8% Medicare surcharge tax.[45] See previous discussion, titled "3.8% Medicare Tax," in the Long-term Capital Gains (IRC §1221 and §1231) subsection of this chapter.

Installment Sales. A property owner's gain realized from the disposition of that property through an Installment Sales Agreement, allowing the Purchaser to make payments to the Seller of the Purchase Price over a period of years, will be allowed to spread the gain realized from the sale over that same period of years. Being able to defer the realized gain over the payment period may offer tax advantages to the Seller or, if the Seller is a partnership or other pass-through entity, for the partners or other equity participants in the selling entity. If the Installment Sales Agreement does not specify an interest component in the installment sales payments to be made by the Purchaser, the Internal Revenue Service may impute a rate of interest and interest component to the installment sales payments, which will change the nature of the gain realized by the Seller. Since the sale of a long-term capital asset is afforded more favorable tax treatment than the receipt of interest income, it is in the Seller's best interest to specify that portion of the installment sales payments received between the amount representing the purchase price for the property and the component representing interest on the amount of the Purchase Price being deferred through the installment sales payments. However, just as the Internal Revenue Service has the power to impute an interest rate, and the attendant interest component of the installment sales payments based on that imputed interest rate, the IRS similarly has the power to scrutinize the basis upon which the parties have agreed, in the Installment Sales Agreement, to allocate the payment of the principal amount of the Purchase Price and the interest component.

Notes

1. Jacobs, Jane, *The Nature of Economies*, Modern Library, a Random House imprint, New York, NY (2000), pgs. 110–111.

2. National Commission on Fiscal Responsibility and Reform, *The Moment of Truth: Report of the National Commission on Fiscal Responsibility and Reform*, December 1, 2010. Found at www.fiscalcommission.gov/sites/fiscalcommission.gov/files/documents/ TheMomentofTruth12_1_2010.pdf

   In the weeks and months to come, countless advocacy groups and special interests will try mightily through expensive, dramatic, and heart-wrenching media assaults to exempt themselves from shared sacrifice and common purpose. The national interest, not special interests, must prevail. We urge leaders and citizens with principled concerns about any of our recommendations to follow what we call the Becerra Rule: Don't shoot down an idea without offering a better idea in its place.

3. For a discussion on some of the causes and consequences of the 2008 Great Recession, see Chapter 9.

4. In the worlds of corporate finance and investing, "debt" and "equity" are generally referred to as "bonds" and "common stock" but the concepts are identical. The following discussion, excerpted from Graham and Dodd's classic treatise, *Security Analysis*, proves instructive in understanding the fundamental differences between debt and equity, *"and everything in-between"*:

Securities are customarily divided into the two main groups of bonds and stocks, with the latter subdivided into preferred stocks and common stocks. The first and basic division recognizes and conforms to the fundamental legal distinction between the creditors' position and the partner's position. The bondholder has a fixed and prior claim for principal and interest; the stockholder assumes the major risks and shares in the profits of ownership. It follows that a higher degree of safety should inhere in bonds as a class, while greater opportunity of speculative gain – to offset the greater hazard – is to be found in the field of stocks. It is this contrast, of both legal status and investment character, as between the two kinds of issues, which provides the point of departure for the usual textbook treatment of securities.

Graham, Benjamin and David L. Dodd, *Security Analysis: Principles and Techniques*, McGraw Hill, New York, NY (2009). *Discussions in both this chapter, and the chapter that follows on financing transactions, will return to the general themes presented in Graham and Dodd's treatise.*

5. Again, reinforcing the "inherent tautology" of this textbook and teaching real estate law through the framework of The Development Process, and without getting too far into the weeds at this juncture about fundamental Contract Law principles like "offer and acceptance" and "due consideration," if you and a friend are at a football match (as in soccer), and because you don't have $10 your friend offers to buy a beer for you (because that's what beers cost at major sporting venues in the United States these days), premised upon your promise to pay your cash-flush friend back that $10 the next day, even though you did not technically "borrow" the $10 from your friend and then pay for that $10 beer yourself, that $10 nonetheless represents a one-day loan, without interest. In other words: debt. However, you would have to know Contract Law in the state in which the football stadium is located to determine, with certitude, whether this scenario actually constitutes a legal debt, which requires that, at some juncture, you are or will become familiar with Chapter 7.

6. Melnick, Richard, "Tax Considerations in Real Estate Transactions." *Guest Lecture*, Foundations of Real Estate Development, FINA-6290–012, October 29, 2014.

7. For information regarding the legal theory of "corporate personhood," see related materials on the companion website to the textbook.

8. For information regarding the relationship between the Interstate Commerce Clause of the U.S. Constitution as it relates to the rights of individual states to enact and enforce their own state laws provided they're neither intended nor administered in a manner that limits interstate commerce, see the related material on the companion website for the textbook.

9. The voting rights of shareholders in a C Corporation may vary from state to state.

10. Massachusetts General Laws, Chapter 156C, Massachusetts Limited Liability Company Act, Section 22. Emphasis added.

11. For additional material on the joint-and-several liabilities of general partners, see related materials on the companion website for this textbook.

12. See Chapter 11 for a general discussion about the law of principal and agent, as well as related material about the authority of general partners to legally bind each other in related material on the companion website for this textbook.

13. Except in the case of the District of Columbia, which under its Unincorporated Business Tax ordinance requires general partnerships to file returns for and pay taxes on its gross receipts from activities in the District.

14. Official Code of Georgia Annotated, §14–8–2(6.1) (2010).

15. Uniform Partnership Act (1997), National Conference of Commissioners on Uniform State Laws, Chicago, IL, adopted at NCCUSL's Annual Conference Meeting in Its One-Hundred-And-Fifth Year, San Antonio, TX, July 12–July 19, 1996, and approved by the American Bar Association, San Antonio, TX, February 4, 1997 (1997), pgs. 10–11.

16. For cases illustrating how the 704(b) Special Allocations work, see related materials in the companion website for this textbook.

17. No taxpayer ever fully eludes the payment of federal taxes. However, there are a number of strategies for deferring into future years the obligation to pay taxes.

18. The IRS's passive activity loss rules interpreting the provisions of the Tax Reform Act of 1986 relating to the limitation of partnership losses from tax-advantaged transactions (aka "tax-shelter" deals) is provided on the companion website for this textbook.

19. Zwick, Gary A., "Partnership Interests in Estate and Trust Administration." *Cleveland Bar Journal* Vol 78, No. 8 (June 2007), reprinted by the author at www.walterhav.com/pubs/GAZ%20Article%20in%20Cleveland%20Bar%20Journal%20(00600032).PDF.

20. Internal Revenue Service Regulations, *§ 301.7701–3 Classification of certain business entities.*

21. Additional information regarding real estate investments trusts (REITs) is provided in the last Feature Box in Chapter 9 regarding the creation of Empire Real Estate Trust, a REIT that became the owner of the Empire State Building through a share exchange with the prior owner, Empire State Building Associates, and in additional material developed for the companion website for the textbook.

22. FTSE EPRA/NAREIT Global Real Estate Index Series, as of June 3, 2015. Found at www.ftse.com/products/indices/epra-nareit.

23. FTSE EPRA/NAREIT US Super Liquid Index Fact Sheet, May 29, 2015. Found at www.ftse.com/Analytics/FactSheets/temp/b4b94f32-c747–46de-a27a-3eb8795a7f91.pdf.

24. Internal Revenue Code §856(a)(1).

25. Internal Revenue Code §856(a)(2).

26. Internal Revenue Code §856(a)(3).

27. Internal Revenue Code §856(a)(4).

28. Internal Revenue Code §856(a)(5).

29. Internal Revenue Code §856(a)(6).

30. Internal Revenue Code §856(a)(7).

31. Internal Revenue Code §857(a) and §§ 561 through 565.

32. Internal Revenue Code §856(c)(1).

33. Internal Revenue Code §859.

34. Internal Revenue Code §857(a)(1).

35. IRC §511.

36. For additional material regarding this requirement, see the companion website for the textbook.

37. As of March 31, 2015, for example, TIAA-CREF had an over $2 billion Net Asset Value in its Real Estate Securities Fund. Audited Schedules of Investments, TIAA-CREF Funds, Real Estate and Fixed-Income Funds, March 31, 2015.

38. American Bar Association's Tax Section Comment Letter to the Commissioner of the Internal Revenue Service dated January 19, 2010, regarding "Comments Concerning Partnership Allocations Permitted Under Section 514(c)(9)(E)." Found at www.klehr.com/C7756B/assets/files/News/ABA%20Section%20of%20Taxation%20Comments%20Concerning%20Partnership%20Allocations%20Permitted%20Under%20Section%20514(c)(9)(E)2.pdf.

39. Reg. § 1.514(c)-2(b)(1)(i), -2(c)(2).

40. See, e.g., ABA Tax Section Asks for Changes in Guidance Regarding Effect of Notice 90–41 on Acquisition Indebtedness, 91 Tax Notes Today 13–11 (January 16, 1991) (hereafter referred to as the "ABA 90–41 Comments"); N.Y. State Bar Says UBTI Rules Carry Too Big a Stick, 91 Tax Notes Today 70–30 (March 29, 1991) (hereafter referred to as the "NYSBA 90–41 Comments"); California Bar Suggests Elimination of Qualified Allocation Rules, 92 Tax Notes Today 117–146 (June 5, 1992); AICPA Criticizes Proposed Regs as Unnecessarily Complex, 93 Tax Notes Today 87–21 (April 21, 1993); NYSBA Submits Report on Debt-Financed Income Regs, 93 Tax Notes Today 94–21 (Apr. 30, 1993) (hereafter referred to as the "NYSBA Prop. Reg. Comments"); NYSBA Submits Report on Taxation of Pension Funds, 97 Tax Notes Today 34–39 (February 20, 1997).

41. Whether and how the IRS will allow deductions for expenses incurred in pursuing a business opportunity, whether or not the taxpayer is deemed to be "in the business" of real estate development, is addressed on the companion website for the textbook.

42. As a general principal, a taxpayer is allowed to off-set gross income received by the aggregate amount of expenses incurred, directly and indirectly, in the production of that gross income.

43. Deductions for depreciation, as well as the amortization of expenditures for intangible assets, such as intellectual property, are governed by specific sections of the Internal Revenue Code and IRS Regulations promulgated thereunder. More detailed information regarding the depreciation of capital assets and amortization of non-capital expenditures is provided on the companion website for the textbook.

44. The specific tax treatments of ground lease payments is discussed in the companion website for the textbook.

45. 26 C.F.R. §1.1411–10(g), effective December 2, 2013.

CHAPTER 9

Financing real estate transactions

The most colossal miscalculation of the 1920s was the Empire State Building, which remained three-quarters empty for a decade after its opening in 1931 and did not turn an annual profit until 1950. The isolated tower at Thirty-fourth Street and Fifth Avenue remained the world's tallest building until the 1970s. Far from the clustered highrises near Grand Central, the Empire State was extraordinary in its size and siting, but was in every other way a standard speculative development. Excellent documentation exists for many aspects of the project, and this rich record allows us to see how economic considerations affected every aspect of its design. Indeed, because the site was so large, 197 x 425 feet, the building did not even fill the maximum zoning envelope on its lower floors. The Empire State demonstrated the principle of form follows finance better than most skyscrapers.[1]

In *Form Follows Finance: Skyscrapers and Skylines in New York and Chicago*, author Carol Willis, an architectural historian and the founder and executive director of The Skyscraper Museum in New York City, makes a cogent and well-documented argument that it is neither lofty design inspiration nor marketing hubris that accounts for the appearance of the magnificent skyscrapers and skylines of Chicago and New York, respectively; the form of these buildings and skylines are a function of the nuts and bolts of how these buildings are financed. Willis's thesis is well articulated in the evolution of the Empire State Building, from conception to completion, although the building's saga from completion and occupancy to profitability might lead one to conclude that the ultimate plan for financing and constructing the final design for the building was, itself, ill conceived.

Whether that assessment is accurate is addressed in a series of feature boxes that appear throughout this chapter, as many valuable lessons can be learned from the history of the Empire State Building, from Idea Generation – the first Sub-Phase in the Project Conception Phase of The Development Process – in 1928, to the present-day Ownership and Property Management Phase. See, for example in this regard, the first Empire State Building feature box, "Empire State Building, 1929: Raskob and du Pont's Investment Letter to Bail Out Floyd Brown's Purchase of the Waldorf-Astoria Hotel and Develop The Empire State Building in Its Place," as well as the penultimate Empire State Building feature box, "Empire State Building, 2009: Repositioning New York City's Largest Commercial Building: The 'Greening' of The Empire State Building," regarding the Empire State Building's Ownership and Property Management Phase.

As stated in Chapter 2, one of the earliest Sub-Phases in the Project Conception Phase of The Development Process is Develop Exit and Funding Strategies: How Will "the Idea" Pay Off? This Sub-Phase provides, in pertinent part, as follows:

A Developer should never embark upon The Development Process without first knowing, or at least having an inkling, about the Exit Strategy: The specific manner in which the Developer will receive compensation or otherwise extract value from the Project in a way that properly compensates the Developer for the value created.

Through the lens of the history and ongoing ownership and property management of the Empire State Building, as described in a chronological series of feature boxes describing critical periods in the development and changes in ownership of the operating property, Chapter 9 provides critical insights – through hindsight – about how developers go about implementing their funding strategy. These Empire State Building feature boxes collectively demonstrate how, as the financing mechanisms became increasingly sophisticated, and as different sources of equity and debt to financing real estate transactions became available, a property's ownership and management was able to optimize gross incomes and maximize profitability. It is clear, from the Empire State Building example that, as time passed, each new phase in the conveyance of ownership interests and/or control of the property was undertaken in a manner that was increasingly consistent with the goals and objectives for the Project. Through adherence to The Development Process as a framework for the development and financing of real estate projects, it is hoped that with each step forward the Developer will get closer to fully realizing, and benefiting monetarily from, its Exit Strategy. This chapter should be read in conjunction with Chapter 8, which also addresses legal issues relating to the creation and operation of Development Entities, the management and tax advantages of different ownership structures, and the rights and liabilities of parties to real estate development transactions.

As Carol Willis's book makes clear, however, having a clear Exit Strategy has often been *a lesson learned in hindsight*, as ambitious real estate developers and investors have not always proceeded so pragmatically as opposed to, as the saying goes, "flying by the seat of their pants."

The men who erected and owned the Empire State Building did not originate the project. In 1928, an architect and developer, Floyd Brown, contracted to buy the famous but fading Waldorf-Astoria Hotel on Fifth Avenue and Thirty-fourth Street for $14,000,000, the highest price recorded in the city that year. In December, the *Real Estate Record and Builders Guide* published a rendering by the architects Shreve and Lamb Associates for a mixed-use building containing about 2,000,000 square feet of rental space with the lower twenty-five floors devoted to shops and lofts and the top twenty-two to offices. Through this publicity, Brown hoped to attract major tenants or investors whose commitments would help him meet his next $1.5 million mortgage payment; when these failed to materialize, he defaulted. Intrigued by the site, Brown's banker, Louis Kaufman, approached his longtime associates Pierre S. du Pont and John J. Raskob, two of the country's richest men. On August 28, 1929, Raskob sent a letter of understanding to Kaufman outlining their proposed participation.[2]

Contrast architect and builder Floyd Brown's approach to developing what he envisioned would eventually become one of Manhattan's largest commercial buildings, starting with his purchase of the Waldorf-Astoria Hotel as the Subject Site for realizing this vision, with the Phases and Sub-Phases in The Development Process, as described in Chapters 2 and 3, respectively.

Identify and Secure Take-Out (Permanent) Financing Commitment (Figure 2.44). As suggested elsewhere in this chapter early in the Project Conception Phase of The Development Process, the Developer should have formulated its Exit Strategy, which, in turn, should inform its Funding Strategy. (See Project Conception Phase, Sub-Phase titled Develop Exit and Funding Strategies: How Will "the Idea" Pay Off?) The Exit Strategy should determine to what extent the Developer will continue to participate in the ownership and management of the Project after the Project has reached and maintained Stabilization (as defined in the Project Completion and Stabilization Phase of The Development Process). The Developer's Exit Strategy may run the gamut from an outright sale of the Project to a Buyer identified very early in The Development Process, to continuing to own or hold an ownership interest in the Project, deriving periodic Management Fees in consideration of the Developer providing Property Management Services to the Project, receiving periodic distributions of Distributable Cash from the Development Entity, and receiving additional, episodic distributions of Distributable Cash upon strategic refinancings of the Project's Permanent Financing. Whatever the mechanism for realizing the Developer's Exit Strategy, it will also serve as the exit strategy for the Construction Lender. Accordingly, the form of the commitment from the entity providing the Take-Out Financing for the Project, its form and substance must be satisfactory to the Construction Lender, which will be relying on that Take-Out Financing Commitment in making its own commitment for the Construction Loan.[3]

From the accounting in Willis's *Form Follows Finance*, Brown didn't appear to have planned out his next few steps following his acquisition of the Waldorf-Astoria Hotel, much less given too much thought to his ultimate Exit Strategy for the Project as he conceived it (as depicted by the Shreve and Lamb Associates rendering). As the excerpt from *Form Follows Finance* suggests, it appears only by happenstance that du Pont and Raskob became financially involved in the redevelopment of the hotel through Brown's banker, when Brown defaulted on the mortgage on his acquisition of the Waldorf-Astoria property.

By way of further contrast with how Brown went about developing and marketing "the Idea" (see Project Conception Phase of The Development Process in Chapter 2), Chapter 3 provides even more details about the critical importance of developing an Exit Strategy, as well as a concomitant Funding Strategy, as early as possible in The Development Process, and certainly *well before actually taking title to the Subject Site*. Absent unlimited resources paired with unlimited foresight about the future of real estate markets and submarkets, no Developer would act as precipitously as Brown did in 1928.

Develop Exit and Funding Strategies. Just as with the selection of the Project Delivery Method, crafting the Developer's Exit Strategy, as well as the Funding Strategy for the Development Entity and the Project, respectively, has wide-ranging implications for many critical steps in The Development Process. So, while completing this task may not have any short-term implications for the Developer in the early part of the Project Conception Phase, every Phase of The Development Process will be impacted, starting with the Negotiate Acquisition and Development (A&D) Financing Commitment of the Project Conception Phase (see this Sub-Phase). The type of funding coming into the Project and/or the Development Entity, if it's already been created, whether equity, debt, a combination and/or hybrid of the two, and how those investments in the Project are expected to be paid a return and repaid will be expressed initially in the Developer's Exit Strategy and Funding Strategy, respectively. Each participant in the Acquisition and Development (A&D) Financing will have tax implications from the nature and extent of their investment (see Chapter 8 in this regard), and will insist that the documentation evidencing their investment, in whatever form, reflects their investment intent and return expectations (see, in this regard, Chapter 9). Additionally, the Preliminary Development Budget pro forma of the Project Conception Phase should reflect both the Exit Strategy and the Funding Strategy, respectively.[4]

Brown's strategy, if it may be imbued with such lofty forethought, research, and analysis rising to the level of an actual "strategy," was to commission an architecture firm of some repute, specializing in commercial buildings in Manhattan, to develop a modestly detailed program and a charcoal rendering, in the prevailing style of the time, of what Brown's new building might look like when completed. This approach might best be described as a very soft marketing campaign: Brown expected his phone would be ringing off the hook with inquiries from prospective tenants and investors, respectively, based on the article appearing in the *Real Estate Record and Builders Guide* in December 1928.

As elaborated in some detail in Chapters 2 and 3, respectively, in order to secure financing of any kind – equity, debt, or some hybrid or combination of the two – *a development project must be financially feasible*. The process of determining a Project's "financial feasibility" is an iterative one that very much mirrors The Development Process itself. Brown, however, didn't appear to be quite so methodical, or analytical, as to undertake such analysis before purchasing the Waldorf-Astoria Hotel. The fact that the Empire State Building was ever built is remarkable, as will be demonstrated in the Empire State Building feature boxes that follow. However, hindsight being 20/20, its ascension as one of the most profitable and successful commercial office buildings in the world now seems to have been inevitable.

Chapter outline

Chapter introduction
The evolution of equity and debt for real estate projects
The role of banks in financing real estate transactions
The rise of institutional private equity
The demise of the savings and loan industry and emergence of capital markets financing

Chapter introduction

Obviously, there are all sorts of reasons, good and bad, why a deal might be brought to you. It's important to understand these motives up front. Some of my best deals were brought to me because people knew I would include them as partners in the deal, and they wanted a chance to be on the equity side. (One of the big lures of real estate is the relative ease of becoming an equity owner, since each project has its own legal structure and is run as a separate business.) By contrast, if they took the deal to a big company, there'd be little chance of that big company allowing a small player to participate in a meaningful way in the ownership structure.[5]

In teaching real estate development and finance to undergraduate finance majors, William Poorvu's *The Real Estate Game: The Intelligent Guide to Decision-Making and Investment* has been a valuable companion to a traditional real estate development textbook. In this single paragraph excerpted from the book, Poorvu raises – mostly indirectly – a number of critical questions, the answers to which impact tremendously the financing of real estate transactions. Reframing the excerpt from *The Real Estate Game* from the perspective of the Developer, rather than from Poorvu's perspective as the real estate investor, the following are just a few of the questions that might provide a frame of reference for the Developer in thinking about *how, when, why and from whom* to bring money into The Development Process:

1. Who should the Developer consider bringing into the transaction during the Project Conception Phase of The Development·Process?
2. Should the Developer only be seeking a necessary infusion of early stage capital – more along the lines of a passive investor – or seek to attract a stakeholder interested in investing capital, knowledge, credibility, and expertise (or some combination thereof)?

3. When should the Developer begin the process of vetting potential, early stage investors in the Project, and how much cultivation will such prospects require to be converted from having potential interest in the Project to being ready to contribute capital to it?
4. How will bringing an equity participant into the Project during the Project Conception Phase change the decision-making process for the Developer throughout the balance of The Development Process?
5. If the potential real estate investor is only interested in a relatively short-term investment to help the Project get off the ground, and does not want to be exposed to or involved in the evolution of the concept or the decision making for the Project going forward, what's the best way to meet the investor's specific goals while still characterizing this short-term investment as equity?
6. How will the presence of an early stage equity investor impact raising additional funding for the Project, both debt and additional equity, if necessary?

One of the most valuable lessons students and readers should take away from this chapter generally, and the foregoing questions specifically, is the critical importance of understanding, with complete certitude, what each investor's goals are when considering making an investment in a real estate development project. It does not matter how deeply the Developer believes in the Project if the Developer is trying to talk an investor into an investment structure or mechanism that does not satisfy that investor's goals and objectives in making an investment in the Project. In point of fact, Floyd Brown appeared so passionate about his idea for the Waldorf-Astoria site he plunged ahead with complete confidence as to the merits of the transaction, but little clue about how to finance it or whether it would make him money as conceived. These and many other issues regarding the financing of real estate transactions are answered in this chapter.

Turning back to what is arguably the most important and most compelling question for a Developer to answer in seeking to finance a real estate transaction: *What does my investor want out of this deal?*

WHAT DETERMINES CAP RATES? BY PETER LINNEMAN

In corporate finance, equity valuation is summarized by the price-earnings (P/E) ratio, which is the ratio of a firm's value (e.g., stock price per share) divided by its earnings. In real estate, valuation is generally described by the capitalization rate (familiarly, cap rates), rather than income multiples. The concept of the cap rate is simply the inverse of the traditional valuation multiple. That is, the cap rate is the income return of real estate, and is defined as stabilized net operating income (NOI) divided by the value of the property (purchase price, either anticipated or actual). The real estate industry's usage of cap rates reflects its historic linkage to the bond market, as real estate derives its income from future tenant promissory income streams. So just as the bond market commonly quotes yield, as opposed to multiples, when describing bond values, the real estate industry generally refers to cap rates.

The cap rate (C) for a stabilized property can be shown to theoretically equal the discount rate (r) for the property's cash stream minus the perpetuity growth rate (g) of those cash streams.

$$C = r-g.$$

The discount rate (r) is equal to the **real long-term risk-free rate** (Rf), plus **expected economy-wide inflation** (p), plus the **operating risk of the asset** (o), plus the **liquidity premium** associated with the asset's illiquidity versus the risk free rate (l):

$$R = Rf + p + o + l.$$

The expected **long-term cash-flow growth rate** (g) is expressed as the expected **real cash-flow growth rate** (c) plus **economy-wide inflation** (p):

$$G = c + p.$$

Thus, basic algebra reveals that the cap rate is theoretically defined as:

$$C = Rf + o + l - c.$$

Note that economy-wide inflation cancels out, as it is an equal component of both the risk-free rate and expected long-term cash-flow growth. Thus, inflation does not theoretically affect cap rates per se, as inflation increases both the discount rate and the cash-flow growth rate by the same amount. The cap rate is therefore equal to the real long-term risk-free rate, plus the property's operating risk and liquidity premiums, minus the real perpetuity expected cash-flow growth rate.

In analyzing these four components, the real perpetuity expected cash-flow growth rate (c) is the least volatile component of the cap rate. This is because "perpetuity" is, by definition, a very long time. The property-specific operating risk component (o) is tied closely to the macro or regional economy and is generally counter-cyclical. Specifically, *cap rates tend to fall due to a decline in operating risk as the economy moves through the recovery phase of the business cycle.* Turning to interest rates, *historically, the real long-term risk-free rate (Rf) has been fairly constant at 200–250 bps*, but has been abnormally low, and at times, even negative during the financial crisis. This reduction of 200–275 bps is historically unique, reflecting both the extraordinary flight to safety during the financial crisis, as well as unprecedented monetary policy activism. As the real return rose by about 100–150 bps since July 2013, it created upward pressure on cap rates, which was observed in both REIT and high-quality private asset pricing. However, *our assessment is that the major movements of cap rates are attributable to changes in the liquidity premium (l). This component is highly counter-cyclical, plunging as the economy and capital markets boom and skyrocketing when they contract.*

In 2015, we were among a minority that believes that cap rates, and equity multiples in general, will basically hold, even as interest rates rise. As support for this position we note that when value multiples were at similar levels in late 2006 and early 2007, the short-term rate was 5.3% and the 10 year yield was at 4.7%. That is, we know that low cap rates (and high multiples) can coexist with high interest rates. But for this to be the case, there must be an increased flow of funds, particularly of debt.

People correctly argue that, all other things being equal, a rise in interest rates should cause cap rates to rise by increasing the weighted cost of capital. But it is important to understand that "other things" do not remain equal as interest rates rise. In particular, as interest rates rise from artificially low levels, borrowers have a reduced incentive to borrow, while lenders have a notably increased incentive to lend. *This incentive to lend manifests itself by changing "other things," including offering higher loan-to-value ratios, slower amortization, longer periods of interest-only payments, reduced covenants, narrower debt spreads, reduced underwriting standards, etc.* These factors result in an increased flow of debt as rates rise from artificially low levels. This results in a reduced weighted cost of capital and more investor money chasing a limited supply of NOI and properties, resulting in higher prices. This was the case in 2006–2007, when high interest rates stimulated a dramatic flow of debt.

In 2015, there was an extraordinary amount of liquidity pent up in the largest money center banks. Hence as interest rates rise, these banks will notably increase lending incentives in order to increase the volume of loan originations. The resulting flood of debt, based on our research, will more than offset any negative impact of higher interest rates on cap rates.

The problem is that when the flow of debt eventually comes to an end, the process dramatically reverses. The contraction of debt is felt dramatically in the real estate sector, even when real estate is in supply-and-demand balance. This is because mortgage loans are roughly 60% of the real estate capital stack. As lenders pull back on originations, prospective buyers, as well as owners seeking to refinance, are negatively and dramatically affected. If they are unable to refinance, existing owners face a capital shortfall, which is simply too large to be "instantaneously" filled. And to the extent it is filled, it is with expensive equity rather than cheap debt. This causes the cost of capital to temporarily skyrocket, forcing transactions to halt. As transactions cease, and loans default, the only transactions occurring are at temporarily depressed values to opportunistic equity buyers. These low value marks (i.e., high cap rates), in turn, further discourage lending, creating a feedback loop.

Given real estate's high overall leverage, even a 5–10% cyclical pullback in outstanding debt is simply too large to be absorbed without a severe impact on liquidity and pricing. This phenomenon underscores the fact that the flow of debt funds – more so than interest rates – is the dominant determinant of real estate pricing, as even very low rates cannot offset the absence of debt in terms of the weighted averaged cost of capital.

The Fed's artificially low interest rate policy has resulted in a lot of frustrated "would be" investors. These are people and firms who would like to borrow at these low rates, but find that they are not credit worthy, and hence are unable to get loans. Most have become so frustrated that they have stopped trying. As the Fed allows rates to rise, we will see an upward movement along the debt supply curve, and lenders will have greater incentive to lend. Thus, higher interest rates result in more funds flowing to borrowers. The result will be fewer frustrated "would be" borrowers, more outstanding debt, and a great flow of debt that will offset any impact of rising interest rates on cap rates (and equity multiples). Hence, it is not hard to understand why even as rates rise from artificially low levels, more debt will be issued.

The foregoing discussion of cap rates was provided by Professor Linneman for use in the textbook at the author's request. Emphasis in the above text was added by the author.[6]

No matter how good "the Idea" is or how adept the Developer is at exploring it fully and improving upon the Idea throughout the early phases of The Development Process, if the Developer is unable to secure necessary financing along the way – and assuming the Developer is unable to fully finance the Project out of its own capital, eschewing the OPM (Other People's Money) that is typically the lifeblood of all real estate development activities – the Developer's Idea will forever remain just that: An idea. The financing of real estate transactions is the difference-maker between thinking and doing; between conceptualization and execution. Without the right amounts and type(s) of financing at critical moments in The Development Process, all of the Developer's early efforts during the Project Conception Phase will all be for naught. See The Evolution of Debt and Equity in this regard.

By the same token, however, depending on the Developer's negotiating leverage – or lack thereof – and level of desperation to see the Idea through to its logical conclusion, it is possible for the Developer to give up far too much control over, and to retain far too little equity in, the Project to reap the benefits originally envisioned in crafting and evolving the Idea. In this regard, it's entirely possible for a Developer to shepherd the Idea through The Development Process and, once the Project has entered the Ownership and Property Management Phase, look back and ponder "where did I go wrong on this Project," not because the Project is not a success but because the Developer did not manage to retain a sufficient ownership stake in the Project and decision-making authority going forward to justify the effort expended getting the Project across the finish line. That is why the Exit and Funding Strategies, as introduced in Chapter 2, are intended to identify the "specific manner in which the Developer will receive compensation or otherwise extract value from the Project *in a way that properly compensates the Developer for the value created*." [Emphasis added.]

As stated in Chapter 2, one of the earliest Sub-Phases in the Project Conception Phase of The Development Process is Develop Exit and Funding Strategies: How Will "the Idea" Pay Off? This Sub-Phase provides, in pertinent part, as follows:

> A Developer should never embark upon The Development Process without first knowing, or at least having an inkling, about the Exit Strategy: the specific manner in which the Developer will receive compensation or otherwise extract value from the Project in a way that properly compensates the Developer for the value created.

Chapters 2 and 3, respectively, provide students and readers with a roadmap for how the Developer should go about implementing its Funding Strategy in a manner consistent with the Developer's goals and objectives for the Project, and that fulfills the Developer's Exit Strategy. This chapter provides a comprehensive survey of how and from where funds may be secured to fund real estate transactions, as well as a solid understanding of the legal and regulatory framework through which such funding becomes available, along with specific examples of ownership and financing structures through the Empire State Building feature boxes. Chapter 9 should be read in conjunction with Chapter 8, which also addresses legal issues relating to the governance of and rights and liabilities of parties to real estate development transactions.

THE EMPIRE STATE BUILDING, 1929: RASKOB'S AUGUST 29, 1929, INVESTMENT LETTER TO BAIL OUT FLOYD BROWN'S PURCHASE OF THE WALDORF-ASTORIA HOTEL AND DEVELOP THE EMPIRE STATE BUILDING IN ITS PLACE

First, it is important to reiterate that John Raskob's 1929 letter:

1. was sent to Louis Kaufman, and not to Floyd Brown, who had purchased and owned, subject to a purchase mortgage held by Kaufman's bank, the Waldorf-Astoria Hotel, and that Brown was in default of the promissory note, putting Brown's title to the property in jeopardy.
2. was *not* proposing to financially bail out Brown but *to financially bail out the development opportunity* to create Manhattan's largest-ever commercial building on the hotel site, with Baskom and his investment partner, Pierre S. du Pont, having a controlling interest in the project going forward and providing a substantial amount of the funding.

During these discussions, an important change of program was explored: transforming the project into a major office tower. Raskob's letter included a sheet of figures comparing the projected costs and income of two alternatives: fifty-five and eighty-story buildings. The fifty-five-story scheme would contain 29,000,000 cubic feet, cost $45,000,000, and generate an income of $5,120,000 – the equivalent of a gross return of 11.4 percent. The eighty-story building added 330,000 square feet of rentable space, producing an overall income of $6,300,000, and promised a gross return of 12.6 percent. Such numbers were persuasive arguments for greater height.[7]

In Raskob's August 28, 1929, letter to Kaufman, du Pont and Raskob's conclusion about the best development program to pursue (see, in this regard, Chapter 2, Project Conception Phase, Preliminary Program Sub-Phase, Revised Preliminary Program (for Hypothetical, 300-unit Multifamily Rental Project) Sub-Phase, and Updated Program Sub-Phase, respectively, and the same Sub-Phases under the Project Conception Phase in Chapter 3).

> Our present tentative feeling is that we should be able to build a building, the cubicle content of which will be about 34,000,000 feet at $1.00 per cubic foot *including all charges of every kind such as interest, cost of demolition, architect and builder's commission, fees paid for securing mortgages, rental fees, etc. etc.*, which would mean a total cost of not more than $34,000,000, which added to the land cost of $16,000,000 would give a total cost of $50,000,000.[8]

The excerpt from Raskob's letter to Kaufman is instructive for several reasons. First, the precariousness of the language, as author Willis suggests, reflects Raskob and du Pont's caution in undertaking this Herculean project and, consequently, could have made their commitment to Kaufman unenforceable as a matter of law. As it ends up, Raskob and du Pont went forward with their scheme to build the Empire State Building on the site of the Waldorf-Astoria Hotel and, consequently, the legal enforceability of the letter never had to be tested.

Second, it should be of interest to the student and reader to be exposed to the litany of Project Budget expenses Raskob provides in the August 28, 1929, letter to Kaufman, which have been placed in bold for the convenience of students and readers. Note, however, that this letter states "including all charges of every kind" and concludes with ". . . etc. etc., . . ." such that the clear intention of Raskob and du Pont in sending this letter to Kaufman appears to be that the ". . . total cost of not more than $34,000,000, . . ." is intended to and must cover all expenses that would be included in Total Development Cost (see, in this regard, Chapter 2, Project Conception Phase, Preliminary Development Budget pro forma Sub-Phase, and the same Sub-Phase under the Project Conception Phase in Chapter 3).

In her discussion in *Form Follows Finance* of the decision by Raskob and du Pont to become involved in the financing, with Kaufman and, eventually, others, of what became the Empire State Building, Willis includes a set of financial calculations that was attached to the Raskob letter, which includes a handwritten note found in du Pont's copy of the letter that presumably did not appear on Kaufman's copy of the Raskob letter. The attachment itself enumerates the debt financing for both the fifty-five-story and eighty-story schemes developed by Raskob and du Pont, in response to the fifty-story scheme Brown conceived, presumably with the assistance of his architects, Shreve and Lamb Associates.

	56 Storeys [sic]		80 Storeys [sic]
Land	16,000,000		16,000,000
29,000,000 on [sic] ft. @ $1.00	29,000,000	34,000,000 cu. ft. @	
		$1.00 (25 addtl storeys [sic] 80 x 240	34,000,000
Total Cost	45,000,000		50,000,000
1st. Mtg. (5½% — 2% S.F.	25,000,000		27,500,000
Balance	20,000,000		22,500,000
2nd Mtg (6½% with 20% of Com.) (Stk as bonus)	10,000,000		12,500,000
Balance	10,000,000		10,000,000
Pfd. Srk [sic] (7% with 80% of Com. Bonus)	10,000,000		10,000,000

As far as the structure of Raskob and du Pont in Raskob's direct participation in the financial arrangement contemplated by Raskob's letter of August 28, 1929, in a footnote to *Form Follows Finance*, Willis offers the following insight:

> A copy [of the Raskob letter] in Pierre du Pont's files includes his handwritten annotations of the sums to be paid by the different investors (lower right); of the $10,000,000 of equity (preferred stock), du Pont and Raskob were to contribute half, with the remainder to be raised by Kaufman and his associates. For the $12,500,000 needed for the second mortgage, du Pont and Raskob would jointly underwrite $1,250,000, Kaufman et al. an equal amount, and the remaining $10,000,000 [would] be taken by the Chatham and Phoenix affiliate. There is extensive archival material on financial aspects of the Empire State Building at Hagley [Museum and Library, Wilmington, Delaware, Longwood MS 229–15, Box 1 of 5, file 26] in the papers of John Jacob Raskob and Pierre S. du Pont.[9]

The evolution of equity and debt for real estate projects

Everyone Can't Be the Winner. Despite what your soccer coach and team parents, including your own, may have told you on your U-9 recreation league soccer team, *everyone can't be* "the winner." In real estate financing, as in all sports competitions, there has to be a winner, and then there's all the "not-the-winners."

In understanding the difference between debt and equity, this is a *critical concept*. In the world of real estate finance, as well as in matters of corporate finance, this is commonly referred to as "priorities," because this is not so much a zero-sum game, as it is in the World Cup, of one winner and all the not-the-winners. *Everyone is competing for the largest share of the value of an asset at the highest priority level*, with the remaining claims, after the first-priority claims have been satisfied, competing for the remainder value of a diminishing asset until that asset is no more; it is possible, within this regime of hierarchical priorities, that perhaps some claims will not be satisfied at all (i.e., a total loss), because the collective claims with higher priorities will have exhausted completely the value of the underlying asset. *This is not a competition for a single trophy*, in which everyone else who competed goes home emptyhanded. Apologies to those students and readers who, after grasping this concept, may never look at their U-9 "You're a Winner!" soccer trophies the same way again.

When it comes to understanding the "Order of Priorities," as it is referred to in disputes involving competing claims to an asset or assets, debt gets repaid first out of the full value and equity gets paid last out of any remaining value after all debt claims have been satisfied. If there is not enough value in the underlying asset for all debt holders to recover 100% of what they're owed, then generally speaking no equity value remains. Among other reasons, this is because there may be an enormous range of claims just among first-priority creditors. Similarly, there may be a tremendous range of claims of competing and/or different priorities between a First Deed of Trust, for example, and a Developer's equity interest (which will generally be prioritized last, because the financial world believes the Developer must have the most "skin in the game").

Because *debt always has a higher priority than equity*, debt is generally cheaper; sometimes substantially so. A Project might have a loan at an 8% APR, for example, and have equity that commands a 20% return, because the equity component has a higher likelihood of loss as a consequence of its priority position relative to debt.

Except for temporary periods of "excessive exuberance," in which lenders demonstrate a willingness to provide financing on greater than a 1:1 loan-to-value (LTV) ratio and to fight over prospective borrowers, eliminating the need for Developer's equity, financing for real estate development transactions has traditionally required some combination of debt and equity. As indicated earlier, because their risk profiles are fundamentally different, debt may be much less expensive and, as a consequence, *Developers are always biased toward highly leveraged transactions*. Conversely, and depending on the interest rate environment at the time (e.g., are rates relatively high or relatively low in the cycle; is access to credit easy or constrained; are high LTVs commonplace or nonexistent), and the demand for equity to help finance real estate transactions, it's a question of whether equity will be expensive . . . or really expensive. See Professor Linneman's explanation of cap rates regarding the economic and other conditions causing cap rates to rise or fall, and their impact on real estate transactions generally.

In the not-too-distant past, Developers and those who brokered financing for real estate transactions would seek to attract and assemble the optimal combination of debt and equity for a specific real estate development project or acquisition. So finding both lenders and investors not already connected, in some way, to a Project and/or its Developer is nothing new. Technically, whether from a wealthy individual who includes or would like to include the real estate asset class (see, in this regard, Chapter 1) in her investment portfolio or from a syndication of investors choosing to do so, as was the case with Larry Wien in creating Empire State Building Associates (see, in this regard, Empire State Building, 1961: Empire State Building Associates' Syndication and Purchase of the Empire State Building), both reflect "private equity." However, it is the institutionalization of private equity, the pooling of capital in a managed fund with specific investment parameters and return expectations, that has, in many ways, transformed the way in which real estate transactions are financed.

The role of banks in financing real estate transactions

Banking Act of 1933. After the stock market crash, the Banking Act of 1933, commonly referred to by the names of its two congressional co-sponsors as the Glass-Steagall Act (Glass-Steagall), was deliberated to address financial stability concerns. These negotiations would resolve questions surrounding the financial sector's ability to provide consumers reliable sources of credit while providing sound market conditions. Furthermore, these negotiations would address many additional financial stability concerns. But the main persistent financial problem was how to provide dependable sources of credit to consumers while prohibiting risky financial lending behavior. The more credit banks provided to consumers, the more risky lending behaviors increased. The second problem in the financial sector was the question of insured deposits, or whether or not bank deposits should require the mandatory backing of insurance.

Even though many policy makers favored the separation of commercial and investment banking, some continued to remain highly skeptical of deposit insurance. The Federal Deposit Insurance Corporation (FDIC) and its insurance back stop were debated. Supporters of deposit insurance argued for the prevention of excessive depositor withdrawals from banks. They claimed banks would become more risky without insurance-backed deposits. The skeptics argued that banks would increase their risks due to the simple existence of insured deposits and its government backing. Skeptics went on to argue that if banks failed, the U.S. government and its citizens would be responsible for the assumption of failed banks and their accumulated debt.

Ultimately, the Banking Act of 1933 was enacted by Congress and signed into law by President Franklin Delano Roosevelt after the Great Depression. It was a direct response to the origins of the Great Depression. Its prime objective was to separate commercial banking and investment banking and to prevent banks from buying or selling securities; these were the major causes of the Great Depression. Glass-Steagall "prohibited national banks from purchasing or selling securities except for a customer's account." It prohibited any member bank of the Federal Reserve System from being affiliated with a company that engaged in "the issue, floatation, underwriting, public sale, or distribution of securities."

"THOSE WHO DISREGARD HISTORY ARE DOOMED TO REPEAT IT," . . . OR SOMETHING LIKE THAT

"Those who cannot remember the past are condemned to repeat it"[10]

George Santayana

I often remind myself of this quote from George Santayana's *The Life of Reason: The Phases of Human Progress, Vol. 1* (1905), which is misquoted more often than not – my favorite version opens this feature box – because it serves as a reminder that my students rarely have any historical context for many of the events that have shaped real estate development and finance, and finance in general, into the second decade of the twenty-first century. For example, in preparing to teach Principles of Real Estate to senior finance majors at George Mason University in the fall 2015 semester, I recognized that most of them were thirteen or fourteen years old when the Great Recession of 2008 occurred. They may have, perhaps, felt the effects of the crash of capital markets, prompting a crash in the residential real estate market, through their parents and their friends' parents but, beyond that, it might as well be some obscure piece of U.S. history. These students, and most likely the majority of students and readers using this textbook, have even less knowledge and understanding about the Great Depression of 1929, although several of the Empire State Building feature boxes throughout this chapter hopefully serve to provide some context for that truly cataclysmic event.

In order to help rectify this omission in the learning of most students pursuing an undergraduate or graduate degree in finance, real estate finance, and/or real estate development, several substantive sections of this chapter are devoted to explaining some of these seminal events in the United States, and exploring the aftermath of primarily federal statutes and regulations that came after, in an attempt to prevent a repeat of history. The only way to truly understand the contemporary regulatory environment impacting the financing of real estate transactions is to embrace this history.

The Banking Act of 1933 established the regulatory authority of the FDIC. Also during this time, the U.S. Securities and Exchange Commission (SEC) was established through the Securities Exchange Act in 1934 (see discussion regarding the four most significant federal acts passed following the Great Depression elsewhere in this chapter). The Banking Act of 1933 required deposit insurance of all FDIC member banks. The Act guaranteed depositor accounts against losses. In 1934, FDIC member bank accounts insured up to $5,000. Among other things, the Banking Act of 1933:

- established the FDIC as a temporary government corporation (The Banking Act of 1935 made the FDIC a permanent agency of the government and provided permanent deposit insurance maintained at the $5,000 level;
- gave the FDIC authority to provide deposit insurance to banks;
- gave the FDIC authority to regulate and supervise state non-member banks;
- funded the FDIC with initial loans of $289 million through the U.S. Treasury and the Federal Reserve, which loans were subsequently repaid with interest;
- extended federal oversight to all commercial banks for the first time;
- separated commercial and investment banking;
- prohibited banks from paying interest on checking accounts; and
- allowed national banks to branch statewide, if also allowed by state law.

Sections 16, 20, 21, and 32 of The Glass-Steagall Act were specifically crafted in response to the Great Depression. The separation of commercial and investment banking was expressly provided in these four sections.

Section 16 prohibited national banks from purchasing or selling securities except for a customer's account (i.e., as a customer's agent) unless the securities were purchased for the bank's account as "investment securities" identified by the Comptroller of the Currency as permitted national bank investments. Section 16 also prohibited national banks from underwriting or distributing securities. Section 16, however, permitted national banks to buy, sell, underwrite, and distribute U.S. government and general obligation state and local government securities. Such securities became known as "bank-eligible securities." Section 5(c) of the 1933 Banking Act (sometimes referred to as the fifth Glass-Steagall provision) applied Section 16's rules to Federal Reserve System member state-chartered banks.

Section 20 prohibited any member bank of the Federal Reserve System (whether a state chartered or national bank) from being affiliated with a company that "engaged principally" in "the issue, flotation, underwriting, public sale, or distribution" of securities.

Section 21 prohibited any company or person from taking deposits if it was in the business of "issuing, underwriting, selling, or distributing" securities.

Section 32 prohibited any Federal Reserve System member bank from having any officer or director in common with a company "engaged primarily" in the business of "purchasing, selling, or negotiating" securities, unless the Federal Reserve Board granted an exemption.

These four sections of the Banking Act of 1933 helped maintain years of financial stability following the Great Depression. However, in the 1960s, Glass-Steagall was already coming under attack, due to the lack of competition within the financial services sector. This lack of competition was viewed as a negative consequence of the banking sector's constraining regulatory framework. Starting in the early 1960s, federal banking regulators began interpreting provisions of the Glass-Steagall Act to permit commercial banks and especially commercial bank affiliates to engage in an expanding list and volume of securities activities.

Relationship banking

It wasn't all that long ago, before the beginning of the S&L Crisis, referenced earlier and described in greater detail later, that the majority of lending transactions involving real estate development took place between a Lender and a Borrower who knew each other well – sometimes very well – providing financing on development projects in the same jurisdiction as the location of the bank. This has commonly been called "Relationship Banking," and, for the most part, it's waved bye-bye following the crash of the real estate market in the late 1980s, leading to the demise or subsequent acquisition of a large number of savings and loan or "depository" institutions as a consequence. To better understand what Relationship Banking was, and how it operated, students and readers may find a scene from the holiday classic *It's a Wonderful Life* for guidance, in this instance offered up in the context of the aftermath of the Great Recession of 2008:

> To get a better idea why the Obama Administration's efforts to stem the home foreclosure crisis have failed at both ends of the problem, you need only go back to that great scene in Frank Capra's classic, *It's a Wonderful Life*, where protagonist George Bailey (Jimmy Stewart) is on his way out of Bedford Falls with his new bride and high school crush, the former Meg Hatch (Donna Reed). The newlyweds are heading toward the train station to leave on their honeymoon when Meg notices a commotion outside the Bailey Bros. Building & Loan Association, founded by George's revered but now deceased father, Henry, and Henry's bumbling brother, Billie.
>
> The "commotion" is actually a run on the bank. George – bless his heart, and with the full encouragement of the new Mrs. Bailey – hops out of Ernie's cab to see if he can quell the growing crowd assembling outside the locked doors of the Building & Loan. With his usual calm George assesses the situation, asks Uncle Billie to unlock the doors to let the gathering mob into the Building & Loan, and then proceeds to talk (most of) them out of closing their accounts and being refunded the value of their shares.
>
> George patiently explains to his anxious Association members that he can't give each of them 100% of the value of their Bailey Brothers Building & Loan Association shares because the funds from those shares have already been loaned out to worthy borrowers so they can afford to build or buy houses in the community. States George from behind the teller counter:

"[In your best Jimmy Stewart inner monologue voice] . . . you're thinking of this place all wrong. As if I had the money back in a safe. The, the money's not here. Well, your money's in Joe's house . . . that's right next to yours. And in the Kennedys' house, and Mrs. Macklin's house, and a hundred others. Why, you're lending them the money to build, and then, they're going to pay you back as best they can. Now what are you going do? Foreclose on them?"

Just as George appears to be making progress, however, a now former Association member comes running into the Building & Loan pronouncing that Old Man Potter (Lionel Barrymore), who owns the bank and every other business in Bedford Falls, is offering to buy Bailey Brothers Building & Loan shares at 50 cents on the dollar (in an obvious effort to take advantage of the situation by running George Bailey out of business). Saving the day, and confirming that George has indeed made a life-changing decision in his choice of mates, the new Mrs. Bailey, with $2,000 in cash in her purse for their honeymoon, offers the money to the anxious Association members filling the building lobby. George then adroitly parses out their honeymoon money in the smallest increments he can persuade folks to accept under the circumstances.

The scene tells us much about what went wrong with the residential real estate market nationwide. It is more than merely nostalgic to long for such elegant simplicity in the manner in which deposited funds were invested in things such as home mortgages. However, the only thing quainter than that scene in *It's a Wonderful Life* is the idea of a bank or other financial institution originating, owning, and servicing the same mortgage. And therein lies the rub for efforts by the Treasury Department to help right the residential mortgage ship of state through the Making Home Affordable mortgage modification program and the Legacy Asset Recovery program.[11]

After the S&L Crisis, and for reasons explained later in this chapter, it would eventually become an extreme rarity for a Developer to have a business and personal relationship with someone who holds a mortgage on a property of that Developer, and rarer still for both parties to live and work in the same jurisdiction. Borrowers may still have relationships with their Lenders, but those Lenders almost never hold onto the commercial mortgages they originate.

1980s savings and loan crisis[12]

The accumulation of government debt during the run-up to and following the commencement of the S&L Crisis in the late 1980s – primarily due to the fact that so many of these institutions were federally insured (or at least their depositors funds were) – had a profound impact, long after the events that occurred and their resolution, on real estate markets. This is discussed in several different sections of this chapter, inasmuch as there were reform efforts targeting banking specifically, as well as targeting capital markets. They are treated separately in sections that follow.

In 1979, savings and loans (S&Ls), which were also known as thrifts or depository institutions, were offering depositors higher-than-average rates of return for their customers' deposits. This was because of the actions of the Federal Reserve over a number of years, in an effort to control the negative impacts of inflation on the U.S. economy.

Paul Volcker, chairman of the Federal Reserve at the time, and the Federal Reserve Board of Governors, had raised the Fed Funds rate once again, this time raising it to 20 percent, to head off the country's stagflation, a condition where the economy is stagnant (i.e., in a period of low growth) but prices are nonetheless rising (i.e., inflation). Due to these interest rate increases on deposits, locked for long terms, S&Ls were paying excessive rates of interest and losing money on their deposits. In the early 1980s, S&L failures began to increase exponentially. The administration's solution was to deregulate the S&Ls and real estate markets while increasing the insurance deposit limit to compensate for Savings and Loan losses. The FDIC insurance deposit limit increased from 40,000 to 100,000. However, the deregulation of S&Ls and real estate caused S&Ls to increase risk taking. This exacerbated S&L failures across the country.

The U.S. government, through the Federal Home Loan Bank and the Federal Savings and Loan Corporation, was assuming failing S&Ls and their toxic real estate assets. By 1989, the Financial Institutions Reform, Recovery, and Enforcement Act (FIRREA) was established to address these S&L concerns. FIRREA created these regulatory changes:

The Federal Home Loan Bank Board (FHLBB) was abolished. The Federal Savings and Loan Insurance Corporation (FSLIC) was abolished, and all assets and liabilities were assumed by the FSLIC Resolution Fund administered by the FDIC and funded by the Financing Corporation (FICO). The Office of Thrift Supervision (OTS), a bureau of the U.S. Treasury Department, was created to charter, regulate, examine, and supervise savings institutions. The Federal Housing Finance Board (FHFB) was created as an independent agency to replace the FHLBB, that is, to oversee the twelve Federal Home Loan Banks (also called district banks) that represent the largest collective source of home mortgage and community credit in the United States. The Savings Association Insurance Fund (SAIF) replaced the FSLIC as an ongoing insurance fund for thrift institutions (like the FDIC, the FSLIC was a permanent corporation that insured savings and loan accounts up to $100,000). SAIF is administered by the Federal Deposit Insurance Corporation. The Resolution Trust Corporation (RTC) was established to dispose of failed thrift institutions taken over by regulators after January 1, 1989. The RTC will make insured deposits at those institutions available to their customers.

The Office of Thrift Supervision (OTS), currently managed under the U.S. Treasury, was in charge of declaring S&Ls insolvent. Once S&Ls were declared insolvent, The Resolution Trust Corporation (RTC) took over their assets. The RTC was a new organization authorized under FIRREA. It was responsible for the management and liquidation of S&Ls and their portfolios of toxic real estate assets. The RTC sold very large – at least at the time – portfolios of nonperforming real estate assets on which potential purchasers submitted bids, thereby establishing the pricing for these non- and underperforming assets. Many of these prospective purchasers competing for these portfolios relied on private equity funds to back up their purchase offers to the RTC. By purchasing these debt instruments in bulk, at fractions of their aggregate face value, private investors with money invested in participating private equity funds stood to make extremely high returns on their investments. Through this process, the RTC was able to close or resolve the assets of 747 institutions with approximately $394 billion in total assets between 1989 and 1995.

Additionally, the RTC strengthened insurance deposit funds while it increased regulatory supervision. RTC duties also included supervision, investigation, and examination of financial institutions. FIRREA, through the efforts of the RTC and other provisions of the thrift reform legislation (including a makeover of appraisal requirements used for approving and underwriting S&L loans secured by real property), consolidated the S&Ls' regulatory framework to resolve major oversight issues concerning S&L risks. Ultimately, depositors were made whole under federal insurance on their deposits; some of the S&Ls bailed while others closed. Some S&L executives were criminally prosecuted and went to jail, unlike the aftermath of the 2008 financial crisis, discussed elsewhere in this chapter, which made the S&L Crisis pale by comparison.

Federal efforts, through FIRREA, to bail out those Thrifts which could be resolved had a seemingly astonishing price tag, although in hindsight the resolution of so many financial institutions seems to have come relatively cheaply:

> With interest added, realistic estimates of the tab easily exceeded $500 billion in ten years, or more than one trillion over several decades, enough by some calculations to add $13 billion a year in

interest – forever – to the national debt. In 1990 and 1991, with estimates of the bailout's ultimate costs reaching into the trillions, the Bush administration abandoned any pretense of limiting taxpayer liability. It was generally accepted that the public would foot most, if not all, of the cost.[13]

EMPIRE STATE BUILDING, 1931–1941: THE DECADE OF THE "EMPTY STATE" BUILDING

The Empire State Building opened for business on May 1, 1931, having been constructed in thirteen-and-a-half months, a construction record that has never been matched, much less exceeded.[14] The Project's Development Team, which included Shreve and Lamb Associates – which had prepared the original sketch and program for Waldorf-Astoria Hotel purchaser Floyd Brown – as Project Architect, and Starrett Brothers and Eken as General Contractor, was given a directive by the Project's ownership: *You have eighteen months from the architect's first sketch until the opening of the building on May 1, 1931.*

The reason for the extraordinarily tight time frame and, in particular, the *hard opening date* of May 1 was a function of the financial projections supporting the project's financial viability. In New York City at the time, commercial office tenants only entered into one-year leases, and all such leases terminated on April 30, and new leases commenced on the next day, May 1. If the Empire State Building missed its projected opening date, the entire building would likely remain vacant for an entire year, with no gross rental income to offset its operating expenses and its carrying costs, such as real property taxes, insurance, and interest on the various components of its complex financing structure (See Empire State Building, 1929: Raskob and du Pont's Investment Letter to Bail Out Floyd Brown's Purchase of the Waldorf-Astoria Hotel and Develop The Empire State Building in Its Place.).

As stated in the epigraph for this chapter, the timing of Floyd Brown's purchase of the hotel property on which the Empire State Building would be constructed, as well as Raskob's investment letter of August 28, 1929, could not have been worse. *"The . . . Empire State Building . . . remained three-quarters empty for a decade after its opening in 1931 and did not turn an annual profit until 1950."* In addition to other market infirmities from which the building suffered, less than a month after the date of the Raskob letter, the United States suffered the greatest economic collapse in its history.

> During the 1920s, the U.S. stock market underwent rapid expansion, reaching its peak in August 1929, a period of wild speculation. By then, production had already declined and unemployment had risen, leaving stocks in great excess of their real value. Among the other causes of the eventual market collapse were low wages, the proliferation of debt, a weak agriculture, and an excess of large bank loans that could not be liquidated.
>
> Stock prices began to decline in September and early October 1929, and on October 18 the fall began. Panic set in, and on October 24 – Black Thursday – a record 12,894,650 shares were traded. Investment companies and leading bankers attempted to stabilize the market by buying up great blocks of stock, producing a moderate rally on Friday. On Monday, however, the storm broke anew, and the market went into freefall. Black Monday was followed by Black Tuesday, in which stock prices collapsed completely.[15]

While the onset of the Great Depression, less than five months before construction of the Empire State Building commenced on March 17, 1930, presented some advantages for the Project,[16] it wreaked havoc on the building's occupancy for the first ten years after its completion on May 1, 1931.

> It's not as if the Crash had come without warning, especially in real estate, where there was a known building cycle, a known correlation between boom and bust. Major financial panics, or crashes, as Professors George F. Warren and Frank A. Pearson pointed out, came one to four years after a building cycle reached its peak. When the vacancy rate is low, several years are required to build the buildings that will satisfy the market. With that momentum come bigger and bigger office buildings, with the largest of them frequently erected near or after the peak of the building cycle. The big latecomers are the ones that sow the seeds of their own destruction.[17]

In *Form Follows Finance*, Willis suggests that, in addition to the precipitous decline in demand for office space in Manhattan after the Black Tuesday market crash marking the beginning of the Great Depression, Raskop and du Pont's revenue assumptions, as reflected in the attachment to Raskop's August 28, 1929, letter, may have been more than overly ambitious. Among other things, in projecting gross rents from leasing Raskop assumed a 90% occupancy (or, on the flip side, 10% vacancy) rate for the building, without any provision for an absorption schedule of any kind. In his book, *The Empire State Building: The Making of a Landmark*, author John Tauranac chronicles occupancy rates for commercial office buildings coming online in Manhattan in 1929, even before those buildings were topped out, suggesting a robust leasing market at the time.

> The average office building in the twenties opened 52 percent rented, and usually took five years to reach 90 percent. That was considered normal, and the original financing had to take those five lean years into account. Although there was already the beginning of a glut on the market in 1929, some buildings were doing extraordinarily well. The unfinished New York Central Building stood at 80 percent rented early in the year, the unfinished Chanin Building at 40 percent. The Adler Building at 530 Seventh Avenue, which replaced the Pictorial Review Building, would not be ready for occupancy until 1930, but by June 1929, it was already fully rented from the second to the thirtieth floors. And Louis Adler had found a major tenant for the main floor. The Chatham Phoenix Bank would occupy twenty thousand square feet of space in a specially built banking concourse, which would make it the largest banking quarters in Midtown. Adler had only the top three floors of his thirty-three-story building to worry about.[18]

However, arguably none of these examples proved apt comparables for the Empire State Building, which did not open until May 1, 1931, and which represented an unprecedented volume of available commercial space coming to the market in the middle of 1931. As Willis explains it:

> In theory, one simply calculated how many square feet of rentable space could be constructed with the available budget, then multiplied that number by the average rental rate (less the percent for vacancies). Repeating this formula for bigger and smaller buildings provided a means of comparing rates of return. Judging market rents was problematic, though, since so many different factors could affect desirability. Given its size and its location outside the popular office districts, the Empire State Building had

no comparable model for guidelines. The initial estimate of annual rent was $6,300,000, which, under the formula described, would have produced a gross return on equity of approximately 12.6%.

In January 1932, eight months after the Empire State Building's grand opening on May 1, 1931, Al Smith, president of the Empire State Building Company, appeared before New York City's Board of Taxes and Assessments to contest its new valuation of the completed building at $42 million, up from the previous $14 million valuation, based solely on the value of the Waldorf-Astoria Hotel site, because the Empire State Building was still under construction in 1931. In that hearing to contest the valuation, Smith sheepishly admitted that the Empire State Building was *less than 25% leased* and, based on the gross rents, the Board of Taxes and Assessments had grossly overvalued the building based on its actual gross revenues.

By December 31, 1931, the Empire State Building held so few tenants that it earned the nickname the "Empty State" Building among New Yorkers. It lived up to its "Empty State" Building nickname into the mid-1940s. The last significant, street-level retail space was not leased until December 1937, six years and seven months after the building's opening. By 1944, the Empire State Building had finally reached 85% occupancy, 5% below the targeted 90% occupancy Raskob had projected for its first year of operations in his calculations for the financing of the project.

The rise of institutionalized private equity[19]

The history of private equity traces a series of economic cycles starting in the middle of the twentieth century and continuing to the present day. The origins of the modern private equity industry began in 1946, continuing through five major periods characterized by three major boom-and-bust market cycles. The first period of private equity, from 1946 through 1981, was categorized by relatively small volumes of private equity investment, fledgling organizations, immature markets, and limited awareness of and familiarity with an emerging private equity industry. The second cycle, from 1982 through 1993, was characterized by the dramatic surge in leveraged buyout activity financed by high-yield but poorly underwritten debt instruments and ending with the near-collapse of the leveraged buyout (LBO) business in the late 1980s and early 1990s, due to the evaporation of investments in unrated, very high-risk (i.e., "junk") bonds. This cycle also saw the collapse of the savings and loan industry (the S&L Crisis), primarily due to overleveraged real estate development funding and poor underwriting standards for real estate development financing, which had little to do with private equity and everything to do with overleveraged real estate transactions.

The third cycle, from 1992 through 2002, emerged out of the detritus from the S&L Crisis, including the collapse of real estate values viewed as artificially inflated by the ready availability of financing with extremely shallow loan-to-value ratios; the insider-trading scandals; and the consequent recession that commenced in the early 1990s. This period saw the creation of more sophisticated and a greater number of institutionalized private equity firms, which ultimately fueled, and then led to, the massive dot-com bubble in 1999 and 2000. The fourth cycle, from 2003 through 2007, came after the bursting of the dot-com bubble, when LBO's returned with a vengeance, reaching much greater sizes. The further institutionalization of private equity was represented by the Blackstone Group's 2007 private equity initial public offering (IPO).

The fifth and current cycle started in 2007 and continues to the present. It is, of course, characterized by the collapse of capital markets in the fall of 2008, the subsequent crash of real estate markets – first residential for-sale, then commercial – and a very slow and painful recovery. See the section on The 2008 Wall Street Crash That Took the Real Estate Market with It.

During the period leading up to the Tax Reform Act of 1986, much of the "private equity" financing real estate development was raised through syndications, interest in which was generated more by the availability of pass-through deductions for tax attributes such as interest expense and depreciation of real estate assets than by a focus on long-term returns from these investments. Perceiving what it viewed as rampant abuse of such "tax shelter investments," which, among other things, were having a negative impact on collections of federal income tax from individual real estate investors, in the Tax Reform Act of 1986 Congress closed off the availability of tax-shelter benefits through the passive-activity loss rules added into the Internal Revenue Code. See, in this regard, Chapter 8, Operational Tax Issues section, Limitations on Deductions subsection, Passive Losses/Tax Shelters.

In addition to the ready availability of very high LTV loans being made available to real estate developers by depository institutions (i.e., savings and loan associations), the popularity of real estate tax shelter deals among taxpayers in the higher marginal tax brackets was also bidding up the "value" of potential projects, primarily because those investors were much more enamored by the projected pass-through tax losses in the early years of these partnerships than by the fundamentals of the underlying projects. See the Empire State Building, 1931–1941: The Decade of "The Empty State" Building box regarding the importance of real estate equity investors understanding the fundamentals of a development project, including underlying assumptions regarding lease-up, **Vacancy Rates**, and market position.

By the close of the 1980s the United States began to enter a recession brought on primarily by the S&L Crisis, described in greater detail in a previous section in this chapter. A significant volume of commercial real estate loans – including acquisition and development, or A&D, loans for subdivisions developments of for-sale housing – went into default, risking the financial health of numerous depository institutions, which ran afoul of their regulatory requirements. Accordingly, in 1989 Congress passed the Financial Institutions Reform, Recovery, and Enforcement Act of 1989 (FIRREA). Among other things, FIRREA provided the enabling legislation for the new Office of Thrift Supervision (OTS) and the new Resolution Trust Corporation (RTC). The RTC's mission was to help "resolve" troubled assets held by thrift institutions regulated by federal agencies, such as the Office of the Comptroller of the Currency (OCC) and the Federal Deposit Insurance Corporation (FDIC), in hopes that these institutions could remain solvent or be liquidated in the most orderly and least disruptive manner possible. These were, by and large, community and regional financial institutions that were far removed from the investment banking activities of Wall Street.

The S&L Crisis and the resolution or attempted resolution of troubled real estate assets and their attendant S&L-held debt through FIRREA and the RTC left a void in commercial banking, as it stood at the time, resulting in significant changes in the future of commercial real estate lending. Wall Street investment banks recognized the opportunity to purchase troubled loan portfolios from the RTC and through other means at very high discounts, with a view toward restructuring or foreclosing on millions of dollars in nonperforming loans, adding value to and stabilizing the underlying assets. The end game (or Exit Strategy) for the purchase of these troubled loan portfolios was to ultimately sell the investments – either the debt or their underlying asset at a premium relative to their allocated purchase cost in the portfolio. Through this experience with these first "opportunity funds," Wall Street investment banks began the wholesale restructuring of the real estate capital markets, creating potential flows of capital into commercial real estate the like of which no one had ever seen before. Investment banks began issuing new real estate loan portfolios that were subsequently securitized and sold to investors on the secondary market. These commercial mortgage-backed securities (CMBS) became the backbone of real estate development production. Thereafter, real estate private equity developed as an independent asset class in the 2000s and has experienced significant growth in recent years. However, as explained in the section titled The 2008 Wall Street Crash That Took the Real Estate Market with It, the abuse of CMBS inevitably led to the Great Recession of 2008.

The 1990s Dismantling of Critical Section of Glass-Steagall.[20] During the early 1990s, the efficacy of Glass-Steagall was strongly contested in John Dugan's report, Modernizing the Financial System: Recommendations for Safer, More Competitive Banks. Dugan was undersecretary of the Treasury for domestic finance in 1992 and served in the Department of the Treasury from 1989 to 1993. He also served as Comptroller of the Currency from August 2005 until August 14, 2010. This report became known as The Green Book, and, although not law, its ideologies paved the way for future changes to the U.S. banking system. When regulatory changes were eventually achieved and began to impact real estate markets in the 1990s, values began to increase. The Green Book's main initiatives were to allow banks to expand into multiple states without incurring additional regulatory oversight; allow relatively safe commercial banks to merge with riskier investment banks and insurance companies; and allow commercial firms – General Electric, Sears – to purchase banks.

In 1999, portions of the Glass-Steagall Act were repealed under the Gramm-Leach-Bliley Act (GLBA). The GLBA repealed Sections 20 and 32 of the Glass-Steagall Act, not Sections 16 and 21. The GLBA also amended Section 16 to permit "well-capitalized" commercial banks to underwrite municipal revenue bonds (i.e., non-general obligation bonds), as first approved by the Senate in 1967. Otherwise, Sections 16 and 21 remained in effect, regulating the direct securities activities of banks and prohibiting securities firms from taking deposits. After March 11, 2000, bank holding companies could expand their securities and insurance activities by becoming "financial holding companies."

President Bill Clinton's signing statement for the GLBA codified the established argument for repealing Glass-Steagall Sections 20 and 32 in stating that this change, and the GLBA's amendments to the Bank Holding Company Act, would "enhance the stability of our financial services system" by permitting financial firms to "diversify their product offerings and thus their sources of revenue" and make financial firms "better equipped to compete in global financial markets." These statements not only turned out to be ill-considered but the repeal of these sections of the 1933 Banking Act proved, at least in part, responsible for the undoing of the entire financial services sector in those activities by investment banks that contributed to or caused directly the financial crisis of 2008.

The result of these statutory and attendant regulatory changes ushered in by the Clinton administration during the president's second term was that large banks could expand securities, insurance, and leveraged-transaction activities like investing in and trading derivatives. It allowed the assembly of investment banking and commercial banking activities under one roof. Additionally, under GLBA, the repeal of the uptick rule allowed investors to short the stock market much like they had during the Great Depression. Shorting transactions were, arguably, the single, largest underlying cause of the capital markets crash in 2008. The uptick rule is defined in the following way:

> Rule 10a-1(a)(1) provided that, subject to certain exceptions, a listed security may be sold short (A) at a price above the price at which the immediately preceding sale was effected (plus tick), or (B) at the last sale price if it is higher than the last different price (zero-plus tick). Short sales were not permitted on minus ticks or zero-minus ticks, subject to narrow exceptions.

Kansas City Federal Reserve President Thomas Hoenig, in a 2011 speech to the Kansas Bankers Association, explained factors resulting from the repeal of significant portions of Glass-Steagall:

> There were two pieces of legislation that facilitated our migration toward too big to fail . . . Interstate Banking and Branching Efficiency Act of 1994, permitted banks to grow across state lines, and the Gramm-Leach-Bliley Act, which eliminated the separation of commercial and investment banking. Since 1990, the largest twenty institutions grew from controlling about 35 percent of industry assets to controlling 70 percent of assets today.
>
> Once Section 20 and 32 of Glass-Steagall were abolished, banks were permitted to cross state lines adding additional concerns due to the concept of preemption. Preemption, a legal doctrine, said that "the federal government's authority prevailed over state rights in business conflicts" ("Preemption," 2013). Preemption allowed less regulation for large investment banks due to the federal government's establishment of authority in such areas. The OCC now had full command of regulatory results pertaining to investment banks.[21]

According to reporter Zach Carter, whose article quoted from Thomas Hoenig's speech:

> Between 1995 and 2007, the OCC issued thirteen public enforcement actions against national banks on consumer protection issues, for the more than 1600 banks it regulates. Over that same period, zero public actions were taken against the eight largest national banks, even though these banks were at the heart of the predatory lending mortgage explosion.[22]

The federal bailout of the financial services industry after the Great Recession of 2008 primarily centered on the concept of "Too Big to Fail": The belief that a handful of the very largest U.S. financial services institutions had become so large, and so integral to the U.S. domestic and global financial systems, that the failure of just one might lead to the collapse of the global economy. Despite "Too Big to Fail" resolutions, which have been comprised of trillions of dollars in taxpayer-funded bailouts and other monetary system supports to help prop up the largest financial service companies, tight credit conditions continued to prevail. Such conditions, and their tight credit symptoms, have impeded real estate transactions, real estate recoveries, and therefore the recovery of the entire U.S. economy.

EMPIRE STATE BUILDING, 1951: NEWLY FORMED EMPIRE STATE BUILDING CORPORATION BUYS EMPIRE STATE BUILDING IN SALE-LEASEBACK TRANSACTION WITH PRUDENTIAL, SEPARATING LAND AND BUILDING OWNERSHIP

The Empire State Building has been a complex, and oftentimes convoluted, business enterprise from its very inception. This observation is just as applicable *to its ownership and financing structures* over the more than eighty years since Raskob's August 28, 1929, letter, as it is to the organization and composition of its building volumes and overall form, as addressed in detail by Willis' *Form Follows Finance*. The project to develop a massive commercial building on the site of the deteriorating Waldorf-Astoria Hotel, located at Thirty-fourth Street and Fifth Avenue in Midtown Manhattan, at a time when most commercial office buildings were located much closer to the Grand Central Terminal, Penn Station, and the Port Authority bus terminal, in hindsight appeared extremely ill conceived. However, the ultimate success of the undertaking had significantly more challenges than merely a poor choice of location.

The project almost failed before even getting off the ground, when architect and builder Floyd Brown defaulted on the second mortgage payment on his $16 million acquisition of the site of the Waldorf-Astoria. Yet, through a lot of maneuvering and financial engineering (see **The Empire State Building, 1929: Raskob and du Pont's Investment Letter** box, which includes the original development budget for the undertaking, excerpted from the attachment to Raskob's 1929 letter), the Empire State Building was completed in record time, and at a much lower cost than its original projection, thanks to the excess supplies of construction materials and labor caused by the almost complete secession of demand for such things as a direct consequence of the Great Depression.

According to Willis' account in *Form Follows Finance* – which is generally corroborated by Tauranac's *The Empire State Building: The Making of a Landmark* – the Empire State Building did not become profitable until 1950. The seemingly insurmountable difficulties encountered by the Empire State Building in trying to become fully leased – as detailed in the **Empire State Building, 1931–1941: The Decade of The "Empty" State Building**" box, explain, at least in part, why the Empire State Building remained under the same ownership until 1951, the first year after reaching profitability.

Inasmuch as commercial buildings are generally valued by applying a capitalization rate to its Net Operating Income, the lower the amount of gross rent generated by the Empire State Building, the lower the purchase price it could command. Accordingly, trying to sell the building before it demonstrated robust and stabilized rents could result in its owners receiving far less than the Empire State Building could potentially fetch after full lease-up was well-demonstrated (i.e., not only that the building could achieve so-called full occupancy, but that it could remain fully occupied for an extended period of time). So it was that after John P. Raskob passed away in October 1950 (six years after the death of Al Smith), in 1951 the Raskob Estate entered into a purchase contract, brokered by George A. Hammer, a vice president with the New York City brokerage and property management firm Charles F. Noyes Company, to sell Raskob's majority interest in the Empire State Building to Realty Associates, a syndicate led by Roger L. Stevens of Detroit, which was eventually taken over by the Crown family of Chicago, whose patriarch, Henry Crown, had become one of America's wealthiest industrialists.

Not long after his death, two of Raskob's sons were appointed to the Empire State Board, but theirs was not to be the pride of wearing the mantle, of continuing the tradition. Theirs was to sell, and it did not take long. Their father had already held preliminary negotiations with Chicago's Colonel Henry Crown, but Crown felt that the Empire State Building was too rich for his blood, too much to take on individually, and he bowed out. By the end of May 1951, the blandly named Realty Associates Securities Corporation had made a $50 million offer.

The buyers of the Empire State Building in 1951 were all out-of-towners. Two of the buyers, Roger L. Stevens and Alfred R. Glancy Jr., were from Detroit. The third, Ben Tobin, was from Hollywood, Florida. Glancy, forty-three, the son of the former head of the Pontiac Division of General Motors, was a vice president of the National Bank of Detroit. Tobin owned the Hollywood Beach Hotel and the 1,100-room Hollenden Hotel in Cleveland, and served as the president of the Bank of Hollywood. Roger L. Stevens, only forty-one, embarked on a second career as a Broadway producer, with *Peter Pan* already under his belt. A director of the American National Theatre Assembly, and a member of the Playwrights Company, he would go on to be a major force in arts management and to head the Kennedy Center in Washington. Two years before the Empire State deal, the three men had acquired Realty Associates, which brought them the Brooklyn Paramount Theater, the Printing Crafts Building, and a substantial interest in the Taft Hotel.[23]

It is instructive to understand fully how this transaction – which, once closed, would become the highest-cost commercial real estate transaction in the world – came about. Before his death, Raskob had instructed his executors that as soon as a credible purchase for the Empire State Building, in excess of $50 million, could be generated, they were to negotiate a contract of sale and dispose of the property. The transaction occurred through a series of coincidental events, starting with Hammer and Charles F. Noyes Company being engaged to conduct an appraisal of the Empire State Building. Through the valuation process Hammer came to know confidential information about the operating performance and condition of the building, as well as pending transactions that had not yet been made public (such as the forthcoming radio tower lease, which would add approximately $600,000 per annum in revenue).

Learning that Raskob's executors were looking for a disposition of the building at a target sales price in excess of $50 million, Hammer started quietly looking for suitable buyers *before* the executors made any public efforts to formally list and market the property for sale. Shortly thereafter, Stevens' newly acquired Realty Associates negotiated an exclusive option for the syndicate to negotiate for the purchase of the controlling interest in the Empire State Building held by Raskob's estate. Within approximately two weeks after that, the parties entered into a contract of sale.

One truly unique aspect of the proposed purchase of The Empire State Building was the way Realty Associates structured the transaction. As part of its financing of the acquisition of the Raskob majority interest in the Empire State Building, Realty Associates created a sale-leaseback structure, with Prudential Insurance Company of America ("Prudential") purchasing title to the land on which the building had been constructed (i.e., the old Waldorf-Astoria property), and taking back from Prudential a long-term ground lease for the land on which the building sits. In other words, in purchasing title to the Empire State Building land and entering into the sale-leaseback transaction, Prudential was purchasing a long-term revenue stream, as well as the residual value of the land after the expiration of the final extension of the ground lease. Additionally, Prudential provided mortgage financing for Realty Associates' purchase of the building itself from Raskob's estate.

As described by Tauranac:

> Realty Associates did not enter into the deal alone. They made an equity investment of $13.5 million, but the Prudential Life Insurance Company bought the land for $17 million, which would provide handsome returns from a long-term ground lease of $1.02 million yearly, and the insurance company put up most of the balance with a $15.5 million mortgage. The Raskob estate stayed in to the tune of about $4 million.[24]

As mentioned earlier, Henry Crown, one of America's wealthy industrialists, through the Crown family businesses, ultimately became the sole owner of the Empire State Building following the Realty Associates' transaction orchestrated by Stevens and Hammer. This is indeed ironic because, prior to Stevens entering the picture and finding Stevens' syndicate,

Crown and Raskob had negotiated a sale, but the former balked at the latter's $50 million price tag. As Tauranac noted in *The Empire State Building: The Making of a Landmark*, however, Crown and Raskob each got their way, albeit after the latter's death, with Raskob's executors securing a $51 million sales price (although the additional $1 million went to fees and commissions and not the estate's bottom line), and the Crown family achieving 100% ownership of the building from Realty Associates for substantially less than the $50 million sales price that caused Crown to walk away from the negotiating table with Raskob.

> Despite the profitability of the building, the Stevens group was in over its head. Clancey and Tobin sold out to Chicago's Colonel Henry Crown. Stevens, however, did not sell to Crown immediately. According to Peter L. Malkin, the building's managing partner in the mid-1990s first offered to sell the building to Lawrence A. Wien, who analyzed the building and made an offer. Stevens did not take the offer. Instead, Stevens took the price Wien had concluded was appropriate, and without a word of appreciation, Stevens used Wien's figures as a basis for an offering to Crown, who bought out Stevens's interest at the rate of Wien's offering price.
>
> In October 1954, Crown became the second person to own the building personally. He purchased the building for $ 49.5 million, which on paper looked like a loss for the sellers, but which was viewed as a gain because of operating profit and depreciation. According to real estate writer Richard J. Anderson, real estate operators benefited from federal tax laws that permitted substantial depreciation deductions on improved real property. And under accelerated methods of depreciation first allowed in 1954, realtors could take the highest possible write-offs in the early years of ownership.[25]

This transaction would set the stage for the first large-scale realty syndication in the United States, through the creation of Empire State Building Associates in 1961, as well as marking the beginning of the lasting legacy of Lawrence Wien, his son-in-law, Peter L. Malkin, and Wien's grandson, Anthony E. Malkin, Chairman and Chief Executive Officer of Empire Realty Trust, the current owner and property manager, in the long-term ownership and operation of the Empire State Building into the present day. See Empire State Building Feature Boxes Empire State Building, 2009: Repositioning New York City's Largest Commercial Building: The "Greening" of The Empire State Building, and Empire State Building, 2013: Empire State Building Associates "Transitions" to REIT Ownership through Empire Realty Trust, respectively.

EMPIRE STATE BUILDING, 1961: EMPIRE STATE BUILDING ASSOCIATES' SYNDICATION AND PURCHASE OF THE EMPIRE STATE BUILDING

In the 1951 transaction, described in the preceding Empire State Building Feature Box, the Empire State Building Corporation, a New York corporation formed for that purpose, purchased from the Estate of John P. Raskob all of the interests in the Empire State Building. This transaction was structured as a Sale-Leaseback with the Prudential Insurance Company of America, Inc. In 1961, a small number of real estate investors decided to embark on a transaction to bring ownership of the Empire State Building back to New York City, from Chicago, where the Crown family lived and its businesses were headquartered. In order to pull this purchase off, which would be the largest purchase price to date for a single commercial building, the principals leading this transaction would turn to a financing mechanism that would be unique in its application to the purchase of real estate: A public syndication of up to 3,000 "Participation Units," valued at $10,000 each, in an effort to raise up to $39 million of the $65 million purchase price.

> In 1961 came the third change in ownership, when the building and the leasehold upon the land were purchased from Henry Crown by a syndicate called Empire State Building Associates for $ 65 million, a sale that earned a place in the record books. Together with the $ 17 million previously paid by Prudential for the land, the total of $ 82 million was the greatest sum ever paid for a building, and the negotiations were commensurate with the price. The purchase was initiated by Lawrence A. Wien, who had created Empire State Building Associates. He had been interested in the property ever since his "appraisal" for Roger Stevens in 1954, after which he and his broker, Harry Helmsley, had maintained contact with Crown, who on several occasions had indicated interest in selling, only to change his mind and back out. What finally precipitated the sale came when Crown learned that Congress might amend the tax code by taxing long-term capital gains at the substantially higher rate of ordinary income tax as of January 1, 1962. In September 1961, he agreed to sell, with one major proviso – that the sale be consummated by the end of 1961. The transaction kept batteries of lawyers, accountants, tax experts, and title insurance companies hard at work for the rest of the year. The contract and exhibits ran over four hundred pages, with about one hundred legal documents that had to be signed in precisely the right order. Eight dry runs were required before the final signing took place in the board of directors suite of the Prudential Insurance Company of America in Newark, New Jersey. It took from midmorning until midafternoon.[26]

In addition to creating Empire State Building Associates as the vehicle for raising up to $39 million as part of the purchase price for the Empire State Building from the Crown family, Larry Wien also created the Empire State Building Company, together with his partner in a number of successful real estate transactions in New York City, Harry Helmsley, and a few other investors. This is important to understand because not only was the ownership of the building to continue to be separated from the ownership of the land on which the building stands, but the ownership of both of those things was to be separate from the operation and management of the building, which was potentially very lucrative given the size of the building's rent roll.

> Empire State Building Company is a joint venture among Lawrence A. Wien (25% interest), Harry B. Helmsley (25%), Cargo Despatch, Inc. (37 1/2%), a wholly owned subsidiary of American Hawaiian Steamship Company, the principal stockholder of which is Mr. D. K. Ludwig, Darien, Connecticut, and Martin Weiner Realty Corporation (12 1/2%), owned by Mr. Martin Weiner, Paterson, New Jersey.[27]

The public offering by Larry Wien et al. of up to 3,000 Participation Units of $10,000 each in Empire State Building Associates is best understood by reviewing the description from the Prospectus describing the offering to potential investors in the venture.

GENERAL NATURE OF THE OFFERING

A. DESCRIPTION OF THE TRANSACTION

1. EMPIRE STATE BUILDING ASSOCIATES ("Associates"), 60 East 42nd Street, New York, New York, is a general partnership consisting of Lawrence A. Wien, Henry W. Klein, and Peter L. Malkin. Upon completion of the transactions described below Associates will own a net lease (herein called the "Master Lease") of the Empire State Building, 350 Fifth Avenue, New York City and the land thereunder. This lease, with renewal privileges, will run for approximately 114 years to January 5, 2076.
2. Associates' acquisition of the Master Lease will result from the following transactions. Associates has contracted to purchase the Empire State Building, and the ground lease of the land underlying the building. The contract price is $65,000,000, and a $4,000,000 deposit has been made thereunder. The transaction is scheduled for closing on December 27, 1961 (the "closing date"). In addition to the contract price, Associates will make disbursements of $3,000,000, for various fees and expenses as hereinafter described. These will include profits to Mr. Wien and Harry B. Helmsley, who initiated the transactions. Thus, the total cost of closing the transactions will be $68,000,000.
3. Associates proposes to obtain the $68,000,000 as follows:

    $29,000,000 by causing the building to be sold to The Prudential Insurance Company of America ("Prudential"). Prudential already owns the land and is the lessor under the existing ground lease, having purchased the land in 1951 for $17,000,000. Upon acquiring the building, Prudential will execute the Master Lease of the land and building to Associates. The Master Lease will replace the former ground lease and will provide for the payment of an annual rent by Associates? 13,000,000 by a Leasehold Mortgage? and 26,000,000 through the sale to the public of that amount of the Participations being offered hereby. However, the mortgage may be a smaller amount or there may be no mortgage at all (see page 11). In the latter event, the maximum amount of $39,000,000 of Participations will be sold hereunder. Each partner in Associates will sell Participations in his partnership interest equal to one-third of the amount required. Associates will, therefore, acquire the Master Lease for $39,000,000. The $39,000,000 will be derived either from the proceeds of the sale of Participations and a Leasehold Mortgage, or from the sale of Participations alone.
4. The Participations will become effective on January 1, 1962. Thereafter the purchasers of Participations will share proportionately in the ownership of the partnership interests in Associates.
5. Associates will not operate the property. Simultaneously with the purchase, it will execute a net Sublease of the entire premises to Empire State Building Company (the "Sublessee"), with the same term and renewal privileges as in the Master Lease. Empire State Building Company is a joint venture composed of Mr. Wien, Mr. Harry B. Helmsley, and two corporations owned by others (see page 14.)
6. The Sublessee will agree to pay all expenses of operating and maintaining the property and also to pay Associates an annual net rent (the "basic Sublease rent") which, if paid, will enable Associates

    (a) *to pay the Master Lease rent and to make any Leasehold Mortgage payments?*
    (b) to defray administrative costs? and

(c) to make monthly cash distributions to each participant equal to $900 per year on each $10,000 Participation. Reference is made to Page 13 for a discussion of possible increases in distributions to participants and accompanying reductions in the basic Sublease rent which may occur in the future as and when Associates' Master Lease rent or mortgage requirements reduce. The tax treatment of the estimated cash distributions to participants is discussed at Page 18.

7. *Associates has the right to assign the Master Lease and be relieved of future liabilities thereunder. Since the Sublessee will have a corresponding right of assignment under the Sublease, the investment offered hereby should be judged primarily on the basis of the income-producing capacity of the property.*[28]

The complexity of this real estate financing transaction, which would cause its own set of problems for the son-in-law and grandson of Larry Wien, Peter Malkin and Anthony Malkin, respectively, in the second decade of the twenty-first century in their efforts to create Empire State Realty Trust, a publicly traded real estate investment trust or REIT, in an effort to recapitalize the financing and change the ownership structure of the Empire State Building. See Empire State Building, 2013: Empire State Building Associates "Transitions" to REIT Ownership through Empire Realty Trust.

The unintentional creation of resilient fundamentals[29]

Although the Great Depression and Great Recession were different, their resulting regulations and its respective outcomes remain relevant today. Comparing regulations of the Great Depression with the regulations of the Great Recession of 2008 validates this claim. The comparison of past regulation to present regulation allows insights into the regulatory frameworks failures and successes. The representatives who crafted the Banking Act of 1933 built a strong regulatory framework without foresight of just how successful their laws would become. One example of Glass-Steagall's enduring success was its separation of commercial and investment banking. Its subsequent removal assisted in the resurfacing of redundant risks which were a major cause of both crises. Although this cyclical trend of reoccurring risks justifies the vigilant inspection of the regulatory framework, any attempt to alter its durable regulatory structure, and its proven laws, must be treated with the utmost suspicion.

The demise of savings and loan associations and the emergence of capital markets financing

The S&L Crisis, in many material respects, marks a critical turning point in how commercial real estate transactions are financed in the United States. The source of the funds available to loan to commercial real estate transactions changed most dramatically, from the aggregate proceeds of thrift customers' savings deposits, which were then loaned out by loan officers, reporting to internal loan committees to secure their approvals (the S&L model), to a broader and much, much deeper, more innovative, and flexible money source: capital markets.

Wall Street investment banks began issuing commercial mortgage-backed securities (CMBS) in $100 million, $200 million, and even larger bond offerings, providing funds for commercial real estate mortgages. These same Wall Street investment banks also issued similarly sized residential mortgage-backed securities (MBS), providing a continuous flow of capital to fund mortgages for residential sales. At the same time, private equity firms were amassing billions of dollars through private equity offerings, creating an unprecedented source of equity direct investments in commercial real estate development projects.

It is critically important for developers, for whom the capital markets and private equity funds have become their principal source for both debt and equity financing of their projects and refinancing of those projects, to understand the complex regulatory framework within which these sources of debt and equity financing have been created. That regulatory framework is described, in some detail next.

The federal regulatory framework facilitating and limiting capital formation for real estate investments[30]

President Franklin D. Roosevelt was inaugurated in 1933, just over three years after the stock market crash of 1929 and beginning of the Great Depression. In his presidential campaign and once in the White House, Roosevelt argued that *restructuring the economy* was the only solution to prevent another crisis, as well as to avoid a prolonged depression. To this end, he promoted to Congress and helped pass a series of regulatory reform legislation, for which his administration promulgated and finalized administrative regulations. Roosevelt's reforms for restructuring the U.S. economy included:

- the Securities Act of 1933, broadly regulated the securities industry.
- the Securities Exchange Act of 1934, creating the Securities and Exchange Commission (SEC).
- the Investment Company Act of 1940.

All three of these critical pieces of legislation, and their implementing regulations, as well as additional, related statutes and regulations, including Regulation D and the Dodd-Frank Wall Street Reform and Consumer Protection Act, are discussed next.

Securities Act of 1933

The Securities Act of 1933 (Securities Act) was the first federal statute governing the sale of securities. Prior to this, the sale of securities was primarily governed by state laws or Blue Sky Laws. However, the stock market crash of 1929 raised sobering concerns of how markets were regulated. In an effort to bring back stability and investor confidence in the overall system, Congress enacted the Securities Act of 1933. The statute has two main goals:

1. to make uniform and ensure more transparency in financial statements constituting offers to sell securities to investors, enabling them to make informed decisions about their investments, by requiring a registration process for such securities before being offered to the public; and
2. to establish laws against misrepresentation and fraudulent activities in the securities markets.

Registration Process. Absent an exemption specified in the act, securities to be offered for sale and/or sold to the public in the United States must be registered under the Securities Act of 1933 by filing a Registration Statement with the Securities and Exchange Commissions (SEC), which was created by the Securities Exchange Act of 1934, described later. In addition to requiring the registration of securities for public sale, the Securities Act that each offer and sale registered securities also be registered. Accordingly, a prospectus is required to be filed with the SEC as part of the issuer's Registration Statement.

The SEC prescribes the relevant forms on which an issuer's securities must be registered. Regardless of whether securities must be registered, *the Securities Act makes it illegal to commit fraud in the offer or sale of securities.* The Securities Act also provides a federal cause of action for defrauded investors, providing them with grounds to sue for recovery under the Act. Among other things, registration requires:

- information about the management of the issuer;
- information about the securities (if other than common stock);
- financial statements certified by independent accountants;
- a description of the securities to be offered for sale.

Registration statements and the prospectuses required to be incorporated therein become public shortly after they are filed with the SEC. Registration statements are subject to SEC analysis for compliance with all disclosure requirements under the Act.

Exemptions from the registration requirements include:

- private offerings to a specific type or limited number of persons or institutions;
- offerings of limited size;
- intrastate offerings;
- securities of municipal, state, and federal governments (e.g., bonds).

Like all federal legislation, the Securities Act of 1933 contains the framework for this new regime for the capital markets. The details about how the Act is implemented are contained in countless federal regulations, promulgated administratively and then put into final form.

Rule 144. Rule 144 under the Securities Act of 1933 permits the sale of restricted and controlled securities *without registration*, under limited circumstances. In addition to restrictions on the minimum length of time for which such securities must be held and the maximum volume of such securities permitted to be sold, the issuer must agree to the sale. These are the conditions that must be met for these securities to be sold:

- the prescribed holding period must be met;
- there is an adequate amount of current information available to the public regarding the historical performance of the security;
- the amount to be sold is less than 1% of the shares outstanding and accounts for less than 1% of the average of the previous four weeks' trading volume;
- all of the normal trading conditions that apply to any trade have been met;
- if wishing to sell more than 500 shares or an amount worth more than $10,000, the seller must file a form with the SEC before the sale;
- notice of resale has to be provided to the SEC if the amount of securities sold in any three-month period exceeds 5,000 shares or in an amount in excess of $50,000 (Securities Act of 1933).

Regulation S. Regulation S, promulgated under the Securities Act, defines when an offering of securities is considered to be executed in another country and, therefore, is not subject to its registration requirements. The regulation includes two safe harbor provisions: an issuer safe harbor and a resale safe harbor. Each Regulation S offering is subject to two general conditions:

- the offer or sale must occur in an offshore transaction, meaning the seller reasonably believes the buyer is offshore at the time of the offer or sale or the transaction occurs on certain designated offshore securities markets; and
- that no directed selling efforts are made in the United States by the issuer, a distributor, any of their respective associates or any person acting on behalf of the issuer.

Securities Exchange Act of 1934

In contrast with the Securities Act, which regulates the registration and public sale of securities, the Securities Exchange Act of 1934 (Exchange Act) regulates the secondary market:- Sales that take place after a security is initially offered for sale by the issuer. The Exchange Act operates rather differently from the Securities Act. To protect investors, Congress created a mandatory disclosure process that is designed to force companies to make public information that investors would find pertinent to making investment decisions on an ongoing basis, including whether to hold or sell a particular security. In addition, *the Exchange Act provides for direct regulation of the markets on which securities are sold and the participants in those markets* (industry associations, brokers and dealers, and issuers). The Exchange Act endeavors to protect investors by making sure information is available. However, it also protects investors by prohibiting fraud and establishing severe penalties for those who defraud investors, as well as those who engage in certain trading practices, such as insider trading, that take advantage of information to which most investors do not have access.

Among its many important reforms to the capital markets, the Exchange Act established the Securities and Exchange Commission (SEC or, simply the Commission), charging it with responsibility for regulating the securities markets (something the SEC has done with very mixed effectiveness in the more than eighty years it's been in existence). The Exchange Act initially empowered the Commissions to enforce only the Exchange Act. However, the Commission's powers have been greatly expanded since 1934, and they have been extended to include enforcement of the Securities Act, the Sarbanes-Oxley Act of 2002 (SOX), and other federal statutes governing the capital market. One important function of the SEC is to make sure that companies meet the Exchange Act's disclosure requirements. Registered companies must make periodic and episodic (i.e., event-driven) filings with the SEC, making that information readily available to all investors through EDGAR, its electronic, online document system. In general, reporting companies (i.e., those companies with registered, publicly traded securities and of a certain size) must file periodic reports (10-K annual reports; 10-Q quarterly reports), and episodic or "current" reports reporting the occurrence of any specified events (Form 8-K), in accordance with the filing requirements of the Exchange Act.

Many market participants are also subject to SEC regulations and reporting requirements under the Exchange Act. These "market participants" include all exchanges on which registered securities are traded, such as the New York Stock Exchange and NASDAQ (formerly known as the National Association of Securities Dealers Automated Quotation System but now simply referred to as "NASDAQ") must register with the SEC.

Investment Company Act of 1940

Following the Securities Act and the Exchange Act, the Investment Company Act of 1940 (ICA) was enacted in an effort by congress to define and regulate investment companies. As public companies, Funds were already subject to the disclosure and antifraud provisions of the Securities Act, and mutual fund distributors already were regulated as broker-dealers under the Exchange Act. However, unlike other types of corporations, a mutual fund is basically a large pool of liquid assets. Additionally, most mutual funds are managed externally and have no employees of their own. Therefore, unlike other corporations, mutual funds are managed by outside entities and individuals that may have conflicting loyalties and obligations. The other federal securities laws mostly rely on disclosure and antifraud provisions to address potential abuses. This Act was a recognition by Congress that in the case of the unique conflicts presented by mutual funds, disclosure and antifraud protection weren't sufficient.

The Investment Company Act of 1940 is comprehensive in specifying the types of entities that must register as "an investment company," with the SEC. The Investment Company Act forces every company that falls within the Investment Company Act's definition of "an investment company," summarized below, to register unless there is a recognized statutory exclusion, based upon the company's specific activities, under the Investment Company Act or other SEC relief from the act is available. The definition includes not only traditional mutual funds but also affects companies not commonly thought of as investment companies, which may have never had any intention of doing business as "an investment company." The scope of the Investment Company Act ensures that shareholders in any entity that devotes significant assets to investing in securities will receive its protection. The definition of investment company includes:

- any company that engages primarily, or proposes to be engaged primarily, in the business of investing, reinvesting, or trading in securities;
- any company that is engaged or proposes to be engaged in the business of issuing face amount securities of the installment type, or has any such certificates outstanding (this provision has little relevance today); and
- any company that is engaged or proposes to engage in the business of investing, reinvesting or trading in securities, and owns or proposes to acquire investment securities having a value in excess of 40% of the company's total assets (exclusive of government securities and cash items) on an unconsolidated basis.

Section 7 of the Investment Company Act restricts the activities of unregistered investments companies, and prohibits, among other things, the public offering of securities and engaging in interstate commerce. The Investment Company Act also affects almost every aspect of investment company operations.

The statutory objectives of the Investment Company Act in general, are:

- ensure that potential investors and fund shareholders receive timely and accurate information that promotes informed decision-making;
- prohibit self-dealing, in which people or entities related to a fund use the fund to their own advantage; the sale or purchase of property to or from the fund; borrowing by the fund from an affiliate or vice versa;
- regulate joint transactions in which the fund and fund affiliate(s) are parties; transactions in which a fund affiliate receives other than ordinary broker's compensation for acting as agent for the fund in connection with the purchase or sale of property by the fund;

- ensure that purchases by a fund of securities during an underwriting in which a fund affiliate is one of the underwriters. Ensure that fund assets are valued fairly;
- protect the physical custody of fund assets; assets be held with a qualified U.S. bank or, in accordance with SEC rules, with a U.S. broker-dealer, a U.S. central depository, or in highly-regulated self-custody; and
- ensure that officers and employees with access to assets must be bonded, prevent unsound or excessively complex capital structures, and severely limit borrowings by the fund (Investment Company Act of 1940).

There are specific enforcement measures available to the SEC in making sure that the goals of the Investment Company Act are continuously satisfied by those covered by it. Among other things, the Investment Company Act calls for comprehensive recordkeeping by each fund, and gives the SEC the authority, without advance notice and at any time to inspect these books and records at the fund's location. Financial reports that accompany reports to shareholders must be certified by an certified public accountant that has been approved by fund shareholders. The Investment Company Act goes beyond state law and imposes a number of additional conditions and requirements on fund boards.

Over more than seventy-five years since its enactment, the Investment Company Act has adapted to changing circumstances and the evolution of securities markets. This was made possible because the Investment Company Act provides the SEC with broad authority to find exemptions from its provisions in situations that were not predictable in 1940. However, this any such exemption from the coverage of the Investment Company Act must be based on a finding that the exemption is consistent with the protections the Act seeks to afford those investors the Act was intended to protect. Consequently, the industry has been able to develop a diversity of products and services not contemplated in 1940, while the Investment Company Act has been able to fulfill its statutory purpose and objectives.

Investment Advisers Act of 1940. A companion statute to the Investment Company Act, the Investment Advisers Act of 1940 (the Investment Advisers Act) was enacted in 1940 to regulate fund managers. The Investment Advisers Act authorizes and empowers the SEC to monitor finance professionals, and those who hold themselves out as such, who, for a fee, advise investors, including individuals, pension funds, and institutions on how and where to investment their funds. The Investment Advisers Act was designed to regulate investment advisers but, more specifically, to keep track of those in the industry and their methods of operation. The Investment Advisers Act does not provide a regulatory regime specifying or requiring qualifications for becoming "an investment adviser." It does, however, require registration for those conducting investment an advisory business.

The Investment Advisers Act requires the registration of virtually all investment advisers, defining an investment adviser as "any person who, for compensation, engages in the business of advising others, either directly or through publications or writings, as to the value of securities or as to the advisability of investing in, purchasing, or selling securities, or who for compensation and as part of a regular business, issues or promulgates analyses or reports concerning securities." Whether or not a person is considered to be an investment adviser under the Investment Advisers Act generally depends on three things:

- the type of advice offered;
- the method of compensation; and
- whether or not a significant portion of the adviser's income comes from offering investment advice.

The Investment Advisers Act mandated that all persons and firms receiving compensation for serving as an investment adviser must register with the SEC. However, there are three general exceptions to the registration requirement:

1. investment advisers whose clients all reside in the same state as the adviser's business office and who do not provide advice on securities listed on national exchanges;
2. investment advisers whose clients are solely insurance companies; and
3. investment advisers who had fewer than fifteen (15) clients in any previous twelve-month period.

The Investment Advisers Act was amended in 1996 with the Investment Advisers Supervision Coordination Act (the "Supervision Coordination Act").Basically, the 1996 enactment requires the SEC to supervise and register those investment advisers managing $25 million or more in client assets. Those managing less than this amount are to be registered with and supervised by state law. If an investment adviser managing client assets of $25 million or less resides in a state that does not require registration, that investment adviser must then register with the SEC.

Under the Investment Advisers Act securities may be defined as "including but not necessarily limited to notes, bonds, stocks, mutual funds, money market funds, and certificates of deposit". The term "securities" does not generally include commodity contracts, real estate, insurance contracts, or collectibles such as works of art or rare stamps and coins. Even those who receive finder's fees for referring potential clients to investment advisers are considered to be investment advisers.

In general, the Investment Advisers Act excludes those professionals whose investment advice to clients is incidental to the professional relationship. The Investment Advisers Act provides an exemption for "any lawyer, accountant, engineer, or teacher whose performance of such services is solely incidental to the practice of his profession." "*Solely incidental*" is the key phrase If professionals are not to be considered investment advisers under the Investment Advisers Act:

- they must not present themselves to the public as an investment adviser;
- any investment advice given must be reasonably related to their primary professional function; and
- fees for the "investment advice" must be based on the same criteria as fees for the primary professional function.

Banks, publishers, and government security advisers are also excepted from the Act. Financial planners may, under certain circumstances, be considered financial advisers under the Investment Advisers Act.

Under the Investment Advisers Act, investment advisers must register using Form ADV, which requires the disclosure of such information as:

- educational background,
- experience,
- exact type of business engaged in,
- assets,
- information on clients,
- history of any legal and/or criminal nature, and
- type of investment advice to be offered.

Registered investment advisers are required to update their ADV form annually and file operating reports with the SEC or state regulatory agency. Generally, advisers cannot receive compensation based on the performance of the investment advice provided and are prohibited under the Investment Advisers Act, from engaging in excessive trading or profiting from market activity resulting from their advice to clients.

These four federal statutory and regulatory market reforms – the Securities Act of 1933, the Securities Exchange Act of 1934, the Investment Company Act of 1940, and the Investment Advisors Act of – were the subject of significant criticism from both participants in the securities markets as well as issuers and their professional advisers, such as attorneys and accountants, regarding the regulatory burdens they imposed, particularly their impact on small businesses. Some claimed this regulatory compliance burden was solely responsible for the increasing inability of small businesses to raise capital for growth and development. Based on this continuing critique, the SEC conducted an extensive study, which revealed that the registration requirements and the exemption structure of the Securities Act *disproportionately affected small businesses seeking to raise capital* through the sale of securities. One SEC study confirmed that the cost for registration requirements was substantially higher for small businesses than for large ones.

The SEC's primary purposes in promulgating Regulation D were to simplify and clarify the existing exemptions from registration, to expand the availability of such exemptions, and to align state and federal exemptions in order to facilitate capital formation consistent with the goal of investor protection under the Securities Act.

Regulation D

Regulation D was first adopted by the SEC in 1982 to facilitate capital raising efforts by small businesses. The three (3), transaction-based exemptions under Regulation D, comprised of Rule 504, Rule 505, and Rule 506, respectively, accomplish this goal by providing guidelines that allow companies to raise money through the private offering and sale of securities without having to go through the tedious, complex, and expensive process of registering securities for sale to the public, through filings therefore with the SEC (these are often referred to as "Reg. D Offerings").

Rule 504. Rule 504 provides an exemption for the offer and sale of up to $1,000,000 of securities in a twelve-month period. General offerings and solicitations are permitted under Rule 504 as long as they are restricted to accredited investors. The issuer need not restrict purchaser's right to resell securities. In the United States, in order to be an "accredited Investor" for purposes of Regulation D and Rule 504, an individual must have a net worth of at least one million US dollars ($1,000,000.00), *not including the value of one's primary residence* or have annual income of at least $200,000 for the last two years (or $300,000 of joint, annual income if the individual is married) and have the expectation to make the same amount in the current year.

Rule 505. Rule 505 provides an exemption for offers and sales of securities totaling up to $5 million in any twelve-month period. Under this exemption, securities may be sold to an unlimited number of accredited investors and *up to thirty-five unaccredited investors* who do not need to satisfy the sophistication or wealth standards associated with other exemptions. Purchasers must buy for investment only, and not for resale. The issued securities are restricted, in that the *investors may not sell for at least two years* without registering the transaction. General solicitation or advertising to sell the securities is not allowed. Under Rule 505, the SEC must be notified within fifteen days after the first sale of the offering. Also, financial statement requirements apply to this type of offering.

Rule 506. A company may raise an unlimited amount of capital if it doesn't use general solicitation or advertising to market the securities; sale of securities may be made to an unlimited number of accredited investors and up to thirty-five others. Unlike Rule 505, all non-accredited investors, either alone or with a purchaser representative, must be sophisticated – they must have sufficient knowledge and experience in financial and business to enable them to evaluate the specific characteristics of the prospective investment; seller must be available to answer questions by prospective purchasers; financial statement requirements are the same as for Rule 505 offerings; and purchasers receive restricted securities, which may not be freely traded in the secondary market after the offering has concluded.

Rule 504, Rule 505, and Rule 506 offerings are subject to Rule 503, which requires issuers to file a Form D Notice of an Exempt Offering of Securities. Rule 503 also requires that the Form D Notice of Exempt Offering be filed within fifteen days after the first sale of securities in the offering. The date of first sale is the date on which the first investor is contractually committed to the investment, without any right to cancel same. Privately held companies that raise capital are required to file a Form D with the SEC to declare exempt offering of securities. Many of these filings show investments in small, growing companies through venture capital and angel investors, as well as certain pooled investment funds.

Prohibitions Against Fraud in Securities Transactions. The federal statutes and their applicable regulations, referenced above, as well as common law in each state pertaining to the offering and sale of securities, provide generally applicable antifraud provisions. The prevention of fraud in the offering for sale and sale of securities is one of the main purposes of the securities laws enacted in the United States since the Securities Act of 1933 was passed by Congress. For this reason, most of the antifraud provisions of the U.S. securities laws *apply to all issuers of securities*, whether or not such issuers are otherwise required to register under any of the applicable, federal securities acts, and whether or not provisions of such acts other than the antifraud provisions apply to such issuers. Professionals interested in raising private capital should be aware of potential fraud claims, even constructive fraud claims based on negligence, during every phase of forming and operating their funds.

The Securities Act requires that, absent an exemption, all offers and sales of securities must be registered with the SEC. Because private equity funds are offering and selling securities when they solicit investors into their funds, such offers and sales must be registered with the SEC, unless an exemption is available. Primarily because of the attendant costs, the public disclosure obligations, and the ongoing compliance obligations that flow from registration, such funds have strong incentives not to register their offers and sales of interests in their funds if an exemption from registration is available to them.

Registration may be avoided for private equity funds through a number of exemptions available to such companies. By far the most common exemption relied upon to avoid registration under the Securities Act is the private placement exemptions under Regulation D. The SEC provides guidance, under Regulation D, as to what constitutes a private placement of securities. As previously mentioned, Regulation D has different criteria for exemption depending on the size of the offering and to whom made.

Historically, issuers have been able to raise billions by taking advantage of the Regulation D exemption. In 2012, the SEC conducted an analysis of the information extracted from Form D filings received by the SEC since the beginning of 2009. This analysis was conducted in order to determine the amount and nature of capital raised through unregistered offerings claiming Regulation D exemption, and to provide some perspective on the regulatory burden on U.S. capital markets. In 2008, the SEC began requiring Form D filings to be made electronically, and in a structured data format, which enabled large-scale statistical analysis for the period from early 2009, when this requirements was imposed, through the first quarter of 2011.

Some of the main findings from the SEC's study of Regulation D filings include:

- The market for unregistered offerings is very large;
- Prior reports on the analysis by the Office of Inspector General show $1.2 trillion between 2000 and 2001.
- More recently, $609 billion in private placement offerings were made during 2008.
- In 2009 and 2010, based on information extracted from all electronic Form D filings, private offerings totaled $587 billion and $905 billion, respectively.
- In 2011, the first quarter reflected aggregate private placement offerings of $322 billion, corresponding to an annualized rate of $1.3 trillion.
- Real Estate issuers represent 8.4% of the total, exceeded only by healthcare, technology and pulled fund investment.
- In 2010, Regulation D offerings exceeded debt offerings as the leading offering method in terms of aggregate amount of capital raised in the United States thus more likely to represent new investment as opposed to refinancing of existing investment.
- The amount of capital raised through Regulation D offerings may be considerably larger than what is disclosed on Form D because no closing filing is required.
- Rule 506 was the most-used Regulation D exemption (55.4%)
- The median Regulation D offering is small in size: Approximately $1 million.
- Consistent with the original objective of Regulation D to target the capital formation needs of small business, there have been a large number of smaller offerings: 37,000 unique offerings since 2009.
- There has been a shift from public to private capital-raising over the past three years, due to both a decline in public issuances and an increase in private issuances: Public issuances fell by 11% from 2009 to 2010 while private issuances increased by 31% over the same period.

EMPIRE STATE BUILDING, 2009: REPOSITIONING NEW YORK CITY'S LARGEST COMMERCIAL BUILDING: THE "GREENING" OF THE EMPIRE STATE BUILDING

Despite its status as the most iconic commercial building in the United States, as well as one of the best-known skyscrapers in the world, at the turn of the century the Empire State Building was a little worn and looking a little shabby. Its rent roll was dominated by smaller tenants of little fame or notoriety, and the building's energy efficiency, in a market where things like LEED certification were effective marketing tools, was sub-par. To paraphrase an old saying, it was a nice place for tourists to visit but you wouldn't want to have your office there.

Empire State Building Associates, the entity formed by Larry Wien in 1961 to finance and execute the purchase of the Empire State Building from the Crown family, determined it was time for a make-over, to support a comprehensive plan to reposition the building in the greater New York City commercial real estate market generally, and the Midtown Manhattan market specifically.

As reported by The Real Deal, New York City's daily covering the commercial real estate industry, in 2011:

> The Empire State Building may have been the world's most famous office building, but in the New York real estate industry, it was becoming famous for the wrong reasons.
> Lately, however, that's begun to change.
> In January, Malkin, 48, inked a gargantuan, 483,000 square foot lease with LF USA, a division of the Hong Kong-based consumer products trading firm Li & Fung. It was the largest deal for New York City office space in two and a half years. Other new tenants include the German fragrance company Coty Inc.? Skanska, the Swedish construction company? the Federal Deposit Insurance Corporation? Turkish Airlines? Lufthansa? and Air China. More than 300,000 square feet worth of additional deals are "under discussion – serious discussion," Malkin said.
> What's more, space that was renting for $26.50 a square foot in 2006 is now going for more than twice that in some parts of the building.
> It's all part of a $550 million effort to rehabilitate both the structure and the reputation of the legendary skyscraper, and replace the rabbit warren of mom-and-pop tenants, dentists and cobblers renting space with a roster of less than 200 larger leasees, some of which have already signed multi-floor, long-term deals that should ensure the financial stability of the building for decades.[31]

All told, Empire State Building Associates spent approximately $550 million on the make-over, including extensive energy efficiency improvements, such as replacing all of the building's windows with much-more energy efficient, custom-made, replacements matching the design of the originals; rebuilt chillers in the building's basement; a new elevator system, and a host of other upgrades, eventually earning the building a LEED-Gold status.

This substantial renovation and repositioning of the Empire State Building offers an excellent example of how a portfolio developer with an aging asset, if willing to make the capital investments necessary, may dramatically improve a building's long-term prospects for greater profitability, making it in the owner's best interest to continue to hold, and profit from, the asset.

Dodd-Frank Wall Street Reform and Consumer Protection Act

The Great Recession of 2008 constituted the largest economic disruption the United States had experienced since Black Tuesday on October 29, 1929, marking the start of the Great Depression. The reverberations were felt around the world. Trillions of dollars in investment value was lost in the stock market, with a concomitant and equally precipitous drop in residential and, subsequently, commercial real estate market values; millions of Americans lost their jobs. Unemployment climbed to more than 10% and did not come down to below 5% until January 2016, seven and a half years after the recession's onset.

Much of what went wrong in the U.S. economy that triggered the crash of capital markets in the Fall of 2008, was caused by unrelenting greed in the subprime mortgage markets, which eventually translated to a proliferation of engineered financial instruments like CDOs (collateralized debt obligations) and Synthetic CDOs (which are almost impossible to explain even to seasoned capital markets professionals). Because the velocity at which Wall Street demanded more and more product – i.e. residential subprime mortgages to back $100 million and larger subprime mortgage-backed securities (MBSs) – the more lax with underwriting standards (if there were any operating at this point) and the more aggressive with things like teaser-rates and extremely high LTVs the loan originators became, fueling speculative purchases of for-sale homes to be devoted to rental housing or in hopes of being flipped.

Not unlike what had happened in the years leading up to the S&L Crisis housing prices were being artificially driven up, based on nothing more than the easy availability of purchase money mortgages on terms too favorable to pass up. When the financial markets collapsed, real estate values followed. In some markets, home values dropped by as much as 50% of what they had "appraised" for six to twelve months earlier. It was as if no one who had been around in the mid-to-late 1980s before the depository institutions collapsed in the S&L Crisis had learned any lessons from the experience. The total cost of the federal government's, taxpayer-funded bailout of the financial services industry exceeded several trillion dollars when all subsidies and market supports are calculated, including the Federal Reserve's quantitative easing strategies to keep interest rates artificially low. (For more details about the specifics of what caused the Great Recession of 2008, see *A Finance Major's Guide to "The Big Short,"* the book by Michael Lewis chronicling the events that led up to the collapse of the financial markets in 2008, on the companion website for the textbook.

In a post-Great Recession effort to regulate the U.S. financial system and prevent a future financial crisis of such epic magnitude, President Obama signed the Dodd-Frank Wall Street Reform and Consumer Protection Act of 2010 (commonly referred to simply as "Dodd-Frank") into law on. Dodd-Frank represents the most far-reaching reform of the U.S. financial system since the reforms spearheaded by President Roosevelt after the Great Depression.

Dodd-Frank was designed to prevent the excessive risk-taking that led to the financial crisis that came to a head in the Fall of 2008; to provide protections for American families; and to create new consumer protections to prevent mortgage companies from exploiting naïve and vulnerable consumers. Additionally, Dodd-Frank has extensive implications for private investment funds, private fund managers and private capital-raising. The Act consists of 16 distinct sections, addressing all areas of financial regulation. Significant elements of Dodd-Frank include:

- Creation of a new independent regulatory agency – the Consumer Financial Protection Bureau – intended to serve the interests of consumers of financial products and services.
- New regulations – including "stress tests" for investment banks – designed to reduce the risk that taxpayers will be required to bail out large financial institutions.
- Creation of an overall financial council that will have oversight of the financial system and is intended to identify and address systemic risks posed by large, complex companies and products.
- Increased regulation with respect to over-the-counter derivatives, asset-backed securities, hedge funds, and mortgage brokers.
- A requirement that public company shareholders have a nonbinding vote on executive compensation and authorization for the SEC to adopt rules granting shareholder access to public company proxy statements for shareholder director nominees.
- New regulations for transparency and accountability of credit rating agencies.
- Strengthened ability of regulators to pursue financial fraud, conflicts of interest, and manipulation of the financial system.

Dodd-Frank amended the Investment Advisers Act of 1940 to require registration of many fund managers. It requires the SEC to establish reporting and record-retention for many managers of private funds. It also requires the SEC to develop an exemption solely for advisers to private funds which have assets under management of $150 million or less.

Among other things Impacting private capital-raising, Dodd-Frank adjusted the net worth requirement in the "accredited investor" definition currently found in Regulation D. The SEC is directed to further review the definition of an "accredited investor" in Regulation D for possible updating at periodic intervals. Additionally, Dodd-Frank contains a provision which requires the SEC to adopt rules that disqualify "bad actors" from engaging in offerings and sales of securities under Rule 506 of Regulation D.

Finally, Dodd-Frank adopts a version of the Volcker Rule to prohibit a banking entity from acquiring or retaining any equity, partnership or other ownership interest in, or sponsoring any, hedge fund or private equity fund.

The Volcker Rule. Also impacting the formation and fundraising of private funds is Dodd-Frank's inclusion of a modified version of the Volcker Rule. It is an amendment to the Bank Holding Company Act of 1956 and prohibits any banking entity from engaging in sponsoring or investing in a hedge fund or private equity fund, subject to certain exceptions. For purposes of this prohibition, "hedge fund" and "private equity fund" mean an issuer that would be an investment company or similar funds determined by the appropriate regulatory authorities. To "sponsor" a fund means to serve as a general partner, managing member or trustee of a fund, in any manner to control a majority of the directors, trustees or management of a fund, or to share with a fund, for corporate, marketing, promotional or other purposes, the same name or a variant of the same name. Dodd-Frank specifies that certain activities are excluded from the Volcker Rule's prohibitions. One of these exclusions is for the sponsoring of, and investment in, a hedge fund or private equity fund so long as certain requirements are met.

In addition to the federal legislation, outlined above, that was enacted and signed into law in 2010, in reaction to the Great Recession of 2008, detailed above, Congress passed and President Obama signed into law on April 5, 2012, the Jumpstart Our Business Startups (JOBS) Act, sometimes referred to simply as "the JOBS Act." Whereas the 2010 legislation was intended primarily to prevent bad things from happening again – such as the largest economic recession since the Great Depression – the JOBS Act was intended to free up capital and encourage business start-ups in hopes of providing a significant boost to what was almost universally viewed as a sluggish recovery from the 2008 financial crisis.

The JOBS Act has several key components. It is comprised of six titles:

- Reopening American Capital Markets to Emerging Growth Companies,
- Access to Capital for Job Creators,
- Crowdfunding,
- Small Company Capital Formation,
- Private Company Flexibility, and
- Growth and Capital Expansion.

For more information on crowdfunding, which is increasingly providing equity investments for real estate developers nationwide who might be viewed as too small to garner interest from Wall Street private equity firms, see the following Feature Box, Crowdfunding: The Future of Real Estate Investment, by Nicole Lane. For more information generally about the JOBS Act, see related information on the companion website for the textbook.

CROWDFUNDING: THE FUTURE OF REAL ESTATE INVESTMENT, NICOLE LANE [32]

Crowdfunding Defined

Crowdfunding, peer-to-peer lending and micro-financing are buzzwords in today's media cycle but each of them are monikers for the same concept. Crowdfunding is a method of raising small amounts of capital through the collective efforts of a large pool of individuals (the crowd). The capital is raised primarily online via social media and web based platforms that have been created for the linking of investors and those with interest in the project or product.

Crowdfunding can be divided into three categories: donation based, rewards based and equity.[33] One of the first successful donation based crowdfunding efforts was accomplished in 1997 when fans raised $60,000 to fund British rock band Marillion's U.S. tour.[34] Rewards based funding provides t-shirts, club membership, VIP attendance at an event or public recognition for donation. The equity model, which will be the focus of this section, provides investors shares in exchange for their investment.

A short history of crowdfunding

While the Internet has made Crowdfunding a household name in the past decade, its beginnings stretch far into the past. In the 18th century, Jonathan Swift created the Irish Loan Fund, which provided loans to impoverished families in rural areas.[35] The pioneer of peer-to-peer lending is cited as 2006 Nobel Peace Prize winner Dr. Mohammad Yunus, whose program in Bangladesh provided financing to entrepreneurs who were unable to qualify for traditional bank financing and eventually lead to the creation of the Grameen Bank.[36]

Over time, peer-to-peer funding websites have grown with the most notable being Kickstarter, whose platform raised $480 million from 3 million individuals to fund projects or "$1,315,520 pledged a day or $913 a minute.[37]" Kickstarter is just one of hundreds of platforms used to raise capital and is an excellent indication of the industries far reaching grasp and potential capital gold mine. According to Massolution, an advisory firm specializing in crowdsourcing, the industry has grown significantly in the past decade reaching $16.2 billion in capital raised in 2014, a twofold increase from $6.1 billion in 2013 and is estimated to double again in 2015 to $34.4 billion[38].

Securities Act of 1933

The Jumpstart Our Business Startups Act (also known as the "JOBS Act") was signed into law April 5th, 2012 In order to understand the significance of the, it is important that one review the state of affairs prior to its existence. Before the 1929 stock market crash, few limitations existed on who could invest and how much could be invested. In response to the Great Depression, the Securities Act of 1933 was enacted with a twofold purpose: 1. Provide transparency and improve disclosure by requiring registration with SEC so that investors had access to information necessary to make informed decisions and;2. Establish laws to prevent misrepresentation and fraudulent activity in the market[39]. Additionally, it created a ban on general solicitation or advertising publicly that a company is seeking capital. In order to improve transparency, companies were required to file an offering statement with the SEC in order to offer securities, and were subject to registering and meeting requirements at the state level as well, creating a cumbersome process.

Essentially, the Securities Act of 1933 created a barrier between investors and those seeking capital. The ban on solicitation encompassed not only media advertising but also anyone the entrepreneur did not know, which would make discussing a potential offering at a cocktail party illegal. A piece of legislation known as Regulation D, was a loophole provided to business seeking to issue securities but this also, imposed strict regulations that limited what the lay person could invest as a form of protecting citizens creating two categories of investors: accredited and non-accredited.

According to the SEC website, an accredited investor falls into one of two major categories: Put items 1 and 2 into list form 1. Institutions: bank, insurance company, registered investment company, charitable organization (with assets exceeding $5 million), an employee benefits plan and 2:

"a natural person who has individual net worth, or joint net worth with the person's spouse, that exceeds $1 million at the time of the purchase, excluding the value of the primary residence of such person. . . . [or] with income exceeding $200,000 in each of the two most recent years or joint income with a spouse exceeding $300,000 for those years and a reasonable expectation of the same income level in the current year."[40]

The U.S. Securities and Exchange Commission (SEC) recognized the prohibitive nature of the current state of affairs stating: "Cost-effective access to capital for companies of all sizes plays a critical role in our national economy, and companies seeking access to capital should not be hindered by unnecessary or overly burdensome regulations."[41]

The Jumpstart Our Business Startups (JOBS) Act changes everything

The JOBS Act allows companies to raise as much as $1 million per year from individual investors and eliminates the accredited investor requirement. This expands the pool from 258,000 active accredited investors to 233.7 million potential investors according to Fundable.com[42]. Investors who have a net worth or annual income of less than $100,000 may invest the greater of 5% or $2000 and those with net worth or annual income at or above $100,00 may invest 10% of their annual income.

Rule 506(c) allows private companies to publicly raise funds (using public channels, such as broadcast TV, social media platforms, such a LinkedIn, and online blogs). It places no restriction on who an issuer can solicit, but an issuer faces restrictions on who is permitted to purchase its securities. Additionally, issuers must make reasonable efforts to verify accreditation of investors using tax returns or third parties for verification. Finally, Rule 506(c) requires companies to file within 15 days of the first sale of securities. Other proposed amendments include changes to Regulation A which would allow companies to raise up to $50M in securities under this new simplified filing. A final proposed change would be to allow the solicitation and sale of deals in all 50 states without seeking approval from each state individually.

Effect on the real estate industry

Since the implementation of these changes, the real estate industry has taken advantage of this new capital source. According to Crowdnetic, three real estate development PIPRs (private issuers publicly raising) accounted for $17 million in recorded capital commitments between September 2013 and February 2014 making the industry the leader in crowdfunding investment. A Massolution study reports that in 2014 alone that number increased to a total of $1 billion raised via crowdfunding and invested in real estate in the United States alone with an estimated $2.5 billion to enter the market by end of 2015.[43]

Equity crowdfunding allows unsophisticated investors to invest in real estate just as Real Estate Investment Trusts attempted to do when created. The new method offers investors a chance to fund projects in their own neighborhood as seen with companies such as Fundrise, which is based in Washington, D.C., but has a national, online presence and sponsors real estate development projects nationwide. Rather than invest in a company's strategy as one did with REITs, an individual can invest in a physical asset and gain access to multiple asset classes in various locations. Additionally, the individual avoids high middleman fees associated with purchasing stock in REITs.

Developers now have access to a unique network of investors who are seeking to invest directly in such projects. For its part, through its crowdfunding platform for real estate investing, Fundrise has invested over $10 million, including a project in Washington, D.C.'s up-and-coming Shaw neighborhood that raised $100,000 from 100 investors in the first hour and a half of the offering posting to the company's website. This company allows investments of as little as $100 and provides short-term maturities of one to five years.

Expect More Regulation

The question has been raised as to how companies prevent fraudulent activity when advertising to such a wide base of potential investors whom they have not researched. An article in Entrepreneur magazine discusses some of the proposed regulation to protect consumers with the common theme from those who issued public comments to the SEC regarding regulation being: "the websites administering equity crowdfunding (or the "portals") will be saddled with so much responsibility; they won't be able to effectively function[44]." For starters, the proposed SEC rules address web based platforms that connect the business owners with interested investors and recommend that the owner of the portal shall be held liable for any fraudulent activity by entrepreneurs who solicit funding. Further portals would be viewed as issuers and thus would be banned from providing advice to its users despite being held liable if those users lost their investment especially important considering the new regulation allows unsophisticated investors to participate. This regulation would create high levels of risk and costs of doing business making it nearly impossible for small startup companies that have created investment platforms to survive. Overall, this would provide fewer choices to investors, thus returning them back to the dark ages of a small pool of investors. Much hangs in the balance as the SEC finalizes regulations on what is seemingly the next generation of real estate investment.

Development Entity and Transaction deal structures that facilitate the use of crowdfunding for financing real estate development

Real estate crowdfunding is being used for every asset class from multi-family and retail to even the high barrier to entry hotel asset class. In some cases such as the Hard Rock Hotel Palm Springs, whose owner was the first existing hotel to offer shares, returns are not the only benefit with investors receiving discounted room rates, an exclusive pool side cabana and upgraded rooms.[45]

Much like traditional real estate investing, crowdfunding platforms structure each deal as separate LLC.

Understanding the Financing of Real Estate Transactions in the Context of The Development Process: Outline of the Steps in the Process. Sample documents, related current Case Briefs, and detailed explanation and legal analysis related to the selected entries in the outline are provided on the companion website for the textbook.

EMPIRE STATE BUILDING, 2013: EMPIRE STATE BUILDING ASSOCIATES "TRANSITIONS" TO REIT OWNERSHIP THROUGH EMPIRE REALTY TRUST

In one form or another, the Empire State Building has been in the control of Lawrence Wien, one of New York City's most successful real estate developers in the twentieth century, and his family, since Larry, together with his son-in-law, Peter Malkin, and Henry W. Klien, formed Empire State Building Associates, a general partnership that negotiated for the purchase of the Empire State Building from the Crown family. The transaction, which also involving landowner Prudential Insurance Company of America, in a transaction valued at $85 million in 1961. After the passing of his father-in-law, Peter Malkin assumed the helm of Empire State Building Associates and Malkin's son – Wien's grandson – Anthony Malkin, who is now the CEO of Empire Realty Trust, a real estate investment trust formed in 2011, which in 2013 completed a litigious conversion of Empire Building Associates "Participation Units" into shares of ERT. In addition to the Empire State Building, ERT owns a number of smaller and less-remarkable commercial real estate assets in New York and Connecticut.

    The Malkins pursued the REIT transformation of Empire State Building Associates into Empire Realty Trust because they believed that, by operating as a REIT, the ownership and property management of the Empire State Building would have much greater flexibility, particularly in its ability to raise capital through the REIT, if needed. A minority group of holders of the Participation Units in Empire State Building Associates, which had been acquired in the original, 1961 offering arranged by Wien – some of whom had inherited their units from the original purchasers, objected to the transaction, which they saw as diluting the value of the interests they held.

One of the most interesting aspects of this "conversion" of the old ownership form into the REIT is that the legal form of the former made the creation of the latter problematic. The legal wrangling over whether or not ERT could do what it proposed to do through its initial offering of shares in ERT lasted almost two years, from 2011 until 2013, when the last legal hurdle was eliminated. The issues relating to dilution and valuation of the Empire State Building Associates Participation Units were complicated and, as a consequence, complicated the creation of the REIT out of the existing entity. In the end, Participation Units originally issued in 1961 for $10,000, which at the time represented the life savings of those New Yorkers who wanted to "own a piece" of the world's most famous skyscraper, were estimated at a value of approximately $320,000 but ultimately had an exchange or redemption value of about $234,000. The majority of the Participation Units were voluntarily converted by their respective units into shares in the newly formed REIT.

Notes

1. Willis, Carol, *Form Follows Finance: Skyscrapers and Skylines in New York and Chicago*, Princeton Architectural Press, New York, NY (1995), pg. 90. Footnotes and figure references in the original intentionally omitted; emphasis added in the first instance.

2. Ibid., pg. 90. Footnotes and figure references intentionally omitted.

3. Chapter 2 (Figure 2.30).

4. Chapter 3, Project Conception Phase. Emphasis in original.

5. Poorvu, William J. and Jeffrey L. Cruikshank, *The Real Estate Game: The Intelligent Guide to Decision-Making and Investment*, The Free Press, a Division of Simon & Schuster Inc., New York, NY (1999), pg. 55.

6. Dr. Peter Linneman is a Principal and Founder of Linneman Associates and Professor Emeritus at the Wharton School of Business, University of Pennsylvania. He is the author of a leading textbook on real estate finance: Real Estate Finance and Investments: Risks and Opportunities. Linneman Associates publishes the highly acclaimed industry newsletter, The Linneman Letter. www.linnemanassociates.com. Students and readers are encouraged by the Author to Follow Dr. Linneman on Twitter: @P_Linneman.

7. Willis, *Form Follows Finance*, pgs. 90–93.

8. Ibid., pg. 93. Footnote omitted; emphasis added.

9. Ibid., Note 86, pg. 193, with information in brackets taken from Note 85, pgs. 192–193.

10. Santayana, George, "Reason in Common Sense," pg. 284, from *The Life of Reason: The Phases of Human Progress* 1 (1905).

11. Smirniotopoulos, Peter, "Fixing the Mortgage Mess: Why Treasury's Efforts at Both Ends of the Spectrum Are Failing." *The New Geography*, October 23, 2009. Found at www.newgeography.com/content/001124-fixing-mortgage-mess-why-treasury%E2%80%99s-efforts-both-ends-spectrum-are-failing.

12. Portions of this section of Chapter 9 have been adapted from the following student Final Paper in the author's graduate course, Foundations of Real Estate Law, in the Master's of Real Estate Program at Georgetown University (MPRE-690, MPRE-601–01, Spring 2013): Ressler, Paul, "Too Big to Fail: U.S. Financial Regulatory Framework & Real Estate." April 23, 2013, cited elsewhere as Ressler, "Too Big to Fail."

13. Day, Kathleen, *The S&L Hell: The People and the Politics behind the $1 Trillion Savings and Loan Scandal*, W. W. Norton, New York, NY (1993), pg. 375.

14. Excavation for the Empire State Building began on January 22, 1930, and construction began on March 17, 1930 (St. Patrick's Day). With a completion and opening date of May 1, 1931, the Empire State Building took thirteen months and fifteen days from start to finish of construction.

15. History.com, "This Day in History." October 29, 1929: Stock Market Crashes. Found at www.history.com/this-day-in-history/stock-market-crashes.

16. Grigonis, Richard, "The Empire State Building's 80th Anniversary." *InterestingAmerica. com*, February 11, 2011. Found at www.interestingamerica.com/2011–02–04_Empire_State_Building_at_80_by_R_Grigonis.html:

    Thanks to the economic catastrophe of the Great Depression, the estimated $43 million dollar construction project not only came in ahead of schedule, but also for the amazingly low cost of $24,718,000. The cost of the whole project including the land and demolition of the Waldorf-Astoria was $40,948,900.

17. Tauranac, John, *The Empire State Building: The Making of a Landmark*, Cornell University Press, Ithaca, NY (2014), pg. 272; Kindle Edition, 2014–03–21, at Kindle Location 5095.

18. Ibid., pg. 273; Kindle Edition, 2014–03–21, at Kindle Location 5112.

19. Portions of this section of Chapter 9 have been adapted from the following student Final Paper in the author's graduate course "Foundations of Real Estate Law," in the Master of Real Estate Program at Georgetown University (MPRE-690, MPRE-601–01, Spring 2013): Corea, Juan Camilo, "Federal Statutory and Regulatory Changes in the Post-Great Recession Recovery of the U.S. Real Estate Market: How Expanding Capital Formation While Limiting Debt Availability Will Impact Real Estate Development Projects." April 5, 2013.

20. Portions of this section of Chapter 9 have been adapted from the following student Final Paper in the author's graduate course, Foundations of Real Estate Law, in the Master's of Real Estate Program at Georgetown University (MPRE-690, MPRE-601–01, Spring 2013): Ressler, "Too Big To Fail."

21. Carter, Zach, "A Master of Disaster." *The Nation*, January 4, 2010.

22. Id.

23. Tauranac, *The Empire State Building*, pg. 340; Kindle Edition, 2014–03–21, at Kindle Location 6419–6434.

24. Ibid., pgs. 341–342; Kindle Edition, 2014–03–21, at Kindle Location 6451.

25. Ibid., pg. 342; Kindle Edition, 2014–03–21, at Kindle Location 6468.

26. Ibid., pgs. 349–350; Kindle Edition, 2014–03–21, at Kindle Location 6611.

27. $39,000,000 of Participations in General Partnership Interests in *Empire State Building Associated*, Prospectus dated October 31, 1961, subsection 2. The Lessee, Section VI of the Prospectus: *Operation of the Building Under Sublease*, pg. 11/32.

28. $39,000,000 of Participations in General Partnership Interests in *Empire Stat Building Associated*, Prospectus dated October 31, 1961, subsection 2. The Lessee, Section I. General Nature of the Offering, A. Description of the Transaction, pgs. 3/32 through 4/32.

29. Portions of this section of Chapter 9 have been adapted from the following student Final Paper in the author's graduate course, Foundations of Real Estate Law, in the Master's of Real Estate Program at Georgetown University (MPRE-690, MPRE-601–01, Spring 2013): Ressler, "Too Big To Fail."

30. Portions of this section of Chapter 9 have been adapted from the following student Final Paper in the author's graduate course, Foundations of Real Estate Law, in the Master's of Real Estate Program at Georgetown University (MPRE-690, MPRE-601–01, Spring 2013): Corea, Juan Camilo, "Federal Statutory and Regulatory Changes in the Post-Great Recession Recovery of the U.S. Real Estate Market: How Expanding Capital Formation While Limiting Debt Availability Will Impact Real Estate Development Projects." April 5, 2013, cited elsewhere as Corea, "Federal Statutory and Regulatory Changes."

31. Piore, Adam, "Empire State of Mind." *The Real Deal*, April 1, 2011.

32. Nicole Lane is a 2015 graduate of Georgetown University's Master's of Professional Studies in Real Estate, in the Georgetown's School of Continuing Studies, and a former student of the author's Spring 2013 Semester Foundations of Real Estate Law course (MPRE-690, MPRE-601–02, Spring 2013). Ms. Lane also served as the author's Research Assistant for a research study into conflicts of interest in commercial leasing undertaken by the Center for Real Estate and Urban Analysis (CREUA) at The George Washington University, where the author serves on the MBA faculty in the Finance Department of the GW School of Business. The author served as Research Director, Lead Author, and Project Manager for the study and owns and has the copyrights for all published materials. These include "Conflicts of Interest in Commercial Real Estate Transactions: Who Represents the Tenant?" CREUA, The George Washington University, Washington, DC, November 2014, and "Who Represents the Tenant in Commercial Leasing Transactions." CREUA, The George Washington University, Washington, DC, March 2015.

33. Business Alliance for Local Living Economies, 2013.

34. Fundable, 2014.

35. Fundable, 2014.

36. Clark, 2011.

37. Kickstarter, 2014.

38. CrowdSourcing, 2015.

39. Investopedia, 2010.

40. SEC.

41. SEC, 2014.

42. Fundable, 2014.

43. Grout, 2015.

44. Clifford, 2014.

45. Brandt, 2014.

10

Private actions creating public benefits

When government officials needed additional funds in the decades prior to the 1980s, they simply increased taxes or introduced new taxes. However, by the 1980s, that approach was no longer working. It was about this time that government officials earnestly began exploring alternative ways to finance and deliver services and needed facilities. Privatization began to emerge as the most effective way to deliver services. In addition, governments around the world began to sell state-owned companies to the private sector. [1]

Real estate projects required that the public work hand-in-hand with the private sector. That was different from basically transferring the delivery of services from the public sector to the private sector. For many services, it was clear that the private sector could deliver services faster and cheaper than the public sector. For most real estate projects, neither party could independently structure and implement the finance, design, development, and operation of a facility. The word privatization simply did not apply to real estate. Many public-private real estate projects will not proceed beyond conceptualization if left to one or the other of the parties. These projects require a collaborative effort: a fair and reasonable sharing of the risks, responsibilities and costs. [2]

As real estate development projects in the twenty-first century continued to grow in scale, scope, complexity, and risks, particularly Mixed-Use projects in transitional urban cores of the United States' largest cities, what was still a somewhat novel but emerging concept in 2000, when John Stainback published Public/Private Finance and Development, public/private partnerships became much more commonplace. What had truly been the exception up to that point – the "PPP" or "P3" – was rapidly becoming the rule, at least for the continued transformation of the urban cores in the United States' most populous urbanized areas.

Chapter outline

Chapter introduction
What, and who, is "the government?"
Privately Owned Public Spaces (POPS)
Public takings for private purposes: *Kelo* and the state of public takings for private projects
Tax increment financing

Chapter introduction

Indeed, not to undermine or take away from the thrust of Stainback's book, which may have been the first devoted to the subject of P3s, there has always been a certain amount of interdependence between the private sector and the public sector when it comes to real estate development. Through zoning and Land Use Controls, the public sector has the final word on *what* gets built *where* and, through the local jurisdiction's adopted building code, *how* it gets built. See Chapters 4 and 5, respectively.

Similarly, the provision of the infrastructure necessary to the construction and operation of a building generally must rely on the availability and accessibility of electricity, water, natural gas, sewer service, fire protection, emergency services, refuse collection, and high-speed cable or fiber-optic service. Some of these services have historically been provided directly through municipally controlled and funded departments or divisions, such as the local fire department and the department of public works. Water and sewer services, as well as a few others, are often provided through public utilities or state-authorized agencies that are neither owned nor controlled by the local jurisdiction. Still other, private-sector services, such as high-speed cable or fiber-optic services, must rely on public right-of-ways to give a new building project access to such services. In such ways, there is an implicit public/private partnership between a local jurisdiction and the developer of each and every real estate development project to be built in that jurisdiction.

And yet, the kind of P3 to which Stainback devotes his book is much more intentional; much more project-specific than the implicit partnership between developer and local jurisdiction alluded to in the preceding paragraphs. Public/Private Partnerships generally rely upon specific agreements between a local jurisdiction and the Developer or Development Entity, granting rights and imposing responsibilities and liabilities on the respective parties. While not couched exclusively in terms of Public/Private Partnerships, because the range of potential local government supports for private-sector development are not so limited, this chapter covers a very wide range of government actions intended to confer specific benefits on qualifying private-sector real estate development projects, with specific benefits – including but not limited to increased real property and sales tax revenues and local job-creation – flowing back to the public sector.

Private Actions Creating Public Benefits, and Public Actions Creating Private Benefits, are two sides of the same P3 coin. This chapter could arguably be titled either way: Each party contributes; and each party benefits. For the Developer or Development Entity the question comes down to this: How much will it cost, and what is the value of the concomitant benefit(s)?

What, and who, is "the government?"

Chapter 4 goes into great detail about the roles and powers of local government, and how those roles and powers are distinguished from the roles and powers of states, the juxtaposition of which is the fundamental conflict between Dillon's Rule and the Cooley Doctrine. See Chapter 4 generally, and the Subsection *Dillon's Rule vs. The Cooley Doctrine* in the Local Governments as Creatures of State Government section of Chapter 4 for specifics regarding the allocation of these roles and powers.

However, an important subject not addressed in Chapter 4 so that it could be explored in much greater detail in this chapter is: *What and who is "the Government?"* As will be demonstrated throughout this chapter, the lines between the public and private sectors are oftentimes intentionally blurred, as local and state governments seek to "off-load" some traditional roles of government onto the private sector, dovetailing with the private sector's interest in and desire to have greater control over the scope, extent, and quality of services provided to the users and guests of their real estate development projects.

From public/private partnerships, discussed below; to special taxing districts – such as tax increment finance (TIF) and community facilities districts – allowed to assess and collect taxes to fund specific, primarily public purposes; to separately taxed management and similar districts that, in many instances, fulfill many of the services of traditional local governments; there is a very wide range of entities and activities that need to be examined in order to answer the question: *What, and Who, Is "the Government?"* This chapter reviews the broad range of state statutes and local ordinances that enable the creation of these quasi-governmental entities that facilitate real estate development projects, including very large-scale master-planned communities to Mixed-Use urban projects.

The Impact and Growth of Public Private Partnerships (P3s). The central premise of Stainbach's book is that, since the 1980s, public/private partnerships have played, and will continue to play, a pivotal role in how governments accomplish their policy goals and objectives, particularly where the growth and prosperity of U.S. cities is concerned.

Unilateral versus bilateral approaches to private actions creating public benefits

Sometimes, these "Public Benefits" are *unilaterally created* by governments to serve as inducements to get the private sector to "do the right thing," as a matter of public policy. Regional, mass-transit projects, which have been proven to have enormous and lasting impacts on the jurisdictions and localities they serve, provide an excellent example of public policies creating development inducements that encourage private-sector actions and investments.

> Eisenhower's Mass Transportation Survey's proposal to save [Washington, DC] by merging it into a broader metropolis had been visionary yet relatively uncontroversial. Who could oppose city-suburb cooperation? In contrast, the National Capital Transportation Agency, once it became active during the Kennedy administration, proposed a much more divisive program: *save the city by rejecting freeways*. Such a reversal illuminates a broader shift in federal transportation policy under Kennedy and Johnson. Though powerful, pro-highway members of Congress remained in place, as did key officials in the Bureau of Public Roads and the District of Columbia government, executive branch officials did begin to fight the freeways authorized under Eisenhower. Their battleground was Washington, and their weapon was rapid transit.[3]

The subway system that now serves the Washington Metropolitan Area, including the District of Columbia, two counties in Maryland (Montgomery and Prince George's, receptively), and two counties and two independent cities (Arlington County and Fairfax County, and the City of Alexandria and the City of Falls Church, respectively), is operated by the multi-jurisdictional Washington Metropolitan Area Transit Authority (WMATA). Washington's metro system was originally conceived by the National Capital Parks and Planning Commission (NCPPC) created by President Calvin Coolidge in 1926, and the National Capital Transit Agency (NCTA), created by the United States Congress in passing the National Capital Transportation Act of 1960.

As suggested in the quote excerpted above from Zachary Schrag's book, *The Great Society Subway*, which chronicles the conception and evolution of what later came to be known as "Washington's Metro system," or "Metrorail," the pursuit of developing an underground subway system in Washington, D.C., was borne of a desire to avoid relying upon new freeways as a means of connecting the District of Columbia with its surrounding communities in Maryland and Virginia, respectively. In this way, the many voices and perspectives involved in the ultimate decisions and actions necessary to create and operate Washington's Metro system helped the Nation's Capital avoid the very destructive, urban impacts suffered by many U.S. cities through the Urban Renewal movement of the early 1960s, which forced new interstates through the middle of existing communities and rending the fragile urban fabric in the process, in the name of better connecting cities with their surrounding suburbs. Ironically, such response to the "white flight" of the 1960s, trying to keep suburbanites connected with the urban centers they fled, further destroyed the low-income, minority communities that suburb-bound whites left behind, cordoning these communities off with massive below-grade, at-grade, and elevated highway structures.

The creation and subsequent, incremental expansions of Washington's Metro system provide an excellent learning laboratory for how public policy directly impacts real estate development, even in the absence of an express Public/Private Partnership, serving as a primary example of how public policy can lead real estate and economic development. The first, major expansion of Washington's Metro system, into neighboring Arlington County, led to one of the best and longest-lasting examples of how local government land use and planning creates private-sector development incentives, in the guise of Arlington's visionary master-planning effort in legislating the land use patterns for the areas immediately surrounding each Metro Station planned for County.

This scenario repeated itself, once more, in Fairfax County, Virginia, starting in 2004 with a decision by the Commonwealth of Virginia to create the state's first-ever Public/Private Partnership for a transportation initiative, to develop Washington's Metro system's new Silver Line, which will eventually connect the existing Orange Line's East Falls Church Metro Station with Dulles International Airport in Loudoun County, Virginia.[4] Silver Line plans called for building and opening a total of eleven new stations, starting with four new stations in the Tysons Corner area, plus one new station in Reston in its first phase, with the remaining stations, and the Silver Line's terminus at Dulles, to be completed in the second and final phase of the ambitious mass transit project. See also Chapter 5.

Concurrently[5], the Fairfax County Board of Supervisors embarked upon an ambitious, long-range planning process intended to use the four, planned Metro Stations there to serve as the catalyst for transforming the Tysons Corner area – the poster boy for suburban sprawl characterized by Euclidian zoning practices of the early 1960s segregating different use types and putting commercial office uses onto isolated "corporate campuses," earning the area a featured spot in Joel Garreau's book, *Edge City* – into a series of interconnected, walkable urban places, including the Tysons Corner Shopping Center.[6]

Fairfax County completed its planning process with the adoption, in 2010, of the Tysons Corner Urban Master Plan. Subsequently, on July 25, 2014, WMATA opened the first five stations on its new Silver Line.

In furtherance of their self-interest in making sure these transformational changes would actually take place in the Tysons Corner area, exiting property owners, as well as large-scale developers with the expertise and resources needed to help fulfill the vision of an urban-scaled, walkable, and transit-connected Tysons Corner participated actively in Fairfax County's long-range planning process through the Tysons Corner Urban Center Task Force,[7] seeking a new land use code that would, among other things, prioritize pedestrians and human connectedness over the single-passenger automobiles that had dominated the land use patterns there for the past fifty years. At full build-out, the areas subject to the Fairfax County master plan will have 113 million square feet of space. See End Note vi, below, for details.

In several of the typologies identified and studied by The George Washington University's Center for Real Estate and Urban Analysis (CREUA), to which reference is made in earlier chapters of the textbook, a strong correlation exits between those typologies and their connectivity to mass transit systems, such as WMATA's Metrorail system in Washington, D.C. and the Massachusetts Bay Transportation Authority (MBTA) subway system in Boston (affectionately referred to as the "Tube" or, simply "the T"), respectively. One need only consider the increasing consolidation of aggregate property values located within WalkUPs, and the preponderance of WalkUPs (77%) that have existing or are installing rail transit to understand the critical nexus between rail transit systems and property values:

> Regionally significant and local serving WalkUPs are likely to be the *major generators of real estate growth in the future*. Although no fiscal impact analysis has yet been undertaken for the D.C.-area WalkUPs, *their contribution to total government tax revenues in the region is expected to be many times the proportion of land they consume*. In Arlington County, for example, the share of property tax assessments from the county's seven regionally significant WalkUPs is five times the amount of the land the WalkUPs occupy. *Fiscal impact studies throughout the country indicate that WalkUPs tend to produce a significant net surplus* (tax revenues minus costs of service), subsidizing the local serving areas of the jurisdiction.[8]
>
> Thirty-three of the 43 regionally significant WalkUPs, or *77 percent*, have rail transit or are currently installing rail transit. Two addition [*sic*] WalkUPs (Reston Town Center and Bailey's Crossroads) have rail transit planned within the next decade, *raising the total to 81 percent*. Eight WalkUPs have no rail service and none planned. Statistically, there is no proven causal connection between rail transit and the development of walkable urban places. However, *the high percentage of WalkUPs with rail suggests that it is an important factor*. As the WalkUPs without rail demonstrate, however, it is possible to develop walkable urbanism without rail.[9]

In addition to the case being made indirectly by CREUA in its ongoing research and analysis of walkable urban places throughout the United States, there have also been several, recent studies drawing direct correlations between real property values and direct access or proximity to mass transit systems. Specifically, a 2013 study prepared by the Center for Neighborhood Technology, commissioned by the American Public Transit Association (APTA) and the National Association of Realtors (NAR), found that:

> Across the study regions, the transit shed outperformed the region as a whole by 41.6 percent. In all of the regions the drop in average residential sales prices within the transit shed was smaller than in the region as a whole or the non-transit area. Boston station areas outperformed the region the most (129%), followed by Minneapolis-St. Paul (48%), San Francisco and Phoenix (37%), and Chicago (30%).[10]

Because the CNT study covered the period directly after the onset of the Great Recession, the comparables of property values within and outside the "transit shed," compared relative losses in property values, with significantly smaller loses in property values within the transit shed than outside of it.

Additionally, in an August 2011 study for the Center for Housing Policy, which involved a literature review recently completed studies on public transit's impact on adjoining and nearby property values (which, of course, predates the CNT study, referenced above), author Keith Wardrip posits that it may be difficult to draw any quantitative conclusions because of the variability of other factors:

> As discussed below, the findings of this review suggest the impact of transit on housing prices depends on a number of mediating factors including housing tenure and type, the extent and reliability of the transit system, the strength of the housing market, the nature of the surrounding development, and so on. In a metro area with a strong housing market and a reliable transit system that effectively connects residents with jobs and other destinations, the price premium may well be much higher than average.

It is also important to underscore that effects may vary for different stations within a single market. Averages can hide a lot of variation, and transit stations may have little or no impact on housing prices in certain neighborhoods but a very large impact in others. Both researchers and policymakers should be attuned to this possibility.[11]

Presumably, in central business districts, where land values tend to be the highest, the impact of proximity to public transit is much more pronounced than in more residential areas, even if served by public transit, where development densities tend to be much lower.

Another way that the public sector – particularly at the local level of decision-making – implements statutes, ordinances, and their respective, related regulations in a manner benefitting both the public and private sectors is through cooperation and collaboration before such statutes, ordinances, and regulations are promulgated or finalized. This is the bilateral approach to Private Actions Creating Public Benefits, or Public Actions Creating Private Benefits (depending on one's perspective on the subject).

This bilateral approach is clearly present in some of the seminal steps in the addition of the Silver Line to Washington's Metro system, as described earlier. Both the P3 created by the Virginia Department of Rail and Public Transportation (DRPT) through its Comprehensive Agreement with the Dulles Transit Partnership (DTP) to construct the Silver Line (see End Note iii, below), with considerable federal and state funding contributions through WMATA, and the private-sector's active participation, through the Tysons Urban Center Task Force's considerable contributions to the Urban Tysons Corner Comprehensive Plan of 2010, reflect the bilateral approach to Private Actions Creating Public Benefits.

In some instances, private-sector experience and vision serves as the catalyst for subsequent public-sector decision-making. This is often the case where the public sector uses the public solicitation process – Requests for Information (RFI); Requests for Qualifications (RFQ); Requests for Proposals (RFP) – to elicit private-sector solutions to public problems. This was clearly the case with the Washington Navy Yard project in southeast Washington, DC. In that case, the private sector recognized the tremendous potential of the fallow Washington Navy Yard as a redevelopment site of considerable scale and river-front views and direct access to the Anacostia River. However, were it not for the initiative of the National Capital Planning Commission's long-range planning for federal assets, such as its extensive inventory of historic and other operational buildings in the District of Columbia, including buildings on the Washington Navy Yard complex, the private sector may not have been in a position to start formulating redevelopment plans for the site in response to the Request for Qualifications from the General Services Administration (GSA), which ultimately led to a selected developer and its redevelopment proposal.[12]

GSA's selection of Forest City Washington as the Developer for the Southeast Federal Center (which project has been renamed "The Yards") confers on the Developer a truly unique development opportunity within the District of Columbia, while also providing opportunities benefiting the public sector, such as the consolidation and relocation of staff and offices of the U.S. Department of Transportation in two, new office buildings on The Yards site. As a result of the long-range planning efforts of the National Capital Planning Commission, nearer-term planning by the District of Columbia Office of Planning; the public procurement process undertaken by the GSA, and the subsequent negotiations among these government entities and the Developer, a once largely fallow, contaminated federal property is rapidly becoming an office, retail, residential, and recreational amenity for the Southeast waterfront and the District as a whole.[13]

Emerging Trends in Public/Private Partnership. If anything is evident from the "white flight"[14] from U.S. cities that commenced following the end of World War II, and its attendant explosion of suburban and exurban development, it is that nothing accelerates real estate development like public infrastructure projects:

> Cities had lost substantial populations of both residents and day-time workers to the suburbs, beginning with the "white flight" from city centers in the 1950s, spawning the precipitous growth of suburbs throughout the United States. In the auto-dominated world of the suburbs, each use could be, and usually was, segregated: Bedroom communities here; strip and community shopping centers over there; office parks over there; and so-on-and-so-forth. The birth of the national interstate highway system; new methods for constructing relatively inexpensive single-family detached houses (e.g. the shift away from horse-hair plaster, applied by craftsmen, to the new invention known then as "sheetrock"); low-interest-rate mortgages made available to G.I.'s returning home from the war; these things all contributed to an explosion in bedroom communities away from cities, which remained – for a time, anyway – the employment centers of their respective regions. Once a critical mass of workers had relocated to the pristine, new suburbs, employers and services followed.[15]

Making the suburbs more accessible and developable through the interstate highway system, for example, was a key component in the predominant development pattern in the United States for five decades. As stated in Chapter 2:

> In the fifty or so years of suburban and exurban commercial development in the United States, certain types of real estate development activities became very formulaic and, therefore, somewhat immune to specific development risks: Bedroom communities of single-family detached homes; neighborhood strip shopping centers providing community serving retail; surface-parked, garden-apartment projects; speculative and build-to-suit office buildings in a corporate office parks; warehouses in industrial parks; and the ubiquitous, enclosed, regional shopping mall.

However, as the United States' aging infrastructure has required resources beyond the capacity of federal, state, and local governments – or, at least, beyond the political will to provide such funding – new forms of public/private partnerships have emerged, in some respects supporting and promoting sprawl development patterns.

> Despite its fundamental and multifaceted role in maintaining national growth and economic health, infrastructure in the United States has not received an adequate level of investment for years. Political dysfunction, a challenging fiscal environment, greater project complexity, and the sheer size of the need across different sectors are forcing leaders across the country to explore new ways to finance the investments and operations that will grow their economies over the next decade.
>
> Part of this exploration means new kinds of agreements between governments at all levels and the private sector to deliver, finance, and maintain a range of projects. Beyond simplistic notions of privatization, the interest is in true partnerships between agencies, private firms, financiers, and the general public. Many nations already successfully develop infrastructure in this manner today.
>
> These public-private partnerships (PPPs) are alternately framed as a panacea to all of America's infrastructure challenges or a corporate takeover of critical public assets. In reality, they are neither. A well-executed PPP is simply another tool for procuring or managing public infrastructure – albeit a new and increasingly popular one. The growing interest can be attributed to a number of factors, including tightening budgets, increased project complexity, better value for money, the desire to leverage private sector expertise, and shifting public sector priorities. However, this surge of interest is not matched by broad public sector understanding of the PPP landscape.[16]

Privately Owned Public Spaces (POPs)[17]

Another emerging area in which the lines between the private and public sectors are increasingly blurred is in the proliferation of privately owned public spaces or "POPS." Until the Occupy Wall Street movement took over Zucotti Park in New York City in the Fall of 2011, the average citizen, and perhaps a majority of active developers, most likely did not pay much attention to whether the seemingly public parks they frequented (or, in the case of developers, some of their competitors had developed) were actually owned by the public.

While the Occupy Wall Street protesters may have mistakenly believed Zuccotti Park was owned and operated by the City of New York and, therefore, subject to all of the laws and regulations governing the use and enjoyment of open public space in the city, it later turned out that Zuccotti Park was one of more than 520 POPS in New York City. More important to the Occupy Wall Street protestors and their movement, however, was that, *as a condition of its creation*, Zuccotti Park was required to remain open twenty-four hours a day, seven days a week (i.e., 24/7). Accordingly, there was no legal basis for removing the protestors, or having them removed by police, because the park was never allowed to be closed. Had Zuccotti Park been a traditional, publicly owned park managed and maintained by the City of New York, it most likely would have been closed at dark or at a specific time, such as 10:00 pm, and the New York Police Department would have had legal grounds to remove all protesters and their accoutrement.

Zuccotti Park is owned and managed by Brookfield Office Properties. Originally named Liberty Park, it was developed by U.S. Steel as part of the company's entitlements relating to the removal of the Singer Building and the City Investment Building, to clear the way for the construction of the U.S. Steel Building. That demolition and construction relied upon height and density bonuses secured, in part, in consideration of the company's obligation to construct, manage, and maintain the new Liberty Park on the site of the City Investment Building.

Liberty Park became the property of Brookfield Office Properties when it purchased the U.S. Steel Building from United States Steel. In 2001 the park was heavily damaged by falling debris from the terrorist attacks on the World Trade Center buildings on September 11, 2001, and after an $8 million redesign and construction, Brookfield renamed it Zuccotti Park, after the company's chairman, John C. Zuccotti, who had also been the chairman of the New York City Planning Commission. U.S. Steel offered to create, operate, and maintain the park as part of its original development entitlements for the U.S. Steel Building. The park is unusual in several different respects, among them the fact that Liberty Park (now Zuccotti Park) is free-standing, rather than abutting an office tower, as was the norm for POPS in the city. Zuccotti Park is located at 165 Broadway between Broadway, Trinity Place, Liberty Street, and Cedar Street, in lower Manhattan.

As students and readers of this textbook should already be aware, New York City passed the country's first, comprehensive zoning ordinance, The New York City Zoning Resolution of 1916. See Chapter 5. In keeping with the city's status as the pioneer of land use regulation in the United States, the evolution of New York's post–World War II land use regulation also ushered in the United States' modern-era obsession with the 1960s urban public plazas (see Unintended, or at Least Unanticipated, Consequences of the 1916 Zoning Ordinance and A Skyscraper for the Modern World: Lever House, the Seagram Building, and the Time-Life Building in Chapter 5) and, eventually, the advent of privately owned public spaces.

As early as 1948, the New York City Planning Commission began efforts to replace the Zoning Resolution of 1916, both as a means of streamlining it (the ordinance having fallen victim to thousands of piecemeal amendments since its 1916 adoption) and in order to bring it into its post-World War II context. The first effort, involving a review by Harrison, Ballard, and Allen, an architectural firm, failed to garner sufficient political support as a springboard for revising the existing ordnance. A second reform effort, undertaken by Planning Commission James Felt with the support of New York City Mayor Robert Wagner, Jr., himself a former NYC Planning Commission Chair, who had appointed Felt as Commission Chair, was undertaken in 1956, and another architectural firm – Voorhees Walker Smith & Smith – was commissioned, and funded, to undertake another review of the 1916 ordnance (the "Voorhees report").

> After two and half years of study, the Voorhees firm released its report, *Zoning New York City: A Proposal for a Zoning Resolution for the City of New York*, containing a full draft of a new zoning resolution along with explanatory text.[18]

The Voorhees report, and its attached draft of a proposed, new zoning code for New York City was adopted, with some modifications, by the Planning Commission's Board of Estimate on December 15, 1960, and became effective one year later, on December 15, 1961 (the "1961 Zoning Resolution"). New York City's twenty-first-century skyline is very much a reflection of the changes made by the 1961 Zoning Resolution, as amended over the intervening decades.

> The height and setback controls of the new Zoning Resolution ushered in a dramatic modification of the prevalent wedding cake typology of earlier decades. As described in the Voorhees report, the 1916 Zoning Resolution "was written in large measure to cope with the problem of keeping building from robbing other buildings or the public streets of adequate light. In attempting to solve this problem, a fixed geometric setback plane was established above a specified height, which has the now familiar limitation of producing rigid and complex building shapes which are not only uneconomic to construct but inefficient to use."[19]

See, also, in this regard, the discussion in A Skyscraper for the Modern World: Lever House, the Seagram Building, and the Time-Life Building in Chapter 5. That section of Chapter 5 suggests, among other things, as follows:

> The collision in the early 50s of Manhattan's building boom in the International Style with the 1916 Zoning Resolution turned out to be a happy accident. The rule in the 1916 Zoning Resolution allowing only a tower form above a specified height, with a volume no larger than 25% of the lot area (which was intended to define the volume and form of a tower on top of the wedding cake of a building), found a completely different application in the austere and monolithic forms of the International Style, which used the 75% of the lot area for grandiose public plazas or low-rise building elements that made their monolithic towers even that much more impressive.[20]

Clearly, the 1961 Zoning Resolution was both a reaction to a number of factors and forces emerging in the United States following the conclusion of World War II, as explained in Chapter 5, as well as a response to the clamor from the real estate development, design, and construction industries for a zoning code that promoted more modern buildings that could better accommodate and adapt to such forces. And, as always, there was the financial imperative to allow landowners and building developers to extract an ever-increasing yield from the properties in Manhattan, which had its antecedents in the Equitable Building of 1915, which led, unintentionally to the 1916 Zoning Resolution. See, in this regard, Chapter 5, Defending the Value of Light, Air, and Views: How Manhattan's 1915 Equitable Building served as the catalyst for New York City's, and the United States', first, comprehensive zoning law section.

Interestingly, one of the areas in which the 1961 Zoning Resolution offered the most dramatic changes to the 1916 Zoning Resolution was in its provisions allowing density and other development bonuses resulting in higher overall yield or FAR (Floor Area Ratio, expressed as a ratio of the gross square footage of a constructed building to the land area of the parcel of real property on which that building is constructed) in exchange for the provision of privately owned plazas open to the public; what has evolved over the years since into privately owned public spaces. So, in essence, these provisions in the 1961 Zoning Resolution reflected a codification, of sorts, of what developers and their architects were already doing consonant with the 1916 Zoning Resolution, as reflected in buildings such as Lever House, the Seagram Building, and the Time-Life Building, discussed in Chapter 5.

In his book focusing on POPS in New York City, Professor Kayden chronicles the evolution of the public plazas provisions in the 1961 Zoning Ordinance over several, distinct periods. He addresses not only the original provisions providing for "plazas and arcades" as enacted in the zoning law[21] but the morphosis of those original provisions, first in expanding the definitions by acknowledging new types of public spaces and arcades, such as elevated and below-grade or "sunken" plazas (1968–1973)[22]; and the creation of special purpose districts for the provision of POPS (1967–1973)[23].

Additionally, the 1961 Zoning Ordinance gives the city's Board of Standards and Appeals (through its general powers under the 1961 Zoning Resolution to grant "variances" and "special permits"), and the Planning Commission, respectively, certain latitude, which in its exercise over the years has permitted customized POPS. These "one-off" spaces, which have arisen out of developer proposals seeking variances from height, density, and other limitations by offering idiosyncratic public amenities that did not fit under any of the codified POPS parameters contained in the zoning code as it evolved after 1961, resulted in spaces accessible to the public but which the public's legal right of use has not been, in all instances, a *condition* of the grant of the variance(s) or special permit through which the applicant sought relief from the 1961 Zoning Code, such that some may appear to be POPS but legally are not.[24]

The companion website for the textbook contains a discussion about the essential elements of what makes what would otherwise be a developer or property owners open space a POPS, as well as further consideration of how the Occupy Wall Street movement, and its prolonged occupation of Brookfield Office Properties' Zuccotti Park, has brought public attention to the existence of POPS, as well as perhaps focusing much more acute attention within the development community on the pros and cons of securing selected relief from zoning regulations such as height, massing, and density limitations by offering to create a privately owned public space on the Subject Site.

Public takings for private purposes: *Kelo*[25] and the state of public takings for private projects

Introduction[26]

There is absolutely nothing new about states, or local jurisdictions relying on the constitutions or statutes of the state in which they are located, making use of the power of eminent domain under the Fifth Amendment of the U.S. Constitution, taking private land for public purposes. The Fifth Amendment states as follows:

> No person shall be held to answer for a capital, or otherwise infamous crime, unless on a presentment or indictment of a Grand Jury, except in cases arising in the land or naval forces, or in the Militia, when in actual service in time of War or public danger; nor shall any person be subject

for the same offence to be twice put in jeopardy of life or limb; nor shall be compelled in any criminal case to be a witness against himself, nor be deprived of life, liberty, or property, without due process of law; nor shall private property be taken for public use, without just compensation.[27]

There's a lot packed into the Fifth Amendment, including a defendant's right against self-incrimination, as well as what's known as the "double-jeopardy" clause. Devotees of television crime dramas like the "Law & Order" franchise are not doubt much more familiar with these hallmarks of the Fifth Amendment.

However, the final clause of the Fifth Amendment – commonly known as "the takings clause" – is the one of greatest interest to local jurisdictions and the developers and Development Entities with which they hope to partner in the removal of urban blight and attendant creation of a more valuable and lucrative tax base. The takings clause provides that "no person shall be . . . deprived of life, liberty, *or property*, without due process of law; *nor shall private property be taken for public use, without just compensation*." [Emphasis added.]

In the case of purely public projects, ones where the project will be created, owned, and operated by a governmental entity – such as is the case with a public road or highway, a railroad right-of-way, a water treatment facility, or the installation of power lines for the local public electric utility – the "public use" portion of the Fifth Amendment is easily met, and the only issue to be resolved is what constitutes "just compensation." It was not, however, until after the Urban Renewal[28] movement in the United States in the early 1960s, spearheaded by the U.S. Department of Housing and Urban Development, that local jurisdictions started to get creative in partnering with private-sector companies to secure private land in the path of Urban Renewal that would be redeveloped for new, privately owned real estate development projects intended to revitalizing their surrounding communities.

What, in essence, had been a very straightforward analysis in applying the takings clause of the Fifth Amendment up to that point suddenly presented a very different set of circumstances, in which private parties were going to be active participants in the redevelopment of land local governments had taken from other private parties in the name of Urban Renewal. This evolution in the cases brought to the courts a paradigm shift in challenging what constitutes a permitted "taking" of privately-owned property for "public use." Before introducing the Supreme Court's 2005 *Kelo* decision, it is instructive to better understand the history of challenges to the takings clause of the Fifth Amendment.

The Supreme Court's ruling in *Berman v. Parker* (1954)

Fifty years before its ruling in the *Kelo* case, the Supreme Court took up the issue of the condemnation of private property that was not blighted but was located in a largely blighted neighborhood slated for demolition and "revitalization," in a unanimous (8–0) ruling on the constitutionality of District of Columbia Redevelopment Act of 1945, which was an Act of the United States Congress, which exercises a substantial amount of oversight over the affairs of the Nation's Capital. The act at issue was passed in an effort to eliminate blighting factors or causes of blight in the District of Columbia.

"Blight" is defined as physical deterioration, vacancy, and/or environmental hazards. By 1950, the District of Columbia government had developed a comprehensive plan to revitalize a large-scale area of southwest D.C. A survey of the targeted area indicated that "*64.3% of the dwellings were beyond repair, 18.4% needed major repairs, and that only 17.3% [of the existing dwelling units] were satisfactory.*" The survey also stated that "*57.8% of the dwellings had outside toilets, 60.3% had no baths, 29.6% lacked electricity, 82.2% had no wash basins or laundry tubs, 83.8% lacked central heating.*"[29] Under the revitalization plan, the entire area would be condemned to facilitate the construction of streets, schools, and other public facilities as well as *selling portions of the area to private developers* for the construction of new, modern housing, primarily for low-income residents.

The property that was the subject of the *Berman* case was a department store in the target area owned by Mr. Berman. By all accounts, Mr. Berman's department store was not blighted, and presumably served the impoverished, minority community in which it was located. Mr. Berman's department store was nonetheless condemned under the authority of the DC Redevelopment Act of 1950, as it was located in the midst of other deteriorated structures around it. In its unanimous opinion the Court explained that *"community redevelopment programs need not, by force of Constitution, be on a piecemeal basis – lot by lot, building by building"*[30] but instead should be viewed from a broader perspective.

In its *Berman* ruling, the Supreme Court made clear that it is not within the Court's jurisdiction to determine the efficacy of the overall redevelopment plan and whether it serves the City's "public purpose" as this judgment instead lies with the legislative body of the particular municipality in question. Such unwillingness of the Court to, in effect, exercise a legislative or executive prerogative in ruling on a constitutional issue such as the applicability of the takings clause is consistent with its past, and future rulings on the matter, as seen in the majority opinion of the *Kelo* Court:

> We do not sit to determine whether a particular housing project is or is not desirable. The concept of the public welfare is broad and inclusive. . . . The values it represents are spiritual as well as physical, aesthetic as well as monetary. It is within the power of the legislature to determine that the community should be beautiful as well as healthy, spacious as well as clean, well-balanced as well as carefully patrolled. In the present case, the Congress and its authorized agencies have made determinations that take into account a wide variety of values. It is not for us to reappraise them. If those who govern the District of Columbia decide the Nation's Capital should be beautiful as well as sanitary, there is nothing in the Fifth Amendment that stands in the way.[31]

Hawaii Housing Authority v Midkiff. Thirty years after its unanimous ruling in Berman, the Supreme Court once again took up the constitutional application of the Fifth Amendment's takings clause in *Hawaii Housing Authority v Midkiff*, 467 U.S. 229, 83–141 (1984). In the Midkiff case, the Supreme Court considered whether the Hawaii Housing Authority's eminent domain action against a landholder, Frank E Midkiff, qualified for the "public use" requirement, and whether the Authority's compensation formula constituted "just compensation", under the takings clause.[32]

Hawaii presented an unusual set of circumstances, in the context of the Fifth Amendment's takings clause, because in the *Midkiff* case the condemnation action was taken under the Hawaii Housing Authority's statutory powers pursuant to the state's Land Reform Act of 1967.[33]

In an 8–0 decision favoring the Housing Authority, the Supreme Court ruled that while the compensation formula was unconstitutional, regulating oligopoly was a classic example of states exercising their police power. The Court's ruling provided, in pertinent part (at pgs. 243–244):

> The mere fact that property taken outright by eminent domain is transferred in the first instance to private beneficiaries does not condemn that taking as having only a private purpose. Government does not itself have to use property to legitimate the taking; *it is only the taking's purpose, and not its mechanics, that must pass scrutiny under the Public Use Clause.* And the fact that a state legislature, and not Congress, made the public use determination does not mean that judicial deference is less appropriate. [Emphasis added.]

The Court's unanimous decision in the *Midkiff* case not only set the precedent that the takings need not be specifically intended for public use (just public benefit) but also that courts should not tell legislatures what to deem "public use" – this interpretation of public use was an authority vested in the legislative branch by the Fourteenth Amendment.[34]

The Supreme Court's 2004 *Kelo v. City of New London* Decision

As will be demonstrated, below, the Court's decision in the Berman case set the stage, nearly 50 years later, and twenty years following *Midkiff*, for the Court's next opportunity to consider the limits of the Fifth Amendment's takings clause, in *Kelo v. City of New London*.

Kelo **Case Context.** The City of New London, Connecticut, is a seaport situated at the convergence of the Thames River and the Long Island Sound in southeastern Connecticut. At the turn of the nineteenth century the city was the world's third busiest whaling port, which made it attractive for other shipping and manufacturing businesses. New London is the home of the U.S. Coast Guard Academy and was at one time the home of the Naval Underwater Sound Laboratory (which created and continually improved the Navy's sonar systems), a research facility of the Naval Undersea Warfare Center (NUWC) headquartered in Newport, RI. Both the Coast Guard Academy and the Underwater Sound Laboratory were located at Fort Trumbull in New London, a decommissioned military installation comprised of a thirty-two-acre site. The Underwater Sound Laboratory in New London employed over 1,500 people, many of whom lived in or near New London. In 1996, however, the Navy closed the Underwater Sound Laboratory in New and its activities were merged with the Naval Underwater Systems Center in Newport.

Long before the Navy's decision to close the Underwater Sound Laboratory, however, New London had already suffered from years of economic stagnation and decline due to the loss of many of the shipping and other manufacturing businesses that had been attracted to the City in the first place, leading a state agency in 1990 to designate the City a "distressed municipality," giving the City access to certain state incentives and resources for revitalization.[35] By 1998, the City's unemployment rate nearly doubled that of the state, and its population dropped to only 24,000, the lowest it had been since 1920.[36] At its peak in 1960, New London's population exceeded 34,000 residents. These dire economic circumstances led state and local officials to target Fort Trumbull as an area in need of economic revitalization. To this end, a local private, nonprofit group, the New London Development Corporation (NLDC), developed a large-scale development plan for the area.

It is important to note, at this juncture, that the kinds of struggles the City of New London was experiencing in the early to mid-1990s, and the type of large-scale revitalization effort the City saw as its salvation, have been occurring throughout the postwar United States since white flight started taking not only residents but commercial, industrial, and institutional interests out of the country's urban cores. Cities have been engaged in a stiff competition with their surrounding jurisdictions for decades, trying to attract real property and economic development that would contribute positively to their respective tax base. Only since the beginning of the twenty-first century have cities started to gain traction in competing to expand their residential and commercial populations. Accordingly, the "critical mass" approach of the City of New London, described below, to the overwhelming consequences of economic decline, through comprehensive redevelopment master planning, and the critical roles local jurisdictions play in devising and implementing such redevelopment plans, cannot be overestimated. The efficacy of such plans, however, which ostensibly were vindicated by the

Court's 5–4 decision in *Kelo*, were greatly constrained by how the individual right's activists at the state level influenced forty-nine out of fifty state legislatures to take action to constrain the state's power to exercise eminent domain powers.

The Fort Trumbull Municipal Development Plan. In May 1998, the New London City Council approved the redevelopment boundaries of the Fort Trumbull Municipal Development Plan (MDP), one of the largest redevelopment projects in the history of the City, encompassing more than ninety acres of land. There were two catalysts for the Fort Trumbull MDP:

1) The Naval Undersea Warfare Center's 1996 closure of the Navy Underwater Sound Laboratory; and
2) The 1997 announcement by Pfizer Inc., a major, international pharmaceuticals manufacturer, of the planned development of a $350 million Global Research and Development Headquarters on an abandoned 24-acre site adjacent to and immediately south of the Fort Trumbull site.[37]

The fundamental premise underlying the Fort Trumbull MDP was that natural spin-off business from the new Pfizer headquarters project, such as a marked increase in demand in New London for hotel facilities from non-locals coming to the area to do business with the pharmaceuticals giant, as well as the eventual co-location of other companies doing business with Pfizer in its research and development activities would generate economic activities benefiting the City. As part of the City's commitment to Pfizer, in support of Pfizer's plans to create the $350 million R&D campus in New London, was the promise that approximately 115 existing, privately owned, working-class homes, would be replaced with an upscale 250-room hotel, up to eighty new residential units (both rental and owner-occupied), 450,000 sq. ft. of new office space, the National United States Coast Guard Museum, a river walk providing public access along the shoreline, and parking to accommodate these "improvements"[38]. As the Court noted regarding the MDP:

> The [New London Development Corporation] intended the development plan to capitalize on the arrival of the Pfizer facility and the new commerce it was expected to attract. In addition to creating jobs, generating tax revenue, and helping to "build momentum for the revitalization of downtown New London," the plan was also designed to make the City more attractive and to create leisure and recreational opportunities on the waterfront and in the park.[39]

The new project was expected *"to generate between 1,700 and 3,150 jobs and between $680,544 and $1,249,843 in property taxes revenues"*[40] compared to the City's pre-MDP tax base of $350,000. In addition to the City's substantial commitment to comprehensively redevelop that area immediately adjacent to the proposed Pfizer R&D headquarters, the State of Connecticut also agreed to support the undertaking by providing $78 million for the project. Additionally, Pfizer received an 80% tax abatement for ten years, of which the state agreed to pay 40% to New London.[41]

By early 2000, the MDP was approved by all local and state agencies and the redevelopment project began in earnest with the city council authorizing the New London Development Corporation (NLDC), its nonprofit development entity created in 1990 to facilitate the revitalization of New London, to purchase or, if necessary, acquire through condemnation the properties making up the 90-acre area to be redeveloped in accordance with the MDP. The NLDC was able to successfully negotiate and effect the purchase of most of the real estate in the Redevelopment Area, with the exception of a few homeowners who fought for their homes all the way to the U.S. Supreme Court.

Petitioner Susette Kelo had lived in the Fort Trumbull area since 1997 and had made extensive improvements to her house, a modestly sized pink home set in the New London character. In her own words,

> I was lucky enough to find a great deal on a house with a terrific view of the Thames River, the Long Island Sound, and the Atlantic Ocean, in New London, Connecticut. I spent every spare moment fixing it up and making it the kind of home I had always dreamed of. I'm sure you've heard the expression "location, location, location." Well, this was the wrong location, even if I didn't know it yet.[42]

Ms. Kelo was joined by eight others including petitioner Wilhelmina Dery who was born in her Fort Trumbull home off of Walbach Street in 1918 and had lived there her entire life. This house had been in the Dery family for more than 100 years and her son lived next door in the home he received from his family as a wedding gift. Even though there was no allegation that any of these properties were in poor condition, they were nevertheless condemned because they were located within the boundaries of the development project.

On June 23, 2005, the Court, in a controversial 5–4 decision, ruled that private economic development is a public use under the Fifth Amendment. The Court also ruled that governments can exercise eminent domain to take title to and remove homes in the path of such private development. Private property activists who had followed *Kelo* carefully were apoplectic about the majority opinion in the case. In point of fact, it was not the ruling itself but the legislative backlash it caused that has had the most remarkable impact on large-scale redevelopment projects in which the public sector partners with private-sector developers.

Justice John Paul Stevens, who rendered the majority opinion for the Court, famously remarked a number of years later:

> The opinion for the Court in Kelo v. City of New London, Connecticut is the most unpopular opinion that I wrote during my thirty-four year tenure on the Supreme Court. Indeed, I think it is the most unpopular opinion that any member of the Court wrote during that period.[43]

However, unlike its pivotal precedent, *Berman v. Parker*, the states' respective reactions to the *Kelo* decision went in exactly the opposite direction: Forty-three states have enacted stronger protections against the broad exercise of eminent domain in condemnation proceedings, limiting what each state, itself, may deem to be a "public use" under the Fifth Amendment's takings clause. It is challenging, at best, to identify another Supreme Court ruling the potential impact of which has been so quickly and almost universally "overturned" through state legislative actions. Absent the majority opinion in *Kelo*, the interpretation of the takings clause, applying *Berman v. Parker* and *Midkiff*, was fairly settled, giving local jurisdictions tremendous latitude in working cooperatively with private-sector developers, either through public/private partnerships or development agreements, in applying their powers of eminent domain to undertake large-scale urban revitalization projects.

Understanding the difference between "public use" and "public purpose": the lower court's ruling in *Kelo*

In December 2000, the petitioners filed a cause of action in the New London Superior Court, claiming the condemnation of their properties was an unconstitutional taking of private property, in violation of the takings clause of the Fifth Amendment. In essence, the petitioners argued that the taking of private property through condemnation, to give that property to another private party, did not meet the second component of the takings clause: Public purpose. However, the Superior Court, after a seven-day trial, ruled that the City, through the NLDC as "its development agent in charge of implementation," could exercise eminent domain and seize the properties within the boundaries of the MDP as the City's redevelopment scheme was deemed a "public use." In making this determination, the Superior Court focused on the distinction between private and public *use* rather than on the larger question of whether "economic development" constituted a "public use." The following distinction between public and private may be instructive:

> The controlling question is whether the paramount reason for the taking of the land, to which objection is made is the public interest, to which private benefits are merely incidental, or whether the private interests are paramount and the public benefits are merely incidental.[44]

The Superior Court determined that benefiting private parties was not the primary purpose of the City's MDP, ruling that the primary motivation in City's exercise of its power of eminent domain was to further the city's development by leveraging Pfizer's commitment to develop its $350 million R&D headquarters.[45]

The appellate court ruling: Upholding economic development as a *de facto* "public use." The plaintiffs and defendants each appealed the Superior Court's ruling to the Connecticut Supreme Court in December 2002, which eventually upheld the lower court's ruling on March 2004. In its 4–3 decision, the Connecticut Supreme Court, relying primarily on language in Chapter 132 of the State's Municipal Development Statute, which deemed an economic development project as a "public use" and in the "public interest." The appellate court, in reviewing the facts found in the Superior Court decision, held that "reasonable attention and thought" had been given in determining that the takings of the properties in Parcel 3 were "reasonably necessary" to achieve the City's intended public use and that the takings were for "reasonably foreseeable needs." [46] The Connecticut Supreme Court further held that:

> . . . economic development plans that the appropriate legislative authority rationally has determined will promote municipal economic development by creating new jobs, increasing tax and other revenues, and otherwise revitalizing distressed urban areas, *constitute a valid public use* for the exercises of the eminent domain power under either the state or federal constitution."[47]

As with the Superior Court's ruling, the Connecticut Supreme Court again concluded that the development project was primarily motivated by public interest and not private gain, even though the City's plan did not specifically open the condemned properties to use by the general public. Even the Justice who wrote the dissent, Peter Zarella, concurred that:

> "[T]he record clearly demonstrates that the development plan was not intended to serve the interests of Pfizer, Inc., or any other private entity, but rather, to revitalize the local economy by creating temporary and permanent jobs, generating a significant increase in tax revenues, encouraging spin-off economic activities and maximizing public access to the waterfront."[48]

Appeal to the U.S. Supreme Court: "Public Use" vs. "Public Purpose." Following the Connecticut Supreme Court ruling, plaintiffs petitioned the U.S. Supreme Court in 2004, on the grounds that it presented a constitutional question, repeating their argument before the trial and appellate courts that the implementation of the Fort Trumbull MDP violated the "public use" requirement of the takings clause. After hearing oral arguments from the parties on February 22, 2005, the Supreme Court ruled in favor of the City of New London on June 23, 2005. The majority opinion of the Court, authored by Justice John Paul Stevens, expanded the definition of "public use" and, in so doing established broad parameters for the exercise by local jurisdictions of the takings clause in revitalization and redevelopment projects in which private interests are also involved.

One of the core arguments in Justice Stevens' majority opinion is that the definition of "public use" does not specifically mean that the condemned properties are to be put directly to use by the public. In other words, the scope of "public use" is not limited to properties that are actively used by the general public, i.e., a highway, railroad, public park, or water treatment facility. Instead, the majority opinion states the "*Court long ago rejected any literal requirement that condemned property be put into use for the general public.*" [49] Drawing on previous Supreme Court rulings, Justice Stevens expounded on this line of reasoning:

> Indeed, while many state courts in the mid-19th century endorsed "use by the public" as the proper definition of public use, that narrow view steadily eroded over time. Not only was the "use by the public" test difficult to administer (e.g., what proportion of the public need have access to the property? at what price?), but it proved to be impractical given the diverse and always evolving needs of society. Accordingly, when this Court began applying Fifth Amendment to the States at the close of the 19th century, it embraced the broader and more natural interpretation of public use as "public purpose." . . . We have repeatedly and consistently rejected that narrow test ever since. [50]

In summary, as to the "public use" test of the takings clause as interpreted in the majority opinion of the Supreme Court in the *Kelo* case, the Court applied a broader "public purpose" test in interpreting the Fifth Amendment in the context of the exercise of eminent domain. As the Court makes clear, however, in making this interpretation clarion in the majority opinion, the Court is not breaking new ground but merely summarizing the evolution of prior interpretations of "public use."

A second, major component of the Court's opinion in *Kelo* is the considerable deference courts must give to a state's or local jurisdiction's interpretation of what constitutes a "public purpose": "*Without exception, our cases have defined that concept broadly, reflecting our longstanding policy of deference to legislative judgments in this field.*"[51]

The Supreme Court has been very vocal in its reluctance to supplant the intentions and interpretations of its nine justices for the judgment of state legislatures, municipal legislative bodies, and executive and administrative officials of local and state governments in a variety of contexts: What constitutes a "public purpose" is among the questions as to which the Court has refused to second-guess the authors of such determinations. "*With the local situation the state court is peculiarly familiar and its judgment is entitled to the highest respect.*"[52] In the context of the Supreme Court of Connecticut's determination that the Fort Turnbull MDP did, indeed, serve multiple public purposes, the majority of the Supreme Court's justices chose not to exercise their own judicial discretion to revisit the question of whether the City of New London's assertion that the Fort Trumbull project would benefit the City and thus provide a public purpose was valid. Instead, it was only their position to rule if the City's interpretation of the "public use" requirement of the takings clause was in keeping with the historical precedence set forth in previous rulings. The exercise of such judicial deference toward a state or local jurisdiction's determinations in eminent domain cases dates at least back to *Berman v. Parker*.

> Just as we decline to second-guess the City's considered judgments about the efficacy of its development plan, we also decline to second-guess the City's determinations as to what lands it needs to acquire in order to effectuate the project. 'It is not for the courts to oversee the choice of the boundary line nor [*sic*] sit in review on the size of a particular project area.[53]

Dissenting Opinions and the Implications of the *Kelo* Ruling. It is a fair assessment of the majority opinion in the *Kelo* case that the rationale for the ruling was sound, well-reasoned, and firmly grounded in Court precedent, particularly the *Berman* and *Midkiff* cases. However, for whatever merit the opinion of the Court may be recognized, it is important to bear in mind that Kelo was a 5–4 decision, garnering a concurring opinion from Justice Kennedy, a dissenting opinion from Justice O'Connor, in which Chief Justice Roberts, and Justices Scalia and Thomas, joined, and a separate minority opinion from Justice Thomas. For a "super-minority" of the Justices on the *Kelo* Court (four out of nine), the implications of the majority opinion were too far-reaching to ignore, resulting in the two dissenting opinions.

Dissenting Opinion of Justice Sandra Day O'Connor, in which the Chief Justice, and Justices Scalia and Thomas, joined. While the petitioners in *Kelo* argued that the Fort Trumbull MDP, in its execution through the condemnation proceedings, violated the "public use" test under the takings clause, the petitioner in *Berman* disputed the validity of the condemnation of Mr. *Berman*'s department store because it amounted to "taking from one businessman for the benefit of another businessman."[54] It is the use of the power of eminent domain to transfer private property from one owner to a new, non-public owner to which Justice O'Connor took exception in her dissent. Just after the Bill of Rights was ratified in 1798, Supreme Court Justice Chase in *Calder v. Bull* determined that:

> An Act of the Legislature (for I cannot call it a law) contrary to the great first principles of the social compact, cannot be considered a rightful exercise of legislative authority. . . . [A] law that takes property from A. and gives it to B: It is against all reason and justice, for a people to entrust a Legislature with such powers.[55]

In the opinion of Justice O'Connor, the *Kelo* ruling abandoned the fundamental premise of a private right to property expressed in *Calder v. Bull*: The axiom of limiting government power in the contravention of private property rights. According to Justice O'Connor's minority opinion, the ruling in *Kelo* set a very dangerous precedent whereby economic development plans can and will endanger the rights of individual property owners, which deserve to be protected from overreaching acts of government.

The premise of Justice O'Connor's dissent may be expressed as follows:

> Under the banner of economic development, all private property is now vulnerable to being taken and transferred to another private owner, so long as it might be upgraded – i.e., given to an owner who will use it in a way that the legislature deems more beneficial to the public – in the process. To reason, as the Court does, that the incidental public benefits resulting from the subsequent ordinary use of private property render economic development takings for "public use" is to wash out any distinction between private and public use of property – and thereby effectively to delete the words "for public use" from the Takings Clause of the Fifth Amendment.[56]

In his paper, Will Holliday offers the following assessment of Justice O'Connor's dissenting opinion in *Kelo*:

> O'Connor's reasoning is sound and her concern real: that one of the restrictions of the takings clause had become virtually obsolete in the wake of the *Kelo* ruling. The "*public use*" safeguard that, coupled with "*just compensation*," which promotes stable property ownership had become stripped and thus had opened the doors to "*excessive, unpredictable, [and] unfair use of the government's eminent domain power.*"[57] Complete deference to legislative rulings that delineate what is "public" and what is "private" had eliminated any check on the system. Put differently, the Supreme Court had failed to provide a distinction between "*public*" and "*private*" that states and municipalities would have to uphold. Because "*nearly any lawful use of real private property can be said to generate some*

incidental benefit to the public"[58] there is no restraint or restriction on the eminent domain power. As such a state could rule any private undertaking as serving a public purpose and hence due to Kelo, all properties became liable to condemnation.[59]

In many respects, trying to reconcile the opinion of the Court with Justice O'Connor's dissenting opinion requires one to determine what deliberative body is in the best position to make a determination of what should constitute "public use" or even "public purpose." Clearly, in including the takings clause in the Fifth Amendment, the framers of the Constitution envisioned some set of circumstances in which a state or municipal government may have a need to take private property to be devoted to a public use. As cities grew in size and complexity, for a variety of reasons what constitutes public infrastructure projects also grew in size and complexity. The Constitution, by intention, is a dynamic document, intended to be interpreted by the Supreme Court to meet the needs of a modern democracy while still preserving the foundational principles upon which the nation was founded. There are so very many things the framers could *not* have contemplated over the ensuing 200-plus years, such that modern-day courts must endeavor to apply contemporary fact patterns, customs, and practices to the literal meaning of the words contained within the Constitution in order to divine the correct outcome.

Justice O'Connor's dissenting opinion, while seemingly meritorious on its face, raises an entirely different set of questions; perhaps more questions than it answers.

- To what extent should the private property rights of one or a few persons supersede the needs of tens of thousands of residents, particularly when each property owner is guaranteed "just compensation" for the real property that is taken?
- Under difficult economic circumstances, aren't economic development goals and objectives just as important as other public welfare and safety priorities, such as providing clean water or electrical service (which the Court has consistently ruled as constituting "public use")?
- Is condemning private property, for example, to make way for a privately owned hospital that, by law, must admit all patients regardless of their ability to pay for services to its emergency room any less of a "public use" than a waste treatment facility run by a municipal, district or regional authority?
- There are many Supreme Court decisions in which the Court defers to legislative intent and authority; why should the interpretation of what constitutes a valid "public use" as determined by the legislative body having authority over the jurisdiction, be subject to a reinterpretation by nine Justices?

It is a criticism of the *Kelo* ruling by Justice O'Connor's dissenting opinion that the facts of the case presented the Court with an opportunity to create a clearer definition of "public use," thereby allowing the Court to establish much clearer parameters within which a state or municipality may exercise eminent domain. But that sounds remarkably like legislating rather than exercising a necessarily circumspect judicial interpretation within the bounds of prior precedent. While the Court's opinion accepted a "*natural interpretation of public use as 'public purpose'*", the dissenting opinion defined "public use" much differently:

> The most natural reading of the [takings] clause is that it allows the government to take property only if the government owns, or the public has a legal right to use, the property, as opposed to taking it for any public purpose or necessity whatsoever.[60]

But, in the twenty-first century, should a nineteenth- or even an eighteenth-century perception of "public use" prevail in a system that relies upon the Judicial Branch to consider the Constitution as a dynamic document? The dissenting opinion applied what is frequently referred to as a "strict constructionist" interpretation of the express language in the takings clause, specifically requiring that the consequent "use" of condemned property would must be that it becomes part of the public domain, to be used and employed by the public. But does "use" require that every citizen be able to avail herself of such public domain in all instances? Do they need to be able to enjoy such use regardless of their actual ability to do so?

Instead, the *Kelo* ruling, as characterized by the dissenting Justices, established that the public did *not*, in fact, need to "use" the repurposed, condemned properties so long as such reuse constituted a "public purpose. "This departure from a much more limited interpretation of "use," in the eyes of the dissent, merely equated to the giving of one property to that of another. The danger, expressed in the dissenting opinion, in allowing the taking of private property under the "public purpose," is that those with less political influence and lower socioeconomic standing will be adversely affected by the *Kelo* ruling. However, this is not unlike suggesting that the monuments on the National Mall should be redistributed throughout the country in a way that's much more geographically equitable, so that a larger percentage of citizens may "use" them on a daily basis because potential users of these monuments are currently constrained in their ability to enjoy them because they must travel to the nation's capital to do so.

The dissenting opinion in *Kelo* argued that the aftermath of the Court's decision would provide those in higher political standing to apply pressure to the local government on the scope and boundaries of a redevelopment plan that may result in the condemnation of homes belonging to those with less influence. However, that same argument may be applied to the making of laws in the United States Congress generally, as those with power and influence over legislation, who are financially able to hire lobbyists to do their bidding, have always been in a more favorable position to exercise political influence than those of lesser means.

In the words of Justice O'Connor:

> The consequences of today's decision are not difficult to predict, and promise to be harmful. So-called "urban renewal" programs provide some compensation for the properties they take, but no compensation is possible for the subjective value of these lands to the individuals displaced and the indignity inflicted by uprooting them from their homes. Allowing the government to take property solely for public purposes is bad enough, but extending the concept of public purpose to encompass any economically beneficial goal guarantees that these losses will fall disproportionally on poor communities. Those communities are not only systematically less likely to put their lands to the highest and best social use, but are also the least politically powerful.[61]

It is not that Justice O'Connor's concerns in this regard are wholly without merit. The question, however, is whether duly elected legislative bodies are in the better position than the courts to develop such plans, and to be kept in check by the voters most affected by such projects (or by doing nothing to remove blight, improve economic conditions, etc.).

Another focal point of the dissent rests in the judgments of past rulings whereby the Court upheld the use of eminent domain to relinquish harm from the area in question. In *Berman*, the blighted area of southwest Washington, DC, was creating a negative social and economic impact on the city as a whole. In *Hawaii Housing Authority v. Midkiff*, 467 U.S. 229 (1984), twenty-two landowners owning 72.5% of the fee simple title to land in the island of Oahu created an oligopoly in landownership, which unfairly manipulated the residential fee simple market, inflated land prices, and injured the public welfare.[62]

The *Midkiff* ruling further expanded the definition of public use beyond the more limited definition of blight removal provided in *Berman*. Yet in both, unanimous rulings, the Court upheld the government's assertion that the condemnation proceedings were necessary to eliminate a threat to public health, which is a legitimate "public purpose" in-and-of itself: Eradicating the sources of socioeconomic harm.

> [I]n Berman through blight resulting from extreme poverty and in Midkiff through oligopoly resulting from extreme wealth. . . . the relevant legislative body had found that eliminating the existing property use was necessary to remedy harm. [63]

In contrast to these precedent-setting Supreme Court decisions, the dissenting argument goes, Susette Kelo and Wilhelmina Dery's respective homes were not a source of harm, and yet the *Kelo* ruling upheld the condemnation of these homes. Of course, that argument does not fully recognize that, at least in the *Berman* ruling, the petitioner's property was similarly not a source of the blighting conditions the redevelopment act sought to ameliorate: It was merely "in the way." As a result of the majority opinion in Kelo, the dissenting Justices claim the Court further expanded the definition of public use by eliminating the "harm" requirement presented in *Berman* and then in *Midkiff*, again ignoring the fact that the subject property in *Berman was not, in fact, blighted*.

The aftermath of *Kelo* and its potential impact on urban revitalization projects

While it is fair to say that the Supreme Court's ruling in *Kelo* case granted states and their municipal governments even broader powers of condemnation authority to effect the removal of blighting conditions and/or improve economic conditions, more than ten years later the holding has been largely overshadowed by how the vast majority of states responded to it. Concerned about the adverse impact the precedent of Kelo would have on private rights in real property, and lobbied heavily by property rights activists who had been following the *Kelo* case vigilantly, states began to adopt stricter laws pertaining to the use of eminent domain. The expansions of the takings clause effected primarily due to the Supreme Court's holdings in *Berman v. Parker* and *Midkiff*, respectively, were very quickly being clawed back following the holding in *Kelo*, primarily due to the *"unprecedented backlash in public opinion, citizen activism, legislative changes, state court decision, and lessons learned from the New London case."* [64]

Five years following the *Kelo* ruling, forty-four development projects involving the condemnation of privately owned land and private parties participating in the "re-purposing" of that land were rejected by citizen activists, forty-three states enacted stronger laws to protect private landowners against "eminent domain abuse," and nine state high courts limited the use of eminent domain for private development.[65] This strong, decisive, and almost immediate reaction against the *Kelo* ruling is contrary to the aftermath of the *Berman* ruling where *"no doubt emboldened in part by the expansive understanding of 'public use,' . . . cities 'rushed to draw plans' for downtown development"*[66], displacing families at a startling pace. Of the displaced families after the *Berman* case

> 63 percent of those whose race was known were nonwhite, and of these families, 56 percent of nonwhite and 38 percent of whites had incomes low enough to qualify for public housing. [67]

Thirty-four of the highest state courts rendered decisions in accord with the Court's new interpretation of the taking clause following its ruling in *Berman*, supporting urban renewal or slum clearance projects in what became known as the "Negro removal." [68] Fifty years later, public sentiment, fueled by the media, overwhelmingly rejected the *Kelo* ruling, with polls consistently showing an 80 percent disapproval rating of the case's purported, negative impact on private property ownership.[69]

As a former law partner of mine, who is now Chief Justice of the Virginia Supreme Court, was very fond of saying, "bad facts make bad law." It is fair to say that at least some of the public outrage over the *Kelo* decision was because home owners were able to personalize the outcome. A common refrain among those outraged by the outcome of the case was (and still is): *"[al]though citizens are safe from the government in their homes, the homes themselves are not."*[70] But adding fuel to the fire of national discontent with the *Kelo* ruling was the fact that the entire redevelopment project was a complete failure. The private-sector developer of the revitalization project that required the City of New London to acquire or condemn personal residences near the future home of Pfizer's new, $350 million R&D headquarters could not secure the necessary financing for the project. Pfizer, in 2009, completely abandoned its part of the project, moving the operations it had previously located to the Fort Trumbull site to offices it already maintained in nearby Groton, Connecticut. Even Justice Stevens, after his retirement from the Court, speaking to the University of Alabama School of Law in November 2011 acknowledged *"that [lack of] post-decision development may suggest that there were significant deficiencies in the proposed plan."*[71] These are the kinds of circumstances that make citizens extremely suspicious of grand government visions for ambitious revitalization projects, particularly when they involve taking people's homes and giving the land to other private interests, such as developers.[72]

In his paper, Will Holliday offered the following post-mortem analysis of what transpired on the ground in New London – or, more specifically, didn't transpire – after the City received a complete vindication in the Court's *Kelo* ruling, as well as on the potential longer-term impacts that may be caused by nationwide, negative reactions to the decision:

> About a year after the homes were razed, "the city terminated the development agreement after much controversy and many time extensions given to the chosen developer."[73] The proposed Coast Guard museum has been put on an indefinite hold and in November 9, 2009 Pfizer announced that it would be closing its research and development headquarters and would be leaving New London forever. In a project that was anticipated to bring jobs to the area and create economic growth by building on the momentum of the presence of the pharmaceutical giant, the sad reality is that the area has become barren and the State of Connecticut taxpayers have lost more than $80 million towards an area that may never become what it once was.
>
> Although the Fort Trumbull project was a failure, the reaction to the Kelo case may yet prove more harmful than the dissenting Justices could have envisioned but for different reasons. The dissent expected the ruling would empower the states to abuse eminent domain power, as was the case with Berman, but instead the ruling did just the opposite. This dramatic polar shift that occurred in the wake of the ruling, I would argue, may prove more disastrous.
>
> With land becoming more scarce and older properties occupying the majority of the core urban landscapes, especially in major metropolitan urban cores, large-scale revitalization projects are needed to breathe life back into depressed urban environments and, in turn, benefit communities at large. The condemnation of properties through eminent domain now requires time, money and legal expertise.

The urban legend or, perhaps, Hollywood myth, about real estate developers is that they're high-flying risk-takers. Nothing could be farther from the truth, however. In fact being a successful real estate developer, and having and maintaining reliable sources of project finance (both equity and debt), require being exceedingly careful, diligent, and – above all – risk-averse. One of the most effective strategies for risk aversion is to avoid uncertainty whenever possible. As suggested earlier in this section on the eminent domain is that since the U.S. Constitution was first adopted by the North American colonies, things like city building and economic development have become increasingly complicated. As urban planners, city officials, and elected leaders have searched for increasingly creative yet fiscally sound methods for financing improvements to city life, the more innovative solutions have increasingly relied on partnerships – both formal and informal – between the public sector and the private sector (the theme that runs throughout this chapter). As public officials search for new ways to share the risk of ever more complex and multilayered development projects while also attracting the private sector to create and underwrite certain aspects of urban revitalization projects, these needs, wants, and desires on the part of the public sector will inevitably collide with the private sector's propensity for risk-aversion. What was once a reliable capability the public sector could bring to the table on the creative transactions – the ability to condemn property in the name of a public good has, in the aftermath of the *Kelo* decision, become fraught with uncertainty. Even the mere prospect, much less the actual threat, of prolonged and expensive litigation by well-funded private property activists may interject sufficient uncertainty into the likelihood of the success of the undertaking as to have a chilling effect on undertaking the transaction in the first place.

A natural response by the private sector to the rising tide of such uncertainty, more than ten years after the *Kelo* ruling, is to require the local jurisdiction to undertake the assembly of private property not under its control, but necessary to the jurisdiction's ambitious revitalization plans, well before the private sector becomes formally entangled in the transaction. Such precondition, while perfectly consistent with developers' natural risk-aversion tendencies, in-and-of-itself may place a formidable, prohibitive obstacle to the local jurisdiction's well-intentioned and even well thought-out plans for a better future benefiting its future property owners, residents, and guests. So, as Will Holliday suggested in his paper, the unthinkable future resulting from the Court's *Kelo* decision may not be the unwelcome, adverse social consequences portended in Justice O'Connor's dissenting opinion but the real possibility that so many, potentially worthwhile urban revitalization projects never get started, because the barriers to entry are just too high.

Financing sources for the kinds of complex, Mixed-Use, mixed-tenure, multi-phased urban development projects – the equity investors and construction and permanent lenders developers need to secure before anything in The Development Process can happen in earnest – are *even less willing* to subject themselves to unusual risks. If a complex project cannot overcome known legal obstacles, a promised return on investment or favorable interest rate may not be sufficient to overcome the attendant costs of taking on delays associated with overcoming challenging legal issues, such as whether or not the condemnation of necessary, privately owned land parcels will withstand a constitutional legal challenge.

A second, somewhat related challenge to ambitious and complex urban revitalization projects in the wake of the *Kelo* ruling, is that developers go to great lengths to avoid any hint of negative publicity for their projects (especially when such negative publicity may indeed by warranted). Public condemnation hearings regarding a private developer, directly or indirectly becoming the beneficiary of a public process intended to take real property away from private citizens runs the risk that the public will perceive the project, and the developer, negatively, possibly making other government decisions required to be made through a public hearings or other open and accessible process increasingly problematic, increasing the uncertainty about that project's ultimate fate. In a funding environment in which there is a dwindling number of sources with the capacity and understanding necessary to take on such complex transactions, and an increasing number of potential transactions chasing such funding, why would equity investors and debt providers choose any transaction fraught with uncertainty?

Finally, the aftermath of the *Kelo* case has injected sufficient uncertainty about the legitimacy and duration of condemnation proceedings that future projects requiring condemnation proceedings to secure the requisite site area and location may be subjected to a larger-than-usual number of "hold-outs" in the negotiating process, leveraging their final selling prices by threatening a constitutional challenge to the condemnation action should their price demands not be met in the negotiations. Moreover, an increasing threat of such increase in the number of hold-outs and the magnitude of their demands for "just compensation" could cause developers to unwisely scale-back the audacity of their urban revitalization plans, potentially jeopardizing the favorable impact the project will have on the surrounding community. It has been suggested, in this latter regard, that the size, scope, and overall ambition of urban redevelopment plans have shrunk in the wake of the *Kelo* ruling, with local jurisdictions and/or their development partners intentionally excluding parcels to avoid the legal issues associated with displacing privately owned homes.

Legal Obligations of Applicants to Support or Provide Infrastructure Improvements as a Condition of Securing Necessary Development Entitlements. Whether they're referred to as "exactions," "proffers" or "public benefits," as part of the land use approvals process local jurisdictions endeavor to create legal obligations from developers to off-set what are perceived as the negative impact of development on existing "users" of the jurisdiction, including its residents, businesses, and visitors. These are oftentimes referred to as "conditions" of development, meaning that the right to develop the specified project is "conditioned" upon a list of commitments to which the developer commits in order to secure project approval. In this way, these "conditions" are not unlike the developer commitments to provide POPS under New York City's 1961 Zoning Resolution in exchange for relief from the zoning codes limitations on height, massing, and density, although they are not nearly as formulaic as what's contained in the 1961 Zoning Resolution.

There is a more expansive discussion about these conditions in Chapter 4, offered in the context of the District of Columbia's Public Benefit Agreements zoning requirement, which provides the broader context in which this discussion should be considered. Public benefits and other "conditions" of the entitlement process are generally limited to things the developer can and must do on the Subject Site (also known as "on-site improvements"). The discussion of the evolution of privately owned public spaces as an incentive for developers, above – including examples of developers bargaining with the Board of Estimates or Planning Commission, using their discretionary authority to provide relief to developers from height, massing, and density limitations in exchange for providing a POPS not contemplated under the plazas and arcades provisions in the 1961 Zoning Resolution – may be instructive to understanding this "exchange" of promises between a developer and the local jurisdiction in situations in which the proposed development is not by right (which is almost always). However, such conditions or "public benefits" are not always limited to on-site improvements, and in cases where the developer is required to make or fund improvements outside of the boundaries of the Subject Site, it is, in essence, doing work normally reserved for the local jurisdiction.

The companion website for the textbook offers the following, three examples, from three different jurisdictions, of developer concessions offered to and accepted by the local jurisdiction as part of the entitlements process:

Proffers. Commonwealth of Virginia: Robinson Terminal North, City of Alexandria

Off-Site, Public Transportation Improvements. District of Columbia: Gallery Place, Downtown, Washington, DC.

Direct Improvements to Streets and Sidewalks (City of Houston). Texas: Post
Midtown Square, Houston

Tax increment financing

Introduction. A tax increment finance (TIF) district is, essentially, an artificially declared
boundary created within a local jurisdiction, in accordance with a state statute providing
therefor, with the purpose of providing the mechanism for and authority to collect incremental
increases in the real property taxes assessed within that boundary (the "TIF District") over a
Base Amount of real property taxes determined when the TIF District is created. Essentially, the
Base Amount is what the local jurisdiction is collecting on the aggregate value of real property
within the TIF District.

TIF Districts are created for the purpose of generating a revenue stream that is measured
by the incremental real property taxes accrued and collected from within the TIF District during
the term of the TIF Bonds. The annual, incremental real property taxes within the TIF District is
projected for the entire term of "TIF Bonds," so that the present value of that projected revenue
stream may be used to determine the aggregate amount of the TIF Bonds to be offered for sale,
and which revenues are to be pledged to secure payment of the annual debt service on the TIF
Bonds and pay the annual administrative fees and other expenses of operating the TIF District,
as well as to provide for the periodic curtailment over time or lump-sum payment through sinking
fund contributions and investments, on the tax-exempt bonds issued by the TIF District.

TIF Bonds are issued by the TIF District to fund specified, public improvements to be
made within the district, in an amount such that the principal amount of the TIF Bonds will be
fully defeased (paid off) within their specified maturity. The TIF Bonds and the infrastructure
improvements they fund are generally undertaken in support of a large, catalytic real estate
development planned within the TIF District, the impact of which will be so dramatic and
transformative that it is expected to favorably impact the real property values within the TIF
District. This is, quintessentially, the public financing monetization of the axiom "all ships rise
with the tide."

Procedurally, the chronology of how a TIF District and its attendant TIF Bonds come into
being is that a Developer or Development Entity, which may be a purely private company or
a public/private partnership, proposes a truly catalytic project in a predominantly or partially
distressed commercial area. The Development Entity is willing to fully finance and assume
the risks regarding undertaking the Project but is unwilling or unable to finance the public
improvements surrounding the Project that will be necessary to make it a success.

While local jurisdictions often have a variety of funding tools to provide all or some portion
of the needed improvements surrounding the Project – such as the local jurisdiction's
annual allocation of federal Community Development Block Grant (CDBG) funds from the
U.S. Department of Housing and Urban Development (HUD) – there are often political and
administrative complications presented in funding such targeted public improvements. The
creation of a TIF District and subsequent issuance of TIF Bonds, while involving some public
processes for approval, tend to be less politically fraught than using more broadly available
funding mechanisms, such as federal CDBG funds, because the financing of the TIF Bonds
is tied directly to the success of the proposed Project, and the overall improvement to its
surrounding area or community, which improvement will inure fully to the local jurisdiction after
the expiration of the term of the TIF Bonds.

TIF Bonds are intended to fall within the general category of "Revenue Bonds" or "Conduit
Bonds," as contrasted with a jurisdiction's "General Obligation" or "GO" bonds, because

bondholders are limited in their security for repayment of the TIF Bonds upon defeasance, and for annual or periodic debt service and annual management and operating fees of the TIF District to the incremental real property taxes to be collected by the TIF District. However, unless there is a specific prohibition in the TIF authorizing statute prohibiting the local jurisdiction from providing monetary or credit support for the TIF Bonds, a local jurisdiction may guarantee the annual debt service, payment of administrative and operating fees, and repayment in full of the aggregate, principal of the TIF Bonds. In cases in which the local jurisdiction views the transformative Project is critical for the TIF District's and/or the local jurisdiction's fiscal health and well-being, it would not be unusual for the local jurisdiction to provide one or more types of guarantees if necessary to allow the TIF Bonds to secure a favorable credit rating to improve the selling price of the bonds and, therefore, lowering the yield on the TIF Bonds (the relationship between the ultimate sales price of bonds against the face-rate on which interest will be paid based upon the nominal value of the TIF Bond). [74]

History, evolution and rationale of tax increment financing[75]

California enacted the country's first TIF statute in 1952, authorizing the use of tax increment finance districts to provide matching funds for federal urban renewal plans. As the federal government decreased its funding of urban redevelopment projects in the 1970s, an increasing number of states enacted TIF District authorizing statutes to provide an alternate tool for financing local redevelopment. In California, after the passage of Proposition 13 on June 6, 1978, limiting how and how much local units of government in California could raise from real property taxes for general operating revenues and other uses, such as public school funding, the use of the existing TIF District statute proliferated.[76] Popularity of TIF Districts increased once again during the 1980s and into the 1990s, as the result of a tide of voter opposition to new taxes that swept the country, and yet more states enacted TIF District statutes to make the financing technique available in jurisdictions where new taxes to support such development were not politically palatable. TIF Districts and their attendant TIF Bonds provided a way of supporting redevelopment projects without increasing taxes (or even trying to do so), and could generally be enacted without impacting a city's debt limit or financial stability.[77]

Following Einstein's axiom to make things as simple as possible, but no simpler, a tax increment financing is an artificial mechanism for reallocating real property taxes between the local unit of government legally entitled to assess and collect those taxes and specific expenses attendant a redevelopment project within the boundaries of the TIF District. TIF Districts are arguably nothing more than political expedients because they allow local elected officials to avoid having to explain devoting a disproportionate share of collected real property tax revenues on a very specific geographic area within the boundaries of the local unit of government. The counterargument to this, of course, is that both the TIF District, and its attendant TIF Bonds, allow the local unit of government to front-load the financing of essential infrastructure improvements in a designated redevelopment area without disproportionately burdening the jurisdiction's general operating funds or adding to its General Obligation (GO) bond issuance. The corollary argument to this is that without the offer to create a TIF District facilitating the issuance of TIF Bonds, a Development Entity may not be willing to undertake the proposed, catalytic redevelopment project and bring private-sector equity and debt financing necessary to the realization of the project.

As of 2011, forty-nine states and the District of Columbia had TIF District enabling statutes, Arizona being the only exception. However, in February 2012, the 2011 Budget Act, passed in 2011 by the California Legislature but stayed from being enforced pending the outcome of the litigation referenced in the following paragraph, became effective,[78] eliminating the state's 427 redevelopment agencies, each of which constituted a TIF District under the 1952 enabling statute.

> As part of the 2011 Budget Act, and in order to protect funding for core public services at the local level, the Legislature approved the dissolution of the state's 400 plus RDAs. After a period of litigation, RDAs were officially dissolved as of February 1, 2012. As a result of the elimination of the RDAs, property tax revenues are now being used to pay required payments on existing bonds, other obligations, and pass-through payments to local governments. The remaining property tax revenues that exceed the enforceable obligations are now being allocated to cities, counties, special districts, and school and community college districts, thereby providing critical resources to preserve core public services.[79]

The California Redevelopment Association sued to challenge the 2011 Budget Act, and on December 29, 2011, the Supreme Court of California ruled in favor of defendant Ana Matosantos, the state's Director of Finance, upholding the newly enacted statute.[80] As of 2008, California had over four hundred redevelopment agencies in cities such as San Diego, Los Angeles, and Oakland, with an aggregate of more $10 billion per year in TIF District revenues and over $674 billion of assessed land valuation. A majority of these TIFs promoted urban development, although some did so through stadium and other sports facilities projects, which other funded entertainment and shopping venues. However, tensions between the state and local governments, and also between local governments and redevelopment agencies, over the issue of the "diversion" of real property tax revenues to these redevelopment districts and from schools and other public purposes ultimately led to the end of TIF in California. As Danny Stover stated in his paper:

> TIF is so widely used in California that in recent years, the tax-increment flow to redevelopment agencies has been around $6 billion – some 12 percent of the entire property tax revenue in the state. Because of complicated school equalization requirements in California, the state must backfill every dollar that school districts lose to TIF. Since schools get 50 percent of the property tax that means the state is subsidizing redevelopment to the tune of $3 billion a year. When you're staring at a $25 billion budget deficit, that's real money. That's why California Gov. Jerry Brown – a former big city mayor who used TIF effectively in Oakland – eliminated it.[81]

Chicago has perhaps made more extensive use of TIF Districts than any other major city in the United States. By some estimates, the City of Chicago proper has more than 160 TIF Districts within the city's boundaries, with tax annual, aggregate TIF District receipts in the hundreds of millions of dollars; approximately 10% of the city's total property tax revenue. The program has been such a significant tool for promoting urban renewal projects and increasing property tax revenues that it prompted Mayor Richard M. Daley to claim in 2007 that TIF was "the only game in town" and Chicago's "only tool" for promoting economic development. As a consequence, however, much like the state of California, Chicago recently come under public scrutiny in connection with the city's alleged overuse and abuse of TIF Districts, and the revenues they generate. The following is an excerpt from the January 2012 Chicago report, *Cleaning Up Tax Increment Financing*:

> Every year, $500 million worth of property tax revenue collected in Chicago flows into funding pools shielded from public scrutiny and democratic control – the bank accounts of the city's Tax-Increment

Financing (TIF) districts. That money – 10 percent of Chicago's annual property tax revenue – is intended to promote development in struggling areas of the city, but the fashion in which it has been handled in the past – without full transparency, democratic oversight, or accountability for the recipients of funds – has opened the door to misuse of public money.

Chicago Mayor Emanuel, vowing to reform the City's TIF process, convened a panel to recommend improvements to the manner in which TIF Districts are designated, and how they operate once created. The panel's recommendations appear well-intentioned but perhaps do not go far enough to make any real improvements. Among other things, criticisms of the panel's recommendations include: The recommendations do not correct the fundamental problems with Chicago's TIF program; the recommendations do not rein in the overuse of Chicago's TIF Districts; the recommendations fail to prevent TIF District abuses, such as aggregating revenues that are then used to support projects unrelated to the underlying purpose of the TIF District; and the recommendations do not require the kind of transparency and accountability for which taxpayers have been clamoring.

As suggested in the paragraph introducing the evolution of TIF Districts in California, above, TIF Districts oftentimes take public spending deliberations outside the normal channels of political discourse about municipal budget decision-making. The general lack of public transparency and fiscal accountability in the creation and operation of TIF Districts has resulted in the public backlash over this funding technique. However, many cities and states have tightened legislation in recent years to curb abuses resulting from the prior lack of control, public disclosure, and monitoring of the TIF Districts.

TIF structure

Very few local jurisdictions in the United States have a single real property tax regime. Moreover, it is very common for a single real property, regardless of typology (i.e., single-family detached, attached, or multifamily), to be situated in multiple "local jurisdictions." These may include the local municipality, a school district, a park district, and a water district, for example. Cities that are also creatures of county government may collect property taxes but have to share the proceeds with the county government (or vice versa). Property taxes are generally levied on a parcel of real property by determining that property's "assessed value," and then multiplying that assessed value to a real property taxation or "mil" rate, generally expressed as a percentage or dollars and cents on each $100 of that value. For example, a single-family detached home with an assessed value of $250,000 located in a jurisdiction with a mil rate of $1.10 would be taxed at $2,750 ($250,000 assessed value ÷ $100 x $1.10 = $2,750).

As stated in the introduction to this section, the TIF District is authorized and empowered to collect the *incremental increases in the real property taxes* assessed within the TIF District boundaries over a *Base Amount* of real property taxes determined when the TIF District is created. The Base Amount is generally determined to be the amount of real property taxes the local jurisdiction is collecting on the aggregate value of real property within the TIF District. Using the example provided in the preceding paragraph, and assuming that the mil rate remains constant over time, if the Base Amount for this single-family detached property is $2,750, and the assessed value of that property increases from $250,000 to $325,000, the local jurisdiction would still receive its $2,750 in tax revenue from the property. However, the TIF District would receive the incremental increase in property taxes of $825 ($325,000 assessed value ÷ $100 x $1.10 = $3,575, minus the Base Amount of $2,750 = $825). It should be noted that the property owner in a TIF District is paying the exact same amount in real property taxes as would be paid without the TIF District; the TIF District simply reallocates the amount of real property taxes collected between the local jurisdiction and the TIF District. Of course, that means the local jurisdiction is receiving less gross tax revenues to provide its basic services to the entire jurisdiction.

Since real estate taxes are often the primary source of funds for education, and school taxes are a dominant share of County property taxes, there is pressure to lessen the impacts on school funding. California, Florida, Illinois, New York, and Wisconsin now exempt taxes that would otherwise go to school districts. Kentucky allows school districts to elect to withdraw their source of TIF revenues and Ohio makes provision for payments in lieu of taxes if the TIF is not approved by local school district.

In some cases, TIF that relies solely on a real estate tax does not yield enough revenue to justify use of TIF in the first place. In light of this, and, given the increasing pressure against diverting real estate taxes from school districts, a growing number of states are supplementing TIF revenues with sales taxes. The volatility of sales taxes and the potential for competition for sales taxes by municipalities within a region, however, have caused concern as well. In fact, both California and Illinois have disallowed or phased out the use of sales taxes for TIF. In addition to real estate and sales, other taxes such as hotel, entertainment, utility, and employment taxes, and other local option taxes are also used by a smaller group of states.

TIFs are generally authorized by state statutes and implemented by local governments. However the process is typically initiated by a local jurisdiction, subject to local government approvals. TIF District enabling legislation is generally comprised of the following, essential components:

1. Local unit of government makes a finding of need for redevelopment of a certain area;
2. Working with a firm that specializes in sizing TIF Districts, the jurisdiction proposes the initial TIF District boundaries;
3. Local unit of government promulgates ordinance to create a redevelopment authority that will have specific responsibilities and powers for the redevelopment activities within the proposed TIF District;
4. Newly formed redevelopment agency prepares redevelopment plan, which must be approved by the local unit of government and may require community participation and/or public hearings process prior to approval;
5. Redevelopment agency determines Base Year against which the tax increment will be measured;
6. Redevelopment agency enters into an agreement for each redevelopment project within the TIF District, which agreement sets forth any improvements to the district to be undertaken by the redevelopment agency in support of that redevelopment project;
7. Redevelopment agency issues TIF District revenue bonds, the net proceeds from which will fund the public portions of the redevelopment projects; and
8. Redevelopment agency pays debt-service on the TIF District Bonds using the incremental increase in property tax revenues over the Base Year property taxes in the TIF District, which are deposited into a Reserve Fund for that purpose.

In creating a TIF District its sponsor and proponents must determine it will be project-specific or district-wide in scope. Both approaches have been successful in rehabilitating and revitalizing designated areas but each has distinct differences that should be considered before making the final decision.

Project-Specific TIFs. A Project-Specific TIF District is appropriate when a single property or project will serve as the catalyst for the area's revitalization. These tend to be complex, large-scale undertakings, including hotels, sports and entertainment venues, and mixed-use projects. Generally, the TIF Bond net proceeds are needed to supplement a substantial private-sector investment in a transformative or catalytic project. See, for example, the Akridge Company's Gallery Place Mixed-Use project located in Washington, DC's Downtown BID, in the Case Studies presented on the companion website for the textbook. The net TIF Bond proceeds for a Project-Specific TIF District are used financially to support the project through public infrastructure improvements such as public transit improvements, street lighting, streetscape improvements, water and sewer infrastructure improvements, curbs and sidewalks, and structured parking. Project-Specific TIFs are generally approved more quickly than District-Wide TIF Districts because fewer parties are involved.

District-Wide TIFs. District-Wide TIF Districts often involve both multiple parties and a much larger geographic area, requiring higher costs, greater community focus and input, a collaborative process among landowners, developers, and community stakeholders, and much more elaborate due diligence. This approach may involve complex and expensive land assemblages that the developer or other project sponsor is unwilling to undertake without the commitment of TIF Bond financing to take on the public improvements necessary to support the investor-driven components. However, with the increases in complexity, project scale, and geographic coverage, District-Wide TIFs tend to have commensurately greater impacts than just a Project-Based TIF. Large land assemblages may help achieve a scale of transformation necessary to attract large, anchor businesses that may help improve and shape the economic viability of the surrounding community well beyond the District-Wide TIF's boundaries. For an example of the pros and cons of District-Wide TIFs, see Forest City's Mesa Del Sol master-planned community outside of Albuquerque, New Mexico, in the Case Studies presented on the companion website for the textbook.

However, the creation and management of District-Wide TIFs are not without their challenges, as the process may lead to frustrated and outspokenly negative citizens residing in the proposed TIF District boundaries, some of whom may be requested or required to relocate from within those boundaries to make way for the new development to follow. Additionally, citizens who live and work outside the TIF District boundaries may be impacted negatively by the undertakings, including feeling they've been left out of the benefits of the district, inconvenienced by construction activities that may take years to complete, and that real property tax dollars that ordinarily would be used to fund jurisdiction-wide public services and improvements are being devoted to benefit a small proportion of the residents and their properties within the district.

Examples of special purpose taxing and management districts. The companion website for this textbook includes Case Studies of the following projects throughout the United States, highlighting a variety of statutory special districts facilitating large-scale, private-sector development:

Community Facilities (aka "Mello-Roos") Districts (California). University Hills workforce housing for the University of California, Irvine, Orange County, California.

Community Development Associations (Commonwealth of Virginia). Cameron Station, City of Alexandria, Virginia.

Metro Districts (Colorado). Highlands Ranch Metropolitan District, Highlands Ranch, Colorado.

Management Districts (Texas). Midtown Management District, City of Houston, Texas.

Tax Increment Revitalization Zones or "TIRZ" (Texas). Midtown Redevelopment Authority/Tax Increment Reinvestment Zone Number Twoaka the "Midtown TIRZ," Midtown Houston, City of Houston, Texas.

Public Improvement Districts (New Mexico). Mesa Del Sol, City of Albuquerque, New Mexico.

Business Improvement Districts (District of Columbia). Downtown Business Improvement District, Washington, D.C.

Notes

1. Stainback, John, *Public/Private Finance and Development: Methodology, Deal Structuring, Developer Solicitation*, John Wiley & Sons, Inc., New York, NY (2000), pg. 13.

2. Ibid., pg. 14.

3. Schrag, Zachary M., *The Great Society Subway (Creating the North American Landscape)*, Johns Hopkins University Press, Baltimore, MD (2006); Kindle Edition (2006–08–02), Kindle Locations 1018–1023. Emphasis added.

4. Chapter 5 provides, in pertinent part, as follows:

   The impetus for considering what Tysons Corner might become if it was properly re-planned and redeveloped was the June 10, 2004, decision by the Commonwealth of Virginia's Department of Rail and Public Transportation (DRPT) to enter into a Comprehensive Agreement with the Dulles Transit Partnership (DTP – the first agreement of its kind for a transit project by the Commonwealth of Virginia under the Public-Private Transportation Act PPTA of 1995 – for the creation of the Silver Line, extending the D.C. Area's Metro rail system farther West, from its West Falls Church Station out to Dulles International Airport. Although funding for the Silver Line would need to come from a variety of sources, including the District of Columbia, the State of Maryland, and the federal government, among others, it would not have been possible absent the agreement between DRPT and DTP.

5. In fact, the eventual re-planning of the Tysons Corner area began long before this point in time, although the creation of the Comprehensive Agreement between Virginia's DRPT and DTP entered into between these parties in June 2004 (see Note 4, above) served as the catalyst for the push eventually resulting in the transformational 2010 Comprehensive Plan changes. The Amendment No. 2007–23, FAIRFAX COUNTY COMPREHENSIVE PLAN, (2007 Edition), Tysons Corner Urban Center, Amended through 6–22–2010, at Page 4 provides, in pertinent part, the following planning history of this effort:

   In 1990 the Board authorized a study of the Tysons Corner Urban Center and appointed a 24-member task force to work with staff on this planning effort. This task force included representatives of local businesses, developers and civic associations. The resulting Plan Amendment, as adopted by the Board in 1994, incorporated concerns of the community, applicable countywide goals, and the overall objective to develop Tysons as the "downtown" of Fairfax County. A key feature of the 1994 Plan was the location of three Metrorail stations in Tysons. These stations were expected to serve as the catalyst to transform the area from a suburban to an urban area.

   Over the next ten years, county, regional, state and national officials worked to ensure that Metrorail through Tysons would become a reality. The final Environmental Impact Statement (EIS) for this project identified four transit stations in Tysons, versus the three stations in the 1994 Plan. As a result of the greater certainty of Metrorail's alignment and station locations, in 2004 twenty proposals for redevelopment in Tysons were submitted under the county's Area Plan Review (APR) process. Since the Comprehensive Plan had not been revised to account for the specific locations of the four stations, the Planning Commission deferred all rail-related APR nominations to be reviewed in a Special Study of the Tysons Corner Urban Center.

6. Chapter 5 provides, in pertinent part, as follows:

   At completion, what Fairfax County has denominated "Urban Tysons Corner" will be comprised of over 100,000 residents, 200,000 jobs, and approximately 113 million square feet of commercial development, including the redevelopment of existing properties at the time the Urban Tysons Corner Comprehensive Plan was adopted. Using 2000 Census data by way of providing an order-of-magnitude reference, the projected 2050 employment in Urban Tysons Corner would make it the 7th largest Central Business District (CBD) in the country, just behind Philadelphia, Pennsylvania, with approximately 220,000 jobs in its CBD. The District of Columbia's CBD, according to the same 2000 census ranking of CBDs, represented 382,400 jobs.

7. See the first paragraph of the quote in End Note v, above.

8. Leinberger, Christopher B., *The WalkUP Wake-Up Call: D.C.*, Center for Real Estate and Urban Analysis, The George Washington University School of Business, Washington, DC (2012), pg. 7. Footnotes intentionally omitted; emphasis added.

9. Ibid., pg. 18. Emphasis added.

10. Becker, Sofia, Scott Bernstein, and Linda Young, *The New Real Estate Mantra: Location Near Public Transportation*, Center for Neighborhood Technology, Chicago, IL, commissioned by American Public Transportation Association and National Association of Realtors (March 2013).

11. Wardrip, Keith, "Public Transit's Impact on Housing Costs: A Review of the Literature." *Insights' from Housing Policy Research*, Center for Housing Policy, Washington, DC (August 2011), pg. 2.

12. See, e.g., NCPC's 1992 Master Plan for the Southeast Federal Center, cited in the U.S. General Services Administration's (GSA) Request for Qualifications (RFQ) for Development of the Southeast Federal Center, pg. 2:

   GSA, working closely with the District of Columbia government ("District Government") has developed a draft Illustrative Plan (IP). The purpose of the IP is to provide a framework for the creation of a land use strategy for the SEFC in which GSA will consider comments and alternatives in response to this RFQ. GSA is in discussions with the District Government with respect to the District Government's participation in site infrastructure financing and development of this land use strategy. *Based on past plans and studies (including the 1992 Master Plan for SEFC as approved by the National Capital Planning Commission* ["NCPC"]), the IP includes information on the SEFC site, its development potential and existing conditions from past plans and studies, and reflects GSA's proposed approach to site development. [Emphasis added.]

13. Dingfelder, Sadie, "Navy Yard on Track to be D.C.'s Most Densely Populated Neighborhood." *The Washington Post*, January 9, 2016.

14. As stated in Chapter 4:

   Although white flight is believed to have begun in major U.S. cities in the late 1940s, it was not until better computing power and demographic methodologies in the late 1950s allowed for any kind of precise analysis of the 1950 U.S. Census regarding changing demographics between cities and their suburbs by identifiable racial components. This white flight was exacerbated by the race riots in various U.S.

cities in the mid-1960s, culminating in riots occurring in approximately 125 U.S. cities following the assassination of Dr. Martin Luther King, Jr., on April 4, 1968.See Chapter 4, subsection titled "But, first, a brief history lesson," in *Local Governments as Creatures of State Government* Section.

15. Chapter 1: Real Estate as an Asset Class, Real Estate Assets Classes Subsection, *Mixed-Use Development* description.

16. Sabol, Patrick and Robert Puentes, *Private Capital, Public Good: Drivers Of Successful Infrastructure Public-Private Partnerships*, The Brookings Institution, Washington, DC (December 2014). Footnotes omitted.

17. The author acknowledges the work of Yama Sekander, one of his graduate students in real estate law, selected portions of whose Final Paper for the course, based on the author's Problem Statement "When Bad Things Happen to Good People" dated April 26, 2013 (Georgetown SCS, FREL 610–02, Spring 2013), provided some of the legal research and analysis upon which some of the discussion in this section of the chapter is based.

18. Kayden, Jerold S., *Privately Owned Public Space: The New York City Experience*, John Wiley & Sons, New York, NY (2000), pg. 9. Footnote in the original omitted.

19. Ibid., pg. 10.

20. Chapter 5.

21. Kayden, *Privately Owned Public Space*, pgs. 11–12.

22. Ibid., pgs. 12–13.

23. Ibid., pgs. 13–15.

24. Ibid., pgs. 15–16.

25. *Kelo v. City of New London*, 545 U.S. 1158 (2005).

26. The author acknowledges the work of Will Holiday, one of his graduate students in real estate law, whose Final Paper for the course, *"Kelo's Aftermath and The Impacts on Large-Scale Revitalization Projects"* dated April 26, 2013 (Georgetown SCS, FREL 610–02, Spring 2013), provided some of the legal research and analysis upon which some of the discussion in this section of the chapter is based.

27. Fifth Amendment, Constitution of the United States of America.

28. The Urban Renewal movement in the United States has a very checkered history, with many critics of its largely negative social and displacement impacts on lower-income communities of color earning it the pejorative moniker "Urban Removal."

29. *"Berman* v. Parker." last modified October 20, 2012. Found at http://en.wikipedia.org/wiki/Berman_v._Parker.

30. *Kelo v. City of New London*, 545 U.S. 1158 (2005).

31. *Kelo v. City of New London*, 545 U.S. 1158 (2005) [citing *Kelo v. City of New London*, 268 Conn. (2004)].

32. The author acknowledges the work of Ben Luke, one of his graduate students in real estate law, whose midterm paper for the course, *"Unbreak My HART: Honolulu's Rail Line Fiasco and Eminent Domain"* dated February 13, 2013 (Georgetown SCS, FREL 610–02, Spring 2013), provided some of the legal research and analysis upon which some of the discussion about *Hawaii Housing Authority v Midkiff*, 467 U.S. 229, 83–141 (1984) is based. That paper provides, in pertinent part regarding the Supreme Court's *Midkiff* decision, as follows (pgs. 3–4):

The issue of eminent domain in the state of Hawaii has been one chronicled by a history of broad government interpretation regarding the definition of public use and one that has also left considerable authority in the hands of county governing boards and city councils regarding the valuation of condemned properties. Traditionally, the Hawaii state legislature has been predominantly lenient in allowing local governments and courts to determine both what constitutes a "public use" as well as the degree to which a citizen may be compensated.

33. Ibid., pg. 4:

Under the act, those parties leasing single-family lots on more than 5 acres were entitled to file an application with the Hawaii Housing Authority (HHA) to request a condemnation of the property so that they might purchase the land (either through negotiations with the landlord or at prices determined through the condemnation trial) following a public hearing discussing the land's "public use" and pending approval from the HHA. When landlords and lessees inevitably failed to come to terms and the HHA was forced to establish a value, the landlords filed suit with the Ninth Circuit Court and won, after which the HHA then appealed the decision to the US Supreme Court in *Hawaii Housing Authority v Midkiff* (1984).

34. Ibid. According to the paper's author, Ben Luke:

While the court's decision had even greater national implications, the first use of eminent domain in Hawaii had been vast and potent, solidifying the Hawaii State government's complete autonomy in formulating their own procedures and scope of public condemnations.

35. *Kelo v. City of New London*, 545 U.S. 1158 (2005).

36. Ibid.

37. Pfizer already had a large, corporate presence in the nearby town of Groton, CT.

38. "New London Development Corporation now RCDA." last modified January 2013. Found at www.nldc.org/sec/4.

39. *Kelo v. City of New London*, 545 U.S. 1158 (2005).

40. Rutkow, Eric, "Kelo v. City of New London." *Harvard Law Review*, Vol. 30 (2005), pg. 262, accessed February 2, 2013, Found at doi: www.law.harvard.edu/students/orgs/elr/vol30_1/rutkow.pdf.

41. Institute for Justice Report, "Five Years After Kelo: The Sweeping Backlash Against One of the Supreme Court's Most-Despised Decisions." June 2010, pg. 6,. Found at doi: http://ij.org/report/five-years-after-kelo/.

42. Kelo, Susette, "The Government Stole My Home." *Cato Institute* (2009), accessed February 2, 2013. Found at doi: www.cato.org/sites/cato.org/files/serials/files/policy-report/2012/8/cpr31n2–3.pdf.

43. Justice John Paul Stevens (Ret.), "Kelo, Popularity, and Substantive Due Process." *Alabama Law Review* 63.5 (June 2012), 941–956.

44. 26 Am. Jur. 2nd, Eminent Domain, § 55 (2004); sell also, *Hawaii Housing Authority v Midkiff*, 467 U.S. 229, 83–141 (1984).

45. It should be noted that the City's condemnation of privately owned properties located in Parcel 4a were deemed unreasonable due to the lack of compelling evidence that this

parcel was necessary to fulfill the purposes of the MDP. However, for petitioners Susette Kelo and the Dery family, whose respective homes were located in Parcel 3, the City's condemnation of those properties was upheld by the Superior Court.

46. *Kelo v. City of New London*, 545 U.S. 1158 (2005).

47. Ibid. [citing *Kelo v. City of New London*, 268 Conn. (2004)]. Emphasis added.

48. Ibid.

49. *Kelo v. City of New London*, 545 U.S. 1158 (2005).

50. Ibid.

51. Ibid. Emphasis added.

52. Ibid.

53. *Kelo v. City of New London*, 545 U.S. 1158 (2005).

54. Ibid. [citing *Kelo v. City of New London*, 268 Conn. (2004)].

55. *Kelo v. City of New London*, 545 U.S. 1158 (2005) [citing *Calder v Bull*, 3 U.S. 286 (1798)].

56. *Kelo v. City of New London*, 545 U.S. 1158 (2005).

57. Ibid.

58. Ibid.

59. Holliday, Will, "Kelo's Aftermath and the Impacts on Large-Scale Revitalization Projects." April 26, 2013 (Georgetown University School of Continuing Studies, Foundations of Real Estate Law, 610–02, Spring 2013). Footnotes in the original.

60. Ibid.

61. Ibid.

62. Holliday, "Kelo's Aftermath and the Impacts on Large-Scale Revitalization Projects."

63. Ibid.

64. "Five Years After Kelo."

65. Ibid.

66. *Kelo v. City of New London*, 545 U.S. 1158 (2005).

67. Ibid.

68. Ibid.

69. "Five Years After Kelo."

70. *Kelo v. City of New London*, 545 U.S. 1158 (2005).

71. Justice John Paul Stevens, "Kelo, Popularity, and Substantive Due Process."

72. In a case of history repeating itself, the District of Columbia government, in 2012, won its final eminent domain case, brought against it to prevent the condemnation of privately owned properties necessary to move forward with the Skyland Town Center public/private partnership redevelopment project. Then, in late 2015, the project overcame what appeared to be its final hurdle: Settlement of an action to enforce a 1997 covenant prohibiting the operation of a supermarket or pharmacy within close proximity a national grocery chain store, Safeway, located across the street from the future Skyland Town Center location. Inasmuch as the centerpiece of Skyland Town Center was a Walmart, which sells both groceries and operates pharmacies in its stores, the covenant issue also needed to be resolved. The similarity to the *Kelo* decision is that the benefits of the

Skyland Town Center redevelopment project was sold by the District to its residents, promising to bring a Walmart to a largely underserved population in northeast DC. In order to make the project possible, however, the District needed to acquire – through purchase or condemnation proceedings – numerous locally owned businesses, including a retail store, fast-food restaurants, and a laundromat. Ironically, in early 2016, Walmart announced it would be scaling back on the opening of new stores in the District, including the anchor store for Skyland Town Center and another one also requested by the District government for northeast, to provide much-needed retail to another underserved, primarily minority community. Walmart's commitment to open the two stores in northeast D.C. was made in exchange for the District's development approvals for three other Walmarts in much more affluent D.C. neighborhoods. Walmart had completed and opened the three other Walmarts elsewhere in the District, and claimed that lower-than-expected sales at those stores were a factor in its decision not to open the two northeast stores:

> To get approval to build three stores in wealthier parts of the city, Walmart promised to build two in underserved neighborhoods. So they built the three they wanted. Then, last week, Walmart told city officials that it had made "fresh assumptions" about the profitability of stores slated for black working-class neighborhoods and decided not to build them.
>
> Milloy, Courtland, "Walmart Backs Out of D.C. Deal Citing Costs, and City's Poorest Pay the Price." *The Washington Post*, January 19, 2016. See, also, Neibauer, Michael, "D.C. Wins Last of the Skyland Shopping Center Eminent Domain Cases." *Washington Business Journal*, December 12, 2012; Neibauer, Michael, "D.C., Safeway Ink Skyland Deal. Here's What That Means for the Wal-Mart-Anchored Project." *Washington Business Journal*, October 7, 2015.

73. Ibid.

74. In other words, a $1,000 TIF Bond with a 5% face-rate of interest, which sells at a discount of $950, has a higher yield for the bondholder, and as well as a higher interest cost for the Issuer relative to the gross proceeds received from the sale of that bond. A bondholder who receives an annual interest payment of $50 on an investment of $950 (the actual purchase price) is actually realizing a return on or yield from that bond of 5.263%. That might seem an almost insignificant difference but when the bond purchase is scaled up from $1,000.00 to $100,000 or $1,000,000 the increased yield of twenty-six basis points becomes significant.

75. The author acknowledges the work of Danny Stover, one of his graduate students in real estate law, whose final paper for the course, "A 'TIF' Story," dated April 13, 2013 (Georgetown SCS, FREL 610–01, Spring 2013), provided some of the legal research and analysis on which the discussion of tax increment finance (TIF) district bond financing in this section of the chapter is based.

76. Lefcoe, George, "The Demise of TIF-Funded Redevelopment in California." *The Planning Report: Insider's Guide to Planning and Infrastructure*, August 24, 2014, pg. 2.

77. As noted above, absent a prohibition in the authorizing statute precluding a local jurisdiction from providing credit support for TIF Bonds, depending upon the political will behind the catalytic Project warranting the creation of a TIF District it would not be unusual for the local jurisdiction to provide a guarantee, limited guarantee of payment, or even moral obligation to prevent a default on the TIF Bonds. Such credit supports

for a revenue bond, while not necessarily impairing the credit rating of a unit of local government, could constitute a contingent liability on its financial condition. Ratings agencies that rate the credit worthiness of public entities have specific rules regarding the proper disclosure of contingent liabilities created by providing credit support to revenue bonds and other forms of conduit financing.

78. One component of the 2011 Budget Act, Assembly Bill 1X27, which would have allowed California's redevelopment agencies to continue to operate provided 20% of the revenues collected to be remitted to the state to fund schools and other public services traditionally provided by local units of government, was struck down as unconstitutional by the California Supreme Court in the Matosantos case, with the Court finding as follows:

> A different conclusion is required with respect to Assembly Bill 1X 27, the measure conditioning further redevelopment agency operations on additional payments by an agency's community sponsors to state funds benefiting schools and special districts. Proposition 22 [specifically Cal. Const., art. XIII, § 25.5, subd. (a)(7)] expressly forbids the Legislature from requiring such payments. Matosantos's argument that the payments are valid because technically voluntary cannot be reconciled with the fact that the payments are a requirement of continued operation. Because the flawed provisions of Assembly Bill 1X 27 are not severable from other parts of that measure, the measure is invalid in its entirety.
>
> (*Cal. Redevelopment Assoc. v. Matosantos*, 53 CAL. 4TH 231, 267 P.3D 580, 135 CAL. RPTR. 3D 683 (2011), pg. 3.)

79. California Department of Finance, Redevelopment Agency Dissolution web page, as of January 28, 2016. Found at www.dof.ca.gov/redevelopment/.

80. *Cal. Redevelopment Assoc. v. Matosantos*, 53 CAL. 4TH 231, 267 P.3D 580, 135 CAL. RPTR. 3D 683 (2011).

81. Stover, Danny, "A 'TIF' Story" April 13, 2013 (Georgetown University School of Continuing Studies, Foundations of Real Estate Law, 610–01, Spring 2013).

CHAPTER 11

Property management and leasing

This is the unsexy part of the real estate business. Real estate war stories tend to focus on the dramatic buying and selling of properties, the against-the-odds creation of new buildings, or the inspired reuse of old ones. The reason for this bias . . . is that rewards in the real estate game (as in other games) come from *creating value*. In most cases, creating value involves change.

Operations aren't quite the opposite of change, but they're close. Operations involve growing or defending your margins (or in the worst case, minimizing the shrinkage of your margins).

Operations are rarely heroic. Few real estate moguls find convincing ways to brag about how they fixed a leaky roof, placated an impossible tenant, or restriped the parking lot to accommodate four more cars. But even though discussing operating issues is unlikely to make you the center of attention at a real estate cocktail party, your ability to manage properties effectively will have major impact on your short- and long-term cash flow.[1]

And, so, Professor Poorvu introduces his students and readers to the unglamorous world of Property Management. Ironically, in contrasting *the sexy part of the real estate business* – the creation of value through developing a new commercial building or repositioning an existing, older building into something better tailored to its contemporary real estate market – Professor Poorvu doesn't draw the student's or reader's attention directly, in the opening of the chapter on Operations in *The Real Estate Game*, to the critical nexus between the latter and Property Management.

Business people generally, as well as students of business, are presumably well-acquainted with the axiom of profit-taking: Buy Low; Sell High. This axiom is no less applicable in the world of real estate development and finance as it is in the stock market. There is one, additional axiom equally applicable to both market sectors as well: The role of active management (or, in the case of the real estate business: Property Management).

One of the heroes – or anti-heroes, depending upon one's perspective – in Michael Lewis's *The Big Short*[2] is physician turned equities investor turned hedge fund manager Michael Burry. Before starting his hedge fund, Scion Capital, almost by accident, Burry was the quintessential value investor. A disciple not so much of Benjamin Graham and his devoted disciple, Warren Buffett, but more in line with Buffett's somewhat vitriolic partner, Charlie Munger, Burry was an assiduous researcher in order to find value investing opportunities (see Chapters 1 and Chapter 9 regarding the influence of Charlie Munger on Michael Burry's investment philosophy, respectively). Although not exclusively so, many of the indicia of the existence of potential value had its foundations in poor management of the publicly traded companies in which Burry sought to make an investment.

The same is the case in real estate investment. More often than not, the bargains in commercial real property are a consequence of lax to extremely poor Property Management protocols and practices. Those very unsexy Property Management activities – diligent, consistent, and prudent property maintenance, repair, and replacements; maintaining the appearance and functionality of the building and grounds; great customer services skills in meeting and exceeding tenants' expectations; and market-sensitive lease renewals and originations – are, as Poorvu suggests, critical to maintaining a property's value, including its short and long-term cash flow. As the idiom goes, "one owner's trash is another man's treasure." One property owner's inept Property Management becomes the next Owner's opportunity to build great value.

Chapter outline
Chapter introduction
Commercial Leasing
The commercial real estate services industry
Commercial Lease Agreements
Brokers and Agents, and the Law of Principal and Agent
Potential Conflicts of Interest in the CRES Industry
Property Management
Duties, Liabilities, and Obligations of Property Owners
Generally
Mixed-Use Properties
POPS: Privately Owned Public Spaces
Property Management Agreements

Commercial Leasing

The commercial real estate services industry[3]

The U.S. commercial real estate services (CRES) sector generally. From approximately 2004 until the end of 2013 (the period covered in the *CREUA Conflicts of Interest Research Study Report* regarding the growth and consolidation of the CRES sector), CRES firms have grown in size, geographic reach, breadth of services offered, and overall importance to and involvement in various aspects of the development and financing of commercial properties, both domestically and internationally. They have become increasingly global, and the more Landlord-focused. CRES firms have expanded their tenant representation capabilities primarily by acquiring U.S. national, regional or local tenant-only brokerages: Local firms become or are swallowed-up by regional or national firms, while national firms have become or are swallowed-up by international firms. In 2013 the five largest, full-service CRES firms were involved in 150,461 commercial property transactions[4] generating more than half a billion dollars in commercial property transaction revenues[5] ($553.3 million in the aggregate). The five largest, full-service CRES firms also generated more than *$16 billion* in aggregate, total revenues in 2013.[6] As demonstrated by the table, below, excerpted from Appendix D to the CREUA Conflicts of Interest Research Study Report, there is a substantial disparity between the size and scale of the five largest, tenant-only CRES firms, and the five largest full-service CRES firms, operating in the United States in 2013.

The table at the beginning of Appendix D is reproduced here for convenience.

Table 11.1 Profiles of the largest full-service and tenant-only commercial real estate services firms

	Company	Service	Ownership	2013 Rev. ($ billion)	Leasing Volume (# of transactions)	Leasing Value ($1,000)
1	CBRE Group	Full Service	Publicly Traded	7.2	54,225	223.2
2	JLL*	Full Service	Publicly Traded	2.49	35,669	115
3	Cushman & Wakefield	Full Service	Privately owned	4.46	15,000	162.1
4	Colliers International	Full Service	Publicly Traded	1.31	42,100**	53
5	NGKF***	Full Service	Publicly Traded	0.57	N/A****	N/A***
6	Savills Studley*****	Tenant-only	Publicly Traded	0.23	3,467	58
7	Cresa	Tenant-only	Privately owned	0.24	8,400	8.5
8	Fischer & Co.	Tenant-only	Privately owned	N/A	N/A	N/A
9	Johnson Controls (JCI)	Tenant-only	Publicly Traded	N/A******	N/A	N/A
10	Mohr Partners	Tenant-only	Privately owned	N/A	2400	1

* Formerly Jones Lang LaSalle.

**Including lease and sale transactions.

*** Newmark Grubb Knight Frank

**** Newmark Grubb Knight Frank's financials was reported in BGC Partners' annual report. Leasing transactions and dollar volume of transactions are not enclosed in BGC Partners' annual report.

***** Depending on how the various Savills Studley offices are operated, and the extent of the exchange of information between the Studley tenant-only brokerage staff and the full-service Savills staff on a regular basis, characterizing Savills Studley as a "Tenant-only" CRES may not be and entirely accurate characterization of the firm's operations in the United States.

****** The portion of JCI's annual revenues attributable to CRES is very small compared with either total revenues or revenues from the core business to which such revenues relate, i.e., Building Efficiency. Revenues from CRES activities are included within segment revenue reported under Global Workplace Services, one of five reportable business segments of the company's Building Efficiency core business. However, this reportable business segment only includes but is not comprised exclusively of, revenues from providing occupier services for domestic U.S. customers. The majority of JCI's global revenues are from the sales and maintenance/service of products, primarily equipment and equipment components.

Recent trends in the U.S. CRES sector

The Consolidation Trend in the CRES Sector. As referenced elsewhere in the CREUA Conflicts of Interest Research Study Report, in a February 2012 report in CoStar News, CBRE's CEO Brett White made clear that the market dominance of the top two full-service CRES firms in the United States, JLL and CBRE, would continue into the foreseeable future.

> Both JLL and CBRE expect to continue to capture market share in a highly competitive leasing conditions [sic] in most world markets.
>   "This business is *rapidly consolidating down to a very small number of players*," CBRE's [CEO Brett] White said, adding *that the two largest firms [CBRE and JLL] are "going to capture the vast majority of the available share going forward."*
>   "That trend is absolute, and I suspect that *the mid-tier firms and the smaller firms, you're just going to see them lose more and more share every quarter and every year."*[7]

Assimilation of Tenant-Only CRES Firms into Full-Service CRES Firms. In the span of six years, three large, tenant-only CRES firms – Julian Studley, The Staubach Companies, and Newmark Real Estate Company, Inc., have been acquired by much larger, global, full-service CRES firms, removing a substantial component of tenant-only representation from the CRES sector in the United States, by making formerly tenant-only agents employees of full-service CRES firms:

a. Julian J. Studley, the first tenant-only brokerage firm in the United States, was founded by its namesake in New York City in 1954. When it was acquired in 2012 by Savills, LLC, a global, full-service CRES firm, Studley had twenty-five offices in the United States and 400 commissioned brokers and 175 support staff.
b. The Staubach Companies, founded in 1977 by former Dallas Cowboys quarterback Roger Staubach as a tenant-focused CRES firm, was acquired by JLL (formerly known as "Jones Lange LaSalle") in July 2008. At that time Staubach had fifty offices in North America and 1,100 employees.
c. In 2011 Newmark & Company Real Estate, Inc., a tenant-focused CRES firm formed in 1926, merged with U.K.-based, full-service CRES firm Knight Frank, creating Newmark Knight Frank. Two years later, Newmark Knight Frank which was purchased by BGC Partners in 2012. In 2013 BGC acquired Grubb & Ellis, a full-service, U.S.-based CRES, creating Newmark Grubb Knight Frank.[8]

Anatomy of commercial development transactions

In order to fully understand and appreciate the various ways in which a CRES firm might represent the interests of a Developer or Property Purchase and Owner, as the case may be, one must first understand significant milestones in The Development Process (in the case of the development of a commercial property) and in the strategic acquisition of a portfolio property (in the case of the selection and acquisition of commercial properties).

Developing and implementing a strategic vision

For most regional and national Developers and Property Purchasers and Owners, respectively, the development or acquisition of an individual property will not be undertaken as a one-off transaction. Rather, these actions are generally one component of an overall real estate strategy. An understanding of geographic and asset class market dynamics, as well as the availability of debt and equity financing for various types of properties in different markets, is critical to developing a Strategic Vision. Identifying the options, if not actual sources, for the debt and equity financing necessary to implement this Strategic Vision is also a critical component of formulating a strategic approach to either development or acquisition of commercial properties.

Search, identification, and selection

In the case of the development of a commercial property, the Developer is seeking suitable land for development or redevelopment (in the case of real property that is under-developed based on the current improvements on that property). In the case of the acquisition of a commercial property or portfolio of properties, the Property Purchaser and Owner is seeking existing, operating commercial properties, generally within specified geographic markets and submarkets (e.g., the central business district (CBD) in Washington, DC) and representing specific sub-classifications of commercial properties, including but not limited to general office, Mixed-Use, retail, hospitality, and industrial. Inasmuch as some of the best-suited properties may not be listed for sale, this requires an intimate knowledge of the markets in which such properties are being sought on behalf of the Developer or the Property Purchaser and Owner, respectively.

Property pricing

Whether it is determining what is an appropriate price for raw or underdeveloped land on which commercial improvements are planned as a means of extracting additional value from the site or the acquisition of an operating commercial property that may not be optimally positioned in the marketplace, the common denominator is the same: What is the projected net operating income (NOI) from the improvements or repositioned commercial property once it is fully leased. While the sales comparable method continues to be an acceptable methodology for valuing real property, in appraising or evaluating the "as built" value of commercial property, applying a capitalization rate to the projected NOI is the commonly accepted standard in commercial real estate. So, in other words, *everything comes down to the rent roll*. The entire financing structure, including meeting equity investors' return models and satisfying lenders' loan covenants and debt service and repayment of principal requirements all depend on the leases. Consequently, effectively pricing a commercial property, whether making that determination on behalf of the seller or the prospective purchaser requires an intimate knowledge of the commercial leasing market. This requires up-to-the-minute data on completed transactions, as well as general knowledge about transactions in the pipeline and the demand for particular property sub-classifications.

Securing project financing

Even if the sources or potential sources of debt and equity financing are identified in the creation of a Strategic Vision, and regardless of whether expressions of interest are provided, in advance, by any such sources, actually securing Project-specific hard financing commitments from those sources may rely upon established relationships between each such source and the Developer or Property Purchaser and Owner, respectively, *or someone representing them in the transaction*. Additionally, a firm understanding of what terms and conditions are, at that time, commonly required by debt and equity providers, respectively, depending upon the scope and nature of the specific financing component being sought (e.g., a construction loan or debt financing for an operating commercial property with a stabilized rent stream), is critical to managing the carrying costs of a Project.

Property listing

For a commercial property that is going to be developed, the identification and engagement of a Listing Broker may begin as early as the concept development phase of The Development Process – if the Developer is getting strategic advice from the Listing Broker – but certainly not later than Closing on the construction financing for the project, so that pre-leasing may begin in earnest long before the building is completed and ready to receive a certificate of occupancy. Large, multi-floor tenants may begin their search for new premises 36 months or longer in advance of when they need to relocate, taking into account the time increments most likely to be required for the search, lease negotiation, and tenant build-out in a new building. In the case of the acquisition of an operating commercial property, the leasing strategy may be integral to repositioning that property or at least to assure that the NOI on which the purchase price is based will be preserved, if not enhanced, following its acquisition by the Purchaser. Depending on what the prospective Purchaser has planned for its new acquisition, the pre-leasing process may parallel that of new construction of a commercial office building, as would be the case of an existing, operating commercial building that can only be repositioned in the marketplace through a combination of façade and gut-and-rebuild interior improvements. For an operating commercial property not requiring such extensive improvements, the Listing Broker's focus may be on some combination of renewing quality leases that could command a market rent upon renewal while allowing to expire, upon lease termination, those leases where the current tenants may not be able to renew at market. Depending on the size of the commercial property and the termination dates of extant leases, the Listing Broker may be in a somewhat constant state of marketing the property, including to existing tenants where lease renewals are favorably viewed.

Property management

Some purchasers of commercial property believe that property management is the key to everything: Poor property management creates acquisition opportunities in an otherwise constrained market and excellent property management adds considerable value to a commercial property. While excellent property management cannot make up for physical infirmities in a commercial building, such as extensive deferred maintenance or out-of-date electrical, mechanical, and conveyancing systems, it can mitigate the impact upon existing tenants of such capital improvements being made. Property management is responsible for the timely collection of rents and assessments under each lease, and to the efficient, day-to-day operations. The best way to think about property management is that its main goal is to preserve and enhance a commercial building's principal asset: the rent roll.

Property sale or refinancing

Every commercial real estate enterprise, whether a development project involving new construction or the portfolio acquisition of an operating property, begins, or at least should begin, with an exit strategy: How does the Developer or the Purchaser/Property Owner expect to extract value from its efforts at the end of a period of time? With the exception of a **Fee Developer**, whose sole compensation is the agreed-upon development fee, the value created through the development of a property through new construction or acquisition and operation comes upon the sale or refinancing of that property. A good way to distinguish these two options is to analogize them to beef cattle and sheep. Beef cattle can be slaughtered only once; sheep may be shorn every season. The rate at which lease values rise in a particular market from year-to-year, as well as prevailing commercial, long-term interest rates, will largely determine how often a commercial property may be efficiently refinanced, although refinancing is just as likely to be determined by the expectations or requirements of equity investors and long and short-term (if any) lenders in the project.

The Role of the CRES Sector in commercial real estate transactions

The Increasing Importance and Involvement of CRES Firms in the Development and Purchase of Commercial Properties. As detailed in Appendix D: Profiles of the Top Ten Commercial Real Estate Services (CRES) Firms, to the CREUA Conflicts of Interest Research Study Report, just over the past nine years, CRES firms have grown in size, geographic reach, breadth of services offered, and overall importance to and involvement in various aspects of the development and financing of commercial properties, both domestically and internationally. They have become increasingly global, and the more Landlord-focused CRES firms have expanded their tenant representation capabilities primarily by acquiring U.S. national, regional or local tenant-only brokerages: Local firms become or are swallowed-up by regional or national firms, while national firms have become or are swallowed up by international firms. In 2013, the five largest, full-service CRES firms were involved in 150,461 commercial property transactions[9] generating more than half a billion dollars in commercial property transaction revenues ($553.3 million in the aggregate).[10] The five largest, full-service CRES firms also generated over $16 billion in aggregate, total revenues in 2013.[11] Whereas the traditional role of a CRES firm 40 years ago may have been to simply act as the Listing Broker for a single Developer or Property Owner with a single commercial property, today a full-service CRES firm might be involved in one or more of the following functions on behalf of Developers and Property Owners with multiple properties, all of which services are enumerated above in subsection III.A.1. However, only one of the services enumerated next is specific to tenants:

a. Developing and Implementing a Strategic Vision
b. Search, Identification, and Selection
c. Property Pricing
d. Securing Project Financing
e. Property Listing
f. Representing Prospective Tenants in the Property[12]
g. Property Management
h. Property Sale or Refinancing

Commercial lease agreements

In *The Real Estate Game*, Professor Poorvu uses a typical commercial property lease as the framework for teaching students and readers about the importance of effective property management. Employing this framework is a helpful way for students using, and readers of, this textbook to better appreciate both the general structure of a typical commercial property lease, as well as a window into the world of Property Management. Also, in this way, he endeavors to arm his students and readers with the basic framework that can be applied to the idiosyncrasies of the different property classifications within the real estate asset class, because Property Management differs markedly among them.

In many ways, commercial lease agreements are emblematic of the essential axiom presented in the chapter on Contracts: *What happens in vagueness stays in vagueness.* In order to avoid ambiguity, commercial lease agreements tend to very detail-oriented, in the same ways, and for the same reasons, that Purchase and Sales Agreements are. See, in this regard, Chapter 7. Accordingly, disputes over commercial lease agreements tend to raise one of three, basic issues:

1. What does the lease say?
2. To the extent there is any ambiguity in the relevant provision or provisions of the lease, how should they be interpreted in the context of the dispute(s) raised?
3. To the extent the lease is silent or ambiguous in its applicability, what do applicable statutes, common law, and case law say regarding the dispute(s) raised?

While real estate lawyers go to great lengths to make sure real estate contract documents such as commercial lease agreements address all likely scenarios and eventualities, and are compensated handsomely to do so, inevitably reasonable parties – much less unreasonable parties – are going to have disagreements in interpreting their rights, duties, and mutual responsibilities under such documents.

Professor Poorvu, in his chapter in *The Real Estate Game* on "Operations," offers the following listing of commercial lease agreement sections or major clauses as his framework to understanding Property Management as a function of lease administration and building operations:

The parties	*Eminent domain*
The commencement date	*Default by tenant*
Building and premises	*Default by landlord*
Use of the premises	*Security deposit*
Term: original and extended	*Subordination, estoppel certificates*
Base and additional rent	*and nondisturbance*
Parking	*Subletting and assignment*
Tenant's	*obligations Consents*
Landlord's obligations	*Condition of premises*
Compliance with laws	*Tenant improvements*
Environment	*Landlord's work*
Insurance	*Broker*
Damage to premises	*Miscellaneous*

Many of the specifics of how these lease provisions or clauses manifest themselves in the discharge of Property Management functions are addressed functionally in the Property Management section under the Duties, Liabilities, and Obligations of Property Owners, Generally, subsection, below. Additionally, recent cases addressing specific legal issues arising out of the Property Management function are provided in the Supplementary Materials on companion website for this textbook under Property Management and Leasing. By way of introducing the student and reader to commercial lease agreements, the following is a summary of each of the key sections of a typical commercial office lease, with a brief explanation of how each section defines, describes, and/or prescribes the conduct of each of the parties. Students and readers should note that the following summary is more expansive than what's contained in Professor Poorvu's chapter on Operations.

Parties. The Parties to a commercial property lease are generally limited to the Tenant (i.e. the business entity that will be occupying the "Premises") and the Landlord, which is the Ownership Entity that holds legal title to the Building in which the "Premises" are located. Even in the case of a Development Entity that is a portfolio developer (i.e., is developing commercial properties with the intention of holding onto them in a portfolio of real estate assets), as part of securing the Permanent Financing for the Project, it is possible that the Ownership Entity may be different from the Development Entity as a function of the type and nature of the equity and debt components comprising the Permanent Financing. See Chapters 2, 3, 8, and 9 for more detailed information about the specifics about how the Developer selects a Development Entity, as well as regarding Permanent Financing.

In addition to the Parties, however, there are a number of other players who will be involved in the commercial lease agreement but will not have privity of contract with the Tenant. These include Landlord's Counsel, the Listing Broker for the Building, the Tenant Broker representing the Tenant, and the Property Management Company. Landlord's Counsel, the Listing Broker, and the Property Management Company act as agents on behalf of the Landlord or Ownership Entity, while the Tenant Broker acts as an agent for the Tenant. For more on the Law of Principal and Agent, see that section.

Commencement date. Every commercial property lease should have a beginning date and an ending date, negotiated and agreed to by the parties. The Commencement Date is critical for, among other things, determining the first date on which the Tenant may take occupancy of the Premises, as well as determining the beginning of the period for which Tenant is responsible for the payment of rent, as well as any other periodic charges due under the Lease Agreement. The Commencement Date is also the reference point for the termination of the Lease Agreement (unless otherwise terminated earlier, as described in the section governing Defaults By Tenant, described below), which occurs at the end of the Original Term following the Commencement Date.

Building and premises. A precise description of the Premises is critically important because Tenant's obligation to pay rent and other charges under the Lease Agreement, and the calculation of all such amounts, are based on the total number of square feet comprising the Premises. How leasable space is measured and calculated has been an ongoing issue between Landlords and Tenants for as long as Landlords have been leasing commercial space. There is no acceptable method of calculating the number of square feet with respect to which a Tenant is required to pay Basic Rent and various additions and supplements thereto, and the prevailing method of calculation may vary from Landlord to Landlord and from market to market.

An accurate description of the Building is important for similar reasons, as each Building is essentially comprised of three components: Leasable Space (i.e. the aggregate of all of the Premises contained therein); Common Areas, like building entrance lobbies, floor corridors, and restrooms serving multi-tenant floors; and Building Services Areas (such as interior mechanical rooms, storage rooms, rooftop areas containing HVAC equipment, and the like), which are not open and available to Tenants, visitors, and guests. For example, each Tenant in a Building is required to pay its ratable share – based on the number of square feet comprising the Premises as a percentage of the total Rentable Square Footage of the Building – of Common Area Maintenance or "CAM" charges. CAM charges are generally assessed against the Premises once every twelve months, based on the line items in the Operating Budget for the Building representing the Landlord's cost of maintaining the Common Areas.

Use of the premises. The most common and most benign activity that might take place in a commercial office building is what is typically referred to as "General Office Use." Beyond that, things may get a little more complicated. A General Office Use is pretty much what the lay person might expect: White collar professionals in the professional services sectors (think "lawyers, accountants, and lobbyists, oh my!"); offices and conference rooms along the window walls; cubicles throughout the interior space; library or resource/research room; copy room; server room; file storage; employee lounge with kitchen. Neither the number of Tenant's staff nor the power demands is overly intense; the same goes for the office equipment. Architects and engineers offices, public relations and communications firms, and trade associations, and the like, fall into this same category. By contrast, another category of use, Medical Office, increases the intensity of use (with patient visitations eclipsing the average number and frequency of visitors to the Premises), the weight of equipment the load for which the floors must be adequate, and the power demands to run that equipment. Retail and Restaurant uses, which are generally limited to the ground or subterranean floors of a Building, although rooftop restaurants are not unheard of, would also constitute separate and distinct uses from General Office.

There are at least four, good reasons why the Commercial Lease should be required to fully disclose the Tenant's intended use of the Premises. First, the Landlord has an interest in assuring the quiet enjoyment (see below) of the Premises by all of the other Tenants in the Building, as well as their respective staffs, visitors and guests. Finding that a Tenant is engaging in a use of the Premises that's not disclosed specifically and approved by Landlord in the Lease Agreement, and which use threatens the quiet enjoyment of other Tenants, would be grounds for both a cease-and-desist notice to the Tenant to cease such unauthorized use immediately, as well as constituting grounds for finding the Tenant in Default under the lease and moving forward with termination proceedings.

Second, to the extent the Landlord, or more particularly the Listing Broker for the Building, has carefully selected Tenants whose respective uses of their Premises are synergistic, or at least not in conflict with one another, allowing a Tenant's deviation from such disclosed uses may help the Landlord preserve the cash flows it projects from each such tenant. A good example of this may be found in the case of the typical convenience/sandwich shop commonly found in many downtown office buildings and a business services store, such as a FedEx/Kinko's. Although the former's "use of the Premises" is arguably a limited service carryout, it is not uncommon for these Mom-and-Pop businesses to expand the range of services offered, such as photocopying, faxing, and similar business services. If offering such services contravenes any non-compete provisions in the Lease Agreement of the business services Tenant, Landlord's allowing another Tenant to engage in competing business services could put the Landlord in Default under the Lease.

Third, depending on the nature of the use, it could violate one or more local ordinances or regulations, putting both the Tenant and the Landlord in legal jeopardy. For example, a Medical Office use providing physical and occupational therapy services might decide that offering massage services would be a logical, and lucrative, extension of services already offered consistent with its described use of the Premises. However, many local jurisdictions regulate how, where, and when massage services may be offered as a matter of zoning law. Even if the massage services being offered are purely therapeutic, and wholly consistent with Tenant's other services performed, they may nonetheless violate local law.

Fourth and finally, different Tenant uses often have very different financial and profitability profiles. While the Landlord might not object, at first blush, to the Tenant engaging in new uses neither specified nor contemplated in the Lease Agreement, had such additional uses been disclosed up front, the Landlord may have been inclined to charge a premium rent for allowing them. In such circumstances, the Tenant subsequently adding additional uses of the Premises not included within those specifically described in the Lease Agreement may deny the Landlord valuable, additional rent under the lease.

Term: Original and extended. Depending upon the extent and cost of Tenant Improvements (see below), the Original Term, sometimes referred to as the "Initial Term," of a commercial lease may be anywhere between five and twenty years, in five-year increments. This will be an important subject of negotiations between Landlord and Tenant, and will depend on various factors at the time of the lease negotiations and at any time during the requested Original Term, including but not limited to:

On the Landlord's Side:

Whether the Base Rent reflects a Landlord's versus a Tenant's market;
Landlord's plans to sell the Building or refinance its underlying debt;
Any planned or anticipated capital improvements to the Building; and
Any planned or anticipated market repositioning of the Building during.

On the Tenant's Side:

Importance to Tenant's business and/or image of the Building location;
Importance to Tenant's business and/or image of the Building itself;
The potential disruption to Tenant's business of relocating;
Tenant's ability to expand or contract the Premises during the term; and
Tenant's ability to sublet portions of the Premises.

In a Tenant's market (meaning leasing terms are favorable to tenants), a Tenant whose business has a solid history of growth may want to lock in what it perceives to be a favorable rental rate for an extended period of time, provided other provisions in the Lease Agreement will allow it to expand into contiguous new space, even if the rental rates on such expansion space have to be at the prevailing market rents as of the time such expansion spaces are negotiated, usually through a Right of First Refusal and/or Options clauses in the lease allowing Tenant to do so. On the other hand, in a Landlord's market, reflecting conditions that are the opposite of the Tenant's market (e.g. limited supply of comparable commercial space, with rents reflecting such constrained supply at a time of high demand), the Landlord may want as long of an Initial Term as the Tenant is willing to take on. On the positive side for the Tenant, the longer the Initial Term and the higher the Base Rent, the more generous the Landlord may be able to be in setting the budget to Tenant Improvements. See the section on Tenant Improvements.

Base and additional rent. Base Rent is expressed as a dollar amount per square foot based on the square footage of the Premises (as described in the Lease Agreement), paid to Landlord, in accordance with the Lease, in twelve equal monthly payments. Any and all other charges Tenant is required to pay under the Lease Agreement are included in the definition of "Additional Rent" so that, among other reasons, failure to pay any component of Additional Rent will constitute an Event of Default giving rise to the same Landlord remedies as if the Tenant failed to pay the Base Rent. Additional Rent includes but is not limited to (i) increases in the Base Rent under the Escalation Clause in the Lease Agreement (see below); (ii) amounts required to be paid for off-Premises storage space in the Building; (iii) Common Area Maintenance Charges; (iv) any additional charges for things like having HVAC services beyond the Standard Operating Hours of the Building; and (v) any Rent and Additional Rent on expansion space Tenant may lease and occupy during the Original and any Extended Lease Tem.

Escalation clause. To make sure the benefit of its bargain in agreeing to a Base Rent is not eroded by inflation, the Lease Agreement contains an Escalation Clause increasing the Base Amount each year by a specified percentage or according to an index that tracks inflation. Escalation Clauses are compounding, such that each year's Base Rent plus the escalator becomes the new floor to which a new escalator is applied. Fixed escalation clauses have historically been somewhere between 2% and 3%. An indexed escalation clause is a much more accurate mechanism for maintaining the current value of Landlord's Base Rent.

Payment of rent and additional rent. The mechanics of how, when, and by what means Landlord is entitled to receive Rent and Additional Rent is spelled out specifically in the Lease Agreement. For example, the Landlord may require Tenant to pay its rent only to a lockbox as opposed to the Property Management company directly. Payment of rent clauses are important because Tenant's failure to properly pay rent in accordance with this clause may constitute an Event of Default under the Lease Agreement, possibly triggering Landlord's remedies.

Parking. Most, if not all, commercial office buildings in urban downtown contexts have below-grade parking garages, although the garage is usually operated as a concession by a parking company. The Lease Agreement will guarantee Tenant a specified number of parking space in the Building's garage but does not guarantee the Tenant a specific price for parking "in the building" unless, as an inducement to get Tenant to enter into the Lease Agreement, the Landlord has paid-down the price of parking in a separate agreement with the parking concession operator in order to give Tenant a guaranteed parking rate for a specified period of time. In less-intensively developed downtown office markets where surface parking lots are the norm, Tenants and their employees, contractors, clients and guests may have more options for parking, which, among other things, may act as a constraint on prevailing parking rates.

Common areas maintenance (CAM) charges. What constitutes a Common Area Maintenance or CAM charge is defined the Lease Agreement. It is in the Landlord's interest to have an extremely flexible definition of CAM Charges, while it's in the Tenant's best interest to have a very strict definition. It is always in the Landlord's interest to be able to pass as much of the operating expenses of the Building, including expenses that are much more aligned with capital costs, to the Tenant, because this improves the Building's profitability. From an operating lease and accounting perspective, however, CAM Charges should not include any expenses that improve – rather than merely maintaining – Landlord's capital asset. Some of the most frequent, and sometimes extremely costly, disputes between Tenants and Landlords in commercial buildings arise over the interpretation and administration of the CAM Charges clause in the Lease Agreement.

Building operating hours. Generally speaking, a commercial building will have Monday through Friday operating hours, excluding designated holidays, that mirror typical business hours in the market, with a few hours added on the front and back ends. For example, In a market where the normal practice is for commercial office businesses to be open from 9:00 a.m. to 5:00 p.m., a Building Operating Hours will typically be from 7:00 a.m. to 7:00 p.m. This means, among other things, that Premises in the Building will have heat or air conditioning, depending on the season, during this period of time, as well as readily available business services, such as the ready availability of the Property Manager, a staffed Security Desk in the Building lobby, and a larger, on-call Building Maintenance staff on-site. Some Buildings offer limited Saturday hours as well, such as 8:00 a.m. to 2:00 p.m., to accommodate office workers whose responsibilities involve working on weekends. Having Building Operating Hours that match Tenant's work culture may be an important financial issue because the Lease Agreement will generally allow for the Tenant to have building services, particularly HVAC services, for a specified dollar amount per hour. This per-hour charge will vary depending upon the size and configuration of the Premises simply *because it costs more money to heat or cool a larger Premises than a smaller one*.

A Tenant proposing to occupy a significant percentage of the total leasable square footage in the Building may negotiate for the right to have signage on the outside of the Building, possibly very prominently located depending upon what percentage of the Building's leasable space is represented by that Tenant's Premises. In a Building in which the vast majority of Tenants have Premises representing 5% or less of total leasable space, a Tenant whose Premises accounts for 10% or more the Building's total leasable space may be able to negotiate for Building signage. Depending on demand for signage among competing Tenants, Landlord may be able to charge Tenant for such signage, as Additional Rent, provided Tenant receives an exclusive right to have its signage on the Building. Conversely, in a Tenant's market, a large user – one comprising 20% or more of the Building's leasable space – may be able to demand, and receive exclusive Building signage, paid for and maintained by the Landlord, as part of Tenant's Base Rent. Beyond issues relating to cost, the Landlord has a critical interest in controlling all aspects of the aesthetics of Tenant signage, as such signage potentially impacts how the Building is perceived by current Tenants and their employees and clients, as well as by prospective Tenants and the Building's equity investors.

Tenant's obligations. The Tenant's fundamental obligations are (i) to pay in full all Base Rent and Additional Rent as and when due, (ii) to occupy and use the Premises in accordance with the use or uses stated in the Lease Agreement, (iii) to occupy and use the Premises in accordance with any and all other rules and regulations of the Building to which all Tenants are subject (e.g. not violating any prohibitions against excessive noise; not posting signs in office windows); and (iv) to comply with any and all other affirmative requirements set forth in the Lease Agreement, such as refraining from unauthorized subletting of all or some portion of the Premises and delivering any and all Subordination, Attornment, and Non-Disturbance Agreements (see below) as and when requested to do so. Tenant's Obligations may also include providing Landlord with Tenant's consent without unreasonably delaying, conditioning or refusing to provide same where such consent is required under the Lease Agreement. Generally speaking, Lease Agreements do not create hierarchies among Tenant's legal obligations thereunder, such that Tenant's violation of what may seem to be a "lesser-obligation" to Landlord may be treated the same as nonpayment of rent, triggering an Event of Default and all of the same Landlord remedies.

Landlord's obligations. Landlord's essential obligation to Tenants are (i) to operate the Building in accordance with the Lease Agreement and (ii) not disturb Tenant's "quiet enjoyment" of the Premises. Because Landlords control the form and substance of the Lease Agreement – the rationale being that Landlord has multiple Tenants but Tenant only has one Landlord, such that administrative efficiency dictates that Landlord not have to administer dozens of different leases – the Lease Agreement generally treats the Landlord fundamentally differently from the way it treats Tenants in the event of a failure to perform Landlord's Obligations.

Compliance with all laws. This is a very broad undertaking for any party, and the Compliance with All Laws clause in a Lease Agreement is usually softened with language such as "to the best of [the Party's] knowledge" or an expression of best efforts. This is one of several clauses or sections in a Lease Agreement that should be mutual or "mirror-image." That is whatever it is that's asked or expected of Tenant under the Lease Agreement should be applied with equal force, and equal consequences for non-compliance, to Landlord. The rationale for such a clause or section in a Lease Agreement is that it may provide the non-breaching party with the opportunity to terminate the lease based upon an Event of Default. For example, if Landlord is operating an illegal gambling operation in the basement of the Building, Tenant may not want to remain in the Premises because being associated with the Landlord and the Building may reflect negatively on Tenant and Tenant's business. The same applies to the Landlord and other Tenants in the Building if Tenant is engaging in illegal conduct.

Environmental regulatory compliance. As environmental regulations have grown in scope and applicability to commercial, as opposed to industrial, buildings, requiring that both Landlord and Tenant covenant and warrant that each will, at all times relevant to the Lease Agreement, be in full compliance with all federal, state, and local environmental regulations. From how refuse is handled and disposed of, to mandatory, Building-wide recycling ordinances, to how the Building's mechanical systems are maintained, to how exterior walkways are kept free from ice and snow, there may be an environmental regulation with which Landlord must comply. Depending on enforcement mechanisms available to the environmental regulator having authority over the specific infraction, repeated violations could cause the entire building to be shut down unless and until the violations are remediated and fines paid. Accordingly, Tenant may need to be able to declare an Event of Default in the event such non-compliance is discovered, possibly well-before regulatory agencies get involved and threaten Tenant's quiet enjoyment of the Premises.

Insurance. Both Landlord and Tenant should be required to have the Building, and the Premises, respectively, covered with adequate insurance. The "adequacy" of insurance coverage in each case will be addressed specifically in the Lease Agreement, both as to the types and breadths of coverage provided, as well as the minimum value and possibly also deductibles charged under such insurance. For example, Landlord will want Tenant to have adequate coverage to be able to continue in business, in the Premises, after a catastrophic event, including Business Interruption coverage so that, among other things, Tenant is able to continue to pay Basic Rent and Additional Rent to Landlord during any displacement of Tenant's business from the Premises. Similarly, Tenant will need to be assured that, in the event of a catastrophic event, Landlord has the necessary resources to fully restore the Building, whether Tenant's Premises is directly or indirectly impacted. However, the extent of the insurance coverage required to be issued to and maintained by Landlord will depend, in part, on the clause or section in the Lease Agreement regarding Damage to Premises, addressed next.

Damage to building or premises. This section in a Lease Agreement addresses the Landlord's obligation to restore the Building and/or Premises after a catastrophic event, such as a fire, flood, earthquake or tornado. This is distinct from the Insurance section, which addresses coverage requirements and policy parameters. However, in the event a substantial percentage of the Building or Premises is damaged, or if the extent of the damage is such that there are significant structural problems as a result, the Landlord wants to have the option of either making the repairs necessary to fully restore the Building or claim the Building's a total loss, take the insurance proceeds, and walk away from the Building. The threshold for giving the Landlord this option may be as little as 25% of the Building, and may also provide alternative mechanisms for what triggers Landlord's prerogative, such as a minimum amount of time necessary to fully restore the Building. For example, this clause may provide that if the damage caused by a catastrophic event requires that more than 25% of the Building be restored or if such restoration will require more than six (6) months, regardless of the percentage of the Building impacted by the catastrophic event, the Landlord may terminate the Lease in its discretion, without any further obligation to the Tenant thereunder. This is a fairly standard clause in a Lease Agreement. Accordingly, Tenants need to make sure they carry business interruption and similar insurance coverages to protect Tenant's business in the event this lease provision is triggered.

Eminent domain. The Eminent Domain provision is somewhat similar to the Damage to Building or Premises Lease section on the "catastrophic event," and is actually a government entity initiating a condemnation proceeding against the Building. If the Building is condemned, then obviously the Landlord can no longer fulfill its obligation under the Lease Agreement, which is terminated. This is similar to the impossibility of performance argument in Contract Law. For more information about impossibility of performance and other defenses to claims for contractual performance, see Chapter 7. For more information about the law of eminent domain and the condemnation of real property, see Public Takings for Private Purposes: The Supreme Court's 2005 *Kelo*[013] decision and the state of public takings for private projects in Chapter 10.

Representations and warranties. During the lease negotiation process, the Landlord and Tenant each make statements to the other, some of which rise to the level of serving as an inducement for entering into the Lease Agreement and/or upon which one party relies to its detriment in entering into the Lease. In order to make the failure of any such statement to, in fact, be true, Landlord and Tenant reiterate and exchange such statements in the form of written representations and warranties. The parties' respective Representations and Warranties are important because they exist separate-and-apart from the Landlord's and Tenant's *other* obligations and commitments under the Lease Agreement, such that the mere violation of any one representation and warranty may constitute an Event of Default under the Lease Agreement, giving rise to the exercise of remedies by the party aggrieved by such breach. For example, Tenant may be required to represent and warrant that financial information provided to Landlord during the lease negotiation process was valid and complete. Should it later turn out, after Tenant has taken possession of the Premises, and the fact that Tenant's payments of Basic Rent and Additional Rent have all been timely made in accordance with the Lease Agreement notwithstanding, that Tenant withheld or misrepresented critical financial information, Landlord would be able to notify Tenant of an Event of Default based upon a breach of Tenant's Representations and Warranties. Similarly, if the ongoing ownership and management of the Building by Landlord had been the subject of the parties' lease negotiations, to the point where Tenant insisted that Landlord provide among its Representations and Warranties that Landlord has no intention of selling the Building, and it later turns at that at the time the Lease Agreement was executed by the parties that Landlord had signed a Letter of Intent or Purchase and Sale Agreement to sell the Building, Tenant would be able to notify Landlord of an Event of Default for based on Landlord's breach of one or more Representations and Warranties, the remedies for which could allow Tenant to terminate the lease.

Default by Tenant. This section of the lease details the specifics of Landlord's remedies if Tenant commits an Event of Default. Because, as pointed out above, the Lease Agreement for all Tenants in the Building is provided by, and drafted by its real estate counsel in favor of, Landlord, Landlords' remedies against Tenant for an Event of Default tend to be multifaceted, comprehensive, and oftentimes draconian in their potential impact, including but not limited to eviction of Tenant from the Premises and the imposition of costs of collection in addition to all outstanding monies owed under the Lease Agreement, including accrued but unpaid Base Rent, Additional Rent, and any penalties and fees specified in the Lease Agreement.

Default by Landlord. This section of the lease details the specifics of Tenant's remedies if the Landlord commits an Event of Default. Because the Lease Agreement is Landlord-friendly, Tenant's remedies against Landlord for an Event of Default are rarely as effective or draconian in their potential impact as are Landlord's remedies against Tenant in an Event of Default, which include eviction of Tenant from the Premises (clearly, Tenant is not empowered to evict Landlord for a building it owns and manages). An illuminating example regarding the lack of parity between how remedies work to cure an Event of Default by Landlord versus an Event of Default by Tenant is that most Lease Agreements do not allow a Right of Set-Off. This means Tenant *must continue to pay* Base Rent and Additional Rent to Landlord even if Landlord is denying Tenant the fulfillment of Landlord's Obligations. Absent a negotiated agreement between the parties, only a court of competent jurisdiction can assess a monetary penalty for Landlord's Event of Default, and even then Tenant will have only the same rights as any litigant that has secured a money judgment against another party, unless the judge orders that Tenant be allowed to off-set *the obligation to pay Base Rent and Additional Rent against such money judgment.*

Parties to a Lease Agreement are generally entitled to two things upon or after the occurrence of an Event of Default: Notice of the alleged Event of Default and a reasonable opportunity to cure that default. Much like the familiar thought experiment "if a tree falls in the forest, and there's nobody around to hear, does it still make a sound," Lease Agreements often raise the question: "If the party who breaches a provision in a lease agreement doesn't receive notice of the occurrence of the alleged breach by the aggrieved party, is there still an Event of Default?" Generally speaking, the occurrence or mere existence of an alleged Event of Default under a Lease Agreement is discernable from objective facts: Tenant either did or didn't pay a particular month's Basic Rent and Additional Rent; Landlord either is or isn't providing adequate heat, cooling and light in accordance with the Lease Agreement; Tenant either is or isn't operating its business in the Premises in accordance with the permitted use(s) set forth in the lease. And while there may always be questions of fact to be determined by a judge or a jury – for example, Tenant did, in fact, place its rent payment in the mail but it's not clear whether Tenant also properly addressed the envelope and affixed the required postage, or whether Landlord or Landlord's agent for collecting rent received and properly processed that payment – the mere fact of the existence of an alleged Event of Default, in and of itself, may not trigger any obligations, liabilities, and/or rights of and between Landlord and Tenant. If Tenant is not aware of an alleged Event of Default, its occurrence might as well not exist. The party alleging the occurrence of an Event of Default under a Lease Agreement must provide Notice to the other party in accordance with the notice provisions specified in the lease, either in the Notice and Opportunity to Cure section of the document or in a separate section of the lease describing any and all forms of communication (does an email count?), as well as the delivery method (is it required to be a form, such as certified mail, requiring a delivery signature?), that constitutes "valid notification" under the Lease Agreement. Depending upon how valid notification is defined in the Lease Agreement, such "delivery" of the Notice of an Event of Default starts the Opportunity to Cure Period, during which Tenant may either challenge the validity of the alleged Event of Default or, if valid, take steps to cure such Default.

It is instructive for students and readers to understand that, while there may be very valid reasons why a Landlord or Tenant may deliver the other a Notice of Event of Default, triggering an Opportunity to Cure Period under the Lease Agreement, these parties may, during the Term of the lease, experience other forces completely unrelated to the actual performance of the other party that may prompt an effort to terminate the lease without further obligation. The most common reason for either party of a commercial lease to seek to terminate it is that the "benefit of the bargain" reflected in the Lease Agreement no longer reflects economic realities in the commercial real estate market. A Building saddled with what, under current market conditions, is an underpriced Lease Agreement will be considered by the Landlord as underperforming, even if the current value of what is now a bargain lease was built into the Landlord's Cash Flow Projections at the time. Similarly, a Tenant occupying Premises at a premium price per square foot under current market conditions will be operating its business at less than optimal profitability than it would if the Tenant could move into new office space at a more favorable, market-based, price per square foot.

Security deposit. The Security Deposit is intended to protect Landlord against costs for which Tenant is contractually responsible under the Lease Agreement but, for whatever reason, Tenant is unable, unwilling or unavailable to pay (or at least pay promptly or without judicial intervention). The security deposit is usually equal to one or two month's Base Rent; it may or may not be required to be deposited into an interest-bearing trust or escrow account;

it is not to be applied to the last month's rent at the end of the lease term or any extension(s) thereof. The Security Deposit section of the Lease Agreement describes the procedures Landlord must follow in assessing any damages to the Premises for which Tenant is liable and notifying Tenant of Landlord's intention to use all or some portion of the Security Deposit to compensate Landlord for such assessed damages.

Tenant's quiet enjoyment. Tenant's *primary right* under the Lease Agreement is to freely enjoy its occupancy and use of the Premises without being disturbed by Landlord. The legal concept of a tenant's "quiet enjoyment" in its use of real property for which it has paid a Landlord dates back to English Common Law. Indeed, the term "Landlord" refers to the Lord of the land in feudal times.

Subordination, Non-Disturbance, and Attornment Agreement. In the event the Landlord decides to sell the Building or refinance the Mortgage through which the Building serves as security for Landlord's debt against the Building, the existing mortgagor, in the case of a refinancing, or the Buyer's prospective mortgagor, in the case of a sale of the Building, will require that each Tenant in the Building execute a Subordination, Non-Disturbance, and Attornment Agreement or "SNDA" Agreement. The SNDA Agreement is distinguished from an "estoppel certificate," the completion, execution, and delivery of which precludes the Tenant from later denying the stipulations set forth therein. Signed SNDA Agreements from all of the Tenants in the Building provide the financial institution with the comfort that there are no pending or latent claims against the Landlord of which the financial institution does not have knowledge. The SNDA Agreements section of the Lease Agreement creates a legal obligation on Tenant to complete, sign, and deliver an accurate and thorough SNDA Agreement any time it is requested of Tenant.

Indemnification and hold harmless. The Indemnification and Hold Harmless section of a commercial lease is another area of mutual legal responsibilities that, because the Lease Agreement is prepared by Landlord's counsel, nonetheless is more likely to be one-sided or skewed toward the Landlord and against the Tenant. In reality, however, consistent with the legitimate rights, obligations, and liabilities of the two parties, the Indemnification and Hold Harmless section should follow the mirror-image rule of contractual liabilities. Basically, this section of a commercial lease provides that one party will "indemnify and hold harmless" the other party for any legal liability that the other party might suffer despite the fact that the party giving the indemnification and agreeing to hold the other party harmless was in the best position to avoid any such legal liability arising in the first place. For example, a Tenant will generally be held accountable for the actions of its employees, agents, contractors, and assigns. If the Building has a bank on its ground floor, and one day one of Tenant's employees robs that bank, should the bank subsequently sue the Landlord because the Landlord, through the lease, allowed the bank robber access to the Building, the Landlord could interpose the Indemnification and Hold Harmless section of Tenant's Lease Agreement to require Tenant to defend Landlord in such lawsuit. If Tenant's efforts to indemnify Landlord by defending against the lawsuit fail, and a judgement is found against Landlord for the actions of Tenant's employee-turned-bank robber, Landlord could require Tenant to pay the amount of any monetary judgment awarded to the bank, under Tenant's obligation to "hold Landlord harmless" from such money judgment. The ubiquity of the Indemnification and Hold Harmless section of a commercial lease is a reflection of not only how litigious business has become, but the common practice of plaintiff's attorneys to "sue everyone who might be remotely liable" for the cause of action, and let the process and proceeding sort out who's legally liable and who isn't.

Subletting and assignment. Landlords have several, distinct interests intended to be protected through the Subletting and Assignment section of a commercial lease. One such interest is preserving Landlord's confidence in Tenant's ability to operate its business profitably in the Premises and Tenant's ability to timely pay Base Rent and Additional Rent as and when due. Additionally, Landlord wants to preserve the primacy of its right to increase rents when market conditions warrant, and that primacy may be subrogated if a Tenant is allowed to sublet a portion of the Premises or assign the balance of the lease at a more favorable rate than Tenant's current, escalated Base Rent. Finally, the required notice to Landlord by Tenant in order to seek the required consent from Landlord under the Subletting and Assignment section of the Lease Agreement may serve as a bellwether for Landlord that perhaps Tenant is struggling to meet its obligations to Landlord under the Lease Agreement and/or that market conditions may create an opportunity for Landlord to take space back from Tenant by reducing the square footage of the Premises in order to re-let such space at then-current market conditions. By the same token, in taking on a substantial amount of space over a Term of five years or substantially more, Tenant will seek the maximum flexibility under the Lease Agreement in its ability to sublet all or some portion of the Premises or assign the Lease Agreement to a new Tenant, subject to Landlord's consent (see below), which "shall not be unreasonably withheld, delayed or conditioned."

Consents. As suggested in several of the explanations above of other sections typical of a commercial lease in an active, urban market, there are a number of instances specific to various sections of the Lease Agreement requiring that Tenant secure Landlord's affirmative written consent before Tenant may proceed with a specified activity. A very specific example is provided, above, in the discussion of the Subletting and Assignment section of a typical commercial lease. However, additional areas in which Landlord's affirmative written consent may be required before Tenant may proceed involve the Use section (i.e. changing Tenant's permitted use or uses of the Premises), the Tenant Improvements section (see below, in this regard), and the Parties section (such as a change in the ownership of Tenant that, because of other sections of the Lease Agreement, such as the Representations and Warranties section, would be rendered breached absent securing such affirmative, written consent). It should be noted that a consent may be secured and relied upon *only if* the subject matter of the requested consent does not rise to the level of something requiring that the Lease Agreement be amended by the Parties (in which case *both* parties' signatures, and not just the Landlord's, would be required to effect such change).

Condition of premises. In the case of a Tenant taking over Premises in the Building in their existing condition, without requiring that Landlord undertake, or requesting that Tenant be permitted to undertake, substantial Tenant Improvements (see below), the condition of the Premises at the time Tenant may take occupancy will be precisely described in the Tenant Improvements section of the Lease Agreement. Under the more common scenario in central business districts of mature office markets, Tenant is more likely to required that Tenant Improvements be made by Landlord (and priced into the Base Rent), such that the Condition of Premises upon Tenant taking possession of the Premises is likely to be described, in great detail, in any attachments, such as Construction Drawings, referenced in the Tenant Improvements section of the Lease Agreement, to which Landlord and Tenant have agreed before the Lease Agreement is finalized and duly executed. In the case of a Tenant agreeing to occupy the Premises in "as-is condition," if the Premises are occupied by another Tenant at the time Tenant inspects them but before the current Tenant has vacated the Premises, Tenant will want, expect, and require that Landlord assure the condition of the Premises as of the time the Lease Agreement provides Tenant has the legal right to take possession of the space. Among other things, such requirement as part of the Condition of Premises section in the Lease Agreement will protect Tenant from any damage caused by the existing Tenant in moving out of the Premises.

For some of same reasons benefiting the Tenant as described earlier, the Landlord has a valid interest in receiving possession of the Premises in an agreed-upon physical condition at the natural termination of the Lease upon the expiration of its Term, and any extensions thereof, or in the event Tenant needs or is required to vacate the Premises earlier than such termination date. Specific issues relating to the Condition of Premises upon Tenant's vacation of the Premises and return of possession to Landlord include (i) the removal of any fixtures, and remediation of any damages to the Premises caused by such removal (whether the installation of any such fixtures was permitted or not by Landlord through the Lease Agreement), and (ii) the removal of any Tenant Improvements, whether undertaken by Landlord or by Tenant, and whether approved by Landlord in advance or undertaken by Tenant without the advance notice and written consent of Landlord, as may be required under the Lease Agreement. Again, as suggested at the beginning of this section, it has become increasingly unlikely that tenants in mature, major urban office markets, paying premium Base Rents, will occupy new Premises without first requiring Landlord to make Tenant-specific Tenant Improvements (making the Condition of Premises somewhat of a moot point), Landlords nonetheless like to have the flexibility of being able to market finished space in as-in condition. That only works if such Premises are returned to Landlord in good condition, reasonable wear-and-tear expected.

Tenant improvements. As discussed in the section on Condition of Premises, more often than not tenants in established markets [e.g., central business districts (CBDs)] in first-tier urban centers want and expect Landlord to undertake specific Tenant Improvements, on a turn-key basis, so that Tenant may move into customized, newly finished space on Day One of the Lease Agreement. In essence, Landlord is capitalizing the cost of such Tenant Improvements, which are amortized over the Initial Term of the Lease Agreement (inasmuch as Landlord has no assurance Tenant will exercise any Extended Terms permitted under the Lease Agreement). Accordingly, in the final analysis Tenant is paying for all Tenant Improvements, and the only question is Landlord's willingness to finance 100% of the cost of those improvements through the dollar-per-square-foot rate expressed in the Base Rent of the Lease Agreement.

Among the many issues Landlord and Tenant must negotiate and resolve in the final version of the Tenant Improvements section of the Lease Agreement are: (i) all of the specifics of the layout, configuration, fixtures, finishes, and overall quality of construction of the Tenant Improvements, which will be comprised of a set of drawings and specifications attached to the Lease Agreement (and which may or may not constitute the Construction Documents from which Landlord's General Contractor will build-out the Premises); (ii) the value of the Tenant Improvements, based on Landlord's contract with its General Contractor for all of the work to be performed in order to complete and deliver the Tenant Improvements; (iii) the duration of the construction and completion of the Tenant Improvements, which – among other things – will impact the Occupancy Date for Tenant to take possession of the Premises, which will be conditioned on the issuance by the building department of the local jurisdiction of a Certificate of Occupancy or "C of O"; (iv) Tenant's rights of observation or inspection while the Tenant Improvements are underway; and (v) Tenant's right to inspect, and right to accept as complete, the Tenant Improvements prior to Tenant's obligation under the Lease Agreement to take possession of the Premises.

Because, as described earlier, the Landlord is capitalizing the cost of the Tenant Improvements and allowing Tenant to fully amortize that total cost through a component of the Base Rent over the Initial Term of the Lease Agreement, the Tenant Improvement section of the Lease Agreement should address what happens in terms of Landlord recouping the capital costs of the Tenant Improvements if the lease is terminated during the Initial Term.

How such situation is resolved in the Tenant Improvements section may depend, at least in part, on who caused or is otherwise responsible for such premature termination of the Lease Agreement. Additionally, either this section or the section in the Lease Agreement governing Tenant's right to extend the Initial Term of the Lease Agreement, may address Tenant's rights to Additional Tenant Improvements to occur prior to such extension or subsequent extensions. The specificity of any language in the Lease Agreement about Additional Tenant Improvements will depend upon the nature of Tenant's right to lease extensions, including whether the Base Rent under a unilateral Tenant Right to Extend is to be negotiated by the Parties in good faith or whether the Base Rent for the Extended Term is determined by reference to an index intended to reflect the then-prevailing market rent.

Landlord's work. Despite the fact that Tenant Improvements will generally be performed by a general contractor with which Landlord has entered into a contract to perform these improvements, the Tenant Improvements, and any other work performed by on or on behalf of Landlord is sometimes referred to in Commercial Leases as "Landlord's Work" and addressed in a separate section. To the extent the Lease Agreement provides a separate section by this title, the section generally relates to Landlord's obligation, and Tenant's right to expect, that any and all improvements to the Premises and/or the Building by or on behalf of Landlord, whether by Landlord's employees, agents, contractors, and assigns, will be performed in a professional and workmanlike manner in accordance with the custom and practice of the marketplace. In the absence of a separate section on Landlord's Work, a statement to this effect may be required of Landlord, by Tenant, in the Representations & Warranties section of the Lease Agreement.

Brokers and Agents. For a very extensive discussion about the role of Brokers and Agents in commercial real estate transactions generally, including with regard to commercial leasing, see the following section, "Brokers and Agents, and the Law of Principal and Agent," later in this chapter.

Jurisdiction and venue. Depending on the case law involving commercial landlords and their tenants in the jurisdiction in which the Building is located, the Landlord may want to secure the Tenant's concurrence in the Lease Agreement to follow the law of another state in the event there are disputes under the lease that the parties desire to resolve through civil litigation. For example, California is traditionally extremely consumer-oriented in it judicial rulings at the local and state level. If Landlord's principal place of business or headquarters is located in another jurisdiction, such as New York City, it may require that the laws of New York will be controlling in interpreting the Lease Agreement. Additionally, the Landlord may further require, for its convenience, that New York City courts will be the exclusive venue for filing any action involving the Lease Agreement. Even if Tenant agrees to such provisions in the Lease – particularly if, during the lease negotiations, Landlord advises Tenant that the Jurisdiction and Venue section of the document is "non-negotiable," Tenant may nonetheless be able to get a court in the jurisdiction in which the Building is situate to overturn the Jurisdiction and Venue section as being contrary to public policy (see, in this regard, Chapter 7, Selected, Common Law Elements of Contracts section, Enforceability of the Agreement subsection, Contrary to Public Policy paragraphs.

Miscellaneous. Students and readers who are familiar with the phrase "legal boilerplate" may be interested to know that it refers to a host of sections or provisions in any legal agreement – such as a Lease Agreement – which are non-substantive but, rather, go to the mechanics of how the document is interpreted, administered, and enforced. For example, the discussion, above, about the Notice and Opportunity to Cure section of a Lease Agreement may refer to or rely upon a separate lease section titled, simply, "Notice," addressing the specifics of how effective notice may be given by one party to another. Such Notice section would likely appear at the end of the Lease Agreement, among the miscellaneous provisions. The same might also apply to the Jurisdiction and Venue section discussed above. Additional miscellaneous sections might include a Severability section (making clear that, in the event any single section or sections of the Lease Agreement are determined through a civil proceeding to be legally invalid, such invalidity does not render the entire document to be invalid); a Presumption of Validity of Signatures section (stating, in essence, that one party may assume the legal authority of the signatory on behalf of the other party to bind that other party), and an Entire Document section (stating that both parties agree that their entire agreement is reflected in the Lease Agreement, and that no outside documents or oral agreements between the parties relating to the substance and subject matter of the Lease Agreement are binding).

Residential lease agreements – at least those in professionally managed, multifamily rental projects, as contrasted with more ad-hoc properties such as single-family detached, single-family attached, and small, multi-unit residential buildings – tend to be much more homogenized than leases for different premises in the same building. While the configurations and sizes of dwelling units may vary considerably, from studio apartments to three and even four-bedroom apartments well over 1,000 square feet in size, for example, the residential lease agreement across such range of units are largely uniform in their provisions. Size, configuration, floor, location on the floor, and views may all factor into the pricing of a multifamily rental unit but all of the other provisions of the residential lease will be the same from a studio apartment on the ground floor facing the parking lot or garage to a three-bedroom, corner, penthouse apartment with a view of an cultural or geographic amenity.

By contrast, despite the fact that they are located in the same commercial building, leases for premises will be very idiosyncratic, from the original and extended terms of the lease, to the extent, cost, and time required for TI (Tenant Improvements), to the allowance and or limitations on specific uses of the Premises. Another important contrast between residential and commercial leases is that the former rarely extend beyond twelve months in the original term of the residential property lease. Commercial leases, by contrast, generally have a minimum, original term of five (5) years, with multiple, sequential renewal (or extended) terms. Depending upon the aggregate amount of rentable square feet and/ or floors in a building comprising the Premises of a single Tenant, the importance to that Tenant of the particular geographic location of the Building, and the shear logistics of relocating the Tenant to the Premises once completed, the original term of a commercial lease is more likely to be in the range of ten to twenty (10–20) years, with a sequential series of extended, five-year terms thereafter exercisable by the Tenant upon specified or to-be-calculated rent.

As the student or reader might assume based on the foregoing, the residential property lease in a multifamily building is quite different from its counterpart in a commercial office building. Moreover, unlike the latter, where there are no statutes or body of common law intended to protect the rights of tenants – the assumption being that commercial office tenants are sophisticated business people and, consequently, are not in need of such protections – every state has enacted one version or another of the URLTA or Uniform Residential Landlord Tenant Act. Accordingly, the legal framework with which developers, owners, and property managers of multifamily residential buildings is very different from the legal framework within which developers, owners, and property managers operate with regard to commercial buildings.

The latest version of the Uniform Residential Landlord Tenant Act is available on the companion website for the textbook.

Brokers and agents[14] law of principal and agent

Basics of principal and agent

The definitive legal treatise on agency law, the American Law Institute's Restatement of the Law of Agency (hereinafter "The Restatement of Agency)" defines agency as follows: [T]he fiduciary relationship which results from the *manifestation of consent* by one person to another *that the other shall act on his behalf* and subject to his control, and consent by the other so to act [emphasis added].[15]

A relationship between a "principal" and an "agent" may arise, under common law, between two parties based on a specific agreement between them to form such a legal relationship or from the conduct of one or both of those parties without an express agreement. Although the typical, contemporary agency relationships in the context of real estate transactions generally arises through the execution by the parties of specific, written agreements between a "principal" (e.g. a buyer or seller of real property, or a lessee or lessor of real property), and an "agent," other forms of agency occur more often than one might suspect.

For example, a developer who is in the business of identifying, purchasing, and upgrading a particular type of multifamily product (e.g. mid-priced, walk-up or garden apartments with limited common area amenities) to reposition and re-price it in the marketplace, could very easily create an agency relationship with a broker of such properties, simply through their course of conduct with one another over a period of time, without ever having entered into a prior written agreement or even having never discussed the fact that the broker will be acting as the potential buyer's agent in such transactions.[16]

The common law recognizes a variety of types of agency relationships depending upon the facts and circumstances in each instance.

Types of agency. There are six different types of agency:

Actual Express Authority. Principal and agent have entered into an express agreement creating the agency relationship, including describing the scope of the agency.

Actual Implied Authority. Principal and agent have entered into an express agreement creating the agency relationship, and although the scope, extent, and powers of the agency relationship are not expressly stated in such agreement, they may be inferred from the nature of the agency relationship.

Apparent Authority. There is no agreement between principal and agent creating an agency relationship but a third party may reasonably infer from the conduct of the principal that and agency relationship exists between them.

Agency by Estoppel. A principal is estopped from objecting to or denying the veracity of a legal obligation entered into by the agent on behalf of the principal where the principal knew of such agreement as it was being made and failed, nonetheless, to intervene for his own benefit, and the third party reasonably relied on the authority of the agent.

Ratification. Even in the absence of authority granted by the principal to the agent, express or implied, apparent only or by estoppel, if the principal accepts an act committed by the agent in the principal's name, then in so doing, the principal creates an agency relationship by that act of ratification.

Inherent Agency Power. First introduced in the Second Restatement in 1958, and then left out of the Third Restatement of Agency Law in 2006, "inherent agency power" is neither grounded in any grant, express or implied, of agency authority, nor implied by the conduct of one party or the other. Rather, the inherent agency doctrine is one means by which a third party may subject principals to liability for their agents' conduct.

Duties of Agent to Principal. As the reference above, from the Restatement Second suggests, the agent is in a fiduciary relationship relative to the principal. Courts generally place great weight on the responsibilities of fiduciaries:

Fiduciary relationship "A relationship in which one person is under a duty to act *for the benefit of another* on matters within the scope of their relationship. Fiduciary relationships – such as . . . principal-agent . . . require an unusual duty of care."[17] "A fiduciary is: 1 . . . one who owes to another the duties of *good faith, trust, confidence, and candor* . . . 2. [o]ne who must exercise *a high standard of care* in managing another's money or property."[18]

Agency relationships in real estate transactions

Brokers and agents defined. Both "agents" and "brokers" in the real estate industry are licensed professionals according to the state law in the state wherein their principal place of business is located, and according to any other state in which they do business, depending on such other states' laws. The licensure and testing requirements, if and when applicable, for an "agent" are less-onerous than for a "broker." Agents are allowed to engage in commercial real estate services such as office leasing only under the direction and supervision of a licensed broker. Someone who holds a broker's license but is working under another licensed broker in a supervisory role is commonly referred to as an associate broker, to distinguish that associate broker from the role of the supervisory broker having liability over the associate brokers and agents in that office.[19] For a comparison of the testing and licensure requirements for real estate agents and brokers in nine (9) states and the District of Columbia, see Appendix E. Comparison of Disparate Commercial Brokerage Regulatory Frameworks, CREUA Conflicts of Interest Research Study Report, referenced in the section, above, titled "The role of the CRES sector in commercial real estate transaction."

Agency in residential sales transactions. Residential real estate agents, whether agents or associate brokers, are treated as "agents" under the common law definitions for principal and agent, and may also have separate duties, obligations, and requirements under the licensure, testing, and continuing education/re-licensure statutes and regulations in the jurisdiction in which they are licensed as such. In addition to the common law duties of an agent to its principal described above, the state regulatory framework governing residential real estate agents should be consulted. In this regard, see Appendix E. Comparison of Disparate Commercial Brokerage Regulatory Frameworks, CREUA Conflicts of Interest Research Study Report, referenced in the section, above, titled "The role of the CRES sector in commercial real estate transaction."

Agency in commercial sales transactions. Commercial real estate agents, whether agents or associate brokers, are treated as "agents" under the common law definitions for principal and agent, and may also have separate duties, obligations, and requirements under the licensure, testing, and continuing education/re-licensure statutes and regulations in the jurisdiction in which they are licensed as such. Most state statutes do not make any distinction between commercial real estate agents involved in sales versus those involved in leasing. However, many do distinguish between commercial and residential real estate agents. In this regard, see subparagraph 1. Florida, of Subsection IV.C. Basics of Legal Duties of Agents to Principals in Real Estate Transactions, below. In addition to the common law duties of an agent to its principal described in Subsection IV.A. Basics of Principal and Agent, above, the state regulatory framework governing residential real estate agents should be consulted. In this regard, see Appendix E. Comparison of Disparate Commercial Brokerage Regulatory Frameworks.

Basics of legal duties of agents to principals in real estate transactions. The duties an agent owes to a principal in a real estate transaction may be a function of the common law of principal and agent in that state, as interpreted by judicial precedent, or may be codified in the licensure requirements and regulations, by state statute, which may take precedence over common law. This section examines two state statutes – California and Florida – which demonstrate the dichotomous treatment of commercial leasing agents.

BASICS OF LEGAL DUTIES OF AGENTS TO PRINCIPALS IN REAL ESTATE TRANSACTIONS: FLORIDA

Florida law exempts commercial leasing transactions from an otherwise comprehensive listing of duties that commercial real estate brokers owe to their principals. Florida Statutes, Section 475.278 – Subsection (2) sets forth the following duties of a landlord's broker (what is commonly called a "listing broker" and, under Chapter 475 of the Florida Statutes, is referred to as a "transaction broker."

(2) TRANSACTION BROKER RELATIONSHIP. – A transaction broker provides a limited form of representation to a buyer, a seller, or both in a real estate transaction *but does not represent either in a fiduciary capacity or as a single agent* [emphasis added]. The duties of the real estate licensee in this limited form of representation include the following:

  (a) Dealing honestly and fairly;
  (b) Accounting for all funds;
  (c) Using skill, care, and diligence in the transaction;
  (d) Disclosing all known facts that materially affect the value of residential real property and are not readily observable to the buyer;
  (e) Presenting all offers and counteroffers in a timely manner, unless a party has previously directed the licensee otherwise in writing;
  (f) Limited confidentiality, unless waived in writing by a party. This limited confidentiality will prevent disclosure that the seller will accept a price less than the asking or listed price, that the buyer will pay a price greater than the price submitted in a written offer, of the motivation of any party for selling or buying property, that a seller or buyer will agree to financing terms other than those offered, or of any other information requested by a party to remain confidential; and
  (g) Any additional duties that are mutually agreed to with a party.

The foregoing could serve as a fairly comprehensive listing of the duties of an agent to its principal in the context of a commercial leasing transaction. However, in addition to exempting the relationship between a Listing Broker and the Landlord from what would otherwise, under common law, be characterized as a "fiduciary relationship," this section of Florida law further exempts from this comprehensive list of duties owed by a transactional broker to its principal the representation of parties in commercial leasing transactions. Specifically in this regard, Florida Statute 475.278(5) – APPLICABILITY, Subsection (b) – Disclosure limitations. – provides, in pertinent part: "(2) The real estate licensee disclosure requirements of this section do not apply to: nonresidential transactions; the rental or leasing of real property, unless an option to purchase all or a portion of the property improved with four or fewer residential units is given;. . . [emphasis added]."

It is curious that the Florida Legislature, in enacting these provisions, would expressly exempt commercial leasing activities from the same disclosure requirements it imposes on brokers and agents (whether a Transaction Broker or Single Agent as those terms are defined under Florida Statutes Chapter 475) representing parties in a commercial property sales transaction, as well as exempting them from the enumeration of duties. California law, as of January 1, 2015, imposes upon commercial real estate brokers and agents, whether engaged in sales or leasing transactions, the same duties of disclosures to and securing waivers from prospective clients as have long been imposed on residential sales brokers and agents in any situation involving dual agency.

BASICS OF LEGAL DUTIES OF AGENTS TO PRINCIPALS IN REAL ESTATE TRANSACTIONS: CALIFORNIA

What ultimately became California Senate Bill 1171 in the California Legislature during its 2014 legislative session was conceived approximately two years earlier, and subsequently proposed to State Senator Ben Hueso for California's 40th District (D-San Diego) by Jason Hughes, founder and principal of Hughes Marino, one of California's largest, independent, tenant-only CRES firms.[20] Senator Hueso introduced what became S.B. 1171 in the California Senate on February 20, 2014; it was passed by the Senate on May 12, 2014, and by the General Assembly on July 3, 2014; Governor Jerry Brown signed the act into law on August 14, 2014, on which date it was also filed with the Secretary of State of California. The new law takes effect on January 1, 2015.[21] The Legislative Counsel's Digest for S.B. 1171 provides as follows;

> SB 1171, Hueso. Real property transactions: agents: obligations.
> Existing law requires listing and selling agents, as defined, *to provide the seller and buyer in a residential real property transaction, including a leasehold interest*, with a disclosure form, as prescribed, containing general information on real estate agency relationships. Existing law also requires the listing or selling agent to disclose to the buyer and seller *whether he or she is acting as the buyer's agent exclusively, the seller's agent exclusively, or as a dual agent representing both the buyer and the seller.*
> *This bill would extend these disclosure requirements to include transactions involving commercial real property, as defined, including a leasehold interest.*[22]

Testimony in favor of passage of S.B. 1171. In addition to receiving twenty verified letters of support for S.B. 1171,[23] the bill's author, Senator Hueso, offered the following in support of his bill on the Senate floor:

> As written, *the protections outlined in Civil Code Sections 2079.14 to 2079.24 cover only residential real estate transactions and do not extend to commercial real estate transactions.*

> There is *a common misconception* that parties involved in commercial real estate transactions are (1) *sophisticated*; (2) *of equal bargaining power*; or (3) *equally knowledgeable and experienced in real estate as the other party or the brokers involved.* This is not always the case. For example, *a small business owner whose only real estate transaction over the next five years will be his/her office lease is not going to be as sophisticated as a landlord whose primary business is real estate and who is negotiating multiple leases a year with the help of a team of sophisticated professionals.* That business owner is at a severe disadvantage at the bargaining table and *should be educated on the duties or limited duties the licensed real estate professionals involved in the transaction owe to all parties.*
>
> *The objective* of SB 1171 is clear and simple: to educate the parties to all real estate transactions as to the duties and responsibility of a listing agent, selling agent, landlord agent, tenant agent or dual agent.[24]

Testimony in opposition to S.B. 1171. Writing in opposition to S.B. 1171, the California Association of Realtors,[25] which represents both residential and commercial real estate brokers and agents, stated:

> When our association sponsored the original agency disclosure legislation, including the written form requirement that now applies to residential agency, and commercial transactions were deliberately not required to use the same forms as residential transactions. The reason for the different rule is the different level of sophistication and complexity that exist in non-residential transactions. We believed, and experience seems to bear it out, that simply requiring disclosure of multiple agency relationships and allowing commercial practitioners to utilize their own contracts and forms is sufficient to protect the parties.[26]

Potential conflicts of interest in the CRES industry

Analysis of an agent's conflicts of interest in real estate transactions

Unbroken Service and Loyalty. Arguably, an agent's duty of unbroken service and loyalty is an overarching one, from which all other fiduciary duties emanate[27] or, at a minimum, the prism through which such other duties should interpreted and evaluated. Additionally, the Restatement of the Law of Agency (Third) distinguishes between duties of loyalty and duties of performance.

Elements of the duties agents owe to their principals

a. Unbroken service and loyalty;
b. Confidentiality;
c. Full disclosure of information to allow well-informed decisions by principal;
d. Acting in the best interest of the client; and
e. Accountability to the principal.

> . . . duties of loyalty have distinctive functions and consequences, ones distinct from duties and consequences defined by other bodies of law. Within common law agency, an agent owes the principal fiduciary duties of loyalty as well as duties of performance. Although an agent owes both types of duties, distinctive legal consequences follow a breach of a duty of loyalty. These include

but are not limited to an enhanced range of remedies available to the principal. The distinctive consequences triggered by an agent's breach of a duty of loyalty are a helpful vantage point from which to assess whether and how an agent's fiduciary duties of loyalty are themselves distinct from duties defined by other bodies of law – in particular, Contract Law and tort law principles. . . . An agent's fiduciary duties of loyalty serve functions related to but distinct from the agent's duties of performance and that these functions, in turn, assist in identifying how best to resolve questions about the consequences that should follow an agent's breach of a duty of loyalty.[28]

It's conventional to distinguish among an agent's duties. Restatement (Third) of Agency uses the terminology of *duties of performance* and *duties of loyalty*. An agent's duties of performance include the duty to act only as authorized by the principal; to fulfill any obligations to the principal defined by contract; to act with the competence, care, and diligence normally exercised by agents in similar circumstances; and to use reasonable effort to provide the principal with facts material to the agent's duties to the principal. An agent's duties of performance are often defined by agreement between principal and agent.[29]

An agent's duties of loyalty stem from the agent's basic obligation to act loyally for the principal's benefit in matters connected with the agency relationship. An agent's more specific duties of loyalty include *a duty not to acquire a material benefit from a third party in connection with transactions or other actions taken on behalf of the principal or otherwise through the agent's use of position; a duty not to deal with the principal as or on behalf of an adverse party*; a duty not to compete with the principal or assist the principal's competitors during the duration of the agency relationship; and a duty not to use property of the principal, and not to use or communicate confidential information of the principal, for the agent's own purposes or those of a third party. *A principal may consent to conduct by the agent that would otherwise breach a duty of loyalty, but in obtaining the principal's consent, the agent must act in good faith and fully disclose material information to the principal. Although open-ended advance consents to disloyal conduct are not effective*, the fact that a principal may consent to conduct that would otherwise breach an agent's duties of loyalty mitigates the stringency associated with the fiduciary regime of remedies and other consequences that follow breach, as does the agent's power to terminate the relationship.[30]

Confidentiality. An agent is obligated to safeguard his principal's confidence and secrets. *A real estate broker, therefore, must keep confidential any information that might weaken his principal's bargaining position if it were revealed*. This duty of confidentiality precludes a broker representing a seller from disclosing to a buyer that the seller can, or must, sell his property below the listed price. Conversely, a broker representing a buyer is prohibited from disclosing to a seller that the buyer can, or will, pay more for a property than has been offered [emphasis added].

> **CAVEAT:** This duty of confidentiality plainly does not include any obligation on a broker representing a seller to withhold from a buyer known material facts concerning the condition of the seller's property or to misrepresent the condition of the property. To do so would constitute misrepresentation and would impose liability on both the broker and the seller.[31]

Full Disclosure of Information to Allow Well-Informed Decisions by Principal[32]

An agent is obligated to disclose to his principal all relevant and material information that the agent knows and that pertains to the scope of the agency. The duty of disclosure obligates a real estate broker representing a seller to reveal to the seller:

- All offers to purchase the seller's property.
- The identity of all potential purchasers.
- Any facts affecting the value of the property.
- Information concerning the ability or willingness of the buyer to complete the sale or to offer a higher price.

- The broker's relationship to, or interest in, a prospective buyer.
- A buyer's intention to subdivide or resell the property for a profit.
- Any other information that might affect the seller's ability to obtain the highest price and best terms in the sale of his property.

A real estate broker representing a buyer is obligated to reveal to the buyer:

- The willingness of the seller to accept a lower price.
- Any facts relating to the urgency of the seller's need to dispose of the property.
- The broker's relationship to, or interest in, the seller of the property for sale.
- Any facts affecting the value of the property.
- The length of time the property has been on the market and any other offers or counteroffers that have been made relating to the property.
- Any other information that would affect the buyer's ability to obtain the property at the lowest price and on the most favorable terms.

CAVEAT: An agent's duty of disclosure to his principal must not be confused with a real estate broker's duty to disclose to non-principals any known material facts concerning the value of the property. This duty to disclose known material facts is based upon a real estate broker's duty to treat all persons honestly and fairly. This duty of honesty and fairness does not depend on the existence of an agency relationship.

Acting in the best interest of the client[33]

An agent is obligated to obey promptly and efficiently all lawful instructions of his principal. However, this duty plainly does not include an obligation to obey any unlawful instructions; for example, an instruction not to market the property to minorities or to misrepresent the condition of the property. Compliance with instructions the agent knows to be unlawful could constitute a breach of an agent's duty of loyalty.

Reasonable care and diligence

An agent is obligated to use reasonable care and diligence in pursuing the principal's affairs. The standard of care expected of a real estate broker representing a seller or buyer is that of a competent real estate professional. By reason of his license, a real estate broker is deemed to have skill and expertise in real estate matters superior to that of the average person. As an agent representing others in their real estate dealings, a broker or salesperson is under a duty to use his superior skill and knowledge while pursuing his principal's affairs. This duty includes an obligation to affirmatively discover facts relating to his principal's affairs that a reasonable and prudent real estate broker would be expected to investigate. Simply put, this is the same duty any professional, such as a doctor or lawyer, owes to his patient or client.

Accountability to the principal[34]

An agent is obligated to account for all money or property belonging to his principal that is entrusted to him. This duty compels a real estate broker to safeguard any money, deeds, or other documents entrusted to him that relate to his client's transactions or affairs.

How the legal profession handles conflicts of interest

The legal profession has had very clear guidance about identifying, disclosing, and avoiding conflicts of interest. This guidance, which is currently codified in the American Bar Association's Model Rules of Professional Conduct, has been adopted, largely in its entirety, by the state bar organizations of all fifty states and the District of Columbia. State and the District of Columbia bar organizations have authority over, among other things, the licensure to practice law of, and disciplinary actions against, lawyers in each state.[35]

Rules 1.7, 1.8, and 1.9 of the American Bar Association's model rules of professional conduct

These three rules cover conflicts of interest in different contexts, specifically involving a "current client," "prohibited transactions," and conflicts of interest with a "former client," respectively. For purposes of extrapolating this analogy to legal ethics and applying it to the CRES context, the focus will mainly be on ABA Rule 1.7, relating to conflicts of interest with current clients. These rules are simple and straightforward regarding the avoidance of conflicts of interests with existing clients. When interpreted in the context of other Rules of Professional Conduct, these three conflicts of interest rules may be summarized as follows, although their interpretation has been the subject of various disciplinary proceedings and court challenges.

i. A lawyer should always err on the side of "avoiding even the appearance of impropriety" in the representation of a client whose interests might not be zealously represented due to a real or potential conflict of interest.
ii. A lawyer is responsible for identifying and evaluating conflicts of interest that may adversely impact a client being represented by that lawyer, and is further required to do any one or more of the following:

    a. Disclose the existence of the conflict of interest or potential conflict of interest to the client.
    b. If the conflict or potential conflict is deemed to be susceptible to a waiver by the client, then secure a signed, written waiver.
    c. If the conflict or potential conflict is so glaring that it cannot be remedied by disclosure and a written waiver by the client, then the lawyer must withdraw from representation.

Rule 1.7 – Conflicts of interest; current clients[36]

(a) Except as provided in paragraph (b), a lawyer shall not represent a client if the representation involves *a concurrent conflict of interest*. A concurrent conflict of interest exists if:

    (1) the representation of one client *will be directly adverse to another client*; or
    (2) there is a *significant risk* that the representation of one or more clients *will be materially limited by the lawyer's responsibilities to another client, a former client or a third person or by a personal interest of the lawyer*.

(b) Notwithstanding the existence of a concurrent conflict of interest under paragraph (a), *a lawyer may represent a client if*:

    (1) the lawyer reasonably believes that the lawyer will be able to provide competent and diligent representation to each affected client;

(2) the representation is not prohibited by law;

(3) the representation does not involve the assertion of a claim by one client against another client represented by the lawyer in the same litigation or other proceeding before a tribunal; and

(4) *each affected client gives informed consent, confirmed in writing* [emphasis added].

Interpretations of Rule 1.7 of the Rules of Professional Conduct by State Bar Organizations, as the Rule Relates to Real Estate Transactions. Two examples, from North Carolina and Illinois, are provided in feature boxes in this chapter, regarding how state bar organizations have interpreted Rule 1.7 to members of their respective bars, in the context of a lawyer's proposed representation of two parties in the same real estate transaction.

HOW THE LEGAL PROFESSION ADDRESSES CONFLICTS OF INTEREST: NORTH CAROLINA

Whether a conflict is consentable [*sic*] depends on the circumstances. See Comment [15]. For example, *a lawyer may not represent multiple parties to a negotiation whose interests are fundamentally antagonistic to each other*, but common representation is permissible where the clients are generally aligned in interest even though there is some difference in interest among them. Thus, a lawyer may seek to establish or adjust a relationship between clients on an amicable and mutually advantageous basis; for example, in helping to organize a business in which two or more clients are entrepreneurs, working out the financial reorganization of an enterprise in which two or more clients have an interest or arranging a property distribution in settlement of an estate. The lawyer seeks to resolve potentially adverse interests by developing the parties' mutual interests. Otherwise, each party might have to obtain separate representation, with the possibility of incurring additional cost, complication or even litigation. Given these and other relevant factors, the clients may prefer that the lawyer act for all of them.[37]

HOW THE LEGAL PROFESSION ADDRESSES CONFLICTS OF INTEREST: ILLINOIS

In a 1991 ISBA Advisory Opinion on Professional Conduct, the Illinois State Bar Association (ISBA) interpreted Rules 1.6 and 1.9(a) of the Illinois Rules of Professional Conduct as prohibiting an ISBA-licensed attorney from representing a client in a negotiation of a lease against a former client when the representation is of the same or substantially related matter (in this case, commercial leasing of retail premises), unless the former client consents after disclosure. In this instance, an ISBA-licensed attorney, who had previously represented a national mall operator through his former firm, asked ISBA for advice regarding his ability, after leaving that law firm, to represent a national retail tenant in its negotiation of leases with the former client, without the advance, written consent of that former client. Inasmuch as Advisory Opinion 91–11 interprets ISBA's analog to ABA Model Rules of Professional Conduct Rule 1.9, and not Rule 1.7, which relates to concurrent conflicts of interests, it is questionable, given the conclusion in Advisory Opinion 91–11, that ISBA would permit such dual representation contemporaneously, even if both parties consented, in advance, and in writing.

Advisory Opinion 91–11, which was affirmed by the ISBA Board of Governors in May 2010, holds, in pertinent part, as follows:

> The facts before us are very similar in that the negotiation of the lease is a substantially similar matter even though the retail property which is being negotiated is not the same property subject to the prior negotiations. In addition, it appears obvious that the representation of a party in negotiations of the lease would often require the sharing of confidences. It is very likely that the inquiring attorney, through his prior representation of Client X, became aware of certain portions of the lease that were subject to compromise.
>
> Two of our current Illinois Rules of Professional Conduct apply to the present fact situation. Rule 1.9 states as follows:
>
> > (a) a lawyer who has formerly represented a client in a matter shall not thereafter:
> >
> > 1) represent another person in the same or substantially related matter in which that person's interests are materially adverse to the interests of the former client, unless the former client consents after disclosure; or
> > 2) use information relating to the representation to the disadvantage of the former client, unless:
> >
> > > A) such use is permitted by Rule 1.6; or
> > > B) the information has become generally known.
> > >
> > > > Even though the negotiation of the leases may not have been the same matter, it is a substantially related matter and therefore the attorney in this case does have a conflict that can not [*sic*] be cured without the consent of the former client. Since the former client will not consent, the conflict can not [*sic*] be cured and the inquiring attorney must withdraw from representing the new client in connection with the lease negotiation with his former client.
> > > >
> > > > In addition to being a conflict of interest pursuant to Rule 1.9, it also appears that there could be a violation of Rule 1.6(a) if the representation would be allowed to continue. Rule 1.6(a) of the Illinois Rules of Professional Conduct states as follows:
> > > >
> > > > (a) Except when required under Rule 1.6(b) or permitted under Rule 1.6(c), a lawyer shall not, during or after termination of the professional relationship with the client, use or reveal a confidence or secret of the client known to the lawyer unless the client consents after disclosure.
> > > >
> > > > Under the facts as stated, it appears that during his prior employment, negotiating leases for the former client, he acquired certain confidences. Therefore, if the confidences were either used or revealed, without the consent of the former client he would also be in violation of Rule 1.6(a). Since no consents from the former client are forthcoming, it is the Committee's opinion that the inquiring attorney must withdraw from the representation of the new client, as it pertains to negotiating leases with his former client.[38]

Applying the ABA's Rules of Professional Conduct Regarding Avoidance of Conflicts of Interest to the Commercial Leasing Context. If the ABA's Rules of Professional Conduct 1.7, 1.8, and 1.9, respectively and collectively, as they have been adopted and interpreted by state and the District of Columbia bar organizations throughout the

United States, are treated as analogous to the issue of avoiding conflicts of interest in dual-representation in commercial leasing transactions, at a minimum, a rigorous requirement for informed, written consent in advance of the commencement of such representation should be required in all jurisdictions. However, such guidance by analogy necessarily raises the larger issue as to whether such direct conflict of interest is, indeed, susceptible to securing advance written waivers from both the landlord and the tenant, respectively, or is a non-waivable, dual representation scenario where such dual representation should be strictly prohibited. In other words, this raises a fundamental question: *If legal ethics prohibit an attorney or a law firm from representing both the landlord and a tenant in their negotiations of a lease agreement or in a dispute over the interpretation of the terms and conditions of an extant lease agreement, how can the divergent interests of those same parties nonetheless be adequately represented by the same CRES firm?*

Within the research framework of the CREUA Conflicts of Interest research study, as described in greater in the CREUA Research Study Report, the research study resulted in the following general findings, the basis for which, in each instance, are described in detail in various sections of that report, as supported by the Endnotes, Bibliography, and Appendices that follow the body of the report and are incorporated by reference therein.

1. Unlike other U.S. markets, including but not limited to the residential real estate market and the domestic capital markets, *the U.S. commercial leasing market lacks transparency and equal access to the same quantum of information by all parties*. The following are among the factors supporting this finding.

    a. The commercial leasing market is characterized by asymmetric information, leading to inefficiencies and skewing outcomes in favor of those who control the gathering and selective dissemination of that information. Data regarding market characteristics is almost exclusively idiosyncratic to specific CRES firms. Competing CRES firms tout the superiority of their Research Departments as a market differentiator.

    b. There is neither a centralized source nor an industry standard methodology for obtaining, tracking, and reporting critical data comprising "the market" for commercial office space. Contrast this with the Multiple Listing Service (MLS) in the residential sales market, which provides generally accessible and uniformly collected and reported data on residential sales and homes offered for sale. Similarly, the various stock exchanges making up the U.S. market for capital is even more standardized and accessible than the residential market is, primarily as a function of securities laws and regulations governing the capital market intended for the protection and benefit of investors.

2. To the extent there is a unifying influence over the U.S. commercial leasing market, that influence is consistently *supply side oriented or landlord-centric*. The market is driven by the supply of available premises for lease and not by the demand for such premises. As a consequence, the status quo, including asymmetrical information, supports the interests of landlords and their brokers, to the detriment of tenants. Markets always function most efficiently when all information relevant to a purchasing decision – or in the context here, the decision to lease a particular premises, at a specific price, in accordance with detailed terms and conditions, all set forth in a lease agreement – is readily and equally available to all consumers and suppliers of the goods comprising that market. There is little incentive within the current system for the largest participants to create an efficient market for commercial leasing transactions.

3. The CRES profession – which provides an increasingly sophisticated depth and range of professional services to commercial clients, including real estate developers and other

building owners, institutional and other investors, and lenders involved in various stages of commercial property development and ownership, as well as to prospective and existing tenants – *is loosely organized, such that the conflicts of interest issue has not been addressed in any systematic way benefiting tenants*.

   a. Contrast the CRES sector with the U.S. residential real estate market, where a centralized organization – the National Association of Realtors (NAR) – accounts for a majority of residential real estate brokers and agents, providing uniform and comprehensive procedures, requirements, and guidelines for how transactions are initiated and managed, and how the respective parties within that framework are represented.[39]

   b. Licensure requirements vary from state-to-state (see Appendix E: Comparison of Disparate Commercial Brokerage Regulatory Frameworks).

   c. The CRES industry lacks uniform, national standards of practice and professional ethics (see Appendix E: Comparison of Disparate Commercial Brokerage Regulatory Frameworks).

   d. The CRES sector is dominated by a small number (less than ten) of very large, full-service CRES firms accounting for the vast majority of annual, completed leasing transactions (see Appendix D: Profiles of the Largest Full-Service and Tenant-Only CRES Firms).

   e. The CRES industry has openly opposed legislative and regulatory reform efforts seeking to improve the quality of representation provided to tenants through mandatory disclosure of conflicts of interest in dual agency situations. Such public opposition has created at least the appearance that full-service CRES firms dominate the CRES sector, and that they would prefer not to have to make such disclosures before representing a tenant, despite countervailing, common law duties requiring full disclosure of such conflicts.

   f. Relationships between and among various principals in a real estate development or acquisition transaction, or in the course of the normal ownership and management of commercial property – developers, institutional and other equity investors, and lenders of various types – are increasingly complex yet obscured from the public.

   g. Similarly, the roles played by the respective agents of each principal party in a commercial property transaction – including commercial property sales brokers and agents, capital markets advisors, strategic planning consultants, transaction financing brokers representing equity and debt investments, and, of course, Listing Brokers – are sufficiently sophisticated and complex as to be obscured at the level of commercial leasing transactions. Consequently, it may be unrealistic to expect that the average office tenant, which is not in the commercial real estate business, could understand and fully comprehend the potential impact and negative consequences of such relationships for purposes of creating a meaningful and effective system of conflict of interest disclosures and advance, written waivers by all of the parties to these transactions.

4. The *fundamental relationship between landlords and tenants is inherently adversarial*, both in the negotiation and execution of lease agreements and in the tenant's occupancy of the landlord's premises. In other contexts, this has been deemed to be a conflict of interest that *may not be resolved* through full disclosure. In other words, the parties' respective interests are so inherently adverse that the conflict cannot be waived even with the fully-informed consent of both parties. This raises a fundamental question for the profession: If legal ethics prohibit an attorney or a law firm from representing both the landlord and a tenant in the negotiations of a lease agreement or in a dispute over the interpretation of

the terms and conditions in a lease agreement, how can the divergent interests of those same parties nonetheless be adequately represented by the same CRES firm through dual agency?

How conflicts of interest may manifest themselves in commercial real estate transactions

Given the increasing complexities of the real estate development and finance process and, to a lesser extent, the process of acquiring and positioning in the marketplace operating properties, as outlined in Subsection 1 above, and further considering the consolidation that has taken place in the past few decades within the CRES sector, as described in Subsection 2 above, it is perhaps easy to understand how the incidence of conflicts of interest in commercial leasing transactions may be on the rise, the fact that the majority of these conflicts of interest do not give rise to formal legal claims (the reasons for which are also described in this Subsection).

SCENARIO A: Potential conflict of interest scenarios where the leasing transaction is closed by a listing broker and tenant agent employed by the same full-service CRES firm:

The Listing Broker manipulates or otherwise influences the commission on the transaction to be paid to the Tenant's Agent to get the lease closed.

Without manipulating or otherwise influencing the amount and payment of the Agent's commission, the Listing Broker offers incentives outside the commission structure but within the control of the CRES Firm, including but not limited to promised increases in base salary, benefits, and/or future advancement within the firm.

Without manipulating or otherwise influencing the amount and payment of the Agent's commission or otherwise creating specific incentives within the CRES Firm's ordinary compensation structure, the Developer or Property Owner promises the Listing Broker additional property listings if the Subject Property is fully tenanted within a specified time frame, and the Tenant Agent is promised specific opportunities and/or remuneration if such additional property listings are awarded to the Listing Broker by the Developer or Property Owner.

The Tenant Agent shares with the Listing Broker confidential information about the prospective Tenant that is not generally, publicly available, and which the prospective Tenant has shared with the Tenant Agent in confidence, which information may include but is not limited to:

i. The prospective Tenant's current financial condition;
ii. Changes in the Tenant's business or market position that could impact the prospective Tenant's future operating income and, consequently, its ability to pay rent for the Premises or cover Tenant's assumed portion of the overall budget for Tenant Improvements necessary to make the Premises tenantable;
iii. Potential changes in the Tenant's business or industry sector;
iv. The prospective Tenant's simultaneous negotiation of one or more comparable commercial leases as a hedge against not being able to secure from the Listing Broker the terms and conditions the prospective Tenant requires or prefers regarding the Premises.

SCENARIO B: Potential conflict of interest scenarios where the leasing transaction is closed by a tenant agent employed by a full-service CRES firm, which

firm is offered incentives by the developer or property owner if the CRES firm is instrumental in tenanting the property:

The Full-Service CRES Firm is not the Listing Broker on the Subject Property but is actively seeking to secure new business as the Listing Broker for the Developer or Property Owner on other properties, and the Firm creates incentives and/or other inducements to encourage its Tenant Agents to prioritize or otherwise favor the Subject Property with their tenant clients so that the CRES Firm may be successful in securing such new property listings from the Developer or Property Owner.

The Full-Service CRES Firm is not the Listing Broker on the Subject Property but is actively seeking to secure other types of new business from the Developer or Property Owner of the Subject Property, including but not limited to the kinds of services described in Subsection III.B.1, a through d, inclusive, and g and h, inclusive, and the Firm creates incentives and/or other inducements to encourage its Tenant Agents to prioritize or otherwise favor the Subject Property with their tenant clients so that the CRES Firm may be successful in securing such new business from the Developer or Property Owner.

SCENARIO C: Potential conflict of interest scenarios where the leasing transaction is closed by tenant agents employed by more than one full-service CRES firm, where each such full-service CRES firm has provided professional services to the developer or property owner with respect to the subject property:

Roles played by full-service CRES Firms that are not mutually exclusive to another full-service CRES Firm serving as the Listing Broker for the Subject Property:

Developed and assisted in the implementation of a strategic plan that included the development or acquisition of the Subject Property and its subsequent lease-up on financial terms generally consistent with such strategic plan.

Specifically represented the Developer or Property Owner in the development or acquisition of the Subject Property, including providing market research, financial analysis, and rate/period consistent with the investment and financing structure for the Subject Property.

Specifically participated with the Developer or Property Owner in the financing of the development or acquisition of the Subject Property, including but not limited to representing one or more Equity Investors or Lenders necessary to support the Developer's or Property Owner's plans for the undertaking, the satisfaction of which Investor(s)' return and invested capital security expectations or the Lender(s)' debt service and repayment of principal requirements are dependent upon the lease-up of the Subject Property as and when projected by the Developer or Property Owner to the Investor(s) and Lender(s).

What constitutes an actual, and actionable, conflict of interest in a commercial leasing transaction?

The foregoing scenarios, as well as any others that might be hypothesized, do not suggest that in each such instance there will always be a conflict of interest that is resolved adversely to the Tenant. *The potential that a conflict of interest could arise does not automatically mean that one will occur.*

For example, in the scenarios set forth in SCENARIO C, it is entirely possible, as well as plausible, that a Tenant Agent working for a full-service CRES Firm that assisted the Developer or Property Owner by putting together the package of equity investments necessary to finance the Subject Property can subsequently provide her undivided loyalty to the tenant she is representing and fully discharge all of the other duties an agent owes its principal in recommending the Subject Property and also assisting her client in the negotiation of the lease.

By the same token, not every act or omission by a Tenant Agent, regardless of whether it may be deemed to be a violation of an agent's duties to its principal, will be attributable to a conflict of interest resolved adversely to that tenant. Not every act or omission of a Tenant Agent that is potentially harmful to her client will be motivated by some countervailing benefit inuring to that Tenant Agent's full-service CRES Firm that has an opposing interest in the transaction. Sometimes a Tenant Agent does not perform adequately and in their client's best interest due to incompetence, personal interests, or other reasons that do not give rise to an actionable claim for breach of the duty of an agent to its principal arising out of a conflict of interest.

In order to fully and completely understand the intersection between the Conflicts of Interest Scenarios presented in SCENARIO C and, whether or not an actual, actionable Conflict of Interest has actually occurred, the basic principles or Principal and Agent, already addressed in a separate section of this chapter, above, must be understood.

Dual agency in commercial leasing transactions

California's Approach to Protecting the Interests of Commercial Tenants. Not only is dual agency in commercial leasing transactions not treated uniformly by the commercial real estate services or "CRES" industry or the states and localities in which full-service CRES firms deliver their services, including but not limited to tenant agency, *there is disparate treatment under the law and in practice* from office to office in national and global full-service CRES firms with operations in the domestic United States. The passage and enactment in California of S.B. 1171 made sweeping reform in what previously was the dichotomous treatment of residential brokers and agents, on the one hand, and commercial brokers and agents, on the other (the latter not being legally required to disclose conflicts of interest in dual agency situations). Moreover, the decision by the California Second District Court of Appeal in the *Horiike v. Coldwell Banker Residential Brokerage Company* case,[40] may greatly expand the legal liabilities of licensed brokers who oversee agents and associate brokers in the office(s) they manage.

Forcing Commercial Agents to Choose Who They Will Represent. As already suggested above, "single dual agency" relationships in commercial leasing transactions, at least in Virginia as of July 12, 2012, and in California as of January 1, 2015, mean that agents will be compromised substantially in their ability to represent their client's best interests. Although it is far too early to tell in Virginia, and certainly so in California, where the new law, enacted by S.B. 1171, only fairly recently took effect, it is possible, if not likely, that the magnitude of the required disclosures will give prospective clients considerable pause before engaging a single dual agent.

The *Horiike v. Coldwell Banker Residential Brokerage Company* Case. As suggested above, the final outcome in the *Horiike* case may have a dramatic impact on the liabilities of full-service CRES firms, holding that the brokerage firm is liable for the actions of their licensed agents and associate brokers in their representations of clients of the firms.

The Facts in the Horiike Case. The relevant facts in the Horiike case are that Plaintiff, Hiroshi Horiike, was working with an agent (referred to in the case as a "salesperson") of a licensed California broker, Coldwell Banker Residential Brokerage Company (CB), which had the listing of the house which Mr. Horiike was interested in purchasing. Another CB salesperson, working, through CB, on behalf of the seller of the house, materially misrepresented to Mr. Horiike both the actual square footage of the house (overstating it by almost one-third), as well as the development disposition of adjoining lots on either side of the seller's property (representing that no development was planned when that, in fact, that was not the case on either lot). Mr. Horiike closed on his purchase of the house, for $12.25 million in cash, in reliance upon the representations made by the salesperson representing the seller through the broker, CB, including the sales brochure prepared by CB's salesperson working on behalf the seller. The trial court dismissed the case in favor of seller's agent, on the basis that the seller's listing contract and buyer's was with CB, and not with CB's agent, and therefor Mr. Horiike did not have a basis upon which he would sue over the misrepresentations of the CB salesperson.

The Ruling of the California Court of Appeals (Second Appellate Division). The California Court of Appeals, hearing Mr. Horiike's claims that the trial court incorrectly instructed the jury as well as wrongly dismissing his case (by granting the Defendant's motion for nonsuit), held as follows:

> The buyer contends *that the salesperson had a fiduciary duty equivalent to the duty owed by the broker*, and the trial court incorrectly granted the nonsuit and erroneously instructed the jury. We agree. *When a broker is the dual agent of both the buyer and the seller in a real property transaction, the salespersons acting under the broker have the same fiduciary duty to the buyer and the seller as the broker* [emphasis added].

In its opinion overturning the lower court, the Court of Appeals also discussed the forms that were provided to Mr. Horiike by CB, through its salespeople (Mr. Horiike's buyer's agent and CB's seller's agent), and the three different types of agency relationships contemplated in accordance with those forms:

> The parties to the transaction signed a confirmation of the real estate agency relationships as required by Civil Code section 2079.17. The document explained *that CB, as the listing agent and the selling agent, was the agent of both the buyer and seller.* [The seller's agent for CB] signed the document as an associate licensee of the listing agent CB. [Horiike's agent] also signed the document as an associate licensee of the selling agent CB.
>
> Horiike also executed *a form required under Civil Code section 2079.16 for the disclosure of three possible real estate agency relationships*. First, the form explained the relationship of a seller's agent acting under a listing agreement with the seller. The seller's agent acts as an agent for the seller only and has a fiduciary duty in dealings with the seller. The seller's agent has obligations to both the buyer and the seller to exercise reasonable skill and care, as well as a duty of fair dealing and good faith, and a "duty to disclose all facts known to the agent materially affecting the value or desirability of the property that are not known to, or within the diligent attention and observation of, the parties."
>
> *The second type of relationship, which is not at issue in this case*, involves the obligations of an agent acting for the buyer only. An agent acting only for a buyer has a fiduciary duty in dealings with the buyer. A buyer's agent also has obligations to the buyer and seller to exercise reasonable care, deal fairly and in good faith, and disclose material facts.
>
> *The third relationship described was an agent representing both the seller and the buyer.* "A real estate agent, *either acting directly or through one or more associate licensees*, can legally be the agent of both the Seller and the Buyer in a transaction, but only with the knowledge and consent of both the Seller and the Buyer." *An agent in a dual agency situation has a fiduciary duty to both the seller and the buyer, as well as the duties to buyer and seller listed in the previous sections.*
>
> Horiike signed the disclosure form as the buyer and [the seller's agent] signed as an associate licensee for the agent CB.

Real Estate Broker as Dual Agent. When the buyer and the seller in a residential real estate transaction are each independently represented by a different salesperson from the same brokerage firm, does Civil Code section 2079.13, subdivision (b), make each salesperson the fiduciary to both the buyer and the seller with the duty to provide undivided loyalty, confidentiality, and counseling to both?

The Fallacy of "Client Sophistication" as a Defense to Dual-Agency Disclosure Requirements in Commercial Leasing Transactions. In opposing S.B. 1171, the California Association of Realtors made the following argument, which the California legislators did not find compelling, in nonetheless passing Senator Hueso's bill:

> When our association sponsored the original agency disclosure legislation, including the written form requirement that now applies to residential agency, *and commercial transactions were deliberately not required to use the same forms as residential transactions*. The reason for the different rule is *the different level of sophistication and complexity* that exist in non-residential transactions. We believed, and experience seems to bear it out, that *simply requiring disclosure* of multiple agency relationships *and allowing commercial practitioners to utilize their own contracts and forms* is sufficient to protect the parties.[41]

Residential Sales: An increasingly standardized transaction between adverse parties who, in general, are very evenly matched. The fact of the matter is residential purchase and sales transactions are by far much more straight-forward, and less complex, than commercial leasing transactions. As already suggested, information in the residential sales market is much more symmetrical than it is in the commercial sales market. Moreover, due to the relative uniformity of state laws regarding both the duties of agents and the disclosure requirements in the case of conflicts of interest – thanks in part to the efforts of the National Association of Realtors – and the overlay of federal laws where financing from federal agencies and GSEs is involved (e.g., FHA, Fannie Mae and Freddie Mac), the general body of knowledge in the public domain about selling and purchasing a personal residence is applicable to the vast majority of transactions, which have a number of cookie-cutter aspects to them. Finally, buyer and seller sophistication about residential purchases and sales, thanks in part to the success of programming like that provided on HGTV, a cable network devoted to home buying and homeownership, it is very hard to successfully make the argument, as the California Association of Realtors tried to do in opposing S.B. 1171, that residential buyers are unsophisticated and need the protections of upfront, written disclosures of dual agency.

Commercial leasing: an inherently complex and adversarial, one-off transaction, between two parties with vastly different information, knowledge, experience, skill sets, and negotiating power

Among other things, a commercial lease agreement may run in excess of 50 pages. The terms and conditions of a commercial lease agreement contain idiosyncratic legal provisions and plenty of jargon: "subordination, non-disturbance, and attornment," "indemnification," "subrogation," "common area maintenance (CAM) charges," and "events of default." However, based on employment statistics, perhaps the best measure for gauging demand for expertise and sophisticated, professional representation in commercial leasing transactions, only 0.55% of businesses in the United States is engaged in the real estate industry; presumably, the remainder are merely occupying commercial office space but lack the professional expertise.[42]

Additionally, given the inherently complex nature of real estate development, financing, and ownership structures addressed, in great detail, throughout this textbook, it is highly unlikely that the average commercial tenant commencing its search for commercial office space – beginning with the process of identifying and engaging a commercial real estate agent – truly understands the potential for conflicts of interest in hiring an agent employed by a full-service CRES firm. Accordingly, logic and experience dictate that the opposition made by the California Association of Realtors against S.B. 1171, claiming it to be totally unnecessary, could more effectively be used to argue why – in a period where dual residential agency has been long-settled – commercial tenants should not receive at least the same scope and extent of protection as residential buyers receive in considering the engagement of a tenant representative working for a full-service CRES firm.

How the Federal Government Handles Conflicts of Interest in Commercial Leasing Transactions. The United States government is the largest single user of commercial office space in the United States. In addition to the buildings owned outright by the federal government, through the General Services Administration, the federal government leases just under 200 million sq. ft. of commercial office space in the United States.[43] This makes the federal government an extremely unique and valuable tenant client for full-service and tenant-only CRES firms alike, as well as a very attractive prospect for commercial Developers and Property Owners.

Required Disclosures by a Full-Service CRES Firm Proposing to Represent the Federal Government as a Tenant through the GSA. In order to represent the federal government, through the GSA, as its real estate broker, a CRES firm must enter into a National Broker Services Contract administered by GSA's Public Buildings Service, Office of Real Estate Acquisition, Center for Brokerage Services.[44] Section H.5 of GSA's National Broker Services Contract[45] provides, in pertinent parts, procedures regarding the avoidance of conflicts of interest arising out of the organization of the Contractor (i.e. the CRES firm hired to represent GSA through the National Broker Services Contract). The aforementioned provisions in Section H.5 are provided in Exhibit II to the CREUA Conflicts of Interest Study Report. For more information on the GSA's Dual Agency Disclosure Form, see the Feature Box.

THE GENERAL SERVICES ADMINISTRATION'S DUAL AGENCY DISCLOSURE FORM

The Exhibit 7C – Dual Agency Disclosure Statement, referenced in subparagraph (11) of subsection H.5.(d) of the National Broker Services Contract, which is required to be submitted to GSA *in each case in which the Contractor* (e.g., GSA's tenant-agent), upon accepting a Task Order from GSA, *also represents the landlord in a proposed transaction*, provides, in pertinent part, as follows:

EXHIBIT 7C
DUAL AGENCY DISCLOSURE STATEMENT
Acknowledgement and Consent)
GSA Regional CO:_____
Lessor(s):_____
Property Involved:_____
Dual Agency: The General Services Administration's, National Broker Contract, number _____, allows a brokerage firm under this GSA contract to represent both the Government, as tenant, and the owner in this real estate transaction as

long as this is disclosed to both parties and both agree. This is known as dual agency. Under this GSA Contract, a brokerage firm may represent two clients whose interest are, or at times could be, different or adverse. For this reason, the dual agent(s) may not be able to advocate on behalf of the client with the same skill and determination the dual agent may have if the brokerage firm represents only one client. Dual Agency under this GSA contract does not allow the same agent of the Brokerage Firm to represent both parties.

(b) Purpose. The purpose of this clause is to avoid, neutralize, or otherwise mitigate organizational conflicts of interest that might exist related to a Contractor's performance of work required by this contract. Such conflicts may arise in situations including, but not limited to: a Contractor's participation as an offeror or representative of an offeror, in a procurement in which it has provided assistance in the preparation of the Government's requirements and specifications; a Contractor's providing advisory assistance to the Government in a procurement in which the Contractor's firm, or one which the Contractor represents, is an actual or potential offeror; and a Contractor's participation, as an offeror or representative of an offeror, in a procurement where the Contractor has obtained confidential or proprietary information relating to competing offerors as a result of the Contractor's work on prior task orders.

(d) Restrictions. The Contractor agrees:

1. As a condition of its award of this contract and in addition to other requirements of this contract regarding Contractors ethics program and reporting requirements, and the safeguarding of information, to establish a "conflict wall", in form and manner satisfactory to the Contracting Officer. Any such "conflict wall" shall, at a minimum:

   - Inform all members of the Contractor of the existence of the "conflict wall" and the restrictions set forth in this Clause;
   - Ensure the establishment and maintenance, during the term of this Contract, of separate electronic file servers and other electronic safeguards to prevent access to documents, files and information related to Contractor's work under this Contract to other than Contractor personnel working under this Contract, including Contractor personnel representing building owners or lessors;
   - Ensure that paper files and documents are kept, safeguarded and maintained in separate, secure locations that will preclude access to Contractor personnel not working under this Contract, including Contractor personnel representing building owners or lessors;
   - Be maintained at all times during the term of this Contract.

2. To remain subject, during the term of the Contract, to periodic inspection and verification of the "conflict wall" and the processes and procedures to be maintained in connection therewith.

3. To execute, in connection with any awarded Task Order under this Contract, such certifications as the Contracting Officer may deem necessary and appropriate confirming the continuing existence of the "conflict wall" and the processes and procedures included thereunder, including but limited to, Exhibits 7A, 7B, and 7C.

4. That none of the Contractor's personnel, (including without limitation employees, consultants or subcontractors) may participate as both a GSA representative and as a representative of an offeror on a GSA lease transaction. Such ban shall be in effect for the duration of the lease transaction.

5. That none of the Contractor's personnel, (including without limitation employees, consultants or subcontractors), who have a personal financial interest in a potential or actual offeror for a lease transaction, may participate as a GSA representative on that GSA lease transaction.

6. That none of the Contractor's personnel (including without limitation employees, consultants or subcontractors) performing work under this Contract will participate, in any capacity, in providing any advice or representation to a building owner, representative, lessor or other third-party in connection with any GSA leasing transaction in the same market while an individual is performing service under this contract and for an additional period of six (6) months following conclusion of an individual's work under the Contract.

7. That any person performing services under this Contract shall be and remain, during the term of this Contract, ineligible to share in any fees or commissions received by or payable to Contractor by virtue or Contractor's representation of a building owner, representative, lessor or other third-party in a lease transaction involving the Government; provided, any such person shall be entitled to share in any payment made to Contractor under this Contract.

8. That all personnel performing work in connection with an awarded task order under this Contract may be required to execute such Confidentiality and Non-Disclosure Agreements, or other documents which the Contracting Officer, in his/her sole discretion, may require in order to protect the proprietary nature or confidentiality of information provided by the Government or otherwise received by the Contractor in connection with its work under this Contract. Such Agreements or documents may provide that violations of their terms may result in criminal and civil penalties in accordance with, among other laws and regulations, 41 U.S.C. §423. Failure of the Contractor to provide required Agreements or documents under this paragraph from all required personnel may result in termination of Contractor's work under the task order at issue at no cost to the Government. Repeated violations may result in the termination of this Contract.

9. That the Contractor and all personnel performing work in connection with an awarded task order under this Contract are required to execute the agreements contemplated by Section 9.505–4(b) of the Federal Acquisition Regulation, 48 C.F.R. §9.505–4(b).

10. That all personnel performing services under this Contract will treat any and all information generated and received in connection with their work as proprietary and confidential, continue to do so in perpetuity, and disclose and utilize such information only in connection with their work under the Contract.

11. That upon receipt of a task order request, to immediately notify the Contracting Officer of any potential organizational or individual conflict of interest that would prevent or limit the Contractor's ability to perform the work requested. If any such conflict is identified, consistent with the other requirements and restrictions of this Clause, the Contractor shall provide the certification that the conflict wall is in place and any other documents that may be required by the

Contracting Officer pursuant to paragraph (d).3 above. Contractor shall continue performance of the request, unless notified in writing by the Contracting Officer; provided that the Contracting Officer shall have the right to impose such restrictions as he/she deems appropriate on Contractor's performance based on the existence of such a conflict or, if the Contracting Officer determines that such restrictions would not adequately address the conflict of interest at issue, to terminate the Contractor's performance of work under the task order at no cost to the Government. At the lease solicitation phase, Contractor shall provide executed dual agency notifications and agreements from any interested parties affected by the Contractor's performance of work related to the task order. See Exhibit 7C.

12. To immediately notify the Contracting Officer of any organizational or individual conflict of interest discovered during Contractor's performance of work pursuant to a Government-issued task order; provided that the Contracting Officer shall have the right to impose such restrictions as he/she deems appropriate on Contractor's performance based on the existence of such a conflict or, if the Contracting Officer determines that such restrictions would not adequately address the conflict of interest at issue, to terminate the Contractor's performance of work under the task order at no cost to the Government. If at or after the lease solicitation phase, Contractor shall provide executed dual agency notifications and agreements from any interested parties affected by the Contractor's performance of work related to the task order.

13. That in the event that the Contractor knowingly withholds the existence of a conflict of interest from the Government, that the Contracting Officer may terminate this Contract or an individual task order at no cost to the Government; provided that the foregoing shall be in addition to all other remedies and causes of action which the Government may have against the Contractor, including the suspension and/or debarment of the Contractor.

14. *To include this Conflict of Interest clause, including this subparagraph, in all of Contractor's subcontracts at all tiers (appropriately modified to preserve the Government's interests hereunder) which involve the performance of work by subcontractors in support of this Contract.*

15. *That, in addition to the remedies enumerated above, the Government may terminate this Contract for cause in the event of Contractor's breach of any of the above restrictions.*

Property management

Duties, liabilities, and obligations of property owners

Components of Property Management. The following is a listing of the essential, major functions of Property Management. This listing of the Components of Property Management is followed by a detailing listing of the tasks or undertaking of each component. The companion website for the textbook contains cases and legal analysis of disputes between Landlord's and Tenant's, or between Landlord's and third-parties, regarding selected subcomponents of the Components of Property Management:

Building Operations
Building and Grounds Maintenance and Repair
Managing Capital Replacements
Tenant Relations and Tenant Services
Lease Renewals and Terminations; Marketing and Leasing Premises
Monthly Rent Collection and Reconciliation (Accounting)
Allocating and Assessing Pass-Through Costs to Tenants
Regulatory Compliance (federal, state, and local)
Data Collection and Analysis; Periodic Reporting
Each of the foregoing Components of Property Management are further detailed in the subsections below.

Building operations

Keeping the building at a relatively constant temperature

Warm in the winter
Cool in the summer

Making sure all utilities serving the Property are functioning at all times
Establishing and maintaining cleanliness of all common areas
Smooth operation of elevator systems; keeping stairwells clear
Making sure ingress and egress to/from Property flow freely
Providing security when building is open and when it's not
Keeping ancillary/collateral facilities and services operational

Building and grounds maintenance and repair

Maintaining all building systems in good working order
Maintaining all exterior grounds in clean and orderly condition
Scheduling repair work to minimize disruption to operations
Monitoring all service work performed by third parties
Managing building engineer and staff and/or third-party PM contractors
Collect and examine operational logs
Periodic inspections of the common areas and grounds
Periodic inspections of all building systems and capital equipment

Managing capital replacements

Commission/review periodic, useful-life inspections of building systems
Bid, secure, and manage service contracts for capital equipment
Develop and periodically update Capital Improvements Budget
Monitor balance of Capital Improvements Reserve vs. Budget
Research and make recommendations regarding capital replacements

Develop specifications and requirements for capital replacements
Solicit, and review/analysis of, detailed bids for capital replacements
Prepare at least annual reports on capital replacement needs and funds

Tenant relations and tenant services

Periodic "check-in" visits with Tenants to determine/assure satisfaction
Field and address Tenant complaints regarding building operations
Field and address Tenant complaints about their specific Premises
Identify/resolve Premises issues that are Landlord's responsibility
Manage/monitor Tenant Services provided by Landlord's contractors
Arrange/track costs of Tenant services exceeding Lease requirements
Intercede in disputes between Tenant and Landlord's third-party contractors
If necessary, address/resolve disputes between Tenants

Lease renewals and terminations; marketing and leasing premises

Track Lease expirations/automatic renewals in the Property
Provide Leasing Team with sufficient, advance notice of expirations
Contract for and supervise installation of any marketing signage
Tenant Relations and Tenant Services
Support Leasing Team in Lease Renewals
Support Leasing Team in efforts to solicit/secure new Leases
Make sure that at all times the Property is ready to be shown

Monthly rent collection and reconciliation (accounting)

Collect monthly payments of Basic Rent and Additional Rent
Confirm payments received against all amounts owed
Make internal allocations of monthly gross revenue collected
Address all uncollected rent/delayed rent situations
Initiate collection actions necessary per internal protocols
Initiate Notice of Default and eviction proceedings when necessary
Support Landlord's counsel in lease enforcement/eviction actions
Prepare monthly rent collection and reconciliation reports

Allocating and assessing pass-through costs to tenants

Make operating expense allocations between Landlord and Tenants
Track monthly Common Area Maintenance (CAM) expense allocations
Evaluate actual, monthly CAM charges against budget estimates
Make adjustments to projected CAM charges where necessary
Prepare periodic Tenant CAM charge allocations per each Lease

Prepare periodic CAM charge invoices for each Tenant per their Lease
Substantiate validity of all CAM charges and allocation if necessary
Make reconciliations to Tenant invoices when discrepancies identified
Update CAM projections for the coming operating year for the Property

Regulatory compliance (federal, state, and local)

Environmental compliance (EPA, and state and local regulatory agencies)
OSHA and other worker safety regulatory compliance
Local land use regulatory compliance (e.g. Special Use Permit conditions)
Local recycling ordinance compliance, if applicable
Fair Labor Standards Act compliance of all staff
Department of Homeland Security compliance, if applicable
Internal Revenue Service compliance (e.g. independent contractor status)
Fair Housing Act compliance (for multifamily properties only)
Rent control and federal housing assistance regulatory compliance

Data collection and analysis; periodic reporting

Building operating data
Operating costs and third-party contracts
Capital requirements, replacements, and budget data
Tenant services summary reports (including TI activities)
Lease terminations, renewals, and originations
Collection of Basic Rents and Additional Rents
Calculation of CAM charges and Tenant CAM charge payments
Status of regulatory requirements and compliance

Mixed-Use Properties. Mixed-Use Properties, which have become increasingly common in the regeneration of urban downtowns, present unique Property Management challenges because, as suggested early in this chapter, each use type included within a Mixed-Use Project has distinctly different property management requirements. Accordingly, not only must the Developer, during the Project Conception and Pre-Development Phases of The Development Process design specifically for things like separate public entrances and conveyancing systems for commercial office spaces from residential areas, but separate Project Management protocols and SOPs (Standard Operating Procedures) need to be developed and implemented to address the specific needs of each use type. For example, and as suggested, above, in the discussion comparing Commercial Lease Agreements with Residential Leases, the manner in which Property Management functions are discharged and charged to their respective Tenants are completely different, as is each, respective Tenant's ability to challenge the cost and allocation of those services to the Tenant.

POPS: Privately owned public spaces. Chapter 10 contains an extensive discussion about Privately Owned Public Spaces or POPS, and students and readers are encouraged to review that discussion in the context of Property Management. See Chapter 10, Emerging Trends in Public/Private Partnerships, Privately Owned Public Spaces (POPs).

Property management agreements

The relationship between the Property Management Company and the Development Entity will be governed by the Property Management Agreement. In addition to having a defined Scope of Work, the Property Management Agreement will include other essential terms and conditions, including the amount, terms, and mechanics of payment of the Property Management Company's compensation. The Property Management Agreement governs the entirety of the legal relationship between these two parties, with the exception of certain common law principles impacting their relationship in the absence of specific language to the contrary contained in the contract.

The Property Management Company serves in the role of an Agent of the Owner as Principal. For more specific information about the common law and statutory legal relationships between principals and agents, see the Law of Principal and Agent subsection, under the Brokers and Agents section.

Notes

1. Poorvu, William with Jeffrey L. Cruikshank, *The Real Estate Game: The Intelligent Guide to Decision-Making and Investment*, The Free Press, a Division of Simon & Schuster, Inc., New York, N.Y. (1999), at page 191. Bold-faced, non-italics added to original text.

2. Lewis, Michael, *The Big Short*, W. W. Norton & Company, Inc., New York, NY (2010). See Chapter 9 for a detailed discussion of the Great Recession of 2008, it's reflection of the operation of Capital Markets on real estate transactions, and its implications for real estate financing in 2009 and thereafter, in which discussion Lewis's seminal analysis in *The Big Short* plays a pivotal part.

3. This section, as well as several sections that follow in Chapter 11, have been excerpted directly from the author's work, as Research Director, Lead Author, and Project Manager of a research study into conflicts of interest in commercial real estate transactions undertaken by the Center for Real Estate and Urban Analysis (CREUA) at The George Washington University, where the author serves on the MBA faculty in the School of Business's real estate program. Professor Smirniotopoulos owns outright and holds the copyright to this work, including "Conflicts of Interest in Commercial Real Estate Transactions: Who Represents the Tenant?" November 2014, CREUA, The George Washington University, Washington, D.C. hereinafter referred to as the "CREUA Conflicts of Interest Research Study Report." Found at www.academia.edu/9488812/Conflicts_of_Interest_in_Commercial_Leasing_Transactions_Who_Represents_the_Tenant, and "Who Represents the Tenant in Commercial Leasing Transactions." March 2015, CREUA, The George Washington University, Washington, DC. Found at www.academia.edu/11351622/Who_Represents_the_Tenant_in_Commercial_Leasing_Transactions. All end notes provided in this chapter to this material appeared in the original CREUA Conflicts of Interest Research Study Report. Only the end note numbering has changed to conform to the other end notes in this chapter. Accordingly, some references in these end notes relate directly to the CREUA Conflicts of Interest Research Study Report.

4. As noted in Appendix D: Profiles of the Largest Full-Service and Tenant-Only CRES Firms, the five, largest full-service CRES firms – CBRE Group, JLL, Cushman & Wakefield, Colliers International, and Newmark Grubb Knight Frank (NGKF)–do not report the same information or in the same way. Some are privately owned while others are wholly owned subsidiaries of non-U.S. companies. Accordingly, the 150,461 "commercial properties

transactions" number includes 42,100 commercial leasing and sales transactions, without a breakdown between the two. Additionally, the 2013 Annual Report for BGC Partners, Inc., the parent company of NGKF, doesn't provide data on commercial leasing transaction volume or aggregate value. Accordingly, the 150,461 in 2013 commercial property transactions is arguably misstated but is more likely under-reported here, rather than over-reported, because of the lack of 2013 transactions data on NGKF. Finally, in deference to Julian J. Studley's pioneering work as the country's first tenant-only CRES firm, which tenant-focus continued after internal ownership changes and re-branding of the firm in 2003 as simply Studley, Inc., the post-merger firm Savills Studley is included among the largest tenant-only CRES firms in Appendix D. However, it is entirely possible, if not more likely than not, that Savills Studley operates in very much the same ways as the other, five-largest, full-service CRES firms for which summary information is provided in Appendix D. Accordingly, the 150,461 commercial property transactions would be further under-stated by the 3,467 leasing transactions reported by Savills-Studley for 2013 and credited to the five-largest tenant-only brokerage firms.

5. See note xiii, above.
6. See Appendix D: Profiles of the Largest Full-Service and Tenant-Only CRES Firms
7. Drummer, Randyl, "Largest Publicly Traded CRE Services Firms Finish 2011 With Strong Revenues, Earnings." *CoStar News*, February 15, 2012. Found at www.costar.com/News/Article/Largest-Publicly-Traded-CRE-Services-Firms-Finish-2011-With-Strong-Revenues-Earnings/135622. Emphasis added.
8. See Note 19.
9. As noted in Appendix D: Profiles of the Largest Full-Service and Tenant-Only CRES Firms, the five, largest full-service CRES firms – CBRE Group, JLL, Cushman & Wakefield, Colliers International, and Newmark Grubb Knight Frank (NGKF) – do not report the same information or in the same way. Some are privately owned while others are wholly owned subsidiaries of non-U.S. companies. Accordingly, the 150,461 "commercial properties transactions" number includes 42,100 commercial leasing and sales transactions. However, because the 2013 Annual Report for BGC Partners, Inc., the parent company of NGKF, doesn't provide data on commercial leasing transaction volume or aggregate value, the 150, 461 in 2013 commercial property transactions is arguably under-reported here, and not over-reported. Finally, in deference to Julian J. Studley's pioneering work as the country's first tenant-only CRES firm, which tenant-focus continued after internal ownership changes and re-branding of the firm in 2003 as simply Studley, Inc., the post-merger firm Savills Studley is included among the largest tenant-only CRES firms in Appendix D. However, it is entirely possible, if not more likely than not, that Savills Studley operates in very much the same ways as the other, five largest, full-service CRES firms for which summary information is provided in Appendix D. Accordingly, the 150,461 commercial property transactions may be further under-stated by the 3,467 leasing transactions reported by Savills-Studley for 2013.
10. See note xiii, above.
11. See Appendix D: Profiles of the Largest Full-Service and Tenant-Only CRES Firms
12. Contrast this list with that of a tenant-only commercial brokerage firm, for which this is the *only* task undertaken, although there are tenant-only or "occupier-specific" services offered by tenant-only CRES firms but *not* included in this listing.
13. *Kelo v. City of New London*, 545 U.S. 1158 (2005).

14. This section, and several subsequent sections that follow in Chapter 11, have been excerpted directly from the author's work, as Research Director, Lead Author, and Project Manager of a research study into conflicts of interest in commercial leasing undertaken by the Center for Real Estate and Urban Analysis (CREUA) at The George Washington University, where the author serves on the MBA faculty in the School of Business's real estate program. Professor Smirniotopoulos owns outright and holds the copyright to this work, including "Conflicts of Interest in Commercial Real Estate Transactions: Who Represents the Tenant?" November 2014, CREUA, The George Washington University, Washington, DC hereinafter referred to as the "CREUA Conflicts of Interest Research Study Report." Found at www.academia.edu/9488812/Conflicts_of_Interest_in_Commercial_Leasing_Transactions_Who_Represents_the_Tenant, and "Who Represents the Tenant in Commercial Leasing Transactions." March 2015, CREUA, The George Washington University, Washington, DC. Found at www.academia.edu/11351622/Who_Represents_the_Tenant_in_Commercial_Leasing_Transactions. All end notes provided in this chapter to this material appeared in the original CREUA Conflicts of Interest Research Study Report. Only the end note numbering has changed to conform with the other end notes in this chapter.

15. American Law Institute, Restatement of the Law of Agency, Second (1958), pg. 6, hereinafter referred to elsewhere in this Report as "the Second Restatement." The common law of agency is decided as a matter of state law, based on legal precedent in each state on the subject. However, those state courts that have adopted a federal common definition of what constitutes "agency" generally follow the Restatement. *Steinberg v. Mikkelsen*, 901 F. Supp. 1433, 1436 (E.D.Wisc. 1995).

16. See subparagraph 1.c., Apparent Authority

17. Garner, Bryan A., Editor, *Black's Law Dictionary*, Third Pocket Edition, Thomson West Publishing, St. Paul, MN (2006), pg. 289, hereinafter referred to in this Report as *Black's Law Dictionary*. Emphasis added.

18. Ibid., pg. 289. Emphasis added.

19. Regarding licensure and other requirements for agents, associate brokers, and brokers engaged in commercial real estate transactions, including but not limited to leasing, see, e.g., "Texas Real Estate License Act." Texas Occupational Code §1101.002. (2003). Found at www.statutes.legis.state.tx.us/Docs/OC/htm/OC.1101.htm, and "Registrations of Certain Professions and Occupants." *Massachusetts General Laws*. XVI 112 § 87PP. Found at https://malegislature.gov/Laws/GeneralLaws/PartI/TitleXVI/Chapter112/Section87PP.

20. *"Commercial real estate laws have favored landlords for decades. In short, they allowed for commercial real estate brokers to represent both a tenant and a landlord in the same transaction, without any requirement that they notify the parties of their role as a dual agent. By contrast, laws strictly requiring disclosure of this "dual agent" practice have been in place in residential real estate laws for years."*

    Jason Hughes, president and CEO, Hughes Marino, August 24, 2014. Found at www.hughesmarino.com/hughes-marino-blog/sb-1171-represents-major-victory-for-tenants-in-commercial-real-estate/.

21. http://openstates.org/ca/bills/20132014/SB1171/.

22. California Senate Bill No. 1171. Found at http://leginfo.legislature.ca.gov/faces/billNavClient.xhtml?bill_id=201320140SB1171. Emphasis added.

23. Text from one of the twenty letters of support submitted to the California Senate, urging passage of S.B. 1171.

> I have practiced in the commercial/industrial real estate industry for over thirty years. I have been growing very concerned over the increasing incidence of one real estate brokerage representing both sides of a real estate transaction. This practice raises a decided conflict of interest which clashes with the fiduciary duties owed by real estate agents and brokers to their principals. I would support any bill Senator Hueso would introduce that would require commercial real estate agents and brokers to make full disclosure of the conflict of interest that arises when a brokerage firm is representing both sides of a real estate deal. In addition, I urge Senator Hueso to include in any such bill the requirement that in the event of such a conflict the brokerage firm must put in place a security wall that would prevent agents and brokers from disclosing to the other side confidential information which if disclosed would adversely impact their principal.
>
> Examples of the types of problems I have personally observed in a dual representation situation include an agent negotiating with a co-worker agent disclosing how much landlord would be willing to accept less than what is being asked for a leased property.
>
> Another example is a [sic] agent representing a party to a commercial/industrial sale disclosing to the other side how much the seller would accept below the listing price.
>
> I would also recommend that in any bill the Senator introduces there be a provision prohibiting any licensed real estate agent or broker from including in any listing agreement a waiver of any conflict of interest requirements imposed by law.
>
> It is time to close this ethics loophole which only exists for commercial/industrial real estate agents and brokers. I appreciate Senator Hueso's consideration of this much needed legislation.

24. www.leginfo.ca.gov/pub/13–14/bill/sen/sb_1151–1200/sb_1171_cfa_20140731_093509_sen_floor.html. Emphasis added.

25. In its Legislative Program 2013–2014, published September 19, 2014, the California Association of Realtors also stated, opposition to S.B. 1171, that "C.A.R. opposed this measure because it *unnecessarily complicates commercial transactions* [emphasis added]." www.car.org/governmentaffairs/stategovernmentaffairs/legprogram, page 9. It should be noted, in this regard, that *California Business and Professions Code Section 10176(d)* imposes upon commercial real estate brokers a duty to disclose a dual agency relationship; S.B. 1171 merely codified the requirement and method for securing the client's written consent to such dual agency, consistent with the manner in which dual agency is required to be disclosed to residential clients of brokers and agents.

26. www.leginfo.ca.gov/pub/13–14/bill/sen/sb_1151–1200/sb_1171_cfa_20140731_093509_sen_floor.html.

27. DeMott, Deborah A., "Breach of Fiduciary Duty: On Justifiable Expectations of Loyalty and Their Consequences." *Arizona Law Review* 48 (2006), pg. 925:

Writing in 1908, the American philosopher Josiah Royce characterized loyalty as the ethical principle that unifies and animates all other virtues. Royce defined loyalty as "[t]he willing and practical and thoroughgoing devotion of a person to a cause." Loyalty in his account necessarily requires submission of other desires to the object of loyalty, which then guides an actor's conduct.

28. DeMott, Deborah A., "Disloyal Agents." *Alabama Law Review* 58.5 (2007), pg. 1049.

29. Ibid., 1052. Emphasis added; footnotes omitted.

30. Ibid., 1052–1053. Emphasis added; footnotes omitted.

31. Risk Management & License Law Forum, May 15, 2013, "Fiduciary Duties" (hereinafter the "NAR Statement on Fiduciary Duties of Agents." Found at www.realtor.org/sites/default/files/handouts-and-brochures/2014/nar-fiduciary-duty-032213.pdf:

    > A real estate broker who becomes an agent of a seller or buyer, either intentionally through the execution of a written agreement, or unintentionally by a course of conduct, will be deemed to be a fiduciary. Fiduciary duties are the highest duties known to the law. Classic examples of fiduciaries are trustees, executors, and guardians. As a fiduciary, a real estate broker will be held under the law to owe certain specific duties to his principal, in addition to any duties or obligations set forth in a listing agreement or other contract of employment. These specific fiduciary duties include:
    >
    > - Loyalty
    > - Confidentiality
    > - Disclosure
    > - Obedience
    > - Reasonable care and diligence
    > - Accounting

32. NAR Statement on Fiduciary Duties of Agents.

33. Ibid.

34. Ibid.

35. The ABA Model Rules of Professional Conduct were adopted by the ABA House of Delegates in 1983. They serve as models for the ethics rules of most states. Before the adoption of the Model Rules, the ABA model was the 1969 Model Code of Professional Responsibility. Preceding the Model Code were the 1908 Canons of Professional Ethics (last amended in 1963). www.americanbar.org/groups/professional_responsibility/publications/model_rules_of_professional_conduct.html.

36. ABA Rules of Professional.

37. Comment [28], Rule 1.7 Conflict of Interest: Current Clients, North Carolina State Bar. Emphasis added.

38. Illinois State Bar Association, ISBA Advisory Opinion 91–11, November 22, 1991. Found at www.isba.org/sites/default/files/ethicsopinions/91–11.pdf.

39. More than half of all real estate agents in the United States (estimated at approximately 2 million) are members of the National Association of Realtors (1,063,950 as of June 30, 2014), according the N.A.R. membership statistics and information compiled by Association of Real Estate License Law Officials (ARELLO). N.A.R. "Field Guide to Quick Real Estate Statistics" www.realtor.org/field-guides/field-guide-to-quick-real-estate-statistics.

40. California State Legislature, Senate Bill No. 1171, CHAPTER 200, an act to amend Section 2079.13 of, and to amend the heading of Article 2 (commencing with Section 2079) of Chapter 3 of Title 6 of Part 4 of Division 3 of, the Civil Code, relating to

real property transactions [Approved by Governor, August 15, 2014. Filed with Secretary of State, August 15, 2014].

41. www.leginfo.ca.gov/pub/13–14/bill/sen/sb_1151–1200/sb_1171_cfa_20140731_093509_sen_floor.html. Emphasis added.

42. According to 2012 Economic Census numbers from the U.S. Department of Labor, 1,926,027 workers were employed in real estate businesses (NAICS 53: Real Estate and Rental and Leasing), out of a total of 349,561,848 workers employed in all industries.

43. According to the GSA's September 2014 Lease Inventory, the federal government has 197,676,370 sq. ft. of office space under lease currently. Found at www.gsa.gov/portal/content/101840.

44. General Services Administration, National Broker Contract Program portal. Found at www.gsa.gov/portal/content/104481.

45. GSA National Broker Services Contract, Volumes I & II (REDACTED). Found at www.gsa.gov/graphics/pbs/NBC2contract_VOL-I_REDACTED-Signed_21June2010-rs508c.pdf.

80:2 Solution – This is a metric devised by the author to keep the Developer's early, out-of-pocket expenditures to a bare minimum during the Project Conception Phase. Stated as simply as possible, the 80:2 Solution is a quantitative metaphor for a qualitative expression: *"Spend as little money as possible to learn as much as you possibly can."* Literally speaking, the 80:2 Solution means the Developer should expend no more than 2% of the Project's projected Total Development Cost while getting at least 80% of the way to the final formulation of the Project; getting 80% of the way (or more) toward figuring out *precisely what can be developed on the Subject Site and its immediate and long-term value*, before committing further to purchase or otherwise secure legal control of the Subject Site. Of course, getting 80% of the way toward a complete answer is at best an imperfect science. However, the principle of the quantitative metaphor of the 80:2 Solution should always be at the forefront of the Developer's mind during the Project Conception Phase.

Absorption Rate – The pace at which a Project is projected to reach full occupancy, as defined by the Developer, over the period of time beginning with the issuance of a Certificate of Occupancy (C of O) to being fully occupied. For example, a 300-unit multifamily rental building with an Absorption Rate of 15 DUs/month will take twenty months to reach full occupancy. It should be noted, in this regard, that while a Project also has a Vacancy Rate to account for tenant turnover year-over-year (e.g., 5%), which will be used in Pro Forma projections of Project Gross Income, all Projects are expected to be 100% occupied after their completion and issuance of the C of O.

Acquisition and Development (A&D) Financing – Prior to the S&L Crisis of the 1980s, depository institutions engaged in relationship banking would routinely make acquisition and development loans for residential developers or builders to finance a portion of the cost of acquiring land and taking it through the land use approvals process. This was in part to support and maintain the depository institution's business relationship with the borrower but also because the borrower would, with the completion and marketing of the dwelling units being produced, create a potentially lucrative market for the depository institution to make purchase money mortgages to the buyers of the homes being built. Following legislative and regulatory changes at the federal level, put into place to preclude another S&L crisis, very few banks of any type continued this practice of freely making A&D loans. Accordingly, Acquisition and Development Financing shifted from primarily debt-based to almost exclusively equity based transactions.

Agricultural Property – One of a number of property types in the real estate asset class, Agricultural Property is defined as any land, including farm land, ranches, pasture land, and the like, that is specifically designated for and dedicated to the production of food and food-related products, apparel, and the breeding of working animals used in agricultural production, such as livestock (including dairy cows, sheep for the production of wool, beef cattle, and breeding domesticated animals such as dogs), permanent crops (orchards and vineyards), arable land for the production of staples, produce, and crops such as cotton used in the apparel industry. See **Figures 1.20A, B**.

AIA Document Families – AIA Document Sets are organized into "families" or documents relating to the Project Delivery Method being employed by the parties.

AIA Document Sets – The American Institute of Architects or AIA has developed, maintained, and updated a series of contracts relating to the construction of Improvements designed my AIA members, intended to address the legal responsibilities of various parties to such construction. The most commonly known of these AIA Document Sets is the AIA-201 Contract and General Conditions documents, within the Design/Bid/Build family of AIA construction documents.

ALTA – American Land Title Association.

ALTA Preliminary Title Report – The ALTA Preliminary Title Report provides narrative descriptions of the title history of the Property, up to and including the current Seller of the Property, as well as any restrictive covenants, easements, limitations or restrictions upon the Seller's use and possession of the Property. An ALTA Title Survey and ALTA Preliminary Title Report must be read together to get a complete picture about the quality of the title to the Property that is proposed to be conveyed from Seller to Buyer, as well as any constraints on the Buyer's post-Closing use of the Property. For instance, an easement depicted on the ALTA Title Survey may show the physical location or boundaries of such easement, within the legal Property boundaries, but would not explain the nature of the easement, by whom it is held, and its terms and conditions, including but not limited to its duration. Both documents are needed to fully understand the complete impact of any such constraints on the Seller's title to the Property being conveyed to the Buyer.

ALTA Title Survey – The American Land Title Association (ALTA) and the American Congress on Surveying and Mapping (ACSM) provide the standards for "an ALTA Title Survey," which is a prerequisite to secure title insurance on real property. Together with an ALTA Preliminary Title Report (see paragraph, below), the ALTA Title Survey provides a complete picture of the property being acquired, and any recorded claims, including constraints on title and claims of rights of use or possession, against the property. ALTA Title Survey is a scaled map showing the property boundaries, the footprints of all improvements on the property, all means of ingress to and egress from the property, and any and all easements on the property.

American Institute of Architects or "AIA" – The American Institute of Architects or AIA is the professional association of architects in the United States. AIA is a membership organization, and membership in AIA is not a requirement to become a Registered Architect is any state.

Architect/Engineer or "A&E firm" – A Registered Architect, licensed in the state in which the Project is located, an engineer licensed in the state in which the Project is located, or a professional services firm having at least one Registered Architect and one engineer licensed in the state in which the Project is located. Jurisdictions within the same state may have adopted different building codes and may have different requirements for who is required or authorized to stamp construction documents prior to their delivery to the local building department for approval. A structural engineer has different educational, professional experience, and licensure requirements than a Registered Architect. The process for "pulling" building permits in the local jurisdiction in which the Project is to be constructed will determine which professional design and engineering discipline(s) are authorized to sign or "stamp" CDs being submitted for approval.

Asset Allocation – As a principal of investing and portfolio management, asset allocation has as a principal goal spreading the risk of loss in the portfolio through diversification, as well as optimizing returns from one asset class at a time when the return performance of another asset class or classes may not be as robust. While not among the troika of primary asset classes – stocks, bonds, and cash equivalents – real estate is an important asset class for investors. The percentage of an investor's portfolio of assets allocated to real estate will depend upon that investor's tolerance for risk (low, moderate, or high). The risk associated with a particular investment in real estate will be balanced against its potential return to the investor, either through anticipated, periodic cash distributions, projected increases in the value of the original investment, or some combination of the two.

Asset Class – Essentially, "asset class" defines a group of financial instruments with similar characteristics – such as an ownership interest, which entitles the holder to a ratable share of a corporation's assets – that tend to respond in a somewhat similar manner to prevailing market characteristics, and which generally are treated the same under the law. The classification of investments or investment securities has traditionally recognized only two asset classes – equities (i.e., stocks) and fixed-income securities (i.e., "bonds") – with a third class – cash-equivalents – only having been added to the list in the latter half of the twentieth century. Depending on whom you ask, in addition to what were, by the 1970s, the three main asset classes – equities, fixed-income securities, and cash-equivalents – there are two or three additional asset classes recognized by investors and fund managers in the twenty-first century: Guaranteed securities; commodities, and real estate.

Building Code – An essential aspect of a local jurisdiction's Police Powers for the protection of the "health, safety, morals, and general welfare" of its citizens is assuring that buildings, as and after they are being constructed remain standing at all times. In other words, buildings that tend to fall down present a clear and present danger to both the building's occupants and those in the building's general vicinity. Accordingly, local jurisdictions adopt, update, amend, and – most importantly – enforce a local building code. These local building codes are, by-and-large, adopted from one of the several building code organizations that develop them as model building codes. The Building Officials and Code Administrators International (BOCA Code), the Council of American Building Officials (CABO Code), the International Code Council ("International Building Code"), and the International Conference of Building Officials ("ICBO Code") are the most prominent model building codes throughout the United States, although there are a few regional variations in adopted building codes.

Building Department – Every jurisdiction has a building department, in one form or another, charged with responsibility for administering that jurisdiction's building code. This generally means, among other things, having a process for receiving and approving building plans, issuing building permits, and making inspections of workmanship, in accordance with the jurisdiction's building code and the relevant building permit issued, of construction work completed along the way.

Building Inspection – Periodic inspections by a **Building Inspector** with the requisite construction knowledge and experience (e.g., a "plumbing inspector") of incremental phases of construction, to make sure such work has been completed in accordance with the construction permit issued (e.g., a "Plumbing Permit") and in accordance with the jurisdiction's most recently adopted building code.

Building Inspector – An employee of a jurisdiction's building department assigned to make building inspections in that employee's area(s) or expertise.

Certificate of Occupancy or "C of O" – An official document from the building department of the local jurisdiction, issued after the conclusion of a new construction or renovation project, verifying that the building or premises, as completed, is safe for occupancy by tenants, and their employees, visitors, and guests, and by members of the general public. Prior to the issuance of a C of O only the Development Entity's employees, agents, and third-party contractors, including but not limited to the General Contractor and its subcontractors, are permitted inside the Building or Premises, as the case may be.

Change Order or "CO" – Confusion with the acronym for a Certificate of Occupancy is inevitable but the construction industry also refers to a Change Order as a CO. The Change Order process is set forth in several sections of the AIA's A201 General Conditions document, which is discussed in the Supplementary Materials on the companion website under Construction Phase Issues, Documentation, and Claims, along with a discussion comparing differences between the AIA document sets and their counterpart ConsensusDOCS construction contract documents. In addition to the reasons emanating from the RFI process for the GC's submittal of a Change Order Request, Change Orders may also be initiated by the Developer for any number of reasons. Under the A201 General Conditions document, changes may not be made without a written and approved Change Order. Because the Construction Lender is not a party to the Construction Contract Documents and, therefore, there is no privity of contract (see, in this regard, Chapter 7), the Construction Loan Documents should provide protections for the Construction Lender in the Change Order process, including the advance review and approval of any Change Orders, regardless of by whom they are requested, if the cost increases occasioned by such Change Orders are expected to be paid through Draw Requests.

Choice of Entity or Entity Choice – The Developer of a Project is rarely also the Development Entity. Real estate development projects are always undertaken by an SPE – a Special Purpose Entity or Single-Purpose Entity – in order to shield the Development Entity and the Developer from potential claims and losses from other development projects. However, while the use of an SPE to undertake a single, specific real estate development project is universal, the choice of the entity to be used may be as varied as the projects themselves. Accordingly, in each instance, in setting up the Development Entity for a specific project, the Developer will have to make a choice of entity to be used, such as a General Partnership (GP), a Limited Partnership (LP), a Subchapter S Corporation (Sub-S), a Limited Liability Company (LLC), a Limited Liability Partnership (LLP), a Limited Liability Limited Partnership (LLLP), or some hybridization of the foregoing, such as an LLP with an LLC serving as the Managing General Partner. Among other things, the choice of entity will determine, to a certain extent, the legal liabilities and tax treatments of the parties having interests in each, such entity.

Closing – Every complicated transaction involving multiple parties is usually consummated at a "Closing." Transactions typically requiring a Closing include but are not limited to Purchase and Sales Agreements and finding transactions, such as the Closing on Permanent Financing for a Project after it's achieved stabilization.

Commercial Office – One of a number of building types in the real estate asset class, comprised of : any improvements to real property (i.e. "building or buildings") dedicated to "general office use." Depending on local land use and zoning laws and regulations, however, "general office use" varies from jurisdiction-to-jurisdiction. For example, a day-care facility or early childhood development center in the ground floor of a downtown office building may or may not be a by-right use in a Commercial Office property, requiring additional approvals other than a Certificate of Occupancy or C of O as a condition precedent to such uses being permitted. Similarly, many ground-floor retail uses – such as convenience stores, sandwich shops, sit-down restaurants, office supply stores, and apparel retailers – are now the rule rather than the exception in downtown office buildings, although additional legal hurdles may need to be overcome prior to such occupancies and uses being permitted. However, their presence does not change the fundamental use and, therefore, classification, of the building as Commercial Office. See **Figure 1.1**.

Common Areas – Whether in a commercial office building or a residential condominium, the Common Areas are comprised of all of the public spaces in a building or buildings or on the grounds of the Project available for all to use. This would include the main entry lobby, elevator lobbies and corridors on floors above the building entry, public restrooms, and stairwells. In a residential condominium, Common Areas are comprised of similar building features but also community buildings and all outdoor recreation areas. What constitutes "Common Areas" are important in both situations, because the Tenants or "Occupiers" in the commercial office setting, as well as the Condominium Unit Owners in the other, will be burdened by their ratable share of the annual cost of maintaining and, in some instances, replacing furnishings and equipment in, such Common Areas through an annual assessment or invoicing for such charges. In the commercial office setting, this is referred to as a Common Area Maintenance of "CAM" charge.

Community Facilities District – Community facility and analogous districts (e.g. Georgia's Community Improvement Districts or "CIDs," California's Community Facilities Districts or "CFDs," and New Mexico's Public Improvement Districts or "PIDs"), provide the mechanisms necessary to fund the up-front costs of public infrastructure serving a development project through the creation of quasi-governmental authorities with the power to issue public bonds secured by a revenue stream assessed against the owners of properties being developed in such projects.

Consensus DOCS – In 2007 a consortium of twenty construction industry organizations and trade groups decided to challenge the preeminence of the AIA construction document sets by developing its own. Now known as Consensus DOCS, the premise for this undertaking is that form documents for construction shouldn't favor the "Owner" but, instead, should be neutral. For a discussion of some of the differences between key documents in the AIA document sets and their ConsensusDOCS counterparts, see the Supplementary Materials on the companion website under Construction Phase Issues, Documentation, and Claims. Regardless of the source of the contract forms used by the parties, almost all construction disputes involve the interpretation of specific provisions in documents negotiated and entered into by the parties.

Construction Close-Out or simply "Close-Out" – Close-Out takes place at that point at which the General Contractor has notified the Owner, in accordance with their Construction Contract, that the construction is "Substantially Completed." In the case of Horizontal Construction, this means that Vertical Construction may proceed but that there are non-structural issues remaining to be resolved. In the case of Vertical Construction, this means that the building or other Improvements are ready for the issuance of a Certificate of Occupancy or "C of O." The Construction Close-Out process should also produce a Punch-List of minor items the GC needs to address (but which should not preclude issuance of the C of O), and it does not alter the GC's future responsibility to address Warranty Issues in the future.

Additionally, Close-Out may take place without jeopardizing or otherwise impairing the rights of the Owner and the GC regarding any unresolved Change Order issues.

Construction Contract – The legal agreement between the parties involved – depending upon the Project Delivery Method – by which the Owner (aka the Developer or Development Entity) will have the Improvements constructed on the Subject Site, in accordance with the CDs and on a schedule and for a cost agreed to by those parties. The Owner will have privity of contract only with the General Contractor and not with the GC's Subcontractors. Payments to the GC will be in accordance with a Draw Schedule specified in the Owner's Construction Loan, to which the GC is not a party but may be described as a third-party beneficiary.

Construction Documents or "CDs" – Also referring to the Construction Drawings, the CDs are the technical drawings, such as an Electrical Plan and a Reflected Ceiling Plan, and accompanying specifications, from which the GC will build the Improvements for which the Owner has contracted with the GC. In the case of the Design/Bid/Build Project Delivery Method, the selected GC will have based all of its estimates, including those submitted to the GC by its proposed Subcontractors, in determining what the Owner agrees to pay for the completed Improvements.

Construction Lender – The institution, entity or organization providing the Construction Loan to the Developer (aka the "Owner"). Construction lending is fundamentally different from bridge and permanent financing of an operating building, involving an inverse process from how mortgage financing is funded, and presenting a completely different set of risks. Some commercial banks, for example, offer both to their customers. Mortgage lenders, on the other hand, by definition do not offer Construction Loans. Finally, some institutional investors, such as life insurance companies and pension trusts, may offer both a Construction Loan and the Take-Out Financing, which may be comprised of 100% equity investment or some hybrid of equity and debt.

Construction Loan – The source of funds for the construction of Owner's Improvements on the Subject Site, with which the Owner (aka the Developer) will pay the General Contractor in accordance with the Construction Contract, as well as in accordance with the Draw Schedule specified in the Construction Loan Agreement. The Construction Lender will not issue a commitment, much less close on a Construction Loan, with a Take-Out Financing Commitment from a lender and/or equity party that will be prepared and able to provide the funds to pay the full balance of the Construction Loan, including accrued but unpaid interest, as and when due.

Construction Loan Commitment – In order to proceed with the Developer's efforts to secure a General Contractor and negotiate and finalize a Construction Contract, the Developer will need a written commitment from the Construction Lender to fund the Construction Loan. This Construction Loan Commitment will be based on, among other things, a Take-Out Financing Commitment, as well as the Construction Lender's review of the CDs, Bid-Package, and proposed construction contract.

Construction Loan Documents – While the specific terms and conditions of a Construction Loan may be embodied in a single document, such as a Loan Agreement, the Construction Loan is fully documented through a series of related contracts, including a Security Agreement, an Assignment of Collateral, the Borrower's Construction Contract documents, insurance contracts, and performance and completion bonds. These contracts and agreements are collectively referred to as the Construction Loan Documents.

Construction Manager or "CM" – The Construction Manager will oversee the construction process and monitor and administer the various documents governing that process, including but not limited to the Construction Contract, the Construction Documents, and the Construction Loan. There is no "one way" or "right way" for the Owner, aka the Developer, to manage the Construction Phase of The Development Process. A Developer may be "fully integrated," meaning that the General Contractor is either a division or wholly or partially owned subsidiary of the Developer. Alternatively, the Developer may not have a captive construction company but may have in-house capabilities to serve as Construction Manager for the Project. If the Developer does not have such in-house capabilities, however, a third-party Construction Manager may be engaged as part of the Development Team. It is not only possible but recommended that, early in the Project Conception Phase of The Development Process, during the Select Project Delivery Method Sub-Phase, the Developer will have considered all of the options for Construction Management under whichever Project Delivery Method the Developer selected, and made key decisions about how to handle Construction Management, with or without actually engaging a Construction Manager (CM) for the Project at that time and making the CM part of the Development Team. As with most relationships and transactions forged or occurring during the Pre-Development Phase of The Development Process, the engagement of a Construction Manager by the Development Entity will be the subject of a binding written agreement. During the latter part of the Pre-Development Phase of The Development Process, immediately preceding Closing on the Construction Loan and entering into the Construction Contract with the GC, the Developer will need to have the CM engaged and fully on-board, regardless of whether that CM is in-house or a third-party contractor. If a third-party CM is to be engaged, the Developer will need to decide whether to hire a CM only or a "CM at Risk."

Construction Manager at Risk or "CM at Risk" – Because of the multiplicity of parties involved across the various agreements and other documents supporting the construction of the Improvements – General Contractor and its Subcontractors; architecture or engineering firm; Lender and Lender's designee for approving Draw Requests, local building code enforcement officials; surety bond provider – it is critical that the agreement between the Development Entity and its Construction Manager clearly set forth the specific responsibilities of the CM with regard to the construction process, including the review and approval of Draw Requests, as well as how RFIs and COs will be managed. For a Construction Management Contract hiring a CM at Risk, the responsibilities assumed and liabilities incurred by virtue of that position will be spelled out explicitly in that agreement between the Owner and the CM at Risk. Additional and more-detailed information about the CM at Risk is provided on the companion website for this textbook.

Construction Phase – One of the five phases of The Development Process, the Construction Phase is very straightforward: It represents the period during which all of the Improvements are being constructed. It arguably involves the greatest amount of risk for the Project, given the dangers inherent in the construction process itself but also considering the opportunities for conflict between the Construction Documents and their implementation by the General Contractor, potentially leading to delays and cost overruns negatively impacting the Development Budget on which everything is based. Project construction will generally involve both Horizontal Construction, which is comprised of all tasks necessary to prepare the Subject Property for the construction of the Improvements, and then the construction of the Improvements themselves, referred to as Vertical Construction. Depending upon the size, scale, and complexity of the Project, both Horizontal Construction and Vertical Construction may be phased, such that one section or phase of the Project may be completed and ready for occupancy before any other phases are completed, as would be the case with large-scale subdivision development. Horizontal Construction and Vertical Construction may be funded differently, with different draw schedules, conditions precedent, and approvals necessary to make payments to the General Contractor. Additionally, large-scale, Mixed-Use projects may rely upon sophisticated financing techniques for massive infrastructure improvements, such as the creation of a Community Facilities District, to fund all Horizontal Construction costs using bonds. The Construction Documents, the Construction Contracts (including the General Conditions, in the case of the traditional family of construction documents produced by the American Institute of Architects for Design/Bid/Build Project Delivery Methods), and the Construction Loan Agreement govern the conduct, rights, duties, obligations, and liabilities of the various parties during the Construction Phase.

Depreciation – As a general principle of the Internal Revenue Code, a taxpayer is allowed to deduct from gross income all expenses incurred in generating that gross income. However, in addition to general rules applying to the timing and recognition of business expenses, there are specific provisions in the tax code governing certain types of deductions. One of the most common, and by far the largest expense item allowed as a deduction from gross income is the allowance for depreciation, which is applied to the largest single component of the Development Budget: The aggregate expenditures for Hard Construction Costs through the Construction Contract. The allowance for and timing of deductions for business expenses depend, in part, upon the nature of the expenditure. Just because a taxpayer incurs what is otherwise an allowable expense does not mean the full amount of that expenditure may be used to offset gross income in that same Tax Year. The development or purchase of Capital Assets, and expenditures for other long-lived assets, both intangible and tangible, the benefits of which are expected to extend beyond a twelve-month period, are subject to specific rules intended to match up the expenditure over the "life" of the asset acquired through such expenditure. Depreciation and amortization are two, somewhat similar approaches to matching up the recovery of costs for long-lived assets in order to better match the costs up with the income those assets generate over time. It is important to note, however, that the "cost recovery systems" – of which depreciation and amortization are component parts – mandated under the Internal Revenue Code, are not the same as cost recovery approaches mandated by Generally Accepted Accounting Principles (GAAP), either for purposes of generating audited financial statements and/or for meeting the financial disclosure requirements imposed under the Securities and Exchange Act of 1934, to which public companies such as publicly traded REITs are subject. Accordingly, many real estate investment entities must employ two, separate methods for cost recovery purposes in order to comply with both IRS and GAAP requirements.

Design/Bid/Build Project Delivery Method – In the traditional Design/Bid/Build Project Delivery Method, the Developer and the Architect/Engineer work together to take the Idea for the Project from Schematic Design, through Design Development, and to the completion of the Construction Documents, from which competing General Contractors seeking to be selected by the Developer will submit their construction cost estimates or "Bids," in an effort to be selected for the specific work. The foundation of the Design/Bid/Build Project Delivery Method is that, by making the GCs compete with one another, based on experience, cost, and on-time completion of the Improvements, the Developer is being afforded the opportunity to select the best GC for the job. However, there are many benefits to the Project and for the Developer by encouraging the early collaboration of a GC, which the Design/Bid/Build does not allow.

Design/Build Project Delivery Method – In the Design/Build Project Delivery Method, the Developer engages the General Contractor early on by hiring one that specializes in the Design/Build process, meaning the firm not only designs the Improvements in collaboration with the Developer but then executes that design by being the builder as well. This Project Delivery Method precludes the Developer from receiving competitive bids from different GCs, which open competition the Design/Bid/Build Project Delivery Method claims produces the most cost-effective results. However, the Design/Build Project Delivery Method claims to produce a superior end product at the lowest total cost, because the inefficiencies inherent in the GC's ongoing collaboration with the Developer produces a superior result in terms of quality, cost, and delivery time because decisions are made in real time and with all decision-makers participating actively.

Design Team – The Design Team, which is a subset of the Development Team, is comprised of design professionals, such as land planners and landscape architects, building designers and architects, and engineers.

Developer – The individual or legal entity undertaking a Project. Historically, the term "developer" referred to a Land Developer; someone who acquired land and made it available for a certain type and intensity of development. This might entail only taking the land through the Land Use Approval Process or additional work to bring all necessary utilities and other Infrastructure Improvements to the Site. The Land Developer would then sell or otherwise make the Site available for a Builder or Builders to construct improvements thereon. Today it is much more common for a Developer to undertake or orchestrate The Development Process from start to finish. What constitutes "finish," in this regard will depend on, among other things, whether the Developer is a Fee Developer or a Portfolio Developer, and what that Developer's Exit Strategy is.

Developer's Fee – The amount of compensation to which the Developer is entitled, usually expressed as a percentage of Total Development Cost, for the successful completion and occupancy of the Property. The amount of the Developer's Fee, as well as the timing of its payment and whether it will be paid as a lump-sum upon the occurrence of a specific, objectively determined event or paid in installments, over time, upon the successful achievement of detailed milestones, will all be subject to negotiation between the Developer and any equity participants in the Development Entity.

Development Entity – Individual Developers do not undertake real estate development projects in their own name; the same holds true for corporations and other legal entities that engage in real estate development and financing transactions as their primary business. Each development project is undertaken by a separate legal entity, in order to shield the Developer's assets – whether the Developer is an individual, corporation, or other type of organization – from the liabilities of and claims against specific development projects. Projects are undertaken by a Special Purpose Entity or "SPE," which may take many forms, as discussed in Chapter 8. See, also, Choice of Entity. For the sake of simplicity, the textbook refers to the Development Entity in order to distinguish it from the Developer, which or whom is the real driving force behind each Project.

Development Phase – The Development Process is broken down into five distinct Development Phases: Project Conception; Pre-Development; Construction; Close-Out and Stabilization; and Property Management and Ownership. A definition of each is provided in this Glossary. Each Development Phase is, in turn, broken down into Sub-Phases. Each Development Phase ends with a milestone event, ushering in the next Development Phase.

While there is a typical chronology in the commencement of each Sub-Phase within each Development Phase, there is considerable interplay between and among many of the Sub-Phases, such that the entire process within each Development Phase is described as being "linear but iterative."

Development Team – Getting to the 80:2 Solution means engaging third-party professionals very early on in the process, well before the Developer is in any position to know whether the Idea is financially feasible or even viable at all. Hiring professionals means spending money or at least committing to expend funds in the future. In a depressed market for professional services, participation on the Development Team, particularly for an existing or attractive prospective client, may be undertaken as a loss-leader by many professional services firms, particularly if such participation is the best way to assure the opportunity to continue as part of the Development Team as a Project moves from the Project Conception Phase to the Pre-Development Phase. Additionally, for the vast majority of tasks to be undertaken by third-party professional services firms during the Project Conception Phase, there is little to no professional liability incurred. Consequently, covering only actual costs, such as the fully loaded staff costs of all personnel to be involved in the engagement and any out-of-pocket expenses to be incurred, may comprise the threshold for a professional services firm to agree to participate on the Development Team. For most real estate development projects in the Project Conception Phase, the Development Team will be comprised of the following experts: A design or design and engineering firm; a civil engineering or land planning firm; an environmental assessment vendor; a local law firm specializing in zoning and land use in the jurisdiction where the Subject Site is located; a market analysis firm experienced in the market and submarket where the property is located; and a communications and public relations firm. If the Integrated Project Delivery or Design/Build Project Delivery Method is selected by the Developer, the Development Team should also include the Design/Build firm or the General Contractor for the IPD method, as the case may be. Finally, it is prudent, albeit not required, to have the Property Manager and the marketing and pre-leasing experts on the Development Team as well.

Distressed Sale – In a distressed sale situation, the Developer, for whatever reason, isn't given the choice of whether or not to dispose of the Project; the Developer *must* sell the asset. Among other things, a Distressed Sale generally means that the Developer is unlikely to received full value for the Project, and may also have to accept other disadvantageous terms and conditions in order to expedite the disposition.

Distributable Cash – What constitutes "Distributable Cash" will be defined in the documentation that governs the operation of the Development Entity. For example, if the Development Entity is a Limited Partnership, the Limited Partnership Agreement will not only define what constitutes Distributable Cash but also will define how Distributable Cash is to be distributed to all of holders of Limited Partnership Interests. It is important to note that tax attributes for Development Entities that are pass-through entities for federal tax purposes, as is the case with partnership and S Corporation interests, may be completely unrelated to the availability and actual distributions of Distributable Cash, such that the holders of such interest may incur tax consequences from the reporting of allocable tax attributes without the benefit of having received cash distributions from that Development Entity with which to pay tax liabilities incurred.

Downtown Adjacent Walk-Up – Immediately adjacent to downtown, these WalkUPs usually have a lower density than downtown and possess unique character. Downtown

Adjacent WalkUPs have a substantial amount of office space (58%), but they also have significant residential (24%) and four times the relative retail of downtown (4% versus only 1%, respectively). The result is generally a lively, twenty-four-hour environment.

Downtown Walk-Up – Downtown WalkUPs are the original downtown sections of a metro area's principal city. Downtown WalkUPs are dominated by office space (83% of total square footage) and have modest though fast-growing residential (6%). Only 1% of the space is occupied by retail, although one-of-a-kind regional assets (convention center, Verizon Center, museums, etc.) account for 10% of all space.

Draw Request Process – A Construction Loan operates inversely from the way every other loan works. For a mortgage loan, for example, the proceeds from the full amount of the loan is applied to the benefit of the Borrower to pay for real property in the Borrower's name, and then the Borrower is legally required to make ratable (usually monthly) payments of principal and interest. With a Construction Loan, the Construction Lender is making the net proceeds of the loan available to pay for the ongoing costs of construction as they're incurred; the Borrower is not entrusted with the net proceeds of the loan and then expected to pay the GC along the way. The mechanism for making such periodic payments to the GC is referred to as the Draw Request Process. Generally speaking, the GC submits monthly invoices to the Borrower and the Construction Lender, specifying the Percentage of Completion represented by the GC's work incorporated into the Improvements, as well as the value of all supplies and materials securely stored on the Site but not yet incorporated into the Improvements. The Lender verifies that the GC's representation of the Percentage of Completion for that Draw Request is accurate, and makes payment to the GC less a hold-back, which is usually 10% of the requested payment. This hold-back aggregates with each, successive Draw Request, such that, at the time of the GC's Draw Request for the final draw-down from the Construction Loan, the Construction Lender and the Borrower have funds available in the event there are unresolved issues regarding the Substantial Completion of the Improvements.

Draw Schedule – The Draw Schedule generally provides for the GC to submit its Draw Requests at the end of each Calendar month, and allows the Construction Lender a period of thirty (30) days to reconcile the request against the construction records and make a Draw Request payment accordingly.

Entertainment/Restaurant – One of a number of building types in the real estate asset class. Although arguably a sub-classification of either Retail Properties, Mixed-Use Properties (discussed below), or both, the Entertainment/Restaurant classification within the real estate asset class is warranted in the context of real estate law because the intensity of use is so much greater and, as a consequence, involves additional legal hurdles in securing local land use and zoning approvals, as well as additional regulatory compliance in their operation. This classification encompasses everything from the free-standing, fast food restaurant with drive-through service, to white table cloth dining establishments, to night clubs offering food, dancing, and music to stand-alone concert venues. The intensity of the use, in each case, is likely to be addressed in a variety of legal requirements, ranging from where they may be located to specific limitations on their operations. See **Figure 1.6**.

Environmental Protection Agency or "EPA" – A non-Cabinet-level agency of the Executive Branch created on December 2, 1970, by an Executive Order issued by U.S. President Richard M. Nixon, the U.S. Environmental Protection Agency is charged with protecting the environment, and protecting people in the United States from the hazardous consequences of environmental pollution, through administering and promulgating federal regulations authorized by acts of Congress. President Nixon's Executive Order was later ratified by the U.S. House of Representatives and the U.S. Senate, respectively. Although it is not a Cabinet-level agency, the EPA Administrator routinely attends cabinet meetings at the pleasure of the president of the United States.

Etailers – A retailer whose retailing presence exists exclusively or primarily online, in contrast to traditional retailers whose primary or exclusive presence is through physical locations (also referred to as "brick-and-mortar" locations).

Exit Strategy – A Developer should never embark upon The Development Process without first knowing, or at least having an inkling, about its Exit Strategy: *the specific manner in which the Developer will receive compensation or otherwise extract value from the Project in a way that properly compensates the Developer for the value created*. Expressed in its simplest form, the Exit Strategy answers this simple question: How will "the Idea" that forms the genesis for The Development Process pay off? The Developer's Exit Strategy may be somewhat of a misnomer, however, because the Development may not actually exit from the transaction in order to extract and realize value from the Project. Similarly, inasmuch as the Developer most likely will be seeking various sources of equity and debt to fund the Project at various phases in The Development Process, a **Funding Strategy** premised on the Developer's Exit Strategy will be an essential framework for seeking and securing various sources of funding, with a view toward avoiding, to the greatest extent possible, conflicts between different funding sources and their respective, idiosyncratic funding requirements. Even though it is very early in the Project Conception Phase of The Development Process, and knowing that the Funding Strategy will need to evolve as the Idea evolves well into the Pre-Development Phase, having the Funding Strategy as a guide during the Project Conception Phase will be critical to the feasibility and overall success of the Project. The Developer's extraction of value or Exit Strategy marks either the conclusion of The Development Process, in the case of a Fee Developer, or merely one in a series of milestones in the Ownership and Property Management Phase in The Development Process, in the case of a Portfolio Developer. The Developer's formulation of its Exit Strategy, as well as a Funding Strategy consistent with and that supports the Exit Strategy, is one of the earliest Sub-Phases in the Project Conception Phase of The Development Process. The Developer's Exit Strategy generally follows one of several alternative formulations, which are described in Chapter 2.

Fannie Mae – The Federal National Mortgage Association or "Fannie Mae" is a government-sponsored entity, or GSE. Publicly traded and operating under a federal charter, Fannie Mae makes a secondary market in residential mortgages and, as such, contributes to the free flow of capital to fund residential mortgages and support homeownership in the United States by assuring liquidity in the mortgage market.

Fee Developer – A Fee Developer is just what it sounds like: A Developer that undertakes a Project in exchange for a Development Fee upon the completion of the Project or upon the Project achieving stabilized income and expenses, and does not take or retain an interest in the Project after it is conveyed to its new owner. It is possible, however, that a Developer, through its Development Entity, will serve as a Fee Developer, and that the Developer will have an ownership interest in the entity purchasing the Project from the Development Entity (which purchase may be effected through a traditional Purchase and Sale Agreement or through the new owner purchasing all of the interests in the Development Entity). A Fee Developer taking an ownership interest after its receipt of the Development Fee for the Project is not, necessarily make it a Portfolio Developer, however.

Financial Feasibility – A determination of whether a Project is "financially feasible" is made at various points along The Development Process, with the most intense analysis occurring during the Project Conception Phase, well before the Developer makes a financial and/or contractual commitment to proceed with that Project. A Feasibility Analysis is undertaken by the Developer, generally through the collective efforts of the Development Team assembled by the Developer for that purpose, examining every aspect of the proposed Project.

Freddie Mac – Very similar to Fannie Mae, Freddie Mac, as the Federal Home Loan Mortgage Corporation is commonly known, is a government-sponsored entity, or GSE. Publicly traded and operating under a federal charter, Freddie Mac makes a secondary market in residential mortgages and, as such, contributes to the free flow of capital to fund residential mortgages and support homeownership in the United States by assuring liquidity in the mortgage market.

Fully Integrated Real Estate Development Company – A company or enterprise that directly or through subsidiaries and/or affiliated companies engages in all essential aspects of real estate development and finance, including but not limited to serving as the Developer of Projects but also provides construction services or directly engages in construction as a GC, provides property management services, and engages in leasing and sales activities, is referred to as a Fully Integrated Real Estate Development Company.

Funding Strategy – Even though its creation should come very early in the Project Conception Phase of The Development Process, formulating a Funding Strategy in concert with the Developer's Exit Strategy will be critical to the feasibility and overall success of the Project. The Funding Strategy should be expected to evolve as the Idea evolves well into the Pre-Development Phase; however, having the Funding Strategy as a guide during the Project Conception Phase will help keep The Development Process focused and on-track. For information on how the Funding Strategy relates to the Exit Strategy, see Exit Strategy.

General Contractor or "GC" – Put simply, the General Contractor of GC is the builder of the Improvements on the Subject Site. Over the years, GCs have evolved considerably, changing from full-service builders with all of the trades available from within the company's full-time staff; to having a single area of construction expertise, such as framing or erecting a building's shell structure, and sub-contracting out the remainder of the construction trades; to project management companies that execute construction projects, using subcontractors exclusively for all phases and aspects of the construction project.

General Partnership or "GP" – Chapter 8 describes, among many other things, the differences between a "Taxable Entity" and a "Legal Entity." Sometimes, however, they may be one-in-the-same. General partnerships, for example, which are also known simply as "partnerships," have been recognized at common law for centuries and, therefore, do not require a statutory authority for their existence. For example, a general partnership may be determined to exist purely from the conduct of the parties, and without any formal, contractual arrangements between "the partners," The laws creating legal artifices, such as C Corporations and limited partnerships, are a different matter entirely. They are fundamentally different from the body of law determining the tax status, for federal income tax purposes, of, and tax consequences of transactions undertaken by, such "Legal Entities."

General Partnership Agreement – A General Partnership does not require a General Partnership Agreement to exist. However, as discussed in Chapter 7 on Contract Law, ambiguity should be avoided at all costs: *What Happens in Vagueness, Stays in Vagueness.*

Because common law principles will infer a partnership from the conduct of the parties, parties who conduct themselves as partners would be better of having a written agreement than having to learn the many ways in which common law will find the existence of one.

Geographic Portfolio Diversification – Also referred to simply as "geographic diversification," Geographic Portfolio Diversification means that assets of the same class are reasonably well distributed geographically, to mitigate against risk of loss associated with a market downturn in a specific geographic location or region. A portfolio of real estate assets could be reasonably well distributed within a region, among regions, throughout the United States or internationally, depending on the investment parameters and goals of the portfolio.

Go or No-Go Decision – The Project Conception Phase ends with the Developer's "go or no-go decision" about the Project under consideration. If the Feasibility Analysis proves that the Project is not financially feasible, the Developer will make a "no-go" decision and walk away from further pursuing the Project. If the Project is financially feasible but, during the Project Conception Phase, an issue regarding the Seller's possession or marketable title to the Subject Site arises, the Developer may be forced to make a "no-go" decision, the financial feasibility of the Project notwithstanding. A "no-go" decision ends the Project Conception Phase and The Development Process for that Project; a "go" decision means the Developer moves into the Pre-Development Phase.

Greenfield Walk-Up – Often criticized as sterile, Greenfield WalkUPs are situated where major investment has quickly turned formerly undeveloped land into a walkable urban place. Greenfield WalkUPs have among the most balanced product mix. Office (45%) is in balance with rental and for-sale residential (33%), while retail (6%) tends to be urban entertainment and boutiques. The large upfront capital costs required for Greenfield WalkUPs and high market risk mean few will probably be attempted in the next generation.

GSE or "Government-Sponsored Entity" – Financial services corporations created by federal legislation to support the free flow of funds in capital markets. The Federal Home Loan Bank system is comprised of GSE's; for student access to financial aid Congress chartered Sallie Mae as a GSE. However, by far the two, most recognizable GSEs, providing secondary markets in mortgages through the creation and sale of mortgage-backed securities or MBSs, are Fannie Mae and Freddie Mac.

Government – One of a number of building types in the real estate asset class, Government Properties include any and all area of land and facilities owned by any unit of government, whether local, state or federal, and include municipal, state, and federal buildings; parklands and any and all improvements thereon; community centers; recreational facilities and complexes, including local, regional, and national parks; libraries; jails and prisons; vehicle maintenance and storage lots; landfills and garbage collection and disposal facilities, including co-generation plants; and, to the extent owned and funded by a governmental entity, colleges and universities, hospitals and healthcare facilities, and other Special Use Properties described above. See **Figures 1.19A, B**.

Hard Construction Costs or "HCC" – The brick-and-mortar costs of construction in a Development Budget, as distinguished from Development Budget soft costs, such as A&E fees and marketing costs.

Holy Trinity of Real Estate Law – One of the foundational concepts of this textbook is its emphasis on "the Holy Trinity of real estate law," which is comprised of Land Use Law, Contract Law, and Environmental Law. However, each of these disciplines of Real Estate

Law is fundamentally different in the methodology of its application from the other two. Environmental Law, for instance, is a subset of the broader category of Administrative Law: It is focused primarily on compliance with, and avoiding violations of, what are primarily federal environmental laws and regulations. Success in Land Use Law, on the other hand, is a subset of Local Government Law: It is primarily defined by navigating the land use approvals process in the particular jurisdiction in which the Subject Site is located, which in some cases may also involve actively participating in long-range community planning and "visioning" processes to help shape the land use policies of the local jurisdiction, including the "evolution" of its local Land Use Control ordinances.

Horizontal Construction – Horizontal Construction involves everything that is necessary to prepare the Subject Site for Vertical Construction (i.e., everything constructed from the horizontal plane of the land, up). Horizontal Construction, also known as Site Preparation, includes general grading, cutting-and-filling an uneven site, mass excavation; providing for site drainage; accessing, laying out, and providing for all utilities necessary to serve the entire Site (water, sewer, electrical, natural gas, coaxial or fiber-optic cable; telephone lines); excavating for below-grade facilities such as parking garages, basements, and below-grade foundations; grading for and laying out streets, curbs and gutters, and sidewalks. Depending upon the size of the Subject Site and complexity of the Final Program, Horizontal Construction may need to be completed throughout the Subject Site before any Vertical Construction may begin, or both may proceed in phases, with the first phase of Horizontal Construction preceding the first phase of Vertical Construction, and so on. Regardless of the manner and phasing of Horizontal Construction, however, before any Site Preparation work may be undertaken, it must be planned.

Hospitality – One of a number of building types in the real estate asset class, comprised of every business sector relating to (i) travel and (ii) the activities in which travelers engage on their way to, while at, and on their way from their destination. Accordingly, the hospitality industry includes the hotel industry, which is itself comprised of a variety of players, from the international lodging companies like Marriott and Hilton, to the boutique hotel groups, to the interval-ownership industry (formerly known as "time-sharing"), to one-off accommodations including niche hotels and bed-and-breakfasts, to the emergence of new lodging options and new players in the sector through their participation in The Sharing Economy, such as Airbnb. However, the hospitality industry also includes the airline industry, which requires airports and a network of transportation connections to and from airports to function; public and private transportation networks, including taxi cab companies and their emergent competitors – again a function of The Sharing Economy – such as Uber and Lyft; restaurants catering to business and resort travelers; the gaming industry, which creates entire destinations for business and pleasure travel alike; and a network of service providers, primarily driven by online operators, who assist travelers in knitting together all of the components for a successful or enjoyable (or both) trip. See **Figure 1.5**.

Industrial – One of a number of building types in the real estate asset class, comprised of a broad range properties and uses, from generic warehouse space to light industrial/ manufacturing (mostly assembly work), to distribution facilities, to heavy manufacturing including things like smelting ore and refining crude oil. And as the combination of air pollution, noise pollution, tractor-trailer and delivery truck traffic, toxic waste discharge and disposal, and other by-products of such industrial activities increase, depending upon what they are, the greater the zoning, land use, and operational legal barriers are interposed to limit the number and nature of such uses, or exclude some altogether from particular locations.

Technically, a gas station is both a retail and an industrial use; they are generally specifically provided for in zoning and land use codes or grandfathered in as such. Gas stations and consumer storage rental facilities are fairly commonplace industrial-type uses intermingled with or near less-noxious uses such as car dealerships (also primarily a retail activity but with industrial components, such as large service departments) and auto repair facilities. See **Figure 1.16A, B**.

Institutional/Academic – One of a number of building types in the real estate asset class, Institutional/Academic Properties include college and university campuses and their facilities thereon; museums and art galleries; and academic and not-for-profit research buildings and campuses. See **Figures 1.18A, B**.

Integrated Project Delivery Method – Both the Integrated Project Delivery or "IPD" **(Figure 2.49)** and Design/Build Project Delivery **(Figure 2.48)** methods contemplate different levels of collaboration at different times throughout The Development Process, and are contrasted with the Design/Bid/Build Project Delivery Method, in which the General Contractor is treated as an arm's length third party with which the Developer intends to bargain for construction costs and delivery schedule. Under the Design/Build Project Delivery Method, collaboration begins immediately after the Design/Build firm is selected. With Integrated Project Delivery, collaboration begins during Design Development. Among other things, these early collaborations with the GC are intended to better inform the Developer about the proper pricing and timing of construction, and also avoid design mistakes that may increase both costs and the timeframe for construction.

Internal Revenue Code or "IRC" – The Internal Revenue Code of 1984, as amended from time to time; *United States Code Title 26, Internal Revenue Code*. The Internal Revenue Code was, prior to the publication of this textbook, most recently amended on July 28, 2015, upon the 114th U.S. Congress's passage of Public Law 114–38, *An Act To amend the Small Business Act to increase access to capital for veteran entrepreneurs, to help create jobs, and for other purposes*, introduced in the U.S. House of Representatives as H.R. 2499, and amended by the U.S. Senate, and known as the *Veterans Entrepreneurship Act of 2015*.

Internal Revenue Service or "IRS" – President Lincoln and Congress, in 1862, created the position of commissioner of Internal Revenue and enacted an income tax to pay war expenses from the Civil War. Ten years later the income tax was repealed but Congress revived the income tax in 1894, after which the U.S. Supreme Court ruled an income tax unconstitutional in 1895. In 1913, the last state necessary to ratify a constitutional amendment to permit the collection of taxes on behalf of the federal government, passed the Sixteenth Amendment to the Constitution. In the 1950s the name was changed to the Internal Revenue Service. The IRS is an agency within the U.S. Department of the Treasury.

Investors – Equity participants in the Project are commonly referred to as Investors, although sometimes the term is misapplied to providers of debt as well. Investors rarely fall from the sky: Developers actively recruit and cultivate various sources and types of Investors for their Projects (even for Projects far in the future that haven't been conceived yet), and strategically seek out the best fit between specific projects and the investment parameters of these various investors. Sometimes, Developers rely on brokers or full-service commercial real estate services firms to identify and negotiate with prospective investors. The use of such intermediaries may as much rely on a potential Investor's desire for anonymity as on the expertise offered or provided by the intermediary. The Developer most likely will be seeking various sources of equity and debt to fund the Project at various phases in The Development

Process, through the creation and implementation of a Funding Strategy very early in the Project Conception Phase of The Development Process. The Funding Strategy will be premised on the Developer's Exit Strategy, and will provide an essential framework for seeking and securing various sources of funding, with a view toward avoiding, to the greatest extent possible, conflicts between such funding sources and their respective, idiosyncratic funding requirements, and the investment and return parameters for the Project.

Land Use Approvals – There is almost no real estate development project of any consequence that can be performed as a matter of right. In other words, the *mere ownership* of a parcel of land rarely confers on the property owner the right to build whatever the owner wants, which is commonly referred to as "By-Right Development." Accordingly, before the Developer or Development Entity acquires title to the Subject Site, all critical zoning and land use approvals necessary to support the Final Program for the Project must be secured. Taking title to the Subject Property, by making full payment therefore as agreed to between the Seller and the Buyer, without having all necessary local jurisdictional approvals, will put the Project's financing at risk, and may leave the Developer with undeveloped land that is far less valuable than what was reflected in a purchase price that is premised, at least in part, upon what the Developer wants to develop on the Subject Site, as contrasted with what the Developer has the legal authority to develop based on current Land Use Controls. Additionally, if the zoning and land use approvals secured from the local jurisdiction do *not* support fully the proposed Improvements and, as a consequence, the Subject Property ends up with a lower fair market value than its purchase price, the collateral value of the Subject Site and the project value of the completed Improvements, from the perspective of the Construction Lender, may not allow the requested Construction Loan to be underwritten. This is just one reason why Land Use Law is part of the Holy Trinity of real estate law.

Land Use Analysis – As contrasted with the Preliminary Infrastructure Assessment, the Land Use Analysis reviews and assesses a number of characteristics of a property, including but not limited to site conditions such as slope, the presence of still or moving water, biological and cultural resources, known or reasonably predictable soils conditions (in lieu of actual soils testing, normally conducted during the Pre-Development Phase), access and egress issues, and any observable endangered species or endangered species habitats. The Land Use Analysis is the first step in identifying what portions of the potential site may be developed and what portions of that site will or should be restricted in terms of the construction of Improvements thereon. For example, steep slopes present challenges for both the construction of improvements and managing water runoff on a property. Depending on the location, direction of pitch, and severity of the incline of a steep slope, normal grading techniques may not be sufficient and building retaining walls may prove too costly a solution to create more buildable area. The presence of either still or moving water (e.g., a pond or lake or a stream or creek, respectively) may present both flooding and environmental issues. Either may also provide on its shoreline habitats for critical botanicals and/or endangered species. The Land Use Analysis is intended to provide the Developer with a threshold set of constraints on how the Subject Site may be developed with Improvements beyond any that may already be present on the property.

Land Use Approval Process – Every local jurisdiction has its own process for granting Land Use Approvals. The extent, duration, complexity, and likelihood of success of the Land Use Approval Process also depend on the scope and nature of the Land Use Approvals being requested of the local jurisdiction. A waiver, exemption or variance from an existing zoning ordinance is a much less onerous process than requesting a zoning text amendment or a

Master Plan Amendment. In other words, the extent to which what the Developer is proposing with its Project deviates from existing conditions and the current land use development restrictions will determine how much "process" the Developer or "Applicant" for relief will have to endure. Finally, Land Use Approval Processes tend to be very ministerial in nature: The Applicant's strict adherence to procedural rules, such as giving timely and adequate notice to adjoining property owners, is expected. Land Use Approval Processes have been known to proceed for more than a year, only to have an adjoining property owner or other community stakeholder appear at what is supposed to be the "final" public hearing, and complain about not having received the required legal notice. Absent the Applicant's ability to prove – not merely assert – on the spot that the requisite legal notice was, indeed, delivered to the complaining party, in the specified manner – both as to the substance of the notice and the method of its delivery – and meeting the requisite "advance notice" requirements, the entire process may be directed by the decision-making body to go back to Square One and start over.

Landlord – The Owner, or its designated Property Manager, of a commercial rental building, including commercial office and residential, respectively.

Limited Liability Company or "LLC" – The State of Wyoming passed the United States' first Limited Liability Company Act in 1977. More than ten years after its passage in Wyoming, the Internal Revenue Service finally announced that an LLC formed under Wyoming Limited Liability Company Act would be *taxed like a partnership*. Moreover, it was not until 1996, almost twenty years later, that the National Conference of Commissioners on Uniform State Laws would complete drafting of the country's first model act, the Uniform Limited Liability Company Act (1996). In essence a limited liability company or "LLC" are corporations that act like limited partnerships with one, major exception: None of the LLC members, including the Managing Member, assume any personal liability for the debts, obligations and liabilities of the LLC, as partners normally do in a general partnership.

Limited Partnership or "LP" – Although a "Taxable Entity" and a "Legal Entity" may, in fact, be one-in-the-same, the laws creating legal artifices, such as corporations and limited partnerships, are fundamentally different from the body of law determining the tax status, for federal income tax purposes, of, and tax consequences of transactions undertaken by, such "Legal Entity." Legal Entity status is a matter of state law. And while the vast majority of states have enacted laws regarding the formation and operations of Limited Partnerships (LPs) and Limited Liability Companies (LLCs) based on uniform statutes and model codes, the specific provisions of a particular state's statute governing LPs, and not the Uniform Limited Partnership Act (ULPA), for example, are dispositive of whether a valid LP exists. However, whether an LP constitutes a "Taxable Entity" under the partnership provisions of the Internal Revenue Code, and how the owners of interests in that LP will be taxed for federal income tax and estate tax purposes are determined by the Internal Revenue Code and not by the state statutes under which that LP was formed and operates. For example, an LP that for all intents and purposes is organized and operated as a limited partnership, but which was not properly organized under the limited partnership statute will have the Taxable Entity status of a general partnership under the tax code.

Limited Partnership Agreement – A Limited Partnership Agreement that conforms in all material respects with the Limited Partnership Act or similarly named state statute enacted in the state in which the purported Limited Partnership is formed.

Linear but iterative – Real estate development is both a linear process and an iterative process. Because these are procedurally in conflict, The Development Process is described throughout the textbook as "linear but iterative." It is a linear process in that, in each Phase of The Development Process (see Chapter 2), there are certain critical path items that must be completed before other steps may be taken. For example, jurisdictions generally require that an applicant for any type of zoning approval (e.g., a Special Use Permit, Variance, Master Plan Amendment or Planned Unit Development Ordinance) have control of the Subject Property. This is commonly known as "Site Control." The one is a condition precedent for the other. However, in order to get to a point where the Developer will be comfortable securing Site Control (such as the local jurisdiction and/or legal precedent in that jurisdiction define it), the Developer will need to make certain determinations during the Project Conception Phase regarding the suitability of the Subject Property for the Developer's intentions. As demonstrated in Chapter 2, the Sub-Phases during the Project Conception Phase are largely iterative, with plenty of interplay between them as the Developer and the Development Team move toward the 80:2 Solution.

Loan Covenants – Affirmative commitments made by the Borrower in a Loan Agreement, which may include operating covenants and financial covenants, respectively. Loan Covenants for a Construction Loan, for example, could relate to Borrower's strict compliance with the Draw Schedule and Draw Request procedures specified in the Loan Agreement. For Permanent Financing for a completed Project that has reached stabilization, a typical Loan Covenant would be that Borrower will at all times meet or exceed a threshold Debt Service Coverage Ratio, assuring that the Borrower will, at all times, have more than enough revenue to service the debt under the Loan Agreement.

Low-Income Housing Tax Credit or "LIHTC" – A tax credit program originally enacted in the Tax Reform Act of 1986, providing a potential source of project equity for the development and financing income-qualified housing communities that comply with the express provisions and requirements of Internal Revenue Code Section 42, and Treasury Regulations and interpretive rulings of the IRS promulgated thereunder.

Management Period – The term or duration of a Property Management Agreement or contract.

Market Overview or Survey – One area in which the Preliminary Program most likely will benefit is attaching market pricing to the product or products the Developer contemplated when first generating the Idea, and then refined in developing the Preliminary Program. As a hypothetical example, how much should each of the three unit types – 1BR/1ba, 2BR/1.5ba, and 3BR/2ba – command as asking rents in that particular market and geographic submarket? A threshold question, before getting to pricing, however, is: *What is the Market Area for the Project?* Here are some of the questions that may be asked and answered by the Market Overview or Survey:

- From where is the Project most likely to draw potential renters?
- Which existing and planned projects will be viewed by the marketplace as competing with the Developer's proposed Project?
- Is the Market Area one that the target tenants – luxury apartment renters by choice (i.e. individuals and households that can afford to be buyers and owners of for-sale housing but, for various reasons, choose to rent instead) – view as desirable?
- What amenities, unit configurations, and unit sizes does this target audience find most appealing?

Mixed-Use – One of a number of building types in the real estate asset class. Mixed-Use Properties is a classification that has gained in importance and complexity over the past thirty years or so, with interest in this property classification increasing exponentially over the past ten years. Whereas the first fifty years of real estate development in the United States following World War II focused on suburban and exurban development, starting in the 1980s urban planning and real estate development began to refocus attention on the country's urban cores. Cities had lost substantial populations of both residents and day-time workers to the suburbs, beginning with the "white flight" from city centers in the 1950s, spawning the precipitous growth of suburbs throughout the United States. In the auto-dominated world of the suburbs, each use could be, and usually was, segregated: Bedroom communities here; strip and community shopping centers over there; office parks over there; and so-on-and-so-forth. The birth of the national interstate highway system; new methods for constructing relatively inexpensive single-family detached houses (e.g., the shift away from horse-hair plaster, applied by craftsmen, to the new invention known then as "sheetrock"); low-interest-rate mortgages made available to G.I.'s returning home from the war; these things all contributed to an explosion in bedroom communities away from cities, which remained – for a time, anyway – the employment centers of their respective regions. Once a critical mass of workers had relocated to the pristine, new suburbs, employers and services followed. Today, a Mixed-Use Property may run the gamut from a Commercial Office property with ground floor Retail and Entertainment/Restaurant uses, to Town Centers that accommodate and facilitate the interaction among Residential (both Ownership and Rental), Commercial Office (again, both rental and ownership), and Retail, Entertainment/Restaurant uses, to industry specific projects, such as properties combining commercial office, residential, retail, restaurant, and entertainment uses in combination with research, testing, and production facilities promoting medical technology and treatment breakthroughs. New categories of land use and zoning statutes and regulations have been promulgated and adopted to facilitate the creation of Mixed-Use Properties, and this trend may be reasonably expected to continue for the foreseeable future. See **Figure 1.7**.

Mortgage Interest Deduction – Since the introduction of a federal income tax in 1913, taxpayers have been allowed to deduct from their Gross Income interest paid on a mortgage or mortgages taken out against their primary residence. This deduction is currently codified in Internal Revenue Code Section 163. This exclusive tax benefit is believed to be one of the single, greatest incentives for home ownership in the United States, with as many as 67% of U.S. residents having owned a primary residence in 2007, prior to the collapse of the residential and mortgage markets in the United States, resulting directly from the collapse of the financial industry. For commercial properties, mortgage interest expense is one of a number of operating expenses permitted to be deducted under the Internal Revenue Code.

Necessary Authorities – There is a range of quasi-public authorities (e.g., TIF District, Community Facilities District, a Business Improvement District), determined on a state-by-state basis or even a jurisdiction-by-jurisdiction basis, that may also facilitate the overall funding available for the Project and/or providing a range of quasi-public services supporting the Project. This includes tax increment finance (TIF) districts providing a source of Development Budget funding for public facilities serving the Project; community facility and analogous districts (e.g. Georgia's Community Improvement Districts or "CIDs," California's Community Facilities Districts or "CFDs," and New Mexico's Public Improvement Districts or "PIDs"), providing mechanisms to fund the up-front costs of public infrastructure serving the Project; and quasi-governmental authorities that will operate the Project in the same way a Local Governmental Unit (LGU) might otherwise, if one had the broad powers to do so and the Developer was able to get comfortable with that LGU's capabilities and commitment to do so (e.g., Colorado metropolitan districts).

Necessary Entities – Depending on the Exit Strategy and Funding Strategy, respectively, the Developer may need to create certain Legal Entities, including but not limited to the Development Entity, necessary to implement those strategies. The need for creating one or more such Necessary Entities is addressed in Choice of Entity, above, as well as in definitions in this Glossary of typical entity types for the management of the Development Entity or to facilitate bringing equity into the transaction through Investors, such as Limited Partnerships (LPs) and Limited Liability Companies (LLCs).

Net Operating Income or "NOI" – The definition of "Net Operating Income" may be one of the most contentious issues in real estate development and finance. Among other things, it may determine the timing and availability of distributions to equity investors in a Project. It may also be used in a Loan Agreement to determine whether the Borrower has violated one or more Loan Covenants in a Project's financing. There is no objective point of reference to which the parties refer in defining the components of NOI, and the definition of the term in an Agreement of Limited Partnership may not be the same definition used to establish performance criteria in comprising one or more Loan Covenants in a Loan Agreement. While the definition of what constitutes Gross Income and Adjusted Gross Income, respectively, must be encompassed within the definition of Net Operating Income, it is the line items of deductions from Gross Adjusted Income that may prove contentious, particularly if the Developer and/or Development Entity is the beneficiary of any such line-item expenses, such as Development, Leasing, and Property Management Fees, respectively.

Occupancy Rate – The percentage of occupancy the Developer has assumed for the Project once it has reached stabilization. Stated another way, the Occupancy Rate is 100% less the Vacancy Rate. The Occupancy Rate for a Project is expected to be in conformance with the Occupancy Rate for similar property types in the same market or submarket. Among other things, the Occupancy Rate accounts for periods during a twelve-month operating period that dwelling units or premises are vacant as the result of tenant turnover as well as extended periods of vacancy due to reductions in demand for the Property, as well as periods of time during which units or premises are taken off-line for capital improvements or substantial repairs.

Occupier – Commonly known as a "Tenant" or "Lessee," Commercial Real Estate Services firms specializing in representing Tenants are increasingly referring to their clients as Occupiers. This does not seem to have translated to multifamily rental tenants, however, who only in Landlord-friendly markets like New York City are represented by real estate professionals in their efforts to identify and secure a rental unit.

Operating Losses – An Operating Loss occurs when aggregate annual operating expenses exceed operating income. Whether an Operating Loss has occurred will depend, among other things, on the method of accounting – cash basis versus accrual basis – the Development Entity uses to produce its Annual Income Statement. To the extent Operating Expenses include "paper losses," such as the annual deduction for depreciation, Operating Losses may not automatically translate to negative cash flow for the year either.

Opportunistic Disposition – Unrelated to the market value of the Project and other, similarly situated assets in the Developer's portfolio, the Developer may be presented with an unusual, new real estate development opportunity requiring substantial liquid resources, warranting the disposition of currently held and profitably operated portfolio assets to actuate such new opportunity. In the case of such Opportunistic Disposition including the Project, the new opportunity trumps whether the timing and market dynamics at the time impacting the disposition of existing portfolio assets are ideal, based on the return model presented by the new opportunity. Presumably, in the case of an Opportunistic Disposition, the Developer's analysis takes into account both (i) potential loss in value by selling portfolio assets, including the Project, under such circumstances and (ii) the likelihood that the new real estate development opportunity may not pan out in the manner projected that is prompting the Opportunistic Sale.

Option Contract or simply "Option" – One way for the Developer to Secure Site Control at the end of the Project Conception Phase is by purchasing an Option Contract, also known as an "Option," on the Subject Site. The Developer may purchase the Option, which gives the Developer the contractual right to purchase the Subject Site during a specified period of time at an agreed-upon price purchase price. The Option may include other terms favorable to the Developer, such as Seller Take-Back Financing or allowing the Option Payment applied to the Purchase Price specified in the Option Contract. However, unlike a good faith deposit on a Purchase and Sale Agreement, if the Option is not exercised in accordance with its terms and conditions, the Option will expire and the Option Payment made by the Developer to the owner of the Subject Site is not recoverable, even if the Developer has sound reasons for not completing the transaction.

Owner – The party in possession of legal Title to real property and all Improvements thereon. An Owner may have a possessory interest that does not include the underlying real property, however, and still be able to make a return out of such possessory interest. For example, the "Owners" of the Empire State Building for a number of years did not actually own the building or the ground on which it was erected, but have a long-term lease of the entire building. Similarly, real estate entrepreneur Donald J. Trump negotiated and entered into a 60-year lease, with optional extensions, of Washington, D.C.'s historic Old Post Office Pavilion, from the U.S. government's General Services Administration (GSA), with the intention of extensively renovating and upgrading the building's floors and services in order to operate a luxury hotel, under the Trump Hotels flag.

Ownership and Property Management Phase – One of the five phases of The Development Process, this is the operational phase of the Project, and assumes that the Exit Strategy for the Developer, and the Developer's Investors, is to hold the Project as a Portfolio Asset until such time as the capital value of the Project may be fully realized through a Sale or Refinancing of the Project. A Fully Integrated Real Estate Development Company will earn Property Management Fees during the Management Period, as well as benefit from whatever allocations of Tax Attributes, such as Depreciation and Operating Losses, and Distributable Cash are provided for under the Project ownership documents. However, the largest part of the Developer's return on the Project, other than through the Developer's Fee, may be through the distribution of net cash proceeds from a sale or periodic refinancing of the Project. During the Ownership and Property Management Phase all of the duties, obligations, and liabilities of being both a Property Owner and a Landlord must be fully addressed. This includes maintaining all of the Common Areas and keeping them safe and secure, renewing or securing competitive leases for all Premises in the Project, and making Repairs and Capital Replacements consistent with the useful life of each component of the Improvements. The legal obligations during the Ownership and Property Management Phase may range from dealing with slip-and-fall and other tort-related claims and cases arising from activities and conditions on the Project grounds to making sure Loan Covenants under the Permanent Financing for the Project are not violated (such as allowing the Occupancy Rate to fall below a specified level) to properly funding all Reserve Accounts. See **Figure 2.7**.

Permanent Financing – Mortgage debt with a minimum term of five to seven years, and as many as forty years.

Phase I Environmental Site Assessment – There are two essential components of a Phase I Environmental Site Assessment: A physical inspection of the Property and a search of the land records for the Property to determine if there are any prior uses – e.g. it was formerly a gas station; a dry cleaners where certain hazardous fluids were used and dumped; agricultural land on which certain pesticides were used; machine storage and/or repair facility or yard, where PCBs are likely to be present – that would indicate the need for a Phase II Environmental Site Assessment. Based on the collection of this data, the engineering or environmental services firm conducting the Phase I Environmental Site Assessment will make a recommendation that a Phase II Environmental Site Assessment be performed or, alternatively, indicate that there is not a likelihood that hazardous materials are present on the Property based upon its history and current physical condition.

Phase II Environmental Site Assessment – Based on the nature, scope, and extent of historical uses on the Property, as determined from the Phase I Environmental Site Assessment, the engineering or environmental services firm that conducted the Phase I Environmental Site Assessment will take soils, water, and/or air samplings to determine the presence of any hazardous materials on the Property. Based on the testing and analysis of the samples taken, the engineering or environmental services firm conducting the Phase II Environmental Site Assessment will provide an assessment of the presence, location, and severity of hazardous materials found on the property, as well as recommendations for how each hazardous material found may be acceptably mitigated.

Portfolio Asset – Any single, real estate asset held as part of a portfolio of real estate assets developed, acquired or acquired and renovated by the Developer with the intention of holding the asset in the Developer's portfolio of real estate assets.

Portfolio Developer – A real estate Developer that develops operating assets intended to be held in the Developer's portfolio of real estate assets or in a portfolio not controlled exclusively by the Developer but in which the Developer has a substantial interest.

Portfolio Diversification or, simply, "Diversification" – Asset allocation, as an axiom of investing, has as a principal goal spreading the risk of loss in a portfolio through diversification, as well as optimizing returns from one asset class at a time when the return performance of another asset class or classes may not be as robust. While not among the troika of primary asset classes – stocks, bonds, and cash equivalents – real estate is an important asset class for investors. The percentage of an investor's portfolio of assets allocated to real estate will depend upon that investor's tolerance for risk (low, moderate, or high). The risk associated with a particular investment in real estate will be balanced against its potential return to the investor, either through anticipated, periodic cash distributions, projected increases in the value of the original investment, or some combination of the two. the need to differentiate specific types of real property into categories is not merely limited to an investor's perspective on real estate as an asset class but also functions to help Portfolio Developer's and asset managers diversify portfolios of real estate assets as a principal risk mitigation strategy. Just as different asset classes reflect different risk and return investment characteristics, different types of real property within the real estate asset class not only present similar differentials in risk and return because of the very nature of the product type and use, respectively, but the trajectory of The Development Process is often very different for each category of property classification within the real estate asset class. Each property classification is predicated upon particular aspects in the character and use of real property that differentiate its treatment under the law. For example, typical uses for and users of properties falling within the Commercial Office property classification are very different from typical uses for and users of properties in the Industrial property classification. These different uses and users present substantively different legal issues, which may impact the risk of loss during The Development Process. Similarly, as a function of land use approvals, properties classified as Commercial Office are generally not co-located with properties included in the Industrial asset class, presenting further differences in their treatment under the law.

Pre-Development Phase – One of the five Development Phases of The Development Process. In the Pre-Development Phase the process of moving forward with the Project goes from merely conceptual to *buildable and financeable*. Every aspect of the Project that was explored conceptually during the Project Conception Phase has to be taken to a level of sufficient certitude that the Project will be able to move forward. This means, among other things, that the market survey undertaken during the Project Conception Phase will be replaced by a full Market Study; the Schematic Design will go through Design Development, leading ultimately to the creation of a full set of Construction Documents (also referred to as "Construction Drawings" or, simply, "CD's"), and the Land Analysis will be replaced by a formal Site Evaluation Report by the civil engineering firm, from which it will develop Site Construction Plans for all horizontal construction on the Subject Site. The Preliminary Program for the Subject Property – a detailed description of each of the components that will comprise the Project once everything has been completed – must be tested, refined, and finalized. The level of detail of all of the work undertaken by the Development Team must be able to support, among other things, entering into one or more contracts for the construction of the planned Improvements to the Subject Site, as well as securing both acquisition and construction financing to pay for such construction activity. The process for entering into contracts for the construction of the Improvements to the Subject Site will depend, to a great extent, on the Project Delivery Method selected by the Developer and its Design Team (a subset of the Development Team). Whatever the form of Site Control attained by the Developer in order to be able to move the Project from the Project Conception Phase into the Pre-Development Phase – whether an Option Contract or a Purchase and Sale Agreement – assuming a successful Feasibility Study and Due Diligence Period the Developer – or, more likely, a Development Entity (a Special Purpose Entity also referred to as an "SPE") created by the Developer for that purpose, will need to acquire Title to the Subject Site. The Pre-Development Phase will require several Closings, one for the acquisition of the Subject Site, one for the Construction Documents, and one for the Construction Loan (although the latter two may be combined into a single Closing).

Pre-Leasing – Marketing and leasing of Premises or Dwelling Units during the Pre-Development and Construction Phases, respectively, of The Development Process. It is not uncommon for Permanent Financing to be predicated on a specified percentage of the completed Project to be pre-leased before the Permanent Lender will provide the requested Take-Out Financing Commitment, on which the Construction Lender, in turn, relies as a condition precedent for its Construction Loan Commitment.

Preliminary Market Survey – See Market Overview or Survey.

Preliminary Development Budget pro forma – The Preliminary Development Budget pro forma is used to test the financial feasibility of the Idea. The Developer should have enough information from the Market Overview or Survey and from the Preliminary Infrastructure

Assessment Sub-Phases of the Project Conception Phase of The Development Process to know what product type(s) will work best on the Subject Site, and through the Revised Preliminary Program, have an estimate of the total square feet of building or buildings that need to be constructed on the Subject Site. The Developer should be in a position to apply standards in that market for dollars per square feet of hard construction costs (HCC) for each type of product proposed to be constructed, and also apply reasonable assumptions for soft costs and financing costs to be incurred, as well as the Land Cost based on Seller's asking price for the Subject Site. Additionally, the Preliminary Development Budget pro forma, when evaluated in the context of the Preliminary Operating Budget pro forma, will yield valuable insights into the potential profitability of the Project after stabilization, as well as the projected value of the completed Project based on its Net Operating Income.

Preliminary Program – The Preliminary Program represents the Developer's first attempt to quantify the Idea, providing a relatively simple framework for determining the potential scale of the Project and making some very crude, very early projections about costs and gross revenues. The Preliminary Program may be expressed narratively but more often than not is a quantitative, tabular description of the Idea. For example, the Preliminary Program for a multifamily rental project could be narratively described as simply "a 300-unit rental project comprised of one, two, and three-bedroom units." Chapter 2 offers a glimpse at the evolution of the Developer's Program for a Subject Site, highlighting the *"linear but iterative"* nature of The Development Process.

Premises – A demised area within a building, occupying a portion of a floor, and entire floor or multiple floors, that a Tenant is able to occupy and control for its exclusive use through, and subject to the explicit terms and conditions of, a Lease Agreement.

Product-Type Portfolio Diversification – See description of **Portfolio Diversification**.

Pro Forma – A pro forma is a set of financial projections for a proposed Project, predicated on a series of assumptions, which are created as early in The Project Conception Phase of The Development Process as the Developer is able to start making reasonable assumptions about the Project. Project pro formas typically include a Development Budget pro forma and an Operating Budget pro forma, similar to an Income Statement for an operating property. These pro forma documents are intended to provide the framework for the Developer's determination of the financial feasibility of the Project. Like the Preliminary Program, the Development Budget pro forma will go through a series of iterations, with both greater detail and increasing certitude attached to the values and underlying assumptions of the pro forma. This is another excellent example of how The Development Process is both linear and iterative.

Project Completion and Stabilization Phase – One of the five phases of The Development Process, the Project Completion and Stabilization Phase covers the period between the Substantial Completion of all activities that occurred during the Construction Phase and the commencement of normal operations of the completed Project. What constitutes Substantial Completion, as well as the timely disposition of all Punch-List Items, may be contentious and lead to litigation, although it is more likely than not that substantial disagreements between the Owner, the General Contractor, the Architect/Engineer, and the Construction Lender will have manifested themselves long before the General Contractor claims that the Construction Contract has been substantially completed. The Construction Contract should provide required procedures for dispute resolution among the parties. The Project Completion and Stabilization Phase marks the winding down of all construction activity, other than addressing Punch-List Items, and ramping up of the move-in process (assuming that pre-leasing and/or pre-sales activities were vigorously and successfully pursued during the Construction Phase). Getting facilities, such as a Resident Manager's or Sales Office, and all Common Areas, including Project amenities and facilities furnished, equipped, appointed, and fully staffed are critical components of the Project Completion and Stabilization Phase. In the case of rental Projects, including both Commercial Office, Retail, and Multifamily, either the take-out financing or the investment parameters of the intended, ultimate owner of the Project (such as a pension fund or insurance company) will dictate what constitutes an appropriate Stabilization Period, which may be determined by the passage of time, the achievement of specified Occupancy Rates, or some combination of the two. See **Figure 2.6**.

Project Conception Phase – One of the five phases of The Development Process, the Project Conception Phase marks the beginning, or genesis, of every development project. The Developer is seeking to decide what to do, and where. While limiting, to the greatest extent possible, the expenditure of funds (see the 80:2 Solution), the Developer seeks to identify any impediments to a potential project. Any number of obstacles, such as an inflexible zoning code or problematic environmental conditions, may be identified during the Project Conception Phase. Additionally, the financial feasibility or infeasibility will be assessed during this initial Phase of The Development Process. The Project Conception Phase starts with an Idea. The Idea will either blossom following its genesis or die at some point during The Development Process. In a perfect world, if the Idea is going to die, it should do so relatively quickly, as early as possible during the Project Conception Phase; the death of the Idea during the Pre-Development Phase or, worse yet, the Construction Phase, could spell financial disaster for the Developer, as well as for the Developer's Equity Investors and Lenders.

Project Delivery Method – The method by which the Developer intends to have the Project constructed is described generically as the Project Delivery Method. The textbook considers three, competing Project Delivery Methods:

- Design/Bid/Build. See **Figure 2.47**.
- Design/Build. See **Figure 2.48**.
- Integrated Project Delivery (IPD). See **Figure 2.49**.

Each of these, three Project Delivery Methods are described in greater details elsewhere in the Glossary.

Project Gross Income – Income from all sources generated by a Project. In a Pro Forma, this includes projected gross rents before adjusting for a Vacancy Rate, plus any additional revenue anticipated, such as income from a coin-operated laundry room in a multifamily rental building or Percentage Rent from a retail tenant. In an Annual Income Statement, Project Gross Income is comprised of all revenue received ("received" being determined by whether the Development Entity uses the accrual or cash method of accounting). Over the years, Developers and Landlords have become very creative in developing additional channels for revenue generation, such as leasing of rooftop cell towers and fees for additional services performed, such as rental fees for community rooms and surcharges for building-wide cable television and internet access.

Project Viability – See **Financial Feasibility**.

Property Manager – Generally, a property management services company that has entered into a Property Management Agreement for the Property with the Owner.

Property Management Fees – The monthly fees, usually calculated as a percentage of gross rent collected, that compensate the Property Manager for its property management services for the Project, in accordance with a Property Management Agreement entered into by and between the Property Manager and the Property Owner.

Punch-List Items – A list of incomplete or improperly specified and/or installed items determined by a Walk-Through Inspection of the Property after the General Contractor has given the Owner notice of the GC's Substantial Completion of the Project but before a Certificate of Occupancy has been requested. Neither any single Punch-List Item nor the totality of all Punch-List Items should be sufficient in their impact on the Project to preclude a determination of Substantial Completion. The GC should be able to commit to the complete resolution of any and all Punch-List Items within thirty days of the Walk-Through Inspection, with the exception of any fixtures or other items that the Punch-List requires to be replaced but which will not be available from the supplier or vendor within such 30-day period.

Purchase and Sale Agreement or "PSA" – As a means of securing Site Control, the Developer may enter into a Purchase and Sale Agreement (PSA) with the owner of the Subject Site, conditioning its purchase upon a number of subjectively determined events affording the Developer considerable flexibility in determining whether to proceed with the acquisition after more information has been obtained and analyzed. One of the most common such conditions precedent to the Developer's obligation to purchase the Subject Site is the completion of a Due Diligence Period during which the Developer may walk away from the purchase contract, and be entitled to a full refund of its good faith deposit accompanying the execution of the PSA, for any number of reasonable events subjectively assessed by the Developer. Because PSA's are generally structured in this manner, while the good faith deposit will be exponentially larger than the payment for a Purchase Option, the conditions under which the good faith deposit may be refunded to the Developer under a broad range of circumstances makes the PSA the preferred choice for securing legal control of the Subject Site with limited exposure for risk of losing the value of the good faith deposit.

Real Estate Asset Class – In order to understand "real estate as an asset class" one must first understand that the classification of investments or investment securities has traditionally recognized only two asset classes – equities (i.e., stocks) and fixed-income securities (i.e., "bonds") – with a third class – cash-equivalents – only having been added to the list in the latter half of the twentieth century. Essentially, "asset class" defines a group of financial instruments with similar characteristics – such as an ownership interest, which entitles the holder to a ratable share of a corporation's assets – that tend to respond in a somewhat similar manner to prevailing market characteristics, and which generally are treated the same under the law. Depending on whom you ask, in addition to what were, by the 1970s, the three main asset classes – equities, fixed-income securities, and cash-equivalents – there are two or three additional asset classes recognized by investors and fund managers in the twenty-first century: Guaranteed securities; commodities, and real estate. It is instructive to note the components of real estate as an asset class may also be categorized based on other characteristics of real property, including:

- Geographic location
- Broadly defined risk and return parameters
- Susceptibility to particular types of risk
- Manner/method by which cash flow and value are generated
- Regulatory framework within which it is developed and operated

By way of example, geographic location may be an important characteristic for investors in real estate assets. A portfolio of real estate assets may be composed exclusively of a particular use type – say Hospitality – because of the investor's understanding and acceptance of the general risk and return profile of that property type. However, despite making all of its investments in Hospitality properties, such a limited focus on a single property type may be somewhat ameliorated through geographical diversity among the properties purchased. Through the geographic distribution of its assets, such portfolio may achieve a hedge against specific market downturns while other geographic markets rise and thrive. Similarly, the investment focus of another portfolio may be on a mix of income-producing properties that work synergistically when located in "24/7 markets." Since there is a limited number of such 24/7 markets in the United States, with New York City being the prime example, such portfolio would also be driven by the geographic locations of the properties purchased. The main point here is that the traditional property characteristics used to identify, categorize, and define different real estate assets is not, by any means, the only method for categorizing real property but does provide a variety of opportunities and strategies for diversification within a given real estate asset portfolio.

Refinancing – In a refinancing, the Development Entity replaces existing debt with new debt. The assumption is, so long as the term of the existing debt is long enough, that the Development Entity will be able to choose the timing of the refinancing to coincide with a period of low interest rates. The other assumption is that the Project will be increasing in value over time, such that the value of the Project supports a larger amount for the refinancing, which is sufficient to pay down 100% of the outstanding premium amount of the existing financing, plus any accrued but unpaid interest thereon, plus all transaction costs, and still leave a substantial amount of Distributable Cash for the owners of interests in the Development Entity. In this way, the Developer, which is presumed to be the exclusive or a majority owner of the outstanding interests in the Development Entity, will periodically be able to extract the increased value of the Project without having to dispose of any portion of its interest in order to realize that increased value.

Repairs and Capital Replacements – While Common Area Maintenance or "CAM" Charges are intended to cover ordinary and routine maintenance of the Building each year, some repairs and Capital Replacements fall on the shoulders of the Owner. Most capital replacement may be reasonably anticipated based on the average useful lives of equipment, such as the major, operating components of a Building's HVAC system (such as a boiler or hot-air furnace providing a heat source for the system). By establishing and diligently funding a Reserve for Repairs and Capital Replacements, the Owner may fully fund all such necessary repairs and replacements well before they arise.

Request for Information or "RFI" – If the General Contractor or one of its subcontractors finds something in the CDs that doesn't make sense or they don't understand, their primary obligation is to inquire about that item by submitting a Request for Information or RFI to the Architect. This contractual obligation of inquiry is contained in the Construction Documents and is discussed in the Supplementary Materials on the companion website under Construction Phase Issues, Documentation, and Claims, including in a discussion comparing differences between the AIA document sets and their counterpart ConsensusDOCS construction contract documents. Generally speaking, the General Contractor's submission of an RFI starts the clock ticking on the Architect's Response to RFI, which should be intended to clarify the General Contractor or subcontractor's interpretation question about the CDs or, alternatively, providing a correction to the CDs to the extent the RFI has called attention to an error or conflict in the CDs with another section or sections of the CDs. If the Architect's Response to the RFI requires, in the professional opinion of the General Contractor, the General Contractor or subcontractor to use materials, equipment or personnel over-and-above what the GC or its sub put in their cost proposal in response to the Bid Package, based on a reasonable reading of the CDs contained therein, the General Contractor or the subcontractor, through the General Contractor, may request an increase in the Contract Price based on the added materials, equipment, and/or personnel required based on the Architect's Response to the RFI. Of course, as the representative of the Owner, with which the Architect has a separate contract for the architectural services to be performed, the Architect's natural inclination is to take the position, in the Architect's Response to the RFI, that such response is merely providing additional clarification based on the General Contractor's inquiry, and that such clarification does not materially add to the cost to the General Contractor and/or its subcontractor in performing the Construction Contract as it was bid. If, however, the General Contractor is not satisfied with the Architect's Response to the RFI (e.g., the additional information does not clarify the ambiguity of other infirmity with the section(s) of the Construction Documents what are the subject of the RFI in the first place, or with the Architect's position that the Architect's Response to the RFI should not occasion any increase in the Contract Price, the General Contractor may seek such incremental increase in the Contract Price through a Request for Change Order (CO).

Reserve Accounts – The Developer may establish and fund, or be required by a Project's Equity Investors and or Lenders to establish and fund, certain reserve accounts as part of the Operating Budget for the Project. An Operating Reserve, for example, might be established to address any shortfalls in Adjusted Gross Revenue or precipitous increases in Operating Expenses, to provide actual, cash coverage in the event the latter exceeds the former in any given month. A reserve account may also be established to create a fund, over time, for Repairs and Capital Replacements.

Residential – One of a number of building types in the real estate asset class, comprised of housing. The federal government has extensive involvement in various programs involving "housing." These include but are not limited to the regulation of various types of financial institutions making housing-related loans, the U.S. Department of Housing and Urban Development (HUD), the creation of government-sponsored entities (GSEs) such as Fannie Mae and Freddie Mac, and numerous provisions in the Internal Revenue Code relating to housing (including but not limited to the mortgage interest deduction and the low-income housing tax credit program or LIHTC). Consequently, there is a variety of definitions in federal statutes and regulations relating to the Residential property classification. The far simpler, and arguably more functional, definition of Residential property is any place where people live other than on a very temporary or interim basis, so as to exclude, by intention, lodging properties (see Hospitality classification, below), camp grounds, homeless shelters, jails and prisons, and the like. See **Figures 1.2** and **1.3**.

Retail – One of a number of building types in the real estate asset class, comprised of any commercially zoned property engaged in the marketing and selling of consumer goods and services may be considered a Retail Property. This runs the gamut from a stand-alone retail business, such as a 7-Eleven, to community shopping centers to regional mega-malls, and everything in between. Interestingly, the advent and proliferation of online marketing and sales have eliminated some of the brick-and-mortar retail locations, in favor of an online presence plus logistics and distribution networks facilitating the execution of sales transacted completely over the Internet. However, few brick-and-mortar retailers are willing to abandon their physical locations in strong retail markets in favor of an online-only presence, and some online retailers, such as Levenger, have gone from online only to having both physical locations and a virtual, online presence. See **Figure 1.4**.

Sale or Refinancing – For a Developer that, early in the Project Conception Phase of The Development Process, during the Develop Exit and Funding Strategies Sub-Phase, decided to make the Project a portfolio asset, the sale or refinancing of the Permanent Financing of the Project is the event through which the enhanced or increased value of the Project is tangibly realized. Further extraction of increased value over time of the Project may only be realized through the refinancing option. With regard to a sale of the project, such disposition may be Strategic, Opportunistic, or Distressed. For a portfolio owner of operating, commercial real property, the sale of a performing asset would most likely only come about in one of three scenarios: A strategic disposition of the Project; an opportunistic disposition of the Project to support a new, potentially more valuable real estate development opportunity; or a distressed disposition of the Project. In a refinancing, the Development Entity replaces existing debt with new debt. The assumption is, so long as the term of the existing debt is long enough, the Development Entity will be able to choose the timing of the refinancing to coincide with a period of low interest rates. The other assumption is that the Project will be increasing in value over time, such that the value of the Project supports a larger amount for the refinancing, which is sufficient to pay down 100% of the outstanding premium amount of the existing financing, plus any accrued but unpaid interest thereon, plus all transaction costs, and still leave a substantial amount of Distributable Cash for the owners of interests in the Development Entity. In this way, the Developer, which is presumed to be the exclusive or a majority owner of the outstanding interests in the Development Entity, will periodically be able to extract the increased value of the Project without having to dispose of any portion of its interest in order to realize that increased value.

Schematic Design – Schematic Design will show the footprints of all buildings (existing, if applicable, and to be constructed); each point of ingress onto and egress from the property, as well as all internal roads and walkways; surface parking lots and/or parking structures on the site, including all parking lot and garage entryways and exits; and any site amenities, including but not limited to all active and passive-use outdoor spaces. In addition to providing, in plan-view, the first graphic depiction of how the proposed site would be developed in order to implement the Developer's Idea, the Schematic Design also allows the Developer and its planners or designers to test how the potential site meets certain land use requirements and restrictions upon which land use approvals will be conditioned, such as setbacks from public sidewalks and other buildings, and any requirements that a minimum percentage of the total area of a developed property be dedicated to Open Space. The Schematic Design also allows the Development Team to assess how effectively vehicular traffic will be managed on-site, as well as how efficiently vehicular traffic flows into and out of the Subject Site.

S Corporation – An "S Corporation" is not a creature of state statute. In other words, there is no provision under state codes to form an "S Corporation": It is a creature of the Internal Revenue Code that starts out as a C Corporation. In other words, an "S Corporation" is a C Corporation that meets specific requirements set forth in the Internal Revenue Code, and that makes a specific election to be treated under Subchapter S of the Internal Revenue Code as an "S Corporation." Until the advent of a number of relatively new organizational structures that facilitate capital formations and distributions of profits – such as LPs, LLCs, and LLLPs – S Corporations were the preferred organizational structure for limiting the personal liability for equity participants in an enterprise while also allowing all of the tax attributes of that enterprise to "pass through" to those equity participants.

Seller – The owner of recorded Title to a property, whether improved or unimproved, in a Purchase and Sale Agreement for the subject property. Whether a purposed seller of real property is legally entitled and duly authorized to dispose of the property by a transfer of a fee simple interest therein will depend on the legal status and entity type of the Seller. For example, real property that is held in a trust may only be disposed of through sale by the party or parties so identified in the trust agreement, and in accordance with the procedures therefor established in the trust agreement.

Site – The parcel of real property on which a Developer is interested in developing a Project.

Site Control – A party having Site Control is either the record owner of Title to the Property or has a contractual right, through an Option Contract or Purchase and Sale Agreement, to unilaterally become the Owner of the property.

Special-Purpose Entity or "SPE" – A legal entity created expressly for the purpose of undertaking a real estate development project as a means of sheltering the assets of other parties associated with the SPE from exposure to the liabilities to be incurred as a consequence of such real estate development activities. See Choice of Entity, above, regarding various legal entities that may be considered for creating the SPE.

Special-Use Properties – One of a number of building types in the real estate asset class, Special Use Properties include airports; hospitals and healthcare facilities; dedicated sports stadiums and baseball parks; convention centers; performing arts centers; multiuse entertainment complexes designed to host NBA and NHL franchises' home games, A-list concerts, extreme sports events, and WWE spectacles; and publicly financed private utilities facilities, such a water treatment plants and pumping stations. Special Use Properties are increasingly the result of public-private partnerships (P3s), generally require some combination of public and private financing, and are almost always the result of specific statutes and local ordinances permitting them, the specifics for which evolve out of the overall process of negotiating and structuring the P3 arrangements among the key participants and stakeholders. The larger the scale and land area footprint of such Special Use Properties the greater the likelihood that government powers of condemnation may need to be exercised to acquire land from recalcitrant landowners. See **Figure 1.17A, B**.

Stabilization Period – The period of time, usually expressed in months, the Developer has estimated will be required for the Project to reach Stabilized Net Operating Income.

Stabilized Net Operating Income or "Stabilized NOI" – Stabilized Net Operating Income is Net Operating Income or NOI (see definition, above), after the Project has reached Stabilization and for a reasonable period thereafter consistent with Developer's reporting requirements and/or the requirements of the Project's Permanent Lender regarding the threshold period of time the Project must maintain stabilized rents and operating expenses.

Strategic Disposition – A strategic decision may be made to no longer continue to hold the Project, all real estate assets in the geographic market in which the Project is located – in which case other portfolio assets will also be marketed for sale – or real estate assets in a particular real estate asset category applicable to the Project (e.g. hospitality, which tends to be more susceptible to market volatilities than other real estate asset categories). A portfolio Developer may make a strategic decision to divest the Project or a package of properties including the Project either because the Developer foresees problems on the horizon that may negatively impact the future operating performance of each such property in the portfolio to be made available for a Strategic Disposition, or because the Developer perceives the Project and any other related, bundled real estate assets assembled from the overall real estate portfolio for sale have reached a price premium not expected to be seen again for a prolonged period of time. Although these alternative scenarios may sound similar – sell at a peak in value before problems foreseen on the horizon erode that value – these are, in reality, two different scenarios. It is, however, easy to understand how, under certain circumstances, there might be some convergence of these two scenarios.

Strip Commercial Redevelopment Walk-Up – Typical Suburban Town Centers are 18th or nineteenth-century towns that were swept up in the sprawl of the metropolitan area after World War II. Following decades of decline, they have found a new economic role. Suburban Town Centers have relatively less office space than in downtowns or downtown adjacent areas (although offices still occupy 46% of all space), more residential (30%) and significantly more retail (16%).

Substantial Completion – A status of construction completion that, despite the existence or unresolved Punch-List Items does not preclude the Project receiving a Certificate of Occupancy. The Construction Contract may provide a definition of Substantial Completion that is more onerous or rigorous than the local jurisdiction applies in determining whether a C of O may be issued.

Suburban Town Center Walk-Up – These WalkUPs were mid-to-late twentieth-century strip commercial that became obsolete and then evolved into higher density development. Somewhat similar to suburban town centers, Strip Commercial Redevelopment WalkUPs have relatively less office space than in downtowns or downtown adjacent areas (46% of all space), more residential (31%) and significantly more retail (16%). Many of these WalkUPs include regional malls that have been or will be urbanized. This type of WalkUP will be the major focus of walkable urban development over the next generation.

Take-Out Financing – Financing necessary to pay down in full the principal balance of the Construction Loan, plus any accrued but unpaid interest, fees, and charges, with a term necessary to allow the Project to reach Stabilization. Take-Out Financing may take the form of a Mini-Perm (generally not more than three years) or bridge financing, depending upon the terms and conditions of the Permanent Financing Commitment for the Project.

Tax Attributes – Any item of income, expense, deduction or credit under the Internal Revenue Code required to be reported as income, allowed to be used to off-set taxable income or applied as a credit against a tax liability that is attributable to an operating enterprise that is not a reporting entity for federal income tax purposes because all of its tax attributes are passed through to its interest owners, such as is the case with a Limited Partnership (LP), Limited Liability Company (LLC) or S Corporation.

Tenure Type – Sometimes simply referred to as "tenure," Tenure Type refers to the nature of a Tenant's or Occupier's temporal and legal interest in real property. This generally is broken down between those who own real property and those who have a temporally limited right to occupancy of Improvements to real property, commonly known as a "Renter," "Tenant" or "Lessee."

The Development Process – The Development Process[1] is presented as a series of five (5) Development Phases (see **Figure 2.1** and the Appendix), with each Development Phase representing a discrete set of tasks or Sub-Phases, each of which must be accomplished before the Project can move forward into the next Development Phase. Each Development Phase concludes with a critical milestone marking the end of one Development Phase and the beginning of the next one (See, e.g., **Figure 2.2**). Additional descriptions of The Development Process milestones, by Development Phase, are provided in **Figures 2.4** through **Figure 2.7**. A complete summary of The Development Process is presented, in its entirety, in the Appendix, as well as in context in Chapter 2.

Title – A written instrument, including a metes-and-bounds description, evidencing a party having fee simple title to the described real property, and which to be effective must be duly executed by the previous owner of record conveying legal title to said real property *and recorded* in the land records of the local jurisdiction in which said real property is found.

Title Report – An ALTA Title Report provides narrative descriptions of the title history of the Property, up to and including the current Seller of the Property, as well as any restrictive covenants, easements, limitations or restrictions upon the Seller's use and possession of the Property. The ALTA Preliminary Title Report and an ALTA Title Survey, defined above, must be read together to get a complete picture about the quality of the title to the Property that is proposed to be conveyed from Seller to Buyer, as well as any constraints on the Buyer's post-Closing use of the Property. For instance, an easement depicted on the ALTA Title Survey may show the physical location or boundaries, within the legal Property boundaries, but would not explain the nature of the easement, by whom it is held, and its terms and conditions, including but not limited to its tenure. Both documents are needed to fully understand the complete impact of any such constraints on the Seller's title to the Property being conveyed.

Total Development Cost or "TDC" – The sum total of all costs associated with a develop Project, from the Land Acquisition Costs, to the Soft Costs, to the Hard Construction Costs (HCC).

Urban Commercial Walk-Up – Historically local-serving neighborhood commercial, these places declined after World War II but, in recent years, found a new economic role. Urban Commercial WalkUPs in metro D.C. are dominated by residential property (56%) and are marked by more retail (15%) and less office space (20%) than downtown or downtown adjacent. The retail in urban commercial WalkUPs is generally characterized as urban entertainment, such as restaurants and nightclubs, as well boutique shops and furniture and home décor stores

Urban University Walk-Up – In these WalkUPs, universities and other institutional owners, such as medical facilities or government research centers, are the dominant landowners. These landowners gauge the "success" of their development not in terms of rent they may be able to collect, but in their ability to attract talent (professors, students, administrators, etc.). The presence of these anchor institutions can also present opportunities for Innovation Districts to develop. As mentioned above, MIT/Kendall Square is one of the country's leading examples of an Innovation District. University space (classrooms, laboratories, hospitals, general office, and dorms) is the largest use, followed by off-campus housing, both rental and for-sale. Office space represents 17%, showing the commercialization of university research and desire to be near the university campus. Retail is very small (1%), which is an opportunity; only Harvard Square has created a critical mass of retail in this type of WalkUP.

U.S. Department of Housing and Urban Development – A cabinet-level department of the United States government, the U.S. Department of Housing and Urban Development is responsible for a broad range of federal government services, programs, and funding sources – both loans and grants – in support of a range of housing opportunities and the health and growth of the United States' urban areas.

Vacancy Rate – The Vacancy Rate for a Project reflects the total percentage of time, on a proportional basis based on the total, leasable square footage of the Project over a specified, twelve-month period that Premises or Dwelling Units, as the case may be, are not occupied by rent-paying Tenants. The Vacancy Rate is expected to be in conformance with the Vacancy Rates for similar property types in the same market or submarket. Among other things, the Vacancy Rate accounts for periods during such twelve-month operating period that Dwelling Units or Premises as the case may be, are and remain vacant as the result of Tenant turnover, as well as extended periods of vacancy due to reductions in demand for the Property, as well as periods of time during which units or premises are taken off-line for capital improvements or substantial repairs.

Vertical Construction – Construction "from the ground up," as contrasted with Horizontal Construction, which is defined as all construction necessary to support Vertical Construction. With regard to Vertical Construction on underground or at-grade parking structures, the Developer, the funding for both Horizontal and Vertical Construction, the Construction Lender(s), and the Project Accountant will likely collaborate on whether parking structure should be accounted for as part of Horizontal Construction or Vertical Construction.

Walkable Urban Places or "WalkUPs" – Walkable urban places, or WalkUPs, offer a much-more fine-grained understanding of the "Mixed-Use" classification. Walkable urban development or "WalkUPs" are best understood in the context of the predominant development pattern in the United States in the second half of the twentieth century: Suburban Euclidian Development, aka "suburban sprawl." In addition to the functional importance of Mixed-Use Properties as a real estate asset class category, Mixed-Use projects and, more particularly, WalkUPs, comprise an ever-larger proportion of total real estate development, and real estate asset value, in the United States.

Notes

1   The author claims copyright protection, dating back to its first usage in June 2010 in the United States, in the name and concept "The Development Process," and in all graphic depictions of The Development Process throughout this textbook and on this textbook's companion website, as well as in all substantive descriptions and discussions about each Development Phase in *The Development Process*, and each Sub-Phase within each Development Phase.

Bibliography

Aalberts, Robert J., *Real Estate Law*, Eighth Edition, South-Western Cengage Learning, Mason, OH (2009).

American Law Institute. *Restatement (Second) of Contracts*, Washington, DC, May 17, 1979, Kindle Edition.

American Planning Association, *Policy Guide on Smart Growth*, Chicago, IL (2002), found at www.planning.org/policy/guides/adopted/smartgrowth.htm.

Bassett, Edward M., Chairman, *Report of the Height of Buildings Commission to the Committee on the Height, Size and Arrangement of Buildings of the Board of Estimate and Apportionment of the City of New York*, M.B. Brown Printing & Binding Company, New York, NY (December 23, 1913).

Becker, Sofia, Scott Bernstein, and Linda Young, *The New Real Estate Mantra: Location Near Public Transportation*, Center for Neighborhood Technology, Chicago, IL, commissioned by American Public Transportation Association and National Association of Realtors (March 2013).

Benkler, Yochai, " 'Sharing Nicely': On Shareable Goods and the Emergence of Sharing as a Modality of Economic Production," *Yale Law School Legal Scholarship Repository*, January 1, 2004.

Board of Estimate and Apportionment, City of New York, "Building Zone Resolution," adopted July 25, 1916, found at www.nyc.gov/html/dcp/pdf/history_project/1916_zoning_resolution.pdf.

Brennan, Joseph, "HardRock Development Corporations 200 Acre Bay View Development-a New Direction?" Final Paper, Georgetown University, School of Continuing Studies, Master's Program in Real Estate, *Foundations of Real Estate Law*, FREL 601–01, Spring 2013, April 3, 2013.

Bucci, Federico, *Albert Kahn: Architect of Ford*, Princeton Architectural Press, New York, NY (1993).

Buder, Stanley, *Visionaries & Planners: The Garden City Movement and the Modern Community*, Oxford University Press, New York, NY (1990).

Burns, Robert, "To a Mouse, on Turning Her Up in Her Nest with the Plough," from *Poem's, Chiefly in the Scottish Dialect*," Kilmarnock (1786).

Calthorpe, Peter, *The Next American Metropolis: Ecology, Community, and the American Dream*, Princeton Architectural Press, New York, NY (1993).

Calthorpe, Peter, and William Fulton, *The Regional City: Planning for the End of Sprawl*, Island Press, Washington, DC (2001).

Carter, Zach, "A Master of Disaster," *The Nation*, January 4, 2010.

Cohen, Ronnie, and Shannon O'Byrne, "Law, Emotion, and the Subprime Mortgage Crisis," *SOLOGP Magazine*, Vol. 29, No. 1 (January/February 2012), ABA Solo, Small Firm, and General Practice Division, found at www.americanbar.org/publications/gp_solo/2012/january_february/law_emotion_subprime_mortgage_crisis.html.

Conference on Mixed-Use Development, 2006, Press Release dated November 17, 2006, found at www.icsc.org/uploads/research/general/Mixed-use_Definition.pdf.

Connecticut Department of Environmental Protection, *Site Characterization Guidance Document*, Hartford, CT, September 2007 (Revised, December 2010).

Constitution of the United States of America.

Corea, Juan Camilo, "Federal Statutory and Regulatory Changes in the Post-Great Recession Recovery of the U.S. Real Estate Market: How Expanding Capital Formation While Limiting

Debt Availability Will Impact Real Estate Development Projects," Final Paper, Georgetown University, School of Continuing Studies, Master's Program in Real Estate, *Foundations of Real Estate Law*, FREL 601–01, Spring 2013, April 5, 2013.

Cullen, Scott, "Value Engineering," *Whole Building Design Guide*, a program of the National Institute of Building Sciences, last updated 12–15–2010, found at www.wbdg.org/resources/value_engineering.php.

Dalton, Clare, "Book Review: The Death of Contract," *The American University Law Review*, Vol. 42 (1975), 1372.

Day, Kathleen, *The S&L Hell: The People and the Politics behind the $1 Trillion Savings and Loan Scandal*, W. W. Norton, New York, NY (1993).

DeMott, Deborah A., "Breach of Fiduciary Duty: On Justifiable Expectations of Loyalty and Their Consequences," *Arizona Law Review*, Vol. 48 (2006), 925.

Dillon, John F., LL.D, *Treatise on the Law of Municipal Corporations*, James Cockroft & Company, Chicago, IL (1872).

Dingfelder, Sadie, "Navy Yard on Track to Be D.C.'s Most Densely Populated Neighborhood," *The Washington Post*, January 9, 2016.

District of Columbia Office of Planning, *Height Master Plan for the District of Columbia: Final Evaluation & Recommendations*, DCOP, Washington, DC (November 20, 2013).

Drummer, Randyl, "Largest Publicly Traded CRE Services Firms Finish 2011 With Strong Revenues, Earnings," *CoStar News*, February 15, 2012, found at www.costar.com/News/Article/Largest-Publicly-Traded-CRE-Services-Firms-Finish-2011-With-Strong-Revenues-Earnings/135622Duany, Andres, Elizabeth Plater-Zyberk, and Jeff Speck, *Suburban Nation: The Rise of Sprawl and the Decline of the American Dream*, North Point Press, a division of Farrar, Straus and Giroux, New York, NY (2000).

Dupré, Judith, *Skyscrapers*, Black Dog & Leventhal Publishers, Inc., New York, NY (1996).

Fairfax County (VA) Board of Supervisors, *2010 Comprehensive Plan Changes*. The Amendment No. 2007–23, FAIRFAX COUNTY COMPREHENSIVE PLAN (2007 Edition), Tysons Corner Urban Center, Amended through 6–22–2010.

Farber, Daniel, "*Ages of American Formalism*," *Northwestern University Law Review* Vol. 90 (1995), pgs. 89–106.

Farnsworth, E. Allan, *Contracts*, Aspen Publishers, New York, NY (2004).

Ferris, Hugh, *The Metropolis of Tomorrow*, Princeton Architectural Press, New York, NY (1986), a reprint of the 1929 original by Ives Washburn, Publisher, with additional material added.

Fisher, Glenn W., "History of Property Taxes in the United States," *EH.Net Encyclopedia*, edited by Robert Whaples. September 30, 2002, found at http://eh.net/encyclopedia/history-of-property-taxes-in-theunited-states/Forster, Ryan, and Kail Padgitt, "Where Do State and Local Governments Get Their Tax Revenue?," Fiscal Fact No. 242, August 27, 2010, Tax Foundation, Washington, DC, found at http://taxfoundation.org/sites/taxfoundation.org/files/docs/ff242.pdf.

Fisher, Glenn W., *The Worst Tax? A History of the Property Tax in America*, University Press of Kansas, Lawrence, KS (1996).

Garreau, Joel, *Edge City: Life on the New Frontier*, Anchor Books Doubleday, New York, NY (1991).

Gause, Jo Allen, Editor, *Developing Sustainable Planned Communities*, Urban Land Institute, Washington, DC (2007).

Gilmore, Grant, *The Death of Contract*, Ohio State University Press, Columbus, OH (1974).

Glaab, Charles N., *The American City: A Documentary History*, The Dorsey Press, Inc., Homewood, IL (1963).

Gordon, Robert W., "Book Review: The Death of Contract," *Yale Law School, Faculty Scholarship Series* (1974).

Graham, Benjamin, *The Intelligent Investor: A Book of Practical Counsel*, Revised Edition, First Collins Business Essentials Edition, Harper-Collins (2006).

Graham, Benjamin, and David L. Dodd, *Security Analysis: Principles and Technique*, Sixth Edition, McGraw-Hill Companies, Inc., New York, NY (2009)Gratz, Roberta Brandes, with Norman Mintz, *Cities Back from the Edge*, Preservation Press, John Wiley & Sons, Inc., New York, NY (1998).

Greer, Gaylon E., *Investment Analysis For Real Estate Decisions*, Fourth Edition, Dearborn Financial Publishing, Inc., Chicago, IL (1997).

Greer, Scott, *Governing the Metropolis*, John Wiley and Sons, Inc., New York, NY (1962).

Grigonis, Richard, "The Empire State Building's 80th Anniversary," *InterestingAmerica.com*, February 11, 2011, found at www.interestingamerica.com/2011–02–04_Empire_State_Building_at_80_by_R_Grigonis.html.

Guinther, John, *Direction of Cities*, Viking Penguin, New York, NY (1996).

Guthheim, Frederick Albert, *The Federal City: Plans & Realities*, Smithsonian Institutional Press, Washington, DC (1976).

Hakes, Russell A., "Focusing on the Realities of the Contracting Process – An Essential Step to Achieve Justice in Contract Enforcement," *Delaware Law Review, University of Delaware*, Vol. 12, No. 2 (2011).

Hall, Sir Peter, *Cities in Civilization*, Fromm International, New York, NY (2001).

Hamilton, Alexander, James Madison, and John Jay, *The Federalist Papers*, with introduction, table of contents, and index of ideas by Clinton Rossiter, New American Library, Inc. (Mentor Books paperback edition), New York, NY (1961).

Hawken, Paul, L. Hunter Lovins, and Amory Lovins, (2007–10–15), *Natural Capitalism*, US Green Building Council, First Edition, Washington, DC (October 12, 2000); Hachette Book Group. Kindle Edition, October 10, 2007.

Hayward, Mary Ellen, and Charles Belfoure, *The Baltimore Rowhouse*, Princeton Architectural Press, New York, NY (1999).

Hillman, Robert A., "The Triumph of Gilmore's The Death of Contract," *Cornell Law Faculty Publications* (1996), Paper 922.

Holiday, Wil, "Kelo's Aftermath and The Impacts on Large-Scale Revitalization Projects," Final Paper, Georgetown University, School of Continuing Studies, Master's Program in Real Estate, Foundations of Real Estate Law, FREL 601–01, Spring 2013, April 26, 2013.

Hovenkamp, Herbert, and Sheldon Kurtz, *Principles of Property Law*, Sixth Edition, Concise Hornbooks Series, Thomson West, St. Paul, MN (1991).

Institute for Justice, "Five Years After Kelo: The Sweeping Backlash Against One of the Supreme Court's Most-Despised Decisions," Arlington, VA (2011), accessed February 2, 2013, found at doi: www.ij.org/five-years-after-kelo-the-sweeping-backlash-against-one-of-the-supreme-courts-most-despised-decision.

Institute for Local Self Governance, *[California] Municipal Finance Quick Reference* (2004).

Jacobs, Jane, *The Death and Life of Great American Cities*, Modern Library Edition, Random House, New York, NY (1993), originally published in 1961.

Jacobs, Jane, *The Nature of Economies*, Modern Library, a Random House imprint, New York, NY (2000).

Katz, Bruce, and Jennifer Bradley, *The Metropolitan Revolution: How Cities and Metros Are Fixing Our Broken Politics and Fragile Economy*, Brookings Institution Press, Washington, DC (2013).

Kayden, Jerold S., *Privately Owned Public Space: The New York City Experience*, John Wiley & Sons, New York, NY (2000).

LaFarge, Albert, Editor, *The Essential William H. Whyte*, Fordham University Press, New York, NY (2000).

Landmarks Preservation Commission of New York, Record of Decision of Landmark Designation of the Equitable Building, June 25, 1996, Designation List 273, LP-1935.

Lane, Nicole, "Crowdfunding: The Future of Real Estate Investment," *Research Assistant to Professor Smirniotopoulos, Center for Real Estate and Urban Analysis*, The George Washington University School of Business, Research Paper Draft, Fall 2015.

Lefcoe, George (2009-05-06). *Real Estate Transactions, Finance, and Development*, Matthew Bender & Company, Inc., a member of the LexisNexis Group, Dayton, OH (2009; Kindle Edition, May 06, 2009).

LeGates, Richard T., and Frederic Stout, Editors, *The City Reader*, Second Edition, Routledge, New York, NY. (1996).

Leinberger, Christopher B., *The WalkUP Wake-Up Call: Atlanta*, Center for Real Estate and Urban Analysis, The George Washington University School of Business, Washington, DC (2013).

Leinberger, Christopher B., *The WalkUP Wake-Up Call: D.C.*, Center for Real Estate and Urban Analysis, The George Washington University School of Business, Washington, DC (2012).

Leinberger, Christopher B., and Patrick Lynch, *Foot Traffic Ahead: Ranking Walkable Urbanism in America's Largest Metros*, Center for Real Estate and Urban Analysis, The George Washington University School of Business, Washington, DC (2015).

Leinberger, Christopher B., and Patrick Lynch, *The WalkUP Wake-Up Call: Boston*, Center for Real Estate and Urban Analysis, The George Washington University School of Business, Washington, DC (2015).

Lewis, Michael, *The Big Short*, W. W. Norton & Company, Inc., New York, NY (2010).

Luke, Ben, "Unbreak My HART: Honolulu's Rail Line Fiasco and Eminent Domain," Georgetown University, School of Continuing Studies, Master's Program in Real Estate, *Foundations of Real Estate Law*, FREL 601–02, Spring 2013, February 13, 2013.

March, Roy Hilton, "The Making of an Asset Class," *Wharton Real Estate Review*, Spring 2012, found at http://realestate.wharton.upenn.edu/review/index.php?article=229.

Marshall, Alex, *How Cities Work: Suburbs, Sprawl, and the Roads Not Taken*, University of Texas Press, Austin, TX (2000).

Martinelli, Christin, "The Pud Process: Know the Rules, Roles and the Right People," Final Paper, Georgetown University, School of Continuing Studies, Master's Program in Real Estate, *Foundations of Real Estate Law*, FREL 601–01, Spring 2013, April 26, 2013.

Massey, Kathleen N., "Securities Litigation Arising Out of the Financial Crisis: A Survey of Relevant Decisions and Their Implications," *The Investment Lawyer*, Vol. 16, No. 5 (May 2009) (Aspen Publishers).

Mello-Roos Community Facilities Act of 1982, added to the California Government Code by Statutes 1982, Ch. 1451, Sec. 1., California Government Code §§53311–53317.5.

Melnick, Richard J., "Tax Considerations in Real Estate Transactions," Guest Lecture, The George Washington University School of Business, MBA Program, *Foundations of Real Estate Law*, FINA-6290–012, October 29, 2014.

Miller, David Y., *The Regional Governing of Metropolitan America*, Westview Press (a member of Perseus Book Group), Boulder, CO (2002).

Milloy, Courtland, "Walmart Backs Out of D.C. Deal Citing Costs, and City's Poorest Pay the Price," *The Washington Post*, January 19, 2016.

Mills, Edwin S., and John F. McDonald, Editors, *Sources of Metropolitan Growth*, Center for Urban Policy Research, Rutgers University, New Brunswick (1992).

Moeller, Jr., G. Martin, *AIA Guide to the Architecture of Washington, D.C.*, Fifth Edition, The Johns Hopkins University Press, Baltimore, MD (2012).

Moravec, Alexandra Croft, "An Analysis of Planned Unit Development Regulations and Processes in Washington, DC: A Development Risk Management Case Study," University of North Carolina, Chapel Hill, Master of Regional Planning in the Department of City and Regional Planning Thesis Paper (2009).

Mumford, Lewis, *The City in History: Its Origins, Its Transformations, and Its Prospects*, Harvest Book Edition, Harcourt Brace & Company, Orlando, FL (1961, 1989).

Municipal Art Society of New York Report, *Accidental Skyline*, Municipal Art Society, New York, NY (December 2013).

National Capital Planning Commission, *The Height Master Plan for Washington, D.C.: Federal Interest Report and Final Recommendations*, NCPC, Washington, DC (November 27, 2013).

National Commission on the Causes of the Financial and Economic Crisis in the United States, *The Financial Crisis Inquiry Report*, Public Affairs, Perseus Books Group, Philadelphia, PA (2011).

National Commission on Fiscal Responsibility and Reform, *The Moment of Truth: Report of the National Commission on Fiscal Responsibility and Reform*, Washington, DC (December 1, 2010).

Neibauer, Michael, "D.C. Wins Last of the Skyland Shopping Center Eminent Domain Cases," *Washington Business Journal*, December 12, 2012.

Neibauer, Michael, "D.C., Safeway ink Skyland deal. Here's What That Means for the Wal-Mart-Anchored Project," *Washington Business Journal*, October 7, 2015.

New York Times Editorial Board, "Disney Retreats at Bull Run," *New York Times*, September 30, 1994, found at www.nytimes.com/1994/09/30/opinion/disney-retreats-at-bull-run.html.

Norquist, John O., *The Wealth of Cities: Revitalizing the Centers of American Life*, Perseus Books, Reading, MA (1998).

Olmsted, Jr., Frederick Law, "Landscape in Connection with Public Buildings in Washington," excerpted from Moore, Charles, Editor, *Papers Relating to the Improvement of the City of Washington*, Government Printing Office, Washington, DC (1901).

Piore, Adam, "Empire State of Mind," *The Real Deal*, April 1, 2011.

Poorvu, William, with Jeffrey L. Cruikshank, *The Real Estate Game: The Intelligent Guide to Decision-Making and Investment*, The Free Press, a Division of Simon & Schuster, Inc., New York, NY (1999).

Ressler, Paul, "Too Big To Fail: U.S. Financial Regulatory Framework & Real Estate," Georgetown University, School of Continuing Studies, Master's Program in Real Estate, *Foundations of Real Estate Law*, FREL 601–01, Spring 2013, April 23, 2013.

Rusk, David, *Baltimore Unbound: A Strategy for Regional Renewal*, The Abell Foundation, Johns Hopkins University Press, Baltimore, MD (1996).

Rutkow, Eric, *"Kelo v. City of New London,"* *Harvard Law Review*, Vol. 30 (2005), 261–279.

Sabol, Patrick, and Robert Puentes, *Private Capital, Public Good: Drivers of Successful Infrastructure Public-Private Partnerships*, The Brookings Institution, Washington, DC (December 2014).

Sagalyn, Lynne B., *Cases in Real Estate Finance and Investment Strategy*, Urban Land Institute, Washington, DC (1999).

Sarachan, Ronald A., and Daniel J. T. McKenna, "Litigation, Subprime Lending, and the Financial Crisis," *The Philadelphia Lawyer* (Winter 2009).

Schachtman, Tom, *Skyscraper Dreams: The Great Real Estate Dynasties of New York*, Little, Brown & Company, Boston, MA (1991).

Schmitz, Adrienne, and Deborah L. Brett, *Real Estate Market Analysis: A Case Study Approach*, Urban Land Institute, Washington, DC (2001).

Schrag, Zachary M., *The Great Society Subway (Creating the North American Landscape)*, Johns Hopkins University Press, Baltimore, MD (2006).

Sekander, Yama, "When Bad Things Happen to Good People," Problem Statement Final Paper, Georgetown University, School of Continuing Studies, Master's Program in Real Estate, *Foundations of Real Estate Law*, FREL 601–01, Spring 2013, April 26, 2013.

Smirniotopoulos, Peter E., "Fixing the Mortgage Mess: Why Treasury's Efforts at Both Ends of the Spectrum Are Failing," *The New Geography*, October 23, 2009, found at www.newgeography.com/content/001124-fixing-mortgage-mess-why-treasury%E2%80%99s-efforts-both-ends-spectrum-are-failing.

Smirniotopoulos, Peter E., *Conflicts of Interest in Commercial Real Estate Transactions: Who Represents the Tenant?*, November 2014, CREUA, The George Washington University, Washington, DC, hereinafter referred to as the "CREUA Conflicts of Interest Research Study Report," found at www.academia.edu/9488812/Conflicts_of_Interest_in_Commercial_Leasing_Transactions_Who_Represents_the_Tenant.

Smirniotopoulos, Peter E., *Who Represents the Tenant in Commercial Leasing Transactions*, March 2015, CREUA, The George Washington University, Washington, DC, found at www.academia.edu/11351622/Who_Represents_the_Tenant_in_Commercial_Leasing_Transactions.

Stainback, John, *Public/Private Finance and Development: Methodology, Deal Structuring, Developer Solicitation*, John Wiley & Sons, Inc., New York, NY (2000).

Stein, Jay M., Editor, *Classic Readings in Real Estate and Development*, Urban Land Institute, Washington, DC (1996).

Sudjic, Deyan, *The 100 Mile City*, Harvest Original Edition, Harcourt Brace & Company, Inc., Orlando, FL (1992).

Swallow, Erica, "The Rise of the Sharing Economy," *Mashable*, February 7, 2012, found at http://mashable.com/2012/02/07/sharing-economy/.

Tauranac, John, *The Empire State Building: The Making of a Landmark*, Cornell University Press, Ithaca, NY (2014).

Turner, Ralph, *The Great Cultural Traditions*, McGraw-Hill Book Company, New York, NY (1941).

Urban Land Institute, *Housing America's Workforce: Case Studies and Lessons from the Experts*, Washington, DC (2012).

Wardrip, Keith, "Public Transit's Impact on Housing Costs: A Review of the Literature," *Insights' from Housing Policy Research*, Center for Housing Policy, Washington, DC (August 2011).

Whyte, Jr., William H., Editor, *The Exploding Metropolis*, University of California Press, Berkeley, CA (1993).

Willis, Carol, "Drawing Toward Metropolis," included as additional material appended to Hugh Ferris's *The Metropolis of Tomorrow*, Princeton Architectural Press, New York, NY (1986), a reprint of the 1929 original by Ives Washburn, Publisher, with additional material added.

Willis, Carol, *Form Follows Finance: Skyscrapers and Skylines in New York and Chicago*, Princeton Architectural Press, New York, NY (1995).

Wilson, Reid, "The Most Corrupt State(s) in America," *The Washington Post*, January 22, 2014, found at www.washingtonpost.com/blogs/govbeat/wp/2014/01/22/the-most-corrupt-states-in-america.*Zoning Resolution of the City of New York*, enacted December 15, 1961, replacing the 1916 Zoning Resolution.

Zukin, Sharon, *The Culture of Cities*, Blackwell Publishers, Cambridge, MA (1995).

Zwick, Gary A., "Partnership Interests in Estate and Trust Administration," *Cleveland Bar Journal*, Vol. 78, No. 8 (June 2007),), reprinted by the author at www.walterhav.com/pubs/GAZ%20Article%20in%20Cleveland%20Bar%20Journal%20(00600032).PDF.

Index

Note: Figures are indicated by page numbers in *italics*.

cap rates and 317–19; commercial real
estate services and 403; construction,
closing in 87, *87*; debt in 322–31; equity
in 322–31; law and 115–16, 120–1,
123; permanent 51, 66, 82, 98–9, *99*;
private equity in 331–40; questions with
316–17; relationship banking and 326–7;
tax increment 385–90; *see also* loan,
construction
floor area ratio 56, 167, 370
fraud: in inducement, *vs.* in execution 241–2;
in securities transactions 348–9; Statute of
Frauds and 249–50
Freddie Mac 8, 436, 463–4, 479
fully integrated real estate development
company 51
funding strategy *53*, 53–4; law and 111–12

Gallery Place, Washington DC *17*, 384, 390
Garreau, Joel 183–4, 364
Gause v. Clarksville 135
general contractor 48, 54; law and 121–2;
pricing and bidding for *83*, 83–4, *84*; request
for information and 91–2
general partnership 286–7
general partnerships (GPs) 81, 120
geographic location 7
Georgetown, Washington DC *13*
Georgia State Capitol *30*
Georgia Tech University *28*
Gilmore, Grant 231, 232
Glancy, Alfred R., Jr. 335
Glass-Steagall Act 324, 325, 333, 334, 340
goals 105–6, 235
good faith deposit 256–7
go or no-go decision 46
Governing the Metropolis (Greer) 131
government *see* local government; state
government
government properties 28, *30*
government-sponsored entities (GSEs) 8
Governors Island Teaching Garden *31*
Graham, Benjamin 3–4, 38n3, 399
Graham, Ernest R. 173, 177, 179
Gramm-Leach-Bliley Act (GLBA) 333
Great Depression 182, 324–6, 329–30, 333,
335, 340–1, 350–3
Great Recession 67, 241–2, 276, 324–5, 334,
350–1
Green Building Code (Washington DC) 193–4
greenfield WalkUPs 25, *25*
gross leasable area (GLA) 56, *57*, 59, *59*,
64, *64*

habitat conservation 204–5
Hamilton, Alexander 146
Hammer, George A. 335
Hawaii Housing Authority v. Midkiff 372–3, 380
Hawken, Paul 193
health services: as local government power 145
Height of Buildings Acts (Washington DC)
169–74
hierarchies of law 109–10
historic preservation 154, 156, 160, 175,
205–6, 216–17, 226
Hoenig, Thomas 334
Hogan, Thomas E. 201–2
Holliday, Will 378–9, 382
home rule 132, 136, 140
Hoover, Herbert 167
*Horiike v. Coldwell Banker Residential Brokerage
Company* 434–6
horizontal construction 48, 49, 74, 90–1, *91*
hospitality: as asset class 12–13, *15*; residential
vs. 9
housing: as local government power 143
Housing and Urban Development, Department
of 8
Houston 137–9, 151, 385, 390
Hudson Yards Case Study 138, 143
Hunter v. City of Pittsburgh 136
Hutchinson, Dennis 231–2

idea, in development process 42, 45
idea generation 51–2, *52*; law and 110–11
impossibility of performance 245–8, 412
improper persuasion 244
improvements 41, 255
incarceration: as local government power 141
Incentives, laws as 108
income allocation 293, 305–7
inducement, fraud in 241–2
industrial, as asset class 25–6, *26*
inflation 318
infrastructure assessment 60–1, *61*; law and
114–15
Inman Park, Atlanta *9*
institutional/academic, as asset class *28*
insurance: in lease agreements 412
intangible personal property 256
integrated project delivery 54, 56, 79, *80*, 83,
85, 112, 460, 466, 476
interest, taxes and 303
Intergovernmental Panel on Climate Change
(IPCC) 194
Internal Revenue Code: of 1986 274–5;
residential class in 8